EXCAVATION AND
SALVAGE AT
RUNNYMEDE BRIDGE, 1978

EXCAVATION AND SALVAGE AT RUNNYMEDE BRIDGE, 1978:

The Late Bronze Age Waterfront Site

Stuart Needham

with major contributions by

Geraldene Done, John G Evans, Rowena Gale, James Greig, Susan Limbrey,
David Longley and Mark Robinson

and further contributions by

Julie Carr, Anthony Clark, Andrew David, John Evans, Pete Fisher, Andrew Foxon, Ian Freestone, Maureen Girling,
Veryan Heal, Jennifer Hillam, Ian Kinnes, Morven Leese, Eric Robinson and Alan Saville

and line drawings by

Stephen Crummy and Phil Dean

British Museum Press
in association with
English Heritage

© 1991 The Trustees of the British Museum
Published by British Museum Press
A division of British Museum Publications Ltd
46 Bloomsbury Street, London WC1B 3QQ

British Library Cataloguing in Publication Data

Needham, Stuart
  Excavation and salvage at Runnymede Bridge, 1978.
  I. Title
  936.229

ISBN 0 7141 13972

Printed and bound in Great Britain by
The Bath Press, Bath, Avon.

Contents

6

List of Plates

List of Figures

List of Tables

Foreword and acknowledgements

The archaeological work reported in this volume came about as a direct result of observations and actions taken by a local amateur archaeologist, David Barker. It was David in fact who had been instrumental in the initial discovery of the site during the planning stages of the M25, a discovery which led to the first excavation in the winter of 1975/6 under the direction of David Longley, then a Surrey Field Archaeologist (Longley 1980). That excavation (Areas 1 & 2) took place in a long narrow trench hemmed in on the one side by the existing A30 embankment, on the other by the old floodway also serving the A30. Already at the time of excavation a new embankment due to carry the M25 had been brought forward to a point just south of the trench and therefore further excavation at the Late Bronze Age levels in 1976 could only have proceeded in a northwards direction along the narrow extant berm towards the River Thames. Unfortunately the northern end of Area 2 was found to have suffered some severe erosion in antiquity and this led to the deduction, now known to be erroneous, that any prehistoric deposits to the north would have been re-worked by meandering of the Thames. The dark layer found in the new floodway walls to the north-east was assumed to be an erosion deposit. It was against this background of low or nil expectation that the renewed discoveries were made by David Barker in April 1978.

By the Easter of 1978 work had begun on the construction of the foundations of a new bridge, which, along with the 1959–60 bridge, would carry both the A30 and the M25 across the Thames, 10 traffic lanes in all. A substantial iron-piled coffer dam had been driven in along the river bank and a large L-shaped hole had been excavated behind it by the contractors (Figs. 2–3); it was kept drained by six large Univac pumps (6″). The part of the 'L' alongside the river was in the course of receiving the footings of the southern bridge pier, whilst further back other concrete footings were under construction to form a 'launch-pad' on which elements of the bridge superstructure were to be cast before being rolled into position over the pier foundations. Considerable destruction of intact sedimentary sequences, including rich archaeological layers, had then already taken place. However, through the kindness of the contractor, Fairclough Civil Engineering Ltd, and the consultant engineers, Ove Arup & Partners, it was possible to inspect, clean up and record large portions of the standing sections flanking their excavations. This process was invaluable for assessing the best intact areas for a controlled excavation and, furthermore, has provided an enormous amount of information on the alluvial context of the archaeology.

The embankment due to carry the M25 on the approach to the bridge had been brought forward from its 1976 position to a point alongside Area 8, thereby covering Area 2

and adjacent land (Fig. 3). This left accessible for possible excavation a rectangle of land trapped in the angle of the 'L' pit. The eastern part of this land was known to have carried the A30 floodway, at this stage already backfilled, and thus had limited prospects for the survival of the Late Bronze Age land-surface.

David Barker, having noticed dark earth deposits with finds in the walls of the contractor's pit, notified Stuart Needham, who joined him on the site on 16 April 1978. In addition to rich deposits of occupation material, they found a number of worked pile-driven timbers, either *in situ* in the sections, or partly disturbed by the contractors. These timbers had evidently been preserved below the permanent water table, but were now exposed owing to the pumping out of the area behind the coffer dam. The instant impression gained was that the timbers in evidence were associated with prehistoric material and it was considered likely that they were a structure belonging to the Late Bronze Age settlement. On the basis of early observations in Areas 5, 6, and 7 it quickly became apparent that most piles might fall into alignments. These would have been destroyed between Areas 5 and 6, and to the east of 7, although the pile tips were later found *in situ* across Area 4. However, it seemed probable that such alignments would remain largely undisturbed through the body of soil in the angle of the 'L' pit. From the salvage sections it also became apparent that the pile alignments were associated, perhaps along their whole length, with an ancient river channel, the bank of which could be identified just to the south of the piles in major sections.

The prospects of preserved structures, of layers rich in cultural debris and often waterlogged, thereby promising organic remains, of a variety of environmental data, and of a topographic feature perhaps bordering the settlement were compelling reasons for undertaking a controlled excavation.

A case was made to the Department of the Environment via Dr David Bird, Surrey County Archaeologist, and negotiation with the Department of Transport and the contractors ensued. Meanwhile a salvage campaign was mounted by Stuart Needham with David Longley to record as much as possible of the sections, as well as occasional *in situ* deposits (Area 4) around the contractors' pit, before they suffered more damage or became inaccessible. This campaign ran intermittently through May and June with the welcome assistance of Rob Poulton, Martin O'Connell, Phil Dean, Kathleen Needham and occasional other helpers.

A decision in favour of the excavation of Area 6 was finally made towards the end of June with the assistance of Stephen Dunmore, Ancient Monuments Inspectorate, just before the area was due to be covered in concrete. A duration of four weeks was allowed, in which time it was intended to excavate all the Late Bronze Age deposits encountered within Area 6 as well as to sample the Neolithic bearing layers believed to lie somewhat deeper on the basis of finds made during salvage work in Area 4. In the event these goals were realised over a period of four and half weeks. By September Area 6 and the surrounding area had been buried in concrete and sand prior to completion of the bridge abutment to the embankment. It is thought that extensive unexcavated prehistoric deposits probably remain buried under the combined A30/M25 embankment.

The excavations were directed jointly by David Longley and Stuart Needham. They were most ably assisted by a digging team drawn together at short notice, most important amongst whom were Phil Jones, who supervised, and Ann Clark, who gave considerable assistance with paperwork. We particularly wish to thank Richard Bradley, whose quick recognition of the potential of the site caused him to send several Reading archaeology undergraduates to dig. The whole team are to be praised for their devotion to the task in hand, which was illustrated above all by their preparedness to excavate at times until dusk.

We owe a debt of gratitude to David Bird and the Planning Department, Surrey County Council, who handled administrative and financial matters throughout the excavation and continued to give support during the post-excavation programme. The publication volume obviously would be nothing without the hard work of the many specialists. Amongst them we would especially like to single out Maureen Girling for her valuable direction of the on-site sampling for environmental remains and subsequent coordination of the other environmentalists involved up until her untimely death in December 1985. Sadly her own study on the insect remains from the site was barely begun at this time, but fortunately Mark Robinson has been able to work this subject up in a manner that does great credit to Maureen's involvement. We benefited enormously from Maureen's moral support and her interest in the interpretations that were tentatively ventured as the post-excavation proceeded. We also wish to thank Susan Limbrey, James Greig, Tony Clark, Andrew David and Peter Fisher for their active roles on site in their respective fields, and Ian Tyers who undertook much of the laboratory processing of environmental samples.

The post-excavation process was aided immensely by members of the Guildford group – Kathleen Needham, Christine Hendrie, Margaret Sellers and Dorothy Sturley – who took on the task of washing and marking the large assemblage of animal bones. Geoff Carter assisted David Longley in study of the Late Bronze Age pottery, Arnold Aspinall of the University of Bradford kindly arranged for NAA analysis of a selection of pottery to take place, and Julie Carr is to be thanked for various pieces of post-excavation analysis for Stuart Needham. We would also like to acknowledge the considerable assistance of Jacqui Watson and Glynnis Edwards with the early care of the waterlogged wood while it was at the Ancient Monuments Laboratory.

The splendid line drawings in the volume are mostly the work of two illustrators at the Department of Prehistoric and Romano–British Antiquities; Steve Crummy was responsible for all the sections, plans and diagrams; Phil Dean for all drawings of finds with the exception of the worked stone and the wooden stakes, which were done respectively by freelance illustrators, Simon James and Rosemary Walker. Site photographs are those of the directors, while artifacts were shot in British Museum studios by Sandra Marshall and Victor Bowley, the bones by Rex Cooper, the worked timbers by Liza Lawler, and other specialist plates by the respective authors. Much of the weighty manuscript was typed by Judith Cash. Thanks also go to Sheridan Bowman and Denise Longley, long sufferers of plan-strewn floors and the like. We are grateful for all these contributions.

Ian Freestone would like to thank David Peacock and Andrew Middleton for providing samples of Lodsworth stone, and Alan Woolley for the results of his earlier examination of one stone sample from Runnymede. John Wymer gave some helpful comments on the Area 8 burin to Alan Saville. Hilary Sale-Harding efficiently carried out much of the sorting for James Greig, and Lisa Moffett helped him with the identifications of charred grain. He would also like to acknowledge unpublished information from Wendy Carruthers, Mark Robinson and Vanessa Straker. John Evans thanks Rosina Mount for her analysis of *Carychium* shells, and Vivian Evans for doing the extraction and preliminary identifications. Geraldene Done is grateful to Alison Locker and Roger Jones for their kind help with identification of some of the bones.

The excavated assemblage was donated to the British Museum by the Department of Transport.

This report was published with the aid of a grant from the Historic Buildings and Monuments Commission.

S. P. Needham and D. Longley.
December 1989

Summary

This is the second of the final excavation reports on the prehistoric settlement site beside the Thames at Runnymede Bridge, Berkshire (TQ 018718). It covers the archaeological campaign conducted in 1978 during the construction of the bridge to carry the M25 orbital motorway across the Thames. This involved the recording of extensive sections through alluvial deposits as well as the excavation of interstratified settlement deposits of Middle Neolithic and Late Bronze Age periods. Isolated groups of finds of Mesolithic and Late Neolithic age were also recovered from stratified positions. As a result it has been possible to outline a long history of alluviation and changes to the river system during the Flandrian in this part of the valley. The report presents the overall sequence in terms of major accretive units, or alluvial parcels. Sedimentary deposits included both channel sediments and over-bank flood silts. Sequences were investigated to varying depths up to 1.5 m below the present water table.

Permanent waterlogging and the calcareous nature of the sediments led to the survival of diverse and prodigious environmental remains – pollen, plant macrofossils including wood, insects, snails, ostracods, diatoms – and study of these is fully reported for two key sequences relating to the settlement phases of the Neolithic and Late Bronze Age. Different data are seen to shed light on the environment within different spheres around the site; there are detailed insights into the surrounding habitats, both natural and farmed, and a marked decline in woodland between the Neolithic and the end of the Bronze Age is well shown. The data offer rather less information directly on settlement activities, although there are important indications of grain processing and manure-rich middens for the Late Bronze Age. The food economy is documented by a good yield of cereal grain, a large animal bone assemblage and identifications of charred food residues on potsherds. Cattle and pigs were major food sources in both periods, although in the Late Bronze Age there were temporal changes, notably pig becoming more important later on.

The Neolithic deposits recovered in 1978 were all waterlogged, lying either in channel sediments or marshy backwaters. Associated artifact material belongs to the Middle Neolithic and dating (radiocarbon and palaeomagnetic) indicates a calendar date range in the early 4th millennium BC for this activity. *In situ* structures were recorded in salvage operations in Areas 4 and 8, whilst Area 6 yielded only prostrate structural timbers associated with refuse. The structures were based on pile-driven uprights sharpened with stones axes and, in Area 4 at least, had associated brushwood and stones. Important finds included two complete polished stone axes, decorated pottery and a piece of worked bark.

A later group of butchered bone, possibly from a single cow, was dated to between 3300 and 2600 cal BC. During this period after Middle Neolithic occupation there was some regeneration of woodland locally, but grazing probably continued on a lesser scale.

The part of the Late Bronze Age site excavated in 1978 lies on the north-east perimeter of a large settlement. Occupation is represented on the levee and in the edge of a silting river channel both as structures and dense refuse. The deep channel sequence is grouped into 10 stratigraphic units (A–J) and is particularly important for identifying a passage of events and changes in artifacts during the Late Bronze Age occupation period. Changes in the ceramic assemblage are documented and differences from the 1976 assemblage are interpreted as due to functional as well as temporal factors. The history of this perimeter zone begins with vegetation clearance, around 900 cal BC, followed by a piled structure interpreted as the foundations of an enclosure, waterfront 1. This was replaced by a similar structure on new piles later in the 9th century cal BC. Both structures followed a cusping line traced for 50 m and were probably cross-braced to the contemporary river bank behind. The superstructure is deduced to have had a walkway or platform behind a stockade. Laid timbers regarded as hardstandings for beaching boats were added to waterfront 2 around 800 cal BC, but thereafter a peat pool developed and the waterfront went into decline, possibly accompanied by a hiatus in occupation. A later phase of activity may be represented by finds at a higher level, but no structures are attributable to this phase.

On the adjacent bank, or levee, there was an early phase of pits, possibly with a partition fence. One large pit containing a dismembered horse has ritual implications, and the pits are interpreted as being connected with the definition of the site's boundary. Later, a post-built rectilinear structure was erected behind and approximately parallel to waterfront 2. Most of the refuse in this zone probably accumulated around the footings of this structure, which is not viewed as a domestic dwelling despite the abundance of evidence for cooking and perhaps feasting. Other activities could have taken place in the immediate vicinity since a number of crafts are represented amongst the artifact assemblage.

The settlement seems to have had wide contacts; noteworthy from this campaign were quernstones from greensand sources. However, its siting on the river bank is argued to relate more to conceptual values of association with the river than to economic motives as such.

Abbreviations

General prefixes

A	Area
F	Feature
FR	Food Residue sample number
L	Layer
S	Sample
SA	Section or plan drawn during salvage campaign
SF	Special Find
SS	Soil/sediment column sample
WF	Soil/sediment column sample – LBA waterfront zone

Prefixes for artifacts

B	Bone/antler
C	Clay artifacts (including refractories)
FL	Flint
M	Metalwork
NP	Neolithic pottery
P	LBA pottery
S	Stone
SH	Shale
W	Wood

General abbreviations

BC	Calendar date before Christ
BP	Radiocarbon date (uncalibrated) before present (AD 1950)
cal BC	Calendar date based on calibrated radiocarbon measurements
LBA	Late Bronze Age

Abbreviations for dimensions in artifact catalogues

B	Breadth
D	Depth
d	Diameter
E	Extant
L	Length
M	Maximum
T	Thickness
W	Width
wt	Weight

The Contributors

Julie Carr, Department of Urban Archaeology, Museum of London.

Anthony Clark, Guildford, Surrey

Andrew David, Ancient Monuments Laboratory, Fortress House, London.

Geraldene Done, West Byfleet, Surrey.

John G. Evans, School of History and Archaeology, University of Wales College of Cardiff.

John Evans, Department of Mathematical and Physical Sciences, Polytechnic of East London.

Peter Fisher, *formerly* School of Geography, Kingston Polytechnic, Kingston upon Thames.

Andrew Foxon, Hull Museums and Art Galleries.

Ian Freestone, Department of Scientific Research, British Museum.

Rowena Gale, Chute Cadley, Hampshire.

The late Maureen Girling, Ancient Monuments Laboratory, Fortress House, London.

James Greig, School of Biological Sciences, The University of Birmingham.

Veryan Heal, Chulmleigh, Devon.

Jennifer Hillam, Department of Archaeology and Prehistory, University of Sheffield.

Ian Kinnes, Department of Prehistoric and Romano-British Antiquities, British Museum.

Morven Leese, Department of Scientific Research, British Museum.

Susan Limbrey, Department of Ancient History and Archaeology, The University of Birmingham.

David Longley, Gwynedd Archaeological Trust, Bangor.

Stuart Needham, Department of Prehistoric and Romano-British Antiquities, British Museum.

Eric Robinson, Department of Geology, University College London.

Mark Robinson, The University Museum, Oxford.

Alan Saville, Artefact Research Unit, National Museums of Scotland, Edinburgh.

Introduction: the 1978 investigations at Runnymede Bridge

The salvage operation

Conditions for archaeological observation were, almost inevitably, far from ideal during the salvage operation and the availability of areas for study often changed quickly. The sections recorded were generally inclined at angles between vertical and about 45° and so they are not true representations of stratigraphic sequences along precise transects. They were also usually irregular in plan, even where the overall trend was a straight edge to the pit, and the available man-power did not allow more than limited straightening of sections, nor indeed much deepening or lateral extension to follow interesting features. Most energy was given over to cleaning in order to establish layer boundaries, followed by drawing. In places cleaning was incomplete for one reason or another, notably along the upper part of Area 4, where in retrospect it is thought possible that a Late Bronze Age land surface might have survived in parts, although the temporary diversion of the new M25 floodway would have run diagonally across Area 4, truncating some of the upper deposits. Area 8 posed a problem due to the mass of dumped sand poised above the modern turf line, sand which was swept down over the section with each fall of rain.

Thus most parts of the sections that it was possible to clean were drawn to scale and these are mainly published here. A few parts were only sketched, while most of the information in the Area 6 salvage section (which was properly drawn) was superseded by various sections later drawn during the excavation of Area 6. Fig. 4 and Table 1 summarise details of salvage sections and plans.

Nowhere was there time for leisurely consideration, indeed most recording got done just ahead of further devastating contractor's works. Area 8 was completed just before the section base was concealed by a concrete flooring; Area 5 was finished during the rise of water consequent on a breach in the coffer dam – thereafter it was not very accessible; Area 7 became difficult to access owing to shuttering for the launch-pad; and in Area 4 the limited *in situ* deposits were rapidly excavated, and the truncated pile bases planned in the nick of time prior to renewed disturbance by machinery and more concrete-laying. A short standing section at the northern corner of Area 4 (Plate 5) was prepared for drawing, but then destroyed before this could be undertaken.

As salvage work got under way in Area 4 it quickly became apparent that surviving archaeological deposits at the low level reached by the contractors contained only Neolithic finds. This added a new dimension to the proposed excava-

Table 1: Summary of salvage plans and sections

Area	Section	Plan	Published (this volume)	Archive (parts unpublished)
5		SA1	Fig. 8	
5	SA2		Fig. 7b	
5	SA3		Fig. 7a	
6	SA4		Fig. 9 (partial)	Photographs and 1:10 drawing
7	SA5		Fig. 10 (partial)	Photographs and 1:20 drawing
8	SA6		Fig.11	
8	SA7		Fig.12	
8	SA8		—	Sketch in journal
8	SA9		—	Sketch in journal
4	SA10		—	Sketch in journal
4	SA11		Fig.13	
4		SA12	Fig.14	
4A		SA13	—	Sketch in journal
4B		SA14	Fig. 15a	
		SA15	Fig. 15b	

tion, since the earlier work (Areas 1 and 2) had not located any pre-Late Bronze Age material despite a sondage of between 0.60 and 0.90 m into the underlying silt.

The Area 7 section was encountered with a step running the whole way along its top in addition to the ledge at the A7/A8 junction where a pump stood (Fig. 3). This had evidently been cut by the contractors to carry pipes and cables. Unfortunately this made it impossible to assess whether a Late Bronze Age surface, indeed at the southern end also a Neolithic land surface, might have survived there on the eastern edge of the A30 floodway. The upper deposits recorded at the northern end of Area 7 also showed disturbance and this was almost certainly associated with a temporary course of the M25 floodway. This occurred when it was first constructed prior to 1978 (presumably as the embankment progressively buried the previous A30 floodway). To begin with, however, the M25 floodway ran out into the Thames through the original exit (crossed by a footbridge) and this necessitated a 'switch' in the otherwise straight course of the new floodway. This was the course encountered by Longley around 1975/6 (Longley 1980: 11, fig. 9). The walls of the 'switch' were at that time cleaned up to reveal a thin band of darker soil, which is likely to have been a Late Bronze Age horizon, either *in situ* or eroded (discussed in Chapter 1). This deposit would have lain above Area 4 and the new bridge foundations and the line mapped would have clipped the corner between Areas 6 and 7. By the beginning of the 1978 campaign the old floodway exit had been removed to make way for the coffer dam and contractor's pit and a new exit had been broken through to the river in line with the M25 floodway (as seen in Fig. 3).

A number of samples of both wood and sediments were taken during the salvage campaign. These included columns in Areas 8 and 4: from approximately Neolithic sediments (layers 85, 86, 87, 93) in section SA6, probable post-LBA channel silts in section SA9, and a Middle Neolithic–Middle Bronze Age sequence in section SA11 (layers 114–119). A series of spot samples in Area 5 also gave an effective column, while various other spot samples were taken. Many of these samples subsequently went astray or became mixed up and only a minority have been studied. However, it has been possible to obtain valuable radiocarbon ages for the timber structure in Area 4B and a pile in Area 8, to have many further timbers identified to species and to have insect remains from the waterlogged Area 4 column samples studied.

The A30 bridge construction, 1959–60

The 1978 discoveries in Area 5 and 6 in particular suggested that good archaeological deposits, including the pile rows, would have once existed under the A30 bridge foundations. It emerged that archaeological material had in fact been noted by someone working on that construction site in 1959–60. At the time the existence of such finds was suppressed, but some years later a brief written report was supplied to Egham-by-Runnymede Historical Society (Longley 1980: 3). Large quantities of bones, antlers, burnt stones, waterlogged wooden 'stumps' and pottery had evidently been brought up with the spoil, having mainly come from a 'black bed' 30–45 cm thick and some 1.5–1.8 m deep. Some pottery

had been kept for a while and one sherd is sketched in the archive report. This shows a decorated Middle Neolithic rim sherd in keeping with the assemblage now known from the site. Much of the spoil from the 1959–60 foundation trench is said to have been dumped nearby on the river bank, thus accounting for the hummocky nature of the ground in the wooded area immediately south-east of the M25 floodway. Worked flints and potsherds have been retrieved from the ground surface there.

The excavation: Area 6

A controlled excavation took place in Area 6 for a period of 4½ weeks during the month of July, 1978. As explained above the area was located so as to expose undisturbed piles, thought to be set in rows, the edge of the river channel which contained them and a part of the adjacent river bank. The size of the area opened was dictated primarily by the time and labour available. The overburden, which was machined off with a hy-mac, comprised mainly rubble, probably material associated with the construction of the 1959–60 bridge as also were two elongate pits projecting into the western side of Area 6 (F1, F2). Machining ceased when clean undisturbed silt was encountered in the zone of the ancient river channel and when the first signs of occupation soil and finds appeared on the levee, or river bank.

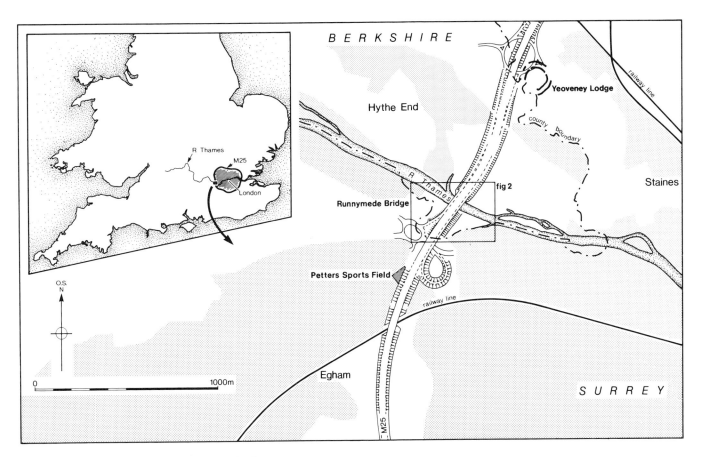

Fig. 1 Location map of Runnymede Bridge, Berks.

In the eastern part of Area 6 the recent backfill of the A30 floodway was also excavated by machine. This was taken down roughly to the original broad 'U' profile of the ditch in the northern part, but south of the pile rows, where it had bottomed onto the thick sterile pre-Late Bronze Age flood silt (L38), machining was continued straight down to the organic layers (L40) in preparation for the search for Neolithic material.

It was decided at the outset to set out a baulk to provide a deep, standing section through channel and bank sediments. This was positioned so as to be more or less perpendicular to the presumed lines of the river and pile rows, but also to capture the longest transect through the channel deposits for which the fullest possible sequence was preserved. This entailed placing it as close as possible to the western edge of the A30 floodway. This baulk remained in place throughout the excavation (it was originally intended to be excavated towards the end) and divided trench 1 from trench 2 (Fig. 5). Additional standing sections were created at intervals along the length of the river channel for the various reasons given below. The locations of these and other major sections are shown in Fig. 5.

After the excavation of Late Bronze Age deposits and cut features had been completed on the levee, a machine was brought back to excavate the underlying silts down to layer 40. This resulted in a roughly coffin-shaped hole across the southern half of trench 1 and an extension into the southwestern corner of trench 2 from the part already deeply dug. These sondages for exploring the Neolithic levels are referred to as trench 1 deep and trench 2 deep. Meanwhile excavation of the deep cultural-bearing sequence in the river channel continued by hand; the approach taken is described below. Late in the excavation the ancient river bank was spaded through to form a continuous section alongside the main baulk (38A and 38B). This involved cutting a slot north-east from trench 1 deep and resulted in the exposure of a little more of the Neolithic deposits.

The sampling of Area 6 for environmental remains, sedimentary studies and dating purposes is described in Chapter 10.

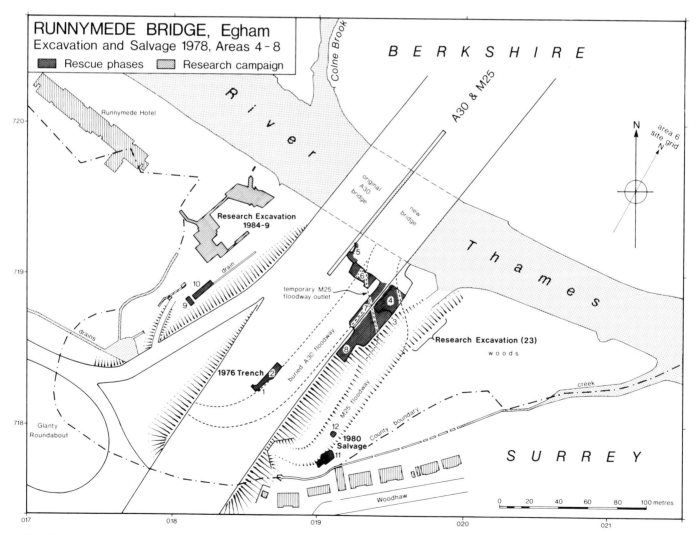

Fig. 2 Runnymede Bridge: site plan (1:2500). Showing Areas 1–2 (1975/6), Areas 4–8 (1978), Areas 9–12 (1980) and research excavations, Areas 13–32 (1984–9).

The site report has been presented as four chapters. The stratigraphic contexts in all the salvage areas are dealt with first as these provide a long sequence of alluvial deposits that give a good framework for the more detailed stratigraphic information derived from the excavation of Area 6; the latter is dealt with in Chapter 2. Relevant contexts and context groups in Area 6 are referred to in Chapter 1 for ease of correlation, while broad stratigraphic evidence from later excavations on the site (1984–89) is drawn in where appropriate. Chapter 3 deals with all types of Late Bronze Age structural evidence in Area 6, and Chapter 4 offers a discussion of the overall sequence of structures and deposits for the Late Bronze Age.

Note on the published context numbers

Because of the complexity of the stratigraphy and the occasional mismatching of excavated layer numbers in separately excavated sequences, it was considered advantageous to apply a new set of context numbers for publication purposes. Layer contexts 1–42, some with subdivisions, cover the full sequence in Area 6, running broadly from latest to earliest. These aid discussion and comprehension of the stratigraphy. Concordance with as-excavated layers is shown in the catalogue of layer-type contexts (Table 2), which also notes when finds are not uniquely assignable to the as-published contexts. The sequence is continued, 43–145, to cover layers identified in the salvage operation; these had not been numbered on site.

Features are denoted by the prefix F and remain numbered as on site; they are unique only to the particular area. The Area 6 cut features are catalogued in Table 5, whilst retrieved timbers are dealt with in Table 4.

Terminology for topographic features

Because of the ambiguity of the term *river bank*, it has been reserved in this report strictly for the immediate land/water interface, that is the sloping face of the land mass that comes into contact with water under normal non-flood conditions. This face itself shifted through time as the bank aggraded. The top of this slope is referred to as the *bank crest*, while the more level surface behind the crest (often called generally the river bank) is referred to as the *floodplain* or *levee*, even though the Runnymede examples are not proven levees in the geomorphological sense. The silts in the originally flowing river channels are collectively referred to as *channel deposits* despite the fact that some of the upper ones are more strictly over-bank flood deposits.

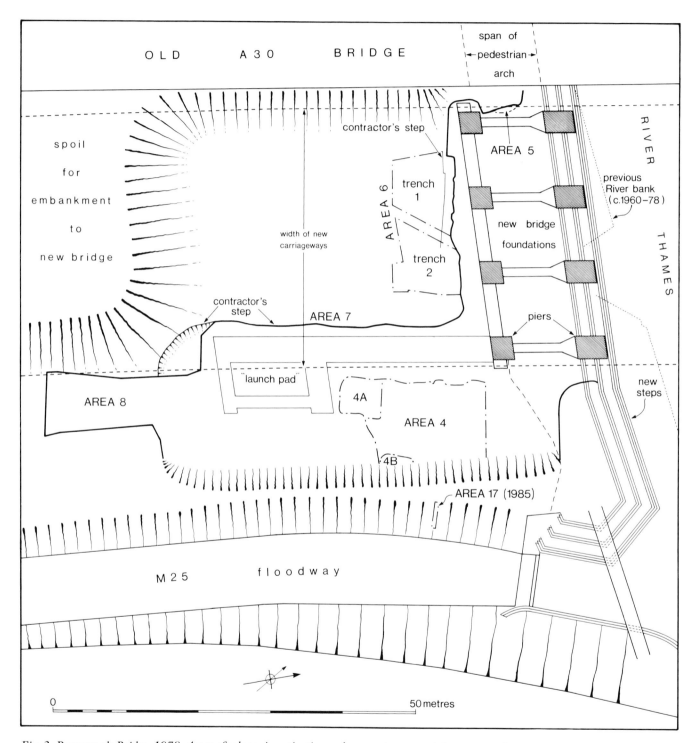

Fig. 3 Runnymede Bridge, 1978. Areas of salvage investigation and excavation around the contractor's pit.

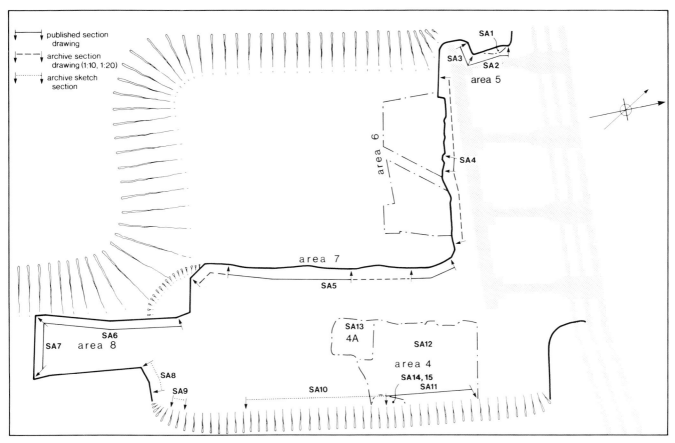

Fig. 4 Runnymede Bridge, 1978. Sections and plans recorded during the salvage operation; those in bold are published in this volume (see also Table 1).

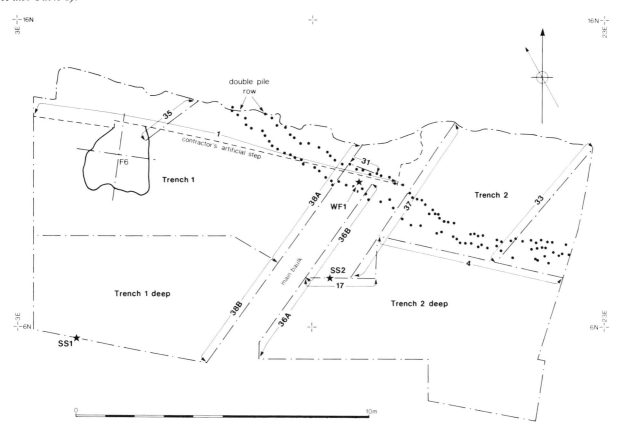

Fig. 5 Runnymede Bridge, 1978. Plan of the excavated Area 6 showing locations of trenches, deep trenches, main sections, pit F6 and sample column positions.

SECTION A:
THE SITE

Summary

Section A is the basic site report for all of the 1978 investigations at Runnymede Bridge. Three chapters describe the recovered evidence and a fourth contains a limited discussion.

Much of the site evidence concerns a long alluvial history which was documented not only in the excavated area (Area 6), but also in long contractor's sections recorded during the salvage campaign. A large number of layers were recorded across the site; these are numbered uniquely (catalogued in Table 2), correlations between deposits in different areas being presented in Table 3a. The alluvial sequence established from the salvage campaign is presented first, providing a long time trajectory in chronological order (Chapter 1). The deposits are grouped into six major accretive units, or *alluvial parcels*, dating from Mesolithic to post-Bronze Age times. A parcel may include both channel and overbank deposits, although any clear breaks between types of sedimentation are used to subdivide parcels. Evidence for human activity stratified within this sequence is described in the appropriate section; most notable are the Middle Neolithic structural and artifact remains, including organics, situated in a damp river's edge setting in Area 4 (parcel 2). A cluster of Mesolithic flints was stratified in parcel 1 (Area 8).

An attempt is made to correlate the LBA deposits exposed in Area 8 with those in other areas in terms of topography and natural alterations. This involves a reinterpretation of the relative chronology of erosion and occupation in the earlier excavated Area 2. It is concluded that *in situ* deposits would probably have extended from Area 2 to Area 6, but would only just have stretched eastwards to the line of the new M25 floodway.

Other dating evidence is introduced as appropriate, including cross-referencing to the Area 6 sequence. The detailed excavated stratigraphy of Area 6 is presented in Chapter 2; it relates to alluvial parcels 2 and 4 and provides the framework for the wealth of environmental results (Section C). The earliest cultural evidence recovered here was a horizon of Middle Neolithic artifacts and structural timbers; all however represent secondary refuse in stream channel deposits against the flank of a mid-channel bar. A group of butchered bones at a higher level are referable broadly to the Late Neolithic, part of a period of little human activity on the site which lasted until the early Late Bronze Age.

Much of Chapter 2 is devoted to a river bank, which aggraded during the phase of LBA occupation. The stratigraphy in the edge of the associated channel follows the formation of a sand/shingle bar, the subsequent silting of a slack behind it, and then the sealing of this system by flood silts. The resulting two-metre deep sequence is divided into ten stratigraphic units (A–J) based on a combination of sedimentary characteristics and significant human interventions. The evidence for LBA activity spans eight of the units (B–I), although definite *in situ* material is only present in six (B–G). Major horizons trapped in the channel edge silts are a mass of burnt vegetation debris (unit B), a midden (units B–C), layers of dense domestic refuse (units E and G) and laid-branch structures (unit F).

In addition, two rows of vertically driven pile foundations survived; the rows were parallel to the ancient river bank and accompanied by a few outlying and inlying piles. The problems and principles of relating pile-driven timbers to horizontally bedded layers are outlined as a prelude to the stratigraphic sequence. Layer discontinuities and, to a lesser extent, drag-lines are used to place the inner and outer pile rows respectively at about the unit C/D interface and unit E. The method of excavation of the pile-bearing silts is also described.

Description of the occupation soil contexts on the levee follows. Although boundaries are not clear cut, there appear to be some distinct deposits present within the small area excavated. These differences can be related to temporal and spatial changes.

LBA structural evidence is dealt with under four

main headings (Chapter 3). In the case of the pile-driven structures, the text draws also on the evidence from salvage Areas 4, 5 and 7 for continuations of the Area 6 waterfront foundations. A 50-metre span may be interpolated as a cusping line in both phases, although the spacing of timbers varies along this span. The horizontal branch structures are argued to have been laid *in situ* rather than being collapsed superstructural elements. An interpretation in terms of hardstandings for supporting boats beached on the foreshore is advanced.

Cut features are classified into five types for convenience, the more important types being sub-classified. Attention is drawn to the main concentrations of fired or burnt clay because of possible derivation from buildings or smaller structures.

Further discussion of the Neolithic settlement evidence is reserved for the final discussion, but for the LBA some interpretation of structural and layer-type evidence is necessary (Chapter 4) prior to the wider considerations of Chapter 25. In particular, suggestions are advanced on the form of the waterfront superstructure, albeit without any surviving remains. Two alternatives are given, both employing platforms and straightforward palisades set above. Features on the crest of the bank are suggested to have performed the role of rear braces. Linked to these reconstructions are the arguments advanced that two debris-rich layers

in the underlying silts were formed during demolition or decay phases of the two waterfronts. The cuspate form of the waterfronts, the outlying posts and the hardstandings outside waterfront 2 are considered in relation to access to the river and overall waterfront function.

On the levee the main set of post-holes is suggested to belong to a rectilinear building, not quite parallel to the waterfronts; a possible square four-post setting situated symmetrically within the latter might belong, or otherwise might represent a distinct structural phase. Some concentrations of surface debris, including burnt clay and burnt flint cobbles, are seen to relate to these standing buildings and are used to argue that much of the surviving rubbish layers is contemporary with them. Despite the evidence for various kinds of activity, function is unclear; use as a dwelling is possible, but not favoured.

An earlier phase is represented by two large pits and a fence perpendicular to the river bank. One large pit is part of a feature complex involving an encircling post ring, another pit, a stake-and-wattle line, a midden deposit, a horse burial, a hearth deposit, and possible deliberate artifact placements. A sequence of acts took place here between units B and F. Further discussion of the significance of this complex is to be found in the final discussion.

Chapter 1
The overall stratigraphic sequence: salvage areas

Introduction

The salvage contexts, which are almost all of layer type, were described at the time of recording, but were not numbered until later. The retrospective numerical sequence continues that for Area 6 (contexts 43–145; Table 2) and uniquely references each context identified. The layers in Areas 7 and 8 (43–97) have been integrated into a single sequence because of the continuous nature of their respective recorded sections, stretching for some 55 m in a line perpendicular (except for a small dog-leg) to the modern river and the valley axis. Areas 4 and 5 have each been numbered separately (contexts 98–123; 124–145), because in both cases observable sections were discontinuous with the sequences in either Area 6 or Area 7/8. However, a number of good correlations between these sequences may be suggested on the basis of similar sediment characteristics and comparable stratigraphic positions; these are shown in Table 3a. It is also possible to suggest some correlation with the earlier excavation of Area 1/2. For each sequence contexts are numbered beginning with the youngest and working back broadly chronologically to the oldest. They are grouped into major accretion units or 'parcels', each of which will correspond to a particular phase or phases of alluviation on the site. There may be a little overlap between the formation of some parcels, but many are shown to be essentially successive either by the superimposition of one parcel on top of one or more others, or more usually by the lateral juxtaposition of one parcel against an erosion line cutting through another. The concept of 'alluvial parcels' has been presented elsewhere (Needham 1989) and is intended to serve as a useful structuring of complex sedimentary data to aid description and interpretation. The numbering of parcels in this report differs from and replaces that presented in Needham 1989. The deposits of all salvage areas may be treated together as six alluvial parcels and, as a separate unit, the Late Bronze Age occupation soil. These units are discussed in chronological order.

Alluvial parcel 1: Mesolithic–Neolithic alluvium; plus Early–Middle Bronze Age channel fill

AREAS 7 AND 8: CONTEXTS 83–97   FIGS. 10 AND 12

Many of the layers in this group are horizontally bedded, but an undulating erosion surface is apparent at the base of 84 and there may have been a major time lapse at this interface, which is used to divide parcel 1A from 1B. Contexts 85–97 belong broadly to the Mesolithic, possibly

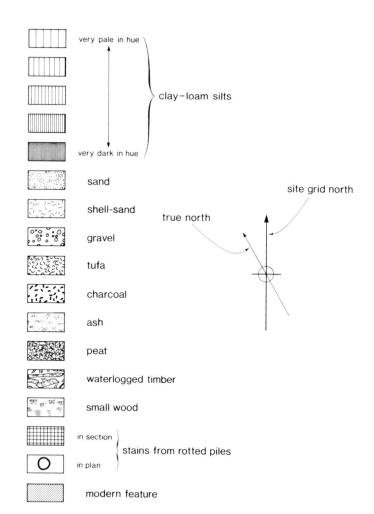

Fig. 6 Key for conventions representing sediment types in the section drawings.

extending into the Neolithic. Low down in the sequence are coarse sediments, the gravel layers (97, 95), but these rapidly give way to very fine sediments suggestive of overbank flood alluvium or quiet, almost lacustrine conditions of deposition (88–93). To the north-east these layers are cut by an ancient river bank underlying parcel 2. To the south-west, however, the relationship with adjacent context 86 is uncertain. Layer 88 is recorded as having merged into 86 immediately above the surviving tips of three piles. It is likely that these piles had extended higher, but that their upper parts were excavated away with spoil by the contractor in the course of creating the slightly inclined section. Concentrations of wood flecks occurring in the section above the pile tips are likely to have been the partially decayed parts of further piles still buried in the silt, a feature familiar in other sections containing piles. There would appear to have been a group or line of piles here: these either formed a pre-existing boundary against which the different deposits 86 and 88 accumulated on different sides, or, more likely, the structure was set at the edge of a steep bank truncating 88, and 86 along with 85 and perhaps 87 represent subsequent channel fill. The existence of channel activity here in this period could help explain the trough form of the later scouring, which probably took place before gravel 84 choked the trough.

The sequence described so far, parcel 1A, can be relatively well dated. A tight cluster of struck flints (A8 F4) and a possible pebble anvil stone (S1) were retrieved from the undisturbed silt of layers 91–92 in the short right-angle section linking Areas 7 and 8. Their clustering (within just a few centimetres) suggests an *in situ* group and the one specific type, a burin, is most satisfactorily placed in the Mesolithic (Chapter 5). Furthermore, the overlying layer 88 is cut by channel action which pre-dates a complex set of silts constituting parcel 2; some of these silts are dated by various means to the 4th millennium cal BC, thereby again suggesting a Mesolithic or earliest Neolithic accumulation for parcel 1A. A final piece of evidence comes from a radiocarbon determination of 4690 ± 110 BP (HAR-6133) obtained from a pile (A8 3B) in a second cluster of three lying 3.7 m to the south-west of the group or line already discussed. In a similar way the bases of these timbers had remained *in situ*, but an unknown upper portion had been destroyed by the contractor. The point of 3B was not far below the drawn section and the pile must therefore have been driven through most or all of layer 93, which would therefore probably predate 3100 cal BC (Chapter 20). Layers 85–87 cannot be related closely to any of the dating evidence, unless it is assumed that they post-date the northern pile cluster and this in turn is assumed to have been contemporary with A8 3B.

Layers 83–84, however, almost certainly post-date all of the piles, including the radiocarbon-dated example, since the one-metre thick bed of dense gravel (84) would have been impenetrable to pile driving and there were no signs of large holes having been dug through it. In fact 84 can probably be broadly equated with an event that left its mark more widely on the site. A bed of dense gravel has been found in later excavations to the north-west; it totally caps a Neolithic land surface that in turn sits on top of silt similar to context 88. The gravel bed is currently dated to the end of the Neolithic or Early Bronze Age. On this basis 83 is likely to equate with part of the long period of alluviation during the 2nd millennium BC represented by, for example, layer 38 in Area 6 (Chapter 2). If this late dating is correct contexts 83 and 84 may not be appropriately grouped with parcel 1 deposits; they are therefore designated parcel 1B. To the south-west layer 83 and the whole of parcel 1 were truncated by channel erosion. That channel then had time to choke (parcel 3) before Late Bronze Age occupation began shortly after 1000 cal BC.

There must be a strong possibility that the piles recorded in Area 8 belonged to one or more Middle Neolithic structures, but the form taken cannot be guessed at from the sections alone. There was certainly occupation of the higher banks at this time nearby and two soil marks (?truncated) which appear to cut into 88 (Area 7, section SA5) could conceivably represent such activity, as might a patch of burnt clay incorporated in river silts immediately to the north (73).

Alluvial parcel 2: Neolithic–Early Bronze Age channel fill/floodplain alluvium

AREA 4: CONTEXTS 114–123; ?AREA 5: CONTEXTS 140–145;
AREA 7: CONTEXTS 62–77   Figs. 7, 10 and 13

This alluvial parcel is also represented by Area 6 excavated contexts 38–42, which provide more detail on the formation and topography of the deposits in one part of the channel (Chapters 2 and 11).

This parcel divides into two main units separated by a phase of severe erosion. The earlier sequence, parcel 2A (64–77; 116–123) is basically channel fill, although there were undoubtedly gross changes in water flow. The lowest deposit (77, 123) is a bed of tufa, seen to be at least 0.5 m thick in places where sections were taken down through piles which penetrated the deposit. The stratigraphic relationship of this deposit to parcel 1 deposits is uncertain, for it could not be followed all the way to the parcel 1/2 interface. It could belong to the main flow phase of the channel subsequently filled with parcel 2A silts, or it could be a relict of an earlier system. Either way, the strong undulations in its surface seen in Area 7 might suggest a phase of erosion prior to the aggradation of channel silts. The tufa is dated only by its relationship to the overlying sediments, which are dated to the Middle Neolithic; a date close to the climatic optimum of the Atlantic period would be appropriate for this type of formation.

The main channel fill is a complex of interleaved silts ranging from fine clay-loams through to coarse shell-sand silts with variable but generally abundant organic detritus. Only a small amount of gravel was deposited on the river bed (72). As is typical of such fills, there is a general trend from predominantly coarser silts low down to predominantly finer ones higher up (66, 116). There is also a trend for the aggradation to proceed from the south-west bank in a north-easterly direction with time. Within this lateral drift certain 'standstills' or minor re-erosion phases may be identified in the form of successive river banks, each facing roughly north-east. Area 7 shows this best: starting at the parcel 1/2 interface, next is the dipping deposit of 68, then the interleaved and dipping sediments of 65. Area 4 also records similarly oriented truncation at the 116/119 interface. Lacking evidence from the intervening land, correlation between the two areas is hazardous; however, if 116/119 and 68 represented one particular bank line, it would be roughly parallel to the southern edge of the mid-channel bar in Area 6 (Fig. 16), leaving a 17 m broad channel between. In this sequence 65 could then represent a later minor gulley erosion through the nearly filled channel; the gulley itself choked with much coarser shell sand, perhaps derived from the still partially exposed bar immediately upstream in Area 6 (41).

The earliest stage fill represented in the parcel 2A sediments is therefore 73–76, deposits which sit against the southern bank of the river and may have trapped some Neolithic occupation debris in the form of burnt clay (base of 73). Close by, the shape of context 75b is perhaps suggestive of a cut rather than a natural feature. Layers 68 and 71 can be regarded as boundary contexts. Layer 72 should be a localised gravel bed of the river in its second (still flowing) stage. Overlying layers 66–70 should overlap to some degree with the Neolithic layers in Area 6 (40–41), but exact correlation is tricky given that channel fill sequences can change rapidly along stream just as they can laterally (across stream). Layer 66, however, may be broadly correlated with 40 in Area 6 and 116 in Area 4. Whether 70 could be coeval with the sand bar in Area 6 (41), or again with the similar grey shelly silts in Area 4 (117–121), is difficult to assess.

The channel fill components of parcel 2 (i.e. below 63 and 115) are fairly well dated by the Area 4B cultural deposits (as well as by Area 6 – Chapter 2). Most important are the cultural layers represented by contexts 117a, 118, 120 and 121 at least, although only parts of 117a, 120c and 121 were extant in Area 4B for hand excavation. These layers contained Middle Neolithic pottery, including many sherds belonging to a single bowl, a certain amount of flintwork, some retouched, two polished flint axes, much animal bone and brushwood. The horizontally laid timber or brush was not obviously worked, but the implication is that it was deliberately laid as part of human activity here. Indeed, the upper layer of wood shows signs of some preferred alignments, especially north-south from pile S1 to S7 and perpendicular to this. There was no indication that any hurdle work was represented, although it is not inconceivable that some of the rods were remains of the basal wattles woven round the upstanding piles to form walls. Mainly, however, the horizontal timbers in both planned levels are considered to be more or less contemporaneous material dumped in order to consolidate wet ground. This dump occurs high in layer 121, the two larger branches at the north-eastern end (one being L3Sa) showing in the section below 120c (Fig. 13). There was only a limited quantity of domestic debris (pottery and bone) mixed in with these contexts. A rather larger quantity occurred in the overlying and brush-free sediment, 117a. This material may in fact be associated with slightly later structures or dumps of material apparent in the section, but not surviving in plan. 120a–b overlaps the structure described and seems to have contained a lot of brushwood. There may be signs of erosion on the northern edge of the 120b structure, for 119 appears to truncate it, and this might explain a still later dump, this time in the form of a dense jumble of wood and cobbles, 118. This dump could almost be an attempt at creating a small embankment to keep back foreshore waves.

Branch L3Sa was submitted for radiocarbon dating but unfortunately no result was forthcoming. Two radiocarbon results exist for piles believed to be associated with the structure(s) described. At least 14 piles were found within and around the brushwood and enveloping silts. Their full upward extent, however, is not known and there is no strati-

graphic basis for assessing the level from which they were driven. The possibility that some were, for example, Late Bronze Age cannot be ruled out. At least four (S1–S4), however, can be assigned a Neolithic date on the basis of either the survival of stone axe facets or the radiocarbon measurements of 4630 ± 70 BP (A4S1; HAR-6132), 4920 ± 80 BP (A4S4; HAR-6128). It seems likely that most if not all of the piles in Area 4B were intimately connected to the brush raft and domestic refuse; indeed there is a certain regularity of spacing along line S3–S8–S9–S4–S6 and again along the parallel line S2–S1–S5, which is persuasive of their close connection.

Further limited *in situ* deposits were hand-excavated in Area 4A (121a) and they produced a reasonable quantity of cultural debris. Although the matrix was similar to that of 121 in section SA11, no physical connection survived the contractor's clearance of Area 4 and therefore no stratigraphic correlation can be made. Many sherds from 121a do, however, belong with some from 117a to form bowl NP5, thus suggesting a broad correlation. In addition to the more common cultural refuse (pottery, bone and flintwork), 121a also yielded a piece of bark, W4 (F89) (plates 17 and 18). This was recovered in rather fragmentary condition but was painstakingly reconstructed by Jacqui Watson to reveal one neat convex edge, inset from which she observed holes believed to be for stitching. Other remarkable finds were the two complete polished stone axes (S2 and S3). These were retrieved virtually from the surface and could have been disturbed by contractors' machinery. Area 4A, like 4B, had several piles penetrating the underlying deposit 123. None, however, is dated either by technology or radiocarbon.

Most of the piles planned elsewhere in Area 4 can be assigned with some confidence to the Late Bronze Age waterfronts and ancillary structures. These are discussed in more detail below (Chapter 3). Most of the cluster between the waterfront rows and Area 4A, however, are more likely to be of earlier origin.

The early suite of deposits in Area 5, contexts 140–145, are clearly remnants of an alluvial parcel which was dissected by and somewhat earlier than parcel 4, the Late Bronze Age river channel. They are most likely to be infill of part of the Neolithic channel/backwater system. They have most in common with the late Neolithic organic silts (40, 66, 116), but their altitude (11.35–12.00 m OD) is considerably lower, levels at which tufa was encountered in Areas 6, 7 and 4. The date of deposits 140–145 is wholly equivocal: they might represent bottom infill of a contemporary channel flowing along the north side of the Area 6 bar or of a later channel which cut into it, or they could even pre-date that bar. None of the branches in silt 145 has been radiocarbon dated. The planned group (Fig. 8) does not show obvious signs of having been deliberately laid, no working was found on the wood and no associated artifacts were retrieved.

As silts built up in the parcel 2A river channel, flow probably became more and more intermittent, to the point where continued aggradation generally only took place under flood conditions, defined as parcel 2B (62–3, 114–115). Flooding could also, of course, have caused erosion. This appears to have happened at the 63/66 interface, for certain dipping structures within 66, the earlier deposit 68, and perhaps also 65 seem to be truncated at this interface. In conjunction with a major hydrological event at this time there was a loss of surviving organics in context 63 and above; the conditions under which the equivalent layer to 63 in Area 6 (39) accumulated are described as 'perennially stagnant' (Chapter 11).

The sequence from dark brown organic silt to beige silt to yellow clay-loam is a feature of Area 6 (40, 39, 38) as well as Areas 4 (116, 115, 114) and 7 (66, 63, 62). These can almost certainly be regarded as simultaneous accumulations over a distance of at least 40 m and probably covering a long period of time. One difference in supposed parallel deposits is the sandiness of layer 39 in Area 6 which was not noted in 63 or 115. This sandiness could be a localised feature derived from the Area 6 sand/shingle bar (41).

Although the parcel 2B silts are bereft of cultural or other dating evidence, they are fairly well bracketed. On the one hand they pre-date Late Bronze Age occupation soil and the Late Bronze Age river channel (parcel 4), which date from approximately 1000 cal BC; on the other, they overlie not only Middle Neolithic material but also a Late Neolithic bone group from Area 6 layer 40 dated between about 3300 and 2600 cal BC (Chapter 20). Broadly speaking they may be referred to the 2nd millennium BC, although accumulation might have commenced a little earlier.

At the section line of Area 7 (if not elsewhere) the prior erosion phase seems to have cut back to the pre-existing bank line (i.e. beneath 75). This was subsequently concealed by flood silt 62, which, as has already been suggested, may eventually have crept over the higher bank presumed to have overlain 88, to be left as 83 in Area 8.

Alluvial parcel 3: pre-Late Bronze Age channel fill

AREA 8: CONTEXTS 78–82   FIGS. 11 AND 12

The sole record of this parcel is in the south-west corner of Area 8, in both the SW–NE and NW–SE sections (SA6 and 7). Different interpretations of the channel are possible relating to its alignment and whether gravel deposit 82 lay within or outside its fill. The latter question is difficult to decide without a deeper section. Layer 80 was noted to overlap 82 in section SA7; however this and overlying layers could merely have filled a hollow or trough at the edge of a channel trapped between the bank (parcel 1, 83–87) and a mid-channel gravel bar represented by context 82. If this was the case, the further extent of the river channel to the south would have been removed by later river action (parcel 5). Alternatively, the gravel of 82 could be viewed as one and the same deposit as 84, which later became dissected by a fairly narrow channel filled with deposits 78–81.

Although gravel bed 82 lay at a somewhat lower altitude than 84, the pronounced undulations at the base of the latter suggest that this phase of deposition took place on a non-planar surface, which may have dipped in a southerly direction.

A preferred solution can be given to the question of channel alignment. The possibility that sections SA6 and 7 just clipped the edge of a north-south aligned channel cutting across the western corner of Area 8 seems unlikely given the established history of channel courses on the site from the Neolithic on. Furthermore, the alternative roughly W–E aligned channel running right into Area 8 finds support in the deposits encountered in Area 2, 40 m to the southwest. There the silt immediately underlying the Late Bronze Age occupation was, as in Area 8 (context 78), notably sandy (Longley 1980: 5, layer 1), which contrasts with the clay-loam character of the subsoil in virtually all other investigated parts of the site. The Area 2 LBA deposits also, towards the northern end, occupied a slight hollow and it seems more than likely that this marked the top of a choked channel which ran through to Area 8 where occupation material 53 also sat in a depression. If the full channel (rather than a sub-channel) was bounded by gravel banks 82 and 84, it would have been around 8 m broad; however, the original crest of the southern bank prior to erosion might have been higher and set further back than the extant top of 82 (13.55 m OD compared with the top of the northern bank 83, 14.15 m OD).

Although the south-eastern face of Area 8 was not recorded, it is thought that it would have presented silts belonging to alluvial parcel 5, which would have truncated parcel 3 before it reached that section (see below). The interpreted channel occupied by alluvial parcel 3 obviously pre-dates the Late Bronze Age, but if the correlation of 83, which it cuts, with 2nd millennium BC silts elsewhere (38 etc.) is correct, then its infilling is likely to have occurred late within that millennium. This would seem to be the earliest of a sequence of channel fills on the southern edge of the explored site unless the parcel 1B deposits do represent a channel fill as discussed above. A succession of bank lines all on approximately the same alignment, but shifting progressively further south-east, can be reconstructed from Area 8 (parcel 5) and later investigations in Areas 11, 12 and 23 (Fig. 136).

Alluvial parcel 4: Late Bronze Age river channel

AREA 4: CONTEXTS 98–113; AREA 5: CONTEXTS 126–139;
AREA 7: CONTEXTS 54–61   FIGS. 7, 10 AND 13

This alluvial parcel also passes through Area 6, where it is represented by excavated contexts 4–30. Discussion of that Area should be referred to for more detail on the sedimentation process, environmental change, the impact of human activity and the date range of the channel fill, which broadly equates with the Late Bronze Age, 1000–700 cal

BC.

All the contexts listed under this heading can be identified as belonging to parallel sequences of silts deposited against a river bank on the south-western side of an ancient river. This north-east facing bank survived to be recorded in section SA4, throughout Area 6, section SA5 (north end) and section SA11.

It cannot be established for how long a river had flowed in this approximate position but a change in flow patterns seems to have caused aggradation close to the bank from about 1000 cal BC. This began with the formation of a gravel and sand bar on top of the basal gravel bed (113, 30, 61), the surface of which dipped gently from Area 6 (12.05–12.15 m OD) eastwards to Area 4 (11.90–12.00 m OD). The bar was a linear formation parallel to the river bank and lying just a few metres into the channel. It is represented by layer 25 in Area 6, 60 in Area 7 and 109–111 in Area 4. The bar reached a maximum height of 12.60–12.70 m OD in recorded sections and created a trough between it and the bank. The steady infilling of the trough is thoroughly described in relation to Late Bronze Age structures in Chapter 2. Correlations between the different sections (Table 3) are reasonably coherent given the distance along the ancient river's edge involved (50 m). These sometimes include minor deposits such as the sandy lens low in the sequence on the slope of the bank (22, 56b). In the trough coarse sandy silts (24/25 etc.) are succeeded by finer silts (20 etc.) before being sealed by a peat layer (9 etc.). This last occurs at altitudes (basal) of between 12.75 and 12.95 m OD in Areas 6 and 7. A deposit at the same level (12.70–13.05 m OD) in Area 4 (102/103) can probably be seen as a lateral equivalent, although one slope (102) was somewhat sandy. Above this there may be a slight discrepancy. Layer 101 preceded a sandy layer (100) and eroded occupation material (99/101 interface); the last two are best correlated with layers 7 and 6 respectively in Area 6; 101 therefore appears to have no equivalent in Area 6.

Area 5 is not so securely correlated to the other sequences. 132–133 may well be the original gravel bed of the river, therefore equivalent to 30, 61, 113. Its upper surface is lower (at 11.75 m OD) than further east (ranges from 11.90 to 12.15 m OD) and it appears to sit in a deeper channel which dips below the level of 11.40 m reached in excavation. Again the interface between 127 and 128 which should equate with that between 20 and 25 further east is 0.20–0.30 m lower. 126 seems likely to be a short-lived variation within the type of sedimentation represented by context 20 and 127.

The parcel 4 river bank reconstructed in plan (Fig. 16) describes a gently concave sweep from Area 5 in the northwest to Area 4 in the south-east. There is a remarkable coincidence between this curve projected north-westwards and the present course of the Colne Brook, a tributary that meets the Thames opposite the site. Clearly that stream itself may have shifted course since the Late Bronze Age, but the connection seems compelling and is taken as probable in the overall consideration of channel changes (Chapter

23). The parcel 4 bank was followed by pile rows throughout its recorded length. These foundations and associated structures are described later. Similar structures to the laid brush and branch structures in Area 6 (F155, F164) may also have occurred at an equivalent stratigraphic horizon in Area 4, where a concentration of slender rods was drawn in the section at the top of 106.

Late Bronze Age occupation soil

AREA 8: CONTEXT 53   FIGS. 11 AND 12

Outside the excavated Area 6 (32–37), Late Bronze Age occupation deposits on an old ground surface (rather than the slope of a river bank) were only encountered in Area 8 during the 1978 campaign. They had probably been truncated from the top of Area 7 and if present in the Area 4 section were not cleaned of spoil.

In Area 6 the underlying surface undulated between about 13.70 and 14.05 m OD, most of this variation being seen along the crest of the bank from north-west to south-east (Fig. 45). Area 8 shows a much larger amplitude of undulation, albeit over a longer distance, which is caused entirely by differences in the underlying deposits. The lowest parts sit in the depression still present at the top of the river channel filled not long before occupation (alluvial parcel 3) and fall to a minimum level of 13.47 m OD. From here the occupation material rises south-eastwards before being truncated by parcel 5, but also shows a sustained rise northeastwards over alluvial parcel 1B where the ground surface peaks at 14.30 m OD. The upper surface of the dark soil follows a similar trend, with levels of 13.65 m at the minimum and 14.40 m OD at the maximum. There is, however, a significant difference in the thickness and colour of the 'occupation soil' between the high and low ground, clearly due to different histories of formation and/or subsequent alteration. The thicker, blacker deposits surviving in the hollow can probably be regarded as *in situ*, whereas there must be a strong possibility that much if not all of the thinner, more washed-out soil on the higher ground has been flood-disturbed. This interpretation is strengthened by the 'trail' of finds which appear to have been redeposited from the higher ground across the top of the depression 6–8 m along section SA6.

A good number of finds, including burnt flint, pottery and animal bone, projected from the sections, especially from the *in situ* layer. Most notable was a large sherd of a decorated fineware vessel (P648). Underneath the occupation soil up to seven features of post-hole-like proportions were observed cutting into the subsoil. These suggest a reasonable density of cut features, perhaps similar to that found in Areas 6 and 2 (Fig. 45; Longley 1980: fig. 3).

The topographic profile underneath the Late Bronze Age soil in Area 2 matches that in Area 8 fairly well. At the base of the channel a level of 13.23 m compares with 13.47m in Area 8. To the south, it rises quickly to 13.62 m (cf. 13.55 m in Area 8), beyond which is a gentle rise to 13.88 m, a part of the profile not present in Area 8. On the other hand the northern bank found in Area 8 must have lain outside Area 2 to the north.

The dearth of features towards the northern end of Area 2, coincident with the deepest part of the depression, was explained by Longley as being due to a phase of erosion which preceded the midden dumping represented by layers 6 and 7 (Longley 1980: 5). Although such erosion is possible the evidence for it is not particularly strong. Firstly there is no sign of differential feature truncation as the topography dips from south-west to north-east. Instead the features just stop at F90 and F91, with the one outlier at F92. If anything, the best case for ground surface truncation is the apparent creation of a scoop underneath layer 3 and F31; yet again the associated post holes show no signs of preferential truncation and one can therefore only assume that platform cutting was contemporary with or preceded the main structure(s) here. Indeed four of the post holes were observed to penetrate layer 3 (Longley 1980: 8, fig. 5). It seems best, therefore, to regard the ground profiles underlying Areas 2 and 8 as little modified from the topography initially encountered by the Late Bronze Age occupants. The dearth of features at the northern end of Area 2 is likely to have much more to do with the functional organisation of the settlement. If Longley is correct in interpreting layer 9 as an erosion deposit, then this would indicate some scouring of the depressed area late in the occupation, or after it, but it did not scour to the base of the midden (layer 7) except perhaps at the very northern end.

Some information regarding the destroyed Late Bronze Age occupation deposits across Area 4 may be gleaned from the Area 3 records of 1975/6. The layer of dark earth recorded in the temporary floodway walls contained pottery and charcoal (Longley 1980: 11–12). Longley suggested that the material had a derived appearance; this might be true in part, but the discoveries in Area 6 not far from the north-western end of Area 3, where the layer was black and fairly thick, now suggest that *in situ* deposits were also present. Furthermore the plotted profile (Longley 1980: 11, fig. 9) shows a clear dipping away of the soil at the north-western end in a break of slope which coincides closely with the Late Bronze Age river bank. Indeed the lie of this layer recalls that of, for example, layer 8 in Area 6. It is possible that the cultural component of river channel layers was becoming less intense eastwards, either owing to erosion or for other reasons. By section SA11 in Area 4 there was no dominant 'dark earth' layer, nor indeed was much occupation debris in evidence at all.

At its southern end the Area 3 layer appeared as 'a very faint grey discoloration' (Longley 1980: 11). This end passed beyond Area 4 and finally faded out somewhere within the existing course of the M25 floodway. If it was present in the Area 4 section SA11 (above the cleaned and recorded part), it seems to have disappeared completely by Area 17, where the only vestige of occupation material may have been occasional charcoal fragments recorded in the sediments

between 13.10 and 13.50 m OD. There is probably little doubt that a Late Bronze Age horizon in Area 3 was severely eroded in its south-eastern sector; what is more difficult to reconcile with other evidence, however, is the impression that this eroded material was basically occupying its original *in situ* position because of the profile linking it to supposed *in situ* material further north. If this was the case then the underlying land-mass had not been removed by the later river action associated with alluvial parcel 5. This would lead to the interpolation of a very strongly concave river bank for parcel 5 which seems difficult to accept as it implies a very pronounced meander (Fig. 16). It is perhaps preferable to see alluvial parcel 2, on which Late Bronze Age occupation sat, surviving only just to the east of section SA11 with Area 17 and the south-eastern tails of Area 3 falling outside it, i.e. in the fill of parcel 5. The early deposits of parcel 2 (Middle Neolithic) were noted to extend for some 7 m south-west of drawn section SA11 and this gives a north-westerly limit to the erosion associated with parcel 5. However, the exact extent and nature of LBA occupation on the south-eastern tip of the site cannot be resolved by existing evidence.

Alluvial parcel 5: post-Bronze Age channel fill

AREA 8: CONTEXTS 46–52   FIG. 11

This parcel is only unequivocally documented in Area 8, though it must have extended into Area 4 in some form, as discussed above. Drawn section SA7 shows at the south-east corner a feature with a steep cut line (F2). Within the available section the feature descended to 1.40 m below the top of the Late Bronze Age deposits. It was possible to chase this feature down to a point where the base was almost level at 12.50 m, but it may still have dipped away further to the south-east. At the time of recording it was thought possible that this was a ditch or other large feature, but subsequent investigations in Area 8 and to the south and east convinced us that it was again due to channel migration. Section SA8 had a sequence of deposits which can be matched up closely with those 15 m to the south-west in section SA7. At the base was an orange gravel, probably equating with 82 overlain by lenses of shelly and organic silt (cf. 79–81?); these all relate to alluvial parcel 3 and earlier sequences and were cut by an erosion line dipping gently eastwards from a highest observable level of about 12.85 m OD at the west corner of the section, down to 12.45 m at a point 2 m east. Above the erosion line was an orange shell sand which may equate with 52 and a dark 'peaty' deposit which probably equates with 51. The latter is thicker and rose a little higher (top at 13.05 m OD) than in F2 (cf. 12.70 m), but in both cases it is immediately overlain by a thin orange sand lens, 50. This is overlain by pale sand, probably 49, at the east end and elsewhere by a light brown clayey silt with lenses of charcoal flecks which corresponds well to the eroded occupation horizon 47. As in F2 this is interlinked with a gravel deposit, 48; in section SA8 the gravel deposit actually tapers into 47 instead of meeting it at a point. The gravel was seen to thicken to over 40 cm depth towards the corner of the section and was identified as having a similar thickness in section SA9. The sequence continues with a thick deposit of pale yellow sand, as 46 in F2.

The steep erosion scarp of F2 was not present in section SA8 but probably existed immediately west of the recorded section. The crest of the bank is unlikely to have lain more than about 2 or 3 m beyond the corner. This allows the interpolation of a channel edge more or less parallel to the south-eastern face of Area 8 (Fig. 16). The line along which this would have continued towards Area 4 is open to uncertainty, as discussed in the previous section.

Dating of the parcel 5 sediments relies heavily on their interrelationship with Late Bronze Age occupation soil 53. It is just conceivable that this bank had cut back to the position observed and had begun to silt up during occupation. However, the nature of the interface lends much more weight to parcel 5 being entirely later than 53. The latter deposit and an underlying post-hole appear to be quite abruptly terminated by F2 whilst the trail of soil (47) spilling into the channel from 53 has a distinctly paler, washed-out character. That this is indeed an erosion deposit may be put into good context by the associated gravel bed 48, which implies a high water-energy event as a likely cause of cutting back and perhaps also some over-bank scouring. The gravel of bed 48 could in part have come from the under-bank gravel body, 82.

It cannot be ascertained how much later than occupation this channel activity took place, especially since the overlying alluvium 45 remains undated. The only find made in parcel 5 silts was an unworked shed antler. Obviously there would be a high risk of residuality in this context.

Alluvial parcel 6: post-Bronze Age alluvium

AREA 8: CONTEXT 45   FIGS. 11 AND 12

A fairly thick deposit of flood plain alluvium (45) was recorded sealing the Late Bronze Age deposits in Area 8, as had been the case in Area 2. Its thickness, including the modern turf, varied between 0.42 m and 1.06 m in Area 8, or 0.45 m and 0.70 m in Area 2. The modern (pre-bridge) ground surface undulated a little, apparently still respecting the course of the parcel 3 channel! The lowest points were 14.45 m OD in Area 2 and 14.55 m OD in Area 8. The highest points were 14.65 m and 14.95 m OD respectively, in both cases to the south of the depression.

Although there appears to have been some scouring of the occupied site towards the end of the occupation or fairly soon afterwards (e.g. Area 6, p. 66), it cannot be assumed that this would have acted evenly across the full 2 hectare area. Neither can it be assumed that the accretion of alluvium would have begun soon after. Occasional Roman sherds have been retrieved (subsequent to 1978) from on or in the LBA deposits and this might suggest that parts of the site at least received no significant covering of alluvium prior to Roman times, thus allowing these sherds to be worked down into the soil profile.

It seems probable on the evidence of Area 3 that the Late Bronze Age occupation surface may also have been well covered by alluvium until recently at the north-eastern edge of the site. The overburden shown (Longley 1980: 11, fig. 9) may, however, include some modern make-up. At the time of excavation alluvium had virtually all been removed from Area 6 by the A30 floodway and other disturbances associated with the first bridge construction.

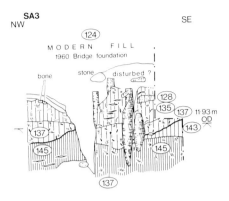

Fig. 7a Area 5: salvage section SA3.

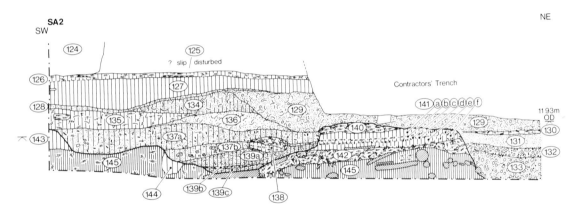

Fig. 7b Area 5: salvage section SA2.

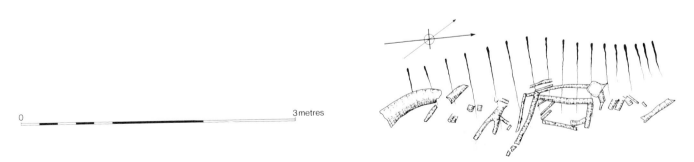

0 ————————————— 3metres

Fig. 8 Area 5: salvage plan SA1 of branches in alluvial parcel 2.

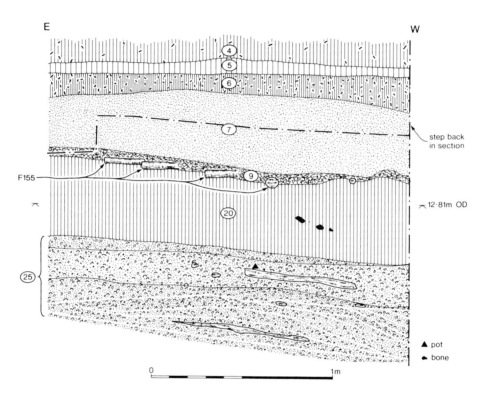

Fig. 9 Area 6: part of salvage section SA4 to show branch structure F155 and overlying deposits.

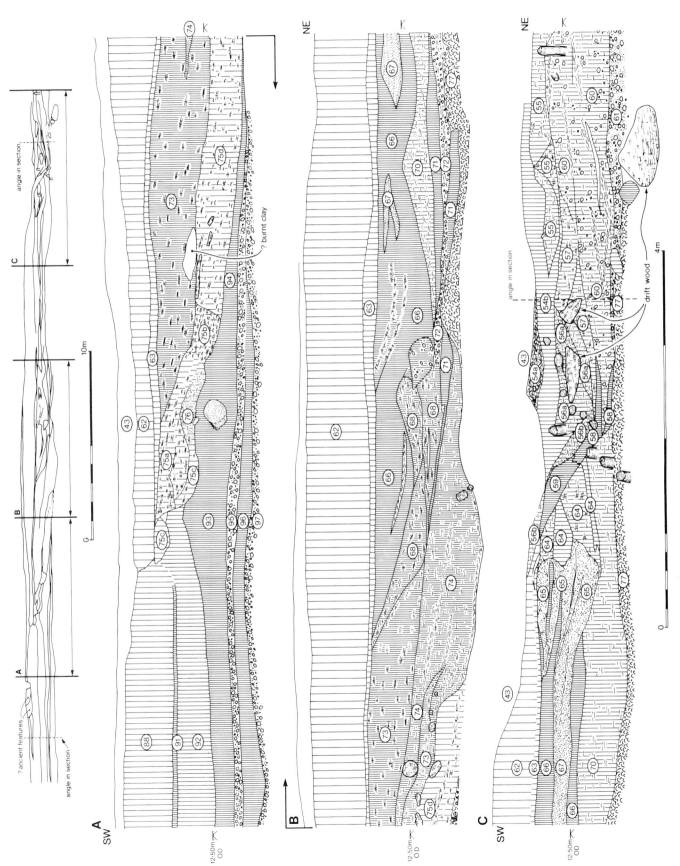

Fig. 10 Area 7: key drawing of salvage section SA5 and full drawing of the three stretches marked there.

36

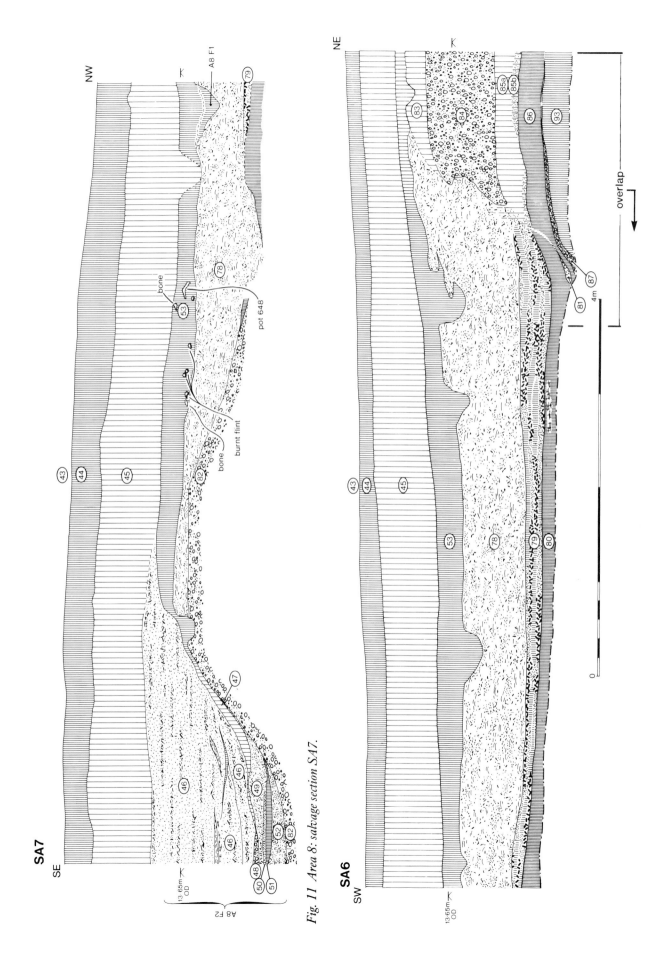

Fig. 11 Area 8: salvage section SA7.

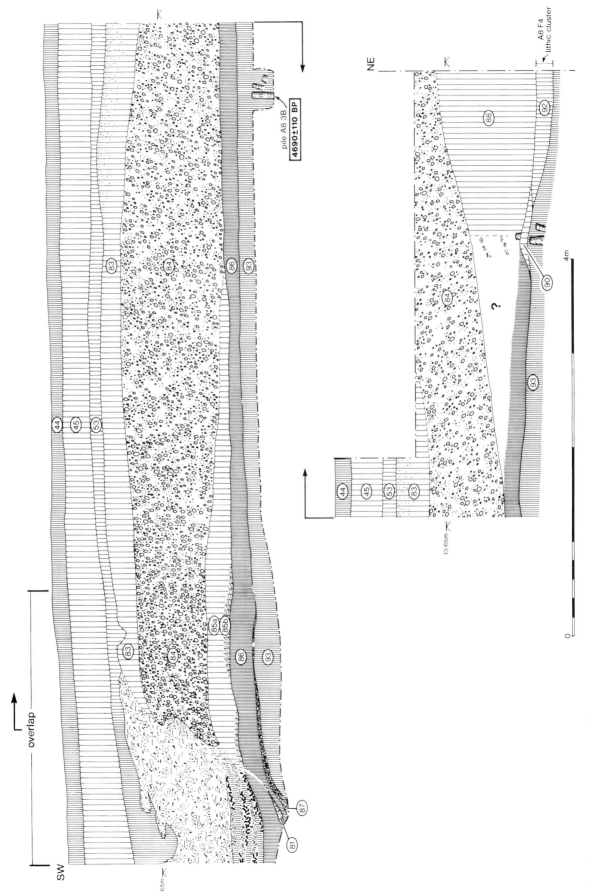

Fig. 12 Area 8: salvage section SA6.

Labels within figure: SW, overlap, 13·65m, 44, 45, 53, 83, 84, 85a, 85b, 86, 93, 87, 81, K, pile A8 3B, 4690±110 BP, NE, K, A8 F4 lithic cluster, 88, 92, 90, 84, ?, 93, 44, 45, 53, 83, 13·65m, 0, 4m

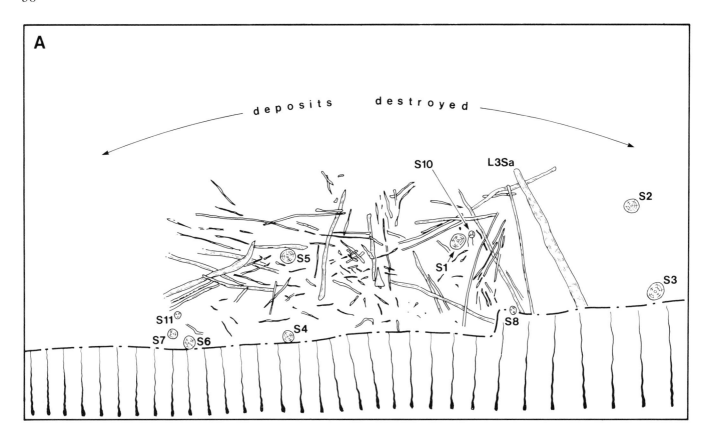

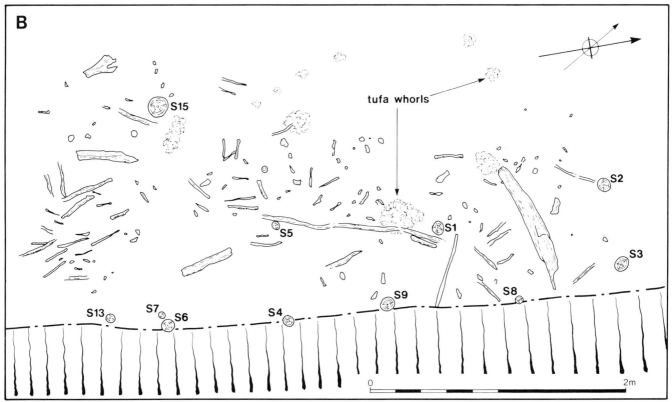

Fig. 15 Area 4B: plans of piles and horizontal timbers at two levels during the excavation of in situ *Neolithic deposits: a) upper level, within layer 120; b) lower level, after most horizontal timbers lifted, layer 121.*

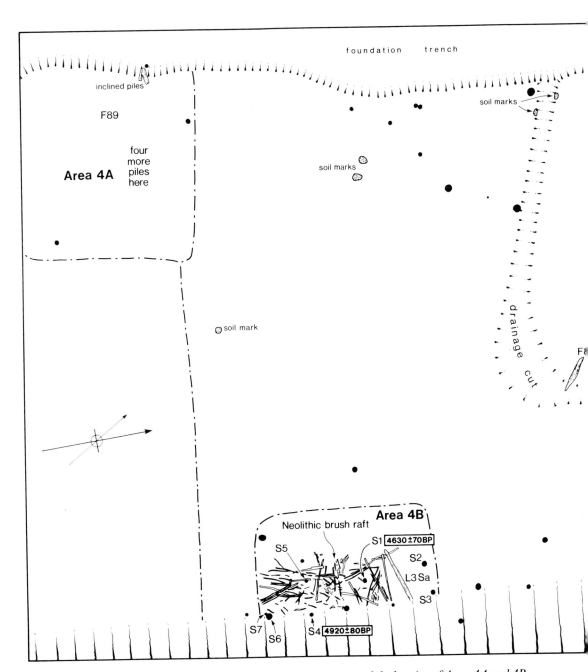

NE

c 12 60m
OD

foundation   trench

inclined piles

F89

Area 4A

four
more
piles
here

soil marks

soil marks

drainage cut

F8

soil mark

Area 4B

Neolithic brush raft

S5

S1 4630±70BP

S2

L3 Sa

S3

S7

S6

S4 4920±80BP

Fig. 14 Area 4: salvage plan showing piles truncated by contractors and the location of Areas 4A and 4B.

Fig. 13

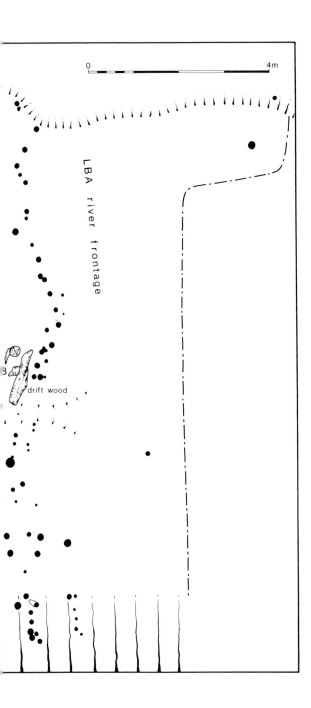

0   4m

LBA river frontage

drift wood

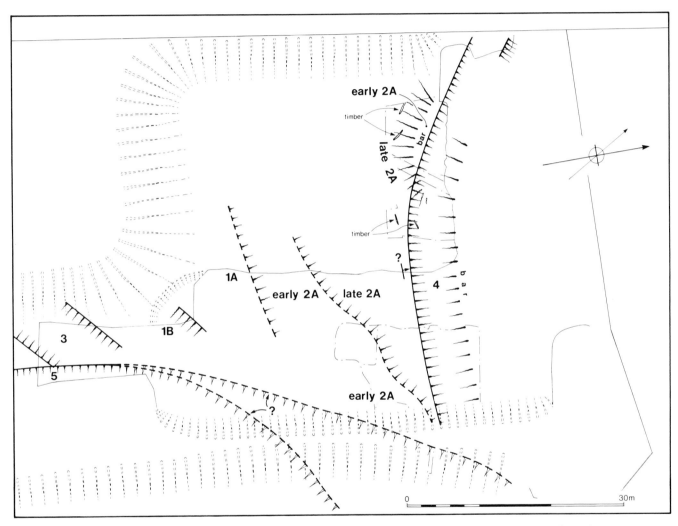

Fig. 16 Interpretative plan showing major topographic features in the prehistoric flood-plain deposits at Runnymede Bridge.

Table 2: Summary of all layer-type contexts recorded in the 1978 campaign.

Published contexts	Layers as excavated	Colour/matrix	Extent	Finds	Relationships, comments, interpretation
AREA 6: EXCAVATION *Overburden and cleaning*					
1	1	Mixed	Mainly tr.1	Yes	Surface cleaning after machine removal of rubble overburden; possibly disturbed tops of contexts 4, 31 & 35a.
2	2	Very variable	Northern edge of tr.1 and main baulk	Yes	Rigorous cleaning of contractor's step along northern strip of Area 6 and section 1 standing above it; cuts across all of the upper channel fill.
3	3	Mixed	Most of tr.2	Yes	Machine excavation of back-filled A30 floodway channel and subsequent hand cleaening of base and walls; cuts through LBA and earlier silts.
Late Bronze Age river channel – upper deposits					
4	4	Light grey-brown clay-loam; sparse charcoal flecks; tapers out and upwards towards SW	Tr.1 & 2	Fair amount of weathered prehistoric material	Top deposit of river channel sequence in north-east part of Area 6; above context 5 – boundary diffuse; post-LBA flood silt with redeposited artifacts.
5	6	Beige slightly sandy clay-loam, paler than 4; gently inclined	Tr.1 & 2	Small quantity of weathered prehistoric material	Above context 6; post-LBA flood silt incorporating a little material scoured off occupation surface.
6	7	Grey-brown clay-loam with shell and charcoal	Tr.1 & 2	Fairly dense finds	Above contexts 7 & 8 – some merging at W end with 8, but still distinctly paler; no cut features recognised in association, therefore likely flood silt with redeposited finds deriving from late deposits no longer present on the bank.
7	9	Pale yellow loose sandy silt; inclined layer, tapered out part way up slope of bank; some lensing in thickest part (tr.2) including localised charcoal band and charred branch (F101)	Tr.1 & 2	Very sparse finds throughout	Above 8a & 9; seals dog skeleton F111/111A and rotted stumps of outer row piles; flood silt post dating demise of waterfront 2.
8a	– upper part 10 – 14A	Dark grey-black sandy clay-loam with much charcoal; some variation in characteristics	Tr.1 & 2 Tr.2 confined by outer pile row	Very dense finds, unweathered and including many joining potsherds and two articulated stretches of vertebra in silt 'trap' immediately behind inner pile row (stumps); many finds only attributable to context 8 generally.	Above 8b & 10; during excavation 8a was not distinguishable from 8b on the upper slope where context 10 did not intervene; localised part of base lying in a depression behind outer piles in tr.2 was excavated as separate layer (14A); occupation soil resulting from midden dumping; late in lifetime of waterfront 2; thin scatter of finds on top of context 9 may equate with 8a.
8b	– lower part 10 – 14 – 14B	Dark grey-black sandy clay-loam with much charcoal	Tr.1 & 2; upper slope Tr.1 lower slope Tr.2 lower slope	Very dense finds including joining potsherds many finds only attributable to context 8 generally.	Above 14a & 14b; on upper slope not distinguishable from 8a during excavation; context 12 is lateral extension of 8b N of inner pile row; occupation soil resulting from midden dumping late in lifetime of waterfront 1.

Table 2: Summary of all layer-type contexts recorded in the 1978 campaign.—*(continued)*

Published contexts	Layers as excavated	Extent	Colour/matrix	Finds	Relationships, comments, interpretation
9	18	Tr.2; exclusively N of outer pile row, which it abutts	Dark brown fibrous peat with sandy patches, charcoal and woody fragments	Relatively modest quantity with notable dog skeleton embedded in top (tr.2) and wooden ladle (W1)	Above 20c; barely extant in tr.1 above 20a; abutts outer pile row; seals timber structure F164 which projects out of 20c; peat pool developing late in lifetime of waterfront 2; situated in longitudinal depression.
10	13	Tr.1 & 2; behind inner pile row	Pale yellow sandy silt; thin lens, thickens eastwards	Very few	Above 8b; lateral extension to N of inner pile row is undoubtedly context 11; river silt trapped behind piles during lifetime of waterfront 2.
11	27	Tr.1 & 2; between pile rows	Pale yellow sandy silt with yellow-green streaks	Few	Above 12; lateral extension of context 10; abutts southern face of outer pile row, apparently having been truncated on N side; interpretation as for context 10.
12	28	Tr.1 & 2; between pile rows	Grey sandy clay-loam with charcoal flecks and localised concentrations	Moderate density	Above 13, 20b, 20c; lateral extension north of inner pile row of context 8b, but drops in small step coincident with inner pile row; may have been a small tail extending beyond outer row but this not differentiated from 20 in excavation; interpretation as for 8b.
12a	28	Tr.2 around outer row piles	As 12.		Merges with 12; mixed silt around outer row piles.
13	38	Tr.1; between pile rows	Yellow-beige sandy clay-loam	Few	Localised lens above 20b; probable lateral extension N of inner pile row of 14a; probably truncated N of outer row; interpretation as for 14a.
14a	– 20 – uppermost 20	Tr.1 Tr.2; S of pile rows extends to crest	Pale yellow sandy silt, generally clean but with localised patches of charcoal flecks, some representing tops of pile pipes; other inner row pile tops appearing as hollows	Few; finds in tr.2 not attributable more closely than 14a-c	Above 14b; distinction with 14b in tr.2 poor and not made under excavation; context 13 is probable extension to N of inner pile row; last of series of 'clean' river silts belonging to lifetime of waterfront 1.
14b	– 21 – middle 20	Tr.1 Tr.2	Light grey sticky clay-loam with charcoal flecks	Very few; finds in tr.2 not attributable more closely than 14a-c	Above 14c; distinction with 14c not made in tr.2 during excavation; slightly darker lens at top of 20b in tr.1 might be extension of 14b N of inner pile row; river silt accumulating without significant rubbish behind waterfront 1 during its use.
14c	– 54A – bottom 20	Tr.1 Tr.2	Light yellow-brown friable silt	Few; finds in tr.2 not attributable more closely than 14a-c	Above 14d – clarity of interface variable; interpretation as for 14b.
14d	– 54B – top 40	Tr.1 Tr.2	Yellow-brown friable silt, with some charcoal flecks and yellowish-green accretions	Few; finds in tr.2 not attributable more closely than 14d-e/20c-d	Above 14e – clarity of interface variable; 20b may be extension to N of inner pile row; interpretation as for 14b.
14e	– 57 on upper slope – mid 40	Tr.1 Tr.2	Mottled brown/light yellow-brown friable silt with some charcoal; somewhat undulating	Relatively few; finds in tr.1 – 14e/20c, in tr.2 – 14d-e/20c-d	Above 22,23a; enters slot associated with F182 in section 38; silt contemporary with beginning of waterfront 1, perhaps associated with construction and incorporating upcast?

Table 2: Summary of all layer-type contexts recorded in the 1978 campaign.—(continued)

Published contexts	Layers as excavated	Extent	Colour/matrix	Finds	Relationships, comments, interpretation
14f	not hand excavated	Tr.1; section 38	Light grey	Nil	Localised lens within 14a; ?linked to 14g.
14g	not hand excavated	Tr.1; section 38	Grey	Nil	Top fill of F182, apparently merges into 14b.
14h	not hand excavated	Tr.1; section 38	Light yellow-brown	Nil	Middle fill of F182, apparently continuous with 14c.
14i	not hand excavated	Tr.1; section 38	Slightly darker than 14h	Nil	Sitting in slot entering F182; wedged between 14e and 14h.
Deposits filling F300 on lip of river channel					
15	19	Tr.1; F300	Yellow sandy clay-loam with charcoal and daub flecks; a little lighter than 14a–b	Few	Above 16a; grades laterally into 14a-b; inwash of river silts into shallow depression left on bank; character slightly different due to erosion of sides?
16a	upper 22	Tr.1; F300	Grey clay-loam with sandy patches and alot of charcoal; thick on western rim	Moderate number	Above 16b, 17; possibly weathered into F300 from dump of soil on side.
16b	lower 22	Tr.1; F300	Beige sandy lens at base of 16a	As 16a	Above 17; may be same deposit as 14c in channel, but there was a small gap between the two.
17	23,25A 26,29	Tr.1; F300	Mixed deposit, generally grey sandy silt with localised clayey lens and much charcoal and daub fragments	Moderate; large clods of burnt clay at very base more likely belonging to 18	Above 18; grades laterally into 14d/e; excavated as four layers, but rather mixed and differentiation generally poor; dumped midden material.
18	30	Tr.1; F300	Mottled yellow-grey clay-loam with charcoal flecking	Few, but noteworthy clods of bright red clay	Above 38; sat in base angles of F300; strong component of underlying natural, presumably initial weathering deposit.
Late Bronze Age river channel – lower deposits					
19	34, 36 37, 41, 45	Tr.1; localised 'midden' area	Very mixed deposit, generally friable grey-brown sandy silts; variation in colour and texture; much charcoal, daub and stones; distinct lens of charcoal within; some woody fragments	Dense finds, especially pottery; specific midden insect assemblage retrieved	Above 24; interleaves with/ grades laterally into 14e & 20c; excavated as five contexts of variable coherence and mainly pretty mixed; midden resulting probably from successive dumpings, but becoming diffused into river silts, especially at edges.

Table 2: Summary of all layer-type contexts recorded in the 1978 campaign.—(*continued*)

Published contexts	Layers as excavated	Extent	Colour/matrix	Finds	Relationships, comments, interpretation
20a	upper 35	Tr.1; N of pile rows	Similar deposit to 20c, but slightly lighter in colour; suggestion of lensing towards base	As for 20c	Above 20c; possibly abutted outer row piles; not separated from 20c in excavation; silt accumulation ?post-dating pile emplacements, but continuing earlier silting type.
20b	upper 35	Tr.1 & 2; between pile rows	Similar deposit to 20c, but slightly lighter in colour; suggestion of lensing in places	As for 20c	Above 20c, but not separated from it in excavation; possibly abutted both pile rows; although very similar to 20a there seems to be a mismatch in lens patterns either side of outer pile row; denticulate interface with 20c due to disturbance or fluctuating water table? probably post-dates inner row emplacement.
20c	- mid-low 35 - 57 on lower slope - mid 40 lower slope - 31, 32 - 64	Tr.1 & 2; N of inner pile row Tr.1; S of inner row Tr.2; S of inner row Tr.1; midden area Tr.1; S of inner pile row	Somewhat mottled grey-brown clay-loam with slight sandiness in places; woody fragments and wood pebbles, charcoal and shell	Moderate; includes near complete pottery bowl (P73)	Above 20d,25; interleaved with 22; abutted 23a at section 38 due to slumping; interleaved/graded laterally into 19; thick lens of silt marking change to finer silt regime, pre-dating both pile rows.
20d	- lower 40	Tr.2; S of inner pile row	Similar to 20c but with bluer hue	Few	Above 24,25b; abutted 23a;c likely silt of same character as 20c incorporating eroded bank material (eg 23).
21a–b	48	Tr.2; extreme N of Area 6	Loose shell-sand silt with some shingle and pockets of organic silt like 20c	Moderate	Interleaved with 20c as two major lenses; represents higher velocity discharge than 20c with which it is broadly coeval.
22	- 58A - 39	Tr.1} S of inner Tr.2} pile row	Clean pale yellow loose sand; thin intermittent lens	Very few	Above 23a; interleaved with 20c in tr.2; brief phase of sandy silt washed onto foreshore, or upcast from pile pits on bank (eg F182)?
23a	- 59 - 43, 70	Tr.1} S of inner Tr.2} pile row	Cleanish beige clay-loam, becoming more grey-brown to N; charcoal flecking	Very few	One deposit with 23b which together entrapped 24; abutted 20c/20d due to slumpage; redeposited clay from river bank disturbed by 'clearance' activity.
23b 23b*	- 69 - 42, 57A, 58	Tr.1 & 2 Tr.1; midden area	Beige clay-loam; variable charcoal contamination from 24	Very few	Above/abutted 27a; also abutted 27c in section 38; interpretation as for 23a
24 24*	- 65 upper slope - 44	Tr.1 Tr.2	Dense mass of charcoal within clay-loam matrix; includes burnt and partially burnt branches	Moderate, especially in midden area where 24* includes virtually complete jar (P33)	Mainly trapped within 23; lateral equivalent of 25b; dense charcoal all along slope of river bank, being product of massive burning of vegetation – ? clearance debris.
24a	- 33 44A	Tr.1; midden area Tr.2	Brown sandy silt	Few	Interleaved with, but mainly overlay 24; a little interleaving with 20d; possibly channel silt lapping slope.

Table 2: Summary of all layer-type contexts recorded in the 1978 campaign.—(continued)

Published contexts	Layers as excavated	Extent	Colour/matrix	Finds	Relationships, comments, interpretation
25a–h	– 50, 66 – 50, 62 66, 67 – 51, 53 56	Tr.1 Tr.2 Tr.1; midden area	Complex of variegated lenses forming syncline alongside bank and anticline further out in channel: white/yellow/grey; silt, coarse shell-sand, shingle and a little gravel; some lenses with much woody material (drift); 25b with fairly dense charcoal	Moderate – includes near intact fineware bowl (P44); finds from upper-most part in tr.2 were probably attributed to 21	Interleaved with but mainly overlay 27; 25b contains lateral extension of charcoal from 24; coarse sediments deposited early in sequence of aggradation in channel edge; likely part of bar.
26	52	Tr.1; midden area	Dark brown peaty deposit, some wood; thin localised lens	Few	Under thin lens of 25; superficially similar to 24 with which ends seemed to merge; possible natural deposit on slight shelf in the bank.
27a–e	– 49 – 55, 60, 61	Tr.1 & 2 Tr.1; midden area	Clay of rich bluey/greeny hues mixed with grey/brown; sand patches, wood lens and a little charcoal; distinct lenses of slightly differing character	Few; some/all may be pressed in from 24/25 above	Partially interleaved with 25; overlay 28/29 or erosion line of river bank directly; incorporates erosion material from bank itself.
28	63	Tr.1; midden area & section 38	Orange sand with some gravel; profile a little convoluted	Few	Above 29 or erosion line of river bank directly; only found in two localised areas – may have been present between.
29	—	Tr.1; section 38	Varied grey-brown banded deposit of silts and shell-sand lenses; profile a little convoluted	Nil (no hand excavation)	Above slumpage fault in section 38; almost certainly slumped part of Neolithic layer 41.
30	—	Tr.2; outside pile rows	Moderately heavy gravel in greyish sandy silt matrix	Nil (no hand excavation)	Lowest deposit reached in river channel away from bank; under 25; graded into silt body close to pile rows; actual bed of river during full flowing phase.

Late Bronze Age occupation surface deposits

Published contexts	Layers as excavated	Extent	Colour/matrix	Finds	Relationships, comments, interpretation
31	5	Tr.1; centre and southern edge	Grey-brown soil	Moderate density, but generally small and weathered pieces	Above 32a, 33a, 34a; below overburden and context 1; silt undisturbed by modern interference, but probably post-Bronze Age overbank silt incorporating eroded LBA finds.
32a	8	Tr.1; 3-5E/5-6N	Dark grey-brown soil; comparatively stone-free	Moderate	Above 32b; abutted 33a; *in situ* LBA occupation soil.
32b	12	Tr.1; 3-5E/5-6N	Dark grey-brown soil; comparatively stone-free	Moderate; includes pot group F295 in SW corner at 32a/32b interface	Above 32c; abutted 33b; *in situ* LBA occupation soil.
32c	15	Tr.1; 3-5E/5-6N	Dark grey-brown soil; comparatively stone-free	Moderate	Above 36 – separated by thin sandy lens; abutted 33c; *in situ* LBA occupation soil.
33a	8	Tr.1; 4-6E/8N, 5-7E/7N, 6-7E/6N, 6-9E/5N	Dark grey-brown soil; even distribution of stones – possibly base of resorting zone	Fairly dense	Above 33b; abutted 32a; LBA occupation soil, possibly minimally resorted by flood action.
33b	– 8 – 12	Tr.1; 3-5E/9N, 3E/8N, 7-8E/8N 8E/7N, 8-10E/6N 4-6E/8N, 5-7E/7N 6-7E/6N, 6-9E/5N	Dark grey-brown soil; stony – concentration of burnt flint cobbles at NW end (F298) and small concentration at 7E/6N	Dense; large bone and potsherds; tops of burnt clay dumps (F297); fill of F15 began to show	Above 33c; abutted 32b; *in situ* LBA occupation soil.

Table 2: Summary of all layer-type contexts recorded in the 1978 campaign.—*(continued)*

Published contexts	Layers as excavated	Extent	Colour/matrix	Finds	Relationships, comments, interpretation
33c	– 8	Tr.1; 6-7E/9N, 9-10E/7N	Dark grey-brown soil; moderately stony	Dense; large bones and potsherds; notable concentrations of burnt clay, F297; base of fired clay bowl F15 within layer	Above 36; abutted 32c; *in situ* LBA occupation soil incorporating debris from pyro-technic activities; deposit contemporary with main post structure.
	– 12	3-5E/9N, 3E/8N, 8E/7N, 8-10E/6N			
	–15	4-6E/8N, 5-7E/7N, 6-7E/6N, 6-9E/5N			
34a	8	Tr.1; 5-7E/10-12N	Dark grey-brown soil with blacker patch on south side; band of moderately dense stones round west and south sides	Moderate	Above 34b; arbitrary spit across the top of fill of F6 before this clear – undoubtedly cuts across different layers but these diffused by flood reworking.
34b	12	Tr.1; 5-7E/10-12N	Dark grey-brown soil with blacker 'ashy' band along S edge and lighter patch at N	Moderate	Above F6L1; probably cut 35b; arbitrary spit across upper fill of F6 crossing different layers which were diffused by flood-reworking; ashy patch probably represents top of F6L4.
35a	5	Tr.1; 3-4E/11-12N	Lightish brown soil	Moderate; finds not separable from 31	Above 35b; occupation deposits possibly altered by flood reworking.
35b	8	Tr.1; 3-4E/11-12N	Lightish brown soil with large lumps of fired clay and only moderate density of stones	Moderate	Above 35c; this layer evidently cut by F6 phase 2, possibly also phase 1; interpretation as for 35c.
35c	12	Tr.1; 3-4E/11-12N	Ruddy-brown soil with alot of comminuted fired clay	Moderate	Above 38; *in situ* LBA occupation soil pre-dating F6 phase 2 and possibly coeval with F300.
36	–8	Tr.1; 9E/8N 8E/9-10N	Patchy brown and black soil mixed with yellow clay-loam of underlying natural	Fairly sparse	Above 38; thin horizon at base of LBA occupation soils, probably incorporating early material trodden/worked into subsoil as well as some material from base of overlying deposit 33c; 32c separated from 36 by thin sandy lens.
	–12	9-10E/7N, 7-9E/8N 6-8E/9N, 8E/10N			
	–15	8-10E/6N, 8E/7N, 3E/8N, 7-8E/8N, 3-5E/9N			
	–16	3-9E/5N, 3-7E/6N, 5-7E/7N, 4-6E/8N			
37a	8	Tr.2; 11-13E/5-6N 12-14E/7N	Dark grey-brown soil	Moderately dense	Above 37b; below 3; *in situ* LBA occupation soil.
37b	12	Tr.2; 11-13E/5-6N 12-14E/7N	Dark grey-brown soil	Moderately dense	Above 38; overlay fill of pit F11; *in situ* LBA occupation soil.

Pre-Late Bronze Age silt sequence

38	17	Tr.1 & 2	Deep deposit of yellowish clay-loam up to 1.30 m thick; comprises bands bedded horizontally with slight variations in colour and texture – some at least due to post depositional alteration (Chapter 11)	Virtually sterile; one struck flake and antler/bone noted	Top surface cut by all LBA features; above 39; overbank flood silt – accumulation broadly datable to 2nd millennium BC.

Table 2: Summary of all layer-type contexts recorded in the 1978 campaign.—(continued)

Published contexts	Layers as excavated	Extent	Colour/matrix	Finds	Relationships, comments, interpretation
39	17A	Tr.1 & 2	Sticky beige silt with shell sand	Sterile	Above 40 – interface undulates gently, 40 having been previously truncated.
40	24	Tr.1 & 2	Dark brown, waterlogged organic silt with plant remains and woody fragments; minor dipping lenses of sand	A few potsherds plus *in situ* Late Neolithic butchery deposit (F125)	Above 41; slow fill in syncline above stream channel deposits.
41a-i	25, 68	Tr.1 & 2	Complex set of interleaving lenses of variable character in broad anticline/syncline formation; dark brown silt similar to 40 predominated towards top, while coarse sediments with sand, tufa lumps and some gravel predominated lower down; many plant remains incorporated	Moderate density – finds only attributable to 41 generally; worked timbers in secondary positions	Above 42; due to difficulties with the water table, not excavated stratigraphically; sand/gravel bar which developed in flowing channel and caught up rubbish from nearby Middle Neolithic activity.
41*	25B	Tr.1 & 2	As 41a-i	Few	Interface zone between 41 and LBA river channel
42	—	Tr.1 & 2	Tufa deposit	Nil	Lowest stratigraphic deposit recorded in Area 6; seen only in limited parts of deep sections.

AREAS 7 & 8: SALVAGE
Post Late Bronze Age alluvium and spoil

Published contexts	Extent	Colour/matrix	Finds	Relationships, comments, interpretation
43	7 & 8	Variable	—	Modern dump for embankments, modern feature fills and other modern disturbance.
44	8	Grey-brown soil	—	Above 45; buried modern topsoil.
45	8	Light grey-brown silt	—	Above 46,53; post LBA silt.

Post Late Bronze Age channel, F2

Published contexts	Extent	Colour/matrix	Finds	Relationships, comments, interpretation
46	8; SE corner	Pale yellow and grey sandy silts with lensing, much shell and possibly some charcoal; lenses of concentrated shell or woody fragments	Unworked antler	Above 47,48; upper fill of channel (?or ditch) edge which truncates LBA occupation soil 53.
47	8; SE corner	Brown clayey; lens dipping steeply down erosion face	—	Merged into 53 at top; lateral equivalent of 48 at bottom end; above 49; erosion deposit fairly rich in soil from LBA layer 53.
48	8; SE corner	Gravel lens	—	Above 49.
49	8; SE corner	Grey shelly sand lens	—	Above 50 and against channel erosion face.
50	8; SE corner	Thin orange sand lens	—	Above 51.
51	8; SE corner	Thin blackish organic-rich lens	Sample taken; no results	Above 52; likely natural accumulation of organic detritus.
52	8; SE corner	Grey sand	—	Lowest fill encountered in channel feature F2; sealed lowest part of erosion face exposed which appears to have truncated LBA occupation soil 53; directly above earlier gravel 82.

Table 2: Summary of all layer-type contexts recorded in the 1978 campaign.—*(continued)*

Published contexts	Extent	Colour/matrix	Finds	Relationships, comments, interpretation
Late Bronze Age occupation soil				
53	8	Dark grey-brown soil at S end, but grading into a paler and thinner grey-brown soil where it rises over gravel/silt bank 83/84 at N end	A few finds of pot, bone & burnt flint	Above 78,83; truncated at SE corner by erosion associated with F2; truncated at N by contractors; associated with several post hole like features cut into underlying deposits; almost certainly *in situ* LBA occupation soil. Late Bronze Age channel fill
Late Bronze Age channel fill				
54a	7; N end	Peat with woody fragments	—	Above 54b; presumably part of peat bed 9.
54b	7; N end	Organic ('peaty') silt	Timber projecting, apparently horizontally	Above 56,57; interleaved with 55.
55	7; N end	Shelliferous silt, many woody fragments	—	Interleaved into 54b; above 60.
56a	7; N end	Shell-sand silts with woody fragments, somewhat variable in exact character	Block of ?driftwood plus 6 timbers projecting – 4 probably upright; potsherd	Sat in hollow above 57,58,59, immediately outside post rows; apparently horizontal inclination of two most northerly timbers likely due to being pulled over by contractor's machines.
56b	7; N end	Orange shelly silt	—	Above 59; against erosion line of river bank.
57	7; N end	Shelly organic silt with many woody fragments	Lump of ?driftwood	Above 58,60; lag deposit on bank side of bar 60.
58	7; N end	Blue clayey silt	—	Graded into 59; interleaved with 60; rested against erosion line of lower bank.
59	7; N end	Brown organic silt	—	Graded into 58; rested against erosion line of upper bank.
60	7; N end	Complex banded body of silt with much shell and gravel, woody lenses and clayey lenses	Outlying upright post	Above 61; interleaved with 58; along with 55, 56, 57, it forms a bar close to the river's edge.
61	7; N end	Gravel in silt matrix; some largish stones; encapsulates clod of organic clayey silt.	—	Rested on base of LBA channel fill which had cut down to tufa deposit 77.
Neolithic – Early Bronze Age channel fill/floodplain alluvium				
62	7	Orangey-yellow clay-loam	—	Top truncated by contractors; above 63; cut by LBA channel (54-61).
63	7	Light brown clayey	—	Merges with 62; above 64,65,66,73,75 – the top of these having been truncated by erosion.
64	7; N end	Variable grey/brown organic silts with shell sand and woody fragments	-	Interleaved with 65; above likely erosion line into 70.
65	7; N end	Lensed deposit, predominantly orange coarse shell sand with brown organic silt bands	—	Interleaved with 64; interleaved at thinner end with 66, 67 - likely erosion deposit washing out from these layers.
66	7	Dark brown organic silt with some shell; incorporates north-dipping lenses of woody material	—	Encapsulates 67; above 68, 69, 70; interleaved with 65; low-energy open water deposit.
67	7	Orange shell-sand silts, some lensing; becomes greyer with woody lenses towards 65	—	Interleaved with 65; within 66.

Table 2: **Summary of all layer-type contexts recorded in the 1978 campaign.—(continued)**

Published contexts	Extent	Colour/matrix	Finds	Relationships, comments, interpretation
68	7; centre	Localised deposits of brown organic silt with variable concentrations of shell and woody fragments; partly mottled	—	Graded into 72; above lower part of 71; lay against erosion line into 73.
69	7; centre	Localised orange shell-sand lens	—	Above 70.
70	7	Grey shell-sand silt	—	Above 71 and erosion interface along top of 77.
71	7; centre	Localised lenses of brown organic silt	—	Encapsulated 72; above erosion interface cutting 74, 77.
72	7; centre	Gravelly and shelly silt lens	—	Within 71; ?graded into 68; with 71 and 68 represents beginning of second phase of channel fill probably after some erosion of phase one fill (73 and beneath).
73	7; centre	Brown organic silt with woody fragments penetrated by thin stake-pipe with orange-clayey fill – not necessarily ancient	Patch of ?burnt clay just above 73/75 interface	Interleaved with 74; above 75; upper part of first phase channel fill.
74	7; centre	Brown organic silt rich in shell and fragments, including branches	—	Interleaved with 73; above 77; at deepest part may sit on base of wood channel.
75a	7; centre	Light grey shelly silt with dense woody lenses	—	Above 75c, 76; ?natural detritus collapsed down, or accumulated against, bank.
75b	7; centre	Light grey shelly silt with much wood	—	Localised block of sediment between 75a and 75d, its sectional form suggestive of a feature fill (cut from 73/75 interface).
75c	7; centre	More clayey light grey silt, some wood	—	Lies against erosion scarp through 88 etc; leads into 76.
75d	7; centre	Light grey silt with shell and wood, some in lenses; includes branches	—	Lateral continuation of 75a/75c; lies over erosion scarp representing ancient river bank.
76	7; centre	Orange sandy silt	—	Localised deposit within base of 75.
77	7; north-centre	Tufa	—	Beneath 70, 71, 72, 74; top of deposit only exposed (above reduced water level); lateral extent strongly suggests this deposit formed early in the lifetime of the channel system filled by 62–76.

Pre-Late Bronze Age channel fill

Published contexts	Extent	Colour/matrix	Finds	Relationships, comments, interpretation
78	8	Pale yellow shell-sand silt	Sterile, except for isolated patch of 'occupation' material with charcoal and struck flake – likely LBA feature base	Beneath 53; above 79; upper fill of channel; possibly the same deposit as underlay LBA levels in Area 2 to SW.
79	8	Lenses of dirty sand and organic silt; layer thickened to N where it sat in slight hollow	—	Above 80.
80	8	Dark brown organic silt with localised dense lens of wood fragments	—	Enclosed 81; lowest fill encountered in channel which cut 82 on S, 83 and below on N; former erosion scarp gentle, latter steep.
81	8	Shingle lens	—	Within 80; dipped down from steep erosion line, presumably eroded material from layer 84.
82	8; S end	Gravelly deposit	—	Top only exposed in section; cut by two channel systems (46–52, 78–81); possible outlying relict of layer 84.

Table 2: **Summary of all layer-type contexts recorded in the 1978 campaign.—(continued)**

Mesolithic – Middle Bronze Age alluvium

83	8; N end – centre	Light brown clay-loam, upper part towards N was more sandy	—	Below 53; above 84; truncated by channel 78–81; likely equates with 2nd millennium BC floodplain silt elsewhere on site (eg 38 in Area 6).
84	8; N end – centre	Orangey dense gravel in silt; thick deposit lain above slight hollow	—	Above 85, 86, 88; likely deposited after hollow scoured through underlying sequence; could be same as gravel bed found in subsequent excavations to W and now dated to circa EBA.
85	8; centre	Yellow silt (85a), with localised white sandy silt at base (85b)	—	Above 86; at N end, where probably truncated, it merged into 84
86	8; N end – centre	Brown clayey silt with woody fragments; mixed blue/brown close to interface with later, but superficially similar channel fill 80	—	Above 87,93; unclear relationship at N end – possibly met 88 at apparent pile line; clusters of woody flecks suggest rotted tops of further piles behind those exposed at foot of inclined section.
87	8; centre	Black-brown wood/peat lens	—	Above 93; mainly *in situ*, S end eroding out into later deposit 80.
88	8; N end	Crumbly orange silt; two possibly ancient features penetrate top (A7), one with silty sand fill, other with 'burnt' clay and wood"	—	Above 91,92; truncated by modern disturbance; top of alluvial silt body truncated by channel action to S (fill 84) and N (fills 62-76); uncertain relationship to 86; likely equates with silt found under Middle Neolithic occupation in subsequent excavations.
89	7; S end	Lens of ?manganese rich silt	—	Within 88.
90	8; N end	Light coloured silt lens immediately surrounding vertical wooden members	—	Under 86,88; above 93; ?lateral extension of 92.
91	7; S end	Thin pale grey horizon	Tight cluster of lithic finds picked from short section between Areas 7 & 8 from layer 91 or 92	Above 92; possible standstill or soil development phase; likely Mesolithic date.
92	7; S end	Orange-grey to brown silt		Above 93; appears to sit in shallow hollow.
93	8; N end – centre	Blue/grey clayey silt with woody flecks	Piles projected from this layer in inclined section	Above 95; graded into 94.
94	7; S end	Brown silt at extreme N end of 93	—	Above 95; probably 93 reworked/altered by later channel action.
95	7; S end	Thin layer of medium-sized gravel	—	Above 96.
96	7; S end	Brown clayey silt with some woody flecks	—	Above 97.
97	7; S end	Gravel	—	Lowest stratigraphic horizon encountered in 1978 campaign; top only exposed in section.

AREA 4: SALVAGE

Late Bronze Age channel fill

98	4; N end	Light coloured clayey silt	—	Above 99; uppermost channel fill recorded in Area 4.
99	4; N end	Grey-brown clayey silt	—	Above 100,101.
100	4; N end	Light yellow sandy silt forming lens down slope of river bank; tails out into a thin band of stones and charcoal flecks at 99/101 interface	—	Above 101,102.
101	4; N end	Grey-brown organic silt	—	Above 102,103.

Table 2: Summary of all layer-type contexts recorded in the 1978 campaign.—(continued)

Published contexts	Extent	Colour/matrix	Finds	Relationships, comments, interpretation
102	4; N end	Shell-sand silt with many woody fragments, particularly at N end	—	Above 104,106; abutted 103; possibly two distinct deposits combined; gap in layer likely caused by former pile extension (since rotted).
103	4; N end	Brown clayey silt with dense lenses of woody material	—	Above 106; abutted 102.
104	4; N end	Localised lens against bank	One rotted pile pipe present	Above 105,106; abutted inner pile row as represented by rotted post pipes.
106	4; N end	Organic brown clayey silt with wood fragments including large pieces and concentration towards interface with 104	One pile of outer row projected	Above 107,108,109; interleaved with 105; abutted inner pile row at ancient river bank; horizontal brush-like wood at 104/106 interface could belong to structure similar to F164 in Area 6.
107a-d	4; N end	Shell-sand silts with variable concentrations of wood fragments; 107b orange	Two piles of outer row projected	Above 111, 112; appeared to enclose 'finger' of 116, presumably secondarily eroded.
108	4; N end	Orange shell sand with some wood flecks	—	Above 109.
109	4; N end	Grey shell sand with a little gravel	—	Above 110; may be lateral equivalent of 107.
110	4; N end	Thick bank of orange-stained gravel in a shell-sand silt matrix	—	Above 113; graded into 111.
111	4; N end	Gravel in grey shelly silt matrix	—	Graded into 110 and, to some extent, 112.
112	4; N end	Mottled blue/brown sticky silts	—	Graded into 111; above 113 and lay against erosion line of bank.
113	4; N end	Large gravel in blue-grey clayey silt	—	Lay against base of old bank cutting through 114 etc; likely basal deposit of this channel fill.

Neolithic – Early Bronze Age channel fill/floodplain alluvium

114	4; centre	Light yellowish clayey silt	—	Top of deposit not seen (covered by spoil); above 115; truncated to N by channel system 98–113.
115	4; centre – S end	Beige clayey silt	—	Above 116.
116	4; centre – S end	Dark brown organic clayey silt with, at N end, small lenses of shell sand and woody fragments	One pile projected	Above 117, 118, 119 – apparently laid after this system had been unevenly truncated by erosion.
117a-c	4; S end	Shell-rich brown silts with woody fragments and lensing; lateral variation – 117a more orange, 117c very shelly	Pottery and bone	Abutted 118; above 119, 120; part of 117a hand excavated (as A4 L2); silt inwash sealing timber brush structure?
118	4; centre	Concentration of stones and wood forming small heap or bank	—	Abutted by 117c; above 119; probably truncated by erosion prior to 116 deposition; almost certainly an artificial structure associated with the brush platform, but unfortunately not excavated.
119	4; centre	Very mixed deposit, grey/brown shell sand and organic silts; localised shelly concentrations and many wood fragments	—	Above 121,122; interleaved with 120.
120a-c	4; centre – S end	Complex lenses of brown clayey silt with variable shell sand and dense bands of wood, much of it evidently brushwood, particularly at top of 120b; also some larger branches	Pottery and bone	Above 121; graded into 119; a little of this deposit beside section at southern end (ie mainly 120c) was hand excavated (as A4 L3); contained brush structure(s) regarded as consolidation material and *in situ* Neolithic debris.

Table 2: Summary of all layer-type contexts recorded in the 1978 campaign.—*(continued)*

121	4; centre – S end	Grey shelly sand with numerous lenses of small woody fragments	Pottery, and bone	Above 122, 123; mainly below brush structure; part hand excavated (as A4 L3).
121a	4A	Grey-brown silt with a number of gravel cobbles	Pottery, bone, flintwork 2 stone axes and worked bark (W4)	Above 123; isolated remnant apparently not disturbed by contractor, but not directly correlatable to layers in the main section; hand excavated (as A4 L1).
122	4; centre	Grey shell sand with wood	—	Above 123.
123	4	White tufa bed made of hard whorls	—	Lowest deposit encountered in A4 – exposed over virtually whole area.

AREA 5: SALVAGE

Modern and uncertain contexts

124	Mottled yellow/brown/blue clay with roots and flint cobbles		Very probably backfill of foundation trench for 1959-60 bridge (A30).
125	Light clay merging downwards into grey clay	—	Possibly in situ material disturbed and concealed by slippage.

Late Bronze Age channel fill

126	Brown silt band with dense woody fragments	—	Above 127; truncated to N by contractor's 1978 trench.
127	Grey-brown clayey silt	—	Above 128; truncated to N by contractor's 1978 trench.
128	Light brown sandy silt, thin lens	—	Above 129, 134, 135; truncated to N by contractor's 1978 trench.
129	Orange-stained shell sand with some gravel	—	Above 130; sealed relict silt mass 140 etc; may have graded into 134,136
130	Shelly silt with wood fragments or charcoal	—	Above 131.
131	Grey sand	—	Above 132.
132	Gravel	—	Above 133.
133	Gravel in shell sand	—	Lowest fill encountered in deepest erosion cut through silt body 140-145
134	Grey shelly silt with some orange-stained	—	Above 135,136; may have graded into 129.
135	Dark grey shelly silt with wood or charcoal fragments	Piles present within	Above 136,137a.
136	Light orange-grey shelly silt	—	Above 137a.
137a	Shelly silt with wood or charcoal fragments	Piles present within	Above 137b.
137b	As 137a, but with large wood fragments	—	Entrapped 138; above 139a.
138	Bands of peat and silt with wood lens	—	Entrapped within 137-9; apparently an eroded clod of deposits 140-142.
139a-c	Grey fine shell silt, with lens rich in wood or charcoal fragments (139b)	—	Basal fill of erosion gully into silt body 140-145.

Silt body pre Late Bronze Age channel – ?Neolithic

140	Very dark peat or organic silt with woody material	—	Above 141; truncated by LBA channel system (126-139).
141	Grey sticky silt with alternating lenses rich in woody fragments	—	Above 142.
142	Very dark peat or organic silt with woody material	—	Above 145.
143	Ruddy brown clayey silt	—	Above 145; truncated by LBA channel system (126-139).
144	Light brown clayey silt pocket	—	Penetrates 145.
145	Dark grey/brown organic silt with woody fragments and concentration of larger branches in northern half	—	Lowest stratigraphic context encountered in Area 5; branches possibly laid as consolidation.

Table 3a: Suggested layer correlations.

Brief description		Area 2	Area 7/8	Area 4	Area 6	Area 5
LBA occupation surface		3, 5–7	53		32–37	
	sandy silt			98, 99	4–6	
				?100	7	
	peat bed		54a	?103	9	
			54b	106	20	?126, 127
alluvial			55	?108	21	
parcel 4			56a, 57	107	24, 25	?128–131, 134–136
			56b		22	
	gravel bar		60	109–111	25	
	bluey clay		58	112	27	
	basal gravel		61	113	30	?132, 133
top of parcel 3		LBA subsoil	78			
	yellow silt		62, ?83	114	38	
parcel 2	beige silt		63	115	39	
	dark brown silt		66	116	40	
	tufa		77	123	42	

Table 3b: Concordance between as-excavated spits and published contexts for the occupation deposits on the levee.

Zone	Grid squares	5	8	12	15	16
				Excavated layer/spit number		
(i)	T1: 3–5E/5N 3–5E/6N	31	32a	32b (+ F295)	32c	36
(ii)	T1: 6–9E/5N 6–7E/6N 5–7E/7N 4–6E/8N	31	33a	33b	33c	36
(iii)	T1: 8–10E/6N 8E/7N 3E/8N 7–8E/8N 3–5E/9N	31	33b	33c, (except 7–8E/N: 36)	36	
(iv)	T1: 9–10E/7N 6–7E/9N	31	33c	36		
(v)	T1: 9E/8N 8E/9–10N	31	36	36		
(vi)	T1: 3–4E/11N 3–4E/12N	35a	35b	35c		
(vii)	T1: 5–7E/10N 5–7E/11N 5–7E/12N	31	34a	34b		
(viii)	T2: 11–13E/5N 11–13E/6N 12–14E/7N	—	37a	37b		

Chapter 2
The excavated stratigraphic sequence in Area 6

The Neolithic sediments: alluvial parcel 2A

CONTEXTS 40–42   FIGS. 17–19, 21–24

The recovery of Neolithic material at a low stratigraphic horizon in Area 4 suggested that it would be worthwhile searching for some corresponding deposits in Area 6. On analogy with Area 4 it was felt likely that any Neolithic material would be stratified beneath the deep yellow clay-loam, layer 38, underlying the LBA occupation surface. The A30 floodway passing through trench 2 of Area 6 gave an early indication of the depth of layer 38 and its evident sterility, in terms of cultural material, and furthermore bottomed into a dark brown organic mud, layer 40, similar to that immediately overlying Neolithic levels in Area 4 (116; Fig. 13).

Consequently, after the excavation of the LBA occupation surface was completed, the southern part of trench 1 and the south-west corner of trench 2 were taken down by machine to the top of layer 40. Excavation then proceeded by spade across the southern half of both trenches (Fig. 5) and by trowel once artifacts were encountered. Layer 40 itself seemed to be as sterile as layer 38 until the surprise discovery of a confined deposit of butchered bone (F125) and a pair of horn cores (87) close by (Fig. 19; Plate 19). Few other finds occurred in layer 40, whereas notable concentrations of cultural material appeared in the underlying and more variable sediments of layer 41. In general terms these equate stratigraphically and culturally with the salvage-recovered finds from Area 4. The pump-reduced water-table allowed excavation to a variable depth approaching one metre below the normal water table at the maximum (11.75 m OD). Over much of Area 6 layers 40 and 41 dipped away below this level, but in localised areas an underlying tufa deposit (42) was reached. This constitutes the starting point for describing the sedimentary sequence.

The tufa exposed in Area 6 could be regarded as the crests of an underlying surface reaching 12.00 m to 12.20 m OD, which corresponds well with the levels observed in Areas 4 and 7. Despite this correspondence, it is possible that some of the tufa 'peaks' in Area 6 were not part of an *in situ* bed, instead being eroded lumps thereof.

The deposits making up layer 41 are variegated bands of silt and sand which gave a systematic anticlinal topography. They are clearly channel sediments which accumulated as a shoal or bar in a stream. The axis of this bar possibly ran roughly from grid square 8E/12N to 12E/9N, based on the horizontal bedding of layer 41 in sections 35 and 38 (Figs. 23 and 24), although it was not possible to demonstrate a link between these respective deposits by excavation. This axis continues eastwards to the tail of the bar

which appeared at around 15E/7N in plan just below the surface of layer 40 (Fig. 19). The deposits can be seen to dip gently towards this tail in the near axial section 17 (Fig. 21) in the expected manner for a bar. They are described in Table 2. A reconstruction of the plan of the bar is shown in Fig. 16, from which it may be seen that its north-east flank was eroded away by the LBA river channel.

As already mentioned, most of the Neolithic finds were stratified in layer 41. Because of intermittent problems with the reduced water table and the consequent difficulty of keeping surfaces clean, the sub-divisions of layer 41 were not excavated in stratigraphical succession, but rather as a single unit. The concentration of the recovered finds, including those planned in Fig. 17, came from a low absolute level, between 11.95 m and 12.15 m OD, but being on the flank of the bar they may be broadly correlated with layers 41a–e. Timber F205 at 12E/9N, although at c.12.63 m OD near the crest of the bar, was nevertheless from a comparable stratigraphic position. On the other hand the few sherds of pottery from the north-east corner of trench 1 will have been in somewhat lower stratigraphic positions, perhaps 41g–i.

Archaeological material from 41 comprised five types: pottery, animal bone, struck flint, burnt flint and worked wood. This material was widespread in trench 1, but was sparse in trench 2. Given the nature of the enveloping sediments and the presence of driftwood in close proximity, concentrations of such material are likely to be the fortuitous result of natural agencies, rather than direct associations of human contrivance. The abraded condition of some of the pottery and all of the definite or possible worked timbers emphasises their subjection to water erosion. All of the material could therefore have lain in secondary contexts, although one should not totally exclude the possibility of an admixture of some primary discards in the assemblage. On this interpretation the artifacts and associated ^{14}C dates of 4930 ± 90 BP (F168); HAR-6131) and 4830 ± 70 BP (F202; HAR-6130) provide a *terminus post quem* for the formation of the deposits. However, the relationship with a date range obtained for layer 41 sediments by the palaeomagnetic method suggests that there was no great time lapse between use and final deposition. The results from column SS2 cover sediments 41c–41i and give an approximate date range of 4200–3650 cal BC (Chapter 21). The upper half of this sequence equates with some of the find-bearing layers in trench 1, probably those incorporating the two radiocarbon dated timbers. Since only the earlier halves of the calibrated radiocarbon ranges (Figs. 132) overlap the palaeomagnetic date range there is little scope for the timbers to be much older than the enveloping sediments. In the case of one timber (F202) there is unlikely to have been more than about a century between felling and ultimate deposition.

The distribution of finds in layer 41 has little significance beyond that of illuminating the hydrological conditions. Four substantial but slender timbers (F168, 184, 202, 205) and a thin branch-like piece (F204) are thought likely to

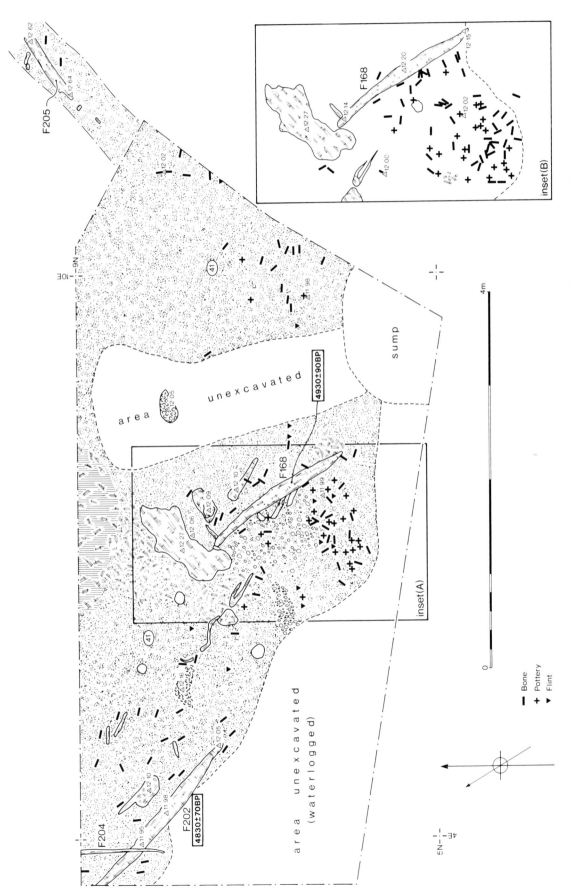

Fig. 17 Area 6, trench 1 deep: the distribution of Middle Neolithic finds within the upper lenses of sand bar 41. Inset B shows the concentration of finds immediately above those in Plan A.

have been worked pieces and in some cases were doubtless originally structural. All were recovered in near-horizontal positions, while three of the larger pieces as well as sundry branches were approximately co-aligned with the axis of the bar, presumably respecting the flow of the current. Only F205 on the crest of the bar was more transverse to its axis, perhaps having been caught high and dry on the sand bank when a flood abated. In this manner fallen trees have been observed to generally follow the stream alignment in fossil river channels of the Trent near Nottingham (Salisbury *et al*. 1984).

The definition of layer 40, which overlay 41, is based on increased homogeneity of deposit rather than a marked change in silt character. This does however represent changed conditions of sedimentation. Layer 40 is a thick deposit of a dark brown organic silt with some sand, a matrix which was also present in 41 interleaved with coarser sediments. It evidently accumulated under less changeable river conditions, probably characterised by slow-moving or still water (Chapter 24) and it built up around the flank and tail of the sand bar (41). In trench 2 it was extensive and may have lain directly on the scoured tufa surface (42), or otherwise incorporated eroded lumps of tufa (Fig. 18); it was restricted to the southern band of trench 1.

The accumulation of layer 40 seems to have coincided with a marked reduction of activity on the adjacent river banks as suggested by its poor yield of cultural material. However the one noteworthy find group from layer 40 may be confidently regarded as an *in situ* deposit in contrast to the layer 41 material. The context in question in fact comprises two bone groups separated by a metre and a half and lying at the same level, *c*. 12.65 m OD. At 18E/5N were two horn cores, while a clustered jumble of butchered bone debris occurred in metre square 19E/5N (Fig. 19). All of the identifiable pieces are cattle and the possibility has been advanced that they belong to a single beast of about three years age (Chapter 18). The spatial integrity and isolation of the deposit calls for explanation, for it is obvious that this is not the accumulation of casually jettisoned refuse over a period of time, but rather derives from a unitary event. A ritual explanation is attractive since the material is clearly not part of an occupation horizon or regular dumping ground, nor can it be viewed as the debris left behind at a transient slaughter site. Furthermore Done has pointed to unnecessarily great expenditure of effort in the butchering. Despite the confined distribution of the two bone groups there were no signs of any containers; in the waterlogged conditions of layer 40 even organic containers should have survived.

There were no artifacts associated with F125 and its cultural position can only be assessed from a radiocarbon measurement on some of the bone, 4270 ± 110 BP (HAR-6136). This gives a two-sigma calibrated date range of 3300–2580 cal BC and the find can be attributed to a Late Neolithic stage. Amongst the little pottery from layer 40 are four feature sherds (46–49), but they are not obviously dif-

ferentiated from the stratigraphically lower assemblage.

Early alluvial parcel 2 is covered by sample column SS1 for sediment and environmental studies. The lowest samples, 170–195 cm, comprise the uppermost lenses of the sand bar 41, including some at least of the Middle Neolithic artifacts. Above this level the samples appear to relate to a post-occupation phase. The important results on the environment and evidence for cultivation are dealt with in the environmental reports and summarised in the conclusions.

The 2nd millennium BC alluvium: alluvial parcel 2B

CONTEXTS 38–39   FIGS. 21–24

At some point after the formation of layer 40, it and the adjacent bar suffered some truncation before the overlying level (39) was laid down. This is most evident from the sandy deposit 41b (Figs. 21 and 23), which is truncated by the interface with 39, implying that it originally rose higher up the flanks of the bar. It may never have capped the bar, however, and reduction of its crest consequently need not have been very severe. The phase of erosion left a surface still undulatory, the height in Area 6 ranging from 12.63 m to 13.00 m OD. Some of this undulation could perhaps be due to differential later compaction of silts. Erosion has been noted at the same interface in some of the salvage areas and a major hydrological event has been inferred (p. 28–9). Across this surface was laid a pale sandy silt (39), the appearance of which contrasted strongly with 40/41, for there is a loss of permanently waterlogged conditions at the 39/40 boundary, although 39 was perennially stagnant (Chapter 11). An overall, if not marked, change in the local water-table is envisaged to have accompanied the change in sedimentation. The sand component of layer 39 included mineral sand as well as shell sand. The sand might have derived from the erosion of underlying deposits.

Layer 38 differed from 39 in the absence of a sand component and superficially it appeared as a homogeneous layer of yellow clay-loam. In detail, however, up to seven zones could be identified in this thick deposit, being characterised by slight differences in colour, structure and iron staining. These variations and their significance are dealt with by Limbrey (Chapter 11).

Finds from layers 38 and 39 are very few; some bone and a single struck flint flake. Dating depends on underlying and overlying deposits. In Area 6 itself, bone group F125 provides a *terminus post quem* of 4270 ± 110 BP (HAR-6136; 3300–2580 cal BC) for the 38/39 interface event. Subsequent excavations in Area 14 have now provided a later date, which nevertheless still underlies the 38/39 horizon: 3770 ± 60 BP, 2460–2030 cal BC (BM-2435; *Radiocarbon* 31, 1 (1989), 17). It is argued by Limbrey that the accretion of L38 was largely arrested a little before Late Bronze Age occupation began, which is best dated to around 900 cal BC. Accumulation of silt to a depth of over a metre took place therefore

Fig. 18 Area 6, trench 2 deep (eastern end): the distribution of Neolithic material and tufa humps low in silt body 40.

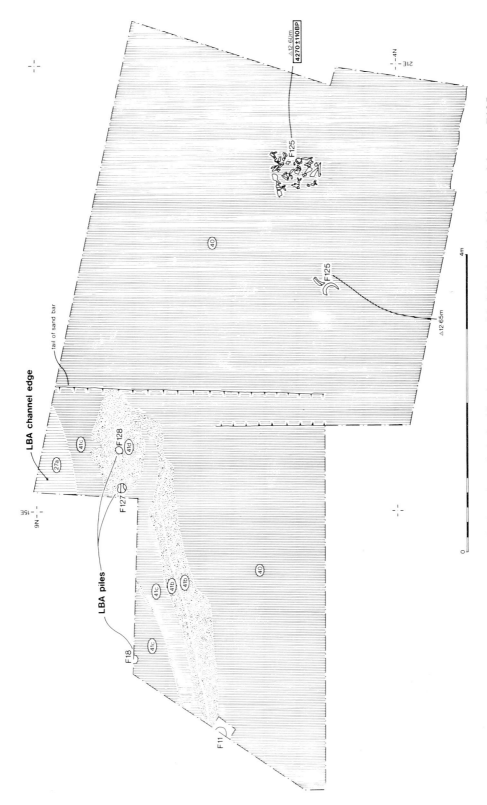

Fig. 19 Area 6, trench 2 deep: plan of surface high within silt body 40, showing Late Neolithic jumble of butchered bones, F125. The crest of the tail of sand bar 41 is also exposed.

during the second millennium BC. This is interpreted as steady alluviation due to over-bank flooding.

Late Bronze Age deposits: general introduction

Considerable quantities of rubbish and a large number of features were recovered in Area 6 in both topographic zones: the river channel edge and the occupied levee alongside. Owing to the good stratigraphy in the Late Bronze Age river channel, structures and material therein can be confidently phased, whereas less stratigraphic information is available for those on the dry bank and phasing thus relies more on circumstantial evidence.

Although the excavated area of the Late Bronze Age deposits is fairly limited, consequently limiting interpretation of full plan and function of structures, it has nevertheless been possible to identify a number of interrelated structural elements and to suggest in some detail a sequence for structures and rubbish accumulations.

The topography of Area 6 should be considered first. Fig. 45 shows interpolated contours at 0.05 m intervals based on a metre grid levelling in trench 1. On the fairly level levee this represents the surface of natural silt immediately underneath all Late Bronze Age occupation soil. The contours describing the steeply sloped river channel edge are not, however, for the base of the channel fill, but instead describe the layer 8/14 interface. In view of the fact that the lower ground on the levee, on the western side of trench 1, generally lacks deep features of post-hole and stake-hole types, it is possible that this surface may have been truncated during occupation. This could have left intact only the shallow bases of once deeper features. If this happened, however, it would appear from the stratigraphy described below to have occurred prior to the formation of the main occupation deposits and thus also the associated deep post-hole structures. An alternative explanation would be that this was an original depression which was quickly filled with rubbish early in the occupation so that features subsequently cut through these deposits barely reached the subsoil. Again, however, the layer evidence in Area 6 does not support such a history of formation. The localised hollow in the north-west corner of trench 1 was potentially due to human landscaping but must date early in the Late Bronze Age sequence.

Both layer- and structure-type contexts are conveniently treated in two parts. The layer systems excavated in the river channel and on the levee were entirely discrete and each poses different problems of interpretation. A similar though more overlapped geographical division exists amongst the structural features. The usual suite of post-holes, stake-holes, pits and miscellaneous scoops penetrated the dry levee and extended onto the slope deposits on the edge of the river channel where these were above the water table. In contrast, a pile-driving technique was adopted for the insertion of footings below water table in the river channel. Occasional piles were inserted into the dry bank, but only after the initial digging of pits through the upper dry silts. Hori-

zontally laid timber structures surviving in the waterlogged channel fill are dealt with in conjunction with the piles.

The Late Bronze Age river channel stratigraphy: alluvial parcel 4

CONTEXTS 4–30   FIGS. 20–25
General principles and excavation method
The channel bordering the north-eastern edge of the settled part of Area 6 has a complex multi-layer fill, which includes gravel, shelly sand, peat and predominantly a clay-loam silt. Although the latter accounts for much of the channel fill, slight changes in texture and marked differences in colour and finds densities give rise to a rapidly changing succession from top to bottom of the feature. In addition to stratigraphic and sedimentological evidence, environmental remains confirm that these deposits are for the most part laid by a continuously or seasonally flowing channel, only towards the top grading into over-bank flood silts.

The detailed sequence of silting, and therefore also of the contained artifacts, is thus relatively straightforward. However the channel silts also contained certain wooden structures, two of which comprise vertically set piles. These are more difficult to relate precisely to the layer sequence and the principles of correlation are described below. This leaves some small uncertainty as to the correlation of the radiocarbon-dated piles to the silt layers. Fortunately two other sets of radiocarbon dates are on stratigraphically bedded timbers tied in directly to the layer stratigraphy.

In order to understand the development of waterfront structures certain stratigraphic principles relating to pile insertion and their effect on channel silting need to be recognised. The stratigraphic horizon at which a pile was inserted will be determined only if a distinction is observed between the silts it had been driven through and those that had accumulated around the standing post. Differentiation might take the form of changed patterns of silting or the contrast between the presence or absence of drag-lines alongside the pile. Careful sectioning of many of the Runnymede piles showed on occasion these characteristic drag lines, which result from silt being drawn down by the physical contact with the driven pile. Where such features could be detected, it is a good indication that pile insertion post-dated the layer or layers exhibiting drag. In plan this can at certain levels produce a halo effect with a ring of different-character silt encircling the timber. This pattern was observed around piles in Area 4 which had been sliced through horizontally by the contractor (Plate 23). However, drag-lines were present only sporadically, and do not necessarily on their own allow individual piles to be positioned in the channel stratigraphy. Overall trends are clear for the pile rows and are supported by silting evidence, whereby the layers following 20c no longer show uniformity on either side of both pile rows. In some cases silts of comparable character do occur both inside and outside the row, but meet at the pile barrier at different levels (e.g. 8b and 12), so that it is difficult to explain deposition in the usual channel formation terms. In such circumstances, whatever the precise correlation of layers either side of a pile row, it is clear that the row was having a noticeable barrier effect on silting patterns and therefore that its insertion preceded the affected layers.

At the time of excavation a lot of importance was attached to the recording of drag-lines in the hope of phasing the piles. For this reason the method of excavating the channel layers was changed once the decayed tops of the piles were unequivocally identified, that is from the top of layers 14a and 12 (11 in trench 2), as recorded in plan (Fig. 26). At this level two narrow zones were strung out, each encompassing a pile row, and excavation then proceeded downwards in the three flanking zones, leaving walls of soil standing round the piles (Plate 21). This allowed foresight of the general channel stratigraphy inside, between and outside the pile rows before exposure of sections across the soil walls at each pile to look for drag-lines and other critical relationships. This method also had the advantage of keeping the piles encased in soil for as long as possible, thereby limiting drying problems. The strategy worked well, although the logistics of excavating between the two soil walls became problematic as the level went down. It was possible to section the soil flanking many piles, either individually or in small groups. All such sections were photographed and some were drawn. In retrospect, however, it is felt that this method of excavation obstructed the correlation of deposits transversely from bank to channel during excavation and this led to slight mismatches in the boundaries defined between layers. Although it is considered unlikely that any important stratigraphic information was lost, by continuing instead to dig the whole of the channel by layers one might have attained a better record of the morphology of each deposit in relation to the pile barriers.

The likelihood of different rates of silting inside and outside a pile row, even where piles are slightly spaced as at Runnymede, is easy to appreciate. Although the barrier is not impenetrable and would allow some silt-bearing water to pass through, the quantity might be of reduced proportion because the many passages were at right angles to the current. Except under flood conditions, when large areas behind the river bank could have been scoured, this restriction could have led at times to greater dumping of silt outside the pile rows. On the other hand, during an eroding phase there would be a reversal, with scouring taking place preferentially along the outer edge of the pile frontage. This latter process seems to have taken precedence in the middle silts at Runnymede. It should be borne in mind that the scouring need not be entirely natural; once a waterfront structure had been erected there may have been reasons for counteracting natural aggradation by dredging, thus maintaining standing water, albeit shallow, at the frontage.

The final principle to be considered concerns the disuse of the pile foundation. The stratigraphic horizon at which a given structure became defunct is more difficult to determine than that at which it was constructed. Regardless of whether superstructure was dismantled or destroyed, or just collapsed owing to rotting at water level, there is in all these events a possibility that part of the embedded piles would project above the contemporary river bed. Any projecting stumps would continue to have some degree of barrier effect on subsequent silting and the phase following may not differentiate itself from the phase of usage until the surrounding silting finally engulfed the projecting stumps. After this point the demise of any barrier effect should allow a natural unimpeded pattern of silting. This stage is seen in the Area 6 channel at layer 7, which extends unbroken across the pile rows. In the absence of other evidence this layer should only be taken as a *terminus ante quem* for the cessation of the pile structures.

A note should be made regarding post-pipes which survived at the top of most piles. These generally took the form of clear soil stains extending the preserved timber by a small height, but were on occasion complete voids above the rotted pile top (Fig. 26). It might be argued that the top of the pipe merely represented the preservation level in the Late Bronze Age, while the slightly lower surviving timber indicated the level of the minimum water table since the Late Bronze Age, and that the defunct stumps could originally have projected higher than either. However, it is hardly fortuitous that stratigraphic discontinuities recur around the pile-pipes but were never observed above them. The top of the pipe can therefore be taken with some confidence as the top of the stump surviving after disuse. The survival of pipes, either as complete voids or filled with overlying soil types, demonstrates the compact and stable nature of the enveloping silt matrix.

Before the waterfront phasing is elucidated in detail, some general observations are useful. All the waterfront structures excavated were constructed, used and abandoned at levels between the top of layer 20c and the base of layer 7. The absolute depth of the intervening silts is not great and might give the impression of a fairly short duration and a large measure of contemporaneity between different structural elements. Radiocarbon dating, however, suggests that this is a somewhat conflated horizon of significant chronological depth (Chapter 20). Weight is added to this through the detailed relationships of the variable silt beds involved. These show that the temporal succession in this zone is partly expressed by horizontal shifts in deposition, in a direction away from the river bank. This new pattern is intimately connected with the presence of the waterfront structures themselves, which probably further exacerbated the normal problems of discontinuity to be expected in an active river channel.

The layers in the channel may be horizontally bedded or slightly undulating, but they slope up at the now buried ancient river bank. The bank itself is fairly steep and, where simply eroded by natural agencies, can achieve a slope of between 40 and 50%. However, in places humanly dug features disturb the crest and associated slumpage at one point has given rise to a maximum slope of 70% at what is effectively a fault line (Fig. 23). The change of river regime which caused this once eroding bank to become a face of aggradation is of some interest and is discussed below (Chapter 23). More important for the moment, however, is the observation that this change took place somewhat prior to Late Bronze Age activity on the site and thereby, through steady subsequent aggradation, gave rise to a highly sensitive chronometer for LBA events and cultural refuse.

The channel fill respects the basic hydrological laws of river systems in that coarse-grained deposits predominate in the lower parts while finer silts increase upwards to become exclusive in the higher levels. Significantly there is also a bed of peat in the upper part of the sequence implying essentially static water conditions. The detailed sequence as excavated is inevitably more complex and is elucidated below. A complete picture of the surviving stratigraphic succession can only be understood by reference to all five major sections taken through the channel edge deposits (Figs. 20–24: sections 33, 35, 36, 37 and 38). This is due not only to localised stratigraphic features of natural and human origin, but also to the vagaries of the modern disturbance in construction work, of which two major features merit comment. The somewhat regular contractor's step, in running along the northern edge of the site, was skew to the ancient channel alignment and it therefore removed a notch from different parts of the silting sequence at each major section line. At section 35 this had destroyed part of the vital interface between the fill of F300 in the river bank and the bordering natural channel silts. In section 38 it had cut the soil stains on top of the outer pile row and surrounding layers such as the peat bed (L9). Section 37 was laid out in order to escape the notching effect, but instead impinged on the edge of the old A30 floodway, which had removed the uppermost sequence. This upper sequence is provided instead by section 36, set back from 37. Finally, section 33 was laid out in order to transect the broadest possible span of the old channel deposits in the excavated area, thereby showing the extent of gravel banking away from the river's edge. Here, however, truncation from the A30 floodway was at its maximum, thus leaving only the below-water-table deposits.

For all but the uppermost sequence, section 37 is most complete and uncomplicated regarding the channel edge and attendant waterfront structures. It best serves for the basic outline. The river channel contexts have been placed in ten groups or *stratigraphic units* labelled A–J, based primarily on the nature of the sediments and also taking account of major anthropogenic events. The matrix of stratigraphic relationships is shown in Fig. 33.

Stratigraphic unit A: the coarse bottom deposits
CONTEXTS 25C–H, 26–30

The lowest stratigraphic unit is that beneath layers 24 and 25b. The silt beds hard up against the bank are repeatedly characterised by a remarkable grey and blue mottled hue

(layer 27c). The blueness may be due to some particular biochemical reaction at the land/water interface. Some of these layers, which are nominally part of the channel fill, nevertheless appear to interleave with considerably earlier (Neolithic) deposits stratified low in the bank itself. It is probable that this kind of 'false stratigraphy' is a recurring feature of river banks with erosion causing undercutting, mixing, slumping and washing out. These would seem therefore to attest an active water-flow, and this is supported by the interleaving beds further away from the bank, which are of a different character. At first the loamy silt (27a–b) is interrupted by lenses of silts with a marked shell-sand component (25c) and sometimes concentrations of wood pebbles (25d). Further out from this horizon, and best seen in section 33, the sandy silt either becomes dominant or, at certain levels, merely a matrix around gravel (25c–h). These coarse variegated deposits suggest deposition in the bottom of the channel by a relatively high-energy water flow. They were seen to overlie a more consistent gravel bed in the north-east of Area 6 (layer 30; Fig. 20). This bed overlay in turn the tufa of mid-Flandrian times (42) and quickly graded into the Neolithic mixed deposits (41) at the foot of the old river bank. The position of this transition is unlikely to be coincidence and the gravel bed 30 should be regarded as the active bed of the LBA channel during full flow, rather than a somewhat earlier deposit being scoured by the LBA river action. How much deeper the channel went cannot be ascertained, but the river bed profile recorded in Area 5 (section SA2) falls away at the northern end to a depth of at least 0.5 m below the lowest point of section 33. It may also be noted that the bluey-grey silt (27c) was still dipping away at the lowest point of the excavation (11.85 m OD) around section 38.

The gravel/sand bar comprising layer 25 has been seen to have extended the whole 50 m length of the recorded channel edge, alluvial parcel 4 (Chapter 1). The fossilisation of this major feature, originally perhaps mobile, suggests an important change in the channel's hydrology. This led inevitably to the major transition seen in sediments after unit B. It also created a linear depression or trough between bar and river bank, about 4 m across. This syncline was at first perpetuated, then gradually eradicated by subsequent silt infill.

Stratigraphic unit B: the clearance horizon
CONTEXTS 23, 24, 24*, 25A–B

The next stratigraphic unit, wherever it survived in the excavated area, was dominated by an extremely distinctive layer. Layer 24 was so rich in charcoal that it appeared absolutely black. In some places this ashy deposit survived as a bed 0.15 m thick. The most concentrated deposits lay consistently on the slope next to the ancient bank and the charcoal content quickly dissipated with distance from that bank. At the western end of the excavated deposit, 24* was distinguished from 24 simply because it contained a concentration of pottery and underlay the midden; in this general zone 24/24* contained a number of branches (F163, F193–F195, F207; Table 4), some clearly burned and one with evidence for working (Fig. 62). Seven radiocarbon measurements were made on young branches and charcoal; five have been combined to give a mean of 2729 ± 32 BP assuming a single age (Chapter 20).

This ash-rich bed suggests a great conflagration on the adjacent river bank and the fact that this roughly corresponds with the earliest occurrence of LBA artifacts in the channel fill has led to its interpretation as the result of massive vegetation clearance in preparation for the occupation. However, the predominance of oak amongst the identified wood and charcoal might suggest that this deposit is not entirely the debris of local vegetation. 'Clearance' is nevertheless a useful label for the event represented by 24.

Closely associated with 24, both overlying and underlying, is a fairly clean silt (L23) with rather sparse charcoal inclusions. The two layers lie above 27 at the edge of the river channel. The basic matrix of 23 is of yellow clay-loam derived directly from the upper bank (38), but this was somewhat dirtied, in particular by inclusions of charcoal. It is hard to escape the conclusion that the formation of this deposit was connected with the adjacent charcoal layer, since 23 often encapsulates 24. It is not difficult to envisage 23 as being bank material slipped or shovelled into the channel by human agency along with the burnt vegetation debris.

Once the thick ashy deposit had come to line the river bank, it probably suffered erosion and reworking. It is easy to appreciate that at times of high water flow in the channel a considerable quantity of charcoal could have been swept away; the deposit may originally therefore have been somewhat thicker than that excavated. Two types of deposit adjacent to 24 bear witness to the process of erosion. The first deposits (25b) continue the line of 24 out into the channel. They are sandy silts quite distinct from the loamy matrix against the bank, and although charcoal is a notable component it is considerably less dense. Further out these sandy beds interleave with gravelly beds (25a) and in fact the sequence represents the final stage of the pattern of silting seen in the lowest stratigraphic unit of the channel fill.

The sudden change in the character of the silts and the density of charcoal inclusions at the boundary between 23/24 and 25b is strongly suggestive that this was roughly the line of the normal water's edge. This ideally explains the continuity of 25a–b from the comparable underlying levels and the apparent reworking of the in-mixed cultural debris, in contrast to the *in situ* character of 23/24 up the slope. Natural reworking of the latter was only implied by the form of its upper surface and presumably derived from abnormally high water flows. This is the second type of erosion evidence and takes the form of localised lenses (24a) still containing charcoal concentrations but which are more silty and interleaved into the top of L24 (best seen in section 37). The silt matrix of these lenses was essentially that of overlying silts 14 and 20.

Stratigraphic unit C: early occupation

CONTEXTS 20C–D, 21, 22 (FOR CONTEXTS 18, 19 SEE MIDDEN, BELOW.)

A relatively homogeneous body of grey-brown silt (20) overlies the clearance horizon in the channel itself, while superficially similar silts up the slope tend to be banded (14). Detailed stratigraphical evidence suggests that these two bodies are not synchronous: the former largely pre-dating, the latter largely post-dating, the first waterfront structure. Although the boundary between the two was not well defined, they will be treated as separate units.

The main element of the pre-waterfront unit was the grey-brown silt (20), which seemed homogeneous for much of its thickness (20c). This particular division is likely to pre-date all pile structures, whereas the upper part (20a–b) should be somewhat later. 20c–d occupy the long-channel gully formed inside the gravelly bar, as described above. Occasional lenses of the sandier underlying beds (25) were interleaved with 20 at the boundary (e.g. section 38), whilst accretion of coarse sediment on top of the bar itself continued intermittently in this unit as two shelly sand lenses, 21a/b (Figs. 20–21; and in plan, Fig. 27A). The upwards trends seen in (a) the fining of the coarser sediments and (b) the predominance of the fine silt type conform to expectations for a naturally silting channel without marked changes in local hydrology. Unworked wood, some of it thought to be drift, some perhaps laid material (Chapter 3), was present throughout the sequence, but an apparent concentration within 20c in trench 2 was planned (Fig. 27A) as a reference for the higher-stratified laid structures.

The pre-waterfront phase of 20 probably tailed out almost 1 m inside the (subsequent) inner pile row, but apparently at this stage did not lap up the slope, where instead a distinctive light yellow sandy silt was deposited (22). In section 37 part of 22 is seen to interleave with the 14/20 interface, presumably through re-erosion. Further west this sandy bed, along with 23, which it overlies, was apparently truncated by the pile-driven feature, F182 (section 38; Fig. 23). The underlying block of silt here is that which had slumped from higher up the bank. This slumpage should have taken place after the accumulation of lower 20 to account best for the vertical abutting of 23a and 20c/d. It should be noted that the associated slip line continued right down to the base of the recorded section; thus the underlying levels 28a and 29 were displaced to lower horizontal positions than their continuations in the intact bank (41). The slump would have been resisted by the mass of silt already laid in the channel and the net effect was to cause some convolution, or buckling, of beds, seen well, for example, in the 27c/28 boundary. Slumpage probably therefore occurred after a period of silting following clearance.

The deposits overlying layers 20c and 22 form the next stratigraphical unit, which is associated with the first timber waterfront structure.

Stratigraphic unit D: waterfront 1
Contexts 13, 14, 20b (For contexts 15–17 see midden, below.)

The construction and use phase of the inner pile row can be reasonably bracketed by the top of 20c and the base of 8b/12. This silting episode comprises silts which are comparatively clean of charcoal and artifacts. It may not be represented outside the outer pile row owing to subsequent erosion.

The surface of 20c appeared in sections to be rather convoluted (Figs. 22 and 23), probably resulting from the disturbance to be expected in pile-driving operations. Layer 14e is the first silt deposit to overlie this horizon and the sandy silt 22. It lies on the slope of the bank inside the main pile line and, in section 38, extends into the upper fill of the pile pit (F182) on the river bank. 14e was so similar in character to the underlying silt 20c that it was excavated as the same context, but in both main sections (Figs. 22 and 23) it appears as the uppermost phase of that silt regime. It is possible that it actually represents up-cast from 20c, perhaps having been excavated from the river bed during pile emplacement, for in section 38, 14e has a hummocky appearance. The inner row piles could have been started off by digging small pits into 20c and 20d, in the manner used on the dry bank.

The precise level of inner pile insertion depends upon the interpretation of a certain feature which was regularly encountered around piles at the 20c/14d boundary (Figs. 22 and 23; mainly photographic records). The feature comprised an encircling cone of the upper and lighter silt type (14d) penetrating into the top of 20c. These are morphologically distinct from more widespread and linear 'root' pipes penetrating the same boundary. Five possible origins for the cones may be raised:

1) Lateral movement of the pile at the river bed after emplacement. This is extremely unlikely as the cones are rather squat and stop quite abruptly; the pile would not be able to bend so much over such a short part of its length.
2) Solution or eddy feature.
3) Drag-lines from the driving operation (as described above). This is a possibility; some downward trails are believed to represent drag-lines, although they tend to be slighter. Note also the clear deformation of silts at pile tips elsewhere (e.g. F273 and F182, section 38).
4) Tamping to consolidate any loosened silt at river bed level. Deliberate tamping of silt around the piles immediately on emplacement might better explain the squat form of the cones.
5) A small dug hole, in order to ensure correct location of pile at the start of the driving operation. This is quite logical and possible, especially given the evidence for the digging of the larger pile-pits on the dry bank.

It is not possible to choose definitively between these origins, but options 3, 4 and 5 are considered most likely. In the case of option 3 or 4, the piles would have been driven from a level above (but not far above) the top of 20c, with lighter covering silts 14d and 20b already *in situ* to become dragged or tamped down. Alternatively, option 5 would allow pile-driving from within the same silts (14d, 20b) or as low as the top of 20c itself. Under this hypothesis the surface silts were compact enough to maintain the dug hole (despite disturbance in the course of construction), which was then filled with an inwash of the lighter silt type. This would also allow 14e to be up-cast from the dug holes, as suggested above.

A *terminus ante quem* for pile construction is provided by a continuous greyer horizon (14b) which was observed in a number of sections to continue uninterrupted right up to a pile, in effect sealing the cones of disturbance. In a few cases there was the suggestion of a lower grey band behaving likewise. Therefore, despite uncertainties, pile row insertion can be stated to have taken place between the beginning and the end of the accumulation of silt 14c–d.

Eight samples were taken from four inner row piles for radiocarbon measurement. They gave a consistent series of results (Chapter 20) and, assuming the timbers represent a single event and were felled within a short space of time, allow a mean date of 2742 ± 28 BP (*c.* 930–870 cal BC) to be applied to inner row construction. As the number of rings in the piles is small the average true age of rings is likely to be no more than 10 years earlier than the actual felling date.

At about the same time the large pile (F182) which had been driven into the bank earlier (L22/14e boundary) appears to have been withdrawn. Although not fully excavated, the profile implies a contained, steep-sided feature. A pit was obviously dug into the river bank crest initially, but the lower profile suggests that it was produced by a sharpened timber the size of the hole, having a diameter of about 0.25 m and driven some 0.5 m deep. The driving of such a substantial timber would readily explain the deformation of the underlying layers, notably 39. That the pile was withdrawn is indicated by the clear layering of the fill (the upper part actually an extension of channel fill 14 a–c) and the complete absence of a post-pipe or any organic remains, even at the base, which just penetrated the water table. Since withdrawal took place before 14c accumulated and thus apparently shortly after insertion of the inner pile row and long before it became defunct, it cannot be regarded as a rear stay for waterfront 1. Instead, it is better regarded as part of the sturdy apparatus that might be required to carry out the pile-driving operation on this sector; in other words, it could have been the support for a substantial pile-driver which was moved on completion of the task.

On the now gentle slope of the river bank, subsequent silts were laid in an even fashion, but three thin beds could be differentiated by colour. In particular the middle deposit, 14b, was slightly greyer, probably as a result of comminuted charcoal inclusions. Both 14b and 14a appear to have equivalent deposits surviving in places outside the inner pile row (but not outside the outer row). The top horizon of 20b is in character with 14b, while 13 is a very clean light-coloured silt similar to 14a (section 38). Assuming these equations are correct, it will be noted that both layers step down a little at the pile barrier in section 38, although a number of other sectioned piles show more of a uniform gradient. In part of trench 2, although not throughout, these northward extensions had evidently been removed by erosion. In section 37 this erosion can be seen to have scarped the top of 14a immediately behind the inner pile row. This gave overlying layer 8b/12 a steep gradient locally, and 12 here could include a remnant of 14b.

The small step between L8b and L12 at pile F117 (section 38) may be understood in conjunction with evidence planned further west, around piles F265, 268, 270. In this area the contractor's step had truncated the channel silts close to the L12/13 boundary. This had exposed the lighter-coloured layer 13 in patches just outside the inner row, while a basal remnant of 12 (which was dipping north-eastwards) survived as a strip further out (Fig. 26). A curious feature, however, was the existence of two or three linear extensions of the L12 deposit, each running back through exposed L13 to abut the pipes above inner piles. Layer 12 must have been filling gullies here. As it seems unlikely that these regular gullies were impressions formed by the collapse of upright timbers from the superstructure, it is proposed that they result from the preferential trapping of silt 14a behind the piles with some washing out through the gaps to create small tongues. Slight gullies preserved between would fall in line with the impeding piles. It should be noted that this was only seen as a localised feature, possibly dependent on very specific pile formation/water current relationships. However, in such a situation a transverse section through the pile and enclosing silts would give the appearance of a small step in the base level of L8a/12. A comparable discontinuity might arise when, as in the case of F117, a pile was set back from the line of its neighbours (F115–6, 304–5).

Stratigraphic unit E: waterfront renewal
CONTEXTS 8B, 12

The next stratigraphic unit is marked by a dramatic increase in the refuse content of the silt. This is seen in masses of charcoal giving a rather black coloration and in large amounts of other debris. This comprises a single layer (8b/12) which, on the slope, merges with a later unit (8a), but lower down, in the vicinity of the pile rows, is isolated by clean overlying silts (10, 11). The part of the layer lying outside the inner pile row (12) tended to be thinner and a little paler, but still incorporated charcoal concentrations (Figs. 23 and 25). L12 also dipped into the gullies extending outwards from certain piles as described above. That 8b and 12 were part of the same depositional event was clear in excavation. The slight step at the pile row itself, as seen in section 38, is unusual and a more uniform gradient, as

seen in section 37, or a step just behind the row, as seen in section 1, were more normal (Figs. 22 and 25). In both cases the southern edge of 12 blended imperceptibly with 8b, even where there was a small but sudden drop due to the underlying topography. The difference in the density of inclusions is explained by the continued projection of the inner piles, as seen from the pile pipes, above this level, (although possibly not far above). The piles were then tall enough to have acted as a partial trap for rubbish ejected from the bank. This effect was superbly illustrated at the upper artifact-rich horizon (8a; below – Plate 39).

One possible explanation for the new, refuse-rich silting pattern might be the effect of a devastating flood which swept quantities of midden material off the adjacent occupied surface, only to be left on the slope (cf. Needham and Longley 1980: 401). However, it may be questioned whether such a process would have redeposited such dense concentrations of charcoal and, furthermore, whether it satisfactorily explains the occurrence of obvious *in situ* debris, such as conjoining pot sherds and groups of articulated bones. To account better for these, it is now considered far more likely that the dramatic change from the preceding levels reflects a difference in access to the river bank. It might be conjectured that the steady accumulation of cleanish silts, into which only a little refuse found its way, implies some form of protection from the garbage-producing occupants, most logically a continuous platform between pile row and river bank. If this inference is correct then layer 8b clearly implies the loss of that platform through collapse or demolition. Indeed it is an attractive proposition to suggest the burning of some of the waterfront structure, thus accounting for the charcoal content of 8b/12. If a former platform had been demolished, then it is not unreasonable to suspect that this deposit also marks the end of the waterfront phase 1 structure as a whole. This ties in well with the dating of the presumed replacement (outer row) which would indicate a lifespan of 50–100 years for the phase 1 structure. This could tally with a typical life expectancy for waterfronts, which, after that order of time, rot at the water line.

On the interpretation advanced, the material in layer 8b/12 could have accumulated over a fairly short period after the demolition of waterfront 1, and before the erection of waterfront 2, assuming that this similarly entailed a platform, as perhaps suggested by the recurrence of clean silts (10, 11). The detailed arguments for phasing of the outer pile row are presented in the next section.

Stratigraphic unit F: waterfront 2 and hardstandings
CONTEXTS 10, 11, 20A; F155, F164

As was the case for the inner row, the silts on either side of the outer row showed a different sequence above layer 20c. This gave the superficial impression at the time of excavation of a stratigraphical horizon similar to that for the inner row. However, detailed analysis suggests that the contemporaneity initially proposed (Needham and Longley

1980: 399) is incorrect. A good case can now be made for the outer row being secondary. For most of the length of the outer row the relationship between silts 8a/11/12 and the piles was lost owing to the contractor's step. The relationships only survived for a short stretch between the eastern end of that step and the western slope of the A30 floodway, that is between piles F314 and F146, and is recorded in sections 1 and 37.

The construction and use of the outer pile row is most obviously bracketed by deposits 20c and 7. A number of outer row piles were observed to have drag-lines of lighter silt penetrating 20c and there can be little doubt that they post-date that layer. On the other hand layer 7 sealed decapitated or decayed pile tops, as seen clearly in section 1, and is therefore a *terminus ante quem* for the disuse of the outer row. The intervening silts are the crucial ones and these show clear discontinuity to either side of the pile row, which must therefore have been creating a barrier effect. The general trend in the lie of the layers is clear. Throughout this sequence they dip gently north-eastwards from bank into channel, but more abrupt changes at the outer pile row resulted either from the loss of a given layer beyond, or its sudden stepping down. Most important in this respect are layers 11 and 8a. Layer 11 abuts a pile in section 37 and shows a steep bluff close to another in the oblique section 1; it must either have accumulated preferentially behind the row or have been preferentially scoured away outside it. There were signs of a small talus of this silt coming through the outer pile row in trench 2 and underlying the hard standing (F164). Layer 8a was laid upon the upper surface of layer 11; basically it also stopped at the pile row, but section 1 shows it stepping down over the bluff and a thin trace of similar material occurred over layer 9 immediately outside the row (see below).

The insertion of the outer pile row seems most likely to have occurred before the layers discussed, that is during or close to layer 12. Only in section 37 is L12 clearly seen in relation to a pile, at which it stops abruptly in a mixed, somewhat distinct clod (12a), possibly exhibiting drag or the in-fill of a cone. This rather suggests that L12 was already in existence, in part at least, at the time of insertion, thus becoming disturbed by contact with the piles. Beyond the outer row L12, already a pale reflection of L8b, quickly faded out; this dissemination could have been caused before or after insertion by lapping waters at this level.

The possibility that pile emplacement preceded L12 cannot be ruled out. In this situation the melée 12a would have to be seen as a result of active erosion during or after L12 deposition. Assuming a slightly lower river bed outside the row at this stage, which is highly likely, an appropriate mechanism would be some sort of swirling round the back of piles which stood exposed to the current in times of spate.

If pile insertion was earlier than L12, it is unlikely on two grounds to have been significantly earlier – for example, contemporaneous with the inner row. Firstly, the mean of seven radiocarbon dates on outer row timbers is 2655 ± 30

BP (*c.* 840–790 cal BC), which is somewhat younger than that for the inner row (Chapter 20). Secondly, with the two rows in simultaneous use certain aspects of erosion are difficult to reconcile. At an early stage, after the deposition of 13, there appears to have been some erosion of its top in areas between the rows, notably in trench 2. The overlying layers 12 and 11 seem to have been protected here, however, and only suffered beyond the outer row.

Discussion of this stratigraphic unit will proceed on the basis of the preferred interpretation, that L12 and outer row pile insertion were closely related temporally. With the deposition of clean sandy silts (L10–11) the barrier effect of pile rows clearly came into play again. This new deposit survived up to a maximum of 15 cm thick behind the outer row, but thinned rapidly as it rose to extend just beyond the stumps of the inner row.

One ramification of the stratigraphic succession deduced above is that outside the pile rows there was potentially a substantial hiatus between the accumulation of layer 20 and layer 9, which immediately overlies. This is due to successive accretions being largely restricted to the zone behind the pile rows. In other words there was a systematic pattern of silts being trapped behind, and not surviving in front of, the piles. From sections, however, localised variations not recognised in excavation can be seen towards the top of layer 20 outside (and inside) the outer pile row. These may partially fill the stratigraphic interval, units D–F.

In trench 1, a lighter coloured silt, 20a, was separated from 20c by a thin slightly darker horizon, suggesting lensing and perhaps a temporary standstill phase (section 38). This band was noted in other sections alongside piles in trench 1 and in one case (F199) three such bands were observed in upper L20. In trench 2, by contrast, a depression continued to run outside the pile rows. The overlying peat in the channel here (L9) and layer 8a behind the outer row are grouped together in the next stratigraphic unit but the peat growth might in its deepest part overlap deposition of 10/11. This is suggested by lenses of silt tipping into its southern edge in the eastern part of trench 2 (section 33). The top of this interleaved sequence was truncated by the A30 floodway, but the location and inclination of the silt lenses is strongly suggestive of extensions from a silt body behind the pile row – logically therefore L11. The clean nature of 10 and 11 suggests that either this was a rapidly dumped silt load or over a longer period cultural refuse was again restricted from entering this area behind the piles.

Two laid timber structures, F155, F164, relate to the stratigraphic discontinuity described outside the outer pile row, since they occurred in the top of layer 20. Although their potential date span is broad (D–F), it will be argued that they probably belong late within this period, that is to unit F.

F155 was a small group of parallel timbers laid east–west which survived on the edge of the contractor's pit at 13E/12N and was first recorded in salvage section SA4 (Fig. 9). It was sealed by some *in situ* peat, layer 9, and lay at a height of 12.77 m OD. F164 has two components (Plates 40–42). First there is a bundle of withies, which were almost certainly coppiced rods; they mainly lay parallel to waterfront 2, occupying the centre of the depression in the silt, but a few rods lay more transverse to this axis. Overlying the rods was the second component, the remnants of at least five similar-sized branches which seem to have formed a lattice, three on one axis (F164/1, 3, 4) and two on another (F164/6, 7). The possible function of these structures is discussed in Chapter 3.

Structure F164 as a whole was centred on the deepest part of the syncline still evident at the layer 20/9 interface (Fig. 28c). Its precise stratigraphic position is as follows: the branches themselves just projected out of silt 20 for about half of their lengths, these projections having been sealed in peat layer 9. Their northern parts were covered under a shallow depth of silt at the top of layer 20. The rod bundle was immediately underneath. It is impossible to say whether the structure was at its original level or had been pushed down a few centimetres into the soft silt owing to use. The latter would certainly be possible if the structure had borne any weight. From two considerations it can be argued that the structure is late in the permissible time interval. Firstly, the structure respected the outer pile row, only lying outside it, and the radiocarbon measurements for F164 and F155 (four results give a mean of 2579 ± 35 BP; *c.* 810–760 cal BC), give a later range than obtained for waterfront 2. Secondly, the southern ends of the lattice branches overlapped a small wedge of pale silt which is thought to be the talus of layer 11 slipping through the outer pile row (as described above). The silt at the top of layer 20 partially covering F164 need not argue against a late date since it is entirely possible that the structure had become a little submerged, whilst it has already been noted that some of the uppermost silt outside the pile rows is likely to have been somewhat later than layer 20c.

The hardstandings are most likely to post-date waterfront 2 construction, though perhaps only by a few decades or less. Again, it seems likely that the waterfront still stood and functioned at that time, although this is impossible to prove. One can, however, point to a reasonable interval of time during the formation of the peat bed (layer 9) before the waterfront foundations finally became buried within layer 7; this allows the possibility of a continuing waterfront after F164 was laid.

Stratigraphic unit G: peat lagoon and waterfront demise
CONTEXTS 8A, 9

Stratigraphic unit G, comprising layers 8a and 9, was clearly terminated by the deposition of sandy silts 7 and, higher up the slope beyond the limit of 7, was still reasonably well differentiated from 6. The character of the deposits was also absolutely distinct from underlying 10, 11 and 20a. Nevertheless there may be some overlap in the deposition of the two units, as mentioned above.

The state of the ground outside the waterfront just before unit G was clearly that of a foreshore which was periodically damp (Chapter 24). That damp conditions prevailed during G is shown by the peat growth of layer 9, this seemingly also indicating a minimal influence from fresh and flowing water. As already mentioned, there were small silt/sand inwashes which became trapped as lenses or pockets in the peat. Some may have eroded off the slope behind the piles, particularly off silt 10/11, or otherwise it had washed over the bar. The peat contained some cultural debris but pottery sherds are not of large size and some may be residual. A wooden ladle bowl was also retrieved from this deposit (W1).

Layer 8a, which was basically confined to the slope inside the outer pile row, was distinct from layer 9 in its matrix and in having dense finds. The relationship of 8a to the waterfront sequence is of importance. Since layer 7 immediately above is a *terminus ante quem* for the dismantling or decay of the superstructure of waterfront 2, layer 8a may well be associated with its demise. Like 8b at a lower horizon, it is extraordinarily rich in charcoal and refuse, in sharp contrast to the intervening silt (10/11). Again one might suggest that the sudden increase in debris resulted in the opening up of the river bank, perhaps formerly covered by a timber platform running back from the outer row. Even if the changing quantities of inclusions from layer to layer have a different explanation, the end of waterfront 2 should be placed somewhere within the deposition of L8a.

The relationship of L8a to the peat bed outside the pile row was established in broad terms. A cross-section between piles F142 and F143 showed 8a to quickly diffuse at a point in line with the pile row, at the same time dipping to meet the southern edge of the peat. In the long oblique section 1 the layer undulates slightly at the same level as in section 37 (*c.* 13.10–13.20 m OD), but then dips suddenly as it approaches the top of pile F314 at a point just behind F313 (which was in front of the section). Layer 8a was then seen to continue the short distance to the east end of section 1, but more importantly extended northwards for the full length of the offset (recorded in photographs only). Its character remained similar, a pale grey matrix with notable charcoal inclusions, and it comprised a thin spread washed across the surface of the peat bed (9). It is possible that this extension existed in weaker form in the nearby section 37 and further east. Layer 8a then overlies, in part at least, layer 9; it could have been a secondary wash-out from the concentrated deposit behind the pile row, in which case formation of 8a and 9 could still have overlapped.

Stratigraphically related to the 8a wash overlying the peat was the complete skeleton of a dog (F111; Fig. 29b; Plate 43). This was partly embedded in peat, but its bones projected up into the silt of L7. It lay in two articulated sections, the entire body and, at 1 m remove, the skull accompanied by a few cervical vertebrae. Apart from the twofold dismemberment, the skeleton lay in undisturbed articulation and was therefore fleshed on deposition and perhaps rapidly covered. There was no sign of a dug feature to suggest formal burial.

Stratigraphic unit H: hiatus?
CONTEXT 7

Following 8a and 9 there was another major phase of clean silt deposition, layer 7, which sealed the projecting stumps of the outer row. This therefore post-dates the termination of the waterfront and was possibly a hiatus in occupation nearby, since finds were extremely sparse throughout the deposit. It seems unlikely that this was an especially rapid inundation for there were lenses of coarser sediments noted within the deposit (e.g. Fig. 22), suggesting different phases of in-washing. Like layers 10/11 earlier, it only spread a little landward of the submerged pile rows and it largely levelled the step formerly present at the outer row by means of thicker deposition outside.

The dating of this (and higher) layers in the channel is difficult. No radiocarbon dates have been attempted either on the dog skeleton (F111) which layer 7 covered, or on a burnt stick stratified within the lowest part of the layer, whilst the few finds are likely to be residual.

Stratigraphic unit I: late occupation debris
CONTEXT 6

This layer, which stretches along the full slope of the bank, contrasts with the stratigraphically adjacent ones in containing a reasonable quantity of finds and charcoal. At first this gave the impression that an *in situ* occupation or midden horizon might be represented. This now seems unlikely on several grounds. The matrix is a flood silt rather than a soil, no features were identified cut into the underlying deposits and the pottery is almost exclusively of small sherd size (Fig. 74), which suggests that it has been redeposited.

This allows for the possibility that much of the material will be residual from earlier phases. However, the pottery assemblage shows trends in this late part of the channel sequence which suggest that the layer 6 assemblage may well reflect a late stage of occupation not represented in other deposits on the site.

This layer is almost certainly due to major over-bank flooding which swept up a lot of cultural debris from the adjacent bank.

Stratigraphic unit J: post-occupation flooding
CONTEXTS 4, 5

The pattern of flooding which resulted in layer 6 seems to have continued with similar layers being deposited still higher in the channel. These had a basically similar matrix, but had lesser quantities of more reduced debris. Erosion of occupation-bearing deposits was evidently still occurring, but the material being reworked may already have suffered erosion and less was available, owing perhaps to the gradual covering of the Late Bronze Age horizon by flood silts.

The addition of layers 4 and 5 raised the edge of the river channel to a height which was probably not far below that of the main river bank. In effect, then, the channel edge became part of the bank.

The midden and the fill of F300

The river channel sequence at the extreme north-west of its surviving extent (around grid 8E/12N) is different from the standard sequence in certain respects. Its distinctiveness was recognised early in excavation, thanks to inspection of the sections alongside, where a good finds density suggested that this zone might incorporate a midden deposit; subsequent environmental work has helped confirm this (Chapter 17). A section was cut through these deposits, again perpendicular to the ancient river bank (section 35; Plate 45; Fig. 24), and formed two unconnected parts, owing to the contractor's step. Correlation with the main river channel sequence is aided by the oblique edge section 1 (Fig. 25), but is complicated by the fact that the upper sequence is essentially the fill of a feature (F300) on the crest of the river bank. This feature is clearly defined by cut edges on three sides, whereas on the fourth its layers are poorly differentiated from the adjacent channel deposits. A similar diffuse boundary separated the 'midden' from channel deposits in the lower sequence. Consequently neither the midden nor the fill of F300 can be regarded as having been dug through the adjacent channel deposits.

The sequence around section 35 shows none of the slumping in section 38, which may well have been localised. the pre-occupation eroding river bank is lined by a thin woody lens (27e), which then became trapped low down by the accumulation of grey silt (27a) and higher by small dumps of sandy and shingly silt (25). Nearby, but not represented in the section, were other deposits matched in the main channel sequence in stratigraphic unit (A): bluey silt (27d) and orange sand (28) reworked from the eroding Neolithic levels (41). This whole suite of layers is overlain by the charcoal-packed layer, 24*, which is essentially the same layer as 24 but is distinguished here because it was affected by the midden above. In the section itself 24* was not associated with clean clay, but immediately to the west there was again a return to the more normal situation with the charcoal debris engulfed in redeposited natural (23). Layer 24, encountered all along the river bank, is interpreted as a clearance horizon (stratigraphic unit B, above). In places this layer made contact with an underlying and superficially similar-looking woody lens, layer 26, which might be the same as 27e lower on the slope. The branches at this level (24*), partly burnt, and partly embedded in unit A silts, have been described elsewhere (Chapter 3). Their thickness allowed them to form a 'trap' for some overlying deposits.

Three bodies of silt overlay layer 24*. At the north-east, alongside the contractor's trench, was a bed of grey silt continuous with 20c, but this quickly merged into, or interleaved with, a mass of more stony and ashy material (19). This was found to be complicated and was excavated as a series of successive dumps with variable clarity. The midden could have either accumulated roughly in step with the contiguous silt bed 20c, or been dumped slightly earlier, its edge becoming eroded and diffused in character as 20c washed up around it. There was little if any time lag, however, since part of 14d overlying 20c survived to seal one edge of the midden. Finally, at the south-west just below F300, was a markedly ashy patch which turned out to be a stake hole (F322); it is possible that a stake pipe continued up through the midden (19).

F300 took the form of a trough-like pit set perpendicular to the river bank. There appears to have been a very slight hump in the centre of its mainly flattish base. The primary fill (18) comprised fairly clean natural yellow silt, which incorporated several fresh-burnt clay lumps of a bright vermilion colour. There is no evidence that these lumps were, for example, daub that had become burnt. The secondary fill of F300 (17) comprises ill-defined layers of mixed stony and ashy soil, not unlike the composition of the midden, presumably a continuation of the same depositional processes and possibly even overlapping in time. As well as rising in section to the south-west these dark deposits also rose steeply on the south-east side to appear in plan behind section 35 (Fig. 30). To the north-east the upper part of 17 abuts, in a diffuse zone, channel silt layer 14d, which overlies 20c and the midden. The secondary fill changes character after a thin lens of pale sandy silt (16b), which equates in matrix and level with 14c (overlying 14d). 16b and 14c are separated by a small gap in the oblique section 1, but need not have been originally, 16b perhaps being a tongue of 14c extending into the feature hollow. Above the sandy lens is a thin tip of grey silt (16a) less stony than below, but presumably it also represents spill from occupation. This and underlying layers in F300 were cut by the upper cone of F6 (section 35). No relationship survived between F6 and the uppermost layer of F300, 15. The dirty natural element of 15 could therefore represent up-cast from the digging of F6. The boundary of 15 on the river channel side with layers 14a–b is diffuse and, as with lower suites, it is considered likely that a dump of deposited natural was lapped by waters depositing 14a–b, or that the latter action incorporated bank-eroded natural. 15 was overlain by grey silt which seemed continuous with the uppermost lip of charcoal-rich layers 6/8a in the channel. Because of truncation in machining, 6/8a filling the top hollow of F300 appeared in plan as a tongue, as suggested for 14c beneath.

A possible interpretation of the diffuse zone boundary between silts 14a–b/15 and 14d/17 immediately below is that some form of barrier existed on that line. This might, for example, have been closely set (but not contiguous) stakes such as those close by (F316, F317, F318, F322) with or without wattles. These would constitute an effective enough barrier to allow silt bodies to acquire a slightly different character either side, but would also allow some mixing through the gaps. If this was the case, the layer correlations between F300 and the adjacent channel nevertheless make

it clear that the silting was keeping broadly in step.

The large pit F6 (see Chapter 3), by cutting F300, gives the late stages to the stratigraphic sequence beginning with the 'midden'. This is especially informative as it allows two radiocarbon measurements for layer 4 within the pit to be seen in relation to the radiocarbon sequence in the river channel.

The midden area produced a reasonable quantity of Late Bronze Age artifactual debris from nominally pre-clearance levels, that is from stratigraphic unit A, a fact which deserves comment if clearance (unit B) is to be seen as equating with the beginning of occupation. Two small sherds of pottery from 27 belong to the near-complete jar (P33) from 24* above. However, there is probably too much pottery of too large a sherd size for all to be regarded as having been pressed into existing silts from the clearance horizon. Some of the debris was caught in layers immediately underlying 23/24 on a slight shelf in the bank profile which layer 26 occupies (Fig. 24). This feature probably extended at least a short distance further north-west (salvage section SA4) and could easily be a product of human interference with the bank at the beginning of activity on the site and prior to the sweeping of burnt debris from clearance into the channel.

Deposits on the Late Bronze Age occupation surface

Late Bronze Age artifact-bearing levels were found to be very close to the base of the modern rubble over-burden and probably in parts in contact with it. In consequence machine clearance impinged variably on the upper part of the surviving Late Bronze Age occupation levels. It is probable that the close proximity of these deposits was connected with the A30 bridge construction of 1959–60, which should also account for dug features F1, F2, F4. Stripping at this time may well have partially and erratically truncated the Late Bronze Age levels.

After machine stripping for the 1978 excavation and further cleaning of the surface by hand (layers 1–3) the occupation surface was clearly delimited from channel fill by a band of light-coloured silt (Plate 46; Fig. 30). This band of underlying natural silt was exposed by the truncation of the angle between the essentially horizontally bedded occupation deposits on the levee and the dipping channel layers. Two large modern features (F1, F2), once emptied, showed that the surviving occupation deposits thickened inland from this edge. In section and in the initial cleaned surface it appeared as a fairly homogeneous grey–brown deposit, although at each planned level some localised variation in colour and finds densities was apparent. Some of these were relatable to stratigraphic horizons, others were spatially determined, and overall it was not usually possible to predict where discrete stratigraphic units would exist during excavation. Consequently the five spits excavated through the deposit were in part arbitrary, in part stratigraphically valid. Detailed 1:20 plans at each spit interface (Figs. 30–32) combined with a system of recording all finds to a metre square allow reconstruction of spatial and sequential relationships between deposits.

The five excavated spits had different distributions. The first to come off was mainly confined to the southern part of trench 1, with a spur running northwards roughly centred on easting 6–8. The second and third spits effectively covered the whole of trench 1 up to the ancient river bank, and also the south-west corner of trench 2, while the fourth and fifth were confined to the southern part of trench 1 where the occupation deposits had survived to the greatest thickness.

The trench 1 occupation deposits can be rationalised as six units, contexts 31–36 (Table 3b). At the top, 31 was lighter grey-brown silt than the underlying levels and had fewer and smaller finds. The extent found in hand excavation covered contexts 32 and much of 33. On analogy with later excavations on the site, it is probable that 31 represented the base of the *upper zone*, thought to be occupation deposits altered by natural agencies (Needham and Sorensen 1988: 124). Below this the deposits are considered to be *in situ* (lower zone). The context found in the central part of the *in situ* occupation deposits was grey-brown with very dense burnt flint and finds. It was excavated in a maximum of three spits (33a–c) but tapered out to the north-east on the river's edge owing to ancient truncation. Burnt clay (F297) lay within the lower parts (33b–c) and can be related to a structure (Chapter 3). Large bones and fair-sized, but scattered, sherds were noteworthy components. Burnt bone fragments occurred around the burnt clay dumps, and a clay bowl structure (F15) was situated within the 33 soil.

Context 32 bordered 33 and occupied the south-west corner of trench 1. It was a blackish soil, comparatively stone-free, although with some variation through depth. It was taken down in three spits (32a–c), the middle one of which contained a confined pot group (F295) against the western baulk. The boundary with 33 was poorly defined, while at its base a thin sandy lens separated 32 from underlying 36.

Context 36 was a thin blackened soil immediately overlying natural clay-loam (38), and often had a patchy coverage over the whole occupation surface owing to localised undulations as well as the first appearance of features cut into the natural. It contained only sparse stones and finds.

In the north-west corner of trench 1 the character of the deposits was again different and two contexts have been inferred. They were divided from the main occupation soils by the modern cut F1 and, continuing a similar alignment, a narrow strip of natural (38) which was already exposed at the beginning of the hand excavation (Fig. 30). Context 34 is now regarded as the uppermost fill of F6, although the feature only became clear against natural after the removal of two spits (34a, 34b). Nevertheless, retrospectively it was clear that more diffuse edges to the pit could be identified from the top of 34, where a crescent of slightly darker,

stonier soil marked the western and southern borders. Although this uppermost cone of F6 had evidently been altered by natural agencies, its survival at all implies that the pit, or at least its recut, cut all of the extant adjacent deposits, notably context 35 to the west. 35 was a distinctive light to ruddy brown soil with fewer stones than occupation contexts in general. It was excavated in three spits (35a–c), the middle of which had frequent fired-clay lumps, while the lower contained many flecks of 'daub'. Since this soil seems to pre-date F6 it would have been contemporary with channel units A–D and it may link with activities around pit F300, which has large fired-clay lumps in its primary fill. Indeed it is noteworthy that 35 occupied a slight hollow (Fig. 45), perhaps dug in connection with F300 and the platform cut into the adjacent bank (under layer 26; Fig. 24). If later deposits had accumulated on top of context 35, then these had evidently later been removed by human or natural agency.

In trench 2 the surviving occupation levels were rapidly truncated to the east by the A30 floodway. What survived in the south-west corner was excavated as two spits (37a–b), and probably equates broadly with 33 and 36 in trench 1.

The sequence of the occupation surface contexts is shown in Fig. 33. Context 35 could not be related to 32 and 33 (owing to F1 intervening), but these last two deserve comment. The boundary between them, although poor, gave no suggestion that one deposit overlapped the other and it is considered more likely that they accumulated broadly simultaneously under slightly different conditions. The main differences are the lack of burnt flint, large bone and fired clay in 32 and the presence of a pot group, which lay as a 'floor', rather than the scattered pot sherds seen in 33. It seems probable that these different material accumulations represented different activity areas, and a measure of support comes from the post-hole analysis. However, the small area of excavation impedes any firm conclusions on the functions of the respective zones.

Any attempt at more detailed correlation depends on a series of tenuous links involving the joining portions of jar 558 in 32a/b and F6 phase 1, the suggested contemporaneity of a fence line with that phase, and the later dating of the main post structure with accompanying debris in 33. This might suggest that 32b–c are earlier than most of 33. This equation would be invalidated, however, if the main post structure overlapped temporally with F6 phase 1, or if the portion of jar from 32a/b was in fact redeposited after disturbance during the phase 2 recutting of F6.

Although the occupation deposits as a whole yielded a good quantity of featured pottery sherds, individual contexts often have only small groups. Overall pot form analysis suggests that the earliest group of pottery in the river channel (units A–D) is barely represented on the levee (Chapter 9), but it remains possible that the small groups from contexts 36 and 35 include material of an early phase. The pottery assemblage from the main contexts (32, 33, 37) has been compared most closely with that from river channel units E–G.

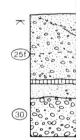

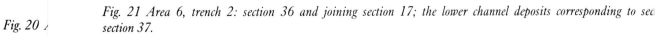

Fig. 21 Area 6, trench 2: section 36 and joining section 17; the lower channel deposits corresponding to sec
section 37.

Fig. 20 /

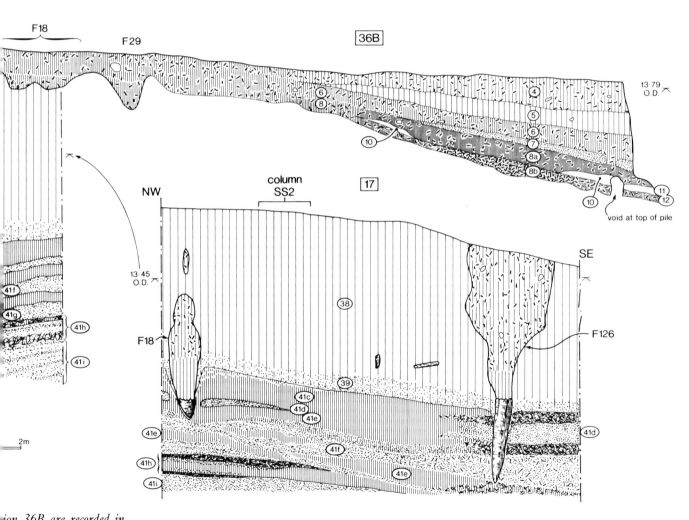

NE

F18

F29

36B

13·79
O.D.

4

6
8

5

6

7

10

8a

8b

10

11
12

void at top of pile

column
SS2

17

NW

13·45
O.D.

38

SE

F18

F126

41c

41d

39

41e

41f

41e

41d

41e

41f

41g

41h

41i

41h

41i

2m

ion 36B are recorded in

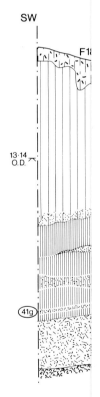

SW

F18

13·14
O.D.

41g

Fig. 22 A

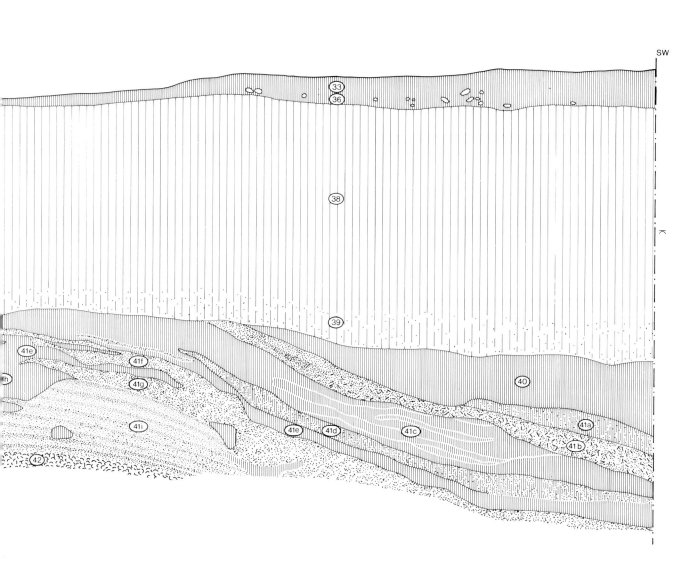

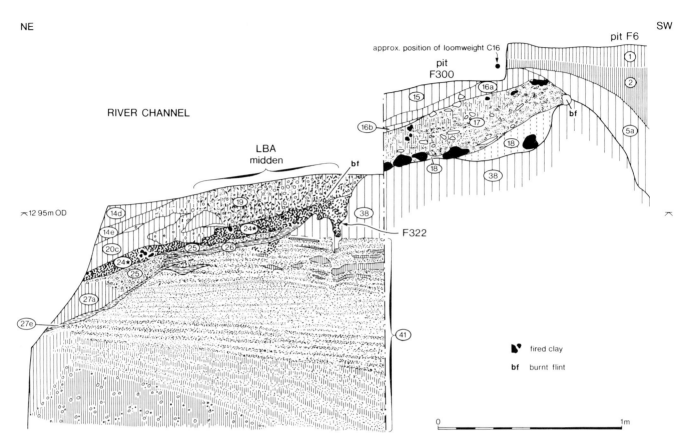

Fig. 24 Area 6, trench 1: section 35, the midden and F300.

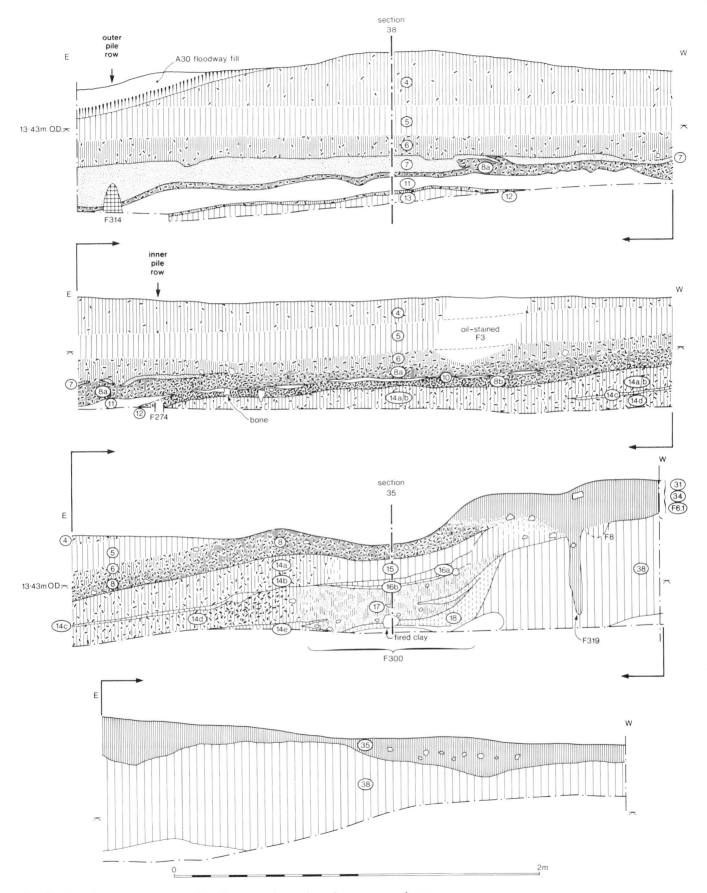

Fig. 25 Area 6, trench 1 and central baulk: section 1, standing above contractor's step.

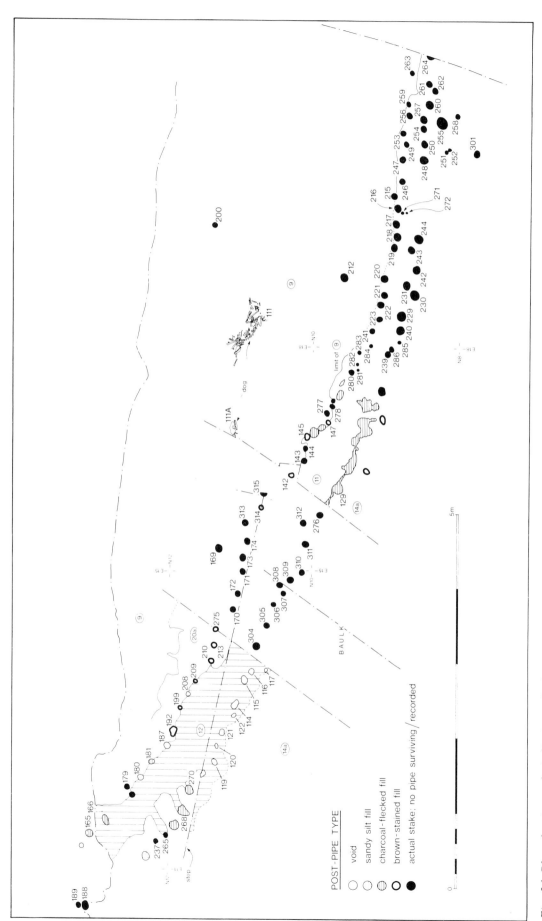

Fig. 26 Plan showing early indications of pile positions, the extent of layers exposed at the time and the position of the dog skeleton, F111. The layers belong to various stratigraphic horizons.

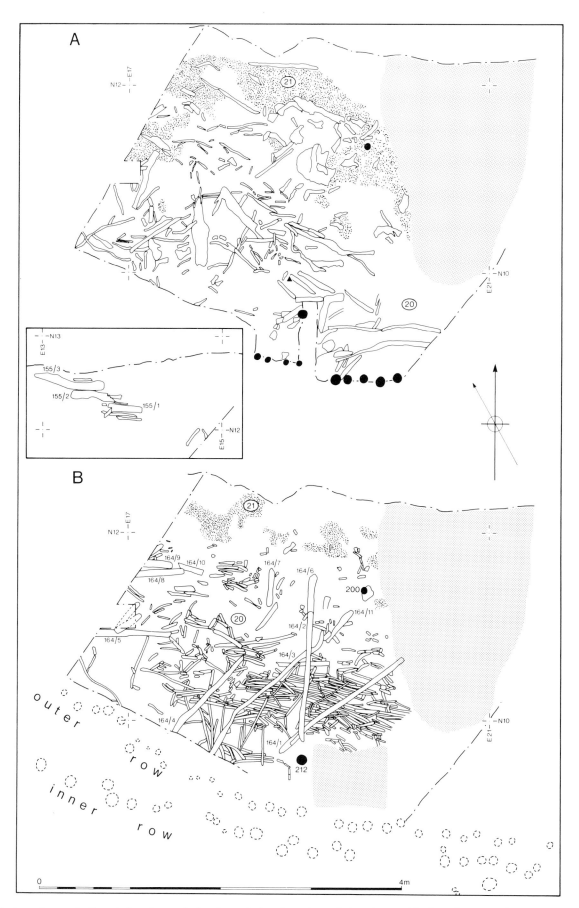

Fig. 27 Area 6, trench 2 and (inset) trench 1: plans of the river channel deposits outside the pile rows. A: wood remains within the upper parts of layer 20; B: the hardstanding of laid branches, F164, and (inset) F155, at the top of layer 20.

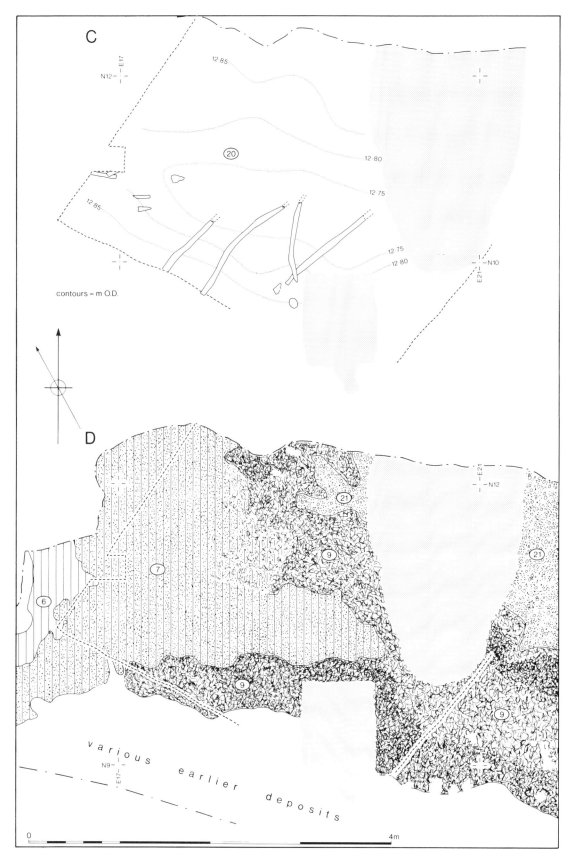

Fig. 28 Area 6, trench 2: plans of the river channel deposits outside the pile rows (continued). C: contouring of the surface of layer 20 after the removal of 9 with the parts of F164 initially exposed; D: layers exposed after removal of the A30 floodway fill – peat bed 9 was reached across most of the trench, while higher layers 7 and 6 were intact on the western flank, although the base of 7 also survived as a spur sitting in the depression in the surface of 9.

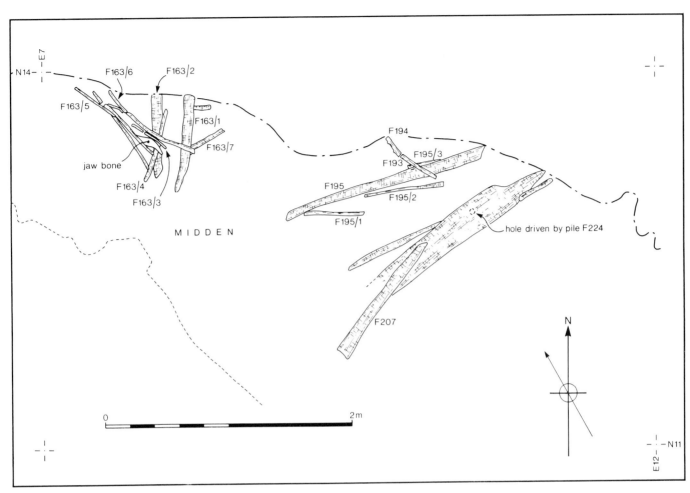

Fig. 29a Area 6, trench 1: timbers in the edge of the river channel around the midden.

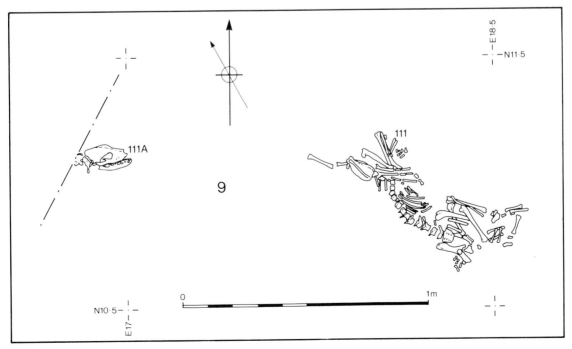

Fig. 29b Area 6, trench 2: detailed plan of the dog skeleton, F111/111A, in the top of layer 9 after removal of layer 7.

Fig. 30 Area 6, trench 1: plan of occupation deposits on the levee after the excavation of the first spit (context 31) and of the river channel deposits after context 5.

Fig. 31 Area 6: plan of the occupation deposits on the levee after excavation of the second spit.

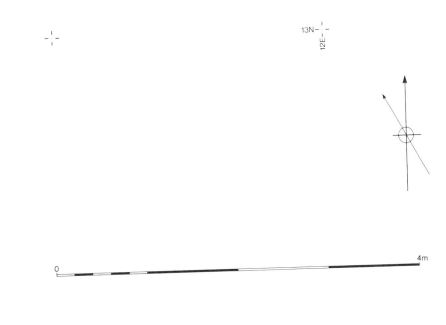

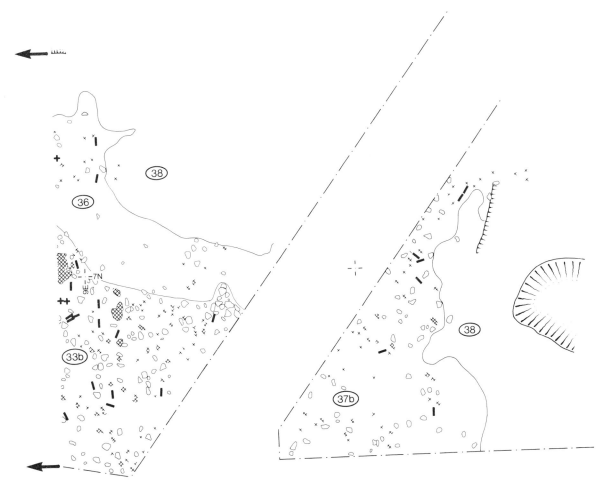

Fig. 32 Area 6, trench 1: plan of the occupation deposits and features as soil marks on the levee after excavation of the third spit.

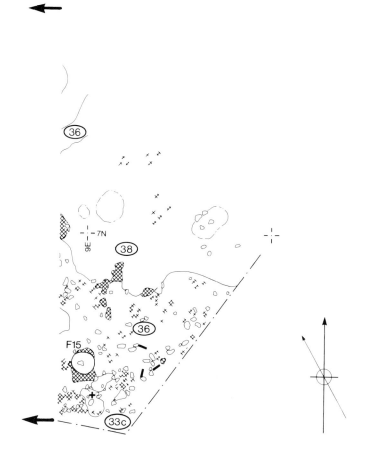

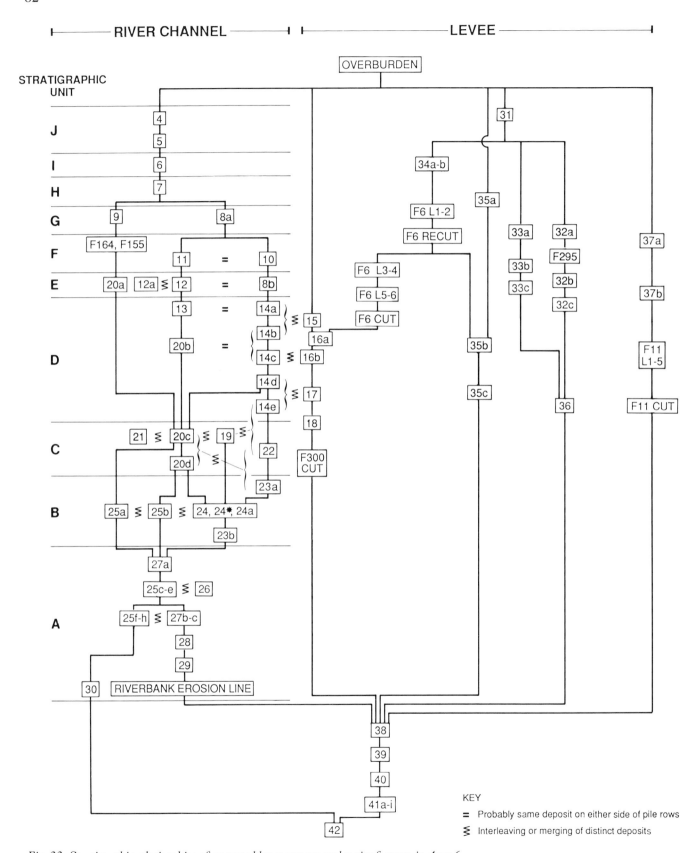

Fig. 33 Stratigraphic relationships of excavated layer contexts and major features in Area 6.

Chapter 3
Late Bronze Age structural evidence

Structural evidence of the Late Bronze Age in Area 6 falls into four categories: preserved pile foundations; other preserved timber constructions; a variety of 'cut' features; and fired-clay remains believed to come from walls and small structures such as hearths. The evidence for the continuation of pile structures in salvage areas 4, 5 and 7 is included in this section. Details of timbers are given in Table 4, of cut features in Table 5 and of fired clay in Table 6.

Pile-driven structures in the river channel (Areas 4, 5, 6, 7)

The great majority of timber piles attributable to the Late Bronze Age were set in the edge of the contemporary river channel (alluvial parcel 4). They were mainly set in two rows, inner and outer (Figs. 34–35). A small number of 'outlying' and 'inlying' posts are all attributable to the Late Bronze Age in Area 6, as should be most of those associated with the channel in Area 4. The two rows follow each other closely, lying a maximum of 1.0 m apart. At first it was thought that the two sets of piles belonged to a single structure (Needham and Longley 1980: 399), but subsequent more detailed evaluation of their stratigraphic positions (above) suggests that they are much more likely to be temporally distinct. The inner and outer rows are attributed roughly to unit C/D interface and unit E respectively. Outlying and inlying piles cannot be phased with any confidence (see below).

The distance between the rows in fact varied along their length, between 0.3 m and 1.0 m and it is better to regard their parallelism as stemming from one having renewed the other, presumably having, furthermore, a similar function. Both respected the line of the contemporary river bank in running parallel to it, but in detail their lines described a series of cusps or bays. This was first picked up during salvage recording in Area 4 and parts of two further bays were subsequently found in the Area 6 segment. That this was a deliberate feature is clear not only from the regularity of cusping but also from the fact that three or four bays have focally placed outlying piles: two bays in Area 4, one in Area 6 and probably one in Area 7. If a focal outlier existed in the western bay of Area 6, it was removed by the contractor's pit. The fact that the outer row echoed the cusping form of the earlier inner row (where both lines survived) suggests that the reason for the cusping persisted, or that the original technique of construction was copied the second time round. It has been argued that waterfront 2, founded on the outer row, was constructed shortly after the demise of waterfront 1, at which time the stumps of

the inner row piles would still have been clearly visible projecting from the silt.

Assuming that outliers were close to central perpendicular axes, as appears to be the case, a continuous cusping line can be reconstructed between Areas 6 and 4, in the manner shown in Fig. 34. This gives bays varying between 6 and 8.5 m across.

The inner pile row: waterfront 1
This is continuous across Area 6 and probably survived across the full width of Area 4. It is presumably represented amongst the Area 7 group of piles. In Area 6 the average spacing is one pile every 0.22 m over the greater portion of the row, but east of section 33 in trench 2 there appeared to be a gap of 1 m before a further eight unexcavated piles (248–264). Behind these piles is a cluster which might be related: including a very stout pile, F255. The row alignment is generally good, with rather gentle cusping forming two bays which meet around piles 308–312.

The piles, where identified, were all made of oak trunks with a maximum of 34 growth rings, but usually between 11 and 23 surviving rings. Maximum diameters are fairly consistent, with most falling between 0.13 and 0.17 m (Fig. 37). Approximate depths of penetration have also been plotted, based on the surviving lengths of piles below the decay line (Fig. 38). This shows that throughout most of the row tips were driven to similar depths, between 1.1 and 1.6 m below water table. There may, however, be an upward trend at the north-west end, perhaps resulting from a correspondingly higher river bed surface at this locality. Approximate angles of inclination have been calculated for fully planned piles and, although these are not precise, they show some significant trends suggesting linkage between sets of adjacent piles, often five to seven in number (Fig. 36). The significance of this linkage is considered below, with suggested reconstructions.

Four piles were used to provide eight samples for radiocarbon dating. On the assumption of a single event these give a mean determination of 2742 ± 28 BP (Chapter 20).

In Area 4 the more southerly pile row entering the east section is assumed to belong to waterfront 1. A fairly continuous row describing two bays can be traced across to the west side. There are some problems in deciding exactly which piles belong in the eastern bay. Close to the section a few piles fall on each side of the interpolated arc: the line appears ragged either because the piles are driven at different angles and the plan records their lower parts, or because there is a gap of some 1.5 m. There is a corresponding gap in the outer row at this point and it may be significant that both gaps coincide with a series of apparently stout posts potentially forming a discrete structure (F44–48; Fig. 14). Although it is possible that this was contemporary with and tied in to the waterfronts, the plan gives the distinct impression that this is a later intrusion, in the construction of which the piles of both waterfront 1 and 2 were dug out. Unfortunately no samples were taken of these piles.

Table 4: Summary of piles and other important wood finds.

Context	Grid E/N	Length (m)	Max. diam. (mm)	Prop. worked	Fig.	Sp	RC	Sample	Comments
Worked Stakes – Area 6.									
Late Bronze Age Inner Pile Row									
Trench 1									
F189	10.3/13.2	0.83	113	1.0	Fig. 40	Q	34(20h) c	D	Top broken.
F188	10.3/13.1	1.40	155	0.6	Pl. 56, Fig. 40	Q			C T*
F224	10.5/12.9	0.68	129	1.0	Pls. 33 & 34, Fig. 40	Q			C; tip driven into large piece of wood.
F225	10.8/12.8	1.01	120	0.9		Q			C(top damaged).
F226	10.8/12.6	1.12	130	0.5		Q			C T
F235	11.0/12.5	1.33	136	0.8	Pl. 55	Q			C T
F236	11.3/12.4	1.47	156	0.4		Q	17(9h) a	HAR-4268 HAR-4413	C
F237	11.4/12.2	1.20	138	0.5		Q	18(10h) b		C(?top damaged). T*
F265	11.5/12.0	1.61	157	0.6		Q			C T*
F268	11.8/11.7	1.56	160	0.6	Pl. 25	Q			C T*
F270	12.1/11.6	1.68	136	0.7	Fig. 59	Q			C T
F274	12.4/11.5	1.30	132	0.6		Q			C T*
F119	12.5/11.4	1.50	150	0.5		Q			C T
F120	12.6/11.3	1.22	148	?1.0	Fig. 59	Q			C T*
F121	12.7/11.1	1.36+	101	0.8		Q			V. tip lacking. T
F122	13.0/11.1	1.24	149	0.7	Pls. 38 & 56	Q			C T
F114	13.2/11.0	1.33	144	0.6		Q			C
F115	13.4/10.9	1.47	167	0.8		Q			C T*
F116	13.6/10.8	1.43+	151	>0.4		Q	23 b		Tip not extracted. T
F117	13.7/10.7	1.56	153	0.7	Figs. 23 & 40, Pls. 27, 29	Q	32 a	HAR-4269 HAR-4277	C T
—	13.9/10.7								
—	14.2/10.6								
—	14.5/10.5								
—	14.6/10.4								
—	14.8/10.4	baulk – not recovered							
—	14.8/10.3								
—	14.9/10.1								
—	15.3/10.1								
—	15.6/10.1								
Trench 2									
F276	15.7/9.9	1.29+	113	—	Figs. 22 & 40, Pl. 28	Q	25 a	HAR-4257 HAR-4275	(Tip half not (retrieved). T
F129	16.0/9.5	1.32	185	0.7		Q			C T*
F130	16.3/9.3	1.41	190	0.8	Fig. 60 & 40	Q			C T
F131	16.7/9.3	1.53	151	0.7	Fig. 40	Q			C T*
F132	16.8/9.1	1.36	142	0.5	Pl. 55, Fig. 40	Q			C T
F134	17.0/9.1	1.23	109	0.6	Fig. 40	Q			C T
F287	17.3/9.0	1.35	163	0.5	Pl. 55	Q			C T
F288	17.4/9.1	1.14	152	0.7		Q			C(?top damaged).
F239	17.8/8.9	1.30+	140	0.5	Pls. 30 & 55	Q			C(v.tip missing). T*
F286	17.9/8.9	1.34	150	0.5	Pl. 30	Q			C T*
F285	18.0/8.8	1.32	149	1.0	Pl.30	Q	17(9h) b	D HAR-4341 HAR-4274	C T
F240	18.2/8.8	1.41	138	0.5	Pl. 37	Q	17(12h) c	D	C (4 parts) T
F229	18.4/8.8	1.28	141	0.7		Q	11(6h) c		C T
F230	18.6/8.6	1.15	150	0.9		Q	18(13h) c	D	4/5 parts (?top damaged) T

Table 4: Summary of piles and other important wood finds (continued).

Context	Grid E/N	Length (m)	Max. diam. (mm)	Prop. worked	Fig.	Sp	RC	Sample	Comments
F231	18.8/8.7	1.11	135	0.7		Q	14(5h) c	D	?C T*
F242	19.0/8.5	1.32	144	0.8		Q			C T
F243	19.2/8.6	1.07	120	1.0		Q	13(6h) c	D	?top damaged
F244	19.4/8.5	1.12	138	1.0	Fig. 60	Q	13 b		C T
F245	19.8/8.3								
F248	20.4/8.5								
F250	20.7/8.5								
F251	20.6/8.2								Very small; behind row
F252	20.6/8.1								Very small; behind row
F254	20.9/8.5								
F257	21.0/8.5	not recovered							
F255	20.9/8.2								Behind row.
F258	21.0/8.0								Behind row.
F260	21.2/8.4								
F262	21.4/8.3								
F261	21.5/8.4								
F264	21.8/8.4								

Late Bronze Age Outer Pile Row
Trench 1

Context	Grid E/N	Length (m)	Max. diam. (mm)	Prop. worked	Fig.	Sp	RC	Sample	Comments
F165	11.4/12.9	0.59	74	0.8	Fig. 40, Pl. 56	Q			C T
F166	11.6/12.8	0.53	82	1.0	Fig. 40	Q			C T*
F178	11.8/12.6	0.50	107	1.0	Fig. 40				?C(top lopped?)
F179	12.1/12.5	0.68	120	0.7	Fig. 40	Q			C T*
F180	12.2/12.3	0.63	82	1.0	Fig. 40	Q			C T
F181	12.4/12.2	0.43	82	?	Fig. 40	Q			C
F187	12.6/11.9	0.45	70	?	Fig. 40			HAR-4272	C
F192	12.9/12.0	0.58	88	0.7	Fig. 40	Q			C
F199	13.1/11.8	0.60	83	1.0		Q			C
F208	13.4/11.6	0.53	82	?1.0	Fig. 40	Q			C T
F209	13.6/11.5	0.54	90	1.0	Pl. 26, Fig. 40	Q			C
F210	13.7/11.4	0.65	115	1.0	Fig. 40	Q	9/10	HAR-4267 HAR-4273	C T
F213	14.0/11.3	0.70	98	0.7	Fig. 40	Q			C
F275	14.3/11.2	0.71	107	1.0	Figs. 23 & 40, Pl. 27	Q			C
F170	14.4/11.1	0.51	85	0.8	Figs. 40 & 41, Pl. 31 & 56	Q			C T
F172	14.7/11.0	0.59	101	0.7	Figs. 40 & 41, Pl. 31	Q			C T
F171	14.9/10.9	0.69	119	0.8	Figs. 40 & 41, Pl. 31 & 56	Q			C T
F173	15.1/10.9	0.65	109	0.8	Figs. 40 & 41, Pl. 31	Q			C T
F174	15.4/10.9	0.82	117	0.8	Figs. 40 & 41	Q			C T
F313	15.6/10.9								
F314	15.8/10.7	baulk – not recovered							
F315	16.0/10.6								

Trench 2

Context	Grid E/N	Length (m)	Max. diam. (mm)	Prop. worked	Fig.	Sp	RC	Sample	Comments
F142	16.0/10.6	1.18	116	0.5	Figs. 22, 40 & 61, Pl. 28	Q	11(8h) c		C T
F143	16.3/10.3	1.01	105	0.5	Fig. 40	Q			C T
F144	16.4/10.1	0.92	110	—	Fig. 40	Q		HAR-4265 HAR-4340	C T
F145	16.6/10.1	1.16	112	0.4	Fig. 61	Q			C T
F146	16.9/10.0	1.09	115	0.5		Q			C T
F277	17.1/9.8	1.03	105	0.5	Pl. 32	Q			C T
F278	17.2/9.7	1.18	83	0.5	Pl. 32	Q	12 b		C T
F279	17.3/9.6	0.85	141	0.6	Pl. 32 & 57	Q			C(?top damaged) T

Table 4: Summary of piles and other important wood finds (continued).

Context	Grid E/N	Length (m)	Max. diam. (mm)	Prop. worked	Fig.	Sp	RC	Sample	Comments
F280	17.3/9.5	0.77	99	0.7	Pl. 32	Q			C(?top damaged). T
F281	17.6/9.3	0.82	106	0.6	Pl. 32	Q			C(?top damaged). T
F282	17.7/9.3	1.18	91	0.6	Fig. 61	Q			C
F283	17.9/9.3	1.06	106	0.6	Pl. 32 & 57	Q			C(?top damaged). T
F284	18.0/9.2	1.04	94	0.5	Pl. 32	Q			?C T
F241	18.2/9.2	0.87	100	0.6	Pl. 32	Q			?C(?top lopped). T
F223	18.3/9.1	1.03	100	0.6		Q	18(8h) a	D	?C T*
F222	18.5/9.0	0.78	92	0.6		Q	15(5h) a	D	C(? top lopped).
F221	18.6/9.0	1.01	110	0.6		Q	15(5h) a		?C.
F220	18.9/9.0	0.92	110	0.5		Q			C (?top damaged). T
F219	19.3/8.9	0.81	111	0.9		Q			?C T
F218	19.4/8.8	0.68	111	0.9		Q	32(20h) a	D	(?top damaged). T
F217	19.6/8.8	0.72	109	0.6		Q	15(6h) a	D	?top lopped. T
F271	19.7/8.7	0.95	70	0.2	Figs. 20 & 62	Q	8 a		CT*Not main support.
F272	19.7/8.7	0.24	47	0.6	Fig. 20	Sa			CT Not main support.
F216	19.8/8.8	0.87	144	0.7	Pl. 57, Fig. 40	Q			C(?top damaged). T*
F215	19.9/8.9	1.14	106	0.8	Figs. 20 & 40, Pl. 57	Q	22(10h) a	D { HAR-4264 HAR-4270	C T
F246	20.2/8.8								
F247	20.5/8.8								
F249	20.7/8.7								
F253	20.8/8.8	not recovered							
F256	21.0/8.7								
F259	21.2/8.7								
F263	21.6/8.6								

Late Bronze Age Outliers and Inliers
Outliers

Context	Grid E/N	Length (m)	Max. diam. (mm)	Prop. worked	Fig.	Sp	RC	Sample	Comments
F169	15.3/11.3	0.29	72	?1.0		Sa			C
F147	17.0/9.7	0.49+	136	—		Q			(Top half only extracted). T
F212	18.9/9.5	0.51	125	0.2	Figs. 40, 42 & 62, Pl. 56	Q			C Oblique point. T*
F200	19.6/11.3	0.28	88	1.0	Fig. 40	Q			C T

Rear 'braces'

Context	Grid E/N	Length (m)	Max. diam. (mm)	Prop. worked	Fig.	Sp	RC	Sample	Comments
F18	12.9/7.6	0.40	122	1.0	Figs. 21 & 40				C
F126	14.7/7.5	0.48	98	1.0	Figs. 21, 45 & 40, Pl. 35	Q			C T
F127	15.3/7.8	not recovered			Fig. 45				
F128	15.8/7.8	not recovered			Fig. 45				
F301	20.6/7.8	not recovered			Fig. 40				

Neolithic timbers (Horizontal, not *in situ*)

Context	Grid E/N	Length (m)	Max. diam. (mm)	Prop. worked	Fig.	Sp	RC	Sample	Comments
F168	7-8/6-7 NW-SE	1.75	227	?one end	Fig. 17	Sa		HAR-6l31	1.3 m recovered; water-worn but one end likely shaped.
F184	19-20/7 WSW-ENE	1.47	153	?1.0	Figs. 18 & 58 Pl. 20	Q	28+(22h)c		Waterworn, but facets still evident. T*
F202	3-4/7-8 NW-SE	2.22	235	?1.0	Fig. 17	Al		HAR-6130	Waterworn, but both ends likely shaped.
F204	3/8 N-S	0.90+	60	—	Figs. 17 & 58	Q	7/8 a		Not all retrieved; waterworn, but worked facets. T*
F205	12/9 SW-NE	1.16	111	—	Fig. 17	Q			Waterworn, no certain facets but likely utilised.

Table 4: Summary of piles and other important wood finds (continued).

Context	Type & grid E/N	Length (m)	Max. diam. (mm)	Prop. worked	Align- ment	Fig.	Sp	RC	Sample	Comments
Area 6: important groups of LBA non-structural wood; worked/felled.										
Clearance horizon										
F163/1	branch 8.2/13.5	0.78	90	—	N-S	Fig. 29a, Pl. 44	?Sa		a)HAR-3752	Truncated by
/2	branch 7.9/13.5	0.66	90	—	N-S	Fig. 29a, Pl. 44	Ac		b)HAR-3751	contractor. Truncated by contractor.
/3	pole 7.9/13.5	0.85	40	—	NW-SE	Fig. 29a, Pl. 44	Q	9		?Truncated by contractor.
/4	pole 7.9/13.4	0.60	40	—	N-S	Fig. 29a, Pl. 44	Q	8		
/5	pole 7.6/13.6	0.88	30	—	NW-SE	Fig. 29a, Pl. 44	Q	8		
/6	pole 7.6/13.6	0.70	30	—	NW-SE	Fig. 29a. Pl. 44	Q	7		
/7	pole 8.3/13.4	0.30	40	—	SW-NE	Fig. 29a, Pl. 44	Co			
F193	pole 10.0/13.2	0.34	30	—	WNW-ESE	Fig. 29a	Q			Likely same piece.
F194	pole 9.8/13.4	0.18	40	—	NW-SE	Fig. 29a	Q			
F195	branch 9.8/13.1	1.70	100	—	WSW-ENE	Fig. 29a	—		a)HAR-3116 b)HAR-3117	
F195/ 1-3	poles around 10/13	0.50 0.65 0.28	40	—	W-E	Fig. 29a	—			
F207	branch 9.7/12.2	1.28	89	0.12	SW-NE	Fig. 29a & 62	Q			Sharpened end. T
Hard standings										
F155/1	branch 13.9/12.2	0.36	80	—	W-E	Figs. 9 & 27b	Q	16		
/2	branch 13.5/12.4	0.45	90	—	W-E	Figs. 9 & 27b	?Q	—		
/3	branch 13.3/12.5	0.76	100	—	W-E	Figs. 9 & 27b	Q	—	a)HAR-3762 b)HAR-3759	Truncated by contractor.
F164/1	branch 19.4/10.2	1.70	70	—	NE-SW	Fig. 27b, Pls. 40–42	Q		a)HAR-3761 b)HAR-3750	Truncated by modern pit.
/2	branch 19.0/10.5	1.40	65	—	N-S	Fig. 27b, Pls. 40–42	Q			Joins F164/6.
/3	branch 18.5/10.3	1.82+	70	—	NE-SW	Fig. 27b, Pls. 40–42	Q			Probably part of F164/11.
/4	branch 17.8/10.2	1.10+	80	—	NE-SW	Fig. 27b, Pls. 40–42	?Q			
/5	branch 17.0/10.9	0.80+	80	—	W-E	Fig. 27b, Pls. 40–42	Q			
/6	branch 19.0/11.3	0.39	90	—	N-S	Fig. 27b, Pls. 40–42	—			Part of 164/2.
/7	branch 18.5/11.4	0.40	60	—	N-S	Fig. 27b, Pls. 40–42	?Q			
/8	branch 17.3/11.5	0.50+	70	—	W-E	Fig. 27b, Pls. 40–42	Q			
/9	branch 17.3/11.6	0.30+	80	—	W-E	Fig. 27b, Pls. 40–42	Q	7		Probably belongs to I64/10.

Table 4: Summary of piles and other important wood finds (continued).

Context	Type & grid E/N	Length (m)	Max. diam. (mm)	Prop. worked	Align-ment	Fig.	Sp	RC	Sample	Comments
F164/10	branch 17.7/11.6	0.30	70	—	W-E	Fig. 27b, Pls. 40–42	Q			Probably belongs to 164/9.
/11	branch 19.3/11.0	0.45	80	—	NE-SW	Fig. 27b, Pls. 40–42	Q	6		Probably part of 164/3.
/12	branch 19.0/10.6	0.60	50	—	W-E	Fig. 27b, Pls. 40–42				

Context	Type & location	Length (m)	Max. diam. (mm)	Prop. worked	Fig.	Sp	RC	Sample	Comments
Worked timbers from salvage (recovered or sampled)									
Area 4 (many others in Area 4 were not recovered, see plan – Fig.14).									
L3 Sa	branch – brush structure Area 4B	—	—	—	Fig. 15, Pls. 12–14	Q	11 a		
S1	pile – Neolithic brush structure Area 4B	—	—	—	Fig. 15	Q		HAR-6132	V. fragmented; indications of working-facets similar to S3 & S4. C T*
S2	pile – Neolithic brush structure A4B	0.76	131	0.6+	Figs. 15 & 58	prob Q			
S3	pile – Neolithic brush structure A4B	0.95	116	0.5+	Figs. 15 & 58		c.19 c		3 portions. T*
S4	pile – Neolithic brush structure Area 4B	0.94+	116	—	Fig. 15	Q	12/13 a	HAR-6128	Fragmented; tip missing; small facets similar to S3. T*
F12	pile; LBA inner row	—	—	—	Fig. 14				Slice only retrieved
F13	pile; LBA inner row	—	—	—	Fig. 14	Q			Slice only retrieved
F14	pile; LBA inner row	—	—	—	Fig. 14	Q	15 c		Slice only retrieved.
F15	pile; LBA inner row	—	—	—	Fig. 14	Q			Slice only retrieved.
F16	pile; LBA ?outer row	—	—	—	Fig. 14	Q			Slice only retrieved.
F18	pile; LBA inner row	—	—	—	Fig. 14	Q	38 c		Slice only retrieved.
F20	pile; LBA inner row	—	—	—	Fig. 14	Q			Slice only retrieved.
F27	pile; LBA inner or outer row	—	—	—	Fig. 14				Slice only retrieved.
F27A	pile; LBA inner or outer row	0.37+	89	1.0	Fig. 14		22 c		2 parts; top truncated.
F28	pile; LBA inner row	0.54+	128	0.9	Fig. 14	Q	14 c		2/3 parts; top truncated, tip missing.
F74	pile; Area 4A	—	90	—	Fig. 14	Fr	18 a		Portion only retrieved.
F83	pile; LBA inner row	—	—	—	Fig. 14	Q			Slice only retrieved.
F88	pile; LBA inner row	—	—	—	Fig. 14	Q			Slice only retrieved.
F88a	?	—	—	—	Fig. 14				
F88A	wood beside LBA inner row	—	—	—	Fig. 14	Al			Large piece of wood with bark noted in places; not obviously used.
F88B	wood beside LBA inner row	—	—	—	Fig. 14	?Q			Not obviously used.
F89	shaped bark; Area 4A	—	—	—	Pls. 17 & 18 Fig. 14	bark			See wooden artifacts catalogue W4.

Table 4: Summary of piles and other important wood finds (continued).

Context	Type & location	Length (m)	Max. diam. (mm)	Prop. worked	Fig.	Sp	RC	Sample	Comments
Area 5									
F292	pile *in situ*	0.90	—	—		Q			Upper part very damaged; inner or outer LBA row. T
F294	branches	—	—	—	Figs. 7b & 8	Sa, Co, Pr,Q			Probably Neolithic age.
Area 6									
F167	pile *in situ* N. edge	0.44	94	1.0		Q			?Top truncated; one of LBA rows. T*
F290	pile *in situ* N. edge	0.68	130	0.9		—			Top possibly truncated; one of LBA rows. T
F291	pile *in situ* N. edge	0.42+	120	1.0		Q			Top probably truncated; one of LBA rows.
Area 8 (NB. total of six piles recorded in section, Fig. 12).									
3B	pile *in situ* W section	0.40+	128	1.0	Fig. 12		40(30h) a	HAR-6133	Pile excavated *in situ*; tip not retrieved; long facets give polygonal section.

Notes:
C – piles retrieved effectively complete to rotted top.
D – sampled for dendrochronological study.
HAR – Harwell reference for radiocarbon measurement (see Chapter 20).
RC – total number of rings extant (number of which are heartwood in parentheses); a, b, c – completeness categories (Chapter 13).
Sp – species of wood (see also Chapter 13).
T – covered by technological study (Chapter 7).
T* – special mention in text of Chapter 7.

There is another gap further along the eastern bay, again in both rows, and this is perhaps due to loss of piles through the deeper truncation there. These gaps result in an average spacing of inner row piles of about 0.38 m, somewhat greater than in Area 6. However, the western bay in Area 4 has an average spacing of 0.34 m and no blatant signs of loss, so the piles may have been a little more widely spaced in this part of the waterfront.

The three southernmost piles in the Area 7 section SA5, at least, seem likely to belong to the inner row. However, in Area 5 it may not be represented. Given that only one tight cluster was present (and assuming a separation between the two rows) it is most likely that those piles belong to the outer row and that the point to the west at which the inner row would have reached the section had been destroyed earlier by the large pit dug for the 1959–60 foundations.

The outer pile row: waterfront 2

This was a continuous line of closely set piles (Fig. 41) across Area 6 with an average spacing of 0.22 m, which is remarkably similar to that for the inner row. The alignment is good, with only small deviations from the two smooth arcs that may be interpolated and which meet in a cusp at piles F313–315. As discussed above, all the piles in Area 5 (section SA3), should belong to the outer row, as probably should some of the northern ones in Area 7, section SA5. The spacing between this and the inner row decreases from 0.7 m in the west of Area 6 to 0.3 m in the east, a close setting which seems to have continued through Area 7 and Area 4 until it began to diverge again towards section SA11. The outer row cannot be traced across the whole of Area 4, apparently giving out in the western bay. As in Area 6, the outer row piles seem generally to be slighter and less deeply driven, and it is possible that the piles in the western bay were entirely removed by the contractor's excavations. Although the two rows seem to have been very close in this segment, it is rather unlikely that the outer row piles were amongst the single line of piles planned, given that the density there matches that of the inner row alone in the eastern bay. From the cusp eastwards to the section about 17 piles are set along the outer row, with an average spacing of 0.44 m. However, the spacing would be somewhat closer but for two gaps, the explanation of which has been discussed above.

Identified piles were all made of oak, usually very young trunks with 10–22 rings, or in one instance 32 rings. Two very slender sharpened stakes (F271, 272) are not considered to belong to the main foundations of waterfront 2, although they may be ancillary; one is oak the other *Salix*. Maximum diameters mostly fall between 0.08 and 0.12 m (Fig. 37) and, being unworked parts of the piles, these values indicate the choice of more slender trees than for the inner row. However, the ring counts indicate a similar age distribution to those for the inner row piles (Fig. 39), and it may be concluded therefore that the trees cut for the outer row grew in an environment less conducive to fast growth, perhaps

on drier or poorer soil. The plot of approximate depths of penetration shows a difference between trench 1 and trench 2 piles. In the former most piles survived to lengths of between 0.50 m and 0.70 m, as compared with 0.90 m and 1.20 m in trench 2 (the shorter ones in trench 2 have all potentially had their tops damaged by the A30 floodway immediately above them). The transition between these trends appears to have occurred under the central baulk. It seems likely that the mean difference of around 0.40 m is due to undulation in the contemporary foreshore, with a higher surface in trench 1. This is partly borne out by a difference of about 0.20 m in the base of layer 8b at the outer row between sections 37 and 38, which can be explained by the presence of silt layer 13 outside the inner pile row in trench 1 but not in trench 2. Again, the approximate angles and directions of inclination of piles seem to group adjacent sets of 6 or 7 piles (Fig. 36) and this can be interpreted in relation to the superstructure (Chapter 4).

Four piles from the outer row were used to provide seven radiocarbon samples. On the assumption of a single event, six results were compatible with one another and give a mean determination of 2655 ± 30 BP (Chapter 20).

Outliers and inliers

In Area 6 four piles can be regarded as outliers which relate to the waterfront structures, while a soil cast with only a wood 'splinter' surviving (F269) may have been a fifth. A further four (F18, F126, F127, F128) were driven into the dry bank, probably after initial digging of a pit; these are categorised below as pit-piles. Finally, at the eastern end of trench 2 there was a cluster of piles and very slender stakes, either just behind, or impinging on, the two pile rows, but of uncertain relationship (F251, 252, 255, 258, 271, 272, 301). Piles in an apparently similar range of positions relative to the waterfronts occur in Area 4, with one in Area 7, but the loss of the stratigraphy leaves the chronology of most of them highly uncertain. Many to the south of the LBA river channel in Area 4 are likely to be Neolithic, as demonstrated for four piles in Area 4B.

As with the main waterfront piles, oak was used, except for F169, which is *Salix*-type. The lengths of those excavated in Area 6 are short, 0.24–0.95 m, but this will be for different reasons. The pit-piles were inserted from a much higher surface and so only the tips penetrated waterlogged ground. The outliers, on the other hand, seem not to have been driven as deeply (with the possible exception of F147) as nearby row piles, suggesting that they bore less load. F212 is also unusual in having an obliquely sharpened point.

Stratigraphic information from the outliers is not terribly helpful. F200 and F212 were truncated before peat layer 9 developed, but penetrated underlying deposits; F200 penetrated layer 25 at least and F212 penetrated most or all of layer 20, as shown by deformation of lenses within the layer (Fig. 42). This allows insertion between units C and G and therefore an association with either phase of waterfront, or on a separate occasion. The phasing of F169 is also determined by the potentially long hiatus at the layer 20/9 interface. F147 was situated only just behind the outer row, to which it could have belonged. However, it leaned in a very different direction to the set of nearby outer piles (Fig. 35) and on these grounds is argued instead to be an outlier of the inner row. The distance of F147 in front of the inner row does conform to a pattern whereby it and three other outliers (F212, F169, F269) all lie between 0.30 and 0.55 m outside one or other of the pile rows. This consistent spatial relationship is about the only guide indicating which waterfront phase they belong to. The axial alignment of F200 and F212 to one of the bays suggests that they might belong together, but on the other hand the close correspondence of bays for the two waterfront phases would create this plan in palimpsest if one focal outlier was associated with each phase.

Although there was obviously a regular pattern of focal outliers in bays, the distances out into the channel varied. F212 was very close to the rows, whilst three were 2 m (Area 7) or 2.5 m (Area 6 – F200; Area 4 – eastern bay) from the outer row. The western bay in Area 4 has two approximately focal outliers about 5 m and 5.5 m out. A pile just in front of the inner row in this same bay could perhaps be a closely set outlier like those in Area 6. Two of the latter kind in Area 6 (F147, F169) are not focal and are situated towards one side of their respective bays.

It seems rather unlikely that any of the outliers were intended to be front braces for the pile rows. Some were too close to the rows, and two of these (F212, F147) were leaning in the wrong direction; those 2 m or 2.5 m away would have to have been angled back sharply, yet F200 at least was not. Those over 5 m away clearly could not have functioned in that way. As already mentioned, the excavated examples were not deeply bedded and therefore their load-bearing or stabilising capacity would seem to be limited. At most they would seem capable of having supported short plank walkways, having acted as mooring posts or display posts.

The four pit-piles in Area 6 form a line 3 m long, well behind the pile rows and oblique to the river's edge. They seem likely to belong together, but it is unclear how they might relate to either the waterfronts or structures on the bank. A line of four or five piles 2.2 m long in Area 4 lies immediately behind the interpreted inner row and could be seen as a similar setting; two of the piles are alternatively grouped with the set which appears to disrupt both waterfront rows (as discussed above).

No outliers or inliers have been radiocarbon dated.

Laid branch structures

Timbers laid on a surface, as opposed to piles driven in, seem to belong to structures at two main stratigraphic horizons. The stratigraphic position of the later group, interpreted as hardstandings on the foreshore (F155, F164), has been fully discussed elsewhere (Chapter 2) as part of the river channel stratigraphy, in which they are attributed to unit F.

F155 was a small group of parallel timbers, laid east–west, which survived on the edge of the contractor's pit at 13E/12N and was first recorded in salvage section SA4 (Fig. 9). It is noteworthy that the closest timbers in trench 2, those running under the main baulk (F164/5,8,9,10 – Fig. 27B) have similar alignment and widths and may be connected more with F155 than the main part of F164. Unfortunately it was not possible to excavate their extension under the baulk. F164 has two components. First there is a bundle of withies which were almost certainly coppiced rods; they mainly lay parallel to waterfront 2, occupying the centre of the depression in the silt, but a few rods lay more transverse to this axis. There was no sign of interweaving to suggest hurdle work, although some rods were very fragmented, which could have led to the loss of that kind of information. Overlying the rods was the second component, the remains of at least five similar sized branches which seem to have formed a lattice, three on one axis (F164/1,3,4) and two on another (F164/6,7). There was no obvious means of securing this structure (pile tips F200 and F212 being believed to belong to the waterfront structures).

The structures under discussion were not obviously collapsed portions of waterfront superstructure, nor indeed parts of other buildings. Yet the alignments make it clear that these were laid formations rather than, say, ejected wood debitage. This suggests, therefore, platforms or consolidation material. Perhaps one likely function, given their foreshore setting, is that of beaching ramps, or hardstandings, for boats. A heavy log-boat or plank-built boat might well sink into the soft mud here on the foreshore and thus be difficult to relaunch. The laid timbers would help prevent such sinking. In the case of F164 there is a temptation to regard the bundle of rods as the crucial element of the structure and the branch merely as weighing-down devices. However, if the hardstanding interpretation is correct, then the bundle merely becomes a foundation to keep the branch lattice proud of the foreshore and capable of supporting a boat by the distribution of its weight.

The majority of the timber identified was of oak, indicating selection, while ring counts suggest use of coppiced wood. Although these structures seem to be a little later than the waterfront 2 piles it is most likely that they were in use during the lifetime of waterfront 2 and thereby represent activities immediately outside the perimeter stockade envisaged.

The material planned at a lower level in layer 20c, beneath F164 (Fig. 27A), was regarded at the time of excavation as a natural accumulation of drift-wood. Much wood in the deposit had a thoroughly water-worn appearance and there doubtless was a drift component, but there are also signs of co-alignment amongst many of the rod-like timbers. Since the alignment does not follow the most obvious water flow, there must be a possibility that remnants of one or more earlier laid timber structures are represented.

94

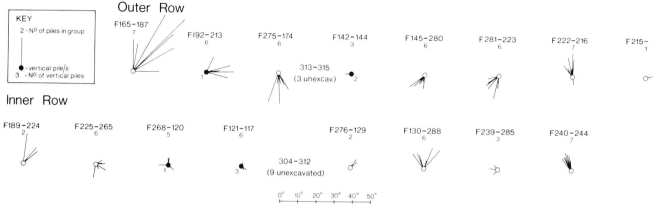

Outer Row

F165-187
7

F192-213
6

F275-174
6

F142-144
3

F145-280
6

F281-223
6

F222-216
7

F215-
1

313-315
(3 unexcav.)

KEY
2 - Nº of piles in group
● - vertical pile/s
3 - Nº of vertical piles

Inner Row

F189-224
2

F225-265
6

F268-120
5

F121-117
6

F276-129
2

F130-288
6

F239-285
3

F240-244
7

304-312
(9 unexcavated)

0° 10° 20° 30° 40° 50°

Fig. 36 Suggested grouping of outer and inner row piles according to trends in their inclinations. Inclinations of less than 2° are treated as vertical and represented by solid circles; angled piles are shown as radiating lines having lengths proportional to their slope angle.

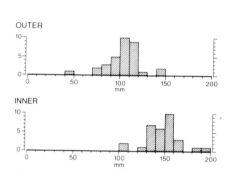

OUTER

INNER

Fig. 37 Maximum diameters of Area 6 piles in the outer and inner rows. Piles worked over their full lengths have been excluded.

Fig. 38 Approximate depths below water table reached by Area 6 piles along the two rows from north-west (left) to south-east. Possibly associated outlying piles are projected onto the rows to show the contrast.

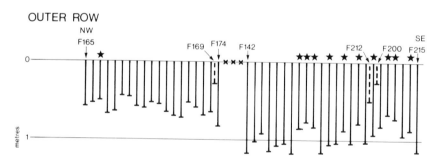

OUTER ROW
NW
F165   F169 F174   F142   F212 F200 F215
SE

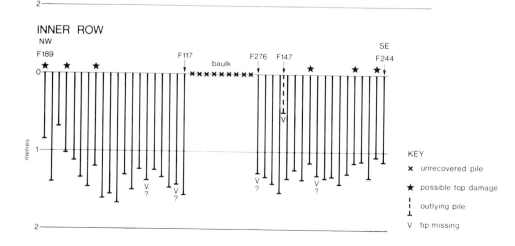

INNER ROW
NW
F189   F117   baulk   F276 F147   F244
SE

KEY
✕ unrecovered pile
★ possible top damage
┊ outlying pile
V tip missing

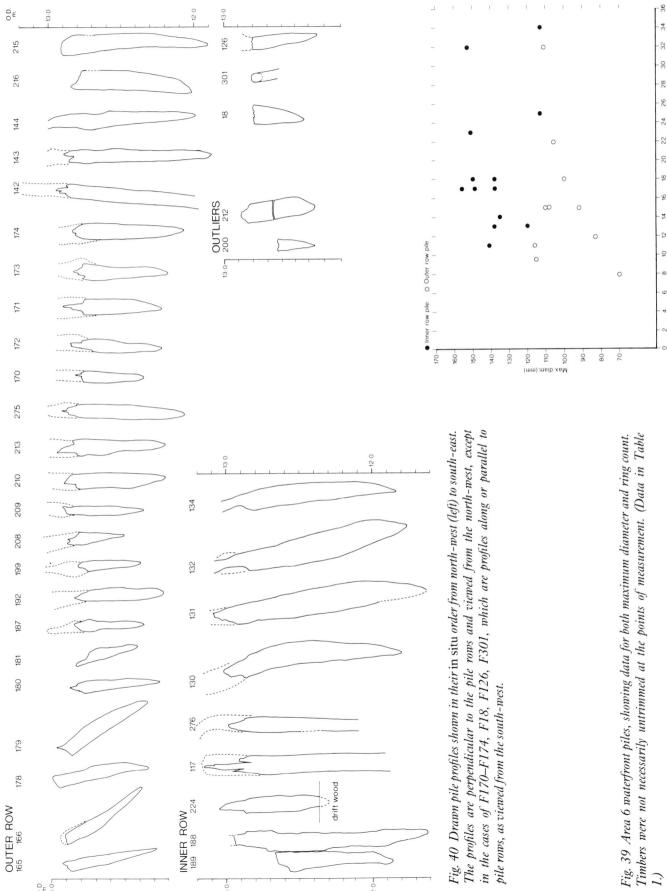

Fig. 40 Drawn pile profiles shown in their in situ order from north–west (left) to south–east. The profiles are perpendicular to the pile rows and viewed from the north–west, except in the cases of F170–F174, F18, F126, F301, which are profiles along or parallel to pile rows, as viewed from the south–west.

Fig. 39 Area 6 waterfront piles, showing data for both maximum diameter and ring count. Timbers were not necessarily untrimmed at the points of measurement. (Data in Table 1.)

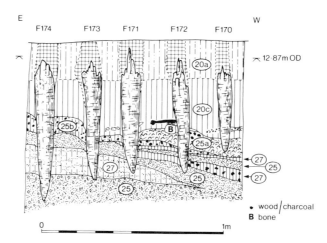

Fig. 41 Area 6, main baulk: section 31 through deposits flanking five outer row piles, F170–F174.

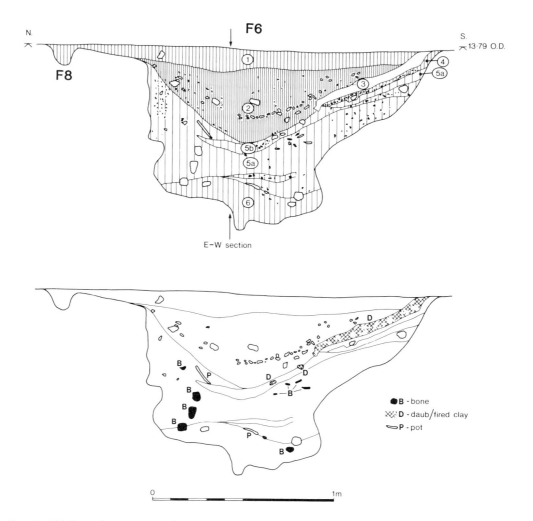

Fig. 43a Area 6: united N-S quadrant sections of pit F6 and the distribution of finds.

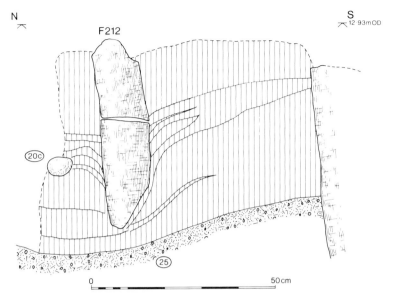

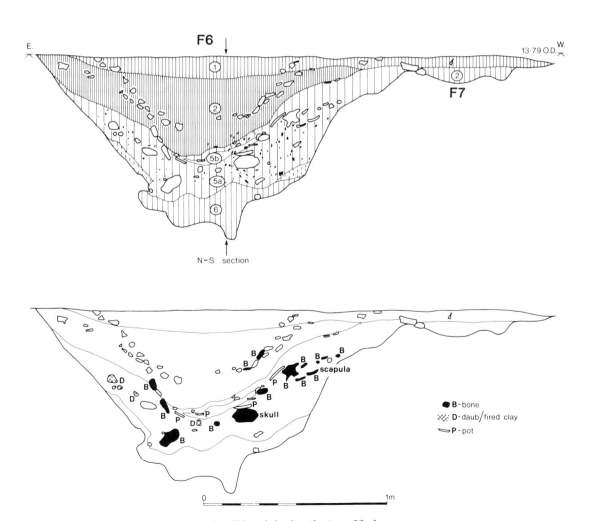

Fig. 42 Area 6, trench 2: section through the deposits penetrated by outlying pile F212.

Fig. 43b Area 6: united E-W quadrant sections of pit F6 and the distribution of finds.

Table 5: Summary of cut features in Area 6.

F no	Grid E/N(m)	Maximum diameter top(cm)	Maximum depth (cm)	Nominal post diameter	Fill characteristics	Finds	Section drawing	Feature classification	Comments
1	4/10	—	—	—	Very mottled blue/green/brown clay	Prehistoric and modern; antler cheek-piece(B14)	—	—	Modern – probably associated with A30 bridge.
2	4/7	—	—	—	Greenish compact clay with ash	Prehistoric and modern; utilised boar's tusk (B11)	—	—	Modern – probably associated with A30 bridge.
3	10/11	—	—	—	Dark stain	—	Fig. 25 A	—	Probably modern oil spill.
4	7/10	—	—	—	Mottled blue/grey clay with orange sand	Prehistoric	—	—	Modern.
5	14/6	102	56	—	Upper: dark brown soil; lower: dark grey soil with some shell mixed with yellow buff clay clods	P, M13	Fig. 44	?P; 'U'base	Possibly prehistoric; truncated by slope of A30 floodway channel.
6 (266) (214) (203)	6/11	205	95	—	L1: brown clayey silt L2a: intermediate from L1 L2b: dark grey silty soil, much C and some D L2c: localised brownish-green in SE quadrant, possibly related to L3 L3: dense orange-red fired clay with some ashy soil L4: dense charcoal in silt; lower part less charcoal rich and browner L5a: only slightly dirty yellow/beige clay-loam L5b: as 5a but more charcoal L6: grey clay-loam with some C	P, B, F, S, BF, loomweight fragment (C16), spindlewhorl (C12) P, B, F, S, BF, whittled antler tine (B12), rib offcut (B6) cut horn core (Chapter 18) ?hone(S177) P, B, F P, B, BF, S P, B, F, S(S170), 2 possible loomweight fragments (not catalogued) P, F, S – hone (S169)	Fig. 43	P(PS)	Probable occupation soil dipping into depression in top of compacted fill. Initial fill after recut; also fills possible sockets F203 and F214. Lens tipped in from south side, truncated by recut. Lens tipped from south side, sealed under L3; C14 results HAR-3112, 3113; large slabs of jar (558) towards base. Disarticulated horse skeleton amongst finds in redeposited natural.
7	5/12	52	9	—	Brown soil with C, BF and burnt clay	P, B, S, F, BF	Fig. 43	M	Primary layer covering base of pit and also infilling post socket in centre of base (F266).
8	6/12	20	10	—	Dark soil	P, B	Fig. 25 A	PH3	Contiguous with F6 on west side; their respective fills merged.
9	6/10	37	6	—	Daub-flecked soil	None	—	M	Possibly intercutting, or part of F319. Shallow depression forming lobe on south side of F6.

Table 5: Summary of cut features in Area 6 (continued).

No.	Date				Fill	Finds	Type	Fig.	Comments
11	12/6	148	126	—	L1: dark grey clayey loam	P, B, S, F	P(PS) – asymmetric conical profile (only half excavated)	Fig. 21	Probably occupation soil dipping into depression in top of compacted fill.
					L2: yellow-brown clay	None			Backfilled natural.
					L3: mottled grey/brown clayey loam, much C	P, B			Charcoal C14 dated: HAR-3118, 3119.
					L4: yellow clay	—			Backfilled natural.
					L5: grey clayey-loam	—			Primary fill, also fills post socket at base.
					NB. Layers 4 & 5 only found after machining to access Neolithic layers.				
12	12/6	33	11	13	Grey/brown loam with C and D flecks	P, B	PH3f	Fig. 44	On periphery of pit F11.
13	12/6	20	9	10	Dark grey/brown clayey loam with C and D flecks	None	PH3f	Fig. 44	On periphery of pit F11.
14	11/5	30	40	20	Dark grey with C	P, B, F, worked bone (B3)	PH1	Fig. 21	Funnel shaped with slight basal expansion.
15	8/5	45	10	—	L1: ash-rich black soil / L2: lightly fired clay lining / L3: grey-brown soil	P, B, BF, D, bronze(M9)	M	Fig. 44	Circular structure with partial clay lining set in low part of occupation soil and also just penetrating natural; L3 may be lateral extension of occupation soil.
15a	11/5	19	4	—	Grey-brown clayey	None	M	—	Against baulk – not fully excavated.
16	11/5	19	5	—	Grey-brown clayey	B	M	—	
17	12/5	82 × 40	32	10	Grey clayey with C and shell, L2 having yellow patches within	P, B, F, spindlewhorl (C11), flint core (FL16)	P or PH1	Fig. 44	Modern pipe driven vertically through NE part.
18	12/7	46	165	12	Dark brown loam with yellow clay flecks; lens in top different	P, B	P(PL) – shallow ledge profile on W lip	Fig. 44	Excavated as deep pit with convoluted profile; later after machining of trench 2 deep tip of pile found directly beneath.
19	6/12	25	7	—	—	D	M	A	At end of linear gully F104.
20	13/7	10	8	—	Dark grey-brown loam	P	M	—	
21	4/6	11	4	—	Brown with C flecks	B, P	M – 'U'base	—	Root activity?
22	5/6	17	4	—	Brown with C flecks	None	M	A	
23	5/5	6	—	—	Grey clay	None	L	—	Probable root hole.
24	13/6	5	14	—	Dark grey-brown clay loam with C and D flecks	None	S	—	
25	13/7	9	6	—	Dark grey-brown clay loam with C and D flecks	None	M	—	
26	13/7	10	5	—	Dark grey-brown clay loam with C and D flecks	P	M	—	
27	13/7	9	6	—	Dark grey loam with C and D	None	M	—	Small slot contiguous with F18.
28	14/7	6	15	—	Dark grey-brown clay loam with C and D flecks	None	S	—	
29	13/7	21	18	—	Dark grey clay loam with C and D flecks	P, B	PH3 – asymmetric conical	Fig. 21	Against baulk, not fully excavated.

Table 5: Summary of cut features in Area 6 (continued).

F no	Grid E/N(m)	Maximum diameter top(cm)	Maximum depth (cm)	Nominal post diameter	Fill characteristics	Finds	Section drawing	Feature classification	Comments
30	5/9	10	6	—	—	P, B, F	A	M	
31	14/7	12	8	—	Dark brown clay loam with C and D flecks	None	—	M	
32	12/6	17 × 8	12	—	Dark brown clay loam with C	None	—	?PH – base irregular	Angled penetration of natural – ?root.
33	11/5	9	7	—	Dark grey-brown clay loam with C and D flecks	None	—	M	Against baulk, not fully excavated.
34	12/5	5	9	—	Dark grey-brown clay loam, C	None	—	S or M ?	
35	13/5	8	—	—	Dark grey clay loam with C and D flecks	None	—	M	Adjacent to steeply pitched modern pipe driven through fill of F17 – also modern?
37	13/5	48	shallow	—	Dark grey clay loam with C and D flecks	P, B	—	M	Against baulk, not fully excavated.
38	4/9	31	4	—	Dark grey clayey with C	P, B, S, D	Fig. 44	M	Probably truncated by shallow end of F2; maximum diameter includes very shallow shelf on E side.
39	5/7	37	11	15	Brown soil with D flecks	B, BF	Fig. 44	PH3f	
40	6/7	60	6	—	Dark grey-brown clayey with C and D flecks	P, B, D	A	M – uneven bottom	Possibly just fill of ground depression.
41	6/8	33	30	12	L1:top 20 cm dark grey with C L2:bottom 10 cm yellower and more clayey	P, BF, S, B, D D, BF	Fig. 44	PH1f	2 sherds of pottery pressed against one side.
42	8/8	20	15	16	Dark grey clayey; C at base	P, B, D	Fig. 44	PH2	Very shallow cone around part of lip not included in diameter.
43	8/6	40	33	14	L1: dark grey-brown clayey with C and D flecks L2: yellow clayey with C L3: grey clayey	P, B BF, P, B	Fig. 44	PH1f	Step in N wall, cone at top; finds from three layers amalgamated together.
44	9/5	38	26	6 × 14?	Dark grey clayey with C	B, BF	Fig. 44	PH1	Ramped, especially on S side which was also penetrated by root or stake hole.
45	9/6	50	24	16	Dark grey clayey with C at E side	P, B, D	Fig. 44	PH1f	Broad cone.
46	10/6	44	36	10-15	Dark grey clayey with C and D flecks	P, B	Fig. 44	PH1f	Probable root gully (F78) runs into N side.
47	5/8	—	3	—	Brown silt	BF	A	—	Probable undulation in natural.
48	3/8	12	—	—	—	None	—	—	Shallow depression.

Table 5: Summary of cut features in Area 6 (continued).

Feature	Grid	Length	Width	Depth	Fill	Finds	Plan	Phase	Comments
49	3/8	10	—	—		None	—	—	Shallow depression.
50	4/8	6	—	—		None	—	—	Shallow depression.
51	7/5	a) 37	21	20	L1: dark grey clayey with C	BF, S, P, B, D	Fig. 44	PH3	3 morphological components: a) main cut at NW end, with fill sequence L1, L4, L2 (top to bottom); b) deeper socket in middle with L1 fill; c) shallow shelf on SE with L2 and L3; Cluster of stones at L1/L2 interface may have been packing.
		b) 10	28	10	L2: yellow-brown clayey, C	BF		S	
		c) 30	5		L3: dark red clayey	None		M	
					L4: black crumbly, much C	BF, P, D, S			
52/61	10/6	50 long	—	—	Grey clayey	None	A	L	Root system? (15 cm wide)
53	7/6	9	9	—	Dark grey clayey with C	BF	—	M ?S	Stake or root?
54	6/6	8	9	—	Dark grey clayey with C	F, B	—	M	Root – split into 2 slanting tapered holes.
55	6/6	10	5	—	Dark grey clayey with C	None	—	M	Double hole – root?
56	6/6	14	4	—	Dark grey clayey with C	BF	—	M	Four depressions – root?
57	7/6	20	11	—	Grey clayey with C	P, BF	Fig. 44	PH4?	Approximately conical.
58	7/5	35	3	—	Red-brown clayey with C	BF	A	M	
59	5/6	16	4	—	Dark grey clayey with C	B, S	—	M	
60	10/8	30	29	15	L1: dark grey-brown clayey with C and D / L2: mixed yellow/brown clayey	P, B, D, shells, pebbles	Fig. 44	PH3f	Layer 1/2 distinction poor.
61	10/6	See F52							
62	10/7	25	31	—	Dark grey clayey with C and shells	P, B	Fig. 44	L	PH2 – 'U' base
63	3/6	(10 wide)	—	—	Grey clayey	B	—	M	Branch-like plan – root system.
64	6/6	18	5	—	Grey clayey with C	BF	Fig. 44	M	
65	6/5	30	4	—	Dark grey clayey	None	Fig. 44	M	
66	8/8	30	7	—	Dark grey clayey with shell	P, B, BF	Fig. 44	M	Root holes ran into N and W sides.
67	11/8	60	27	—	L1: dark grey clayey with D and C	P, B, BF, D	Fig. 44	?P or PH	Complex fill; unclear what overall form, whether multi-phase and whether fully dug.
					L2: grey clayey with D and C towards bottom	P, B, BF			
					L3: brown clayey with C	None			
68	7/7	14	13	—	Grey clayey with shell, especially at top	None	Fig. 44	PH3	
69	9/5	35	35	17	Grey-brown clayey with C	P, D	Fig. 44	PH2f	
70	8/5	13	3	—	Grey clayey	B	A	M	Against baulk, not fully excavated; gully enters N side.
72	8/5	13	5	—	Grey clayey	None	—	M	
73	7/5	18	—	—		None	—	M	?Root hole; against baulk.
74	7/8	20	5	—	Red-brown clayey with C and shell	BF	—	M	Linear gully entered N side.

Table 5: Summary of cut features in Area 6 (continued).

F no	Grid E/N(m)	Maximum diameter top(cm)	Maximum depth (cm)	Nominal post diameter	Fill characteristics	Finds	Section drawing	Feature classification	Comments
75	7/7	a) 5 b) 6	7 / 3	—	Yellow-grey clay with C	BF	—	M	Likely two small root holes.
76	7/7	6	3	—	Yellow-grey clayey with C	BF	—	M	
77	8/7	18	3	—	Brown clayey with D flecks	B	A	M	
78	10/6	80 long 24 wide	4	—	Yellow-grey clayey with C and shell	BF	—	L	Root system?
79	9/7	18	3	—	Grey-brown clayey, C & shell	B	—	M	
80	9/7	13	20	—	Grey clayey with C and shell	P, BF	—	S	Feature possibly not bottomed.
81	8/7	12	5	—	Grey clayey with C	None	—	M	
82	8/7	12	6	—	Yellow-grey clayey with C, shell and D flecks	None	—	M	
83	8/7	60 long	—	—	—	None	—	L	Root gully? 10 cm wide.
84	9/8	43 long	6	—	Yellow-grey with C and shell	B,F	—	L	Root gully? 10 cm wide.
85	8/8	15	8	—	Grey-brown clayey, C & shell	P, B	—	M	
86	10/9	20	39	—	Dark grey clayey with C & D	P, B, F, BF	Fig. 44	S	
87	6/7	5	5	—	Yellow-grey with C & D fleck	None	—	M	
88	11/8	25	7	—	Dark grey clayey with C & D	B, D	Fig. 44	M	
89	9/5	10	8	—	Yellow-grey clayey	None	—	M	
90	6/9	8	—	—	—	D	—	M	Shallow.
91	9/9	18	4	—	Grey-brown clayey	B,D	A	M	
92	7/9	22	6	—	Dark grey clayey with C & D	BF	A	M	
93	7/9	40	7	—	Dark grey clayey with C	P,B,D,BF cobbles	A	M	Mostly shallow, but slightly deeper at S
94	9/9	20	10	—	Grey-brown clayey with C	None	—	PH	
95	9/8	20	10	13	Grey-brown clayey with C	D	Fig. 44	PH2	?Root gully entered W side.
96	7/9	50	35	10-15	Brown clayey with yellow flecks, D, C and shells; occasional stones.	P, B	Fig. 44	PH1	Broad shallow cone around very steep-walled hole.
97	9/10	28	11	—	Yellow-grey clay, C & shell	P, B, BF, D	Fig. 44	PH3f	?Root gully entered it.
98	9/10	21	11	—	Dark grey clayey with C	P	A	M	Probably not bottomed.
99	9/9	9	22	—	Grey clayey with D & C flecks	None	Fig. 44	S	Ran into F19; 18 cm wide.
104	5/12	90 long	5	—	—	P, B	A	L	
105	7/12	7	17	—	Grey clayey with C	None	—	?S	Circular hole, expands with depth; ?not bottomed; penetrated L15 and below.
106	7/10	25	8	—	Dark brown clayey with C & yellow flecks, small stones	P	Fig. 44	M	Lobe off linear gully.
107	12/9	14	23	—	Dark grey sandy clay with C	P,F	Fig. 44	S	Angled down towards SSW; cut into L14a.
108	7/12	6	6	—	Dark soil with C & D flecks	None	—	?S	Cut from top of L15.
109	10/10	26	15	—	Dark grey clayey with C & D	B,F	Fig. 44	PH4	Cut into L14a; asymmetric profile.
110	8/11	a) 38 b) 8	19 / 12	15	Mixed dark brown/yellow clay with C, shell & pebbles	P,B / None	Fig. 44 / —	PH3f / S	Similar fill in both parts.
112	5/12	14	9	—	Slightly darker than natural	P, B	A	M	On edge of linear gully F104.

Table 5 : Summary of cut features in Area 6 (continued).

No.	Context	L	W	D	Fill	Finds		Fig.	Phase	Comments
113	5/12	17	4	—	Brown clayey with rare C	P	—	A	M	Flat-based depression on NW edge of F6.
118	5/11	9	7	—	Brown clayey with rare C & D	None	—	A	M	Small depression into NW lip of F6.
123	9/11	13	4	—	Dark brown clayey with C & D	P, B	—	—	M	Not planned; cut into L14b; irregular.
124	9/11	25 long 7 wide	7	—	Brown clayey with C & D flecks	B, BF	—	—	L	Cut into L14b; dumb-bell shaped; deepest at the ends.
126	14/7	50	125	—	Dark brown clayey with C	P, B, BF	—	Fig. 21	P(PL)	Visible on surface after removal of L8; in fact discovered during deep machining in trench 2; tip of stake *in situ* in base.
154	6/12	—	—	—	—	P	—	—	M	Undulation or root associated with F6.
156	12/9	7	6	—	Dark grey-brown with orange mottling	None	—	—	M	Round bottomed; slightly angled down towards SSE; cuts into L14b.
158	12/9	11	7	—	—	None	—	—	M	Circular; cut into L14b.
159	12/9	7	—	—	—	None	—	—	M	Cut into L14b.
160	11/8	13	7	—	—	None	—	—	M	Cut into L14b.
161	11/9	14	23	—	Dark grey-brown clayey with C & D flecks	P, B	—	Fig. 44	S/PH4	Angled very slightly down towards S; at edge of river channel deposits (L14).
162	9/6	9	3	—	Dark brown clayey with C	B	—	—	M	Cut into L14b.
175	10/11	11	11	—	Dark grey very charcoal rich	B	—	Fig. 44	M/S	
182	12/8	28 (mid)	99	—	Various yellow/brown clays with C	None	—	Fig. 23	P(PL) – pit with sharp pile-driven base profile	Upper part evidently opened out into river channel and filled with silts of Unit D; insertion therefore pre or early D; deposit in top (14g) likely post compaction fill; cut by F302; F182 only discovered when deep slot cut for section.
185	14/7	20	12	—	Dark brown loamy with C	B	—	Fig. 22	M/PH4	Cut L22; fill similar to L14d/e.
203	5/10	20	8	—	Dark grey, much C	None	—	Fig. 44	M	Depression found at interface of F6 L2/5 in SW corner – possible post socket.
211	15/8	7	43	—	Dark, charcoal rich	None	—	Fig. 44	S	Appeared to be sealed by L24.
214	5/10	20	16	—	Indistinguishable from F6L2	P, B, BF, clay object (C5)	—	Fig. 44	PH3	Adjacent to F203 and at same interface.
238	5/11	15	—	—	—	None	—	—	M	Small hollow in NW edge of F6.
266	6/11	10	20	—	Same as F6L6	None	—	Fig. 43	PH	Post socket in centre of base of pit F6.
267	11/11	8	20	—	Brown	None	—	Fig. 44	S	Post pipe of decayed wood.
273	12/11	8	13	—	—	None	—	—	S	Rotted pile tip or impression in L14a.
300	7/12	116 × 60	45	—	Main layers 15–18 (see Chapter 2)	Chapter 2	—	Figs. 24 & 25	P	Trough like feature at crest of river bank opening NE into channel; cut by F6 ph.1.
302	12/8	30	30	7	Brown clayey with C	None	—	Fig. 23	PH1/S	Discovered in cutting deep section; cuts F182; slightly angled down towards SW.

Table 5: Summary of cut features in Area 6 (continued).

F no	Grid E/N(m)	Maximum diameter top(cm)	Maximum depth (cm)	Nominal post diameter	Fill characteristics	Finds	Section drawing	Feature classification	Comments
303	12/8	20	18	10	Brown clayey with C	None	Fig. 23	PH2	Discovered in cutting deep section.
316	8/12	14	—	—	—	None	—	?S	Found below unit B deposits.
317	7/13	22	38	—	Beige clay, charcoal rich	None	Fig. 44	S	Strongly angled down towards SW; sealed by or part of unit B channel fill.
318	6/13	8	—	—	—	None	—	?S/M	Probably below unit B deposits.
319	6/12	8	43	—	Dark soil similar to over-lying deposit	None	Fig. 25	S	?Part of F8; probably post unit D.
320	12/7	35	21	10	Grey-brown clayey	Uncertain (with finds of F11, if any)	Fig. 21	PH3	On NE edge of F11, giving pit a 'lobe' in plan; possibly cut L2 of F11.
321	12/9	7	37	—	Grey, charcoal rich	None	Fig. 23	S	Driven from L14a/8b interface (unit D/E).
322	8/12	20	26	—	Charcoal rich	None	Fig. 24	S	Found after cutting deep section, fill similar to L24 (unit B).

Notes: For feature classification see text (Chapter 3).
Abbreviations: A archive section drawing, B bone/antler, BF burnt flint, C charcoal, D daub/fired clay, F struck flint, P pottery, S stone.

The still earlier horizon of potentially laid timbers comprises a group of branches and withies within clearance (unit B) deposits in trench 1. Under excavation these were thought to be cleared vegetation debris thrown down the bank, but their apparently symmetrical arrangement in relation to the midden and trough F300 above has raised the possibility of some deliberate formation. Overall they define a fan-shaped zone on the slope below F300 (Fig. 48), with one group of branches on the west (F163), another on the east (F193–195, F207). The branches may have been thrown down roughly to define the zone, or perhaps they were more neatly stacked originally, although no pegs were found which could have contained a vertical stack. Most of the timbers involved were oak, with one field maple, one hazel and a possible *Salix*. They fall into two size ranges, 'branches' of 90–100 mm and 'poles' of 30–40 mm diameter, ring counts in the latter group being between 7 and 9.

Two branches were used to provide four radiocarbon samples. Agreement between pairs of results on each of the two branches was poor, but other dates for unit B give a preference to 2800 ± 60 BP (HAR-3751) for F163/1 and 2700 ± 70 BP (HAR-3117) for F195 (Chapter 20).

Post holes and other 'cut' features

Classification

The Late Bronze Age cut features in Area 6 showed a great variation in size and shape. The great majority are thought to be man-made and they are interpreted variously as pits, post holes, stake holes and miscellaneous or nondescript hollows. A minority are considered to have been natural features resulting from roots or burrowing animal activity, as also are certain appendages to man-made features. A few cut features were modern (F1, F2, F3, F4 and the A30 floodway N–S through trench 2). The different classes of LBA feature mainly grade one into another. Each feature has, however, been classified as one of the following to aid analysis and presentation.

Pits, P

Unequivocal pits on the site are large or moderately large (maximum 1.65 m deep). Two specialised sub-types have been defined:

P(PS) pits with post-sockets at their base: F6, F11

P(PL) pits with pile-driven bases (with or without pile tip preserved): F18, F126, F182. By implication F127 and F128 are likely originally to have had similar pits above them prior to modern truncation.

Only two other features may securely be regarded as pits: F5 and F300, the latter being a trough-like feature on the river bank opening into the channel. F5 is not certainly prehistoric. Two possible post holes are regarded alternatively as pits because of anomalous ground plans: F17 and F67.

Post holes, PH

Roughly circular features with depths between about 0.10 m and 0.40 m and maximum surface diameters greater than

about 0.20 m have been classified as post holes. Post pipes were not recognised in excavation, but a nominal post diameter has been suggested for some holes based on the dimensions of the basal part of the feature. The post holes could have carried a range of post sizes from relatively slight to fairly substantial (diameter about 0.20 m).

The post holes have been subdivided according to their shape in profile:

PH1 Steep sides low down with stepped ramp or cone at the top   (F14, F17, F41, F43, F44, F45, F46, F96, F302)

PH2 near vertical sides throughout (F42, F62, F69, F95, F303)

PH3 sloped sides and flat or rounded bottom   (F8, F12, F13, F29, F39, F51, F60, F68, F97, F110a, F214, F320)

PH4 sloped sides and narrow/pointed bottom (F57, F109, F161, F185)

PH unclassified shape (F32, F67, F94, F266)

Additionally:

f   any of PH1–PH3 can have a flat or nearly flat base.

Some examples of PH4, particularly steep-sided ones, might alternatively derive from stakes. Truncated examples of PH1 could, of course, appear as forms PH2 or PH3.

Stake holes, S

These are relatively narrow features with more or less sharp ends; inevitably a number are not certainly stake holes rather than something else:

F24, F28, F34, F51b, F53, F80, F86, F99, F105, F107, F108, F110b, F161, F175, F211, F267, F273, F302, F316, F317, F318, F319, F321, F322

Depths were between 0.09 m and 0.43 m.

Miscellaneous, M

A large number of features are more or less regular, round to oval in plan, but generally shallower than 0.10 m. Few showed clear signs of root or animal origin or disturbance.

In addition to representing emplacements for stakes or posts which barely penetrated subsoil, these could also include truncated features. The broadest examples might be shallow scoops dug to retrieve clay, or for some other purpose.

Linear gullies, L

These describe wavering, curved or straight lines in plan, sometimes with branch-like structure, and are always shallow (less than about 0.08 m). These plans in conjunction with their ephemeral nature suggest that such features were root hollows and burrows. Often they run into other features.

General feature distributions

Although the area of Late Bronze Age occupation surface is too small to expect much in the way of building plans, certain patterns emerge from the feature analysis. These patterns may mainly be conditioned by the adjacent river bank. Within the channel itself are the two rows of closely established for pits F6/F300 and ancillary features and timbers which not only relate stratigraphically to the river channel deposits, but may have been intimately involved with the definition and redefinition of the settlement's boundary. This feature complex lies roughly on an axis running back perpendicular from the river channel and waterfront. The sequence begins around stratigraphic unit B, the episode of clearance (Fig. 48), with the insertion of four small stakes along the river bank (F316, F317, F318, F322) and the placing of several branches and poles down the slope in front (F163, F193, F194, F195, F297). The major branches involved lay in two sets defining a fan-shaped zone or 'chute' on the slope, plausibly a contrived arrangement when viewed in the light of the trough-pit F300 dug at the head of the fan on the crest immediately behind the stake row. This pit was dug prior to its filling during unit D, during which the stakes, possibly with interwoven elements, remained in place. The lightly burnt clay dump, F206, lying just above some of the branches (nominally unit C) could have derived from spoil from the pit. It is likely that little time elapsed during the events described so far. Further evidence that this was a zone defined for some special activity comes from the artifacts and environmental data. During units B and C a midden deposit rich in pottery and midden-liking insects (Chapter 17), in stark contrast to the contemporary flanking silts, accumulated over the fan zone. This pattern of deposition apparently continued (now above the water table, thus depriving us of environmental remains) during the unit D fill of the trough itself. The midden deposits were slightly diffused as river silt encroached around them. During this initial stage, at around the unit C/D interface, waterfront 1 was constructed (Fig. 49); a cusp may have coincided with the feature complex under consideration (Fig. 34).

After the trough pit had become completely filled, and probably also after the main period of use of waterfront 1, a new pit was dug (Fig. 50). F6 clipped the south-western end of F300 and took a very different form, a deep inverted bell with a post-socket in its base. This post obviously relates to an early stage of the pit, but it is not clear whether there was a phase of use in an open state, perhaps as a well in which the post acted as a central support. Perhaps it is more likely that the pit was dug specifically for the largely disarticulated horse burial present in the first-phase infill and the central post merely served as a marker. The first-phase infill was sealed by some large crocks of pottery and deposits interpreted as a redeposited hearth (Chapter 3). These deposits could well relate to rituals associated with the burial. The phasing of this episode at units E–F could furthermore relate it to the replacement of waterfront 1 by waterfront 2 (Figs. 50–51). One of the pottery crocks represented is joined by another segment recovered from the pottery 'floor' F295 located several metres away within occupation soil context 32.

The phase-2 fill of F6, which took place after some subsidence and a little recutting, seems to witness a continuation of the ritual activity implied in phase 1 (Fig. 52). The shallow cone-like pit was probably encircled by several small posts and stakes, two of which stood in a shallow tongue projecting from the south-western side of the pit away from the river. Several 'special finds' were deposited close to a stony horizon which ran through the fill, and while some could be normal domestic losses in the occupation environment, the position and character of others suggests their deliberate inclusion and a relationship to the earlier horse deposit.

Pit F11 has much in common with the first cut of F6 – size, position relative to the river bank, basal post-socket, a rich charcoal deposit within its fill (F11 L3) – and, furthermore, its dating, based on the radiocarbon measurements, is comparable. On stratigraphic grounds it is not late, since it was sealed by the main occupation deposits (37). Unlike F6, however, the excavated half yielded no noteworthy artifacts or animal remains. It is possible that F11 was ringed with posts, especially F12, F13, F32, but the need for caution is suggested by F320, which appears to have been later and is interpreted as belonging with the waterfront (either phase). It is suggested that F6 phase 1 and F11 belong to a particular activity set over a restricted period of time and in this respect it is of interest that a row of modest post holes (F57–F109), although mainly unphasable (F109 post-dates unit D), conveniently bisect the ground between them, as if to define parcels of land (Figs. 49–50). The possible significance of this is examined in Chapter 25.

The main structure identified on the river bank, however, employed fairly deep post-holes. It is likely to have post-dated the early pit-digging period and would have succeeded the possible fence. This structure was situated in trench 1 behind one of the waterfront bays, but could have extended further south outside the excavated area and further east, where truncation in trench 2 would have removed the post holes. The plan recovered is best interpreted as part of a rectilinear building aligned with the river bank (Fig. 51). Three substantial post holes are believed to belong to a four-post structure about 1.5 m square. If this was discrete it would have to belong to a different phase than the rectilinear building. On the other hand, although its posts are set very closely to some in the latter building, it could perhaps belong to it, acting as support for a tower or raised roof portion within the larger structure (Fig. 51). This could have been part of a dwelling, but there is little to support such an interpretation. Instead it appears to have been a focus for contemporary rubbish-dumping, for it is argued that much of context 33 is contemporary (Fig. 52). The associated spreads of burnt clay, other burnt materials, and the *in situ* clay-lined pit (F15) suggest that certain pyrotechnic operations took place close by. The boundary to context 32 may correlate with one edge of this structure and signify a distinct functional zone, resulting in less rubbish generally and the occurrence of the pottery 'floor'. If the post alignment F96–F41–F39 is correctly interpreted as another wall, then the large dump of burnt flint cobbles F298 lies immediately outside on the north-west, although it does just spread around the central end post, F41.

Chapter
The flintwork: N
Neolithic and B

ALAN SAVILLE

A collection of 310 pieces of flir
2.8 kg, was examined from the
and salvage work at Runnymede
from three main areas and are de
headings, arranged in sequence
nant chronology of the pieces inv

Area 8

A small group of 15 artifacts c
be classified as in Table 7.

Table 7: Flints from Area 8, layers

Unretouched flakes
Burin
Miscellaneous retouched pieces

These pieces seem to form
to a lesser extent in general
the Runnymede flints. The t
from the blade forms present
appearance of some pieces i
ochreous staining on their un
the flakes conjoin (Fig. 54,
being successive strikes from
there is definitely more than o
sented by the 15 artifacts, sinc
types of cortex.

The distinctiveness of thi
ever, by the presence of a
fashioned on a blank which
blades present. The burin h
produced by the removal o
transverse truncation at the
This distinctive piece is of
in southern England in late
texts (cf. Mace 1959) and,
accurately a single piece
ascription (i.e. *c.* 10,000–8
the other pieces in this gro
Mesolithic date.

The miscellaneous retou
of two, is an incomplete

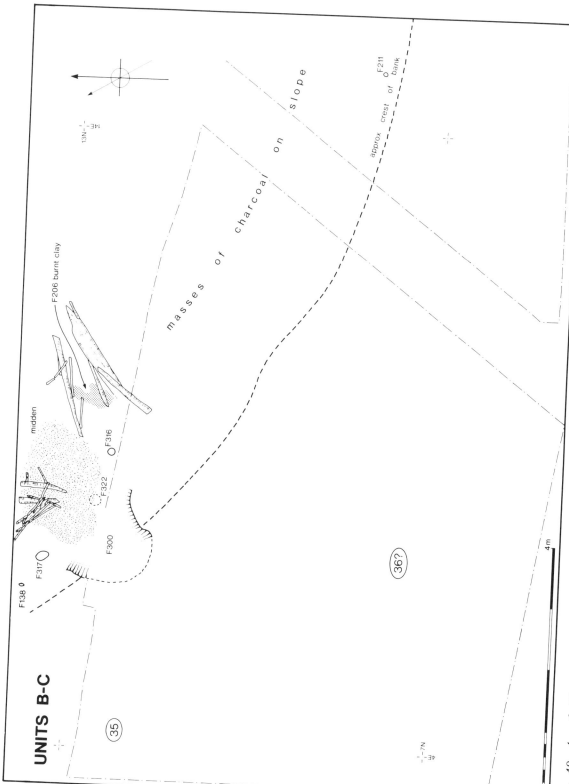

Fig. 48 *Area 8: Phase plan for stratigraphic units B–C, showing the burnt clearance debris, the use of F300 and associated structures, and the accumulation of the midden.*

Runnymede Brid

decorated assemblage of tl
iod. Increasing use of c
deposits dated within the
developments occur durir
changes in bowl forms, th
fineware and coarseware b
reasons – a broadening c
changes in the occurrenc
features. Most pottery o

130

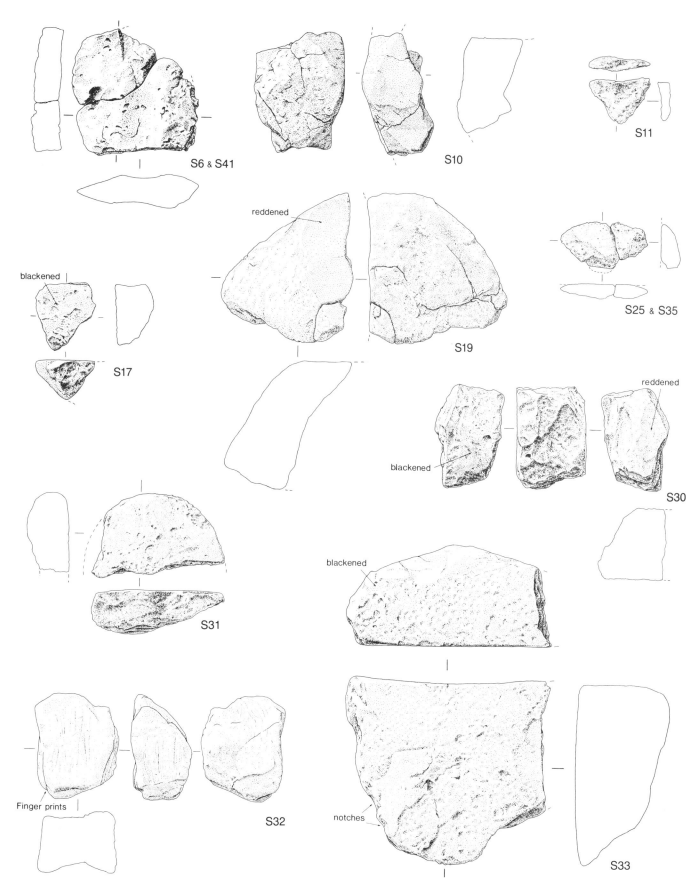

Fig. 56 *Late Bronze Age stone artifacts from Area 6. Scale 1/3.*

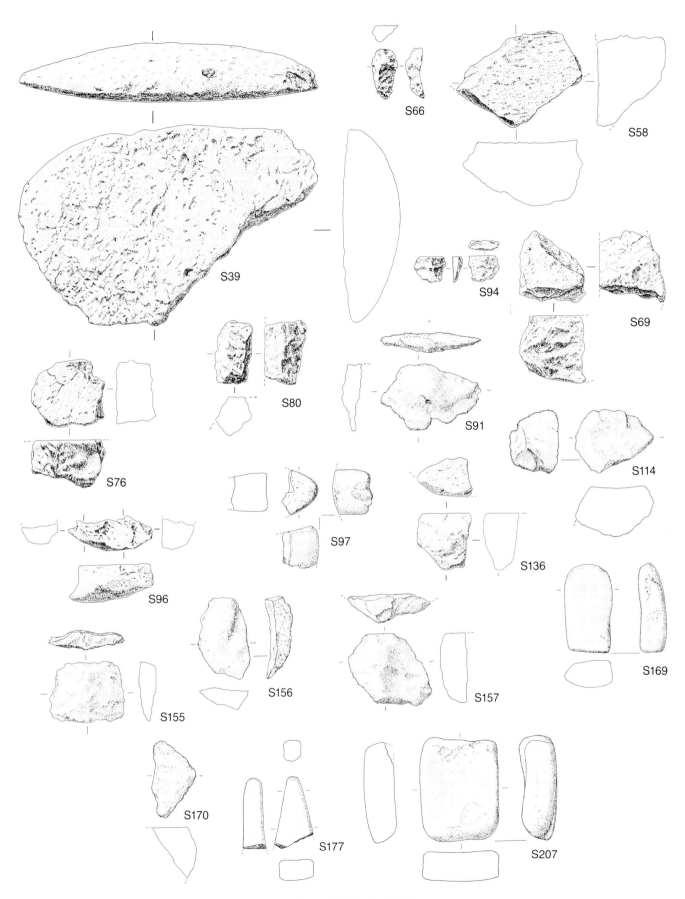

Fig. 57 Late Bronze Age stone artifacts from Area 6 and Area 8 (S207). Scale 1/3.

Chapter 6
The imported stone: Mesolithic, Neolithic and Bronze Age

Morphology and utilisation

All stone material was retained for study with the exception of natural gravel and burnt flint, which was included on plan at each level. The total of 207 stones has been catalogued in archive, catalogue entries for the illustrated pieces appearing in Table 10. The majority are considered to represent some form of human activity, or at least to have been brought in by human agency, since the alluvial deposits at Runnymede are, with the exception of occasional gravel beds, virtually stone-free. Some of the material, particularly the pebble-like pieces, could derive from river gravel deposits at or close to the site, but the majority of the sandstone lumps are likely to have been collected directly from their source areas on the nearby Bagshot Table and further afield. This is undoubtedly the case for the larger blocks of stone.

About 35 fragments show clear signs of having been dressed, worked or utilised, while a further 45 may be worked. In only a few cases are specific artifact types identifiable; nevertheless a broad range of uses may be suggested on the basis of the raw material recovered. The morphological and technological aspects of study need to take full account of the physical properties of the stone, which strongly condition its utility. Discussion of the large LBA assemblage is therefore organised according to broad petrographic groups identified by the writer.

The Early Flandrian and Neolithic stone (Figs. 54 and 55)
Very few stone objects were recovered from Neolithic or earlier horizons. Stratigraphically earliest is the pebble S1 from the flint group F4 in Area 8. The dished face has a dimpled but nevertheless waterworn surface. The face does, however, bear a number of spalls which could have resulted from its use as an anvil stone in flint-working. The pebble shows no indication of use as a hammerstone.

Two polished axes (S2, S3) are the only noteworthy Neolithic stone finds (Plate 51). Both were recovered from the surface of Area 4A in salvage operations and contexts are therefore not secure. Petrological identification by Alan Woolley of S2 as a fine-grained tuff and S3 as a biotite amphibolite similar to group IV suggest origins in Cumbria and Cornwall respectively. The attractive banding and greenish colour of S2 are unusual for products of the Cumbrian axe factories. The surface of S3 has suffered surprisingly bad chemical erosion given the calcareous nature of the local deposits. Only tiny areas retain intact polished surfaces.

Late Bronze Age stone (Figs. 56 and 57)
Most of the stone material is based on various sandstones, which range in durability from hard to extremely friable. For ease of discussion this material may be readily split into three hardness categories; thereafter less common rock types are dealt with. The frequency of pieces of the different lithologies according to context groups and their combined weights are presented in Table 11.

HARD SANDSTONE

About one-third of the material falls into this category, which accounts for virtually all the unequivocally dressed and ground stone. Freestone (below) has identified all but one of 10 sampled examples of this group as Lower Greensand. Twenty-four pieces bear worked faces and may be regarded as belonging generally to querns and grinding stones, although some other functions might be involved. Two large blocks appear to be the major portion of the original objects (S33, S39) and this may also be the case for two joining thin pieces (S6, S41). At least nine fragments have certain or probable edges alongside the worked face, the sides being indicated by form and/or differential weathering (S17, S30, S31, S58, S62, S69, S80, S96, S136, S170). Where sides survive they can be roughly dressed (e.g. S33, S69), fairly evenly dressed (S31) or with a tendency to faceting (S96, S136). A group of six are noteworthy in being flakes which retain a small portion of a dressed face. They are joined by another eight thin flakes, this time lacking any clear working. Many of this flake group (morphological class 'e') bear a more or less pronounced bulb of percussion, which, along with their morphology, would suggest a degree of control in fracture and the possibility of the deliberate detaching of flakes on site to rework stone blocks. This explanation might extend to some of the thicker fragments, which lack any identifying characteristics and therefore could equally be due to accidental physical and thermal stresses.

Reconstructable forms are few. The large block S33 has one dressed and crest-ground face which has a very slight saddle form, while the broadest side has a contrasting surface, which is concave and roughly pecked, with minimal evidence of grinding. The rest of the surfaces, except where fractured, are probably roughly dressed. This is not obviously a quernstone and it is possible that it served as an anvil stone for metalworking. The block could have been set on edge in a block of wood in order that its concave side be used for general hammering and the bordering edges, one a crisp right angle, the other rounded, could be used for bending during forging operations. This could, for example, explain the apparent abrasion and the possible detachment of a chip along the more rounded edge. Alternatively, when set horizontal, the flatter face could have been used for beating out larger objects, even sheet metal in its preliminary stages.

Block S39 appears to be about two-thirds complete, showing a biconvex and fairly slender section in two planes. One face, however, is less strongly convex than the other and

Table 10: Summary catalogue of the illustrated imported stone.

S. No	Context	Grid E N	Date	Unit	Dimensions Lth mm	Wth mm	Bth mm	Wt g	Fig	Rock Type	Section	Morphology	Artificial faces
1	A8F4		Mes		90	85	42	352	54	o		d	

Light orange-brown; localised ochre staining; ? one face roughened by percussion – possible anvil stone; associated with Mesolithic flintwork.

2	A4		Neo		122	71	32	393	55	o	y	axe	a6

Polished stone axe; group VI Langdale rock; greyish-green with attractive lighter banding; most of surface very smooth ground, but a few deeper flake scars survive around the edges; small chip or flaw in the otherwise intact cutting edge; butt and sides carry poorly defined chamfers; overall squat trapezoidal shape with oblique butt.

| 3 | A4 | | Neo | | 174 | 72 | 42 | 731 | 55 | o | y | axe | a6 |

Polished stone axe; very small areas of surface intact – glossy dark green; rest crumbled to rough dull green surface due to erosion (?chemical); cutting edge lost; torpedo shaped with thick oval section and no signs of side facets.

| 6 | A6L27 | | LB | A | 76 | 58 | 21 | 99 | 56 | h | | f | ?a3 |

Joins S41; deep maroon; comes to a thin edge.

| 10 | | | LB | A | 105 | 91 | 52 | 454 | 56 | m | | c | a4, a3/4 |

Very light grey; 1. part of original face shaped with weak Z profile – convex angle is rounded, concave one is crisp – a4; 2. adjacent larger face originally a side (?); polygonal facets with rounded angles between – a3/4; rest fractured; possible small spot of burning; face 1 yellower than most of rest.

| 11 | L24/25b | 11 10 | LB | B | 35 | 52 | 11 | 12 | 56 | h | | e | |

Off-white with yellow ochre staining; possible bulb against one edge.

| 17 | L19 | | LB | C | 61 | 47 | 31 | 60 | 56 | h | | c | a3/5, a4 |

Grey-brown with yellow ochre; essentially trianguloid; n2 – one/two faces; 1. main face flat – a3 with 40% a5; 2. opposite convex face, a4, may be original, as also slightly convex side 3.; 90% of 1 and 20% of 3 are surface blackened.

| 19 | L19 | | LB | C | 155 | 105 | 63 | 865 | 56 | m | | c | a3–4 |

Off-white with yellow ochre; slightly crumbly and fissured stone, probably having suffered some natural abrasion; in two pieces; small part of original ?weathered face has two gentle dished facets – surface layer pink to dull carmine and overlain by thin pale buff lamina; one adjoining face convex and likely original, a3–4; rest all fractures? – one well hollowed, possibly secondary use?

| 25 | L20c | | LB | C | 34 | 28 | 12 | 10 | 56 | cg | | f | a5, ?a3 |

Probably joins S35; pale greenish grey, white and pink; 1. one face with remnant of ground surface, a5; 2. reverse possibly shaped, ?a3.

| 30 | L20d | 10 11 | LB | C | 83 | 57 | 53 | 277 | 56 | h | | b | a3/5, a4/5 |

1. Main face a3/5; 2. opposite parallel face (less surviving) a4/5; 10% red-ochre, thin surface-only coat, limited to 2; 20% blackened, surface only, 1 and 2; possible rough edge also.

| 31 | L20d | 11 11 | LB | C | 111 | 65 | 34 | 235 | 56 | h | y | f | a3/5 |

Light greeny-grey; 1. main face a3/5; 2. reverse face and 3. semi-circular edge both a3(?); short scored groove along part of break.

| 32 | L20d | 10 12 | LB | C | 85 | 67 | 49 | 225 | 56 | ch | | b | |

Chalk block; off-white with black spots scattered over the surface; 1. main face – series of parallel scored grooves over part; 2. adjacent face – grooves all over; 3. reverse face – few miscellaneous short light grooves; finger prints on two corners – ?ancient.

| 33 | L20d | 10 13 | LB | C | 170 | 150 | 80 | 2200 | 56 | h | y | c | a3, a5, a2/5 |

Possible anvil or quernstone? light greenish grey-brown; plano-convex with one flat edge (2); 1. main face – slightly convex on one diagonal, concave on other – a3 with 10% a5; 2. side – concave a2 with very localised a5 (c. 3%); another side and rear face very irregular, but possibly roughly dressed; blackening c. 10% – around one corner; broken edge has crisp apices.

| 35 | 14e/20c | 10 13 | LB | C/D | 52 | 38 | 15 | 27 | 56 | cg | y | f | a5 |

Probably joins S25; pale greenish grey, white and pink; one face largely smooth, flat with fine co-aligned striations; 30% surface grey – ? from burning.

| 39 | L20 | | LB | C/D | 255 | 158 | 49 | 1740 | 57 | h | y | f | a2–3, a4, a5 |

Grey brown; the greater portion of an oval shaped stone of biconvex section, worked all over; 1. good convex profile face in two directions; pecked all over (a2) with localised finer dressing (a4) in centre; 2. gently convex profiles, much very roughly dressed (a2/3) with approximately 40% ground smooth (a5) except for the deep pittings; faint lengthwise striations associated.

| 41 | L18 | | LB | C/D | 104 | 73 | 28 | 224 | 56 | h | | f | a3, a2 |

Join with S6 is a fresh break with only minor abrasion of edges; deep maroon; biconvex section: face 1. convex, a2; face 2. roughly triple faceted; thins to intact sharp edge; opposite edge probably similar prior to chipping.

| 58 | L14 | 12 11 | LB | D | 107 | 73 | 58 | 390 | 57 | h | y | c | a3/5 |

Greenish grey-brown with some orange staining; rock includes small chips of ?hematite; 1. one face worked, gently concave in both sections – coarse dressing (a3) with tiny areas of crests reduced to smooth a5, and striations along the main axis; rest fractured, but opposite face more weathered; blackening of whole of (1) and two adjacent, ?original sides of block.

Chapter 7
The non-lithic artifacts: Neolithic and Bronze Age

The technology of the worked wood and bark

VERYAN HEAL

The great majority of timbers recovered from the site were examined from a technological point of view as indicated in Table 4. The essential details of the recovered piles are tabulated there and a more extensive record is in archive.

Neolithic

The wooden piles from the Neolithic period are in most cases broken into several pieces, usually by recent breaks along their length, though some have fragmented radially as well (e.g. A4 S4). They are all roundwood with hard black heartwood surrounded by paler, fibrous sapwood and their surfaces are eroded. Working traces survive ephemerally in the sapwood and more clearly in the more resilient heartwood. Where the upper ends survive (e.g. A6 F184; Fig. 58) sapwood is eroded, leaving a core of heartwood, this zone of degradation having occurred presumably at the fluctuating surface level of the water. In this case, because F184 was prostrate, this feature presumably reflects degradation during its use in the Neolithic in an upright position. Thus the wood would have had to contend not only with mechanical erosion by the water, but also with attack by biogens which occupy this habitat.

Some of the piles were worked only at the lower end (A4 S3; Fig. 58), the majority of their length being unmodified underbark surface. Where more extensive shaping had been carried out, this was done leaving long shallow facets with signs of tearing, as if the axe had been used to cut into the wood and then to lever and to tear off the unwanted part. At the existing upper ends of the piles it is common for this to have been done tangentially on two chords, leaving the remainder of the circumference unworked and producing a segmental cross-section. Towards the tip the working extends all around the circumference. The point is completed either as a long, shallow, often asymmetrical taper (e.g. A6 F204; Fig. 58) or as a blunt convexly profiled point, cut with many small scooped facets (A4 S2; Fig. 58). The long shallow cuts with tearing were predominantly through the sapwood, occasionally cutting into the heartwood; the shorter, scooped facets in the heart testify to its harder, denser nature, which required 'chipping' away.

The scooped facets are consistent with the use of a relatively thick blade of convex section, characteristic of stone and flint axeheads. The longer, shallower facets in the sapwood would result where the thickness of the blade was used as a lever after striking into the wood. The rotting of the tops of the piles precludes determination as to how

they were driven into position, although the lack of abrasion in the tips and of evidence for fracturing in antiquity suggests easy penetration of the soil, and it is therefore most likely that a wooden mallet was used.

Bronze Age

The piles from the two rows dating to the Bronze Age are similar in general appearance, the heart and sapwood clearly differentiable by colour and texture: the heart forming a dense, dark central column and the sap a soft, stringy, paler outer layer. In most cases the same pattern of decay has occurred as was noted on the Neolithic pieces – the loss of a cylinder of sapwood at the top of the surviving pile, leaving a projecting core of heartwood.

There is bark in place on some piles from both rows; some bark is known to have been lost during excavation, but its absence might in some cases be due to weathering off and water erosion. The unmodified underbark surface which otherwise remains indicates that the piles were used without trimming off the bark. The inner row and outer row both include piles which have impacted during driving – there is a longitudinal crumpling of the fibres without actually fracturing, which occurs where green wood is forced against a harder material. These two factors establish the use of unseasoned wood.

The timbers of the inner row are of similar dimensions, 13–20 cm in diameter in trench 1 and 10–20 cm in trench 2, in both cases the modal average being 15 cm. Their remaining length, of course, indicates more the depth to which the piles were driven than their original length; in the inner row the longest is over 1.5 m. In the outer row diameters are 6–13 cm (trench 1) and 5–14 cm (trench 2), the modal averages being 7 cm and 6–10 cm. Outer row piles remain to a shorter length in trench 1, maximum 80 cm, than in trench 2, maximum 1.20 m (Fig. 38). The generally shorter dimensions of the former reflects original depth of penetration (Chapter 3).

The piles are similarly grown, relatively fast growth with a fairly high proportion of sapwood to heart (see Hillam, Chapter 22 below). The quality of the timber is variable, most pieces being effectively straight, others with bends, bulges, even double bends, knotty and gnarled grain. It would seem that the supply for the inner and outer rows was much the same, though when the outer rows were constructed the trees selected were of smaller diameter, though not of younger growth.

Side branches were removed, some neatly with a few well placed axe blows (F120 – Fig. 59; F274) others less cleanly (F129), or were partly torn where the reaction wood around the knot proved difficult (F239; F271). It is apparent from the knots that the piles were driven so that the upper end in position was also the upper end of the stem in growth. Where the stem had bends and bulges some were left unworked (F286), others were reduced by axe blows (F115), some causing difficulty, owing to reaction wood. One piece with a reversed 'S' curve (F216) was nonetheless finely pointed, though it did impact in driving, presumably owing to the uneven stress in driving.

The sequential nature of the chopping and shaping results in the disfigurement and distortion of working traces, but it is apparent that the blows were directed down the length of the pile towards the tip. Some pieces were worked over the whole (remaining) length: F268, for example, 1.30 m long, of which the point was only the last 30 cm and which included reaction wood which tore in working.

The sapwood bears longer shallower facets than the heart in general, indicating that the sapwood was removed in long slivers. In some cases it was partly levered and torn off, in others it was created by a series of blows in a straight line, leaving a channel of facets (F237). The heart required a sharper angle of blow to cut it effectively and the greater angle of the working of the point also required more wood to be removed over a shorter length, hence the shorter, deeper facets in the heart and towards the tip. In one case this was done too deeply and the blade retracted, leaving a gash (F167).

The pointing varies from quite blunt, lumpy, nosed, and keeled shapes (F231, F239, F265, F188) to fine tapers (F131, F216, F166). Given the relatively soft nature of the sediments in Area 6, the lack of streamlining possibly would not affect driving significantly; indeed there is always a balance to be achieved between fine driving shape and strength derived from blunter points. In most cases the point itself is composed partly of heartwood, in some entirely so (F120 – Fig. 59; F268) and occasionally entirely of sapwood (F223), this last being ill-advised since sapwood is both weaker and more prone to decay. Outlier F212 (Fig. 62) alone had a quite different biface point rather than the usual entire-circumference working. It may have performed a different function, or have been an addition or replacement.

Though relative convexity of blade section can be discerned, the incompleteness of the majority of facets makes detailed analysis of the blade which might have formed them difficult and of dubious value. The facets seem generally to have been made by a blade up to 5 cm across the cutting edge, most facets remaining to a width of 3 to 5 cm. Curved and almost straight edges are indicated, and in one case a blade with a nicked edge, shown by ridges along the facets (F179). The flattish cross-section and blade edge shape are consonant with bronze axe blades of the period; there is no evidence for any other tool being used.

Small wooden artifacts

W1. Ladle bowl or cup, Late Bronze Age; Area 6, layer 9 20.02E/9.56N (SF98) Plate 54; Fig. 63.
Oval in plan with shallow asymmetric U section and simple rounded rim; the asymmetry is probably due to post-deposition distortion; small scallop marks from the shaping on inside and outside; slight cracking and nick out of rim at one end.
On the basis of proportions and small size, most likely to be part of a ladle, in which case a handle would have sprung from the broken end.
Species: probably *Prunus*
L 75 mm; MW 55 mm; MD 29 mm

W2. Worked piece, Late Bronze Age; Area 6, layer 20 18.7E/9.9N (SF93) Fig. 63.
From beneath structure F164. Radially split segment of timber, approximately an eighth of the full round; trimmed by oblique chop marks at both ends; convex face probably the underbark surface; possible axe marks on faces.
It is unclear what function, if any, this would have had, or whether it was an unfinished piece.
Species: *Acer*
L 370 mm; MW 54 mm; MT 43 mm

W3. Worked faggot, Late Bronze Age; Area 6, layer 24 12.2E/11.5N (SF96) Fig. 63.
Small partially charred faggot probably trimmed all round creating sub-D section and blunt nose at one end; other end possibly broken.
Species: *Quercus*
L 173 mm; MW 36 mm; MT 28 mm

W4. Worked bark, Neolithic; Area 4A, layer 121a (F89) Plates 17 and 18.
Thin sheet of bark was found with one neat convex edge – almost certainly cut to this edge in antiquity; possible stitch holes inset from this edge show on radiograph; fragmented on lifting and reassembled in conservation (Jacqui Watson – AML) to the extent shown in the radiograph.
M dimension (as found) 320 mm; W (as found) 275 mm

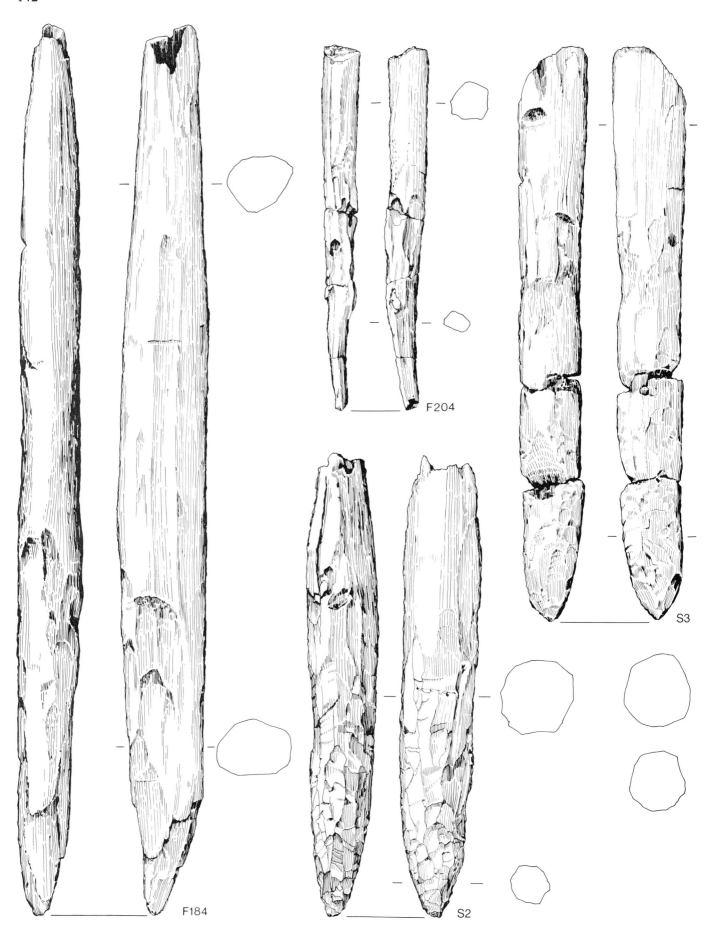

Fig. 58 Neolithic worked wood from Area 4 (S2, S3) and Area 6 (F184, F204). Scale 1/6.

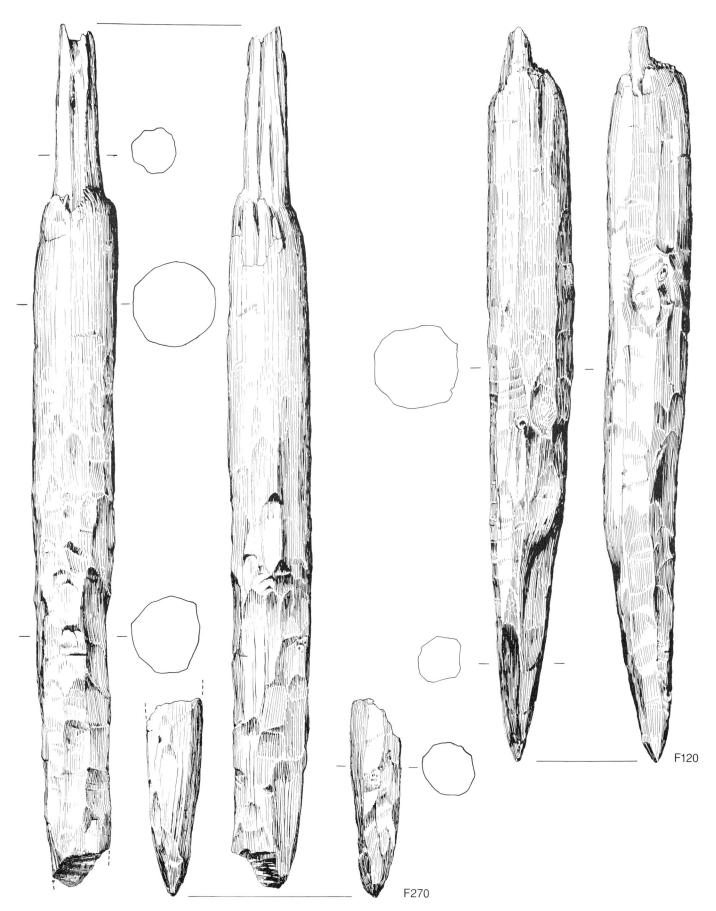

143

F120

F270

Fig. 59 Late Bronze Age wooden piles from the inner row, Area 6 (F270, F120). Scale 1/6.

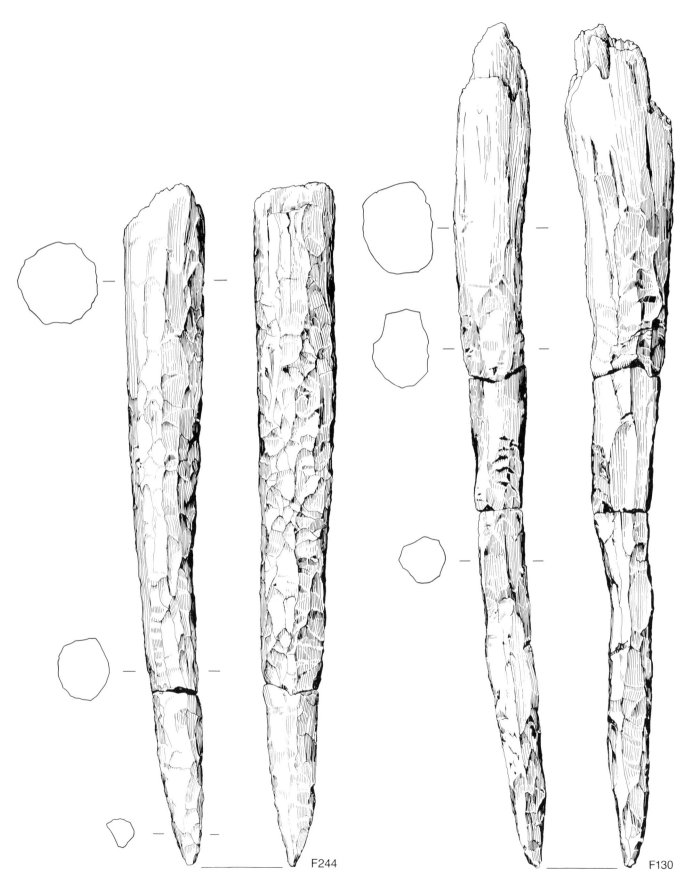

Fig. 60 Late Bronze Age wooden piles from the inner row, Area 6 (F244, F130). Scale 1/6.

F244

F130

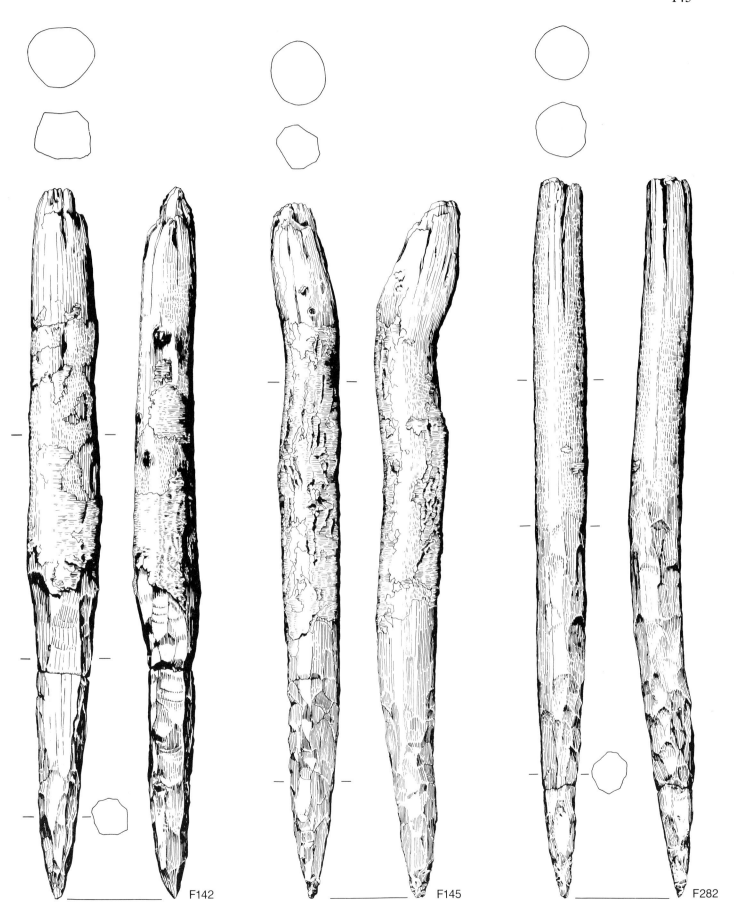

Fig. 61 Late Bronze Age wooden piles from the outer row, Area 6 (F142, F145, F282). Scale 1/6.

146

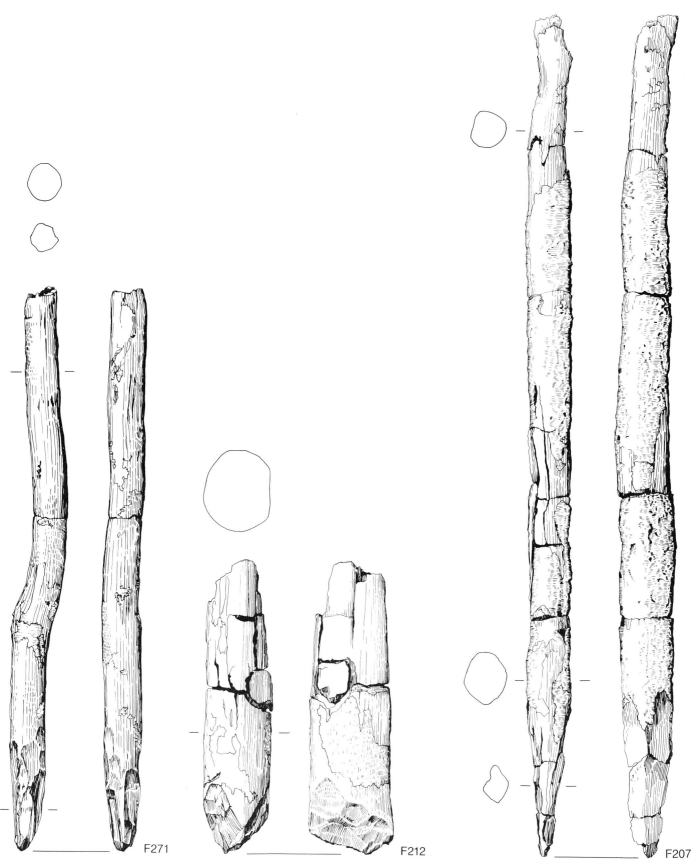

Fig. 62 Late Bronze Age pile outlier (F212) and miscellaneous stakes (F207, F271). Scale 1/6.

F271

F212

F207

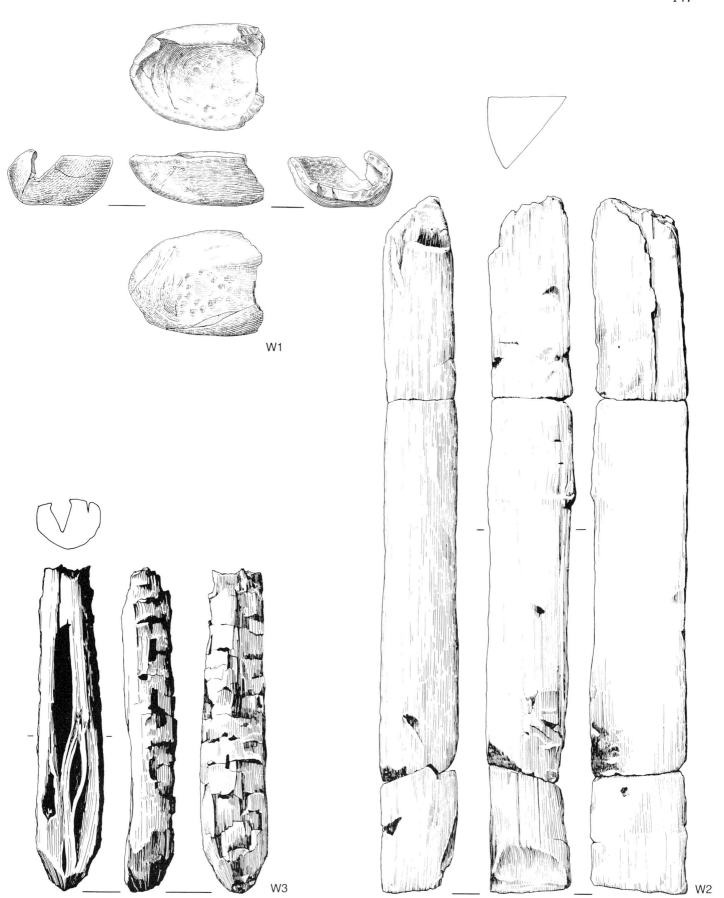

Fig. 63 Late Bronze Age wooden ladle or cup (W1) and other worked wood (W2, W3). Scale 1/2 (W1, W3), 1/3 (W2).

Worked skeletal materials

ANDREW FOXON

Area 4 – probably Neolithic

B1. Bone awl/point; cleaning surface of tufa deposit
(L123) after machine clearance by contractors;
(SF 1) Fig. 64.
Point made on sagittal half of distal end of immature
sheep metapodial; criss-cross striations present on lower
end, but not at tip; whole surface except butt highly
polished, presumably from use.
L 59.5 mm; W 13 mm; wt. 2.5 g

Area 6 – Late Bronze Age contexts

B2. Bone awl/point; layer 25, 18E/11N Fig. 64
Point made on distal end of immature sheep metacarpal;
one face and both sides removed to taper the point;
longitudinal and diagonal striations, but tip mainly
smooth; most of surface polished.
L 66.5 mm; W 19.5 mm; wt. 5.2 g

B3. Bone awl/point fragment; F14, 11E/5N (SF 76)
Fig. 64
Tip fragment of point; bone unidentified; sinuous taper
formed by scraping – many narrow facets discernible;
these create a sub-triangular section close to the tip;
slight polish, especially at tip.
EL 39 mm; EW 8 mm; wt. 0.8 g

B4. Bone point fragment, lodged in drilled metacarpal;
layer 20, 13E/11N Plate 52; Fig. 64
A neat hole has been formed, presumably drilled, into
the anterior face of one verticillus perpendicular to the
line of the shaft; the verticillus is broken away around
the hole; probably a chip had first been detached,
otherwise the drill point would have tended to skate off
the curved surface; a number of scraping marks run
along the shaft.
  The tip fragment of a bone point was found in situ
in the hole, which it fits neatly; the tip is slightly oval
in section and is well polished, but it has no rotary
striations to indicate a drilling action; it is thought
unlikely that this delicate point was part of a weapon or
trap that penetrated the limb of the living animal.
Metacarpal: L 109 mm; W (distal) 20.5 mm;
W (proximal) 18.5 mm; wt. 11.8 g
Point: EL 9.7 mm; Ed 2.6 × 2.3 mm

B5. Bone awl/point; layer 33c, 5.02E/8.02N (SF 71)
Fig. 64.
Small point modified from a segment of long bone; one
end steadily tapered, the other arched; high polish all
over, except in marrow cavity; a few slight facets
discernible.
L 33 mm; W 5.5 mm; B 4 mm; wt. 0.6 g

B6. Rib offcut; F6 layer 2b, 6E/11N Fig. 64.
Offcut from a large rib used to produce bone segment;

the two sides were initially scraped down a little; then
a 'V' cut was sawn in one face, cutting halfway through
the thickness to the cancellous tissue; resultant bevel has
slight cut ledges and a slight sheen; many light
transverse cut-marks and false strokes run alongside;
there are also three on the reverse; 'V' cut presumed to
be one of two, between which a thin segment (half the
thickness of the rib) was detached.
EL 96 mm; MW 20.5 mm; W at cut 15.5 mm; T above
cut 5.8 mm; T below cut 3.0 mm; wt. 11.6 g

B7. Rib offcut; layer 4, 13E/8N Fig. 64.
Offcut from a large rib used to produce bone segment;
one edge scraped a little; marks of periosteum stripping;
'V' cut truncates one face through to cancellous middle
of bone; segment presumably detached between this and
a second cut; tiny fragment of segment still attached
shows main cut and secondary groove; also light
cutmarks just above 'V' cut.
EL 63 mm; W at cut 24 mm; T above cut 9.7 mm;
T below cut 3.5 mm; wt. 8.4 g

B8. Rib polisher; layer 20, Fig. 64.
Large rib fragment with light to moderate polish on one
convex surface; there are copious longitudinal striations
from periosteum stripping, including two very dense
patches on the convex face; sides are faceted by scraping,
at one point this having exposed the cancellous tissue;
transverse broken end slightly eroded, the other is
freshly broken except for protruding piece, which has
an end facet.
L 212 mm; MW 23.7 mm; MT 9.5 mm; wt. 34.5 g

B9. Rib polisher; layer 20, 20E/9N Fig. 64.
Large rib fragment with light polish over much of
surface; dense concentrations of longitudinal marks of
periosteum stripping in hollow of concave face and much
of convex face; ends and sides show heavy grinding and
wear; more spatulate end damaged since use.
L 155 mm; MW 35.7 mm; MT 11 mm; wt. 29.9 g

B10. Incised antler/bone fragment; layer 6, 10E/10N
Fig. 64.
Small fragment with flat face crossed by four light,
straight incisions; two join in a 'V'; presumably
decorative.
EL 14.5 mm; EW 7 mm; wt. 0.2 g

B11. ?Utilised boar's tusk flake; F2 (modern pit), Fig. 64.
Flake of boar's tusk; one end broken; corner broken off
other end, which probably had 'omega' shape – this end
shows wear polish on both faces.
EL 45 mm; MW 29.5 mm; wt. 5.5 g

B12. Whittled antler tine; F6 layer 2b, 6.77E/11.09N (SF
84) Plate 53; Fig. 65.
Tine detached from antler by ringing with deep, slightly
oblique cuts – cut shows facets; virtually whole of surface
and tip end faceted, having been whittled with a fine-
edged tool; limited areas close to tip retain natural

smooth polished surface; piece probably in early stages of manufacturing an antler cheek-piece or other fitting (e.g. tool handle).
L 143.5 mm; d (at cut) 18 × 22.5 mm; d (tip) 8.5 × 9.5 mm; wt. 35.7 g

B13. Worked antler fragment; layer 4, Fig. 65.
Part of polished round-sectioned tine with neat flat end showing light grinding marks; broken end retains tiny corner of a slot with rounded edges and, close by, possibly part of a small, presumably round, perforation perpendicular to slot; possibly part of a cheek-piece or toggle.
EL 26 mm; W 17.5 mm; wt. 2.8 g

B14. Antler cheek-piece fragment; layer 1, 5.38E/10.84N (SF 20; on edge of modern feature, F1) Fig. 65.
Upper (narrower) end of class I antler cheek-piece, broken across the rectangular upper strap slot; part of one peg hole survives on either side; tip cut flat across and whole surface well polished, although in localised areas not entirely removing indications of whittle facets; small groups of striations close to the perforations probably result from manufacture.
EL 80 mm; W at perforation 20 mm; B at perforation 18.5 mm; d top end 9 mm; wt. 13.2 g

Metalwork (Late Bronze Age)

The alloy compositions of the metalwork have been determined by D. Hook in the Department of Scientific Research, British Museum, using X-ray fluorescence analysis and, where possible, atomic absorption spectrometry. These are part of a much larger programme of study on metallurgy at Runnymede; the results and methods of analysis will be described fully in a future volume.

Copper-alloy objects

M1. Socketed knife fragment; layer 1, 6.25E/12.00N (SF18) Fig. 65.
Leaded tin-bronze; patches of dull green patina, rest flaked to light green surface; blade with flattened midrib and hollowed edge bevels inside sharp intact edges; straight end to oval socket with squared sides; blade break ancient, socket fractures probably recent; part of rivet hole survives on one face.
EL 31.5 mm; MW 20.2 mm; MB 7.3 mm; T blade at break 3.5 mm; wt. 8.5 g

M2. Tanged knife fragment; layer 31, (SF 22) Fig. 65.
Leaded tin-bronze; fragments of dark green patina, but most flaked to light green surface; both ends are ancient breaks; blade edges largely intact and backed by hollow bevels flanking rounded midrib; a small hollow in one face may be a casting defect; tang created by blunting stretches of edges – the resulting indents are slightly asymmetric in plan as well as in section with small

flanges raised on one face only; it seems likely that this was a secondary act to rejuvenate a broken blade.
EL 42.7 mm; MW 18.7 mm; W tang at break 13.0 mm; MT 3.8 mm; B flange 2.9; wt. 11.4 g

M3. Ring; layer 33a, 5.38E/8.66N (SF 32) Fig. 65.
Leaded tin-bronze; fragments of grey-green patina, rest flaked to pale green surface; intact ring of sub-triangular section having constant diameter, but one part of circuit possible thinner than that opposite.
d 11.5 mm; B hoop 3.0 mm; W hoop 2.0–2.7 mm; wt. 0.7 g

M4. Penannular ring or link; layer 19, approx. 8E/13N Fig. 65.
Leaded tin-bronze; most of surface covered in thin orange concretion with sand and grit; this and patina flaking to varied green surface; strip with two neat and thin ends indicating a complete object; the strip is flat and expands steadily from one end to the other; a sideways twist at the broader end is probably damage; assuming that the curved form is original, this is likely to have been a plain finger ring or a link for attachment.
Md 19.5 mm; minimum d 15 mm; W terminals 3.8 and 6.8 mm; MT 2.5 mm (including accretion); wt. 1.4 g

M5. Pin-head; layer 32c, 4.18E/6.53N (SF69) Fig. 65.
Leaded tin-bronze; dull green slightly corroded surface with small spots of brighter green; double-moulded head with a flat oval top and a constriction beneath, before the main shank of circular section; fragment gently 'S' curved.
EL 39.6 mm; d head 3.0 × 3.5 mm; d constriction 1.9 × 2.0 mm; Md shank 2.5 mm; d shank break 2.3 mm; wt. 0.8 g

M6. Shank/wire fragment; layer 33b, 8.39E/6.45N (SF48) Not illustrated.
Tin-bronze; rather corroded rod with light green surfaces; in two main parts; apparently had a square section with the suggestion of a slight wavy groove along one face; tapers to one end, but no point survives; could be part of a delicate awl, a pin or a piece of wire.
EL 18.2 mm; MW 2.2 mm; MB 2.2 mm; W narrow end 1.5 mm; wt. 0.2 g

M7. ?Shank fragment/rivet; layer 33b, 6.74E/6.14N (SF57) Not illustrated.
Corroded rod with pale green and purple-brown surface; section circular or sub-square; ends a little irregular; if a complete object it is a small rivet, but more likely a small fragment of wire, pin etc.
L 5.3 mm; d 3.3 mm; wt. 0.3 g

M8. Shank fragment; layer 33b, 8.56E/7.42N (SF45) Not illustrated.
Very small rod with laminar corrosion and pale green surface; ends rounded by corrosion.
EL 6.0 mm; d 2.0 mm; wt. 0.1 g

M9. Sheet fragments; F15 layer 1, 8.94E/5.63N (SF78) Not illustrated.
Dull green surface with dark grey/brown core visible in fresh breaks; in two fragments, the larger (a) with a long convex edge intact, thin and gently curved in profile.
a) EL 14.0 mm; EW 5.5 mm; T 0.6–1.0 mm
b) EL 5.7 mm; EW 3.6 mm; T 0.6–0.8 mm
Total weight 0.2 g

M10. Sheet/blade fragments; layer 4, 14.95E/10.43N (SF26) Not illustrated.
Leaded tin-bronze; pale and dull green surfaces and corroded interior; the three fragments (one in four joining pieces) presumably all belong to one object; all thin significantly to a presumed edge which might survive intact on one side of fragment (a), giving a sharp edge; faces are plain and gently curved in some directions; these could belong to a thin-bladed implement such as a razor or to the thinned edge of a plate of sheet metal.
a) EL 20.2 mm; EW 16.0 mm; T 0.4–2.2 mm
b) EL 14.5 mm; EW 8.8 mm; T 0.3–1.5 mm
c) EL 10.3 mm; EW 9.0 mm; T 0.3–0.8 mm
Total weight 1.2 g

M11. Sheet fragments; layer 33c, 10.14E/6.02N (SF60) Not illustrated.
Pale green surfaces and similar corroded interior; two fragments (each of two joining pieces) presumably belong to one object of roughly constant thickness; one edge of fragment (a) backed by slight flange, while a blunt perpendicular edge may also be intact; fragment (b) has similar flattish edges on a long and a short side; this fragment bends towards one end.
a) EL 8.7 mm; EW 4.5 mm; T 1.0 mm; B flange 1.9 mm
b) EL 10.8 mm; EW 4.0 mm; T 0.9–1.1 mm
Total weight 0.4 g

M12. Sheet fragments; layer 32c, 3.76E/6.23N (SF68) Not illustrated.
Four tiny fragments of thin bronze.
M dimensions 3.8 mm, 3.8 mm, 3.4 mm and 2.5 mm

M13. Sheet fragment; F5 layer 1, 14.45E/6.52N (SF34) Not illustrated.
Chalky green surface; one piece, or possibly two intertwined pieces, of crumpled sheet bronze, probably no original edges.
M dimension 9.2 mm; T 0.5 mm; wt. 0.2 g

M14. Lump (attached to crucible/furnace lining – see entry C1); layer 25, 19.44E/11.22N (SF100) Fig. 65.
Tin-bronze; pale greyish-green 'tabular' lump of bronze with undulating and partly granular surface – possibly grit and sand embedded in the corrosion layer.
M dimension 40.0 mm; MT 3.0 mm; wt. 58.5 g (with clay)

M15. Lump; layer 19, approx. 8E/13N Fig. 65.
Unalloyed copper; brown and green craggy lump with much sand and grit embedded in surface; amorphous shape possibly partly due to corrosion products; likely spill or ingot fragment.
M dimension 27 mm; W 22 mm; wt. 17.2 g

M16. Lump; layer 33a, 5.69E/8.11N (SF35) Fig. 65.
Unalloyed copper; dull green surface with slight dimpling; all edges rough and apparently broken; tapers to one side in cross-section, one face being gently convex, the other flat but with a lip along the thickest edge; at least one porosity hole; the profile of this piece would be consistent with familiar LBA plano-convex copper ingots, but the lip may denote the beginning of a marked upturn on one face which would not conform.
M dimension 22.7 mm; MT 8.2 mm; wt. 9.3 g

M17. Lump; layer 31, 7.83E/6.04N (SF25) Not illustrated.
Leaded tin-bronze; small roughly trapezoid blob of bronze with corroded brightish green and purple-brown surface; no clear form and probably therefore a piece of waste; possibly all corrosion product.
L 16.0 mm; W 9.7 mm; wt. 1.1 g

Lead objects

M18. ?Strip binding; layer 33b, 6.01E/7.72N (SF56) Fig. 65.
Lead with tin (Needham and Hook 1988: 262 no. 6); grey undulating surface, uneven perhaps from damage rather than corrosion; narrow ends both breaks; long edges appear original, one being irregular and rounded in section, the other flat-ended with an inturned flange; the strip is gently curved in long- and cross-section; a short length of rib surviving on the convex face at one end may be an intentional feature, but is not quite parallel to the main axis; a short diagonal rib on the inside face may be accidental; it seems likely that this strip is part of a binding applied to a larger object.
EL 37.5 mm; MW 12 mm; B flange 2.2 mm; wt. 5.9 g

M19. Peg/rivet; layer 4, 14.10E/9.16N (SF30) Fig. 65.
Lead (Needham and Hook 1988: 262 no. 5); surface mainly off-white corrosion layer; central expansion forming a collar dividing ends of roughly equal length; one end pointed and a little bent, the other end rounded with no sign of breakage; circular section throughout; this may be an unused rivet of a pronged type known in bronze and, if so, the blunt end would be closed by hammering when put into use.
L 23.5 mm; d blunt end of shank 3.3 mm; d collar 6.4 × 7.0 mm; d base of pointed end 4.3–5.0 mm; wt. 2.5 g

Shale artifact (Late Bronze Age)

SH1. Bracelet fragment: layer 32b, 5E/6N Fig. 65.
Black polished surface; slight lamination showing; short segment of bracelet with sub-triangular cross-section.
EL 35 mm; MB 6.5 mm; MT 6.5 mm

Clay artifacts (Late Bronze Age)

C1. Crucible/furnace lining (with attached bronze lump, see M14); layer 25, 19.44E/11.22N (SF100) Fig. 65.
Fairly large sherd with large curvature (diameter would be about 22 cm if vertically orientated); slightly hollowed external profile, but perhaps not original exterior surface; broken edges all round show strong laminar construction, probably built up by relining of interior; six laminae seem to be present, each with a very thin surface of either greenish or purple discoloration; basic fabric silty, orange, buff, purple or light grey.
EW 72 mm; ED 56 mm; MT 14 mm; wt. 58.5 g (with bronze)

C2. Mould fragment; layer 33a, 7E/7N Fig. 65.
Abraded sherd of mid-grey sandy fabric, probably inner mould; slightly wedge-shaped section; one face flattish; other with tubular impression inside broad flat area – possibly the matrix and contact face.
EL 22 mm; EW 21 mm; MT 10 mm

C3. ?Mould fragment; layer 32b, 5E/6N Not illustrated.
Abraded sherd with double-layered structure: grey gritless fabric with flat face covered in white 'skin' – possible inner mould; reverse with orange fabric and eroded surface – possible outer mould.
M dimension 26 mm; MT 9 mm

C4. Mould fragment; layer 23/24 Fig. 65.
Dark grey gritless fabric; one thin side, opposite side broken; inner face is evenly concave with probable organic impressions; these likely binding round inner mould valves, and the fragment therefore from an outer wrap.
EL 22.5 mm; EW 15 mm; T 5 mm

C5. ?Metallurgical fragment; F214, 10E/5N Fig. 65.
X-ray fluorescence analysis suggest this is ceramic; purplish-grey sandy fabric with tiny white grits and iron staining; apparently part of a small conical or pyramidal form with a small ancient perforation near the apex; surfaces uneven; conceivably a sprue for pouring a pin or other small bronze.
M dimension 21 mm; W 19 mm

C6. Baked vessel rim; layer 8b, 12.00E/10.73N (SF67) Fig. 65.
Pale orange soft fabric, virtually gritless – perhaps just baked rather than fully fired; poorly moulded shape with rounded rim and strong angle near break.
EL 55 mm; ED 39 mm; MT 18 mm

C7. Spindlewhorl; layer 4, 13.82E/8.77N (SF33) Fig. 66.
Dull grey-brown and lightly flint-gritted fabric; surface with leathery sheen; one side damaged; biconical profile with carination interrupted by continuous row of finger-pinched cusps; upper (illustrated) face has neat dished depression around perforation; rougher and more ephemeral depression at bottom end; straight cylindrical perforation.
Md 35 mm; MT 22.5 mm; d perforation 4.8–5.4 mm; wt. 24.2 g

C8. Spindlewhorl fragment; layer 6, 11.91E/10.74N (SF31) Fig. 66.
Grey-brown grog-tempered fabric; nearly half extant; asymmetric sub-biconical profile; carination interrupted by row of large finger-pinched cusps; slight dished features around top and bottom of cylindrical perforation.
EW 36 mm; MT 30 mm; wt. 19.9 g

C9. Spindlewhorl fragment; layer 32b, 4.64E/6.55N (SF63) Fig. 66.
Dull orange and brown fabric with dense and large flint grits (up to 6 mm); about one-third extant, badly abraded; rounded biconical profile with occasional slight facets.
EW 34 mm; ET 24 mm; wt. 12.1 g

C10. Spindlewhorl; layer 6, 10.15E/10.75N (SF27) Fig. 66.
Dark grey fabric with tiny white grits; grey and light brown smooth surface, semi-burnished in parts; much of one side missing; very asymmetric sub-conical profile with carination close to upper face (as drawn); this has broad shallow dish around conical entrance to perforation; cone retains concentric grooves from ?shaping tool.
Md 38 mm; ET 20.5 mm; Minimum d perforation 6 mm; d perforation entrance 12 mm; wt. 21.9 g

C11. Spindlewhorl fragment; F17, 12.69E/5.26N (SF77) Fig. 66.
Brown and black gritless fabric, slightly laminar; poor condition with top half lacking; black uneven surface; asymmetric sub-biconical profile; extant face has broad dish around perforation.
Ed 40 mm; ET 19 mm; d perforation 7 mm; wt. 17.0 g

C12. Spindlewhorl; F6 layer 1, 5.82E/10.97N (SF97) Fig. 66.
Buff to pale orange fabric with light flint gritting; part of one side lacking; not very neatly shaped hemisphere with opposite face completely dished.
Md 31 mm; ET 21.5 mm; d perforation 6.5–9 mm; wt. 15.3 g

C13. Spindlewhorl fragment; layer 33b, 7.41E/7.14N (SF62) Fig. 66.
Soft silty buff fabric, no grits, but possibly grog; slightly irregular hemispherical form with pronounced depression on opposite face.
EW 21.5 mm; T 23 mm; wt. 6.8 g

C14. Perforated slab fragment; layer 24/25c, approx. 8E/13N (SF91) Fig. 66.
Rough buff surface; fabric grey-brown, slightly flaky structure with moderate flint gritting (grits up to 3.5 mm); intact edge flattish, but with rounded angles; pronounced lips around holes on one face; three holes represented.
EL 64 mm; EW 74 mm; MT edge 20 mm; MT around perforations 25 mm; minimum T 17.5 mm

C15. Perforated slab fragment; layer 20d, 10.2E/11.7N (SF94) Fig. 66.
One intact undulating face; other one entirely lost; grey fabric with moderately dense flint gritting (grits up to 4.5 mm); parts of two or probably three perforations present.
M dimension 67 mm; ET 17 mm

C16. Loomweight fragment; F6 layer 1 and cleaning, 7.42E/11.98N (SF24) Fig. 66.

Friable sandy pale orange and grey fabric with occasional grits and iron-rich inclusions; two joining parts found separately at similar high level in the top fill of pit F6; about half object represented, including part of eroded perforation; top missing; pyramidal form with rounded corners; perforation skew to sub-square cross-section; flat base has slight dimples – ?erosion or irregularities in manufacture.
ED 85 mm; EW 68 mm; EB 67 mm; wt. 237 g

C17. Loomweight fragment; layer 8, 12.66E/9.43N (SF54) Fig. 66.
Light grey/buff/pale orange softish fabric; grog or friable sandstone inclusions, also voids from organic inclusions; surviving rounded corner and part of a perpendicularly aligned perforation suggest a pyramidal loomweight.
ED 69 mm; EW 40 mm; EB 33 mm; wt. 86.5 g

C18. Faced daub; layer 8, 12.98E/10.32N (SF47) Fig. 66.
Very pale pink soft fabric with chalk inclusions, one 8 mm long, flat face slightly whiter than elsewhere; broken reverse contains a 'double' impression: a narrow tube superimposed on and slightly skew to a much broader furrow–possibly wattle impressions.
M dimension across face 54 mm; ET 31 mm

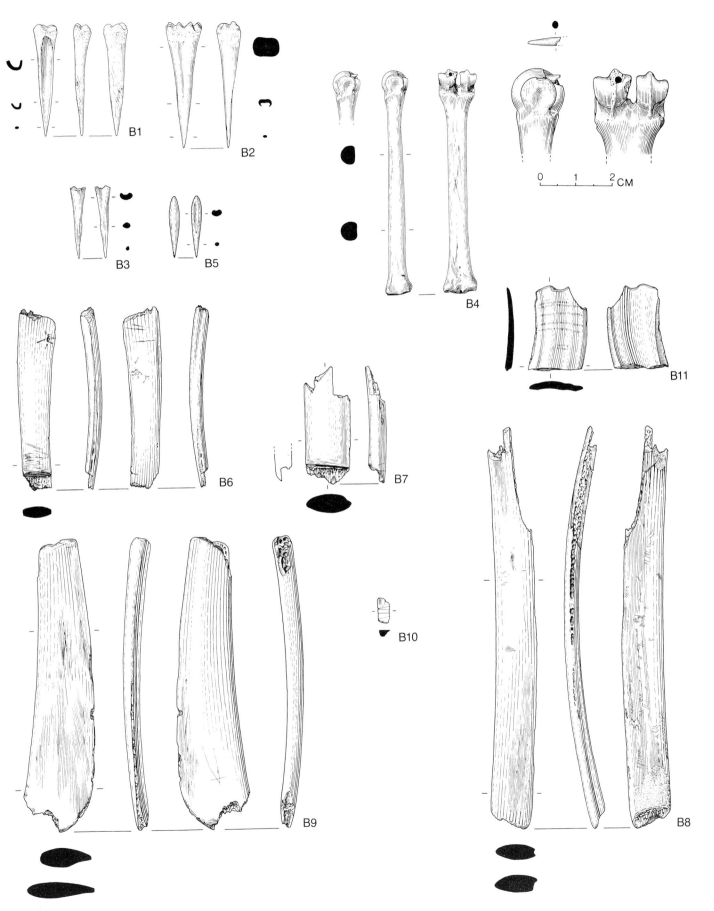

Fig. 64 Bone artifacts in Neolithic, Area 4 (B1), and Late Bronze Age, Area 6 (B2–11), contexts. Scale 1/2.

154

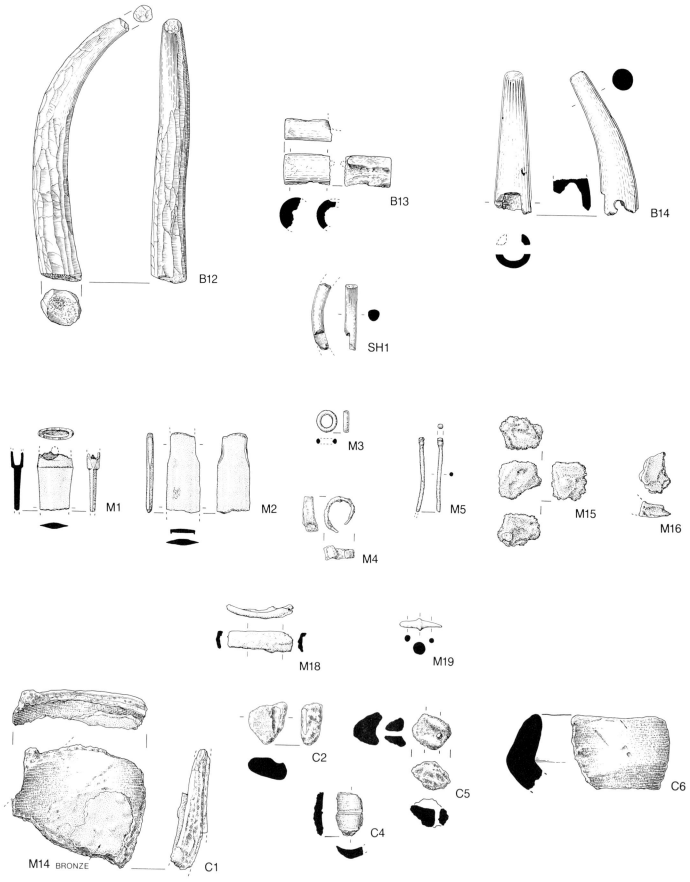

Fig. 65 Late Bronze Age artifacts from Area 6: antler (B12–14), shale (SH1), copper/alloy (M1–5, M14–16), lead (M18–19) and fired clay (C1–2, C4–6). Scale 1/2.

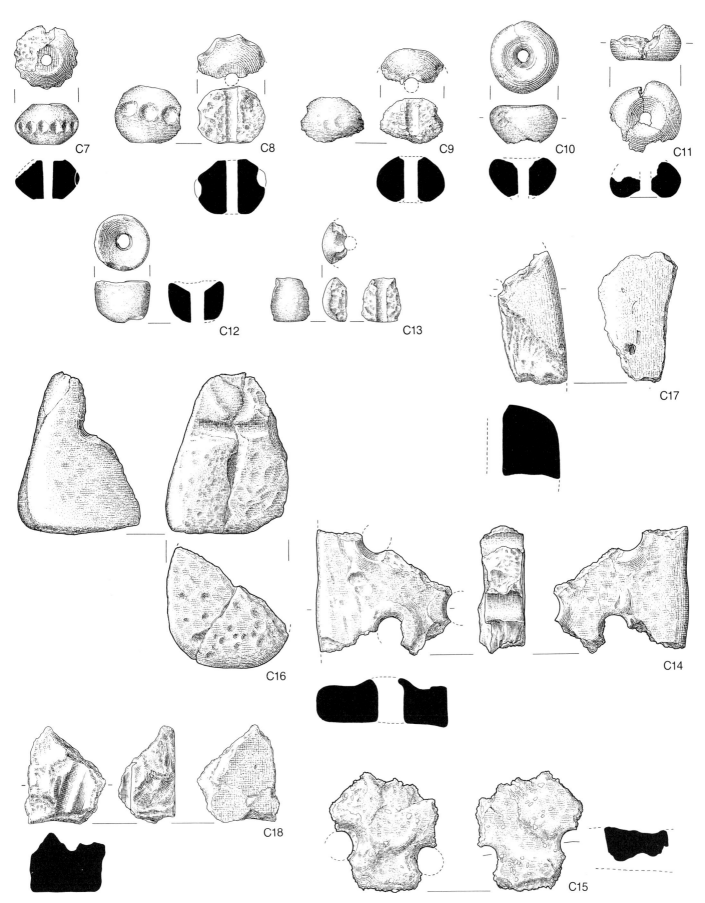

Fig. 66 Late Bronze Age fired-clay artifacts from Area 6 (C7–18). Scale 1/2.

Discussion of the non-lithic artifacts

It is not proposed to enter into any lengthy discussion of specific artifact types here. Most are present in quantities greatly outnumbered by finds made in later excavations on the site and discussion will benefit from consideration of the larger groups in the future. The small finds are representative of an assemblage which is associated with early 1st millennium BC settlements in south-eastern Britain and there have been earlier discussions of some Runnymede material (Longley 1980; Needham and Longley 1980; Needham and Hook 1988).

Amongst the most interesting finds from the 1978 season are those of bone and antler, some for technological reasons. Although not conclusive, the whittled antler tine (B12) seems most likely to have been destined for a cheek-piece. There are a fair number of cheek-pieces now represented on the site, including a fragmentary piece from the top of the same pit (B14), along with many antler offcuts, indicating the production of antler artifacts, doubtless cheek-pieces included. The ringing to help detach the tine and its paring down must have been achieved with sharp, acutely edged bronze knives, two fragments of which were intriguingly also found near pit F6. Knives are, however, one of the more common metalwork types on Bronze Age settlement sites.

Other debitage resulting from the working of skeletal materials is seen in artifacts B4, B6, B7. Object B4 seems to testify to the process of perforation, having an unfinished hole and, remarkably, the tip of the drill still lodged within it. The position of the hole is unusual and it is presumed that a small flake needed to be first detached from the verticillus to prevent the drill point from skating off the bone's surface. A perforation in a similar position on the distal end of a metapodial is known at Grimes Graves (Mercer 1981: 69 B16, fig. 41). It is hard to see what specific function a perforation in this position, rather than at the head of the shaft, would serve.

The rib offcuts (B6, B7) also show a very specific manufacturing technique. One face was evidently deeply cut with two transverse cut marks of V profile. These penetrated halfway through the thickness of the rib and a 'plaque' between was then prised away along the cancellous tissue from the other half. This process was probably geared to the production of thin bone plaques for turning into artifacts as seen at All Cannings Cross (Cunnington 1923: 75, pl. 6) or Staple Howe (Brewster 1963: 123, fig. 69. 1–4), but has also been used to make 'rib knives' in which the pieces seen as offcuts at Runnymede were instead worked into the artifacts (e.g. Cunnington 1923: 80, pl. 7). The other worked ribs from Area 6 show wear and polish to suggest that they functioned as burnishers (B8, B9).

The metalwork from Area 6 is unremarkable in terms of specific types or dating evidence, although it is readily accommodated within the Ewart Park phase to which the previous assemblage has been assigned (Needham 1980). Technologically it is of more interest, with unalloyed copper material (M15, M16), lead or lead-tin objects (M18, M19) and a lump of tin-bronze (M14) still attached to a large crucible or furnace lining (C1), almost certainly a residue of on-site alloying or refining operations. The lead finds from Runnymede are important in being amongst few well associated artifacts of lead and lead-tin in the Bronze Age (Needham and Hook 1988). The analysed cast artifacts are all of leaded tin-bronze, as expected of this phase, except for M6, which is a tin-bronze. Area 6 also yielded four pieces of mould or other refractories (C2–5).

The loomweights (C16, C17) seem to belong to the pyramidal type, now a well established type-fossil for the Late Bronze Age, while the seven spindlewhorls represented (C7–C13) show a surprising diversity of form and fabric, particularly since they all come from mid–late contexts (unit F onwards). In contrast to the weaving equipment, the two perforated slab fragments (C14, C15) come from early contexts (units B–C).

Chapter 8
The Neolithic pottery

Ian Kinnes

This treatment is deliberately brief, in advance of a much larger stratified assemblage with close contextual detail in subsequent work. The catalogue is confined to distinctive feature sherds, with no quantification of the remainder, although all sherds would seem to fall within the fabric groups identified.

Catalogue of the illustrated sherds

The catalogue entries are standardised as follows:
No.: form; decoration; fabric; context.

The numbers refer directly to illustrations (Figs. 67–69); forms have not been typed but are subjective assessments; decoration is described largely by technique since average sherd size for this category (*c*. 12 sq. cm) does not allow of assessment of schema; fabric was identified by macro-examination and is specified below; context is described elsewhere (Chapters 1 and 2).

Abbreviations:

E   external
Ev   everted
I   internal
R   rim
S   simple
Sh   shoulder
T   fabric temper
W   wall
X   expanded

NP1:   EIX; Sh marked; fine incision EI, neck and Sh ovate impressions; TI; A4 L120/121
NP2:   S; T4; A4 L120/121
NP3:   EX; T3; A4 L117a.
NP4:   W; deep stab in ?row; TI; A4 L117a.
NP5:   (Reconstructed bowl); SEv.; TI; A4 L121a and L117a
NP6:   EX; T4; A4 L121a.
NP7:   EIX; R and below fine incision; T2; A4 L121a.
NP8:   X; R impressed herringbone; T2; A4 L121a.
NP9:   Sh slight; light incision; T3; A4 L121a.
NP10: Applied lentoid lug ? on Sh; T3; A4 L121a.
NP11: Sh marked; T3; A4 L121a.
NP12: S; R lentoid impressions, neck vertical row of arcuate impressions; T4; A4 L121a F89.
NP13: EX; R and neck fine herringbone incision; T1; A4 L121a F89.
NP14: I bevel; T2; A4 u/s.
NP15: EX; R fine herringbone incision; T1; A4 u/s.

NP16: EIX; on R deep incision, external bevel fine notching, below R internal incision; T2; A6 L41 sump.
NP17: EX; T1; A6 L41 sump.
NP18: S; T2; A6 L41 sump.
NP19: S; T2; A6 L41 sump.
NP20: S; T1; A6 L41 sump.
NP21: S; T4; A6 L41 sump.
NP22: W; ?reed impressions below diagonal incision; T4; A6 L41 sump.
NP23: W; stabs; T4; A6 L41 sump.
NP24: EX; R ?cross-hatched lentoid impressions; T2; A6 L41 6E/5N.
NP25: Sh slack; T3; A6 L41 6E/5N.
NP26: S; R opposed incised herringbone; T2; A6 L41 6E/6N.
NP27: EX; T1; A6 L41 6E/6N.
NP28: W; fine herringbone point impressions; T1; A6 L41 6E/6N.
NP29: EIX; ?T2; A6 L41 7E/5N.
NP30: EX; deep oblique impressions on R; T4; A6 L41 7E/5N.
NP31: S; below R internal zone of deep impressions: upper tubular, lower blunt point; T1; A6 L41 7E/6N.
NP32: EX; T3; A6 L41 7E/6N.
NP33: S; ?vertical slash from rim; T4; A6 L41 7E/6N.
NP34: W; twisted-cord impressed herringbone; T2; A6 L41 7E/6N.
NP35: Sh slight; T3; A6 L41 7E/6N.
NP36: Sh slight; T2; A6 L41 7E/6N.
NP37: I bevel; T4; A6 L41 7E/7N.
NP38: IX; T2; A6 L41 9E/6N.
NP39: IX; R deep herringbone incision; T2; A6 L41.
NP40: EX; T3; A6 L41.
NP41: S; T4; A6 L41.
NP42: S; Sh slight; T4; A6 L41.
NP43: Sh slight; finely-incised herringbone on neck and body, fine notching on Sh; T2; A6 L41.
NP44: Sh slight; deep impressed notching on Sh; T2; A6 L41.
NP45: Sh marked; T2; A6 L41.
NP46: EX; vertical oval impressions on neck; T1; A6 L40.
NP47: S; T3; A6 L40.
NP48: S; T2; A6 L40.
NP49: Sh slight; T4; A6 L40.
NP50: S; T4; A6 L14e/20c 10E/13N.
NP51: EIX; T1; A6 L8 11E/9N.
NP52: EIX, Sh marked; R light diagonal incisions, neck reserved and filled panels of deep irregular impressions in divided pseudo-herringbone; T1; A8 u/s.

Fabric

Grouping was assessed purely by eye; four groups were established, although relative preservation must allow for some overlap. Tabulation indicates that these perceived divisions have some bearing on manufacture and firing techniques. There is no reason to believe at present that any constituent is other than local to the site but selection of filler would seem deliberate rather than arbitrary. Allowing for differential preservation under variable soil conditions, colour has not, for present purposes, been used as a denominator.

The flint filler largely falls within the crushed to small range; the fine sand, occasionally micaceous, is presumably alluvial; the ferruginous sand, again ?alluvial or in specific local deposits, has a pyrotechnic effect of producing hard, thin fabrics of 'refired' appearance; the vegetable inclusions, thin and flat but not lenticular vacuoles, would seem to be grass or herbage but certainly not shell; manure admixture seems likely. Wall thicknesses broadly confirm these divisions (Table 12) but the present assemblage is too small to test for co-ordination with vessel forms, sizes or decoration.

Affinities

Broadly, the elaborated rim forms and marked shoulders, coupled with an essentially impressed decorative technique, place the assemblage within the regionalised decorated bowl series of the Earlier Neolithic. On current assessment, based on few assemblages and scattered finds, affinities might be found eastwards with Mildenhall (Clark *et al.* 1960), south to Whitehawk (Smith 1956) and north to Whiteleaf (Childe and Smith 1954), whilst a very few sherds recall Ebbsfleet (Smith 1956), although there must be a suspicion that Runnymede, unlike the nearby causewayed enclosure at Staines (Robertson-Mackay 1987), might represent a distinct, and new, regional style (Kinnes in Hedges and Buckley 1978). Although small, the assemblage hints at some difference, presumably chronological, between the A4 and A6 material. The latter would seem to feature a greater variety of vessel form and rim profile, along with a wider range of decorative method and organisation, suggestive of a more developed stage.

Table 12:   Filler types and wall thicknesses for defined fabrics for Neolithic pottery.

| | Filler | | | | Average wall thickness (mm) |
	flint	sand	ferruginous sand	vegetable	
Fabric					
1	X				85
2	X	X			80
3	X	X		X	75
4	X		X		55

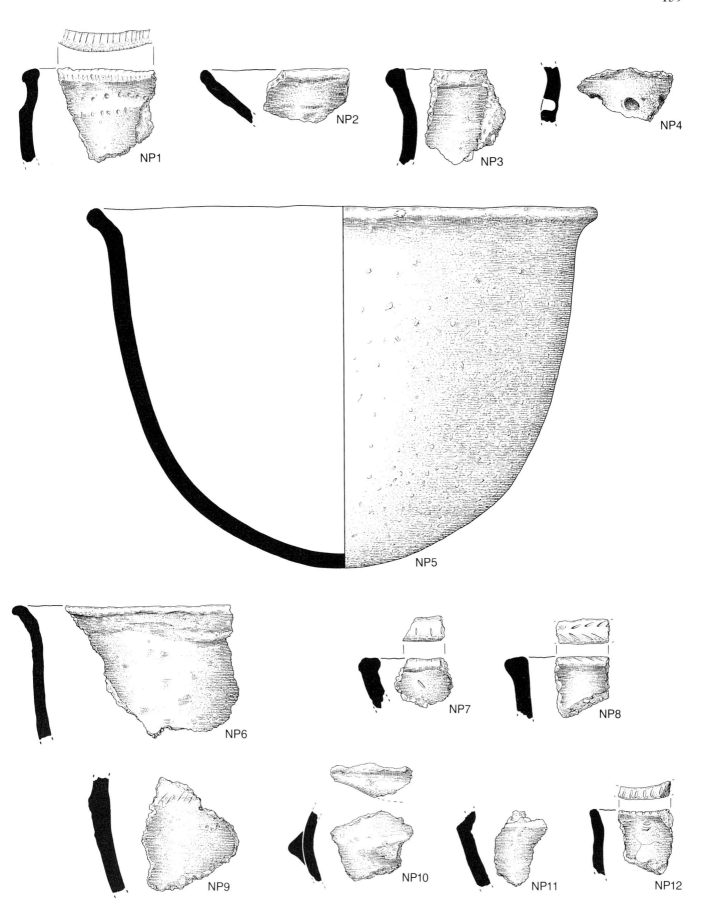

Fig. 67 Neolithic pottery from Area 4 (NP1–12). Scale 1/2.

160

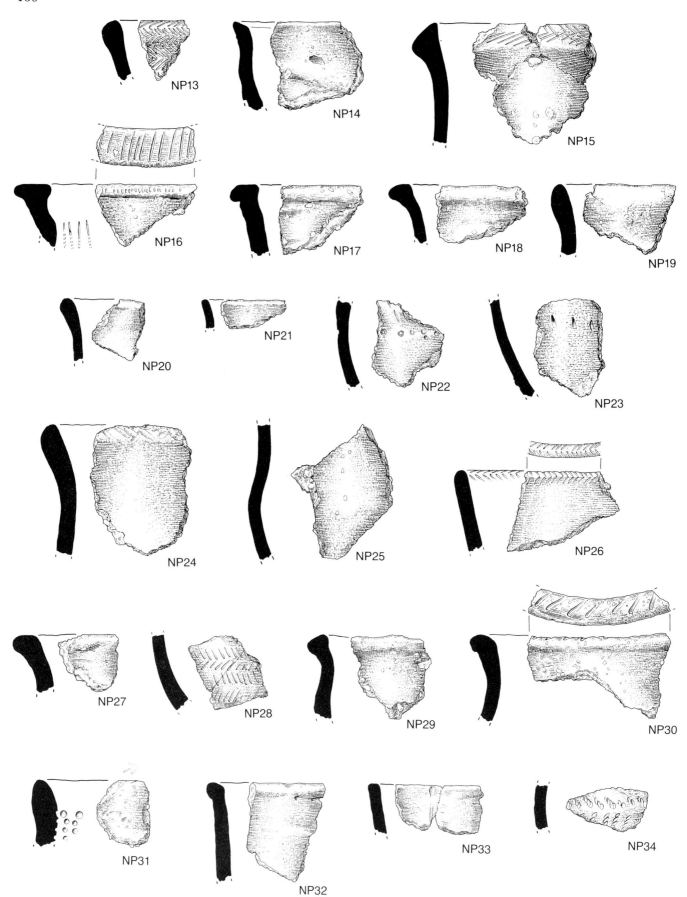

Fig. 68 Neolithic pottery from Area 4 (NP13–15) and Area 6 layer 41 (NP16–34). Scale 1/2.

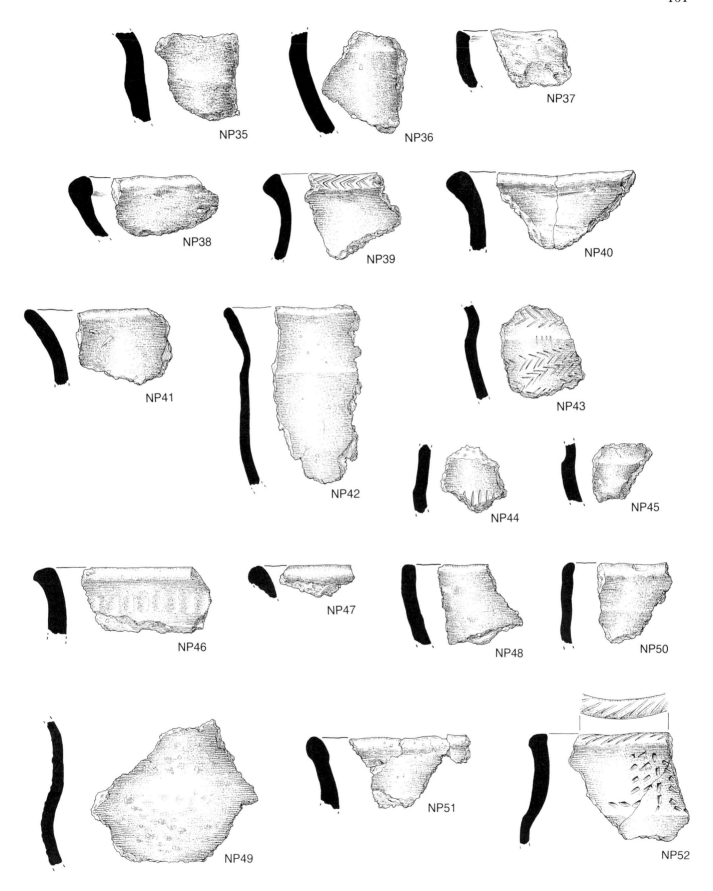

Fig. 69 Neolithic pottery from Area 6 layer 41 (NP35–45), layer 40 (NP46–49), Late Bronze Age contexts (NP50–51) and Area 8 (NP52). Scale 1/2.

Chapter 9
The Late Bronze Age pottery

DAVID LONGLEY

A total of 6886 sherds were recorded from a range of contexts which include a sequence of deposits in the old river channel and a build-up of occupation debris on the adjacent levee. In dealing with such a high concentration of material it was felt that questions might be asked of the pottery beyond those relating to the relatively straightforward association of recognisable vessel types with particular chronological phases in the development of the site. Accordingly, a recording system was employed whereby spatial and stratigraphic variations might be observed in the occurrence of coarse and finewares and in the range of sherd sizes. It was anticipated that this approach might allow a differentiation between, on the one hand, functional areas on the site and, on the other, areas of differential sherd survival – the protected contexts of river mud compared with the expected high breakage levels of trampled floor surface, for example. In practice the relatively small area excavated militated against any clear identification of spatial differentiation of function on the basis of the pottery evidence, although some interesting results were obtained with regard to the character of the material through the stratigraphic sequence. These are discussed below.

A total of 650 featured sherds or groups (rims, bases, shoulders, decorated sherds) were identified in the study; a full catalogue is in archive and a selective catalogue of the 418 vessels illustrated is published here (Table 16).

Type series

With the publication of the finds from the 1976 excavations, a type series was devised to facilitate discussion of the pottery. It was emphasised there that certain vessel forms, distinguished in the series as separate types, might simply arise out of variations on the same basic form and that 'the type series should not be seen as a rigid ordering of the pottery assemblage but, rather, as an aid to the discussion of certain significant combinations of typological features' (Longley 1980: 65). In other words, our desire for classification and the criteria which we select are, to some extent, artificial and are unlikely to reflect accurately the perceptions of the people who made and used the pottery.

The 1976 classification has been retained, in essence, for the purpose of relating the two groups of material and because it still retains some validity. On reconsideration of the assemblage, however, the 28 types and sub-types of the original classification have been rationalised into 9 types (an original version of this modification appeared in an interim report – Needham and Longley 1980). The types are:

1. Cups – vessels sufficiently small and rim forms suitable for them to be considered drinking vessels. A small number of 'cups' were identified in 1976; two possible examples were recognised in 1978. This class includes those identified as 1976 types 2 and 3.

4. Biconical bowls (1976 types 4a and 4b) and bowls with well defined or stepped carinations (1976 type 8). These vessels can have very plain biconical profiles (P74) or can be elaborated with beaded rims and cordons defining the carination (P104).

5. Open bowls (1976 types 5a, 5b, 6, 7a, 7b). These vessels can have slightly globular bodies (P26), sometimes with a beaded or developed rim (P291); they can have slightly out-turning rims (P85) or they can have very plain open profiles (P197, P198).

9. Shouldered bowls (1976 types 9a, 9b). These vessels are really the more shallow, more open, equivalents of the type 12 shouldered jars. To some extent the distinction becomes an artificial one at the point where bowl forms merge into jar forms.

10. This defines a distinctive class of bipartite bowl with tall, often concave, neck above a well defined carination. In 1976 I was struck by the apparent similarity between vessels present at Runnymede and material in the Eldon's Seat II assemblage. Both groups seemed to have an ancestry in more strictly biconical forms with sharply everted rims and furrowed necks (manifested in bronze in association with Ewart Park metalwork at Welby, Leicestershire), through furrowed forms with tall concave necks, until the furrowed decoration was lost altogether (Longley 1980: 68). I now believe the case for the presence of these vessels at Runnymede was overstated, although a handful may be represented in the 1976 assemblage and three examples in 1978.

11. Jars with smoothly curving or S-shaped profiles and a late Urnfield ancestry may be represented by a small number of examples.

12. High-shouldered jars with angular (1976 type 12a) or rounded (1976 type 12b) shoulders. The classification also includes 1976 types 13a and b, which were essentially the same vessels as type 12, and jars with poorly defined shoulders, which were previously classified as type 15.

14. A separate classification has been retained for biconical, rather than high-shouldered, jars although it is accepted that the two categories may merge.

19. Straight-sided jars (e.g. P304) are present though poorly represented.

The frequency of vessel types through the assemblage as a whole is plotted in Fig. 70. An over-confident identification of types was presented in 1976 and a more realistic assessment is now offered in Fig. 70 for comparison. Both groups of material are broadly similar in their composition, with type 12 jars dominating the assemblage. Jars in general outnumber bowls in both instances: in the proportions of 59:41

in 1978 and 55:45 in 1976. The small discrepancy in the proportions of the three most popular bowl forms in 1976 and 1978, types 4, 5 and 9, does not seem significant in view of the numbers involved. While most of the 1976 material might be treated as a contemporary assemblage, however, there would seem to be more scope for identifying a chronological sequence in the 1978 stratigraphy and for considering typological variation in relation to this. These points are discussed more fully below.

Fabric

Most of the pottery is heavily gritted with crushed flint with very little obvious use of other fillers, although a number of sherds display the deliberate addition of quartz sand, while grog and shell are also occasionally present. Colours range from buffs and light greys through a variety of browns and red-browns to black. Irregular firing conditions have resulted in the occurrence of colour variations over the surface of the same pot and while the firing of finer vessels tends to be more uniformly consistent, this is not invariably the case. The vessels are generally well fired, hard and thin-walled in relation to their size.

The lack of consistently recurring variables makes conventional macroscopic fabric sorting difficult. Nevertheless,

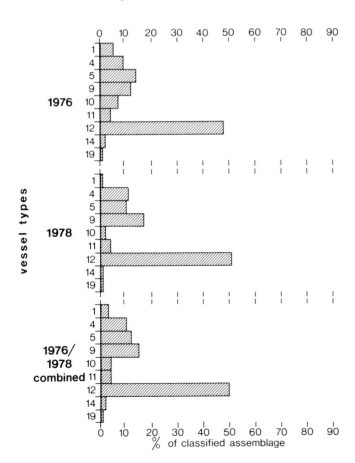

Fig. 70 Frequencies of Late Bronze Age vessel types in the 1976 and 1978 assemblages, separately and combined.

a limited amount of neutron activation analysis has been carried out as a first stage in a programme designed to test certain hypotheses regarding the production and dissemination of pottery in the Thames Valley. Forty-three sherds from the 1976 excavations and 16 sherds from the 1978 season were analysed, together with 17 sherds from the adjacent site at Petters Sports Field, Egham (O'Connell 1986), and 30 sherds from Brooklands, Weybridge (Hanworth and Tomalin 1977). The analysis was undertaken at the School of Archaeological Sciences, University of Bradford, irradiation taking place at AWRE, Aldermaston. Ward's method of cluster analysis was applied to the results, using nine elements: Fe, Co Cs, Eu, Tb, Hf, Th(Pa), Cr and Ce. The results are presented graphically in the dendrogram (Fig. 71). One of the immediately obvious conclusions to be drawn is that there is good separation of the Brooklands and Petters Sports Field pottery, something confirmed by discriminant analysis using these two groups alone. The Runnymede pottery, on the other hand, is dispersed across the dendrogram. A possible explanation of this phenomenon is that, while the Brooklands and Petters communities were using pottery for the most part from limited, perhaps local, clay sources, the Runnymede pottery was reaching the site from a greater variety of sources. Alternatively, the Runnymede potters may have been utilising clays of more varied composition – perhaps a reflection of the river-bank siting.

Most of the Petters pottery is distinguishable macroscopically from the Runnymede fabrics; it is consistently more sandy. At Brooklands this tendency is even more marked and sandy fabrics become the rule locally during the Iron Age, as, for example, at Wisley on the River Wey. One effect of the increasing use of sandy fabrics, at the expense of the use of crushed flint as a filler in the clay matrix, seems to be a relative thickening of the walls of vessels in Iron Age assemblages.

While most of the material from Petters is in a more sandy fabric as described, there are a number of sherds in the earliest contexts on the site which are closely comparable to Runnymede fabrics in the use of flint gritting (Petters fabric A – Needham 1990: 123). One of these, stratified in the lower silts of a large ditch, was included in the neutron activation analysis programme. It is separated by a considerable depth of ditch fill from the context which provided the rest of the analysed material. This latter group clusters tightly in one half of the dendrogram, while the single sherd, stratigraphically earlier and macroscopically distinguishable, can be clearly shown to be of a different clay composition.

Visual fabric-sorting of the Runnymede 1978 assemblage has concentrated on quantifying the selection of grades of flint grit, the density of fillers in the matrix and the presence or absence of surface treatment. These variables were initially categorised as follows:

1 = fine flint grit (less than 0.5 mm)
2 = small flint grit (less than 1.5 mm)

164

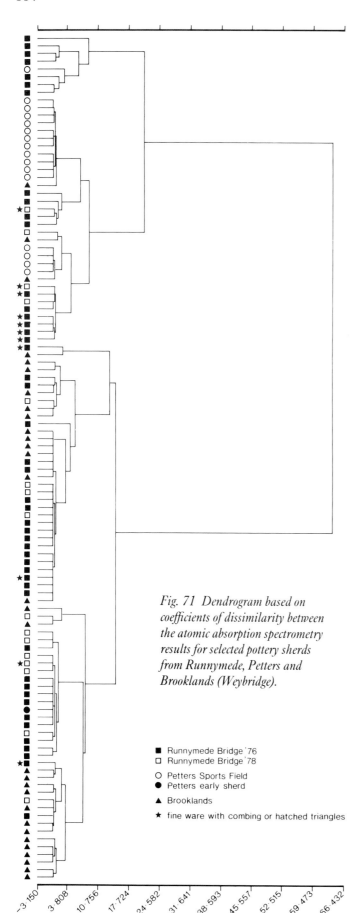

3 = medium flint grit (less than 2.5 mm)
4 = large flint grit (over 2.5 mm)
5 = gritless
(The presence of added quartz grits was also noted and designated '7' in the catalogue.)
 i = sparse density of filler
 ii = medium density
 iii = high density
 a = little or no surface treatment
 b = surface smoothed and even
 c = surface burnished

In practice the categorisation of a particular sherd will generally identify a range of grit sizes present; for example: small/medium (2/3) or fine/small (1/2). Sherds from a vessel in a flint-gritted fabric, then, containing a medium density of fine/small-sized grits with surfaces smoothed and even, might be categorised as 1/2iib. The density of filler is rarely a significant variable, with the vast majority of identifications occurring under category ii.

A preliminary observation to make is that there is a deliberate selection and grading of grits for use in the manufacture of certain vessels and for achieving certain results in the finished product. For example, considering the assemblage as a whole and breaking the fabric classification into six broad categories, reflecting the major distinctions in the association of grit size with surface treatment, we arrive at the associations seen in Table 13.

94% of gritless sherds (category 5) have burnished or smoothed surface finishes. 77% of sherds with fine–small flint grits (category 1/2) have burnished or smoothed surface finishes. In both these instances it appears that a deliberate selection of filler grade has been effected for the production of vessels which were to be further enhanced by surface smoothing or burnishing. Category 2/3 characterises the coarser end of the flint grit range. Only 5% of these sherds have been smoothed or burnished and the vast majority have no surface treatment at all.

This analysis may be extended further to a consideration of the use of certain fabrics in certain vessel forms. Finewares may be defined as those with burnished surfaces or those with smoothed and even surfaces in combination with the selection of fine/small flint grits as a filler. Table 14 charts the occurrence of these fabrics against the vessel forms in which they occur. In general terms it may be seen that more bowl forms were produced in fine (61%) than in coarse fabrics. Jars, on the other hand, are predominantly (84%) coarse vessels. More specifically, certain vessel forms are

Fig. 71 Dendrogram based on coefficients of dissimilarity between the atomic absorption spectrometry results for selected pottery sherds from Runnymede, Petters and Brooklands (Weybridge).

■ Runnymede Bridge '76
□ Runnymede Bridge '78

○ Petters Sports Field
● Petters early sherd

▲ Brooklands

★ fine ware with combing or hatched triangles

Table 13: The associations between grit size ranges and surface treatment in the Late Bronze Age pottery assemblage.

Surface treatment	Grit size		
	5	1/2	2/3
a	4	214	5467
b/c	63	719	258

more likely to be produced in particular fabrics (and to have distinctive decoration applied in association with that fabric – see below). Type 4 bowls are mainly fineware vessels. Type 5 is equally clearly a coarseware type. Type 9 shouldered bowls can occur in coarse and fine versions but more often in finewares. The jar series is dominated by type 12 vessels and the majority of type 12 are in coarse fabrics. Within the assemblage as a whole, on a sherd count rather than on the basis of identifiable vessels, 88% of the total sherds are coarse. It may be that this figure is inflated by the predominance of coarse wares in the larger vessel range, which on breakage might generate more sherds per vessel than smaller fineware bowls. Quantification of the catalogued vessels suggests that a more realistic proportion might be 75% coarse, 25% fine.

Vessels in a fabric containing deliberately added quartz do not seem to constitute a significant element in the assemblage (less than 3% of the total). Nevertheless, there is a progressive increase in the percentage of quartz fabrics through the river channel sequence from less than 1% in the earliest (AB) contexts to 7% in the latest (J). This progression is less easy to discern through the occupation contexts (see Fig. 74), which may not have the same longevity.

Decoration

As was observed to be the case with the 1976 assemblage, a variety of decorative techniques is employed on the pottery. These range from fairly coarse finger-tip and nail impressions on rim, shoulder and body to neater cabling of rims. Stamped circles, combed wavy lines and hatched triangles were also used and a small number of vessels have applied cordons. The relative frequencies of the different decorative treatments are presented in Fig. 72 with the details of 1976 decoration for comparison. The two series are, as might be expected, broadly comparable, with various forms of finger-tipping dominant. One significant distinction, however, concerns the much higher level of combed line and incised line decoration present in the 1976 assemblage. As this is predominantly a decoration applied to fineware bowls (types 4 and some type 9), the discrepancy might be thought to relate to the number of these bowls in the assemblage. In fact this is not the case, as both type 4 and type 9 bowls comprise a higher proportion of the 1978 vessels than of the 1976 vessels.

The main forms of decoration are particular to certain vessel forms. We have already noticed that combed wavy lines, hatched triangles and incised line decoration is to be found predominantly on fineware bowls. Combed lines and hatched triangles, in some instances with white paste inlay surviving, are almost exclusively associated with gritless or virtually gritless dark, burnished fabrics. A variation on the use of combed line decoration occurs on a bowl (P648) from a context away from the main area of excavation (Area 8). On this vessel an arcade of combed arches has been formed above an array of less pronounced arches, all of this above the rounded shoulder of the bowl.

Finger-tip and fingernail decoration is mainly a feature of high-shouldered jars in coarse fabrics. Of classifiable vessels, one type 9 shouldered bowl has finger-tipping on the shoulder and one type 5 open bowl has a finger-tipped rim; the rest are jars. In two instances finger-tipping occurs in association with burnished surfaces but in both instances the flint grit component is coarse. The use of finger-pressed ornamentation is for the most part confined to the rim of vessels, although it is possible that some of the shoulder-

Table 14: The associations between fabrics and vessel types in the Late Bronze Age pottery assemblage.

Fabric		bowls 1	4	5	9	10	jars 11	12	14	19	Totals
Fine	1ib		2	1	1						4
	1ic				1				1		2
	1iib			1							1
	1iic				1						1
	1/2iib		2	1	2		1	1			7
	1/2iic	2	7	1	6	2	1	4			23
	2/3iic				3			5			8
	5c		1		1				1		3
	Totals	2	12	4	15	2	2	10	2		49
Coarse	1ia				1			1			2
	1iia							1			1
	1/2iia									1	1
	2iib				1						1
	2/3iia		2	9	5		2	58	1	1	78
	2/3iib		1	1	1	1	1	2			7
	Totals		3	10	8	1	3	62	1	2	90

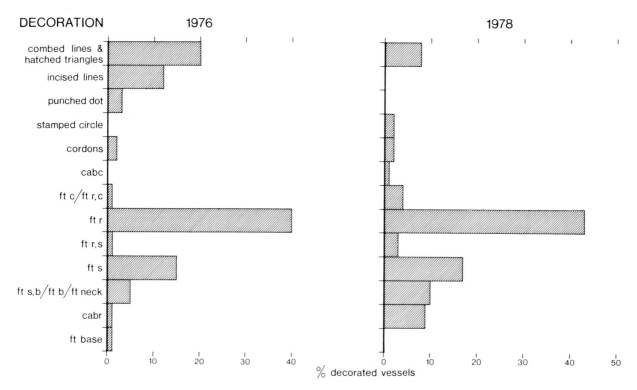

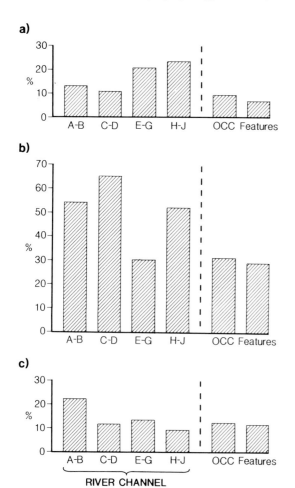

Fig. 72 Relative frequencies of decorative treatment on the 1976 and 1978 Late Bronze Age pottery assemblages. Abbreviations: cab—cabled; ft—finger-tipped; r—rim; c—cordon; s—shoulder; b—body.

Fig. 73 Percentages of a) decorated sherds, b) bowls and c) fineware, in major context groups in the river channel and on the levee.

decorated sherds once belonged with rims that were similarly decorated. This can only be demonstrated in three instances, however. Nine sherds have finger-pressed decoration on the body of the vessel other than a rim, shoulder or cordon.

Cabling, as with finger-tipping, is a feature of coarse jars.

The level of decoration throughout the assemblage as a whole is at about 15%. This is an average value, however, and the proportion of decorated vessels fluctuates, context to context, from around 10% in the occupation contexts generally to 30% in the highest stratified levels in the river channel. These variations are plotted in Fig. 73a and discussed more fully below.

River channel contexts

A and B contexts: P1–P48X, Figs. 76–79.
These contexts comprise the lowest LBA contexts recorded within the river channel sequence. They include a concentration of materials which appeared to the excavators to be a midden in its early stages of formation. Of recognisable types, jars and bowl forms are equally represented: the predominant bowl form is the type 9 shouldered bowl and the predominant jar is the type 12 high-shouldered jar. Approximately 13% of vessels were decorated. Decoration is restrained, being confined to a finger-tipped rim in one instance and a shoulder in another, and two cabled rims – all occurring on type 12 jars. The impression is of a generally plainware assemblage.

A distinguishing characteristic of A and B contexts is the high percentage of medium and large sherds (Fig. 74) together with a relatively high proportion of finewares. This is particularly so on both counts in the area of the midden.

C and D contexts: P48X–P85, Figs. 80–83.
C and D contexts lie above A and B in the river channel and include the upper portion of the midden. Type 12 jars continue to be the most numerous single vessel type in evidence but in C and D contexts bowls now outnumber jars. High-shouldered bowls, however, now give ground to the increasingly popular type 5 open-mouthed bowls and type 4 fineware biconical and flanged bowls. One example of a type 10 bipartite bowl (P70) occurs in one of the unit D contexts. Decoration is confined to approximately 11% of the vessels and is limited to finger-tipping on the rim of type 5 bowls and one type 12 jar. A further vessel displays finger-tipping on the shoulder.

C and D contexts continue to display a significantly high proportion of medium–large sherds.

E, F and G contexts: P86–P175, Figs. 83–88.
These contexts in the river channel represent accumulation during and after the construction of the second pile row. Jars now outnumber bowls and type 12 jars continue to be the most numerous single form, remaining so throughout every context in this group. The level of decoration increases to 21%. The high overall figure is attained, however, by

the high proportion of decorated finewares, with combed line decoration being applied to between 40% and 50% of fineware vessels. Finger-tipping on rim or shoulder provides decoration on about 16% of coarseware vessels, principally type 12 jars. Type 11 jars with smoothly curving profiles make an appearance in E–G contexts, being represented by two examples. One of the rare instances of the identification of a possible cup occurs in this context too.

The proportion of finewares remains, nevertheless, small at around 13%. This compares well with the central phases of occupation build-up on the adjacent river bank (layers 35a, b, c; 32b, c; 33b, c; 37a, b – see Fig. 73c), which additionally provides a closely comparable ratio of small–medium/large sherds (c. 75% small).

H contexts: P175X, not illustrated
Only 21 sherds were recovered from H context and no diagnostic vessel forms were recognised. 18 (95%) of the sherds were small: only one, medium-sized, sherd out of the total 21 was from a fineware vessel.

I contexts: P176–P246, Figs. 88–91.
These contexts, together with J contexts, represent the uppermost deposits in the river channel. The predominant occurrence of small sherds (88% in I and 97% in J) is a severe constraint on the identification of classifiable vessels. Within I contexts bowls and jars appear to be equally represented. Type 5 bowls occur in coarse fabrics, type 9 shouldered bowls occur in finer fabrics with some surface smoothing. The identifiable jars are all type 12. The level of decoration remains high at 22%, principally represented by finger-tipping on rim, shoulder and body – once on rim and shoulder – and by cabling on rims. One body sherd, however, bears combed line decoration and another, one of only two in the total assemblage, has been decorated with stamped circles.

J contexts: P247–P268, Figs. 91–92.
J is the uppermost horizon in the river channel. Small sherds account for 97% of the total 231 recorded, a proportion exceeded only by the uppermost stratified context on the adjacent river bank (layer 31 at 98%). Only two vessels are capable of confident identification: a type 5 bowl and a type 12 jar with finger-tipped body. Other decorated body sherds display finger-tipping on rim, shoulder and body: one has a plain neck cordon. The incidence of decoration throughout J contexts may be estimated at around 30% – the highest of the entire assemblage.

Occupation contexts

Layer 36: P269–P274, Fig. 92.
Layer 36 lies at the base of the stratified occupation sequence on the Late Bronze Age river bank. The proportion of small sherds is relatively high at 85%; nevertheless identifications might be plausibly suggested for four vessels, with bowls

equalling jars. One sherd (P273) may be from a lid. Only one sherd, the finger-tipped rim of a type 12 jar, was recognised as having been decorated; or perhaps two if the supposed lid bears finger-tipping on its upper surface.

One of the type 12 jars appears to have been burnished. This is not a common treatment of type 12 jars. More exceptionally the burnishing of the surface of the vessel has been combined with finger-tipping of the rim. These features occur in combination on one other vessel only – a probable jar rim from F6.4 (P564). In neither case, however, are fine fabrics employed.

Layers 35, 32c, 33c, 37b, 32b, 33b, 37a: P275–P280, Fig. 92; P291–P364, Figs. 93–95; P406–P447, Figs. 97–99; P476–P490, Fig. 100.

These contexts constitute the greater part of the occupation build-up on the river bank. Layers 35, 32c, 33c and 37b are stratified below 32b, 33b and 37a but a case can be made for considering the two groups together as providing a better representation of the character of the Runnymede assemblage. To some extent the stratigraphical distinction might be artificial. The statistics of each group are presented separately in Table 15 and combined in Fig. 74; the discussion will consider the material as a whole.

Jars now dominate the range, with over three times as many jars as bowls. Type 12 jars are by far the most numerous but type 14 biconical jars, type 19 straight-sided jars and a single type 11 'S-profile' jar are also represented. All bowl forms are present, as is one possible cup, and the increase in the variety of vessel types, together with the emphasis on jar forms, corresponds well with the character of the assemblage within E, F and G contexts in the river channel. The relative percentages of coarse- and finewares (87% coarse, 13% fine) are identical in both instances and the percentage of small sherds measured against medium and large is very close in both the occupation contexts under discussion (74%) and in the river channel E–G (75%). Decoration, however, is confined to finger-tipping or cabling (one instance) on the rim, shoulder or body of jars and is restricted to 11% of the total vessels. While this frequency is consistent with the occupation contexts generally, if a comparison is to be made with E–G in the river then attention must be drawn to the much higher (21%) frequency of decoration occurring in E–G contexts, a characteristic which may be chiefly accounted for by the decoration of bowls. In particular the combed line decoration of fineware bowls is a noticeable omission from the repertoire not only of these occupation contexts but of the occupation contexts generally. In this respect it may be observed that the river channel contexts have a consistently higher proportion of decorated vessels (see Fig. 73a).

One type 5 bowl (P406) was in a fine fabric with burnished surfaces – exceptional for this form of open bowl – although it must always be remembered that the type series is simply a convenient ordering of the assemblage and that in practice the distinction between one bowl form and another might

be slight; in this instance the vessel might almost have been classed with type 9 shouldered bowls (see, for instance, cat. P416).

Layers 32a, 33a: P365–P405, 408, Figs. 95–97; P447–P453, Fig. 99.

The upper layers of the river bank occupation deposits contain a relatively high proportion of small sherds. An insufficient number of vessel forms were identified within layers 32a and 33a to establish the continuing currency of the considerable range of types exhibited in the preceding deposits; nevertheless, it seems clear that jar forms continue to dominate. The level of decoration is maintained at around 10% of vessels with cabling on rims and finger-tipping on rims, cordons and bodies.

Pit F6: P539–P611, Figs. 101–104.

F6 is a large pit, recut. The lower, original, fills are clearly dominated by high-shouldered forms, with jars (type 12) in the majority. One identifiable bowl is a high-shouldered type 9 in a fine burnished fabric (cat. P562). Pot P543 might also be classifiable as a bowl. Fine wares are very poorly represented (4%) in the F6 lower fills generally, however. Decoration is sparsely applied, appearing as cabling on one rim and finger-tipping on one shoulder. This represents an estimated 5% level of decoration throughout the range.

The fills of the recut in F6 contain pottery displaying a slight increase in the frequency of decoration (to 7%) and, while jars continue to dominate, the overall impression is of a greater variety in the assemblage. Decoration includes finger-tipped rims and one type 12 jar or bowl with stamped circles on the body (P588). There is a greater percentage of fine wares (15%), too, in the recut fills.

F6 in general contains a higher than average proportion of medium and large sherd fragments (30% in the lower fills, 26% in the recut). This might be expected in the somewhat protected environment of a pit fill, reducing the potential for secondary breakage, but it should be noted that these proportions are not significantly higher than the corresponding river bank occupation surfaces (see Fig. 74).

Layers 34a and 34b: P281–P290, Figs. 92–93.

These contexts occur over the fills of pit F6. The great majority of sherds were small and identifications can be suggested for only two vessels, both of which are bowls, too small a sample from which to draw a valid conclusion. No decorated sherds were recorded (from a total of 230), however, and, as the presence or absence of decoration is not dependent on the size of sherd survival, this might be significant, perhaps reflecting the low frequency of decoration within F6.

Layer 31: P454–P475, Figs. 99–100.

This represents the uppermost stratified context within the levee occupation sequence. The vast majority (98%) of sherds are small and no confident identifications of vessel types are possible. The high incidence of small sherds corresponds well with the equally high proportion of small sherds in the upper layers of the river channel. The frequency of decoration has increased too – occurring as finger-tipping on rims and shoulders and including one plain cordon – and this may also be compared with the increasing incidence of decoration through the river channel sequence. It may be that these contexts with extremely high numbers of small sherd fragments represent derived material, perhaps as a result of water sorting of occupation contexts after inundation by the river. These considerations will be discussed more fully below in relation to the sequence as a whole.

Unstratified overburden and cleaning

Layers 1, 2 and 3: P503–P533, Figs. 100–101.
The material from these contexts can only be used to create a general impression of the character of the latest Late Bronze Age pottery from both the river and the levee. Much of the overburden was removed by machine and there was an element of selectivity in the recovery and recording of material from these disturbed deposits. The statistics may, therefore, overstate the survival of more readily recognisable larger sherds.

Nevertheless, the proportion of small fragments is still very high at 84% and the frequency of decoration (at 19%) is the highest within the levee sequence (the unstratified contexts conflate levee and river channel material but the larger part is spatially disposed over the bank rather than the channel). In reality these contexts might best be seen as an element in the washing out and sorting of levee occupation material by river flood water.

Only one vessel-type might be confidently identified – a type 12 jar in a fine, burnished fabric. Decoration is provided entirely by finger-tipping, occurring on body, rim, shoulder and body together and twice on applied cordons.

General considerations

Dating
An exhaustive discussion of the dating of the pottery was offered for the assemblage from Runnymede Bridge 1976, both with regard to the individual types and the group as a whole (Longley 1980). This attempt to demonstrate the Late Bronze Age currency of vessels which might then have been more commonly regarded as Early Iron Age may now seem unnecessarily laboured. At that time however, it could be argued that 'very little comparable material [was] known from excavated contexts in Britain and still less with any datable associations. Dating [of the Continental material] has often relied on typological considerations.' (Longley 1980: 71). Now the situation has changed dramatically with the excavation of a number of comparable assemblages from southern Britain. In particular, the Runnymede pottery now provides one of the most comprehensive ranges from any

site and one which can be better dated by reference to on-site associations – bronze metalwork and the extensive radiocarbon chronology – than by external typologies. It would seem, then, no longer necessary on the one hand to justify the chronological position of the material or on the other to cite parallels in the hope of fixing that position in the absolute time scale.

Variations and sequence
The character of the 1978 assemblage considered as a whole compares well with that of 1976 (see Fig. 70). The levels of decoration are broadly comparable too with perhaps a slightly higher frequency (20% – revised from the published assessment of 16–22%) in the 1976 range than in 1978 (15%; see Fig. 72). Finger-tipping is more commonly represented in 1978, with a higher level of combed decoration and incised lines in 1976. As these latter two are fineware decorative techniques, the discrepancy might have been explained if there had been a higher proportion of fineware bowls represented in 1976. As this was not in fact the case, other explanations have to be sought. The answer probably lies in the fact that, while the 1976 pottery was treated as a contemporary assemblage, which may remain a valid assumption for the bulk of that material, there would seem to be more scope for identifying a chronological sequence within the 1978 material, with perceptible variations in pottery phase groups, both within the build-up of 1978 river channel deposits and on the levee (Fig. 75).

Type 12 jars are clearly the dominant vessel form through all phases of the sequence. There are, however, fluctuations in the popularity of bowl forms and variations in the ratio of bowls to jars. There are also variations in the proportions of small sherds to medium-sized and large sherds which provide an indication of the character of the context.

The lowest river bank contexts (A–B) are characterised by shouldered vessels with type 9, the shouldered bowl, as the major bowl form. These occur in both coarse and fine fabrics. In no other context group do these bowls achieve such popularity. In units A–B bowls and jars are equally represented; the level of decoration stands at 13%; the group comprises the highest proportion of finewares (22%) of any phase and the highest survival of medium/large sherds (38%). It is likely that unit A–B represents the earliest Late Bronze Age material in the sequence.

During units C–D in the river channel the relative popularity of type 9 bowls decreases with the increasing currency of types 4 and 5. This becomes more clearly discernible in the later river channel contexts E–G and later still in I and J, although the small number of positive identifications in the upper channel, arising from the predominance of small sherds, makes confident assessment difficult. The trend is repeated through the occupation sequence, with shouldered bowls being very poorly represented. It seems possible that what is occurring represents a sort of diversification from the predominant use of shouldered bowls, in both fine- and coarsewares, to the development or, at least, increasing popularity of specifically fineware bowls (type 4) and specifically coarseware bowls (type 5).

The ratio of bowls to jars fluctuates from context to context but, if a pattern can be suggested, it seems to be as follows. Layer 36, the earliest occupation surface on the river bank, and units C–D in the channel share a predominance of bowl forms over jars. In 36 the bowls are type 4; in C–D type 9 are still present but no longer in the majority. The main levee occupation contexts (35 etc.; see above) and the main channel units E–G – occurring immediately above context 36 and units C–D respectively – now display a preponderance of jars over bowls (see Fig. 73b). It seems plausible that material within units C–D in the channel might derive from the same activity which generated layer 36 on the levee and that the build-up during units E–G in the channel is contemporary with the main occupation deposits (35 etc.) on the levee.

There is an anomaly in the occurrence of decoration through the range in that the levee contexts have consistently fewer decorated vessels than the corresponding channel contexts (see Fig. 73a). Nevertheless, a trend emerges which sees the doubling of the amount of decoration through the chronological sequence, both in the channel contexts and on the levee. The increase in the frequency of decoration with time has been recognised elsewhere in the Thames Valley in the development of Late Bronze Age and Early Iron ceramics (Needham and Longley 1980: Fig. 6; Barrett 1980: 307–8) and may be considered to be a general chronological indicator.

With a tendency towards an increasingly decorated assemblage through time and a trend towards the production of specifically fine or coarse vessel forms it may not be surprising to find most of the combed line decoration occurring on fineware type 4 bowls in the later contexts in the river channel. The particularly strong representation of combed and incised line decoration, the level of decoration generally and the range of vessel forms comprising the 1976 assemblage might suggest that the bulk of this material belongs, chronologically, with the later rather than earlier material from 1978.

Sherd size

Individual sherds were quantified by size into three categories, based on a subjective assessment of the character of the assemblage:

small – less than 40 mm across;
medium – less than 90 mm across;
large – over 90 mm across.

Small sherds accounted for 78% of the total, medium sherds 20% and large sherds just 1%. A slightly higher proportion (83%) of fineware sherds fell into the small category, which might be accounted for by the generally smaller, thinner, vessels utilising finewares. In practice, the appropriate distinction is between small sherds and the rest, and the relevant proportions are plotted by context in Fig. 74.

It was thought that the protected environment of the river channel silts might have been conducive to a greater degree of intact sherd survival after breakage than levee contexts where continuing traffic might produce secondary breakage. Furthermore, it was felt that such discrimination might be distinguishable statistically. It may be that this is just what is reflected in the lower river channel (A–B, C–D) and lowest levee contexts, with lower and higher than average percentages of small sherds respectively. The main channel and main occupation contexts, however, are not only closely comparable in the range of vessel forms represented, but also in their proportions of small to medium/large sherds. The upper layers in the channel and on the bank, on the other hand, display an increasingly high percentage of small sherds (small sherds are probably under-represented in the recording of the unstratified overburden clearance) and it may be that we are witnessing here the reworking of the uppermost, and therefore generally latest, deposits on the site, late in the occupation or after abandonment.

Sherd join patterns

STUART NEEDHAM

An extensive search for joins amongst the Area 6 Late Bronze Age pottery was undertaken in the hope that join patterns might help correlate the effectively independent sequences from channel, occupation surface and, indeed, from the pottery-rich pit, F6. It was also hoped to identify the character of any spatial dispersal patterns, although this was conditioned by the shape in plan of Late Bronze Age deposits.

Procedure

The study was conducted in a number of stages. Featured sherds (defined as rim sherds, base sherds, clear shoulder/carination sherds and decorated sherds) were initially selected from all contexts for study by Longley. At this stage joins were sought within each context and many were found. In stage two all the featured pottery was laid out in stratigraphic order within channel and occupation surface sequences respectively (the latter in as-excavated contexts). Next there was a fresh search of all the bulk sherds (over 6000) to look for further joins, especially cross-context ones. For practical reasons sherd comparisons obviously could not nearly approach the enormous number of permutations possible. For the river channel sequence, therefore, attention was focused on stratigraphically close contexts; nevertheless, the featured sherds elsewhere in channel and in occupation contexts were compared when recalled to mind.

A different approach was taken for the occupation and cut feature assemblages. Due to poor phasing on the basis of the stratigraphic evidence alone, it was thought better to compare bulk sherds with all relevant featured sherds in these contexts, regardless of possible temporal and spatial differences. The search consequently had to be a little less intensive than for the river channel material.

Table 15: Frequencies of sherds in Late Bronze Age context groups according to size and fabric.

Context group	small crse	small fine	Sherd size medium crse	medium fine	large crse	large fine	Fabric 5a	5bc	1/2a	1/2bc	2/3a	2/3bc	Qtz	Total no. sherds	Sub-totals coarse no.	coarse %	small no.	small %
A–B	55	10	24	2	3	4	0	0	3	9	78	8	1	98	82	84	65	66
A–B midden	98	33	59	22	7	0	0	0	3	54	159	3	0	219	164	75	131	60
C–D	107	21	62	12	8	0	0	1	5	25	165	14	2	210	177	84	128	61
C–D midden	98	8	31	0	8	0	0	0	1	11	123	10	2	145	137	94	106	73
E–G	586	103	200	16	10	0	1	15	32	85	737	45	10	915	796	87	689	75
H	18	1	2	0	0	0	0	0	0	2	19	0	0	21	20	95	19	90
I	612	64	82	6	7	0	0	0	14	89	632	30	24	771	701	91	676	88
J	203	20	7	0	1	0	0	0	2	25	196	6	16	231	211	91	223	97
Total channel	*1777*	*260*	*467*	*58*	*44*	*4*	*1*	*16*	*60*	*300*	*2109*	*116*	*55*	*2610*	*2288*	*88*	*2037*	*78*
L1, 2, 3	198	23	31	4	6	0	0	0	4	28	163	9	9	262	235	90	221	84
L31	232	17	5	0	1	0	0	2	1	19	230	3	1	255	238	93	249	98
L32a, 33a	388	42	71	8	2	0	0	1	10	51	444	3	17	511	461	90	430	84
L34a–b	168	20	36	6	0	0	0	0	15	22	184	7	13	230	204	88	188	82
L36	77	11	13	2	0	0	0	1	2	7	80	13	0	103	90	87	88	85
L32c, 33c, 35b-c, 37b	409	98	160	8	4	1	0	4	9	73	479	52	16	680	573	84	507	74
L32b, 33b, 37a, F295	763	106	261	28	18	0	1	13	43	122	991	13	35	1176	1042	89	869	74
Total occ. layer	*2374*	*341*	*629*	*57*	*32*	*1*	*1*	*35*	*90*	*340*	*2744*	*106*	*91*	*3434*	*3035*	*88*	*2715*	*79*
F6L1	139	24	52	1	1	0	0	14	6	18	173	6	0	217	192	88	163	75
F6L2	131	39	58	4	2	1	2	9	15	34	158	17	1	235	191	81	170	72
F6L4	43	1	24	7	7	1	0	0	12	9	62	0	0	83	74	89	44	53
F6L5	203	2	51	1	14	2	0	3	32	8	227	3	5	273	268	98	205	75
F6L6	11	0	6	0	1	0	0	0	2	0	15	1	0	18	18	100	11	61
Other features	167	34	28	2	2	0	0	0	3	28	152	15	3	233	197	85	201	86
Total features	*694*	*100*	*219*	*15*	*27*	*4*	*2*	*26*	*70*	*97*	*787*	*42*	*9*	*1059*	*940*	*89*	*794*	*75*
Total layer and features	*2929*	*417*	*796*	*71*	*58*	*5*	*3*	*47*	*154*	*419*	*3358*	*142*	*100*	*4276*	*3783*	*88*	*3346*	*78*
Grand total	4706	677	1263	129	102	9	4	63	214	719	5467	258	155	6886	6071	88	5383	78

172

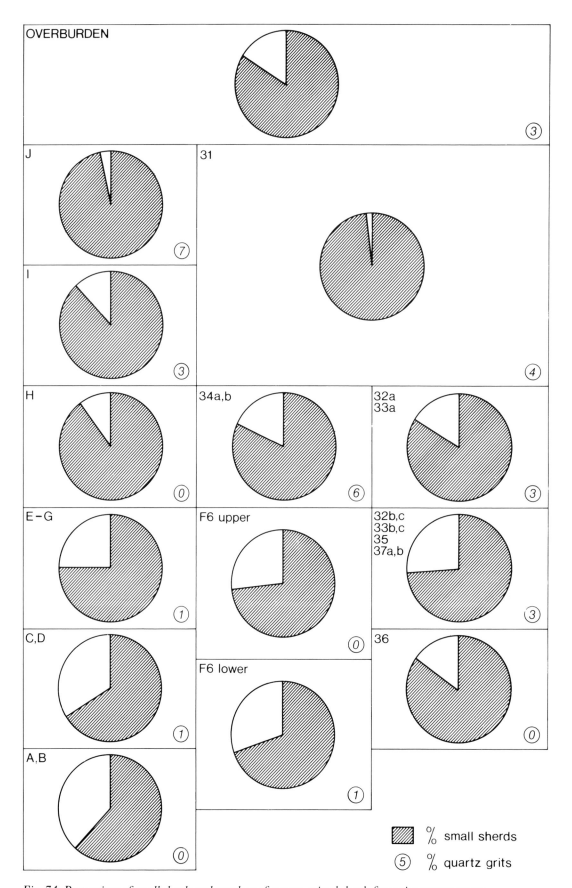

Fig. 74 Proportions of small sherds and numbers of quartz-gritted sherds for major context groups.

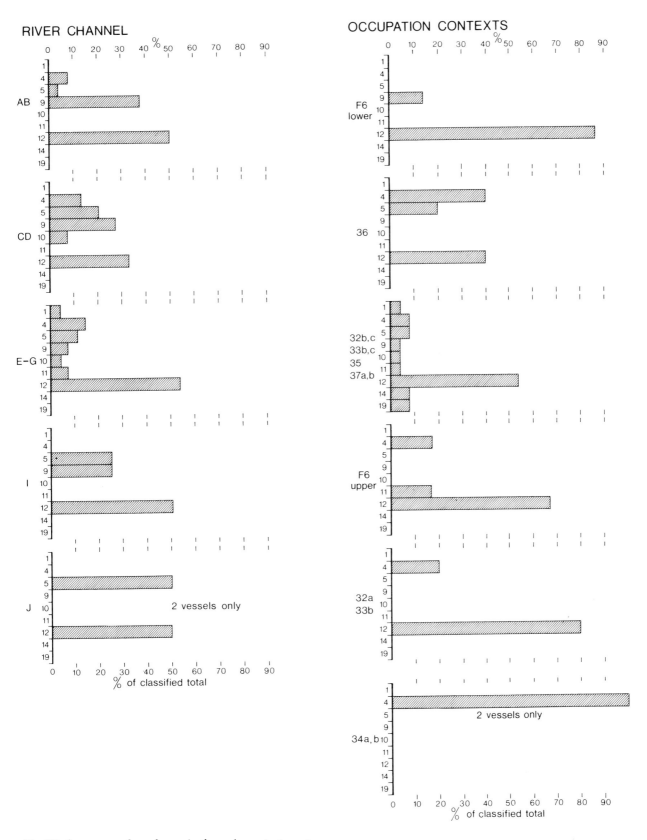

Fig. 75 Occurrence of vessel types in the major context groups.

Table 16: Catalogue of illustrated Late Bronze Age sherds.

No (P-)	Context	Grid E	N	Unit	Type	Decoration	Fabric	Outface	Inface	Core
1	27d			A	9		2/3iia	black	d.brown	d.grey
2	27d			A	9		2/3iia	black	d.grey	d.grey
3	27d			A	?9		2/3iia	black	brown	grey
6	25c			A	?12		2/3iia	l.brown	l.brown	l.brown
7	27	10	13	A	12	cabr	21/3iia	l.or/br	l.or/br	d.grey
8a	27	10	13	A	9		1/2iic	d.br/bl	d.br/bl	d.grey
8b	25c	8	13	A						
8c	24*	10	13	B						
8d	27	10	13	A						
9	27	10	13	A	base		2/3iic	d.gr/bl	d.gr/bl	d.grey
10	27			A	9		2/3iia	black	black	d.grey
11	27			A	?12		2/3iia	black	red/br	l.grey
12	27			A	nd		2/3iia	d.grey	d.grey	d.grey
13	27			A	?12	ftr	2/3iia	black	brown	d.grey
14	27	10	13	A	?12		2/3iia	l.brown	d.grey	d.grey
15	27	10	13	A	12		2/3iia	red/br	d.grey	grey
16	27			A	nd		1/2iib	d.grey	d.grey	l.grey
17	27	10	13	A	base		2/3iia	d.grey	d.grey	d.grey
19	27/26			A	?4		1/2iic	d.gr/bl	d.gr/bl	d.gr/bl
20a	27			A	?9		1/2iic	d.br/bl	d.br/bl	d.grey
20b										
21	26			A	nd		1/2iic	d.gr/bl	d.gr/bl	d.gr/bl
26	24*/25			A/B	5		2/3iia	black	black	black
27	24*/25			A/B	base		2/3iia	d.grey	d.grey	black
28	24*/25			A/B	9		1/2iic	br/bl	d.grey	d.grey
29	25	13	11	A–B	?12		2/3iia	d.grey	d.grey	d.grey
30	23*			B	?12	cabr	2/3iia	black	black	grey
31a	23*			B	4		1/2iic	black	black	black
31b	23*			B						
32	23*			B	base		2/3iia	or/br	or/br	or/br
33	24*	10	13	B	12	fts	2/3iia	red5br	d.grey	grey
35	24/25b	12	10	B	?12		2/3iic	d.grey	d.grey	d.grey
37	24/25b	11	10	B	nd		2/3iic	d.grey	d.grey	d.grey
38	24/25b	11	10	B	nd		2/3iia	d.grey	d.grey	brown
39	24/25b	11	10	B	nd		2/3iia	d.grey	buff	d.grey
40	24/25b	11	11	B	base		2/3iia	buff	black	d.grey
41	24	14	8	B	12		2/3iia	red	red/gr	black
44	25	20	10	A–B	9		1ic	black	black	black
45	25	20	10	A–B	12		2/3iia	bl/br	black	grey
46	25	19	9	A–B	?12		1/2/7ib	grey	l.grey	d.grey
47	25	20	10	A–B	base		2/3iic	black	black	black
48a	24*	10	13	B	9		2/3iic	d.gr/bu	black	black
48b	20c	10	12	C						
48c	19	10	13	C						
49	19	8	12	C	base		1/2iic	buff	bu/gr	red/br
50X	19			C	nd		2iic	bu/br	bu/br	bu/br
51	19			C	12		2/3iia	bu/gr	bu/gr	l.brown
54	19			C	12		2/3iia	buff	buff	l.brown
55	19			C	?12		2/3iib	buff	buff	d.grey
56	19			C	nd		2/3iia	brown	brown	brown
57	19			C	nd		2/3iia	br/bl	br/bl	br/bl
58	20c			C	12	ftrs	2/3iia	d.gr/bl	grey	grey
59	20c			C	nd		2/3iia	black	black	d.grey
60	20d	10	12	C	base		2/2iia	d.gr/brz	d.gr/br	d.grey
60X	20d	19	10	C	?9		1/7ia	grey	grey	grey
61a	20	13	11	C–D	nd		2/3iia	black	black	black
61b	14e/20c	11	10	C/D						
61c	14	11	10	D						
61d	20d	12	10	C						
62a	21	18	11	C	12		2/3iia	or/d.br	br/bl	black
63	21	14	8	C	nd		2/3iia	d.gr/bu	d.gr/bu	black
64	21	17	11	C	nd		2/3iic	or/buff	or/buff	brown
65	21			C	body		2/3iia	orf/buff	or/buff	or/burr
68	14e/20c	12	10	C/D	nd		2/3iic	d.grr/bl	d.gr/bl	d.gr/bl
69	14e/20c	10	13	C/D	nd		2/3iia	d.grey	d.grey	d.grey
70	14e/20c	10	13	C/D	?10		1/2iic	bl/buff	bl/buff	bl/buff
72a	20a–c	20	9	C/D	4		1/2iic	d.gr/bl	d.gr/bl	black
73	20a–c			C/D	9		5c	black	black	black
74	20a–c	19	10	C/D	4		1/2iic	d.gr/bl	d.gr/bl	black
75	20a–c	13	11	C/D	nd		2iic	black	black	black
76	20a–c	19	9	C/D	nd		2/3iia	grey	grey	grey
79	17			D	nd		2/3iia	black	black	black
80a	17			D	5		2/3iia	brown	or/br	black
80b	17			D						
81	16/17	7	12	D	nd		2/3iia	d.grey	d.grey	d.grey
82	16	7	12	D	5	ftr	2/3iia	l.brown	l.brown	brown
83	14	11	10	D	body	fts	2/3iia	bu/br	bu/br	bu/br
84	14	12	9	D	?9		2iib	buff	buff	buff
85	14	15	9	D	5		2/3iia	black	black	black
86a	8b	12	10	E	5		2/3iia	black	black	black
86b	8	12	11	E–G						
86c	8b	12	10	E						
87	8b	12	10	E	12	ftr	2/3iia	br/bl	br/bl	black
88	8b	12	10	E	nd		2/3iia	black	black	black
91a	8	16	9	E–G	9		2/3iic	d.br/bl	d.br/bl	black
91b	8	15	9	E–G						
93	8			E–G	?cup		1/2iic	black	black	black
94	8	11	9	E–G	?10		1/2iic	d.gr/br	d.grey	d.grey
95a	8	13	9	E–G	nd	fts	2/3iia	brown	brown	grey
95b	8	9	11	E–G						
95c	8	12	9	E–G						
95d	6	13	10	I						
96	8	12	11	E–G	nd		1/2iic	d.brown	d.brown	d.brown
98	8	11	11							
				1	E–G	nd	1/2iic	black	black	black
99	8	11	10	E–G	12		2/3iia	d.gr/bl	d.gr/bl	black
101a	8			E–G	11		1/2iic	brown	brown	brown
101b	6	10	11	I						
102	8	11	10	E–G	nd		1/2iic	d.brown	d.brown	d.brown
104a	8	14	9	E–G	4	cl	1/2iic	d.grey	d.grey	d.grey
104b	8	14	9	E–G						
104c	8	12	9	E–G						
104d	2			—						
104e	8	14	8	E–G						
104f	3			—						
104g	U/S			—						
105	8	8	12	E–G	nd	cl	1/2iic	d.brown	black	d.brown
106	8	11	11	E–G	nd	cl	5c	d.grey	d.grey	d.grey
108	8	13	11	E–G	nd		1/2iia	buff	buff	buff
110	8	11	11	E–G	12		2/3iic	buff	buff	brown
112a	8	12	9	E–G	12		2/3iia	grey	l.grey	grey
112b	8	12	10	E–G						
113	8	11	9	E–G	body		2/3/7ia	grey	grey	grey
114a	8	14	9	E–G	11		2/3iib	brown	d.grey	d.grey
114b	8	12	9	E–G						
114c	8	14	9	E–G						
114d	8	14	8	E–G						
114e	6	14	9	I						
114f	6	14	9	I						
114g	6	14	8	I						
114h	8	14	9	E–G						
115	8	14	9	E–G	?4		2/3iia	d.grey	d.grey	d.grey

Table 16: Catalogue of illustrated Late Bronze Age sherds (continued).

No (P-)	Context	Grid E	N	Unit	Type	Decoration	Fabric	Colour Outface	Inface	Core
116	8	12	10	E-G	?5		2/3iia	d.grey	brown	gr/br
119	8	11	11	E-G	nd		2/3iia	or/buff	buff	buff
121	8	7	12	E-G	nd		2/3iia	black	d.br/bl	gr br
123a	8	12	10	E-G	12		2/3iia	buff	d.br/bl	d.grey
123b	8	12	11	E-G						
124c	8	13	11	E-G						
124a	8	14	9	E-G	?12		2/3iia	bu/d.gr	d.grey	d.grey
125a	8	11	10	E-G	12		2/3iia	d.grey	l.grey	d.grey
125b	8	13	11	E-G						
127a	8	11	11	E-G	nd		2/3iia	orange	or/buff	or/buff
127b	6	10	11	I						
127c	6	10	11	I						
128a	8	11	10	E-G	nd		2/3iia	black	buff	buff
128b	8	11	10	E-G						
128c	6	11	10	I						
129a	8	14	8	E-G	?12		2/3iia	gr br	gr br	d.grey
129b	8	14	9	E-G						
129c	8	14	8	E-G						
129d	6	14	8	I						
129e	5	15	9	J						
130	8	12	9	E-G	nd		2/3iia	black	black	black
131a	8	12	9	E-G	12		1ia	or grey	grey	grey
131b	8	11	9	E-G						
131c	8	12	10	E-G						
131d	8	12	10	E-G						
132	8	18	11	E-G	nd	ftr	1/2iia	buff	grey br	d.grey
133a	8	12	9	E-G	nd	ftr	2/3iia	d.brown	brown	d.grey
133b	8	12	10	E-G						
134	8	11	10	E-G	12	ftr	2/3iia	d.grey	d.grey	grey
135	8	11	9	E-G	12	ftr	2/3iia	buff	d.grey	d.grey
136	8	10	11	E-G	nd	ftr	2/3iia	d.brown	d.brown	black
138a	8	14	8	E-G	12	ftr	2/3iia	buff	buff	brown
138b	8	14	9	E-G						
138c	8	14	9	E-G						
138d	8	14	9	E-G						
139	8	13	11	E-G	?12	ftr	2/3iia	d.grey	d.grey	l.grey
140	8	12	11	E-G	body	fts	2/3iia	brown	black	bl/br
141a	8	11	10	E-G	9	fts	2/3iia	bu/br	bu/br	d.grey
141b	8	11	10	E-G						
141c	6	11	9	I						
141d	6	11	9	I						
141e	6	10	11	I						
142	8	11	10	E-G	body		2/3iia	d.brown	d.brown	d.brown
144	8	8	11	E-G	?12		2/3/7iia	or.br	or,br	or,br
148	8	12	10	E-G	base		1/2iic	black	black	black
149	8	10	10	E-G	base		2/3iia	buff	grey	black
150a	8	11	10	E-G	base		2/3/7iib	grey	grey	grey
150b	8	11	10	E-G						
150c	8	11	10	E-G						
150d	6	12	9	I						
151	8	10	11	E-G	base		2/3iia	brown	d.brown	br/bl
157	8a	15	9	G	nd		2/3ia	buff	brown	gr/br
158	9	17	10	G	base		2/3iic	black	black	black
159	9	18	10	G	nd		1ic	black	black	black
160	9	17	11	G	nd		1/2iic	black	black	black
161	9	18	11	G	nd		1/2iib	d.grey	d.grey	d.grey
162	9	18	11	G	nd		1/2iib	grey br	grey br	d.brown
163	9	18	10	G	nd		1/2iic	brown	brown	brown
164	9	18	11	G	?5		1/ib	d.brown	brown	d.brown
165	9	17	10	G	?4	cl	5c	black	black	d.brown
166	9	17	10	G	body	cl	5c	black	black	brown
167a	9	17	10	G	body	cl	5c	black	black	d.brown
167b	6	14	8	I						
168a	9	17	10	G	nd		2/3iia	black	d.brown	d.grey
168b	9	17	11	G						
170	9	17	10	G	?lid		1/2iib	l.brown	bu/br	d.brown
171a	9	17	10	G	12	ftr	2/3iia	bu/br	l.brown	brown
171b	9	18	11	G						
172	9	18	11	G	nd	ftr	2/3iia	d.brown	buff	grey
173	9	17	10	G	nd	ftr	2/3iia	black	d.brown	d.brown
174	9	18	12	G	nd	fts	2/3iia	black	black	black
176a	6	14	9	I	nd		2/3iib	gr buff	d.grey	d.grey
176b	6	13	6	I						
176c	6	14	9	I						
177a	6	13	10	I	9		1/2iib	grey br	d.grey	black
177b	6	12	10	I						
178a	6	14	8	I	9		1/7ib	brown	grey	grey
178b	5	14	9	J						
178c	5	14	9	J						
178d	6	14	8	I						
178e	6	14	8	I						
178f	6	12	9	I						
178g	6	13	8	I						
179	6	9	11	I	nd		1/2iia	grey	grey	d.grey
180a	6	14	8	I	nd		1/7ib	l.brown	d.grey	d.grey
181	6	12	10	I	nd		1/2iic	black	black	black
182	6	14	8	I	nd		2/3iia	d.grey	d.grey	d.brown
183a	6	15	9	I	9		1/2iib	d.grey	d.grey	d.grey
183b	6			I						
187	6	11	10	I	body		2/3ic	d.grey	d.grey	d.grey
190	6	9	11	I	body	cl	lic	brown	brown	brown
191	6	12	9	I	body	sc	2/3iib	buff gr	d.grey	d.grey
192a	6	15	10	I	12		2/3iib	d.grey	d.grey	d.grey
192b	6	15	10	I						
193	6	11	10	I	base		1/2iic	d.grey	d.grey	d.grey
195	6			I	nd		1/2iic	d.brown	d.brown	d.brown
197a	6	13	10	I	5		2/3iia	bl br	bl br	black
197b	6	10	11	I						
198a	6	12	10	I	5		2/3iia	d.grey	buff	d.grey
198b	6	12	10	I						
198c	6	12	11	I						
199	6	12	10	I	5		1/2iib	or.br	brown	brown
205	6	14	8	I	nd		2/3iia	d.brown	d.brown	d.brown
206	6	14	8	I	nd		2/3iia	d.grey	d.grey	black
208	6	14	8	I	nd		2/3iia	d.grey	d.brown	br/bl
211	6	10	11	I	nd		2/3iia	d.grey	l.grey	black
213a	6	14	8	I	nd		2/3iia	d.grey	d.grey	d.grey
213b	3									
214a	6	11	11	I	12		2/3iia	bl/br	or.br	gr/br
214b	6	12	11	I						
215	6	13	10	I	nd		2/3iia	d.brown	black	black
216	6	11	10	I	nd		2/3iia	buff	buff	d.grey
217	6	11	9	I	nd		2/3iia	d.grey	d.grey	brown
218a	6	13	10	I	12	ftr	2/3iia	d.brown	brown	brown
218b	6	12	11	I						
218e	6	9	11	I						
219	6	15	9	I	nd		2/3iia	gr/r br	gr/r br	d.grey
220	6	9	11	I	nd	ftb	2/3iia	brown	br/bl	brown
221a	6	12	10	I	12	ftrs	2/3iia	bl/l.br	l.brown	d.grey
221b	6	12	10	I						
221c	6	12	10	I						
222a	6	16	10	I	12	cabr	2/3iia	buff	buff	black

Table 16: Catalogue of illustrated Late Bronze Age sherds (continued).

No (P–)	Context	Grid E	N	Unit	Type	Decoration	Fabric	Colour Outface	Inface	Core
222b	6	16	10	I						
222c	6	15	9	I						
223	6	11	10	I	nd	ftr	2/3iia	d.brown	br/bl	black
224a	6	14	8	I	nd	ftr	2/3iia	d.grey	d.grey	d.grey
224b	5	14	9	J						
225	6	14	9	I	nd	cabr	2/3iia	d.brown	bu/br	d.grey
226	6	11	9	I	nd	ftr	2/3iia	grey	d.brown	d.brown
227	6	16	11	I	nd	ftr	2/3iia	grey	red br	red br
230a	6	10	11	I	?12	fts	2/3iia	black	bl/br	brown
230b	6	11	10	I						
231a	6	14	9	I	body	fts	2/3iia	d.brown	black	br/bl
231b	6			I						
232	6	12	9	I	body	fts	2/3iia	grey/br	red/br	red/br
233	6	12	9	I	body	fts	2/3iia	red/br	brown	black
234a	6	12	10	I	body	ftb	2/3iia	black	black	black
234b	6	11	10	I						
235a	6	15	9	I	body	ftb	2/3iia	buff	d.brown	black
235b	6	15	9	I						
235c	6	14	8	I						
238	6			I	body		2/3iia	brown	brown	brown
239	6			I	body		2/3iia	brown	brown	d.brown
241	6	12	10	I	base		2/3iia	gr.buff	buff	grey
242	6	16	10	I	base		2/3iia	buff/or	br/grey	d.grey
243	6	10	11	I	base		2/3iia	or.br	black	black
244	6	12	10	I	base		2/3iia	or.br	brown	br/bl
245	6	10	10	I	base		2/3iia	d.or	d.grey	d.grey
247	5	14	9	J	nd		2/3iia	buff	buff	brown
248	5			J	nd		2/3iia	bu/grey	d.grey	d.grey
249	5			J	nd		2/3iib	d.grey	black	black
251a	5	14	9	J	nd		1/2iib	brown	d.grey	d.grey
251b	4	13	8	J						
252	5	14	9	J	nd	ftr	2/3iia	buff	buff	brown
253	5			J	12	ftb	2/3iia	brown	or.br.	d.brown
254	5			J	body	ftb	2/3iia	d.gr/bl	d.gr/bl	d.gr/bi
258	5			J	base		2/3iia	d.grey	d.grey	d.grey
259	4	14	6	J	5		2/3iia	buff	buff	buff
260	4	13	8	J	nd		2/3iia	br/buff	br/buff	black
263	4			J	nd		2/3iia	bu/d.gr	bu/d.gr	d.brown
264	4	13	8	J	nd	ftr	2/3iia	gr.br	bric rd	grey
265	4	14	10	J	nd	ftr	2/3iia	d.brown	d.brown	d.brown
266	4			J	body	fts	2/3iia	br/bu	br/bu	gr.br
267	4	13	8	J	body	c	2/3iia	buff	buff	buff
269	36	5	6		?4		1/2iib	buff	bu/br	d.brown
270	36	3	8		4		2/3iib	buff	or/bl	or/bl
271	36	3	9		nd		2/3iib	black	black	d.brown
272	36	3	8		12		2/3iia	br/or	br/or	d.brown
273	36	8	5		?lid		2/3iia	or.br	orange	orange
274	36	8	5		12	ftr	2/3iic	orange	orange	orange
275	35c	3	12		nd	ftr	2/3iia	or.br	or.br	brown
276	35c	4	12		nd	ftr	2/3iia	or.bl	black	black
277	35b	4	12		nd	?cabr	2/3iia	or.br	or.br	d.brown
278	35b/c	4	12		base		2/3iia	br/bu	brown	d.brown
279	35b	4	12		base		2/3iia	or. br.	or.br	d.brown
280	35c	4	12		base		2/3iia	brown	black	black
281	34b	6	12		?4		1/2iic	buff	grey	grey
283	34b	6	12		base		2/3iic	black	black	black
283X	34b	5	12		base		2/3iia	brown	black	black
284	34a	6	10		?4		1/2iib	grey	grey	grey
285	34a	6	11		nd		1/2/7iib	red	red	black
287	34a	7	10		nd		2/3/7iia	br.gr	grey	d.grey
288	34a	5	11		nd		2/3iia	brown	black	br/bl
289	34a	7	11		body		5a	brown	d.brown	d.brown
290	34a	6	12		base		2/3iia	or.gr	or.gr	or.gr
291	33c	10	6		5		2iib	or.bu	or.bu	or.bu
292	33c	6	7		12		2/3iic	black	black	black
293	33c	6	5		nd		1/2iib	red br	brown	d.brown
294	33c	7	5		nd		2/3iic	buff	buff	buff
295a	33c	8	6		12		2/3iic	br.bl	black	d.brown
295b	33c	7	7							
298	33cc	4	9		nd		2/3iia	grey	grey	grey
299	33c	5	7		nd		2/3iic	d.brown	d.brown	d.brown
301	33c	6	7		nd		2/3iic	brown	d.brown	d.brown
303	33c	9	7		nd		2/3iia	grey	buff	grey
304	33c	9	6		19	cabr	2/3iia	or.buff	or.buff	buff
305	33cc	5	7		nd	ftr	2/3iia	brown	bu/br	brown
306a	33c	6	6		nd	ftr	2/3iia	brown	d.brown	d.brown
306b	33a	7	7							
307	33c	9	6		body	fts	1/2iib	brown	black	black
309	33c	7	6		10		2/3iib	or.buff	or.buff	or.br
310	33c	9	6		4		1/2iic	br/bu	br/bu	br/bu
313	33c	7	5		body		2/3iic	brown	brown	brown
315a	33c	6	9		hndl		2/3iia	orange	grey	orange
315b	33c	6	10							
316	33c	3	8		?14		1ic	grey	black	grey
317	33c	7	5		body		2/3iia	orange	orange	orange
318	33c	4	9		base		2/3iia	orange	gr.br	grey
320	33c	8	6		base		2/3iia	orange	orange	or.br
321a	33b/c	4	7		nd		2/3iib	gr.br	gr.br	d.grey
321b	33b/c	5	7							
321c	4	8								
322a	33b/c	8	6		base		2/3iia	or.br	or.br	brown
322b	33b/c	8	7							
322c	33b/c	6	7							
324	33b	3	8		11		1/2iib	brown	d.grey	d.grey
325	33b	9	6		?4		1/7ib	d.grey	d.grey	d.grey
327	33b	9	5		12		1/2iic	gr/bl	black	d.grey
328a	33b	8	5		nd		?2/3iib	buff	buff	buff
328b	31									
329	33b	4	8		12		2/3iia	black	black	black
333	33b	6	6		nd		2/3iia	d.brown	black	black
3w36	33b	8	5		nd		2/3iia	orange	orange	orange
338	33b	10	6		nd		2/3iia	buff/gr	buff/or	buff/gr
339	33b	6	8		nd		2/3iia	brown	d.brown	d.brown
342	33b	7	5		12		2/3iia	d.brown	br/buff	d.brown
343	33b	3	8		12		2/3iia	d.grey	d.grey	d.grey
345	33b	9	5		12	ftr	2/3iia	or.br	brown	grey/br
346	33b	8	7		nd	ftr	2/3iia	d.grey	l.grey	black
347	33b	7	7		body	fts	2/3iia	br.buff	black	black
349	33b	6	8		?cup		1/2iic	brown	gr.br	gr.br
350	33b	7	6		nd		1/2ib	or.buff	or.buff	gr.br
353a	33b	4	8		12		2/3iia	grey	d.grey	d.grey
353b	32c	5	6							
354	33b	6	6		body		2/3iia	brown	d.brown	d.brown
355	33b	7	6		12		2/3iia	brown	br/bl	br/bl
356	33b	8	5		base		1/2iic	black	black	black
357	33b	7	6		base		5/7b	red/br	red/br	red/br
358	33b	6	7		base		2/3iic	d.brown	d.brown	black
359	33b	7	5		base		2/3iia	buff	buff	buff
360	33b	7	6		base		2/3iia	or.buff	or.buff	or.buff
361	33b	8	8		base		2/3iia	or.br	or.br	black
363	33b	6	6		base		2/3iia	brown	d.brown	d.brown
365	3w3a	8	5		?12		1iia	buff	buff	buff

Table 16: Catalogue of illustrated Late Bronze Age sherds (continued).

No (P–)	Context	Grid E	N	Unit	Type	Decoration	Fabric	Outface	Inface	Core
368	33a	5	8		nd		1/ic	d.grey	l.grey	black
369	33a	4	8		nd		1/2iic	d.gr/bu	d.gr/bu	d.grey
370	33a	7	7		?12		1/2iic	d.brown	black	d.brown
371	33a	8	5		4		1ib	grey	grey	black
372	33a	5	8		nd		1/2iib	or.br	or.br	black
373	33a	10	5		nd		2/3iia	buff	buff	d.grey
373	33a	8	5		nd		2/3iia	d.grey	d.grey	black
375	33a	7	6		nd		2/3iia	or.grey	or.grey	d.grey
377	33a	6	6		nd		2/3iia	black	grey	d.grey
378	3w3a	8	5		nd		2/3iia	buff	buff	buff
379	33a	6	7		nd		2/3/7ia	buff	or.br	d.brown
380	33a	6	7		?12	cabr	2/3iia	or.br	buff/bl	black
381	33a	4	8		nd	ftr	2/3iia	buff/gr	grey	d.grey
382	33a	4	8		nd	ftr	2/3iia	brown	brown	brown
383	33a	10	5		nd		2/3iia	black	d.grey	black
384	33a	6	7		nd		2/3iia	brown	brown	brown
385	33a	7	7		nd		2/3iia	red	or/grey	d.grey
391	33a	8	5		body	ftc	2/3iia	red/br	red/br	d.brown
392	33a	10	5		body	ftb	1/2iia	buff/br	brown	brown
393	33a	7	7		hndl		2/3iia	brown	black	black
394	33a	6	8		body		5b	or.buff	buff	buff
395	33a	6	8		body		2/3iib	grey	black	black
396	33a	7	5		12		2/3iia	oranged	gr.br	o.gr.br
402	33a	7	6		base		2/3iia	black	brown	d.brown
403	33a	6	7		base		2/3iia	or/br	or/br	d.brown
405a	32a	5	5		nd		1/2/7iib	d.grey	d.grey	d.grey
405b	33a	6	6							
406a	32c	3	6		5		1/2iic	d.brown	d.brown	d.brown
406b	33c	6	5							
406c	32c	4	6							
407a	32b	4	5		nd	ftr	2/3iia	gr.br	orange	orange
407b	33b	6	6							
408a	31				12	fts	2/3iia	grey	grey	black
408b	F6L2									
408c	33a	6	5							
408d	32b	5	6							
409	32c	5	6		nd		2/3iia	or.buff	or.grey	brown
413	32c	5	6		nd		2/3iia	d.brown	brown	d.brown
415	32c	4	6		14	fts	2/3iia	bu/d.br	or.br	orange
416	32b	5	6		9		1/2iic	bl/br	brown	bl/br
417a	32b				nd		1/2iib	d.grey	d.grey	d.grey
417b	32, 36	3	6							
417c	32, 36	3	6							
417d	36	3	6							
419	32b	3	6		nd		1/2iia	or.br	brown	brown
422	32b	5	6		nd		2/3iia	or.br	or.grey	or.bl
423	32b	5	6		nd		2/3iia	brown	brown	gr.br
424a	32b	3	6		?12		2/3iia	brown	brown	brown
424b	32b									
426	32b	4	6		nd		2/3iia	d.brown	black	black
427	32b	5	6		nd		2/3iia	brown	d.brown	d.brown
429	32b				?19		1/2iia	grey	grey	grey
430	32b	5	6		nd	ftr	5/7a	gr/br	d.gr.br	gr.br
431a	32b				12		2/3iia	bl/br	d.grey	d.grey
431b	32a	3	6							
431c	32b	5	6							
431d	32c	4	6							
433a	32b				12	ftrc	2/3iia	l.brown	d.grey	d.grey
433b	32b									
433c	32b	3	6							
433d	32b	3	6							
433e	32b	3	6			c				
434	32b	5	6		nd	ftr	2/3iia	d.brown	brown	brown
436	32b				body	fts	2/3iia	gr.br	red br	d.grey
438	32b	4	6		nd		1/2iia	grey/bu	grey/bu	grey
442	32b				body		2/3iia	d.brown	d.brown	d.brown
443	32b	5	5		base		1/2iib	buff/bl	gr.buff	d.grey
444	32b	3	6		base		2/3iia	d.gr/br	d.grey	d.grey
446a	32b	3	6		body		2/3iia	buff	orange	grey
446b	32b									
447a	32b	4	6		base		2/3iia	or.br	d.grey	d.grey
447b	32a	4	6							
448	32a	5	6		nd		2/3iia	d.grey	d.grey	d.grey
450	32a	5	5		nd		1/2iib	black	black	black
451	32a	5	6		body		1/2iib	black	black	black
452	32a	5	6		base		1ib	bl/br	grey/br	brown
453	32a	5	5		base		1/2iib	brown	brown	d.brown
454	31				nd		1/2iic	d.grey	d.grey	brown
455	31	8	8		nd		1/2wiic	d.grey	d.grey	d.grey
457	31				nd		1/2iib	brown	brown	brown
459	31				nd		2/3iia	grey	brown	d.grey
460a	31				nd		1/2iib	d.grey	d.grey	d.grey
460b	31									
462	31				nd		2/3iia	d.grey	d.brown	black
463	31				nd	c	2iib	d.brown	d.brown	brown
465	31				nd		2/3iia	grey	grey	grey
467	31				nd		2/3iia	d.grey	l.brown	d.grey
468	31				nd		2/3iia	d.grey	d.grey	d.grey
471	31				nd	ftr	2/3iia	buff	d.brown	d.grey
472	31				nd	ftr	2/3iia	d.grey	d.grey	d.grey
473	31				body	fts	2/3iia	d.grey	d,brown	black
475	31	8	8		base		2/3iia	or.br	orange	d.brown
476	37b	12	6		nd		5b	d.grey	d.grey	d.grey
477	37b	12	6		nd		2/3/7ib	or.br	grey	grey
478	37b	12	6		nd		2/3iia	brown	brown	brown
479	37b	11	5		?9		1/2iic	br/bl	br/bl	br/bl
480	37b	12	5		base		2/3iia	brown	black	black
481	37b	12	6		base		2/3iia	buff	d.brown	d.brown
484	37a	12	5		nd		1/2iib	d.grey	d.grey	red br
485	37a	11	5		nd		2/3iia	grey	buff	d.grey
486	37a	11	5		nd		2/3iia	d.brown	buff	d.grey
488	37a	12	6		nd		2/3iia	grey	d.grey	red br
489	37a	13	7		nd	ftr	2/3iia	grey	brown	black
490	37a	12	6		body	ftb	1/2iib	red/br	brown	brown
496	32–37				?12	ftr	2/3iia	buff	orange	orange
499	32–37				body	ftb	2/3iia	brown	d.brown	grey
503a	3				12		1/2iic	d.grey	d.grey	d.grey
503b	U/S									
505	3				body	ftsb	2/3iia	l.brown	l.brown	d.grey
507	3				body	ftb	2/3iia	or.buff	d.grey	d.grey
509	2				nd	ftr	2/3iia	d.brown	grey	d.brown
511	2				nd		2/3iia	d.grey	d.grey	d.grey
515	1				nd		1/2iic	d.grey	d.grey	d.grey
516	1				body	ftc	2/3iia	grey.br	d.grey	d.grey
517	1				body	ftc	2/3iia	buff	buff	black
535	F2				nd	cabr	2/3iia	grey	orange	d.grey
538	F5				base		2/3iia	orange	grey	d.grey
539	F6L6				nd		nd			
540	F6L6				?12		2/3iia	d.br/bl	d.br/bl	d.br/bl
541	F6L6				base		2/3iia	buff	buff/bl	or/bl
543	F6L5				9/12		1/2iic	grey/bl	bl/br	grey
544	F6L5				?12		2/3iia	black	black	black

Table 16: Catalogue of illustrated Late Bronze Age sherds (continued).

No (P–)	Context	Grid E	N	Unit	Type	Decoration	Fabric	Outface	Colour Inface	Core
547	F6L5				nd		2iia	black	black	black
548	F6L5				nd		2/3iia	or.br	or.br	or.br
549	F6L5				?12	cabr	2/3iia	buff	or.buff	br/buff
550	F6L5						1/2iic	grey	black	grey
553	F6L5				base		2/3iia	l.br/bl	black	d.grey
554	F6L5				base		2iib	bu/d.gr	buff	grey
555	F6L5				base		2/3iia	d.brown	d.brown	gr.br
558a	F6L5				12		2/3iia	bl/buff	brown	grey/bl
558b	F6L4									
558c	F6L2									
558d	F6L4									
559a	F6L5				base		2/3iia	bl/br	black	d.brown
559b	F6L4									
559c	F6L4									
561a	F6						2/3iia	or/bu	grey	grey
562a	F6L4				9		1/2iic	d.grey	d.grey	d.grey
562b	F6L2									
562c	F6L4									
562d	F6L2									
563	F6L4				12		2/3iia	d.brown	d.brown	d.brown
564	F6L4				nd	fts	2/3iia	brown	brown	brown
566a	F6L2b				nd		1ic	d.brown	d.brown	d.brown
566b	F6L2b									
568	F6L2b				nd		5b	buff	buff/br	d.grey
570	F6L2b				nd		2/3iia	orange	brown	orange
572a	F6L2b				12		2/3iia	black	d.brown	bl/br
572b	F6L2b	7	11							
573	F6L2B				nd		2/3iia	or.br	or.br	grey
574a	F6L2b				nd	ftr	2/3iic	brown	d.brown	brown
574b	F6L2b	6	11							
577	F6L2b				?4		2/3iia	bl/br	black	black
585	F6L2a	6	11		base		2/3iia	bu/d.br	d.brown	black
586	F6L2a	6	11		base		2/3iia	or.br	d.brown	d.brown
588a	F6L1				?12/9	sc	2/3iia	buff/or	buff/or	grey
588b	F6L1	6	11							
589	F6L1	6	11		nd		2/3iia	black	black	black
590	F6L1				?lid		nd	buff/gr	buff	black
591	F6L1				nd		2iib	d.br/rd	d.brown	bl/br
592	F6L1	6	11		?12		2/3iia	brown	grey.br	black
593	F6L1	6	11		nd		2/3iia	l.brown	or/br	grey
595	F6L1				?11		2/3iia	black	black	black
598	F6L1				12		2/3iia	black	black	d.brown
602	F6L1				nd	ftr	2/3iia	black	buff/br	buff/br
604	F6L1				body		5c	grey	grey	grey
608	F6L1	6	12		base		2/3iia	grey	grey	grey
609	F6L1				base		2i/iia	buff	black	black
611a	F6L1				base		2/3iia	brown	black	d.brown
611b	F6L1	6	12							
612	F7L3				5		2/3iia	d.grey	l.brown	d.grey
613	F7L3				nd		2/3iia	buff	l.grey	grey
614	F7L3				9		1/2iic	bl/br	bl/br	grey
615	F7L3				nd		2/3iia	or.br	or.br	or.br
616	F7L3				base		1/2iib	d.brown	black	black
617a	F7L1	5	11		nd		2/3iia	d.grey	d.grey	d.grey
617b	F7L1	5	11							
620	F7				base		2/3iia	d.grey	d.grey	d.grey
622	F11L1				nd		1/2iic	black	black	black
623	F11L1				nd	ftr	2/3iia	brown	d.brown	d.brown
624	F11L1				nd		2/3iia	grey/br	brown	d.grey
626	F17				nd		1iib	or.grey	or.grey	or.grey
628	F37				9		2/3iib	l.grey	l.grey	d.grey

No (P–)	Context	Grid E	N	Unit	Type	Decoration	Fabric	Outface	Colour Inface	Core
630	F41L1				nd		2/3iia	buff	br/red	br/red
633	F43				nd	ftr	2/3iia	brown	brown	brown
634	F43				nd		2/3iia	brown	d.brown	d.brown
635	F43				base		2/3iia	or.br	brown	brown
641	F112				base		2/3iia	or.buff	black	grey
642	F126				?11		2/3iia	red	red	d.grey
643	F154				nd		2/3iia	red/br	red/br	d.grey
644	A6salvage				9		2/3iia	black	black	black
645	A6salvage				body	cabc	2/3iia	brown	or.br	brown
648	A8F1				9	cl	1iic	bl/buff	grey/br	grey
649	A8F1				nd		2/3iia	d.brown	or.br	d.brown

Abbreviations: bl – black, br – brown, bu – buff, d – dark, gr – grey, l – light, nd – no data on pot form, or – orange, rd – red. For fabric classification see text.

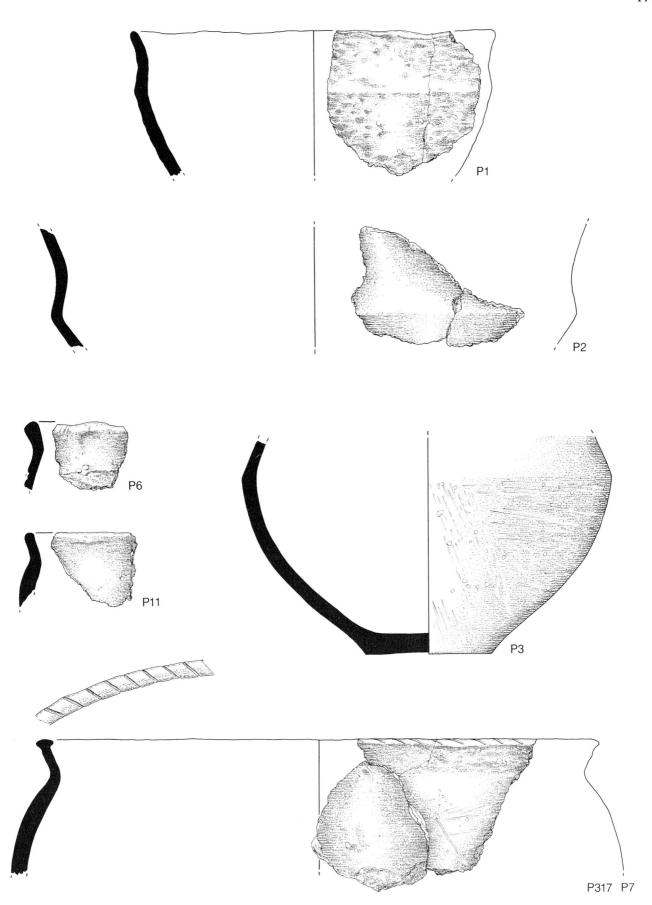

Fig. 76 Late Bronze Age pottery, Area 6, river channel unit A. Scale 1/2.

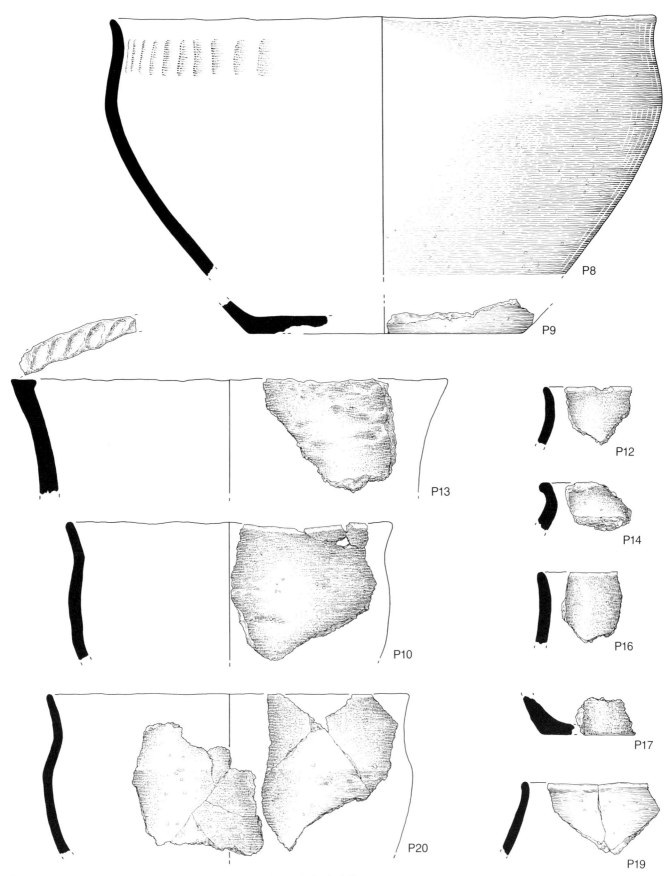

Fig. 77 Late Bronze Age pottery, Area 6, river channel unit A. Scale 1/2.

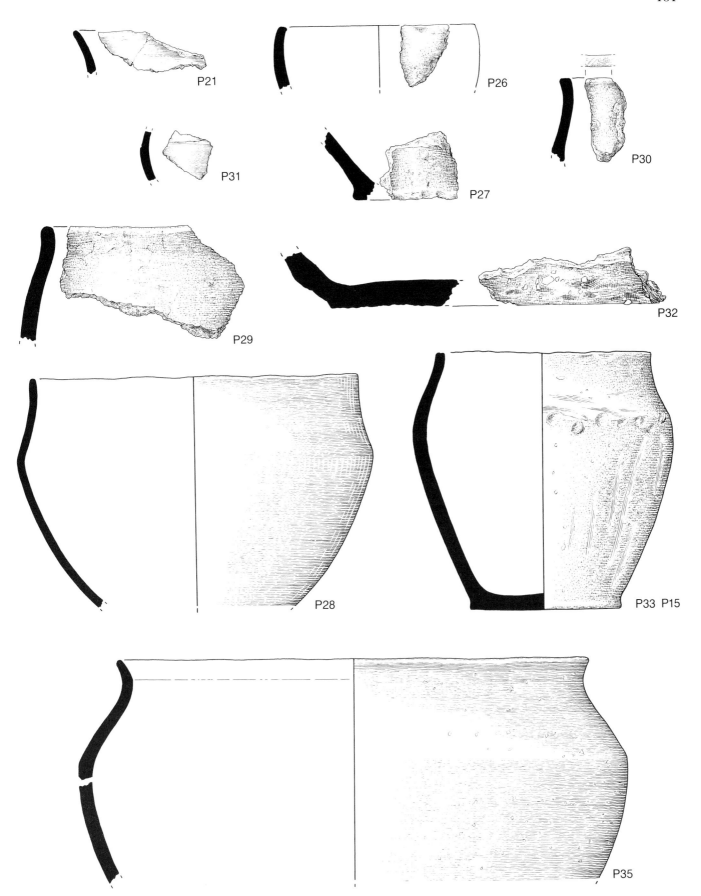

Fig. 78 Late Bronze Age pottery, Area 6, river channel unit A–B. Scale 1/2.

182

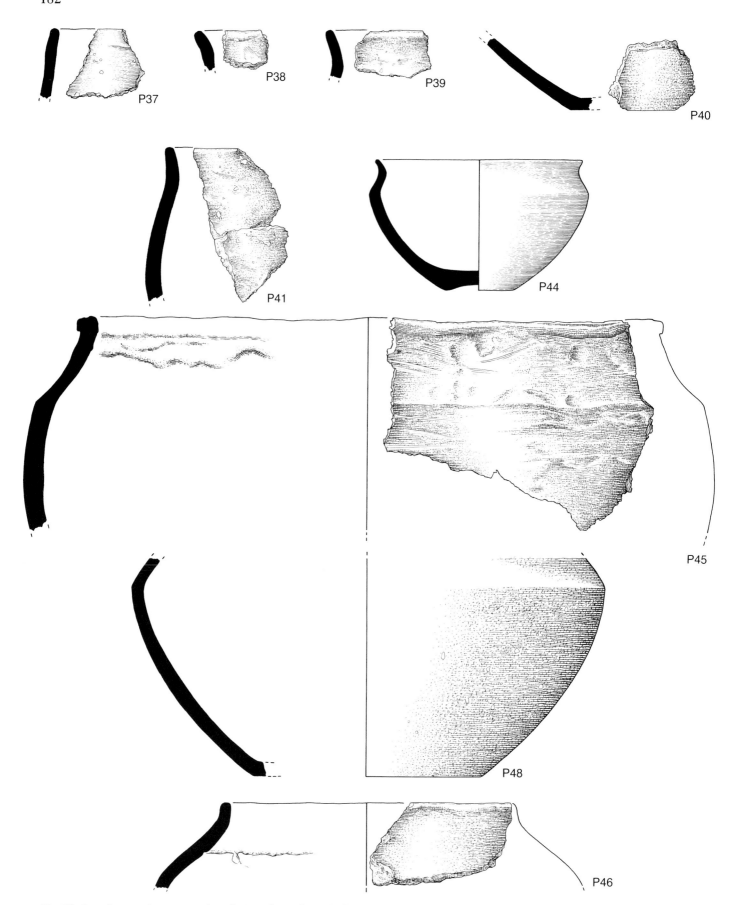

Fig. 79 Late Bronze Age pottery, Area 6, river channel unit B. Scale 1/2.

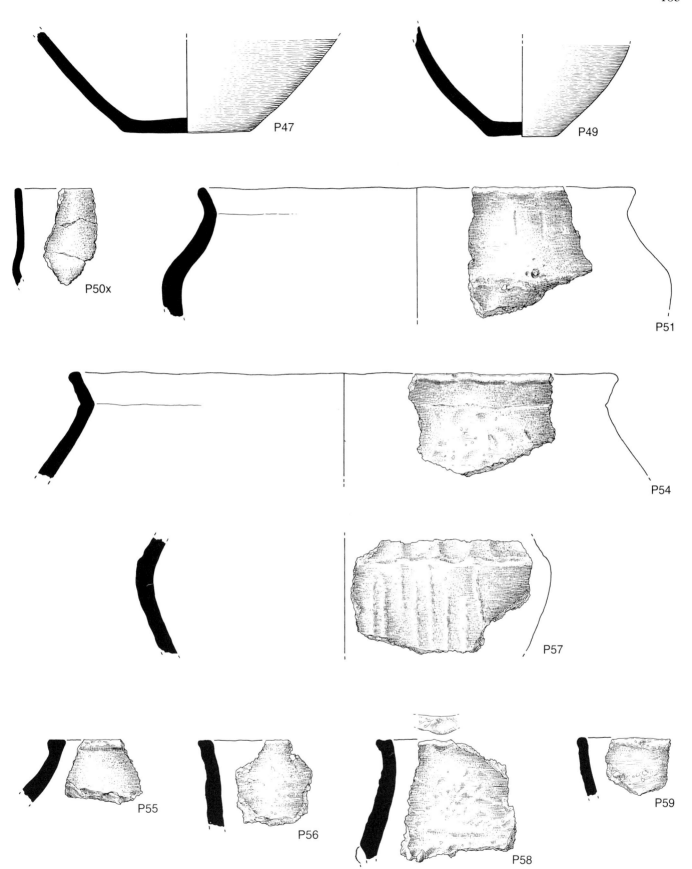

Fig. 80 Late Bronze Age pottery, Area 6, river channel unit C. Scale 1/2.

184

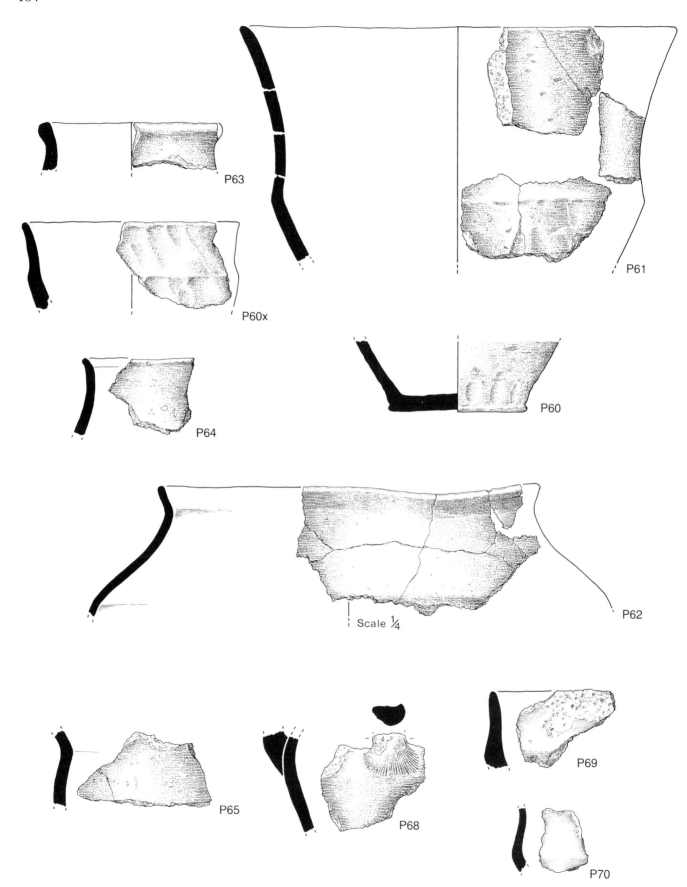

P63

P60x

P61

P64

P60

Scale ¼

P62

P65

P68

P69

P70

Fig. 81 Late Bronze Age pottery, Area 6, river channel unit C–D. Scale 1/2, except P62a, 1/4.

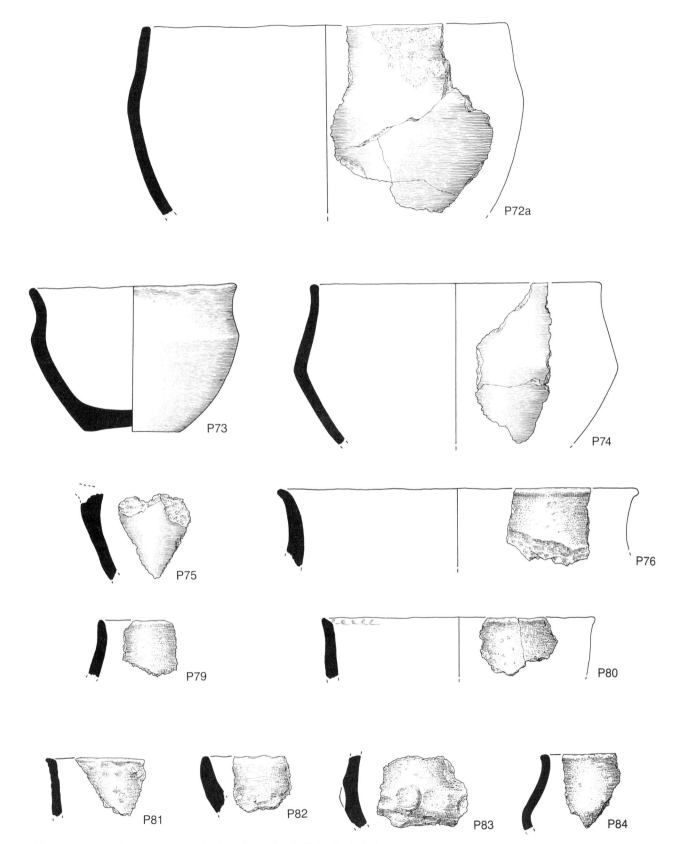

Fig. 82 Late Bronze Age pottery, Area 6, river channel unit C–D. Scale 1/2.

186

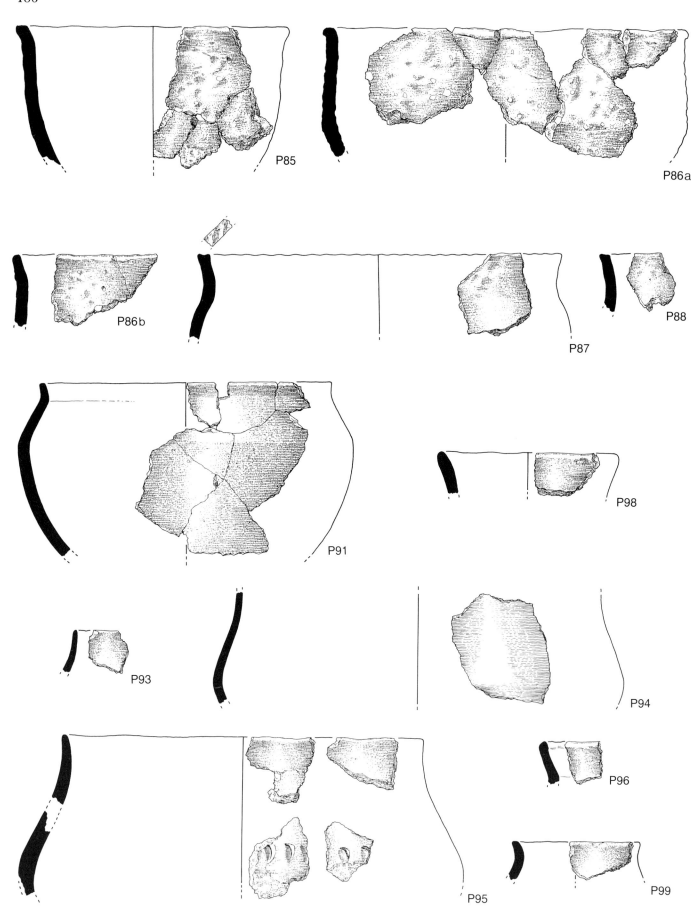

P85

P86a

P86b

P87

P88

P91

P98

P93

P94

P95

P96

P99

Fig. 83 Late Bronze Age pottery, Area 6, river channel unit D (P85), E–G. Scale 1/2.

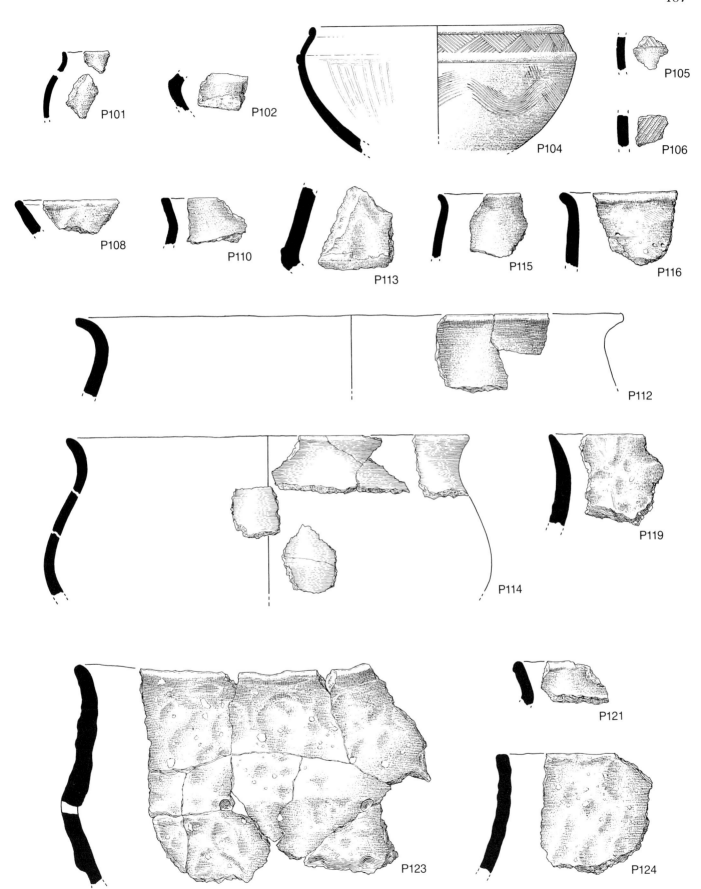

Fig. 84 Late Bronze Age pottery, Area 6, river channel unit E–G. Scale 1/2.

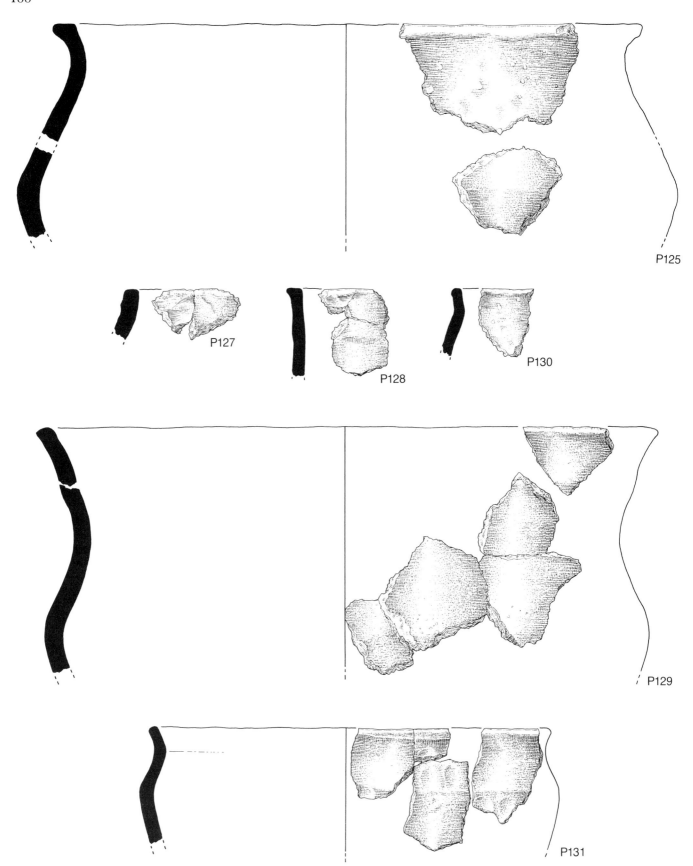

Fig. 85 Late Bronze Age pottery, Area 6, river channel unit E–G. Scale 1/2.

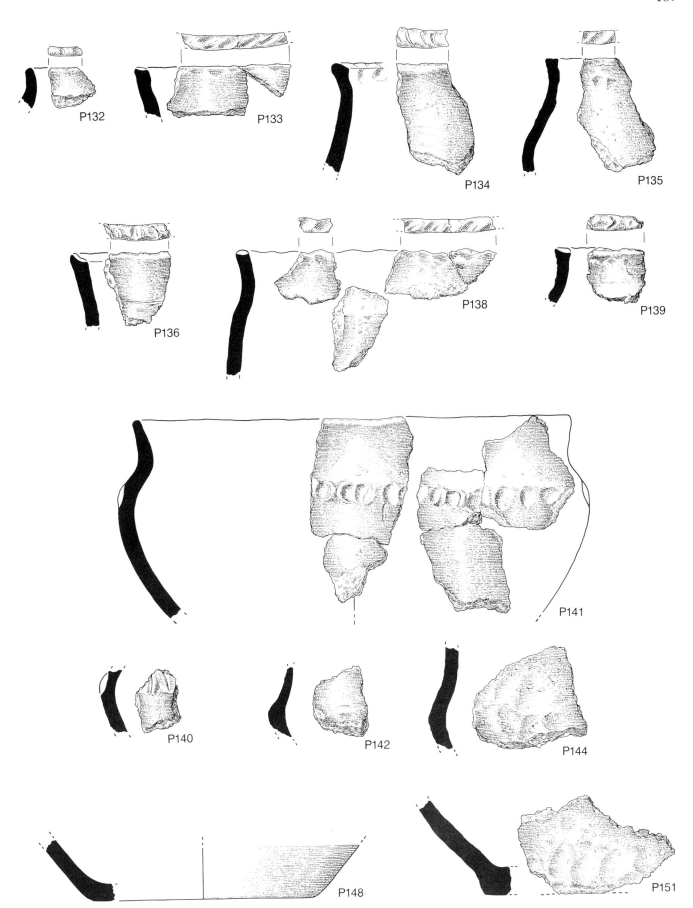

Fig. 86 Late Bronze Age pottery, Area 6, river channel unit E–G. Scale 1/2.

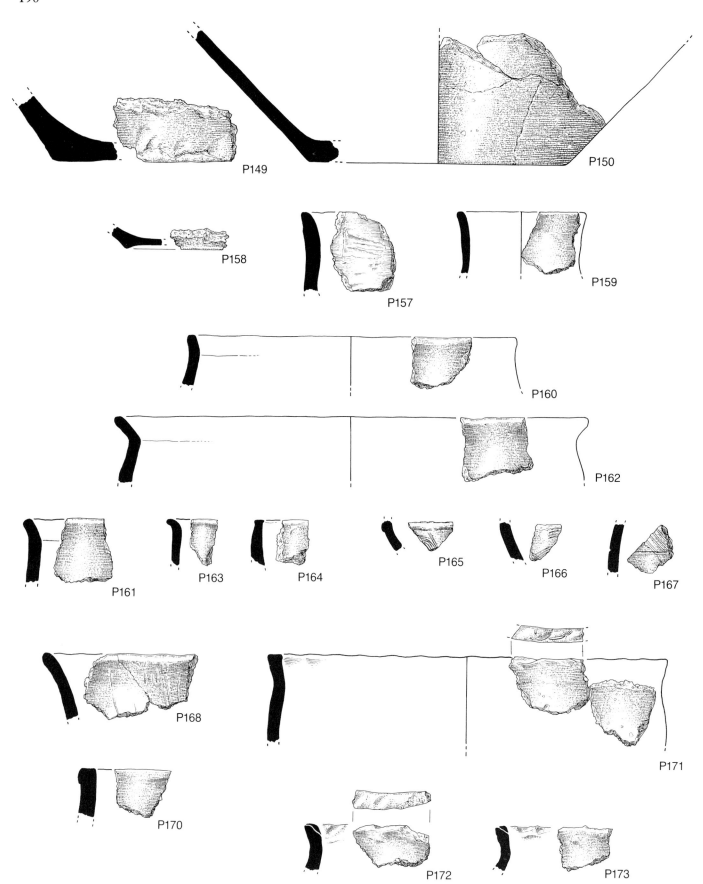

Fig. 87 Late Bronze Age pottery, Area 6, river channel unit E–G. Scale 1/2.

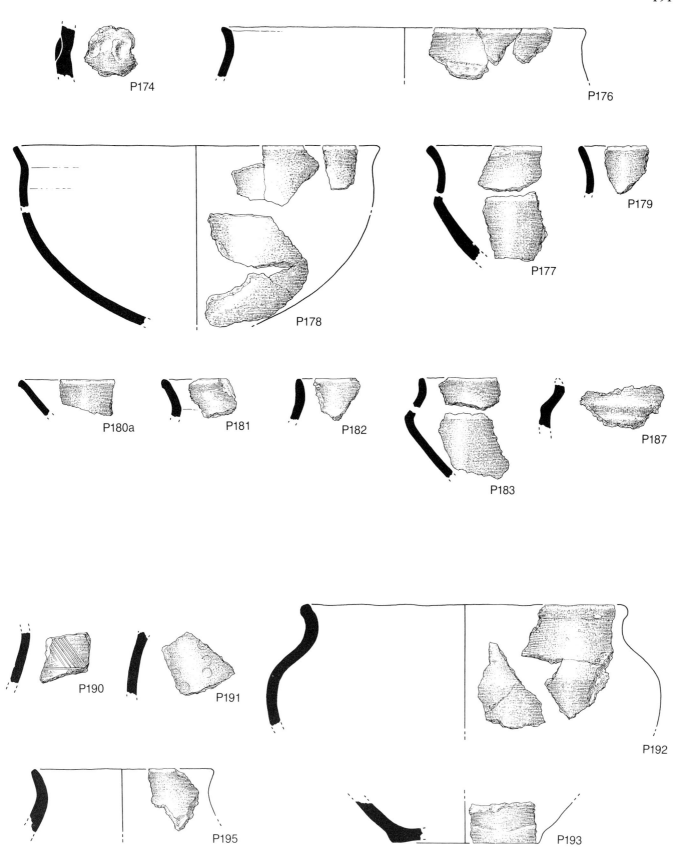

Fig. 88 Late Bronze Age pottery, Area 6, river channel unit G (P174) and I. Scale 1/2.

192

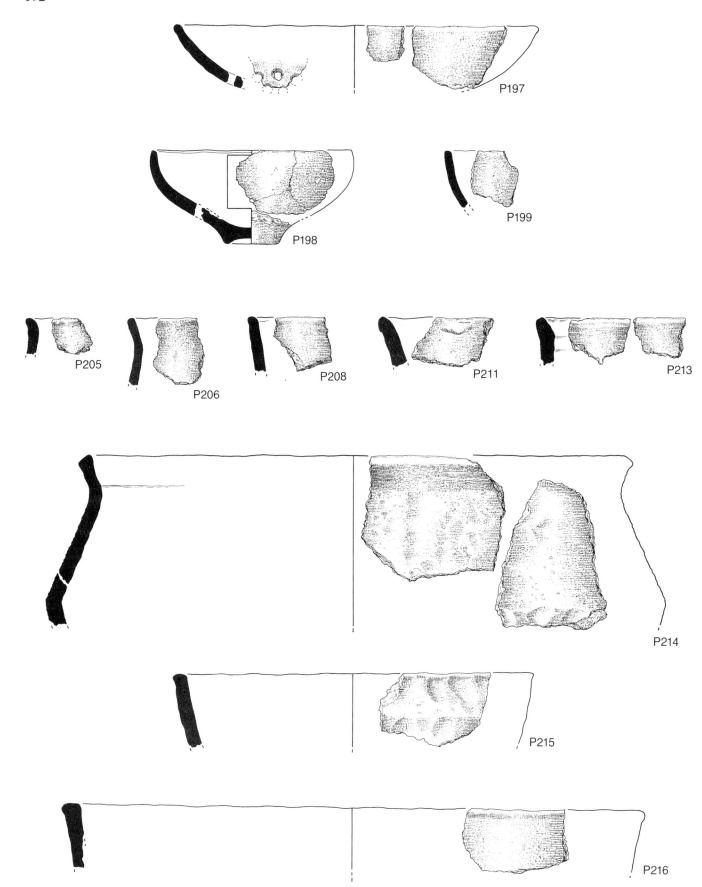

Fig. 89 Late Bronze Age pottery, Area 6, river channel unit I. Scale 1/2.

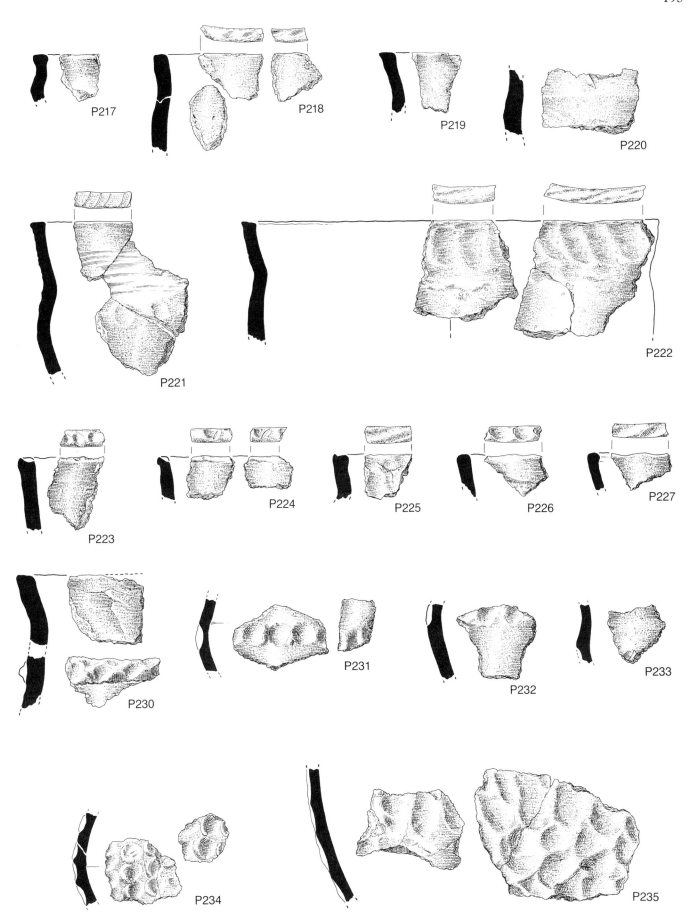

P217

P218

P219

P220

P221

P222

P223

P224

P225

P226

P227

P230

P231

P232

P233

P234

P235

Fig. 90 Late Bronze Age pottery, Area 6, river channel unit I. Scale 1/2.

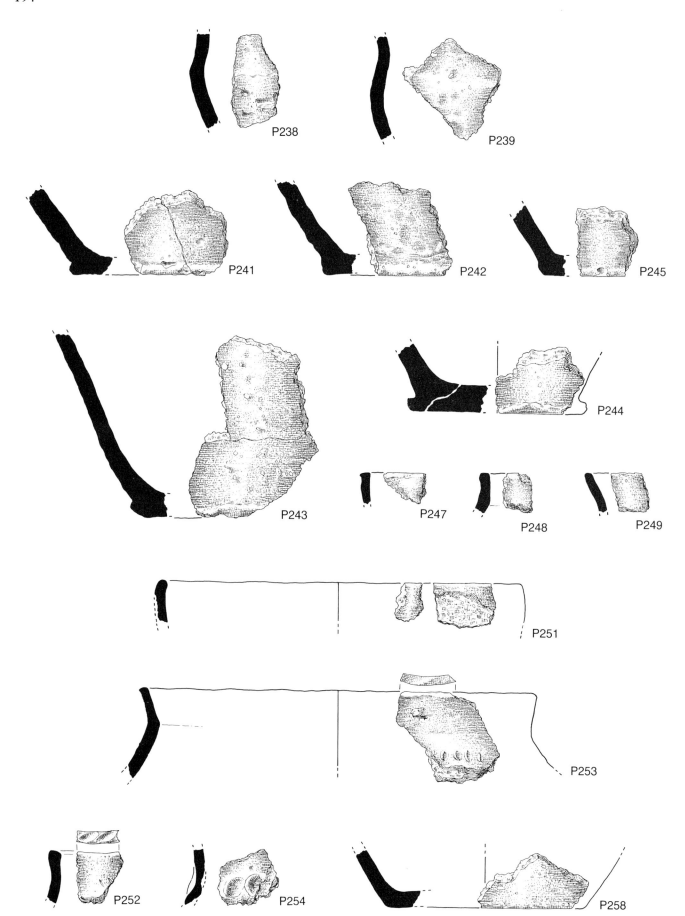

Fig. 91 Late Bronze Age pottery, Area 6, river channel unit I (P238–245), J (P247–258). Scale 1/2.

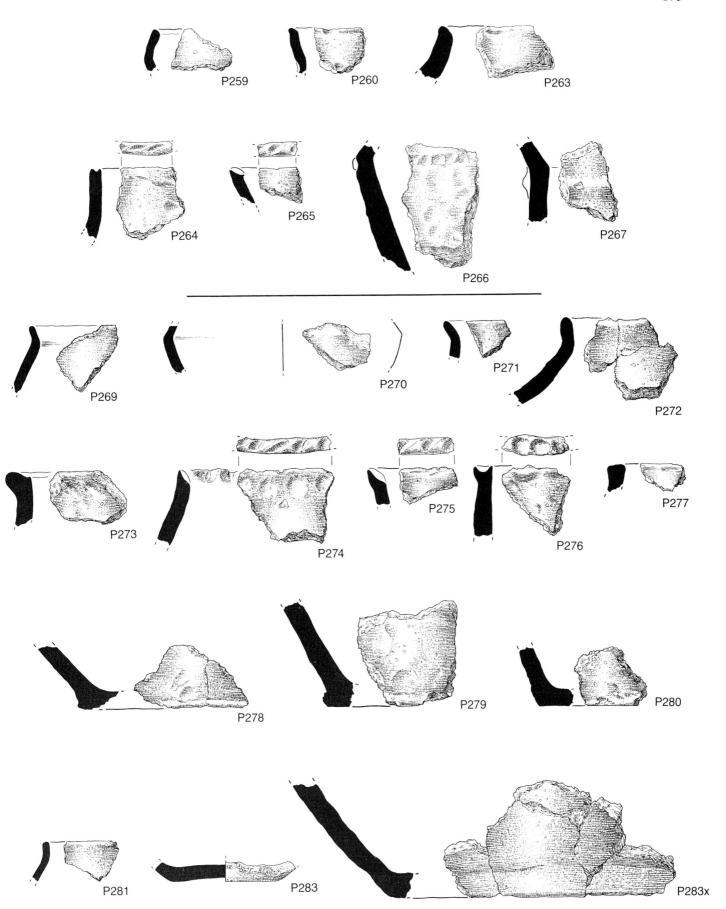

Fig. 92 Late Bronze Age pottery, Area 6, river channel unit J (P259–267); occupation deposits L36 (P269–274), L35 (P275–280), L34 (P281–283X). Scale 1/2.

196

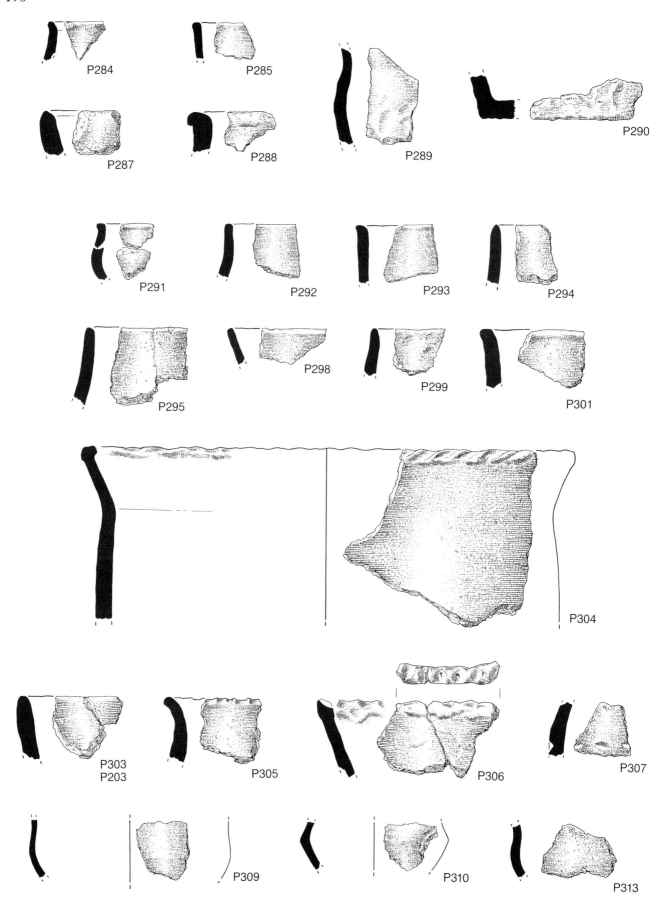

Fig. 93 Late Bronze Age pottery, Area 6, occupation deposits L34 (P284–290), L33c (P291–313). Scale 1/2.

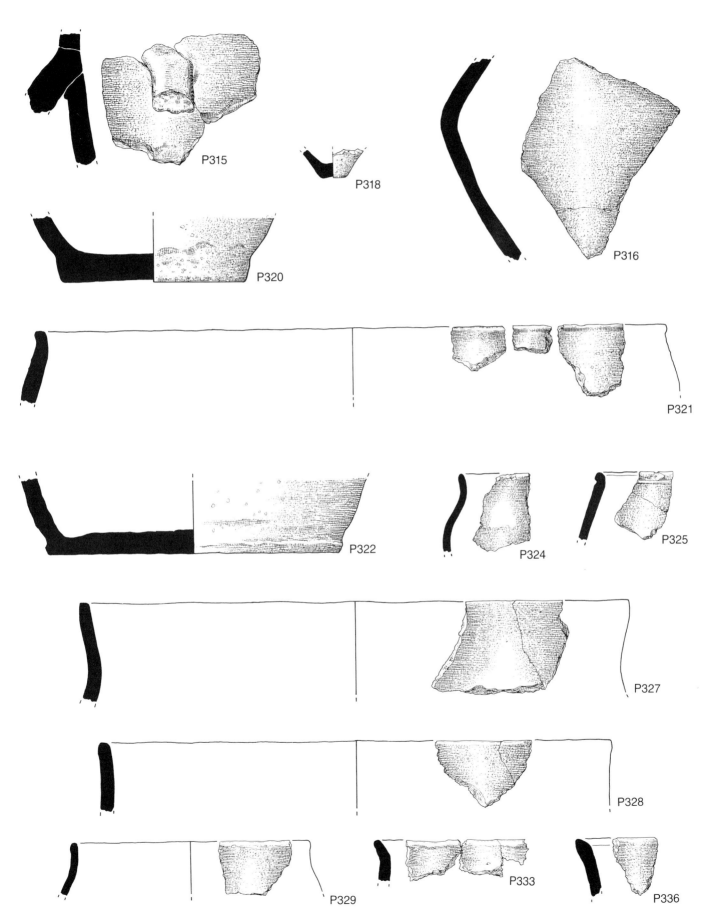

Fig. 94 Late Bronze Age pottery, Area 6, occupation deposits L33b–c. Scale 1/2.

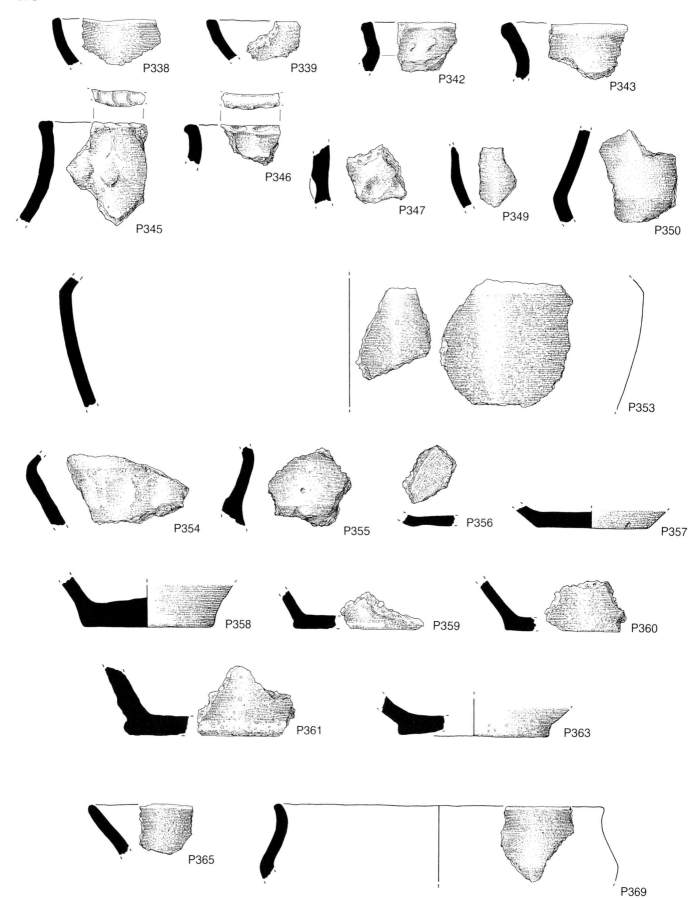

Fig. 95 Late Bronze Age pottery, Area 6, L33b (P338–363), L33a (P365–369). Scale 1/2.

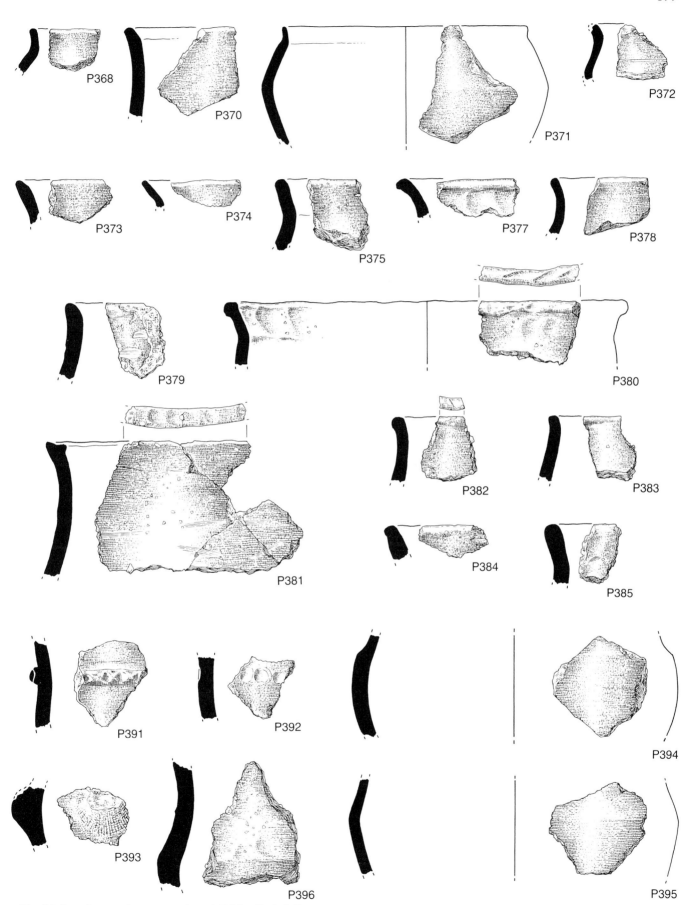

Fig. 96 *Late Bronze Age pottery, Area 6, L33a. Scale 1/2.*

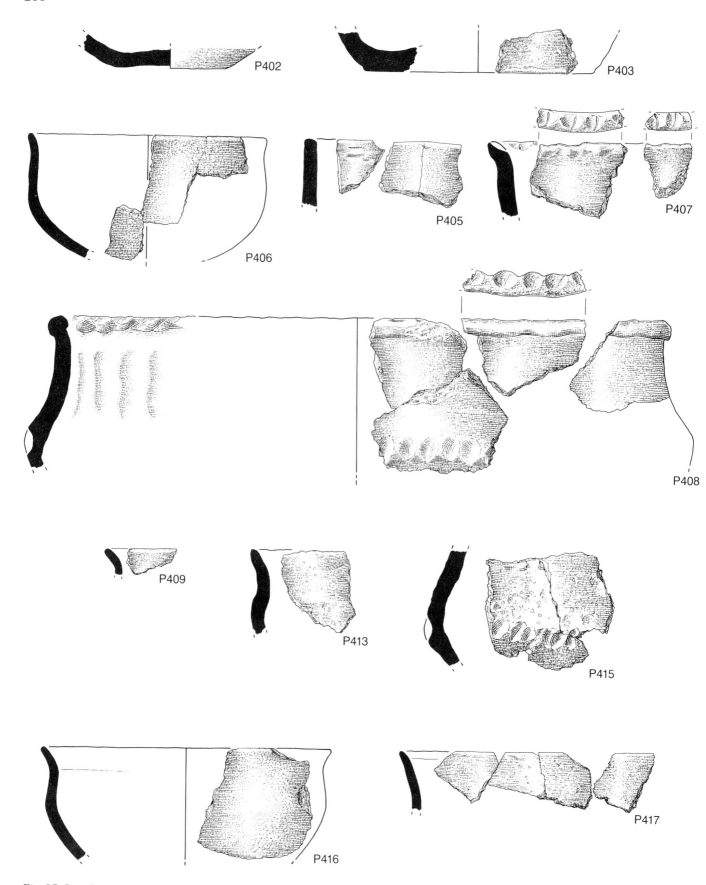

Fig. 97 Late Bronze Age pottery, Area 6, L33a (P402–403), cross-context groups (P405–408), L32b–c (P409–417). Scale 1/2.

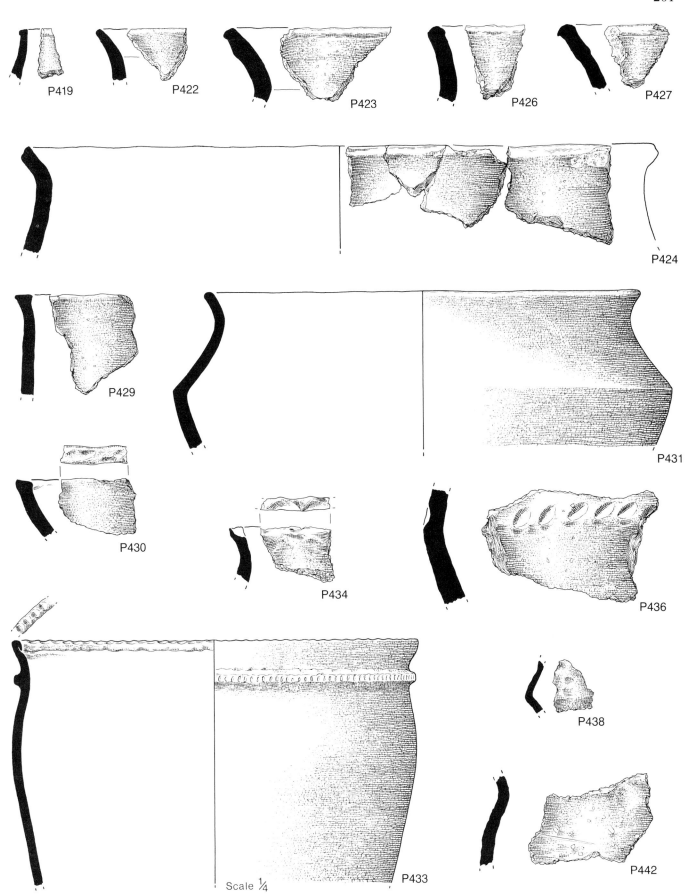

P419 P422 P423 P426 P427 P424 P429 P431 P430 P434 P436 P438 P442 P433

Scale ¼

Fig. 98 Late Bronze Age pottery, Area 6, L32b. Scale 1/2, except P433, 1/4.

202

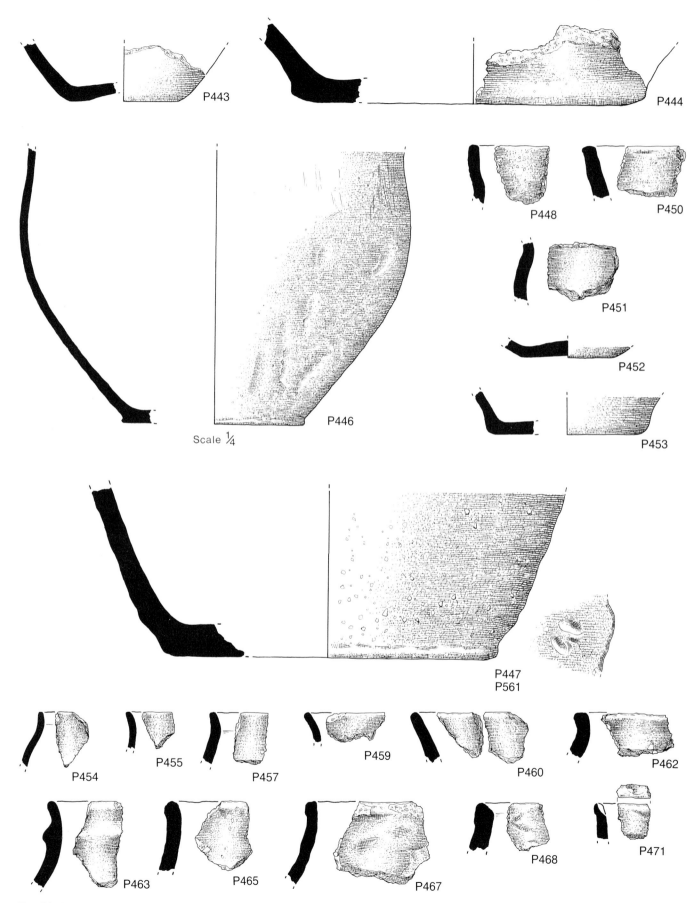

P443

P444

Scale ¼

P446

P448

P450

P451

P452

P453

P447
P561

P454

P455

P457

P459

P460

P462

P463

P465

P467

P468

P471

Fig. 99 Late Bronze Age pottery, Area 6, L32b (P443–446), L32a (P448–453), L31 (P454–471). Scale 1/2, except P446, 1/4.

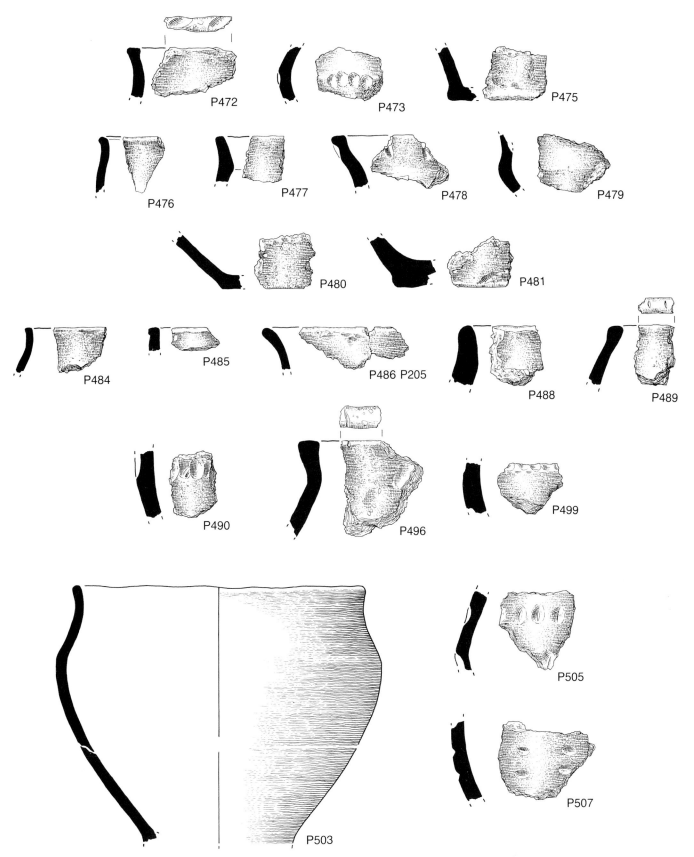

Fig. 100 Late Bronze Age pottery, Area 6, L31 (P472–475), L37 (P476–490), unstratified and poorly phased contexts (P496–507). Scale 1/2.

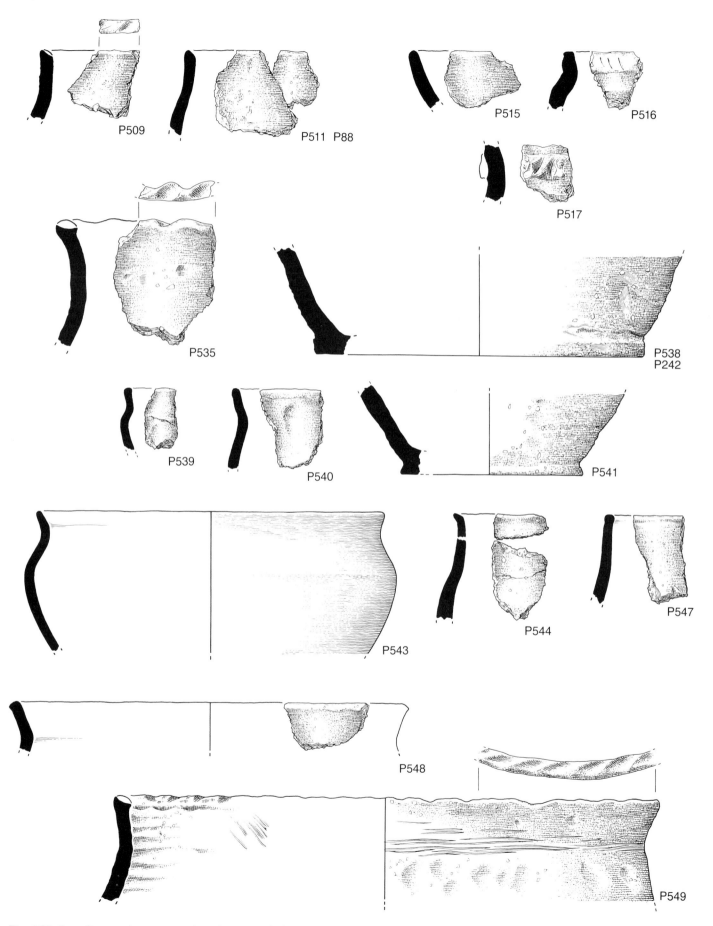

Fig. 101 Late Bronze Age pottery, Area 6, unstratified and poorly phased contexts (P509–538), pit F6 phase 1 (P539–549). Scale 1/2.

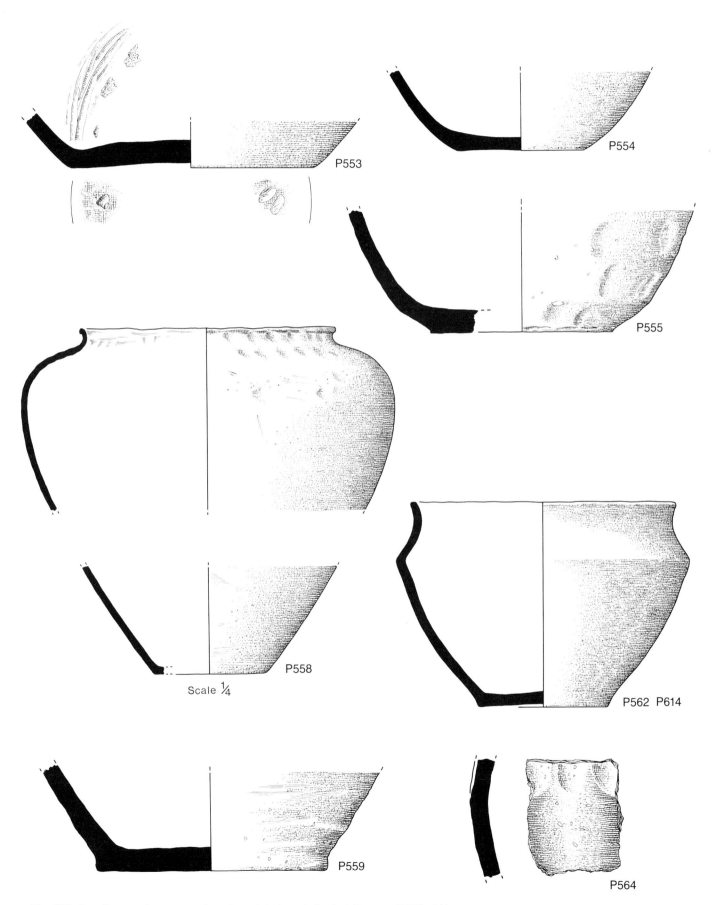

P553

P554

P555

P558

Scale ¼

P562 P614

P559

P564

Fig. 102 Late Bronze Age pottery, Area 6, pit F6 phase 1. Scale 1/2, except P558, 1/4.

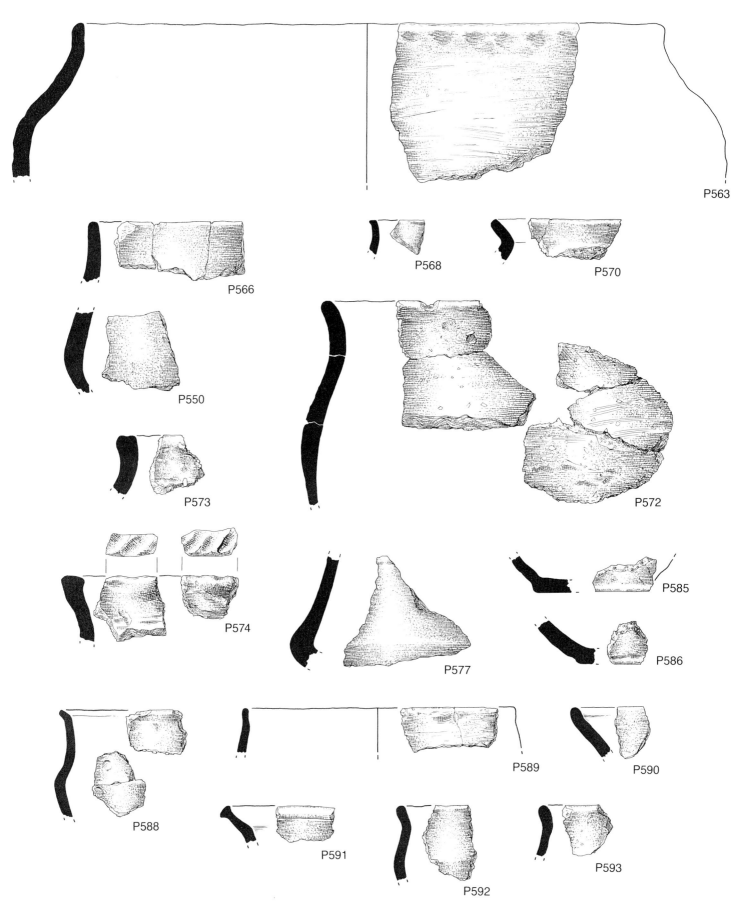

P563

P566

P568

P570

P550

P573

P572

P574

P577

P585

P586

P588

P589

P590

P591

P592

P593

Fig. 103 Late Bronze Age pottery, Area 6, pit F6 phase 1 (P550, 563), phase 2 (P566–593). Scale 1/2.

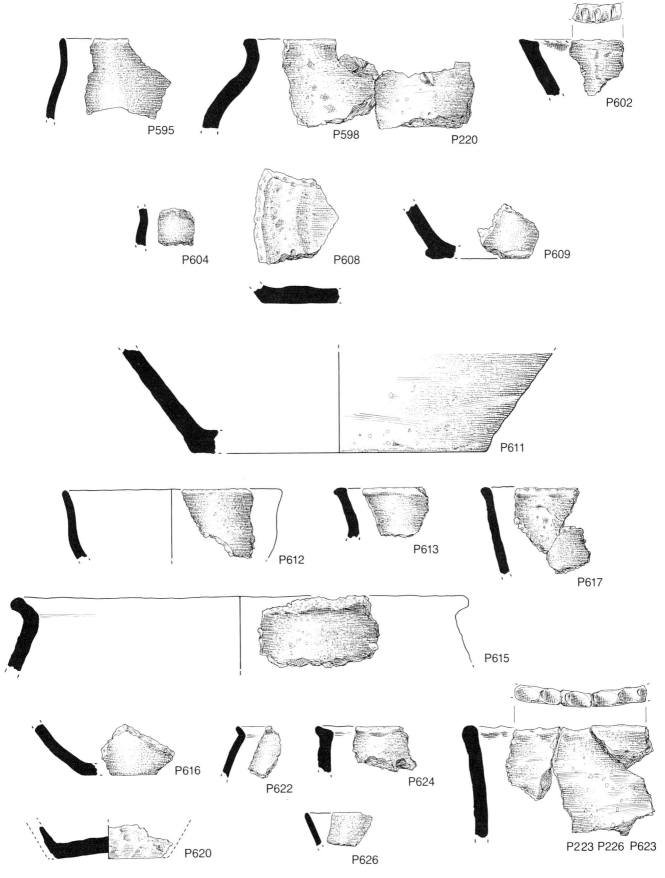

Fig. 104 Late Bronze Age pottery, Area 6, pit F6 phase 2 (P595–611), other LBA features (P612–626). Scale 1/2.

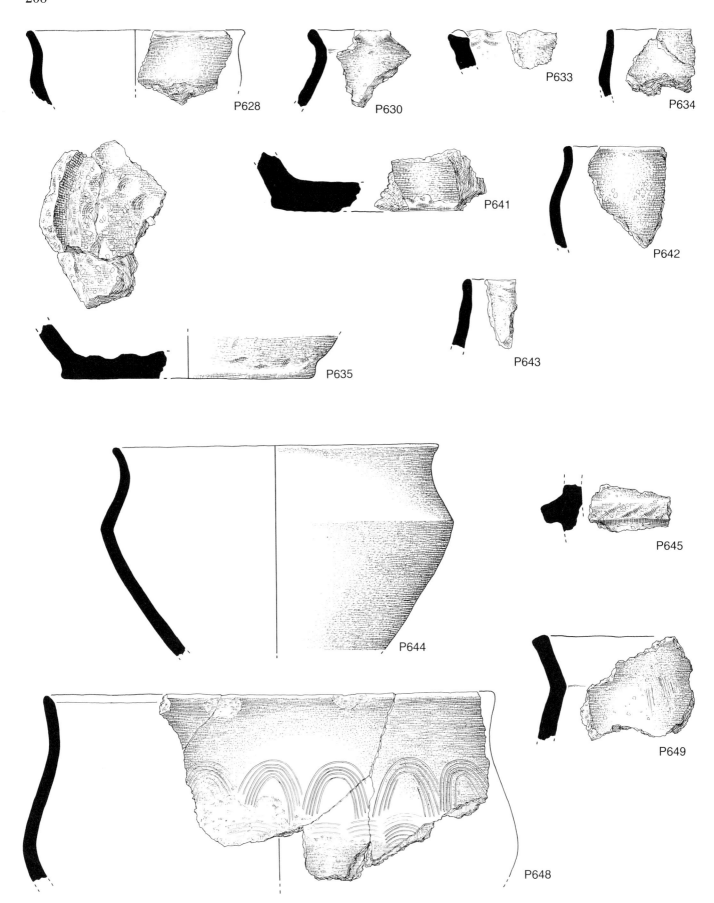

Fig. 105 Late Bronze Age pottery, Area 6, Late Bronze Age features (P628–643), Area 6 salvage section (P644–645), Area 8 salvage sections (P648–649). Scale 1/2.

During this protracted search comparisons were also continually being made amongst the featured sherds from all contexts and more joins or probable belonging sherds were identified. Once the bulk finds were fully worked through, the operation culminated in a systematic comparison between the two featured sherd groups, from the channel and occupation surface. In order to facilitate this the occupation pottery was entirely reorganised into form–fabric groups; each channel 'vessel' was then compared with the relevant groups thus organised.

It cannot be assumed that joins will have had an equal chance of recognition for all classes of pottery. The more distinctive aspects of fabric, surface finish and, to some extent, form in the finer wares undoubtedly enhance the prospects of finding joins or probable belongs. Three categories of affinity were recorded in Table 17 (affiliated sherds are also noted in the archive catalogue): i) joining sherds; ii) non-joining sherds thought almost certainly to be from the same vessel, iii) non-joining sherds thought likely to belong to the same vessel. The last category has not been plotted on the diagrams illustrating spatial and contextual relationships based on the 'join' patterns (Figs. 106–108). Decisions on whether similar sherds should be classified as 'possibly belonging' (category iii) were to some extent influenced by spatial considerations, so that more significance was generally attached when contexts in close proximity were involved.

Implications of the pot joins

The pot joins give some idea of dispersal patterns across Area 6, obviously making allowance for the differential survival of deposits (see below). They are perhaps more important in augmenting the evidence from stratigraphy and pot typology for the correlation of major contexts on the site. In particular, certain relationships can be suggested between the river channel sequence, the occupation deposits and the artifact-rich pit, F6. Joins and sherds thought almost certainly to belong to the same vessel are plotted against a schematic representation of the stratigraphy in Figure 106. Four groups of contexts can be defined as having a number of internal cross-joins:

1. river channel units A–D
2. river channel units E–I
3. occupation deposits south of 10N in trench 1 (zones i–iii; Table 3B)
4. pit F6.

The number of joins connecting any pair of these four groups is variable. Understanding such connections is assisted by assessment of the relative condition of the joining or belonging sherds.

The earliest group of material on the site is probably that from channel A–D. There are no plotted links with higher levels of the channel and two 'possibly belonging' sherds are likely to have been redeposited. One important join, however, links L27 (unit A) with L33c in zone (ii), i.e. low

in the occupation deposits. The sherd from the latter is noticeably more abraded than the conjoining one, implying residuality. This evidence, along with the dearth of links relative to those between the other context groups, would suggest that the early channel sequence is poorly represented on the occupied surface and perhaps only as reworked material.

The mid to late channel deposits exhibit a number of internal links, particularly between L8 and L6. These two layers were in contact with each other up much of the slope of the river bank and both were rich in pottery. Joins are therefore to be expected from portions of vessels occurring close to the excavated layer boundary (which was not clear-cut). Furthermore, a certain amount of redeposition could have taken place from L8 to L6. Fewer joins were found with the overlying layers (L5 and L4), these indicating further redeposition.

Two joins, in both cases between sherds in similar condition, link the mid–late channel with the stratified sequence in pit F6: L8 to F6, phase 1 (F6L5) and L6 to F6, phase 2 (F6L1). Internal links between the two pit phases almost certainly reflect redeposition of pottery from the lower fill (F6L4 and 5) in the phase 2 fill (F6L2), since phase 2 began with a perceptible recut. This disturbance has not led to greater abrasion of the higher stratified sherds.

Cross-links within the occupation deposits are most complex. Although at first sight they seem to traverse the full depth of the deposit, more detailed examination allows a partition into upper and lower deposits, split at the 32b/33b horizon. Two joins appear to cross this boundary (32c–32a, and 33c–33a), but in both cases the uppermost sherd is more abraded and can be regarded as redeposited. Otherwise there are links from the 32b/33b horizon either upwards, defining an 'upper occupation' group, or downwards, defining the 'lower occupation'. Thus contexts 32b and 33b themselves cannot be attributed specifically to one or the other; this is unsurprising in view of the lack of any extensive, clear stratigraphic boundaries within the relatively shallow occupation soil.

Despite the small amount of pottery from context 36, there are three joins with sherds in similar condition in overlying deposits. This suggests that material in this basal, 'dirty natural' horizon often relates closely to that above and is not wholly residual from an earlier phase of activity.

The lower occupation unit is linked by cross-joins to phase 1 of pit F6, and this in turn to channel L8 (units E–G). The upper unit cross-references to pit F6 phase 2, but also to channel unit G (L8a).

In broad terms one could temporally equate mid to lower occupation, F6 phase 1 and channel E–G, and again, upper occupation, F6 phase 2 and channel G–I (Fig. 107). The upper occupation in trench 2 (L37a) is also linked by one join to the latter horizon (L6). So also is the top layer of pit F11, although here relative sherd condition and the pit's stratigraphic position relative to 37a and b (sealed under) suggest that the two sherds in L6 (both joining one in F11)

Table 17: **Record of joining and belonging sherds in the Late Bronze Age pottery assemblage from Area 6.**

For joins/belongs making important links between non-neighbouring contexts, an assessment of relative sherd condition is given.

Fineware and semi-fineware

2 — 61a * 61b =61c = 61d — 60 — 145
8a = 8b * 8c * 8d = 9
16 — 24
20a * 20b — 21
31a * 31b — 93
35 = 36
47 — 75
48Xa * 48Xb * 48Xc — 43
66 — 84
72a = 72b
91a * 91b — 158
93 — 94
95a = 95b = 95c = 95d
97 = 182
101a = 101b
104a * 104b * 104c = 104d = 104e * 104f * 104g = 165 = 166
114d * 114e * 114f = 114a/c/h = 114b = 114g
150a–c * 150d = 150e
167a * 167b
176a * 176b = 176c
177a = 177b
178a * 178b = 178c = 178d = 178e = 178f = 178g
180a = 180b
183a = 183b
191 — 588a = 588b
192a = 192b — 193
307 — 308
328a * 328b — 295a * 295b = 294: 295a–b marginally less abraded
    than 328a–b; 328b in similar condition to, but smaller than, 328a
353a = 353b
379 = 157: both heavily abraded on one side
405a = 405b
406c * 406b * 406a = 406d — 406e (cf. also 417)
416 = 543: no significant difference, mostly unweathered
417d * 417b * 417a * 417c (cf. also 406): sherd condition uniform
431b * 431a * 431c = 431d: mostly unweathered edges, 431b (context 32a) a little abraded
460a = 460b
503a = 503b
553 * 148 — 580 — 327: 553, 148 and 580 in similar lightly abraded
    condition; 580 a lot smaller than 553, from lower fill of same pit
558a * 558d = 558b * 432 = 558c: stretches of light abrasion on all
    sherd groups involved here
562b * 614 * 562a — 562c — 562d: the two sherds 562d are small
    and perhaps more abraded than the rest
566a * 566b
589 — 282
617a = 617b

Coarseware

1 — 10
3 — 4
15 * 33
51 — 52
57 — 67a * 67b
62a = 62b
80a * 80b
81 — 544a = 544b
86a * 86b = 86c = 90X = 90Y = 90Z
88 * 511
108 — 186
112a * 112b = 113
123a * 123b * 123c
124a = 124b
125a = 125b
127a * 127b = 127c
128a = 128b = 128c
129a = 129b * 129c * 129d * 129e
131a * 131b * 131c = 131d
133a * 133b
134 * 638: 134 in fresh condition, 638 more abraded and smaller
137 — 229
138a = 138b = 138c * 138d
141a * 141b * 141c = 141d * 141e — 211
155 — 245
168a * 168b — 206 — 207
170 = 216
171a = 171b — 172 — 173
197a = 197b
198a = 198b = 198c
203 * 303: little abrasion on either, but 303 a small sherd
205 (*) 486: both lightly abraded
214a = 214b = 214c = 214d
218a = 218b = 218c = 218d = 218e
221a * 221b * 221c
222a * 222b = 222c
223 * 623 * 226: 223, 226 both a little more abraded and smaller than
    623, which is in fairly fresh condition
224a = 224b
230a = 230b
231a = 231b
234a = 234b
235a * 235b = 235c
242 * 538: 538 is a little more abraded than 242
251a = 251b
255 — 219
306a * 306b (also cf. 407 etc.): 306a unweathered, 306b more abraded
    all round
315a * 315b
317 * 7: 7 very crisp, 317 slightly more abraded
321a = 321b (*) 321c
322a * 322b * 322c
323a = 323b
407a = 407b = 274 — 275 (also cf. 306): all sherds a little abraded;
    finger-printing a little more abraded on 274
408b * 408a = 408c = 408d: No significant differences in condition

413 – 414
424a = 424b – 572a = 572b
433a = 433c = 433b = 433d * 433e – 381
446a * 446b
447a * 447b * 561a – 561b * 561c – 561d
547 – 596
559c *559a * 559b
560b * 560a – 560c: 560b possibly slightly more abraded than rest
574a = 574b
598 * 220: same condition; very little abrasion despite fairly soft fabric
611a * 611b = 611c
619 – 620
Uncatalogued body sherds:
F6L2 7E 11N * F6L5 SE

Key: *   join   (*) probable join, abraded
       =   almost certainly same pot
       –   possibly same pot

NB: Joins within the same excavated context *and* grid square are not recorded here. Some such joining groups are present here as individual catalogue numbers (e.g. 171a); refer to full archive catalogue.

are residual. In contrast, of the joining sherds in L6 and pit F5, the latter is more abraded.

The overall pattern of relationships based on pot joins ties in well with the established stratigraphic relationships and the two sources give the general phasing outlined in Fig. 107.

The horizontal spatial pattern of pottery joins is shown in Figure 108. The pattern has to be considered in relation to the survival of intact Late Bronze Age deposits, which had a very patchy distribution. The two main concentrations of joins reflect two concentrations of *in situ* deposits, as might have been expected. There does not appear to be any preferred axis to the lines linking each pair of sherds in either concentration. In addition there are a number of linkage lines of between 4 m and 9 m in length and these range well outside the concentrations, in particular linking pit F6 to the south-western corner of trench 1. These longer linkages can run both parallel and transverse to the river bank/ levee alignment.

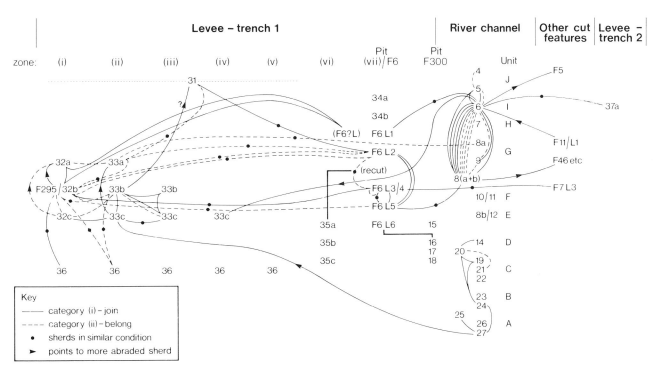

Fig. 106 Cross-context sherd joins for the Area 6 Late Bronze Age pottery shown against a schematic representation of context relationships. Only category (i) and (ii) joins/belongs are plotted.

212

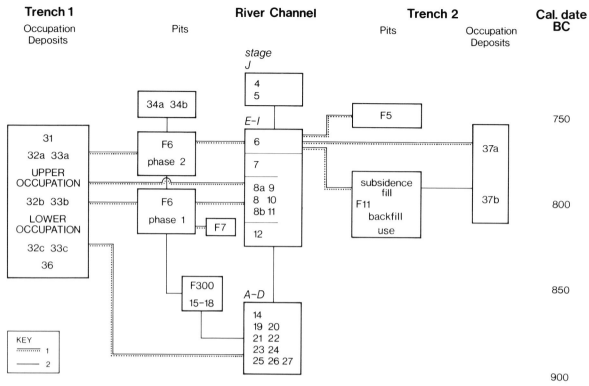

Trench 1
Occupation Deposits

River Channel

Pits

Trench 2
Pits

Occupation Deposits

Cal. date BC

stage
J

4
5

34a 34b

E–I

F5

750

31
32a 33a
UPPER OCCUPATION

F6
phase 2

6

37a

7

32b 33b
LOWER OCCUPATION

F6
phase 1

8a 9
8 10
8b 11

subsidence fill

F11
backfill
use

37b

800

F7

12

32c 33c
36

F300
15–18

A–D

850

14
19 20
21 22
23 24
25 26 27

KEY

·········· 1

——— 2

900

Fig. 107 Simplified interpretation of the phasing of Late Bronze Age deposits in Area 6, based on stratigraphic sequence and pottery joins. Key: 1. temporal relationship suggested by relative condition of joining sherds; 2. temporal relationship based on stratigraphy.

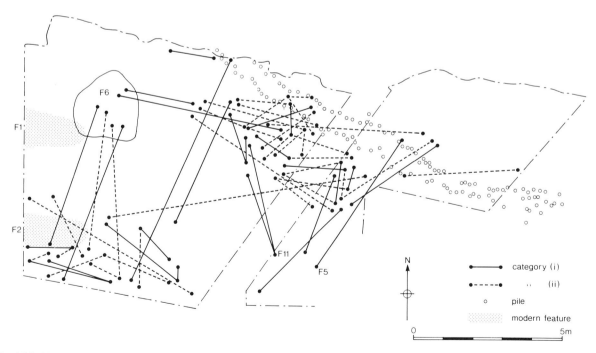

Fig. 108 Horizontal spatial patterning of Late Bronze Age pottery joins in Area 6. Only category (i) and (ii) joins/belongs are plotted.

SECTION C:
ENVIRONMENTAL AND FOOD REMAINS

Summary

A good range of remains relating to the environment and the food economy were found to be preserved on the site, particularly from the waterlogged deposits. In combination these have yielded a stunning array of often unobtainable kinds of information; section C documents the results of their study in depth.

Most of the small biological remains were only investigated from samples from Area 6. Insect remains are, however, reported on for some Area 4 samples, whilst the wood, animal bone and food residue reports all include material from salvage areas (Areas 4, 5 and 8).

Chapter 10 sets out details of the sampling and any subsequent processing carried out centrally. The positions and contextual correlations for three columns in Area 6 are followed by general sampling procedures for the different kinds of data. Lists of the contexts of the particular samples studied by each specialist are, however, given at the beginning of their respective chapters. The same goes for the treatment of samples by the individual specialists.

A vital key to many of the studies in this section is provided by the sediment report in Chapter 11. Two sediment profiles are described and interpreted. These cover the two most important stratigraphic sequences in Area 6, but do not contain all the layer-type contexts encountered. Some additional contexts are covered in a supplementary report on the river channel in Chapter 12. Sedimentary characteristics are identified in the SS1 profile in keeping with a change from Neolithic flowing water, to slack-water silting, to Bronze Age over-bank flooding, and finally soil development prior to LBA occupation. The WF1 profile shows a similar trend from sediments associated with high-energy flow towards over-bank flooding as the river's edge silted up. The particle size statistics given in Chapter 12 should only be treated as approximate values owing to the problem of the high calcareous content of the silts.

Treatment of botanical remains is split between the woody elements (Chapter 13) and the smaller material (fruit, seeds, pollen in chapter 14). Study of the wood remains (both charcoal and waterlogged wood) included counts of growth rings where possible, as well as species identification. Clear selection is demonstrated in the choice of oak for piled foundations and the exploitation of coppiced rods for brush structures. Some changes in the frequencies of species identified from Neolithic to Bronze Age probably reflect changes in the local woodland composition, in particular the appearance of more secondary woodland by the LBA, albeit tempered by anthropogenic factors.

The smaller plant remains (waterlogged and charred) from Runnymede are extremely diverse in species and represent a number of different habitats, although to different degrees. The representatives of different plant communities are described first to provide a framework for the subsequent discussion of vegetational change, cultigens and the various habitats inferred. A significant increase in grassland and other open land is identified between the periods of occupation and the alder carr, which dominated the damper valley floor in the Neolithic, was seriously affected by general woodland decline. There is abundant evidence for grasslands, echoed in the molluscan and insect reports, both damp and dry, and containing various flower species. Plenty of carbonised cereal grain suggests arable cultivation by the occupants, and the strong presence of thorny shrub species leads to the tentative suggestion that hedges divided arable from pasture. Plants, the associated insects and also the molluscs and ostracods give a wealth of information on the kind of flora and fauna supported by the river itself and its banks.

Ostracods were only studied for the WF1 profile, where they survived at depths between 50 and 140 cm.

They suggested the water conditions to have been shallow, quiet and effectively lacustrine, while molluscs and insects point to the presence of flowing water, perhaps seasonally. The molluscs present a fuller picture of changing environments and changing inputs to the site deposits. They survived through most of the WF1 profile, but only the waterlogged part of the SS1 sequence was studied. Analysis shows the presence of mixed assemblages deriving from various aquatic and terrestrial habitats. There are marked changes in the overall balance, whilst some species also show sudden changes in fortune, these factors together being used to suggest which components were autochthonous and which allochthonous, thereby distinguishing the immediate environment from the local backdrop. The degree of assemblage diversity is also considered as having possible environmental implications. Although there are some interesting features not adequately understood, the molluscan assemblages document well changes from watery environments to mud-flats, and then, drier land.

The insect remains are confined to waterlogged sediments, but they nevertheless cover useful chronological spans, as well as some specialised contexts such as a midden and a corvid pellet. In addition to contributing to the overall picture of the local environment, these data are instrumental in documenting a decline in local grazing after the Middle Neolithic settlement phase, and indicating the presence of manure in the Late Bronze Age midden. For analysis the insects are treated in eleven species groups defined by their food and habitats. Tree-dependent beetles give an impression of changing forest character to be tied in with the plant-fossil evidence. Of entomological interest are insect species which are now either extinct or extremely rare in Britain. These and others are introduced into the discussion on climatic change, but no conclusive evidence for such change was found.

The animal bones were studied in the two main period groups – Middle Neolithic and Late Bronze Age – and one small group of the Late Neolithic. In addition to species identification, butchery and palaeopathological aspects of the bones are also considered. Ageing is done on tooth wear and fusion. Cattle, sheep/goats, pigs and dogs were the domesticates present in the Neolithic, alongside a few remains of deer and a flatfish. Horse was added to the domestic range by the LBA, whose large assemblage also includes a small minority of wild species.

Important bone groups in LBA contexts include: most of a disarticulated horse in a pit, stretches of articulated horse vertebrae elsewhere on the site, and a dog skeleton which lay in a peat pool. There is evidence that might point to the stabling of horses and the close confinement of cattle. The age distribution of the sheep/goats is on the young side and the indications are that cattle were also generally killed as young adults. The percentage of pig remains increases through the deep river channel sequence, whilst cattle remains decrease.

The food residue analyses reported in Chapter 19 all relate to the Neolithic. The seven charred residues giving positive results indicate a variety of foodstuffs to be present and illustrate the high potential of such analyses. Negative results from the attached sherds are used to argue against any of the substances having been introduced as pot-sealants.

Chapter 10
The collection and treatment of the environmental samples

Maureen Girling and James Greig

The association at Runnymede Bridge of a Late Bronze Age occupation site and earlier Neolithic layers with water-logged, calcareous organic deposits (also containing charred material) presented a rare opportunity for an archaeological investigation combined with a full programme of environmental studies and scientific dating.

Most of the fieldwork was done while the excavation took place, during the month of July 1978, when there was a pause in the bridge-building to allow the excavation of the exposed site. The site was visited by a number of specialists, a structured sampling programme was decided upon and samples were collected as sections and layers became available. There was no time for leisured consideration.

The sampling was done with two main aims; one was the collection of a representative amount, usually 10–20 litres, of each layer or context over the site, so that it could be studied later, and in the appropriate manner. At that stage it was not known whether plant or insect macrofossils were present, but in hindsight it was a wise course of sampling. Particular sampling areas included those with the appearance of middens, occupation areas, possible hearths and tufa. Further 'spot samples' were taken of objects of particular interest, such as possible dog coprolites (not reported on in this volume), and bird pellets.

The second sampling aim was stratigraphic: to collect samples from profiles which would have a stratigraphic series from the highest to the deepest sediments and which would yield results in a number of specialist fields on plant, insect, mollusc and sediment content and change. Three columns were taken in Area 6 to cover the main stratigraphic sequences present (Fig. 5, p. 23). Others were taken earlier during salvage work in Areas 4 and 8, but little study was possible on these due to shortage of resources and certain sample identification problems. The insects were, however, analysed from a series of samples from Area 4.

The Area 6 columns were as follows:

WF1: This was cut from the north-eastern end of the baulk between trenches 1 and 2, around grid location 14.5E/10.75N, late in the excavation (Plate 58b). The deposits in the column comprise the fill of a river channel and date to the Late Bronze Age. Piles in the outer row at this point had been extracted to allow access to a sequence of silt deposits behind. It was hoped that these silts would be free from disturbance from piles. The column thus provides a record of environmental data from the sediment sequence between the two pile rows. This sequence contains the majority of depositional phases in the Late Bronze Age river channel and all the stratigraphic units defined (Chapter 2) are represented. The layer/sample correlation is shown in Fig. 109. The top of the column lay at 13.77 m OD and was between 0.5 and 1 m behind the drawn east section (38A) of trench 1 (Fig. 5). Some minor collapse at the top of the bluff left by the contractor meant that the column had to be split: WF1a covers depths 0–0.50 m, and is set back (south-west) about 0.25 m from, WF1b, which is the main part of the column, between depths 0.40 and 1.75 m (Plate 58b). WF1a was thus close to, and possibly directly above, the inner pile row, and there may not be perfect layer correlations at the overlap between WF1a and WF1b.

SS1: This column was taken from the south face of trench 1 at around grid location 5E/2.5N. The full sequence exposed at this point covers alluvial silting during the 3rd and 2nd millennia cal BC, with the Late Bronze Age occupation soil at the top (Fig. 109). The stratigraphy is similar (with minor undulations in layer interfaces) to that seen at the south-west end of drawn section 38B (Fig. 23), which was about 4.5 m away. The datum for the environment columns lay at 13.86 m OD on silt underlying the Late Bronze Age deposits. However, only samples from 1.20 m and deeper were recovered for biological remains. This lower part was also sampled for palaeomagnetic measurements. The correlation between archaeologically recorded layers and sample depths is shown in Fig. 109.

SS2: This column lies in trench 2 and was taken from a section through deposits underlying the Late Bronze Age level at around grid location 13.5E/7.75N (section 17 – Fig. 21). The upper part of the sequence (layers 38–39) duplicates part of SS1, but the lower part comprises the channel sediments with Middle Neolithic material which dipped away towards the base of SS1. The datum at the base of the column was 12.37 m OD. Unfortunately the samples taken for biological remains could later not certainly be identified and thus only palaeomagnetic results were obtained from SS2.

The WF1 and SS1 samples taken for various environmental remains were very close to Dr Limbrey's sediment columns and her layer boundaries, measured directly from the respective datums, therefore apply to all environmental studies. Fig. 109 summarises the classes of environmental remains studied at different depths in the columns.

To supplement the columns, numerous 'spot' samples were taken from the archaeological deposits, particularly from the Middle Neolithic levels, the Late Bronze Age occupation surface and the Late Bronze Age midden in the edge of the river channel. These samples were trowelled directly into bags and those studied for remains are listed at the beginning of the respective environmental reports. A further series of spot samples was taken from section 33 (Fig. 20) by Pete Fisher specifically for his sedimentary analysis.

The column in Area 4 was taken from its eastern face and its position is shown on the drawn section (Fig. 13).

216

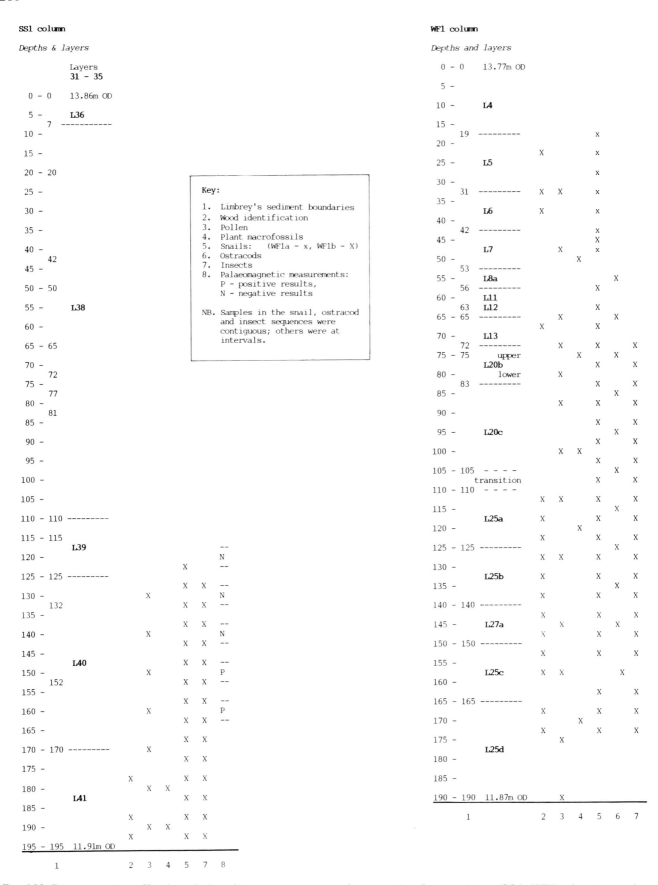

Fig. 109 Diagrammatic profiles through the sedimentary sequences at the two main column positions (SS1, WF1), showing correlations of sample depth with layer contexts. The samples yielding identifiable material of the various environmental categories are shown.

It was 190 cm deep and the lowest sample (170–190 cm) comes from Middle Neolithic silts associated with the brush and pile structure; higher up the sequence probably duplicates that of SS1 in covering 3rd and 2nd millennia cal BC alluviation.

Particular sampling techniques were employed by specialists for the collection of suitable samples:

Sediments: Where possible, in $100 \times 100 \times 250$ mm aluminium monolith boxes, elsewhere in stratigraphic series in polythene bags. The collected samples supplemented field inspection and recording of certain sedimentary sequences.

Geomagnetic: Undisturbed cores set in plaster of Paris.

Pollen: Where possible, vertical monoliths collected in 250 mm aluminium boxes. These samples also provided for the ostracod study and further sedimentological work.

General environmental samples: For macroscopic plant remains including wood, insects, animal bone, molluscs, etc. generally sampled adjacent to pollen monoliths, 3–4 kg collected at 5 cm vertical intervals. Additionally, after the presence of charred grain was indicated by trial sieving on site, waterlogged material from the Bronze Age midden and other occupation layers was trowelled directly into polythene bags by the excavators.

Wood and charcoal: Mainly from archaeological structures or features collected by archaeologists for conservation and other studies.

Animal bone: This was mainly recovered by hand with additions from the sieved samples.

Radiocarbon samples: Came from excavated wooden structures or charcoal concentrations in all but two cases, which were bone groups.

Most samples were individually treated and investigated by their particular specialists. The general environmental samples (both column and 'spot'), however, were initially washed and partially pre-treated at the English Heritage Ancient Monuments Laboratory and the following procedure was adopted:

1. Each sample was weighed and a brief note made of its sediment type.

2. A sub-sample for possible mollusc and/or ostracod work was taken.

3. The remaining sample was soaked in a dilute solution of Sodium carbonate to aid breakdown.

4. The soaked sample was gently disaggregated by hand and washed into a 300 μm sieve. At this stage, all flint (mainly river-borne pebbles), other pebbles, pottery, daub, bones, wood, charcoal over 5 mm long and other objects were removed, labelled and bagged for referral to appropriate specialists.

5. When fully broken down, with the less than 300 μm size fraction washed through the sieve, the samples were drained, returned to a bowl and mixed thoroughly with paraffin (kerosene), and cold water was added to float off the insects and some of the plant remains.

6. The floatant was sorted under a microscope at about $10\times$ for all insects and molluscs. Recognisable seeds and other plant remains were also removed at this stage, although no attempt was made at a thorough sorting of all the plant remains. Instead, the entire floatant, minus molluscs and insect remains, was reserved for sorting by an archaeobotanist.

7. The non-floating residue was tested for insect remains, then divided into halves for sorting by the relevant specialists for plant and mollusc remains. This is essential, as paraffin flotation is meant for insect retrieval and, whilst it will enable the recovery of some seeds and molluscs, other remains do not float.

8. Particular problems, including the possible presence of small seeds less than 300 μm such as *Juncus* (rush), or of easily fragmented biological remains, may be referred to the reserve sample (see 2, above) or the untreated portion of the pollen samples.

The column samples were processed at the Ancient Monuments Laboratory with the assistance of Ian Tyers, as set out above. The residues that did not float were kept, and James Greig later re-sieved them and extracted plant remains to add to those already extracted from the floats, passing them on to John Evans for extraction of the molluscs, particularly the smaller ones.

Chapter 11
The sediments in Area 6

SUSAN LIMBREY

3rd and 2nd millennium BC alluviation (column SS1)

A characteristic of the flood-plain deposits of rivers and streams draining chalk and limestone areas of southern England is deposits of calcium carbonate in the form of tufa, laid down in mid post-glacial times. At Runnymede a layer of tufa, which may have formed in a marsh environment marginal to a channel of the Thames or its tributary, the Colne Brook, is overlain by deposits containing reworked tufa as a component of the sands and gravels deposited in a stream channel. Whether the erosion and redeposition of the tufa indicate a change in fluviatile regime or whether it is simply a minor development in the evolution of the channel pattern cannot be established without the possibility of mapping a larger part of the valley floor of the time, but formation of tufa seems to have ceased by Neolithic times. The sequence of deposits exposed in the excavations shows part of an active and mobile stream system depositing sands and gravels and forming banks or bars behind which finer silts and organic muds could accumulate, giving way to steady deposition from over-bank flooding. The lower part of the sequence shows by its preservation of organic detritus that the deposits have remained within the groundwater table since they were laid down. These deposits show sedimentary structure. As the floodloam built up, however, seasonal fall of water table allowed penetration of air and the establishment of a flood-plain vegetation. Soil processes ensured that organic matter was humified and successive increments of material were incorporated into the soil. The lamination of the earlier deposits is gradually obliterated until no sedimentary structure can be detected. The river has changed from one of low seasonal variability, probably having multiple channels flowing among transient sand and gravel banks bearing ephemeral vegetation, to one of more stable channel pattern in which channels are confined between increasingly high banks, built up by the winter floods of a seasonally variable regime, forming a stable flood-plain surface. By the Middle Bronze Age the frequency of flooding, the amount of deposition, or both were sufficiently reduced for soil formation to gain upon accretion, with the development of a humic topsoil and a site reliably dry enough for occupation. These changes are illustrated by the section described below.

Depths are measured from a local datum, approximately the base of the Bronze Age occupation horizon, 13.86 m OD; the column lies at about 5E/2.5N in the south-west face of trench 1 (Figs. 5 and 109).

Layers 32–36
Occupation soil: Dark grey, 10YR 3/1, sandy clay loam with charcoal, shell fragments and cultural debris, structure compound coarse and fine angular blocky; very strong when dry, very weak when wet; slightly sticky, moderately plastic; swelling.

Layer 38
0–7 cm Merging zone, dark grey soil of the humic horizon and occupation deposits mixed by worm action with the less humic floodloam. Deep worm channels with dark grey soil fill penetrate a further 40 cm below this.

7–50 cm Greyish brown, 10YR 5/2 moist, light greyish brown, 2.5Y 6/2 dry, becoming slightly darker, 20–42 cm, and paler, 42–50 cm; mottles distinct, clear to diffuse, fine and very fine, grey and brownish yellow, 10YR 6/1 and 6/6(dry), mottling increasing from common in the upper 20 cm to many, 20–42 cm, and then decreasing again and becoming paler. Texture is silty clay, becoming more clay-rich downwards, with a sand component dominated by shell fragments. Structure is compound; in the upper 20 cm weakly developed adherent coarse prismatic and very fine angular blocky, then becoming rather better developed fine prismatic and fine angular blocky. Very strong when dry, very weak when wet; consistence slightly sticky, very plastic; swelling. Porosity, about 5% fine macropores.

50–65 cm Similar to above but colour less grey, though still greyish brown, 2.5Y 5/3 moist, light greyish brown, 2.5Y 6/2 dry; fewer mottles than above. Texture silty clay, similar to the upper part above, and structure a little less well developed than immediately above. Strength, consistence and porosity similar.

65–73 cm Darker than 50–65 cm, and mottles rapidly becoming more abundant, coarser and sharper. The mottles now become zones of staining spreading from fine macropores into the matrix, and the pores are lined with thin skins of matrix-coloured clay. Compound prismatic and fine angular blocky structure is moderately developed. Other characteristics remain the same.

73–77 cm Darker still, dark greyish brown, 10YR 4/2 moist, 2.5Y 5/2 dry, with many prominent medium-clear reddish yellow mottles, 7.5YR 6/8 (dry). Structure becomes strongly developed; very strong when dry, remaining strong when wetted until collapsing when very wet.

77–81 cm Similar to 65–73 in colour characteristics, but structure and strength as immediately above.

81–110 cm   Darker again, greyish brown, 10YR 5/2 moist, 2.5Y 5/2 dry, with many prominent medium–clear mottles, reddish yellow, 7.5YR 6/8 (dry), forming continuous concretionary pipes around macropores, which separate from the matrix. Pores have clay linings and some very dark staining on their walls, with traces of root material. Texture clay, finer than above, with very little sand. Very strongly developed compound fine prismatic and fine angular blocky structure; strength as above.

Layer 39

110–125 cm   Colour as above, but from 115 cm becoming paler, with whitening by fine shell sand. Mottling less abundant and less intense, especially below 115 cm, remaining only as diffuse stains, 7.5YR 6/6 and paler, and not forming pipes. Traces of root material increase. Structure becomes less well developed, the secondary, blocky structure being very poorly developed and the prismatic structure weakly developed and adherent. Traces of lamination appear, and macroscopic plant fragments and shell fragments are flat-lying. Whole shells are abundant.

Layer 40

125–132 cm   Rapidly increasing sand content, dominated by shell fragments, giving fine sandy loam texture, with fine laminar sedimentary structure, soil structure dying out. Very dark grey, 10YR 3/2 moist, 5/2 dry, becoming darker downwards, mottling becoming fainter.

132–152 cm   Laminated fine sandy loam, very dark greyish brown, 10YR 3/2 moist, 5/2 dry, with some darker zones. Iron staining in macropores, but not spreading into matrix.

152–170 cm   Similar but with a higher proportion of medium sand and more large organic fragments. Below 142 cm the material oxidised rapidly on exposure, changing from very dark greyish brown, 2.5Y 3/2, to very dark grey, 3/1. Mottling absent, there being no staining in pores.

Layer 41

170–195 cm   Sharp boundary to medium shelly sand.

Synthesis

The deposits described above are divided into two main bodies, the laminated stratified sands below 125 cm, and the fine clayey alluvium above this, in which no sedimentary structure is preserved and in which no changes are sharp or appear in any way associated with sudden changes in the texture of the material being deposited. Changes which occur above 125 cm are visible macroscopically as variation in colour, brought about by differences in organic content and in the size, sharpness, abundance and distribution of ferruginous mottling or staining, and in soil structure. Both these characteristics are functions of aeration conditions in the soil, the development of prismatic structure and the segregation of iron oxides being features of gleyed soils.

Below the soil on which the occupation was established, which is strongly darkened by humus and charred material, in the upper part of the sediments, the mottles are discrete. Their abundance varies somewhat in horizontal zones, but becomes greater downwards, and the mottles become larger and more dominant. In this zone, drainage in summer has been adequate to permit intermittent aeration of the soil via the development of structural fissures as the soil dries. In the lower part of the clayey alluvium, the discrete mottling gives way to intense iron staining spreading into the matrix from vertical macropores, rootholes, some of which contain root residues, and which have an iron oxide-free interior lining. Here aeration has been a function of root respiration rather than by the draining of the soil sufficiently for structural fissures to open. The formation of these iron stains relates to the period of active rooting in that zone, the bleaching of the walls of the pores following when the roots died and their holes became an easy passage for water rising and falling within the deposit.

The deposits are calcareous throughout, with very abundant shell fragments and whole shells. There is no macroscopic evidence of decalcification of the deposits or redistribution of calcium carbonate within them, showing that no intervals in deposition were long enough for any substantial degree of leaching to occur.

Particle size analysis of calcareous sediments is difficult. In order to obtain a dispersed suspension it is usually regarded as essential to decalcify the material, and in doing so the shell content, which is in part a component of the sedimentary material and in part autochthonous, is destroyed. Similarly chalk particles are destroyed, and any material which participated in the deposition in the form of water-stable aggregates derived from calcareous soils will be dispersed. Shell fragments, moreover, have a low specific gravity and a flat shape and therefore do not travel with the particle size class to which they are assigned on analysis. The results cannot therefore be reliably interpreted in terms of water flow characteristics. In these deposits, a very high content of shell fragments in the fine sand grade seriously biases the analyses. It was found to be extremely difficult to achieve a stable dispersion even with decalcification, and an attempt was made to carry out analysis on material treated for removal of organic matter but not calcium carbonate. Results were obtained on some of the samples which were useful for comparison with those on the decalcified material. Because of the difficulties in both analysis and interpretation, particle size results are given only in very broad terms. They are sufficient to characterise the material but not to allow firm conclusions to be drawn about flow conditions during deposition.

TEXTURE OF THE DEPOSITS

Of the stratified sands, in the section sampled only the upper part, layer 40, is included in this discussion of texture. The lower part of this layer was distinctly coarser and more clearly stratified than the upper part. After decalcification and removal of organic matter, which included macroscopic plant material, the remaining sediment consisted of 15% sand, mostly fine, approximately 65% silt and 15% clay. Decalcification has shifted this into a finer size grade – in its untreated state it is dominated by medium to fine shell sand. The upper part of layer 40 is finer and less clearly stratified; after decalcification and removal of organic matter, which together accounted for nearly 60% of the sample, it yielded only 3% sand, of which only a trace was medium and none coarse, about 40% silt and the rest clay. Here, though the decalcification has strongly distorted the picture, we can already see in the remaining material a considerable input of clay, which may have been travelling in coarser aggregates.

With the truncation of the deposits seen in the stratigraphic relationship at the layer 39/40 boundary and the resumption of deposition we see a change in sedimentary environment. In layer 39 the proportion of fine shell sand is much reduced, but there is a substantial non-calcareous sand component, 8%. The deposit now, however, has the character of an organic mud with a high silt content, about 50% and some 40% clay. This deposit fines upwards, losing almost all its sand and some of its silt, becoming about 65% clay. Although macroscopic plant remains are not conspicuous, there is a high amorphous humus content, and reducing conditions persist through much of the fabric, there being only oxidation via the environment of occasional roots, and that dies out downwards. Colour change on exposure to air emphasises prevailing reducing conditions, and together with lack of soil structure development shows that the deposit was never ripened by sub-aerial pedogenetic processes. We have a perennially stagnant situation accumulating predominantly fine material. The sand and silt in the lower part could well be derived from the underlying sand rather than being transported into this quiet muddy pool.

The transition to more terrestrial conditions within layer 38 is gradual, with a build-up of deposits for which the texture of the decalcified material is always dominated by clay and silt; percentages are in the range of 40–60 and 30–40 respectively, sand being between 1 and 11%, predominantly in the fine sand grade. Coarser particles in the form of the larger shell fragments and whole shells become abundant, and there is a considerable content of shell in the fine sand grade. The organic content falls, and the pedogenetic processes of a progressively more terrestrial environment produce the characteristic prismatic structure of a gleyed soil. This structure then becomes less strongly developed towards the top of the deposit as gleying becomes less intense. Oxidation in the lower part is primarily via the respiration of roots of plants adapted to life in waterlogged

soils, and one may envisage a wet, rushy meadow developing. The ground gradually becomes better drained as the deposit builds up, until the upper part, above about 65 cm, is able to enjoy aerobic soil processes in summer.

Variations within the deposit include differences in the intensity of mottling, which may relate to variations in the water table but are not so marked as to override the progressive improvement in drainage, and a markedly more humic zone, ca. 70–77 cm, which probably represents a period when deposition was slower and accumulation of humus relative to mineral sediment could increase. Overall humus levels are low once preservation by anaerobism is left behind (i.e. throughout layer 38), but it is not clear whether this is because of vigorous mineralisation below the zone of active incorporation or because deposition was so fast as to keep relative humus content down.

Formation of a humic soil by the time of the occupation shows a cessation or strong reduction in build-up of mineral sediment, and thus could have been long established by the time occupation occurred. Because of the effect of disturbance and the incorporation of anthropogenic organic residues and charred material, it is not easy to assess the degree of development of the soil, but lack of evidence for decalcification suggests a rather low degree of maturity.

The Late Bronze Age waterfront deposits (column WF1)

The deposits of the waterfront are described as they occurred in a monolith taken in a continuous series of boxes of 10 cm square cross-section. This was the monolith sampled for pollen. The description follows soil survey practice (Hodgson 1976) in so far as this is appropriate; pedological characteristics die out downwards, and concepts such as structure, strength and consistence are not applicable to the lower part of the column. Textures in this description are based on hand assessment. Boundaries between layers are all 'abrupt', that is, change from one layer to the next is via a zone of uncertainty 0.5–2.5 cm deep.

0–19 cm Layer 4
Coarse sandy loam, greyish brown, 2.5Y 4/2–5/2 moist, 2.5Y 6/2 dry, with common fine distinct to diffuse yellowish brown mottles, 10YR 5/6 dry, increasing downwards. The lower 4 cm slightly paler and less sandy. Structure compound strongly developed medium prismatic and fine angular blocky. Less than 5% fine macropores. Very strong when dry, weak when moist; moderately sticky, very plastic.

19–31 cm Layer 5
Silty clay loam, greyish brown, 2.5Y 5/2 moist, light brownish grey, 2.5Y 7/2–6/2 dry, with common fine to medium diffuse yellowish brown mottles, 10YR 5/6 dry. Charcoal fragments. Structure moderately developed fine angular blocky. Less than 5% very fine macropores, which have dark grey and greyish brown clay skins. Very strong when dry, weak when moist; moderately sticky, very plastic.

31–42 cm Layer 6
Similar to layer 5 but with greater admixture of charcoal fragments and stones and fine char, giving very dark greyish brown colour, 2.5Y–10YR 3/2 moist, greyish brown, 2.5Y 5/2 dry, with common very fine sharp mottles, colour as above but fewer. Structure becoming less well developed and soil strength weaker: weakly developed fine angular blocky; very firm when dry, very weak when moist; moderately sticky, very plastic.

42–53 cm Layer 7
Silty clay loam, marbled very pale brown, 10YR 7/3 moist, 7/2.5 dry, and light grey, 10YR 5/2 moist, 6/1.5 dry; few very fine sharp yellowish brown mottles. Scale of marbling is a few mm. Charcoal fragments appear in the bottom 3 cm and mottling increases in the bottom 2 cm to common, diffuse. Marbling is a mixture of material of slightly different texture and humic content. Structure weakly developed adherent coarse angular blocky; moderately firm when dry, very weak when moist; slightly sticky, very plastic.

52–56 cm Layer 8a
Sandy clay loam, with charcoal fragments, dark greyish brown, 2.5Y 4/2 moist, light grey to grey, mixture of 2.5Y 7/2 and 6/1 dry, with many prominent medium diffuse dark yellowish brown mottles, 10YR 4/6 moist and dry. Structure and strength as layer 7.

56–63 cm Layer 11
Silty loam, greyish brown, 2.5Y 5.5/2 moist, 7/2 dry, with common distinct to prominent fine diffuse yellow and very fine sharp yellowish red mottles, 10YR 5/6 and 2.5YR 4/8 moist, 10YR 4/6 and 5YR and 5YR 5/8 dry, the finer mottles being stains in very fine macropores. Structure massive; moderately firm when dry, very weak when moist. Slightly sticky, very plastic. <5% fine macropores, with dark grey clay skins.

63–65 cm Layer 12
Similar to above, with zones of charcoal concentration.

65–72 cm Layer 13
Clay, with a conspicuous white shell sand component. A mixture, on a scale of a few mm, of light greyish brown and pale brown, 10YR 6/2 and 6/3 moist, light grey and light greyish brown, 10YR 7/2 and 6/2 dry, with some darker grey patches and with common distinct fine diffuse mottles and few distinct very fine sharp mottles, as in layer 11. Dark grey clay skins occur in fine macropores, as above. Structure massive; moderately firm when dry, very weak when moist; moderately sticky, very plastic.

72–75 cm Layer 20b upper
Similar to above, but dark grey and more clayey component occurs as lenses and the diffuse mottling concentrates into more intense coarser horizontally zoned bands and is associated with some of the macropores, spreading into the matrix from the pore walls.

75–83 cm Layer 20b lower
Clay loam, overall colour greyish brown to brown, 10YR 5/2–5/3 moist, light grey to light greyish brown, 10YR 7/2–6/2 dry, formed of a mixture of lighter and darker areas, light greyish brown, 10YR 6/2, and dark greyish brown, 10YR 4/2, moist, on a scale of a few mm, with common medium and fine distinct mottles, strong brown, 7.5YR 6/6–5/8 moist, and some redder fine sharp mottles as stains in fine macropores. Structure massive; moderately firm when dry, very weak when moist, slightly sticky, very plastic. Some macroscopic plant remains.

83–105 cm Layer 20c
Clay loam, a mixture of dark grey, 10YR–7.5YR 4/2 and pale brown, 10YR6/3 moist, light grey, 10YR 6/1.5 and 7/2 dry, the components being more clearly separate and the scale larger than in 20b, and the dark, humic component increasing downwards, with common strong brown linings to fine macropores, with some spread of staining from them into the matrix. Structure massive; moderately firm when dry, very weak when moist; moderately sticky, very plastic.

105–110 cm Transition
Thin layers of coarse sand occur, and the pale brown component, which is now clearly sandier than the dark grey material, becomes more clearly segregated into separate thin layers. At the base there is a particularly dark and humic layer.

110–125 cm Layer 25a
Coarse shelly sand with macroscopic plant remains, including wood fragments. The upper 10 cm has loamy sand texture, with a high humic content and slight diffuse iron staining, and a band of finer loamy sand occurs obliquely in the lower 10 cm. In these areas, colours are variable, dark greyish brown, 10YR 4/2 with staining of dark yellowish brown, 10YR 4/6 moist, light greyish brown, 10YR 6/2 dry. Otherwise, the colour is a mixture of variable light to dark greyish brown and the white of the coarse shell sand.

125–138/141 cm Layer 25b
Steeply bedded alternating layers of coarse shelly sand and finer, loamy sand, as above, 2–5 cm thick, with wood fragments and charcoal. Colours as above, according to texture.

138/141–150 cm Layer 27a
Loamy coarse shelly sand, variable, with more and less loamy parts, but not so sharply layered as 25b. Colours as above.

150–165 cm Layer 25c
Slightly loamy coarse shelly sand and fine gravel.

165–190 cm (bottom of column) Layer 25d
Coarse woody detritus with shells in a loamy humic sand matrix. In the upper 10 cm the wood fragments are in the form of rounded 'wood pebbles', below this, twiggy fragments predominate.

Synthesis
The deposits described above fall into two groups, the coarse

sandy material of layers 25 and 27 and the fine loamy and clayey material of layer 20 and above. The sub-units of layers 25 and 27 vary in their texture and in their content of charcoal and wood fragments, and in the column described there is a lot of overlap in their characteristics, but the distinction between 25 and 27 is predominantly in the content of finer material and organic matter giving a loamy matrix to the coarse sand, and in the degree of sharp internal stratification. These characteristics reflect the variability of water flow. In general, both units were laid down by a swiftly flowing, rather variable stream which was redistributing sands and gravels within its channels. The distinctive 'wood pebbles' in the lower area of the deposits could have been derived from a woody peat deposit bordering the stream further up: wood fragments must have been waterlogged to have been deposited with the sands rather than carried away, and their rounded shape suggests wood already softened and then abraded by tumbling in the steam bed.

The abrupt transition to the clay-rich deposits of layer 20 is made by the loss of nearly all material coarser than fine sand and by an increase in clay and humus content. The change occurs within about 5 cm, there being small incursions of coarser sand after the failure of rapid flow as the dominant regime, but these soon cease altogether. The texture of layers 20 to 7 remains fairly uniform, with almost no coarse sand and very little medium sand. Fine sand forms a substantial component throughout, but the deposits are dominated by silt and clay. In the lower part of these fine deposits, however – that is in layer 20 – the texture as expressed macroscopically is formed by a mixture of finer, more organic material and slightly coarser, less organic material, which can just be detected by the naked eye and is clearly apparent under low magnification. In the lowest part of layer 20c, the separation of the two components is most complete, and in general the scale of the mixing becomes finer upwards. It would appear, therefore, that the sediments were laid down under two regimes, one of very quiet water in which clay settled out and humified organic material accumulated, and one in which fine sand silt was washed in by clearer water. The mixing could be due to faunal turbation or the lapping of shallow water. Alternatively, the sorting into the two components could have been produced by such lapping, but this is less likely since the poor degree of aeration of these deposits suggests a depth of quiet water rather than the oxygen-rich environment of shallow, rippling water.

The humic content of the deposits decreases upwards, the colours changing from dark grey and brown moist colours to light grey and very pale brown. At the same time the oxidation conditions change: whereas in the lower part aeration is only via pores and spreads very little into the matrix, in the upper part diffuse areas of oxidation occur throughout the fabric. This implies shallowing water, perhaps intermittent drying out. The zone of better aeration coincides with the depth over which the preservation of the piles fails and wood fragments ceased to be preserved. The occurrence of ostracods also fails at the lower boundary of the better oxidised deposits, which may accord with changes in water depth and continuity of wetness throughout the year. With the loss of humic content the mixture of finer and coarser components is less easily detected. It is particularly strongly expressed in layer 20b upper, but above this is not apparent. With drying conditions, more vigorous faunal turbation could be expected to produce complete mixing.

In the column examined, some of the layers identified in the field by their high charcoal content, and becoming more important towards the dry land, are represented only by thin charcoal-rich layers; layers 8a and 12 cannot be characterised separately except as spreads of charcoal in the sedimentary environment.

The upper layers of fine material, layers 4, 5 and 6, while still low in coarse sand, have an increase in medium sand, showing slightly higher water flow in their deposition. Oxidation is poor in layer 6 but increases upwards, and at the same time soil structural features appear, becoming well developed in layer 4, characteristic of seasonally drying floodplains with vigorous faunal activity. There appears, therefore, to be a transition from deposition in very quiet water, shallowing until drying occurs, to deposition from a stronger flow with more marked seasonality.

In summary, the deposits are those of a stream channel, giving way rapidly to those of a quiet pool or a channel margin protected from the main channel by a bar, by fringing vegetation or by artificial structures in the channel, which fills with sediment brought by intermittent inwash until it shallows and begins to dry out occasionally. The situation then becomes part of a flood-plain subject to seasonal overbank flooding. The changes are in part due to evolution of the site itself and in part to change in river regime, so that the filling up of the channel contributed to the progressive confinement of the river, on this bank at least, while greater seasonal variation of run-off ensured that high flows would break out of the channel and spread over the floodplain.

Chapter 12
Sedimentology of the Late Bronze Age channel deposits in section 33

PETE FISHER

Section 33, like the WF1 sequence, shows the interbedded fluvial deposits of the LBA channel (Fig. 20). However, as it extended further into that channel and contained a few layers not present in WF1, a separate study was conducted.

Description

The deposits here, as elsewhere on the site, were bedded on tufa deposits. The age of calcium carbonate deposition to form the tufa was not investigated. This is superseded by a bed of gravel which extends the length of the trench up to the LBA wooden piling. This gravel is described in field notes as a medium to coarse gravel, reflecting its modal particle size, giving in this case a coarse gravel or cobble maximum size. The deposits overlying this gravel were deposited in a generally U-shaped feature. The oldest deposits (layers 25g, h and f) drape the basal gravel, and reach the top of the section at the point furthest from the Bronze Age piling. Subsequent layers are laid down broadly parallel to the surface of these layers. The particle size varied considerably, with a general sand character incorporating small lenses of gravel-sized material, and interbedded with silty deposits. The most recent deposit (layer 9) was very organic, probably a peat (Table 2).

Grab samples of the deposits overlying the basal medium to coarse gravel were taken, this being the most appropriate method for the shallow section with the varied deposits encountered. In the laboratory the particle size distribution of the samples was measured by a combination of dry sieving of the sand and gravel fractions and pipette analysis of the finer material (Figure 110; British Standards Institution 1975). Summary statistics (mean, sorting, skewness and mode) of the distribution were calculated, using the formulae given by Folk and Ward (1957) and are shown in Table 18. As a by-product of the analyses the carbonate and organic matter contents of the finer samples were also determined (Table 19). From the particle size analyses it is possible to make an estimate of river velocities (Table 19). This assumes the material to have been in transport to this point on the river, and therefore the size can be associated with the flow at transition from transportation to deposition (Hjulstrom 1935). The 95th percentile of size is used to estimate velocity (Cheetham 1976). Unfortunately it is not possible to estimate discharge rates from the available information; it would also be necessary to know the contemporary stream cross-section at least.

Interpretation

The outstanding characteristic of the deposits sampled is their variability: samples with particle size classes from gravel to clay, mean sizes from 2 mm to 0.007 mm are included; all samples are poorly to very poorly sorted; the skewness varies from very slightly negatively skewed (−0.1) to very positively skewed (0.47). Such sorting and skewness values are characteristic of fluvial deposits in general and appear to be unrelated to mean size. The size variability of the samples is therefore the more interesting property. The general trend confirms the field observations mentioned above, and shows a fining upward sequence, indicating a generally reducing flow rate in the immediate vicinity of the piles; a rapid flow rate would have created the basal gravels and relatively stagnant water would have been associated with the upper peats and silts. Stagnant water in the upper part of the sequence is confirmed by the recognition of large quantities of diatoms in the layers 9, 20 and 21a (see below).

It can be inferred from this sequence that the basal gravel, layer 30, is a lag deposit formed at the base of the river soon before or during the Late Bronze Age period. It can also be inferred that the peat, layer 9, reflects the top of the water level in the river at the time of its formation, somewhat later.

Within the sequence up to layer 21, gravel lenses are common. Thereafter, they are relatively scarce. The presence of the gravel indicates dramatically changing flow velocities (and by implication river discharges) at this time. The relatively sudden change from these lower silts, sands and gravels (layer 25) to the stillwater conditions implies that these may have occurred due to a channel cut-off or ox-bow type phenomenon. The implication of this is that during the accumulation of layers 21, 20 and 9 the river only reached the piles during high discharge events (i.e. floods); the rest of the time, the reach within about 2 m of the piles (at least) would have supported stagnant and not open water. It would appear that at least part of the Bronze Age occupation of the site would have been associated with stagnant water against this river bank.

Diatoms

An exhaustive study of the diatoms found has not been made. The most common species found has been identified as *Melosira arenaria* (J Penn, pers. comm.; Marciniak 1973). This species is now believed to be extinct in the Thames, the genus being represented by *M. varians* (F M Speller, pers. comm.). The significance of this change may be due to a number of environmental factors including temperature change and acidity (Batterbee 1984; Round 1957).

Summary

River deposits associated with the period of Late Bronze Age occupation at Runnymede Bridge were investigated.

Table 18: Particle size summary statistics for channel sediments in section 33.

Sample number	Archaeological layer number	Mean size (phi)	Sorting	Skewness	Mode (phi)	Verbal description
1	20	6.96	3.17	0.1	0.68	C
2	9	5.45	2.54	0.44	1.21	SZL
4	21a	4.63	2.6	0.44	1.51	SL
5	25a	−0.55	2.27	−0.1	0.84	SG
6	25b	5.06	3.08	0.45	0.89	SL
7	27a	5.91	3.06	0.47	0.67	CL
8	25a	−1.51	2.32	−0.04	0.67	SG
9	25d	−0.15	2.45	0.23	0.84	SG
10	25e	1.4	1.54	−0.11	1.89	S
11	25f	−1.9	2.08	0.45	0.68	MG

MG–medium gravel; S–sand: SG–sandy gravel: SL–sandy loam; SZL–sandy silt loam; CL–clay loam; C–clay.

Table 19: Velocity estimates and chemical analyses for channel sediments in section 33.

Sample number	Mean size (phi)	95th percentile (mm)	Implied velocity (cm/s)	Organic matter (%)	Calcium carbonate (%)
1	6.96	0.12	0.9	24	36
2	5.45	0.4	3	5	31
4	4.63	0.45	3.2	7	31
5	−0.55	15	90	nd	nd
6	5.05	17	95	8	24
7	5.9	0.2	1.4	8	33
8	−1.14	19	100	nd	nd
9	−0.15	15	90	nd	nd
10	1.4	4	30	nd	nd
11	−1.9	19	100	nd	nd

Velocity is found by using the 95th percentile and the graph of Hjulstrom (1935).

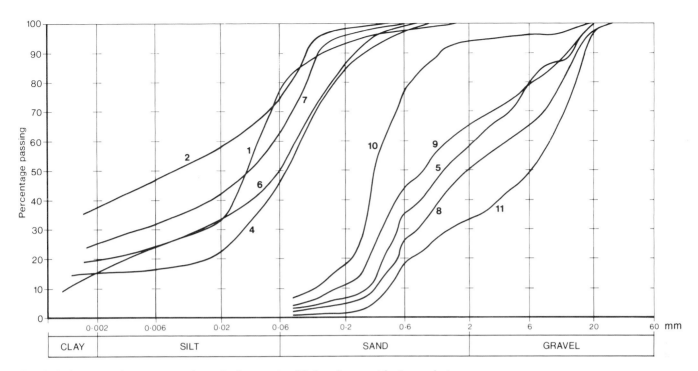

Fig. 110 Sediment characteristics of samples from section 33, based on particle size analysis.

The deposits occupy part of the channel feature, and can be divided into upper and lower deposits. The particle size analyses of the deposits show the earlier, lower material to be anything from gravel to silt, which can be related to a greatly fluctuating discharge. The later deposits, on the other hand, were created by generally slower flow rates, probably culminating in stagnant water and possibly associated with a cut-off channel. This last interpretation is supported not only by the presence of peats but also by the occurrence of diatoms within them.

Chapter 13
The identification of wood remains

Rowena Gale

Introduction Stuart Needham

Wood and charcoal remains from the excavated area were consistently kept for species identification, while the salvage operation only allowed more sporadic sampling. Area 6 yielded a good quantity of wood remains, which fall into five categories: structural timbers, portable artifacts, trimming debris, driftwood and charcoal deposits, the last sometimes very concentrated. All categories apply to the Late Bronze Age material, only some to the Neolithic. The assemblage therefore seemed to offer excellent opportunities for, firstly, contrasting Neolithic and Late Bronze Age species compositions with one another and the respective pollen records and, secondly, examining wood selection strategies against a 'natural' background, especially for the Late Bronze Age. The aims of the identification programme were hindered to some extent by the loss of a wood specialist on the staff of the Ancient Monuments Laboratory in 1978. This led to some delay whilst organising for the work to be contracted out and the consequent deterioration of a small proportion of waterlogged samples.

A cautionary note is perhaps necessary regarding the statistical viability of the species count. The time available for the excavation did not allow detailed recording of all recovered wood, where it was not structural or otherwise significant. Consequently, broken pieces in some context groups may well have derived from a smaller number of *in situ* branches thus leading to some measure of duplication in the figures tabulated. Having said this, the broad trends identified in the results may be regarded as a true representation of the archaeological record.

The range and structure of samples

The samples submitted for identification were woody in structure. The greater proportion consisted of waterlogged wood, with some charcoal and partially carbonised material also present. A few samples of previously wet wood had dried out, with the subsequent loss of cellular structure.

The smaller samples appeared to be unworked and ranged from branches and twigs, many with the bark still *in situ*, to small fragments of wood and loose bark. Worked artifacts were represented by a large number of piles, some over a metre in length and up to 20 cm in diameter. Usually the bark was not present, sometimes having fallen away on excavation. The lower, pointed ends of the piles were consistently in a more stable condition than the upper extremities, which, having been exposed to a more aerobic environment probably with greater moisture fluctuations, had suffered badly from invasive rot.

The waterlogged wood was generally in a very poor condition and varied from being 'spongy' to the touch to crumbly (some samples have disintegrated completely). Fungal hyphae, present in nearly all the samples, had caused a considerable degree of cellular destruction. In addition some samples had also suffered from compression whilst in the ground. The subsequent lack of diagnostic features in some of this material, together with the effects of dehydration, has made the identification of some fragments difficult or impossible (sometimes tentative names have been given).

The carbonised material, on the other hand, was remarkably well preserved, although some pieces were rather friable.

Annual ring counts

An accurate ring count can only be achieved by determining

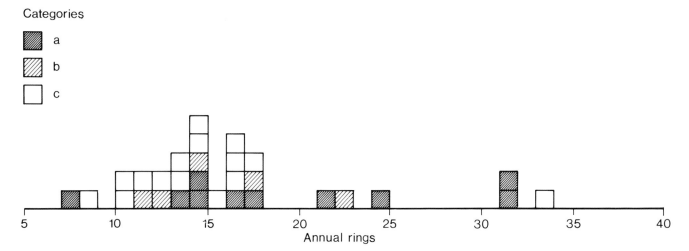

Fig. 111 Distribution of annual ring counts of the oak piles from the inner and outer rows. For definition of categories see the text.

the number of annual growth rings present on the transverse surface from the core of the sample to the vascular cambial region. Many of the Runnymede samples lacked bark and the exposed outer surfaces were often decayed or damaged. Counts were recorded as incomplete when it was evident that some outer rings of sapwood were missing. In some instances when piles had been excavated intact, no ring counts were possible as no true transverse areas were available for examination. In a few samples the heartwood and sapwood were well differentiated and the number of rings in each were noted. The results have been tabulated and divided into different categories to separate the piles with sapwood intact from those with minimal trimmings or damage and those with considerable loss of sapwood (Fig. 111). The categories are defined as follows:

a) either: all sapwood present, with or without bark, or: probably complete to unworked edge – good sapwood presence, but no bark;
b) edge worked at point counted, but clear that little had been removed;
c) either: probably or certainly some ring loss due to trimming or damage, or: no information on completeness.

Sampling and preparation techniques

Where large quantities of fragments came from a particular context they were examined individually, using a ×20 hand lens, and sorted into groups based on the features visible on the transverse surface – e.g. ray width, vessel size and distribution. A representative sample from each group was then prepared for more detailed examination at high magnifications. Occasionally it was obvious that a single sample had fractured into several segments.

WATERLOGGED WOOD

Cubes, approximately 0.5 cm in size, were removed from the samples and, to give support during sectioning, these were frozen for several hours until solid. Thin sections were taken by hand, using a double-sided razor blade, in the transverse, tangential longitudinal and radial longitudinal planes. These were mounted in 50% glycerol on microscope slides. A stereo light-microscope was used for examination at magnifications up to ×400.

DRIED WOOD

Dried samples were revived by boiling in water until soft enough to section and then treated as for waterlogged wood.

CARBONISED WOOD

Fragments were pressure-fractured to expose clean, flat surfaces in the same planes as described above and mounted in Plasticine on microscope slides. These were examined using an epi-illuminating microscope.

The anatomical structure was matched to authenticated reference material.

BARK

The anatomical structure of the phloem and cortical region (bark) of many British trees is very similar and, unless some secondary xylem (wood) is still attached, it is usually very difficult to identify. The morphology of calcium oxylate or calcium carbonate crystals present in most species is of diagnostic value but these rarely survive in archaeological material of this type, and none were found to be present. It was therefore not possible to identify the bark using anatomical methods.

Species represented by woody remains on the site

The identifications are listed in detail in Table 20. Tables 21–23 group the results according to broad context and phase. It is not usually possible to identify to species level, but the early dating of this site suggests that this material arose from native species rather than from later introductions. These have therefore been included in the list of species represented in the woody material from Runnymede.

Aceraceae

Acer campestre L., field maple
A woodland tree often associating with ash or hazel (Rackham 1986), growing particularly on chalk but tolerating most soils. Coppices well.

Aquifoliaceae

Ilex acquifolium L., holly
A slow-growing, prickly-leaved evergreen that casts and tolerates dense shade, and often grows as understorey in oak or beech woods, or in stands in open land and clearings on either acid or calcareous soil.

Betulaceae

Alnus glutinosa (L.) Gaertn., alder
Alder grows on the moist, rich soils of river banks and streams, and also as a woodland tree sometimes mixed with oak. Alder coppices well and, historically, the bark has been used for tanning.

Corylaceae

Corylus avellana L., hazel
When growing as understorey, often with oak, ash or maple, hazel can attain a height of 10 m, with a trunk up to 25 cm in diameter. More usually this species is seen as a shrubby plant of woodland margins, clearings and scrub. The nutritious nuts are only produced on sunlit branches. It is suited to most soils and was one of the most commonly coppiced species; remnants of coppice woodlands still survive.

Fagaceae

Quercus robur L., English oak
A common woodland tree on the lowlands, and dominant on basic loams and clays.

Quercus petraea (Mattuschka) Liebl., durmast oak
A woodland tree, generally with a more northerly and westerly distribution but occasionally mixing with *Q. robur* on the lighter soils in the south. Today old oak woods are found on very acid, infertile soil (Rackham 1986). Oak coppices well and the bark was one of the major sources of tannin.

Oleaceae

Fraxinus excelsior L., ash
A light-demanding tree, frequently colonizing cleared or open areas. The ash population in Britain increased significantly after the 'elm decline', ca. 5000 BP. Although a woodland tree, it also grows in more solitary positions along river banks and in hedgerows. A successful coppice tree.

Rhamnaceae

Rhamnus cathartica L., buckthorn
A spiny, shrubby species growing up to 10 m tall in marginal woodland, scrub and open ash or oak woods, on chalk or clay horizons overlying chalk.

Rosaceae

SUBFAMILY POMOIDEAE

This group includes several species that are very similar anatomically. These are mainly trees of secondary woodland.

Crataegus laevigata (Poiret) DC., may or hawthorn
A small, spiny tree which tolerates shade and often grows as understorey with ash, maple or hazel.

C. monogyna Jacq., may or hawthorn
A spiny shrub or tree often colonising clearings or open land, where it may form scrub.

Both species dislike extremely acid soils and produce edible fruits.

Malus sylvestris (L.) Mill., crab apple
A woodland tree. Fruits edible.

Sorbus aria (L.) Crantz., whitebeam
A tree usually found on calcareous soils, particularly on escarpments and in association with yew. Fruits edible.

S. aucuparia L., rowan or mountain ash
A tree more commonly growing at altitudes up to 1000 m in the north of Britain; probably not native in the south. Fruits edible.

Sorbus torminalis (L.) Crantz., wild service tree
A woodland tree on clay soils, nowadays very rare. Fruits edible.

SUBFAMILY PRUNOIDEAE

Prunus avium L., wild cherry or gean
A woodland tree growing on light, well-drained, rich soils, sometimes occurring on clay overlying chalk and often associating with beech. Fruits edible.

P. padus L., bird cherry
A tree with a northerly distribution, often growing at altitudes up to 620 m.

P. spinosa L., blackthorn or sloe
A large, spiny shrub frequenting marginal woodland and colonising open land, rapidly forming dense thickets. Fruits edible but very sour.

Salicaceae

Populus nigra L., black poplar
A tree of flood-plains and river banks.

P. tremula L., aspen
A tree thriving on rich alluvial soils, particularly in seasonally wet, plateau woods (Rackham 1986).

Salix alba L., white willow
A tree growing on rich, alluvial soils, particularly along river banks and in damp sites.

S. caprea L., goat willow
A smaller tree than the other named species, found in woods, scrub and hedges.

S. fragilis L., crack willow
A tree growing in similar environments to white willow but more tolerant of poor soils. In addition there are many shrubby species of willow.

The anatomical structures of poplar and willow wood are very similar and they cannot be separated on this basis.

Ulmaceae

Ulmus glabra Huds., wych elm
A woodland tree but also growing besides streams on rich, well-drained, alluvial soil.

U. procera Salisb., English elm
A tree of similar habitat to the above. There are several other species which have very localised distributions.

Ulmus was one of the dominant genera in the early post-glacial woodlands but in about 5000 BP the elm populations appear to have been drastically reduced. However, populations re-established, probably encouraged by the regeneration of young trees from root suckers, in addition to the more usual method of seed germination.

Table 20: Wood identifications from Runnymede Bridge.

Species abbreviations
Ac – *Acer campestre*, field maple. Al – *Alnus glutinosa*, alder. Co – *Corylus avellana*, hazel. Fr – *Fraxinus excelsior*, ash. Il – *Ilex aquifolium*, holly. Po – Family Rosaceae subfamily Pomoideae; *Crataegus* spp., hawthorns, *Malus* sp., apple, *Sorbus* spp., whitebeam and rowan. Pr – *Prunus* spp., blackthorn and cherry. Qu – *Quercus* spp., oaks. Sa – Family Salicaceae, which includes *Salix* spp., willows, and *Populus* spp., populars. Rh – *Rhamnus cathartica*, buckthorn. Ul – *Ulmus* spp., elms.

Other abbreviations
C – Charcoal or partially carbonised wood.
W – Undiagnostic waterlogged wood; possibly driftwood but may be associated with waste from worked wood, e.g. trimmings, when occurring in the cultural layers.
ED – Estimated diameter in centimetres.
RC – Annual ring count.

Neolithic

Area 4: Piles: S1 – Qu; S2 – prob. Qu; S4 – Qu;
Brush: L3a – Qu.
Area 5: Branches (? structure): F294a – Sa. (ED11); F294b – Sa. (ED 14); F294c – Co. (ED4); F294d – ? Co. (ED12); F294e – Co. (ED9); F294f – Co. (ED7); F294g – Sa. (ED12); F294i – Co. (ED3.5); 781192:1 – 1Pr, 2Co.; 781192:2 – ?1Sa, 2Qu.; 781192:3 – 3Co/Al.; SA – ?Sa.
Area 6: Piles: F168 – Sa.; F184 – Qu.; F202a – Al.; F204 – Qu.;
Charcoal: L41 – 8Fr(C)
Driftwood: L40 – 21Sa., 16Al.; L40 4E/5N – 1Qu.(C), 1Pr.(C); L40/41 – 2Al., 1Sa., ?1Pr.; L41 – 8A1., 3Sa., ?1A1.; L41 7E/7N – 1A1.; L41 12E/9N – 9A1., F205 – Qu.

Neolithic or Bronze Age

Area 4: Piles: Inner row F13 – Qu.; F14 – Qu.; F15 – Qu.; F18 – Qu.; F20 – Qu.; F28 – Qu.; F83 – Qu; F88 – Qu.
Inner row/outer row: F16 – Qu.; F27 – Qu.; F27a – Qu.
Driftwood: F88A – Al.; F88B – ?Qu.
Area 4A: Pile: F74 – Fr.

Late Bronze Age

Area 5: Salvaged pile: F292 – Qu.
Area 6: River channel, stratigraphic unit:
A) L26 – 2Qu.(C); L25c – 2Qu.(W), 1Fr.(C); L27 – 5Qu.(C), 1Ul.(C), 3Co.(C), 2Al.(W), ?2Al.(W).
B) general: L25a–b 12E/11N – 5Qu,(C), 2Fr.(C), 1Al(C); L25a–b 12E/12N – 7Qu.(C); L25 18–19E/9N 5Qu.(C); L24 12E/10N – 1Qu.(C); L24 11E/11N – 2Qu.(C); L24*/25c – 2Qu.(W); L25 18–19E/9N – 10Qu.(W), 2Fr.(W), 3Al.(W). L25 20E/10N – 1Al.(W).
B) branches: F163 – 5Qu.; F163/1 – ?1Sa.; F163/2 – 1Ac. (ED14); F163/3 – 1Qu.(ED 2.5 RC9); F163/4 – 1Qu.(ED4RC8); F163/5 – 1Qu.(ED3 RC8); F163/6 – 1Qu. (ED3 RC7); F163/7 – 1Co.(ED2); F193 – 1Qu.(ED3); F194 – 1Qu.(ED3); F207 –1Qu.
C) general: L19 – 1Qu.(C); L14e/20c 10E/13N – 3Qu.(W); L20c/23a 10E/12N – 4Qu.(W); L20d 9E/11N – 1Qu.(C); L20d 10E/11N – 1Qu.(W); L20 12E/11N – 1Qu.(W); L20 13E/11N – 4Fr.(C), 9Qu.(C); L20 14E/11N – 3Qu.(C), 1 Po.(W), 1Al.(W); L20 13E/12N – 2Qu.(C); L20 10E/13N – 8Qu.(C); L20 17E/10N – ?2Qu.(C); L20 18E/10N – 1Ac.(C), ?1Po.(W); L20 19E/10N – 1Po.(C); L20 17E/11N – 2Fr.(W), 2Pr.(W), 1Qu.(W); L20 excess soil samples – 4Qu.(C), ?40Qu.(C), 3Pr.(C); L20 17E/10 – 11N – 1Co.(C); L20c/21 – several frags. Qu.(C), few frags. Al.(W).
C) midden sequence: L20c – Qu.(W); L20c 10E/12N – 1Il.(C); L20c 8E/13N – 6Qu.(C); 2Al.(W), 1Co.(W); L19 – 1Qu.(W), 3Al.(W), 8Fr.(W,C), 5Qu.(C), 3Co.(C).
C/D) inner pile row: F114 – Qu. F229 – Qu. F115 – Qu. F231 – Qu. F116 – Qu. F235 – Qu. F117 – Qu. F236 – Qu. F119 – Qu. F237 – Qu. F120 – Qu. F239 – Qu. F121 – Qu. F240 – Qu. F122 – Qu. F242 – Qu. F129 – Qu. F243 – Qu. F130 – Qu. F244 – Qu. F131 – Qu. F265 – Qu. F132 – Qu. F268 – Qu. F134 – Qu. F270 – Qu. F167 – Qu. F274 – Qu. F188 – Qu. F276 – Qu. F189 – Qu. F285 – Qu. F224 – Qu. F286 – Qu. F225 – Qu. F287 – Qu. F226 – Qu. F288 – Qu.
D) general: L13 16E/9N – 4Qu.(C, ED2), 1Fr.(C, ED6); L14 15E/9N – 6Pr.(W); L14 – 1Qu.(W); F206 – 5Qu.(C), 5Co.(C), 1Fr.(C).
E) outer pile row: F142 – Qu. F173 – Qu. F143 – Qu. F174 – Qu. F144 – Qu. F179 – Qu. F145 – Qu. F146 – Qu. F180 – Qu. F181 – Qu. F166 – Qu. F192 – Qu. F170 – Qu. F171 – Qu. F199 – Qu. F172 – Qu. F208 – Qu. F209 – Qu. F210 – Qu. F165 – Qu. F213 – Qu. (F271) – Qu. F215 – Qu. F272 – Sa. F216 – Qu. F275 – Qu. F217 – Qu. F277 – Qu. F218 – Qu. F278 – Qu. F219 – Qu. F279 – Qu. F220 – Qu. F280 – Qu. F221 – Qu. F281 – Qu. F222 – Qu. F282 – Qu. F223 – Qu. F283 – Qu. F230 – Qu. F284 – Qu. F241 – Qu.
F) hardstandings – branches: F155/1 – Qu.(ED10, RC16); F155/2 – ?Qu.(ED?6, C); F155/3 – Qu.(ED7); F164/1 – Qu.(ED7); F164/2 – Qu.(ED4); F164/3 – Qu.(ED7); F164/4 – ?Qu. F164/5 – Qu.(ED6); F164/6 – Insufficient structure to identify but part of 164/2; F164/7 – ?Qu.(ED7); F164/8 – Qu.(ED7); F164/9 – Qu.(ED7, RC7); F164/10 – Qu.(ED8) probably same as 164/9; F164/11 – Qu.(ED6 RC6) probably part of 164/3; F164/12 –Insufficient structure to identify
– poles: F164 – mostly Pr.(C,W), some Fr.(C,W), ED 1–2.5; F164 – 24Qu.(ED 1.5–3, RC 4–8), 2Al.(ED3), 1Co.(ED2).

G)   (+E) general: L8 – 4Qu. (C), 6Ac.(C), 2Po.(C); L9 top 17E/10N –1Qu.(W), 1Co.(C); L9 18E/10N – 1Qu.(C), 1Co.(C), 1Pr.(C); L9 17E/11N – 2Qu.(W), 4Pr.(W); L9 18E/11N – 2Qu.(W), 3Ac.(W), 1Al.(W), 1?Pr.(W); L9 19E/10N – 2Sa.(W), 1Po.(W); L9 17E/10N – 1?Qu.(W), 1Co.(W).

Unphased piles – rear braces: F126 – Qu.
        – outliers: F147 – Qu. F169 – Sa. F200 – Qu. F212 – Qu.

Salvage: F291 – Qu.

Features: F300/L18 (Units C–D) – 5Qu.(C); F6L6 – 3Co.(C), 1Al.(C), 2Qu. (C); F6L4 – Quercus present; F6L3 – 9Qu.(C), 4?Ac.(C), 2Sa.(C); F6L2 – 24Qu.(C), 3Po.(C), 2Rh.(C), 1Pr.(C), 1Ac.(C); F6L1 – 3Qu.(C).

Occupation: L32–37 – 1Co.(C), 2Po.(C).

Artifacts: SF93 – 1Ac. SF96 – 1Qu. ladle/cup SF98 – ?1Pr.

Soil columns:
    SS1 175–180 – 2 fragments of bark; 185–190 – ?2Al.(W); 190–195 – small fragments of bark.
    WF1a 20–25 – 1?Pr.(W); 30–35 – Po.(W); 35–40 – 2Sa.(C).
    WF1b 65–70 – 4Qu.(C); 110–115 – ?Pr.(W); 115–120 – Fr.(C), Pr.(W), ?Al.(W); 120–125 – Qu. (C), Pr.(W), Co.(W); 125–130 – Qu.(C); 130–135 – Qu.(C); 135–140 – Al.(W), Pr.(W); 140–145 – Qu.(W), ?Pr.(W); 145–150 – small twigs too compressed to identify. 150–155 – Pr.(W); 155–160 – Al.(W); 165–170 – Al. (W); 170–175 – Fr.(C), Sa.(W).

Table 21: Summary of Neolithic wood and charcoal identifications by context group, Areas 4, 5 and 6.

	Ac.	Al.	Co.	Fr.	Il.	Pr.	Qu.	Rh.	Po.	Sa.	Ul.
Area 4:											
Piles S1, S2, S4							3				
Brush L3a							1				
Area 5:											
Branches, F294		(1)	6(2)			1	2				3(2)
Area 6:											
Layer 41		18(1)	8				1				3
Worked timbers in											
L41 and L40:											
F168, F184,											
F202, F204		1					2				1
Layer 40/41											
interface		2				(1)					1
Layer 40		16				1	1				21

NB. Abbreviations as for Table 20; ( ) – uncertain identifications.

Table 22: Summary of Late Bronze Age and uncertainly dated wood identifications from Area 4.

	Ac.	Al.	Co.	Fr.	Il.	Pr.	Qu.	Rh.	Po.	Sa.	Ul.
Piles on line of											
LBA waterfront:											
Inner row:											
F13, 14, 15, 18,											
20, 28, 83, 88							8				
Outer *or* inner											
row:											
F16, 27, 27a							3				
Pile in Area 4A,											
F74						1					
Driftwood, F88A,											
88B		1					(1)				

NB. Abbreviations as for Table 20; ( ) – uncertain identifications.

Discussion

Neolithic wood/charcoal

The evidence shows that, although a wide range of tree species grew in the locality, oak was particularly selected for use as piles. Of the eight piles in this phase six are oak, one is willow/poplar and one alder. Oak trunks from young trees, with diameters up to 15 cm, were used whole, with the branches trimmed away and the bark left *in situ*. The sapwood region in young trees of this size is relatively large in comparison to the heartwood. Sapwood is far more vulnerable to attack by external pathogenic organisms than the heartwood, and the risk of attack is increased when points of entry are created, as by de-barking, lopping of branches and exposure at the extremities. In all probability, those building piled structures had no reason to remove the bark, but they may also have known that leaving it in place would help protect the piles from rot.

It is impossible to detect on anatomical grounds whether these timbers were seasoned before use, but the nature of their use was, in any case, very similar to one of the traditional methods of seasoning heart of oak, i.e. steeping in water for several years.

The wood of both alder and willow/poplar is very soft and perishable. When permanently immersed in water alder wood becomes extremely durable and one of its traditional uses is for revetting river banks; the same is true of some species of willow, and these have been used, more recently, for making steamer paddles and water-mill wheels (Edlin 1949).

The brushwood structure associated with the piles in Area 4 also included oak.

Another possible structure, recorded as a mass of branches, was found in Area 5. Although the dominant species appeared to be hazel and willow/poplar, others, including *Prunus* and oak, were also present. It was not possible to count the annual rings, but the estimated diameters ranged from 3.5 to 14 cm, which suggest that this material was not coppice wood but was culled from branches or more mature stems.

An accumulation of waterlogged wood occurred in layers 40–41, but it is possible that this was merely driftwood rather than having been associated with occupation. This included alder, oak, *Prunus* and poplar/willow. Only one context in these layers yielded carbonised wood and, in this material, the only (certain) representative of ash in the Neolithic period.

Late Bronze Age and undated (Area 4)

Eleven piles from the outer and inner rows of the Late Bronze Age waterfront construction were oak, and a twelfth undated pile was ash. Ash timber is renowned for its strength and resilience; however, when used in conjunction with water it is extremely perishable. A small quantity of waterlogged oak and alder, possibly driftwood, was also included in this group from Area 4.

Late Bronze Age (Area 6)

RIVER CHANNEL (STRATIGRAPHIC UNITS A–G)

A   The lowest layers of the river channel included a mixture of waterlogged and carbonised wood, with species such as oak, ash, alder, hazel and elm represented.

B   General: Charred wood, mainly oak, but also some ash and alder, gave an indication of possible land clearance. Some waterlogged wood of similar species was also present.

B   Branches: A group of branches found in close association with each other (F163) included two pieces substantially larger in diameter than the remaining five. One of these, with an estimated diameter of 14 cm, was field maple. The other, which was in very poor condition, was probably willow/poplar. The five rod-like structures were predominantly oak, with one hazel. The estimated diameters of these ranged from 2 to 4 cm, and the annual ring counts from 7 to 9. These measurements, together with the morphology of the material, suggest a possibility of coppice wood and, by implication, a derivation from settlement activities.

C   General: This fragmented material consisted of both waterlogged and carbonised wood. There was a wide range of species present, including oak, ash, hazel, field maple, alder, *Prunus* and the Pomoideae group, and although much of this was charcoal (suggesting a residue from human activity), some could have drifted in the river from a wider catchment.

C   Midden sequence: Fragments of charcoal and waterlogged wood in these layers included oak, alder, ash and holly: the latter carbonised and the only representative of holly from the site.

C/D Inner pile row: 38 posts from the inner pile row were identified; all were oak and of similar description to those previously referred to in the Neolithic section.

D   General: A background of charred and waterlogged fragments contemporary with the first pile structure included oak, ash, *Prunus* and hazel.

E   Outer pile row: 43 piles were sampled from the outer row and, with the exception of one of willow/poplar, these were oak. Species of both willow and poplar would have grown large enough to have provided the timber for this purpose but, as previously stated, willow would have been more suitable.

The annual rings on the piles from both the inner and outer rows were counted where possible and the results are shown in Fig. 111. These indicate the use of young trees ranging from 8 to 32 years of age, with the majority grouped between 12 and 25 years. Maximum diameters are given in Table 4.

F   Hardstandings – branches and poles: A large structure

probably forming a hardstanding yielded a mass of material. The large branches, several lying parallel to each other, had diameters estimated mainly at around 7 cm. Set obliquely to these was a large collection of fragmented poles. A representative sample was examined and showed a predominance of oak, with estimated diameters from 1.5 to 3 cm. Ring counts were possible on 12 of these, with the following results (annual ring counts = RC): RC4 – one sample; RC5 – one sample; RC6 – two samples; RC7 – six samples; RC8 – two samples. In addition, alder and hazel were minimally represented.

A further sample from this context included some partially charred fragments of *Prunus* and ash, with estimated diameters ranging from 1 to 2.5 cm.

G(+E) General: Woody fragments, comprising both charcoal and waterlogged wood (some possibly drift) associated with the peat lagoon which developed in the river channel, included oak, field maple, hazel, *Prunus*, willow/poplar, alder and the Pomoideae group.

UNPHASED PILES

This group included a further seven piles, mainly oak with one willow/poplar. Four outliers, one from the rear braces and two salvaged from the main rows in Areas 5 and 6 make up the total.

FEATURES

Wood from F6 was mainly in the form of charcoal and, although evidently selected and used by the occupants of the site, it is not possible to speculate as to this use. Charcoal included oak, alder, hazel, field maple, willow/poplar and *Prunus*, buckthorn and the Pomoideae group.

OCCUPATION

Background material included fragments of carbonised hazel, and the Pomoideae group.

ARTIFACTS

Wood chosen for these included field maple, oak and probably *Prunus*; the latter was used to fashion a small cup or ladle.

SOIL COLUMNS

SS1: one fragment only of identifiable woody material was available for study from this column, tentatively named as alder; and in addition a few pieces of unidentified bark.

WF1: The WF column was more productive, with a mixture of waterlogged and carbonised materials occurring throughout the column. The bulk of the charcoal was deposited at depths of 35–40 and 135–140 cm. Carbonised material identified as ash was present at the base level at a depth of 170–175 cm.

The concordance between these samples and the river channel stratigraphy is shown in Fig. 109.

Table 23: Summary of Late Bronze Age wood and charcoal identifications by context groups from Area 6.

	Ac.	Al.	Co.	Fr.	Il.	Pr.	Qu.	Rh.	Po.	Sa.	Ul.
River channel stratigraphic unit: A)		2(2)	3	1			9				1
B) general		5		4			32				
branches	1			1			12			(1)	
C) general	1	1+X	1	6+X		5	38+X (42)	1(2)			
midden		5	4	8		1	13				
C/D) inner pile row							38				
D) general			5	2		(6)	10				
E) outer pile row							41(1)			1	
F) hard standings – branches							8(3)				
– poles		2	1	X		x	24				
G) (+E) general	7(2)	1	3			1(5)	7(6)		3	2	
Unphased piles: Rear braces							1				
Outliers							3			1	
Salvage A6 + A5							2				
Features: F300L18 (unit C-D)							5				
F6 L6			1	3			2				
L3 and 4		(4)					9+X			2	
L2 and 1	1					1	27	2	3	2	
Occupation: L32–37			1						2		
Artifacts:	1					(1)	1				

NB. Abbreviations as for Table 20
( ) uncertain identifications; X unquantified but well represented; x unquantified and poorly represented.

Conclusion

Analysis of the sedimentary, molluscan and pollen deposits suggests changes in the environment occurring throughout the Neolithic and Bronze Age phases. This is also borne out by the identification of the woody plant remains from this site.

The material identified from the Neolithic phases of occupation shows a fairly limited range of species compared to the Late Bronze Age, and these tend to represent the larger trees; to a certain extent this may be a reflection of the fact that much less material was available from these early contexts. Certainly oak and ash were present and probably formed woodlands in the near locality of the river. Alder, willow/poplar were probably more confined to the damper soils along the river banks; the absence of poplar pollen (examined by James Grieg) suggests that wood from this species is unlikely. *Prunus* wood, associated with one of the structures, may have originated from cherry but, since blackthorn is the only *Prunus* pollen identified (see Chapter 14) from the site, it seems more likely that the wood is also from this species. Blackthorn dislikes heavy shade, and therefore there is the suggestion that some clearance had already occurred.

Following this, during the Late Bronze Age, a wider range of species is evident, including those associated with the formation of secondary woodland. In addition to the woodland trees of oak and ash, field maple is added, and also other species of lesser stature, some of which can occur in either shade or clearings, such as holly, hazel and some members of the Pomoideae group. The individual members of the latter cannot be recognised by the wood anatomy but some can probably be ruled out: e.g. rowan, on the grounds of its geographical distribution, and both apple and the wild service tree, neither of which is represented in the pollen deposits. This leaves hawthorn and whitebeam, both of which are present as pollen. Buckthorn also suggests marginal woodland or scrub.

The suggestion that much of the original woodland had been cleared by or during the Late Bronze Age also appears to be confirmed by the abundance of young oak trees available for the construction of the waterfront. The piles examined from this phase were all made from trunks of young trees, none being older than 35 years – very young in terms of the life expectancy of oak, which usually survives for several hundred years and can produce a bole several metres in circumference.

A well-established, closed oak woodland will include a high proportion of mature trees and relatively few saplings. A more open woodland encourages the growth of seed germination and sapling growth. Young trees were felled on two separate occasions to provide the piles, and the 78 excavated may represent only a fraction of the total number involved. The inner row has been dated to ca. 920–880 cal BC and it is probable that some 50–100 years elapsed before work started on the outer row, which should have allowed some time for regeneration. It seems likely that these young trees were growing in a fairly open secondary woodland environment.

It is also possible that some form of woodland management was in operation, and indeed the repeated employment of young stems for structures such as the beaching ramp seems to support this. The predominance of seven-year-old stems conforms with the long-established custom of harvesting the rods on a seven-year cycle. The dominant coppice wood appears to be oak. As discussed previously, large numbers of young oaks were felled for building and, unless the roots of these trees were destroyed after felling, they would naturally have initiated coppice stools.

The influence of the elm decline at Runnymede is discussed in James Grieg's pollen report and supported by the absence of woody material until well into the Bronze Age. Although elm wood makes a poor fuel, the timber is extremely strong and very resistant to decay when used under water, thus making a highly suitable wood for piles. The evidence for lack of its use for this purpose may reflect not only its scarcity but also the difficulty of working it (arising from the crossed orientation of the fibres).

Several species represented by pollen on the site are noticeably absent as woody material. These include lime, beech, birch, pine and elder.

It is evident that during the Neolithic and Bronze Ages, selection of timber was related to function. The importance of oak is clearly demonstrated.

Chapter 14
The botanical remains

James Greig

Introduction

The site at Runnymede is one of the richest prehistoric sites available to environmental archaeologists, both in abundance and variety of remains, and this is particularly so with the plant remains. The work on these has proved very time-consuming and had to be fitted in during gaps in other work, rather than being done all at once. The amount of material was so great that only a little work has been possible in some areas, notably the identification of buds and mosses. This report is presented as the best possible that could be completed in the time available, rather than as the ideal.

Laboratory processing

Macrofossils

The WF1b and SS1 column samples of 10–20 litres were sieved, floated with paraffin and sorted for beetle remains at the Ancient Monuments Laboratory by I Tyers under the supervision of M Girling. Plant remains were also sorted out from the beetle floats and stored in alcohol. The non-floating residues were bagged. At Birmingham, these residues were then re-sieved into fractions of >4 mm, 4–1 mm and 1–0.3 mm and were sorted for seeds; there were significant numbers of seeds in the residues because the paraffin flotation is a rather inefficient process for separating plant remains.

The bulk samples that were not processed at the Ancient Monuments Laboratory were subsampled, usually in quantities of 3 or 5 litres. These botanical macrofossil samples were dispersed in water and the plant and other organic material separated by 'washing over': the dispersed sediment was swirled in a bowl of water to help separate the lighter organic remains from the heavier sand and to wash them over into a sieve. The organic material was re-sieved on meshes of 4, 1 and 0.3 mm, giving size fractions of >4 mm, 4–1 mm and 1–0.3 mm for convenience of sorting. The inorganic residue was dried and then floated in water to recover anything organic that had not washed over the first time. Sorting was done in alcohol (and subsequently in water) under a microscope at about 10× magnification, much of the work being efficiently done by Hilary Sale-Harding. The sorts were stored in ethanol to await identification.

Macrofossil identification was done using a reference collection and other published identification criteria (especially those of K.-H. Knörzer), and second opinions were sought from colleagues when necessary. Lisa Moffett helped greatly with cereal identifications.

The macrofossil results from the layer/context samples are given in Table 24 and from the SS1 and WF1b profiles in Table 25; ecological groupings are given in Table 26. The plant records are given in taxonomic order according to the British Flora (Clapham et al. 1962).

List of processed bulk samples

F6 L4 SE: charcoal tip in LBA pit. 1 litre (whole sample), small subsample taken for pollen analysis. Charcoal saved from >4 mm fraction. Other fractions sorted, dried, and floated for charcoal – very little sediment in >4 mm. No residue check as it all floated. Not tabulated.

F15 L1: LBA clay-lined pit. 3 litres sieved. Good amount in each fraction, burnt clay but negligible charcoal. All 4–1 mm fraction sorted. Residue and unsorted material kept. Bronze fragments. Table 24.

L32–37: LBA layer (excavated spit 12) on occupation surface. 5 litres sieved, no plant remains seen, so very small amount sorted. Residue and unsorted portion kept. Not tabulated.

L8: LBA layer in river channel. 5 litres sieved. No waterlogged seeds seen, only a few charred grains. All the 4–1 mm fraction sorted. Residues and unsorted portion kept. Not tabulated.

L20: LBA layer in river channel. About 10 litres sieved. Subsampled for pollen. Table 24.

L14/20 (F130): LBA layer in river channel adjacent to pile F130. 1.5 litres; sample taken for pollen analysis. Table 24.

L24*: LBA layer in river channel underneath midden. 5 litres sieved on 5.6, 4, 1, and 0.3 mm meshes. >5.6: fair quantity of stones, many fire-cracked. Volumes of the size fractions – 5.6–4.0: 35 ml, wood and charcoal; 4.0–1.0: 1150 ml; 1.0–0.3: 600 ml. Subsampled for pollen. Table 24.

L19: LBA midden deposits in edge of river channel. Midden soil, organics, sand, burnt stone, etc. 5 litres soaked in water and then washed on 0.3 mm mesh, then sieved on 5.6, 1 and 0.3 mm meshes. Sand remained behind. Table 24.

L41 top: Neolithic channel sediment. Probably 3–5 litres sieved. Table 24.

L41 F205: Neolithic channel sediment adjacent to timber F205. 4 litres sieved (whole of the sample). A very few seeds, so only about 20% sorted. Residue and unsorted portion kept. Table 24.

L41 6E/8N: Neolithic channel sediment. 0.5 litre (whole sample), subsampled for pollen. No plant material in >4 mm fraction, and very little in other size fractions. All 4–1 mm fraction sorted, residue and unsorted fractions kept. Table 24.

Pollen

The SS1 profile samples came from those originally collected for mollusc analysis (and some for mineral analysis), thanks to Maureen Girling's very thorough work on the site. The pollen samples were taken from the inside of lumps of sediment where possible. The sediment was completely dried out by the time the pollen samples were prepared, although pollen was still well preserved. It is now known that pollen samples should be kept in cold storage for best results.

The WF1b profile pollen samples were taken from the aluminium monolith boxes (250 × 100 × 100 mm) collected on site by James Greig. These were subsampled at 2 cm intervals with a cork borer, from cleaned-back faces of sediment. At first samples were prepared every 16 cm, then every 8 cm. It was intended to prepare a closely sampled pollen diagram, but since the results are uniform and time was short, the WF1b results were left with a wide interval between samples (see Fig. 109).

The archaeological layer pollen subsamples were saved from lumps of the bulk macrofossil samples. Time was too short to count these.

The samples were prepared and counted using usual methods of treatment with hydrofluoric acid, stained with safranin and mounted with glycerol jelly. Pollen preservation was good in some cases, but the SS1 samples were from old dry sediment and it was hard to find sufficient pollen for a count. No pollen was found to be preserved above 32 cm in WF1b.

The identification was done using a reference collection, to which taxa were added to fill necessary gaps. In some cases it was not possible, for example, to prepare pollen of *Dianthus armeria* to check whether this could be identified among the Caryophyllaceae pollen.

The results are drawn out in pollen diagrams (in two parts each) covering the SS1 column (Fig. 112) and the WF1b columns (Fig. 113). The pollen diagrams are drawn with taxa grouped ecologically (forest, woods, open land etc.) and within the groups in taxonomic order (right to left). The pollen percentages are based on a pollen sum of tree + shrub pollen less *Alnus* and *Corylus*, and dry-land herb pollen (insofar as it can be identified). These are drawn in black bars. The pollen taxa not in the pollen sum are drawn in white bars, such as wetland plants and spores. The tree pollen percentages for both columns are drawn in Fig. 114. Taxa not drawn on the pollen diagrams are listed in Table 27.

Some of the possible plant communities interpreted from the pollen and macrofossil results are represented diagrammatically in Fig. 115.

Table 24: Seed lists for bulk or spot samples; Neolithic and Bronze Age

	MN L41	LBA L24*	LBA L20	LBA L14/20	LBA L19	LBA F15
Sphagnum sp. (leaflets)	—	—	—	—	7	—
Chara (oogonia)	—	—	7	—	—	—
Pteridium (frond fragment)	—	10	3	—	1*	—
Ranunculus subg. Ran.	41	100	54	81	13	—
Ranunculus subg. *Ran.*	—	10*	—	—	8*	—
Ranunculus cf. *acris* L.	2	—	1	—	—	—
Ranunculus parviflorus L.	—	—	2	—	1	—
Ranunculus flammula L.	—	—	1	3	—	—
Ranunculus cf. *lingua* L.	—	—	2	—	—	—
Ranunculus sceleratus L.	—	—	3	—	—	—
Ranunculus subg. Batrachium	12	—	48	3	—	—
Thalictrum flavum L.	—	—	4	—	—	—
Ceratophyllum sp.	1	—	—	—	—	—
Nymphaea alba L.	2	—	1	—	—	—
Nuphar cf. *lutea* (L.) Sm.	5	—	1	—	—	—
Papaver cf. *dubium* L.	—	—	—	3	—	—
Papaver rhoeas L. /*dubium* L. /*lecoqii* Lamotte	—	9	—	—	32	—
Papaver argemone L.	—	3	3	1	9	—
Fumaria sp.	—	18	1	3	6	—
Brassica sp.	62	10	13	1	4	—
Thlaspi arvense L.	—	11	2	4	3	—
Barbarea sp.	5	—	29	2	—	—
Rorippa cf. *palustris* (L.) Besser	—	—	—	—	1	—
Rorippa cf. *microphylla* (Boenn). Hyl.	—	—	—	1	—	—
Rorippa sp.	—	5	+	—	—	—
Nasturtium officinale R.Br.	—	—	2	—	4	—
Erysimum cheiranthoides L.	—	—	2	—	—	—
Viola cf. *odorata* L.	—	—	—	—	—	1
Viola sp.	—	7	1	1	1	1
Hypericum cf. *perforatum* L.	1	—	—	—	—	—
Hypericum cf. *tetrapterum* Fr.	1	—	2	—	—	—
Silene alba (Mill.) E.H.L. Krause	—	2	—	—	—	—
Lychnis flos-cuculi L.	2	—	2	—	1	—
Dianthus armeria L.	—	2	—	—	—	—
Cerastium cf. *holosteoides* Fr.	—	2	—	—	—	—
Cerastium cf. *glomeratum* Thuill.	—	—	4	—	—	—
Cerastium sp.	—	—	—	—	1	—
Stellaria cf. *nemorum* L.	2	—	—	—	—	—
Stellaria media tp.	13	85	87	20	37	—
Stellaria palustris Retz./*graminea* L.	—	8	—	8	—	—
Stellaria graminea L.	—	—	—	—	7	—
Moehringia trinervia L.	—	—	1	1	—	—

Table 24: Seed lists for bulk or spot samples; Neolithic and Bronze Age (continued).

	MN L41	LBA L24*	LBA L20	LBA L14/20	LBA L19	LBA F15
Arenaria sp.	—	—	1	2	10	—
Spergula arvensis L.	—	8	—	—	—	—
Caryophyllaceae n.f.i.	—	1*	—	—	2	—
Montia fontana ssp. chrondrosperma (Fenzl) S.M. Walters	—	—	—	—	2	—
Chenopodium cf. *polyspermum* L.	3	—	—	—	—	—
Chenopodium cf. *album* L.	—	347	114	49	280	6*
Chenopodium ficifolium Sm.	—	—	18	8	—	—
Atriplex sp.	5	76	62	16	41	1*
Chenopodiaceae	—	—	—	=52	—	—
Malva sylvestris L. seed	—	1	6	3	—	—
Malva sylvestris capsule fragment	—	1	—	—	—	—
Linum usitatissimum L. seeds	—	14	4	2	8	—
Linum usitatissimum capsule fragments	—	3	—	—	—	—
Linum usitatissimum capsule fragments	—	1*	—	—	—	—
Linum catharticum L.	—	—	2	—	—	—
Rhamnus catharticus L.	—	—	4	—	—	—
Medicago lupulina L.	—	1*	—	—	—	—
Medicago lupulina capsule	—	2	—	—	—	—
Vicia cf. *hirsuta* (L.) S.F. Gray	—	6*	—	—	—	—
cf. *Vicia* sp.	1*	+*	—	—	1*	1*
cf. *Pisum* sp.	2	—	—	—	—	—
cf. *Trifolium repens* L.	—	—	—	—	1*	—
Trifolium cf. *pratense*	—	—	—	—	1*	—
Ornithopus perpusillus L. (cpsl.)	—	—	—	—	1	—
Filipendula ulmaria L.	—	—	—	1	1	—
Rubus cf. *idaeus* L.	—	3	—	1	—	—
Rubus fruticosus agg.	14	43	16	2	15	—
Rubus fruticosus agg.	—	2*	—	—	2*	—
Rubus cf. *fruticosus* agg.	—	—	—	3	—	—
Rubus sp.	—	—	—	1	—	—
Potentilla cf. *sterilis* (L.) Garcke	—	—	1	—	—	—
Potentilla anserina L.	—	4	2	4	—	—
Potentilla erecta (L.)Räusch.	—	1	—	—	3*	—
Potentilla reptans L.	1	9	12	4	7,1*	—
Aphanes cf. *arvensis* L.	1	—	1	—	—	—
Aphanes microcarpa (Boiss. & Reut.) Rothm.	—	1	—	—	—	—
Sanguisorba officinalis l.	—	1	—	—	—	—
Rosa sp.	—	2	—	—	1,1*	—
Rosa/Rubus (thorns)	—	1	2	—	—	—
Prunus spinosa L.	=1	2	1	—	—	=1*
Prunus/Crataegus thorns	—	1	+	—	—	—
Crataegus sp.	+	=1	—	—	—	—
cf. *Crataegus* buds	—	—	7	—	—	—
cf. *Sorbus torminalis* (L.) Crantz	—	—	2	—	—	—
Epilobium sp.	4	—	4	—	—	—
Myriophyllum verticillatum L.	1	—	—	—	—	—
Hydrocotyle vulgaris L.	—	—	—	1	—	—
Torilis japonica (Houtt.) DC	—	1	2	—	3	—
Conium maculatum L.	—	—	16	8	—	—
cf. *Apium nodiflorum* (L.) Lag.	—	—	5	—	—	—
Oenanthe aquatica (L.) Poir.	4?	—	8?	—	—	—
Aethusa cynapium L.	—	22	7	7	13	—
Pastinaca sativa L.	—	19	2	—	9,1*	—
Pastinaca/Heracleum	—	—	—	3	—	—
Daucus carota L.	—	6	1	—	16	—
Umbelliferae	—	23	7	3	3	—
Polygonum aviculare L.	—	54	106	11	60	—
Polygonum aviculare L.	—	4*	—	—	1*	1*
Polygonum lapathifolium s.l.	3	10	7	1	?1	—
Polygonum lapthifolium s.l.	—	1*	—	—	—	—
Polygonum persicaria L.	—	—	—	—	1	—
Polygonum hydropiper L.	—	—	2	—	—	—
Polygonum cf. *minus* L.	—	—	7	3	—	—
Polygonum convolvulus L.	—	40	7	5	—	—
Polygonum convolvulus L.	—	—	1*	—	—	22*
Rumex acetosella agg.	—	3	1	1	7	—
Rumex conglomeratus Murr.	1	—	10	—	—	—
Rumex cf. *conglomeratus* Murr.	—	—	14	—	—	—
Rumex sp.	41	59	67	14	31	10*
Urtica urens L.	—	5	121	34	3	—
Urtica dioica L.	10	19	453	104	53	1
Betula sp.	—	—	4	—	—	—
Alnus glutinosa L.	165	—	48	—	—	—
Alnus catkins	=200	—	—	—	—	—
cf. *Quercus* sp. buds	5	—	1	—	—	—
cf. *Anagallis* sp.	—	1	—	2	—	—
Primulaceae	—	—	—	—	1	—
Solanum dulcamara L.	2	—	12	1	—	—
Solanum nigrum L.	—	1	—	3	2	—
Linaria cf. *vulgaris* Mill.	—	1	6	—	1	—
Scrophularia sp.	1	—	7	—	—	—
Rhinanthus sp.	—	—	2	—	—	—
Verbena officinalis L.	1	—	—	1	—	—
Mentha cf. *arvensis* L.	—	—	5	—	—	—
Mentha cf. *aquatica* L.	—	1	17	—	1	—

Table 24: Seed lists for bulk or spot samples; Neolithic and Bronze Age (continued).

	MN L41	LBA L24*	LBA L20	LBA L14/20	LBA L19	LBA F15
Mentha sp.	3	—	18	1	1	—
Lycopus europaeus L.	—	—	19	—	—	—
Prunella vulgaris L.	1	2	3	1	2	—
cf. Ballota nigra L.	2	—	—	—	—	—
Lamium cf. purpureum L.	—	3	—	—	—	—
Galeopsis segetum Neck.	—	—	—	3	—	—
Galeopsis tetrahit/speciosa	—	2	5	—	—	—
Galeopsis sp.	—	—	—	1	5	—
Glechoma hederacea L.	1	—	1	—	—	—
Ajuga reptans L.	2	—	1	—	—	—
Labiatae	2	—	1	8	—	—
Plantago major L.	3	2	3	2	5	1
Campanula patula L.	—	—	—	—	1	—
Galium aparine L.	—	—	—	—	1*	—
Galium cf. spurium L.	—	—	3	—	—	—
Galium sp.	—	1	—	1	—	—
Galium sp.	—	1*	—	—	—	—
Sambucus nigra L.	53	2	10	6	2	—
Valerianella locusta (L.) Betcke	4	4	2	—	—	—
Valerianella carinata Lois.	—	—	—	2	2	—
Valerianella dentata (L.) Pollich	—	—	—	—	1*	—
Scabiosa columbaria L.	—	—	1	—	—	—
Eupatorium cannabinum L.	—	—	26	—	—	—
cf. Senecio sp.	2	—	—	—	—	—
Tripleurospermum inodorum Schultz Bip.	—	—	—	—	2*	—
Arctium lappa L.	—	—	1	—	—	—
Arctium minus Bernh. s.l.	—	—	1	—	—	—
Arctium sp.	—	—	8	4	—	—
Carduus sp.	1	1	8	—	—	—
Cirsium cf. vulgare (Savi) Ten.	—	—	7	—	—	—
Cirsium cf. arvense (L.) Scop.	—	—	39	—	—	—
Cirsium palustre (L.) Scop./C. arvense (L.) Scop.	—	5	—	—	—	—
Cirsium sp.	5	—	—	3	—	—
Carduus or Cirsium	2	—	—	—	—	—
Lapsana communis L.	—	9	—	—	1	—
cf. Lapsana communis L.*	—	—	—	1	—	—
Leontodon sp.	—	—	2	—	1	—
Picris hieracioides L.	—	5	—	—	—	—
Sonchus arvensis L.	—	—	2	—	—	—
Sonchus oleraceus L.	—	—	2	—	—	—
Sonchus asper (L.) Hill	6	7	31	—	4	—
Taraxacum sp.	—	—	1	—	—	—
Alisma sp.	4	—	6	—	—	—

	MN L41	LBA L24*	LBA L20	LBA L14/20	LBA L19	LBA F15
Sagittaria sagittifolia L.	—	—	6	—	—	—
Potamogeton sp. including P. natans L.	—	1	16	—	—	—
Zannichellia palustris	—	—	14	?	—	—
Juncus sp.	—	—	—	—	20	—
Sparganium sp.	3	—	—	—	—	—
Eleocharis uniglumis/palustris	—	8	4	5	3,1*	—
Scirpus/Schoenoplectus sp.	253	—	24	3	—	—
Schoenoplectus maritimus L.	—	—	—	—	1	—
Schoenoplectus lacustris (L.) Palla	3	3	2	—	2	—
Schoenoplectus tabernaemontani (C.C. Gmel.) Palla	—	1	—	—	—	—
Isolepis setacea (L.) R.Br.	—	1	—	—	1	—
Carex cf. lepidocarpa Tausch	—	—	—	3	—	—
Carex cf. pseudocyperus L.	—	—	2	—	—	—
Carex cf. rostrata Stokes	1	—	—	—	—	—
Carex cf. riparia Curt.	—	28	—	—	—	—
Carex cf. hirta L. + utricle	26	—	6	—	—	—
Carex cf. elata (or muricata)*	—	—	4	9	—	—
Carex cf. disticha Huds.	—	—	1	2	—	—
Carex cf. spicata Huds.	—	—	—	—	—	—
Carex cf. ovalis Good.	—	3	—	—	1	—
Carex sp. n.f.i	—	15	—	—	—	2*
Triticum dicoccum	—	8*	19*	—	—	—
T. cf. dicoccum	—	2*	—	—	—	—
T. dicoccum spikelet forks	—	12*	—	11*	—	—
T. dicoccum glume bases	—	15*	—	—	22*	3*
T. dicoccum rachis fragment	—	1*	—	—	—	—
T. cf. dicoccum rachis fr.	—	1*	—	—	—	—
T. cf. dicoccum rachis node	—	1*	—	—	—	—
Triticum cf. spelta grain	—	1*	16*	—	—	—
Triticum spelta spikelets	—	—	—	—	2*	—
T. spelta spikelet forks	—	44*	—	—	11*	—
T. spelta glume bases	—	62*	—	—	52*	2*
T. spelta rachis	—	5*	—	—	—	—
T. cf. spelta rachis	—	—	—	—	1*	—
T. spelta rachis node	—	1*	—	—	—	—
Triticum dicoccum/spelta gl/b	—	327*	—	—	222*	4*
T. dicoccum/spelta sp/forks	—	12*	—	—	22*	3*

Table 24: Seed lists for bulk or spot samples; Neolithic and Bronze Age (continued).

	MN L41	LBA L24*	LBA L20	LBA L14/20	LBA L19	LBA F15
T. dicoccum/spelta rachis fragments	—	1*	—	—	—	—
T. dicoccum/spelta rachis nodes	—	1*	—	—	—	—
Triticum sp. grain	—	170*	—	—	76*	10*
Triticum sp. glume bases	—	56	—	—	—	—
Triticum sp. glume bases	—	29*	—	—	—	1*
Triticum sp. rachis	—	14	—	—	—	—
Triticum sp. basal rachis	—	1*	—	—	—	—
Secale cereale L. grain	—	1*	10*	—	—	—
? *Secale cereale* L. basal rachis	—	1*	—	—	—	—
? *Secale cereale* L. rachis node	—	1*	—	—	—	—
Hordeum vulgare ?/6	—	1*	—	—	—	—
Hordeum vulgare /6 rachis	—	2*	—	—	9*	—
Hordeum vulgare ?/6 rachis	—	1*	—	—	—	—
H. vulgare ?/2 rachis	—	—	1*	—	—	—
H. vulgare grain	—	10*	—	—	15*	5*
Hordeum sp. rachis	—	7*	—	—	13*	—
Hordeum sp. rachis	—	4	—	—	—	—
Avena sp.	—	—	5*	—	—	—
Avena sp.	—	?	—	—	—	—
? *Avena* flower head	—	1*	—	—	—	—
Cerealia n.f.i.	—	46*	—	—	—	4*
Cerealia culm node	—	—	—	—	3*	—
Bromus sp.	—	—	—	—	25*	=2*
large Gramineae	—	74*	—	—	—	—
small grasses	—	2*	—	—	—	—
Poa sp.	—	—	—	—	2,2*	—
Poa or *Agrostis* sp.	—	—	4	4	—	—
Total (less alder catkins)	844	2176	1883	589	1260	80

Names: Clapham *et al.* 1962, apart from cereals

Cereals identified, or at least confirmed, by Lisa Moffett.

  * = charred remains.

All remains are seeds unless otherwise stated

Table 25: Seed lists for samples from columns SS1 (Neolithic) and WF1b (Late Bronze Age).

	MN SS1 180	MN SS1 190	LBA WF1b 50	LBA WF1b 75	LBA WF1b 100	LBA WF1b 120	LBA WF1b 170	E.
Depths (cm):								
Chara (oogonia)	—	+	—	+	+	1	1	—
Pteridium (frond)	—	—	—	—	2	—	—	x
Taxus baccata L.	—	—	—	—	1	—	—	
Ranunculus subg. Ranunculus	4	+	—	8	8	18	14	x
Ranunculus cf. sardous L.	—	—	—	—	—	—	1	3
Ranunculus flammula L.	—	+	—	—	—	—	—	1.7.1.2
Ranunculus cf. lingua L.	—	—	—	—	—	2	1	1.5.1.1
Ranunculus sceleratus L.	—	+	—	3	—	—	—	3.2.1.
Ranunculus subg. Batrachium	3	+	—	12	6	3	1	1.3.1
Nymphaea alba L.	—	+	—	—	—	1	2	1.3.1.2
Nuphar lutea (L.) Sm.	2	+	—	—	1	2	7	1.3.1.2
Papaver cf. dubium L.	—	—	—	—	1	1	—	3.4.2.1
Papaver argemone L.	—	—	—	1	—	—	—	3.4.1
Fumaria sp.	—	—	—	2	—	—	3	3.3.1.1
Brassica rapa L. subsp. campestris	20	+	—	3	2	2	23	x
Thlaspi arvense L.	—	—	—	5	1	2	—	3.3.1.1
Cardamine sp.	—	—	—	1	—	—	—	x
Barbarea sp.	—	+	—	1	1	?	?	(3.5.2.1)
Rorippa sp.	—	—	—	10	390	—	—	x
Nasturtium officinale R.Br.	—	—	—	1	—	—	—	1.5.1.3
Viola sp.	—	—	—	—	—	1	1	x
Hypericum perforatum L.	—	+	—	4	—	—	—	6.1
Hypericum tetrapterum Fr.	—	+	—	6	2	—	—	5.4.1.2
Silene dioica (L.) Clairv.	—	—	—	—	—	1	2	x
Lychnis flos-cuculi L.	—	+	—	—	—	1	2	5.4.1
Cerastium cf. holosteoides Fr.	—	+	—	—	1	—	—	5.
Stellaria nemorum L.	—	+	—	—	—	—	—	8.4.3.3
Stellaria media tp.	1	+	—	10	7	26	3	3.3
Stellaria cf. neglecta Weihe	1	—	—	—	—	—	—	x
Stellaria palustris/graminea	—	—	—	—	—	3	—	x
Stellaria sp.	—	—	—	4	—	—	—	x
Arenaria sp.	—	+	—	1	—	—	1	(3)
Chenopodium polyspermum L.	—	+	—	5	1	—	—	3.3.1
Chenopodium cf. album L.	—	+	1	74	33	29	25	3.3
Chenopodium ficifolium Sm.	—	—	—	10	1	—	—	3.3
Chenopodium rubrum L./glaucum L.	—	—	—	2	—	—	—	x
Atriplex sp.	—	+	—	15	12	37	14	x
Malva sylvestris L.	—	—	—	1	3	—	—	3.3.3
Linum usitatissimum cpsl. fr.	—	—	—	1	1	—	—	crop
Linum catharticum L.	—	—	—	1	—	1	—	5
? Acer campestre L.	—	—	—	—	—	—	1	
Rhamnus catharticus L.	—	+	—	—	—	—	—	8.4.1
Filipendula ulmaria L.	—	—	—	—	1	—	—	5.4.1
Rubus fruticosus agg.	—	+	—	—	—	—	1	x
Rubus cf. fruticosus agg.	—	+	—	1	—	1	2	x
Rubus sp.	—	—	—	5	—	—	4	x

Table 25: Seed lists for samples from columns SS1 (Neolithic) and WF1b (Late Bronze Age) (continued).

Depths (cm):	MN SS1 180	MN SS1 190	LBA WF1b 50	LBA WF1b 75	LBA WF1b 100	LBA WF1b 120	LBA WF1b 170	E.
Potentilla anserina L.	—	—	—	—	3	—	—	3.7.1
Potentilla cf. *erecta* L. Raüschel	—	+	—	1	1	1	—	5.1
Potentilla reptans L.	—	+	—	2	—	—	—	3.7.2.1
Fragaria vesca L.	1	—	—	—	—	—	+	6.2.1
Aphanes arvensis L.	—	+	—	—	2	1	—	3.4.2.1
Aphanes microcarpa L.	—	+	—	—	—	—	—	3.4.2.1
Rosa sp.	—	—	—	—	—	2	—	x
Rosa/Rubus thorns	—	—	—	—	1	—	—	x
Prunus/Crataegus thorns	—	—	—	2	—	+	3	x
Malus sylvestris L. endocarp	—	—	—	—	—	—	1	8.4
Crataegus sp.	—	+	—	—	1	3	5	8.4
Prunus spinosa L.	—	—	—	—	1	—	1	8.4.1
Lythrum salicaria L.	1	—	—	—	—	—	—	5.4.1.2
Epilobium sp.	—	+	—	—	1	—	—	x
Myriophyllum spicatum L.	—	+	—	—	1	—	—	1.3.1
Myriophyllum sp.	1	—	—	—	—	—	—	
Cornus sanguinea L.	—	—	—	—	—	—	+	
cf. *Chaerophyllum temulentum* L.	—	—	—	—	—	1	+	
Torilis japonica (Houtt.) DC	—	—	—	—	1	—	—	6.2.1
Conium maculatum L.	—	—	—	15	4	2	—	3.5.1 1
cf. *Apium nodiflorum* (L.) Lag.	—	—	—	2	—	1	—	1.5.1.3
Oenanthe aquatica (L.) Poir.	1	+	—	2	?4	—	—	1.5.1.1
Aethusa cynapium L.	—	—	—	3	1	6	3	3.3
Daucus carota L.	—	—	—	—	—	3	—	x
Mercurialis perennis L.	—	—	—	—	—	—	1	8.4.3
Polygonum aviculare L.	2	+	—	5	8	16	5	3
Polygonum persicaria L.	—	—	—	1	6	—	4	3.3.1
Polygonum lapathifolium s.l.	—	—	—	1	—	2	—	3.2.1
Polygonum hydropiper L.	—	—	—	—	—	2	2	3.2.1.1
Polygonum mite Schrank	—	+	—	—	4	4?	—	3.2.1
Polygonum convolvulus L.	—	—	—	—	1	5	2	3.4.2
Rumex acetosella agg.	—	—	—	—	1	3	—	5.1
Rumex conglomeratus Murr.	—	—	—	—	7	—	2	x
Rumex cf. *conglomeratus* Murr.	—	—	—	—	1	—	—	x
Rumex sp.	1	+	—	6	9	9	8	x
Rumex sp.*	—	—	—	1	—	—	1	x
Urtica urens L.	—	—	—	71	26	1	1	3.
Urtica dioica L.	8	+	2	375	103	47	2	3.5
cf. *Humulus lupulus* L.	—	—	—	—	1	—	—	8
Betula sp.	—	—	—	—	1	—	—	8
Alnus glutinosa L.	23	+ +	—	—	7	2	2	8.2.1.1
Alnus glutinosa L. (catkins)	—	+	—	—	—	—	3	8.2.1.1
Alnus glutinosa L. (catkin scales)	—	+	—	—	1	—	2	8.2.1.1.
cf. *Quercus* sp. buds	—	—	—	?	—	—	1	8
Anagallis cf. *foemina* L.	—	—	—	1	—	—	—	3.4

Table 25: Seed lists for samples from columns SS1 (Neolithic) and WF1b (Late Bronze Age) (continued).

Depths (cm):	MN SS1 180	MN SS1 190	LBA WF1b 50	LBA WF1b 75	LBA WF1b 100	LBA WF1b 120	LBA WF1b 170	E.
cf. *Anagallis* sp.	—	+	—	—	—	1	—	(3.4)
Menyanthes trifoliata L.	—	+	—	—	—	—	—	1.7
Hyoscyamus niger L.	—	—	—	1	—	—	—	3.3.4.1
Solanum dulcamara L.	—	+	—	—	1	—	2	x
Solanum nigrum L.	—	—	—	—	1	—	—	3.3
Linaria cf. *vulgaris* Mill.	—	+	—	—	1	—	1	3.3
Scrophularia sp.	—	+	—	3	—	—	1	x
Verbena officinalis L.	—	+	—	—	—	—	—	3
Mentha sp.	1	+	—	5	1	1	—	x
Lycopus europaeus L.	3	+	—	—	7	1	—	1.5
cf. *Satureia hortensis* L.	1	—	—	—	—	—	—	x
Prunella vulgaris L.	—	—	—	—	1	3	—	5.4
Stachys palustris L.	—	—	—	—	—	1	—	5.4.1.2
cf. *Ballota nigra* L.	—	—	—	—	—	1	1	3.5.1.1
Galeopsis tetrahit/speciosa	—	—	—	—	—	2	1	(3)
Galeopsis sp.	—	—	—	—	1	—	—	x
cf. *Glechoma hederacea* L.	—	—	—	2	—	—	—	8.4.1
Scutellaria galericulata L.	—	—	—	—	1	—	—	1.5.1.4
Plantago major L.	—	+	—	1	—	—	—	(3.7.1)
Galium sp.	—	—	—	4	9	—	—	x
Sambucus nigra L.	2	+	2	6	1	8	25	6.2.1.3
Valerianella dentata (L.) Pollich	—	—	—	—	—	1	—	5.2
Valerianella carinata Lois.	—	+	—	—	—	—	—	5.2
Dipsacus fullonum L.	—	—	—	—	—	—	1	3.5
Scabiosa columbaria L.	—	—	—	1	—	—	—	5.3.2
Eupatorium cannabinum L.	2	+	1	5	11	—	—	3.5.2.1
cf. *Achillea* sp.	—	—	—	1	—	—	—	x
cf. *Senecio* sp.	—	+	—	—	?	—	—	x
Arctium lappa L.	—	—	—	13	4	—	—	3.5.1.1
Arctium minus Bernh. s.l.	—	—	—	7	—	—	—	3.5.1.1
Carduus sp.	3	—	—	—	—	—	1	3.4.1.1
Carduus or *Cirsium* sp.	3	—	—	—	—	—	—	x
Cirsium cf. *vulgare* (Savi) Ten.	—	—	—	—	1	3	—	3.5.1
Cirsium cf. *arvense* (L.) Scop.	—	—	—	2	1	2	—	3
Cirsium cf. *palustre* (L.) Scop.	—	—	—	—	2	—	—	5.4.1
Cirsium sp.	—	+	—	—	—	—	—	x
cf. *Lapsana communis* L.	—	—	—	—	—	2	—	3.5.2.2
Leontodon cf. *taraxacoides* Vill.) Mérat	—	—	—	—	1	1*	—	5
Sonchus asper (L.) Hill	—	+	—	2	3	—	—	3.3.1
Alisma sp.	2	+	—	2	3	—	1	(1.5)
Potamogeton sp. including *P. natans*	1	+	—	1	—	4	22	(1.3.1.2)
Zannichellia palustris L.	—	—	—	2	5	—	—	1.3.1.1
Juncus sp.	—	+	—	8	1	—	—	x
Iris pseudacorus L.	1	—	—	—	2	—	1	1.5.1
Sparganium sp.	—	+	—	—	—	—	3	(1.5.1.3)
Eleocharis uniglumis/palustris	—	—	—	—	—	3	1	1.5.1

Table 25: Seed lists for samples from columns SS1 (Neolithic) and WF1b (Late Bronze Age) (continued).

Depths (cm):	MN SS1 180	MN SS1 190	LBA WF1b 50	LBA WF1b 75	LBA WF1b 100	LBA WF1b 120	LBA WF1b 170	E.
Schoenoplectus lacustris L.	2	+	3	4	58	3	145	1.5.1.1
Carex nigra group	—	—	—	—	—	3	—	?
Carex cf. *hirta* L. + utricle	—	—	—	—	3	4	4	3.7.2.1
Carex cf. *disticha* Huds.	—	—	—	—	—	1	—	1.5.1.4
Carex sp.	—	+	—	2	—	—	2	x
Triticum dicoccum glume bases	—	—	—	2*	—	—	—	crop
Triticum cf. *spelta* grains	—	—	—	—	—	+*	—	crop
Triticum spelta glume bases	—	—	—	2*	—	1*	—	crop
Triticum dicoccum/spelta grains	—	—	—	5*	4*	66*	1*	crop
Triticum dicoccum/spelta glume bases	—	—	—	8*	—	—	—	crop
Hordeum vulgare (6 row) rachis	—	—	—	2*	—	—	—	crop
Hordeum vulgare grains	—	—	1*	1*	3*	10*	—	crop
Bromus sp.	—	—	—	3*	2*	—	10*	
Total	100		8	763	750	553	234	

Names: Clapham et al. 1962, apart from cereals.

Cereals identified by Lisa Moffett.

* = charred remains.

All remains are seeds unless otherwise stated.

E = Present day equivalent European plant community represented (Ellenberg 1979).

Most of the WF1b samples seeds came from beetle floats, residues and seeds sorted at London. The SS1 sample is from the original sediment, but taxa are recorded as present (+) abundant (+ +) or absent (—) as there was insufficient time to count the seeds. The SS1 180 cm sample was identified by Mark Robinson – he notes the presence of *Satureia hortensis* with surprise.

Table 26: Combined list of all plant remains from Runnymede Bridge, Area 6.
Arranged according to modern ecological communities (Ellenberg 1979, 1982, 1988). Note The Prehistoric plant communities were not necessarily the same!

SS = SS1 column, MN = Middle Neolithic layer samples, WF = WF1 column, LBA = Late Bronze Age layer samples, E corresponding modern community (Ellenberg 1979).
+ = present, + + present in several samples, + + + present in nearly every sample, * = charred remains, × = no corresponding identifiable pollen type.

	SS pollen	SS macros	MN macros	WF pollen	WF macros	LBA macros	E.
Group 1 WETLAND AND FRESHWATER AQUATIC PLANTS							
pondweed Class; rooted aquatics							
1.3 Potamogetonetea							
Ranunculus subg. *Batrachium*	×	+	+	×	+ +	+ +	1.3.1
Nymphaea alba L.	—	?	+	+	+	+	1.3.1.2
Nuphar cf. *lutea* (L.) Sm.	+	?	+	—	+ +	+	1.3.1.2
Myriophyllum verticillatum L.	+	?	+	+	—	—	1.3.1.2
Potamogeton sp. including							
P. *natans* L.	+ +	+	—	+ +	+ +	—	(1.3.1.2)
Zannichellia palustris L.	—	—	—	—	+	+	1.3.1.1
shore-weed class							
1.4 Littorelletea							
Ceratophyllum sp.	—	—	+	—	—	—	1.4.1
reed and sedge Class; waterside plants							
1.5 Phragmitetea							
Ranunculus cf. *lingua* L.	×	—	—	×	+	+	1.5.1.1
Nasturtium officinale R.Br.	×	—	—	×	+	+	1.5.1.3
cf. *Apium nodiflorum* (L.) Lag.	×	—	—	×	+	+	1.5.1.3
Oenanthe aquatica (L.) Poir.	×	+	?	×	+	+	1.5.1.1
Mentha cf. *aquatica* L.	×	—	—	×	—	+	1.5.1
Mentha sp.	×	+	+	×	+	+	×
Lycopus europaeus L.	×	+	—	×	+	+	1.5
Scutellaria galericulata L.	×	—	—	×	+	—	1.5.1.4
Alisma sp.	+	+	+	—	+ +	+	(1.5)
Sagittaria sagittifolia L.	+	—	—	—	—	+	1.5
Iris pseudacorus L.	—	+	—	—	+	—	1.5.1
Sparganium sp.(*Sparg/Typha* poll)	+ +	+	+	+ +	+	—	(1.5.1.3)
Eleocharis uniglumis/palustris	×	—	—	×	+	+	1.5.1
Schoenoplectus lacustris (L.) Palla	×	+	+	×	+	+	1.5.1.1
Schoenoplectus tabernaemontani							
(C.C. Gmel.) Palla	×	—	—	×	—	+	1.5.1.1
Carex cf. *pseudocyperus* L.	×	—	—	×	—	+	1.5.1.4
Carex cf. *rostrata* Stokes	×	—	+	×	—	—	1.5.1.4
Carex cf. *riparia* Curt.	×	—	—	×	—	+	1.5.1.4
Carex cf. *elata* (or *muricata*)	×	—	—	×	—	+	(1.5.1.4)
Carex cf. *disticha* Huds.	×	—	—	×	—	+	1.5.1.4
Cyperaceae pollen	+ + +	—	—	+ + +	—	—	
sedge mires and fens							
1.7 Scheuzerio-Caricetea nigrae							
Ranunculus flammula L.	×	—	—	×	—	+	1.7.1.2
Hydrocotyle vulgaris L.	—	—	—	+	—	+	1.7.1
Menyanthes trifoliata L.	—	+	—	+	—	—	1.7
Pedicularis palustris L.	—	—	—	+	—	—	1.7

Table 26: Combined list of all plant remains from Runnymede Bridge, Area 6 (continued).

	SS pollen	SS macros	MN macros	WF pollen	WF macros	LBA macros	E.
raised bogs and mires							
1.8 Oxycocco-Sphagnetea							
?*Sphagnum* sp.	+	−	+	−	+	−	
Group 3 WEEDS AND WASTELAND PLANTS							
Cerastium cf. *glomeratum* Thuill.	×	−	−	×	−	+	3
Arenaria sp.	×	−	−	×	+	+	(3)
Polygonum aviculare L.	×	+	−	×	++	++	3
Polygonum aviculare L.	×	−	−	×	−	*	3
Verbena officinalis L.	−	+	+	−	−	+	3
Galeopsis segetum Neck.	×	−	−	×	−	+	×
Galeopsis tetrahit/speciosa	×	−	−	×	+	+	(3)
Galeopsis sp.	×	−	−	×	+	+	×
Cirsium cf. *arvense* (L.) Scop.	×	−	−	×	+	++	3
wet springs							
3.1 Isöetea-Nanojuncetea							
Montia fontana ssp. *chondrosperma* (Fenzl) S.M. Walters	−	−	−	−	−	+	3.1.1.1
Isolepis setacea (L.) R.Br.	×	−	−	×	−	+	3.1.1.1
muddy bank vegetation							
3.2 Bidentetea							
Ranunculus sceleratus L.	×	+	−	×	+	+	3.2.1.1
Polygonum lapathifolium s.l.	×	−	+	×	+	+	3.2.1
Polygonum hydropiper L.	×	−	−	×	−	+	3.2.1.1
Polygonum cf. *mite* Schrank	×	+	−	×	−	−	3.2.1.1
Polygonum cf. *minus* Huds.	×	−	−	×	−	+	3.2.1
spring germinating garden and field weeds							
3.3 Chenopodetea							
Fumaria sp.	−	−	−	−	+	+	3.3.1.1
Brassica sp.	×	++	+	×	+	+	×
Thlaspi arvense L.	×	−	−	×	++	+	3.3.1.1
Erysimum cheiranthoides L.	×	−	−	×	−	+	3.3
Stellaria media tp.	×	−	+	×	++	++	3.3
Spergula arvensis L.	−	−	−	−	−	+	3.3.1
Chenopodium cf. *polyspermum* L.	×	+	+	×	+	−	3.3.1
Chenopodium cf. *album* L.	×	+	−	×	++	++	3.3
Chenopodium ficifolium Sm.	×	−	−	×	+	+	3.3
Chenopodium rubrum/botryodes	×	−	−	×	+	−	3.3
Chenopodiaceae	+	−	−	+++	−	−	
Malva sylvestris L. seed	−	−	−	−	+	+	3.3.3
Malva sylvestris capsule fragment	−	−	−	−	−	+	3.3.3
Aethusa cynapium L.	×	−	−	×	+	+	3.3
Pastinaca sativa L.	×	−	−	×	−	+	3.3.4.2
Polygonum persicaria L.	×	−	−	×	+	−	3.3.1
Urtica urens L.	×	−	−	×	++	++	3.3
Hyoscyamus niger L.	−	−	−	−	+	−	3.3.4.1
Solanum nigrum L.	−	−	−	−	+	+	3.3
Linaria cf. *vulgaris* Mill.	−	+	−	−	+	+	3.3
Lamium cf. *purpureum* L.	−	−	−	−	−	+	3.3.1
Tripleurospermum maritimum (L.) Schultz Bip.	×	−	−	−	−	*	3.3
Picris hieracioides L.	×	−	−	×	−	+	3.3.4.2
Sonchus arvensis L.	×	−	−	×	2	+	3.3.1

Table 26: Combined list of all plant remains from Runnymede Bridge, Area 6 (continued).

	SS pollen	SS macros	MN macros	WF pollen	WF macros	LBA macros	E.
Sonchus oleraceus L.	×	—	—	×	2	+	3.3
Sonchus asper (L.) Hill	×	+	+	×	+	+	3.3.1
'cornfield weeds'							
3.4 Secalietea							
Papaver rhoeas L./*dubium* L./*lecoqii*							
Lamotte	—	—	—	—	+	+	3.4.1
Papaver argemone L.	—	—	—	—	+	+	3.4.1
Papaver cf. *dubium* L.	—	—	—	—	+	+	3.4.2.1
Vicia cf. *hirsuta* (L.) S.F. Gray	—	—	—	—	—	+	3.4.2
Aphanes cf. *arvensis* L.	—	+	+	—	+	+	3.4.2.1
Aphanes microcarpa							
(Boiss. & Reut.) Rothm.	+	—	—	—	—	+	3.4.2.2
Polygonum convolvulus L.	—	—	—	—	+ +	+	3.4.2
Polygonum convolvulus L.	—	—	—	—	*	—	3.4.2
cf. *Anagallis* sp.	—	+	—	—	+	+	(3.4)
Anagallis cf. *foemina*	—	—	—	—	+	—	(3.4)
Valerianella locusta (L.) Betcke	—	—	+	—	—	+	3.4
Carduus sp.	×	+	+	×	+	+	3.4.1.1
cultivated plants							
Linum usitatissimum L. seeds	—	—	—	—	+	+	crop
Linum capsule fragments	—	—	—	—	+	—	crop
Linum capsule	—	—	—	—	—	*	crop
cf. *Pisum* sp.	—	—	+	—	—	—	crop
Triticum dicoccum	—	—	—	—	—	*	crop
T. cf. *dicoccum*	—	—	—	—	—	*	crop
T. dicoccum spikelet forks	—	—	—	—	—	*	crop
T. dicoccum glume bases	—	—	—	—	*	*	crop
T. dicoccum rachis fragment	—	—	—	—	—	*	crop
T. cf. *dicoccum* rachis fragment	—	—	—	—	—	*	crop
T. cf. *dicoccum* rachis node	—	—	—	—	—	*	crop
Triticum cf. *spelta*	—	—	—	—	*	*	crop
T. spelta spikelet forks	—	—	—	—	—	*	crop
T. spelta glume bases	—	—	—	—	*	*	crop
T. spelta rachis	—	—	—	—	—	*	crop
T. spelta rachis node	—	—	—	—	—	*	crop
Triticum dicoccum/spelta glume bases	—	—	—	—	—	*	crop
T. dicoccum/spelta spikelet/forks	—	—	—	—	—	*	crop
T. dicoccum/spelta rachis fragment	—	—	—	—	—	*	crop
T. dicoccum/spelta rachis node	—	—	—	—	—	*	crop
Triticum sp.	—	—	—	—	—	***	crop
Triticum sp. glume bases	—	—	—	—	—	+	crop
Triticum sp. glume bases	—	—	—	—	—	*	crop
Triticum sp. rachis	—	—	—	—	—	+	crop
Triticum sp. basal rachis	—	—	—	—	—	*	crop
Secale cereale	—	—	—	—	—	*	crop
? *Secale cereale* basal rachis	—	—	—	—	—	*	crop
? *Secale cereale* rachis node	—	—	—	—	—	*	crop
Hordeum vulgare ?/6	—	—	—	—	—	*	crop
Hordeum vulgare /6 rachis	—	—	—	—	*	*	crop
Hordeum vulgare ?/6 rachis	—	—	—	—	—	*	crop

Table 26: Combined list of all plant remains from Runnymede Bridge, Area 6 (continued).

	SS pollen	SS macros	MN macros	WF pollen	WF macros	LBA macros	E.
Hordeum vulgare ?/2 rachis	—	—	—	—	—	*	crop
Hordeum vulgare	—	—	—	—	**	*	crop
Hordeum sp. rachis	—	—	—	—	—	*	crop
Hordeum sp. rachis	—	—	—	—	—	+	crop
Avena sp.	—	—	—	—	—	*	crop
? *Avena* flower head	—	—	—	—	—	*	crop
Cerealia n.f.i.	+	—	—	++	—	*	crop
large Gramineae	—	—	—	—	—	*	
Perennial nitrophilous weeds							
3.5 Artemisetea							
Barbarea sp.	×	+	+	×	+	+	(3.5.2.1)
Silene alba (Mill.) E.H.L. Krause	×	—	—	×	—	+	3.5.1.1
Rubus cf. *idaeus* L.	×	—	—	×	—	+	3.5.2.1
Conium maculatum L.	×	—	—	×	+	+	3.5.1.1
Urtica dioica L.	×	+	+	×	+++	+++	3.5
cf. *Ballota nigra* L.	×	—	+	×	+	—	3.5.1.1
Dipsacus fullonum L.	×	—	—	×	+	—	3.5
Artemisia	+	—	—	++	—	—	
Eupatorium cannabinum L.	?	+	—	?	++	+	3.5.2.1
Arctium lappa L.	—	—	—	—	+	+	3.5.1.1
Arctium minus Bernh. s.l.	—	—	—	—	+	+	3.5.1.1
Arctium sp.	—	—	—	+	—	+	3.5.1.1.
Cirsium cf. *vulgare* (Savi) Ten.	—	—	—	—	+	+	3.5.1
Lapsana communis L.	—	—	—	—	—	+	3.5.2.2
cf. *Lapsana communis* L.	—	—	—	—	*	*	crop
pathways and wet bare ground							
3.7 Plantaginetea							
Potentilla anserina L.	—	—	—	—	+	+	3.7.1
Potentilla reptans L.	—	+	+	—	+	+	3.7.2.1
Potentilla type	+	—	—	++	—	—	
Plantago major L.	—	—	+	—	+	+	(3.7.1)
Carex cf. *hirta* L. + utricle	×	—	—	×	++	—	3.7.2.1
Group 5 SEMI-NATURAL HEATHS AND MEADOWS							
Dianthus armeria L.	—	—	—	—	—	+	5
Linum catharticum L.	—	—	—	—	+	+	5
Lotus type	+	—	—	+	—	—	5
Leontodon sp.	—	—	—	—	—	+	5
Leontodon cf. *taraxacoides* Vill. Mérat	—	—	—	—	+	—	5
grasslands (dry acid soils) and heaths							
5.1 Nardo-Callunetea							
Polygala tp.	—	—	—	+	—	—	5.1
Centaurea nigra tp.	—	—	—	+	—	—	5.1
Potentilla erecta (L.)Räusch.	×	+	—	×	+	+	5.1
Rumex acetosella agg.	×	—	—	×	+	+	5.1
Carex cf. *ovalis* Good.	×	—	—	×	—	+	5.1.1
thin communities on sand and stone							
5.2 Sedo-Scleranthetea							
Valerianella carinata Lois.	—	+	—	—	—	+	5.2
Valerianella dentata (L.) Pollich	—	—	—	—	+	—	5.2

Table 26: Combined list of all plant remains from Runnymede Bridge, Area 6 (continued).

	SS pollen	SS macros	MN macros	WF pollen	WF macros	LBA macros	E.
chalk grasslands							
5.3 Festuco-Brometea							
Medicago lupulina L.	−	−	−	−	−	*	5.3.2.1.3
Medicago lupulina capsule	−	−	−	−	−	+	crop
Sanguisorba minor L.	+	−	−	+ +	−	−	5.3
Plantago media L.	+	−	−	+	−	−	5.3
Scabiosa columbaria L.	×	−	−	×	+	+	5.3.2
general grassland communities (moist soils)							
5.4 Molinio-Arrhenatheretea							
Caltha palustris L.	+	−	−	+	−	−	5.4.1.5
Ranunculus cf. *acris* L.	×	−	+	×	−	+	5.4
Thalictrum flavum L.	−	−	−	+	−	+	5.4.1
Hypericum cf. *tetrapterum* Fr.	−	−	+	−	+	+	5.4.1.2
Lychnis flos-cuculi L.	×	+	+	+	×	+	5.4.1
Cerastium cf. *holosteoides* Fr.	×	−	−	×	+	−	5.4
Trifolium repens type	+ +	−	−	+ +	−	−	5.4
Trifolium pratense type	+	−	−	+	−	−	5.4
Filipendula ulmaria L.	+	−	−	+ +	+	+	5.4.1
Sanguisorba officinalis L.	−	−	−	−	−	+	5.4.1
Lythrum salicaria L.	−	+	−	−	−	−	5.4.1.2
Rhinanthus sp.	+	−	−	+	−	+	5.4
Plantago lanceolata L.	+ +	−	−	+ + +	−	−	5.4
Prunella vulgaris L.	×	−	+	×	+	+	5.4
Valeriana type	+	−	−	+	−	−	5.4.1
Taraxacum sp.	−	−	−	−	−	+	(5.4.2)
Woodland clearings, wood margins							
6.1 Trifolio-Geranetea							
Hypericum cf. *perforatum* L.	−	+	+	−	+	−	6.1
woodland glades and hedges							
6.2 Epilobetea							
Fragaria vesca L.	−	+	−	−	+	−	6.2.1
Torilis japonica (Houtt.) DC	×	−	−	×	+	+	6.2.1
Sambucus nigra L.	+ +	+	+	+	+ + +	+ +	6.2.1.3
WOODLAND etc.							
Rosa sp.	−	−	−	−	+	+	8
Sorbus cf. *torminalis* (L.) Crantz	−	−	−	−	−	+	8
cf. *Humulus lupulus* L.	−	−	−	−	+	−	8
Cannabiaceae	+	−	−	+	−	−	
Betula sp.	+ +	−	−	+	+	+	8
cf. *Quercus* sp.(macros: buds)	+ + +	−	+	+ +	+	+	8
(*Salix* type	+ +	−	−	+ +	−	−	8)
alder carr							
8.2 Alnetea							
Alnus glutinosa L. (seeds)	+ + +	+ +	+ +	+ +	+ +	+	8.2.1.1
Alnus catkins	×	+ +	+ +	×	+	−	8.2.1.1
mesotrophic broad-leaved woodland							
8.4 Querco-Fagetea							
Taxus baccata	+	−	−	−	+	−	8.4.3.1
Stellaria nemorum L.	×	+	+	×	−	−	8.4.3.3
Moehringia trinervia L.	×	−	−	×	−	+	8.4
Acer	+ +	−	−	+	−	−	8.4

Table 26: Combined list of all plant remains from Runnymede Bridge, Area 6 (continued).

	SS pollen	SS macros	MN macros	WF pollen	WF macros	LBA macros	E.
Rhamnus catharticus L.	—	+	—	+	—	+	8.4.1
Cornus sanguinea L.	—	—	—	—	+	—	8.4.1
Fraxinus excelsior L.	++	—	—	+	—	—	8.4.3
Prunus spinosa L.	—	—	+	+	—	+	8.4.1
Malus sylvestris L.	—	—	—	—	+	—	8.4
Crataegus sp.	+	+	+	+	+	—	8.4
cf. *Crataegus* buds	—	—	—	—	+	—	8.4
Mercurialis perennis L.	+	—	—	—	+	—	8.4.3
Glechoma hederacea L.	—	—	+	—	+	+	8.4.1
unclassified							
Chara (oogonia)	×	+	—	×	+	+	
Pteridium (frond fragment, spores)	+	—	—	+	+	+	
Polypodium vulgare (spores)	++	—	—	+	—	—	
Ranunculus subg. *Ranunculus*	×	+	+	×	+	+	
Ranunculus parviflorus L.	×	—	—	×	+	+	
Rorippa sp.	×	—	—	×	+	+	
Viola sp.	—	—	—	—	+	+	
Silene dioica (L.) Clairv.	—	—	+	—	+	+	
Stellaria palustris Retz./*graminea* L.	×	—	—	×	+	+	
Caryophyllaceae n.f.i.	×	—	—	×	—	*	
Atriplex sp.	×	—	+	×	++	+	
Chenopodiaceae	+	—	—	++	—	+	
cf. *Vicia* sp.	—	+	—	—			
Rubus fruticosus agg.	—	+	+	—	++	+	
Rubus fruticosus agg.	—	—	—	—	—	*	
Rosa/Rubus (thorns)	—	—	—	—	+	+	
Prunus/Crataegus thorns	×	—	—	×	+	+	
Epilobium sp.	—	+	+	—	+	+	
Pastinaca/Heracleum	×	—	—	×	—	+	
Daucus carota L.	×	—	—	×	+	+	
Rumex conglomeratus Murr.	×	—	+	×	+	+	
Rumex sp.	×	+	+	×	++	++	
Solanum dulcamara L.	—	+	+	—	++	+	
Scrophularia sp.	—	+	+	—	+	+	
Mentha cf. *arvensis* L.	×	—	—	×	—	+	
Ajuga reptans L.	×	—	+	×	—	+	
Galium sp.	+	—	—	++	+	+*	
cf. *Achillea* sp.	×	—	—	×	+	—	
cf. *Senecio* sp.	×	—	+	×	—	—	
Cirsium palustre (L.) Scop. /*C. arvense* (L.) Scop.	×	—	—	×	—	+	
Cirsium sp.	×	—	+	×	—	+	
Carduus or *Cirsium*	—	—	+	+	—	—	
Juncus sp.	—	+	—	—	+	—	
Carex nigra group	×	—	—	×	+	—	
Carex cf. *lepidocarpa* Tausch	×	—	—	×	—	+	
small grasses	×	—	—	×	—	*	
Poa or *Agrostis* sp.	×	—	—	×	—	+	

SS = SS1 column, MN = Middle Neolithic layer samples, WF = WF1 column, LBA = Late Bronze Age layer samples, E = corresponding modern community (Ellenberg 1979).

+ = present, ++ present in several samples, +++ present in nearly every sample, * = charred remains, × = no corresponding identifiable pollen type.

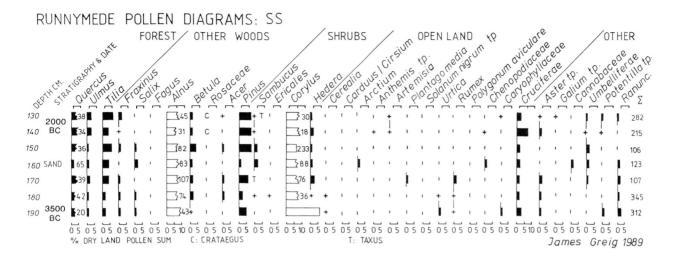

RUNNYMEDE POLLEN DIAGRAMS: SS

Fig. 112 Pollen diagrams for Middle-Late Neolithic sediments in column SS1, Area 6.

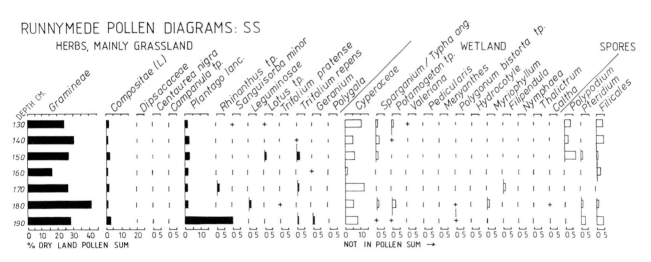

Table 27: Pollen etc. not drawn on diagram.

SS1 profile		WF1b profile				
130 cm		72 cm			190 cm	
cf. *Mercurialis*		cf. *Carpinus*	+		*Mentha* type	+
perennis	1%	*Lamium* type	+		ignota	4%
Alisma	+	Leguminosae nfi	+			
ignota	8%	ignota	4%			
140 cm		80 cm				
Alisma	+	Leguminosae	2%			
ignota	12%	Rosaceae	+			
150 cm		cf. *Anagallis*	+			
ignota	16%	88 cm				
160 cm		cf. *Agrimonia*	+			
Sphagnum	+	ignota	1%			
170 cm		112 cm				
Mentha type	1%	*Rhamnus catharticus*	+			
ignota	7%	Leguminosae	1%			
180 cm		*Mentha* type	+			
Alisma type	+	128 cm				
ignota	3%	Leguminosae	2%			
		Rosaceae	1%			

144 cm		
Lamium type	+	
ignota	9%	
158 cm		
Rosaceae	1%	
174 cm		
Abies	+	
190 cm		
cf. *Onobrychis*	+	
Trichuris	+	

250

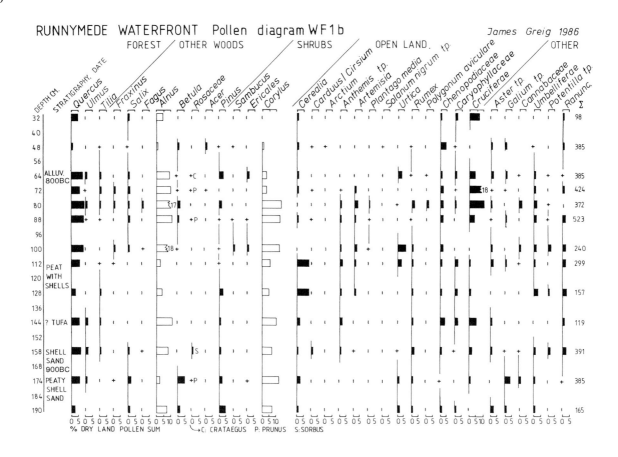

RUNNYMEDE WATERFRONT Pollen diagram WF1b

James Greig 1986

FOREST / OTHER WOODS / SHRUBS / OPEN LAND. / OTHER

% DRY LAND POLLEN SUM → C: CRATAEGUS   P: PRUNUS   S: SORBUS

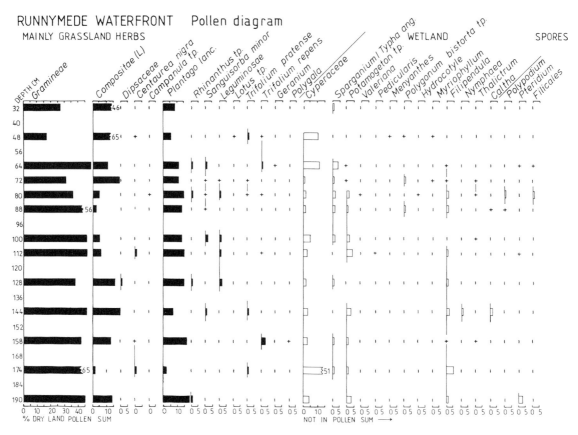

RUNNYMEDE WATERFRONT Pollen diagram

MAINLY GRASSLAND HERBS / WETLAND / SPORES

% DRY LAND POLLEN SUM   NOT IN POLLEN SUM →

Fig. 113 Pollen diagrams for Late Bronze Age sediments in column WF1b, Area 6.

251

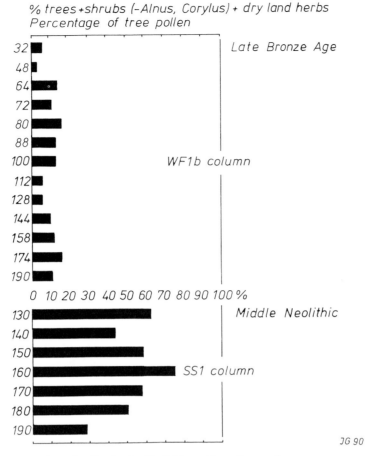

% trees+shrubs (-Alnus, Corylus) + dry land herbs
Percentage of tree pollen

Late Bronze Age

WF1b column

Middle Neolithic

SS1 column

Fig. 114 Percentages of arboreal to non-arboreal pollen for the Neolithic and Late Bronze Age sequences.

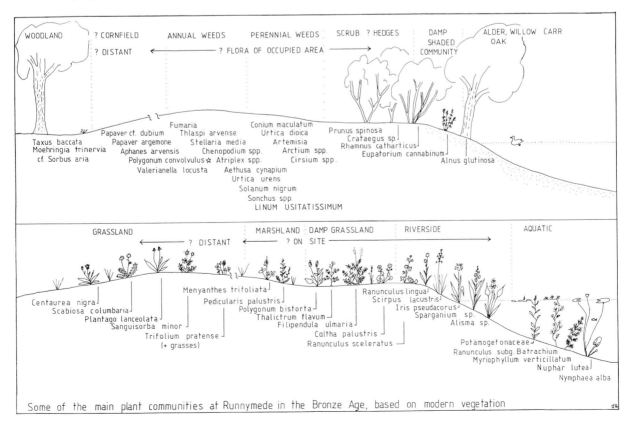

Some of the main plant communities at Runnymede in the Bronze Age, based on modern vegetation

Fig. 115 Vegetational reconstruction for prehistoric Runnymede.

Results

Introduction to interpretation: European plant communities

Interpretation is based on modern European ecological results. This is *just a framework for discussion*, and does not suggest that the kinds of vegetation seen now are the same as those that existed in prehistoric times. The main source of this phytosociological data is that of Ellenberg (1982, rather than the English translation, Ellenberg 1988). Ellenberg's community arrangement (1979) is used here for Table 26. Although based upon central European vegetation of the present day and the recent past, it also applies (although less directly) to the vegetation of adjoining regions such as the British Isles. It is the most useful published source of such data and is already widely used and understood, so this arrangement is adopted here. Although vegetation classification has been done in Britain, very little has been published recently and it is difficult to relate to established arrangements such as Ellenberg's. The broad divisions of vegetation, however, are very similar to the familiar ones described by Tansley (1968) on the basis of earlier, more descriptive ecology.

The phytosociological arrangement divides vegetation according to a hierarchical scheme with names and numbers. There are eight vegetational groups; the ones relevant to Runnymede are: (1) freshwater and marshland plants; (3) weeds and wasteland plants; (5) semi-natural heathlands and grasslands; (6) woodland understorey herbs and shrubs; and (8) broad-leaved woodlands and forests. The groups are subdivided into classes, with names ending in 'etea', which are used in the discussion of the Runnymede results. These classes are in turn divided into orders with names ending in '-etalia', and further into associations with names ending in '-ion', although these fine details are not used here. Crops are not classified, so they are discussed after their weeds (group 3). The discussion follows this order of the plant communities.

Group 1 Freshwater vegetation (Plate 59)

AQUATIC PLANTS (CAN BE COMPARED WITH CLASSES 1.3–1.4 TODAY)

There is a fairly rich aquatic macrofossil flora with *Ranunculus* subgenus *Batrachium* (water crowfoot), *Nymphaea alba* (white water-lily), *Nuphar* cf. *lutea* (yellow water-lily), *Myriophyllum verticillatum* (millfoil), *Zannichellia palustris* (horned pondweed) and Potamogetonaceae (pondweeds) all present in both the Neolithic SS1 (except *Zannichellia*) and Bronze Age WF1b material. There is a substantial pollen record of *Potamogeton* type, as well as scattered records of *Nymphaea*, *Myriophyllum* and *Sparganium/Typha* type in the pollen diagrams (Figs. 112 and 113). These would now be found growing as part of the Potamogetonetalia (1.3) (pondweed vegetation), with rooted rather than fully floating water plants, in still or slow-moving water (Haslam *et al.* 1982).

Ceratophyllum sp. (hornwort) was found only in the layer samples and now belongs in 1.4 Littorelletea, characteristic of slightly stiller water. These plants would probably have grown in the river, by the edge. There are no signs of free-floating plants here to suggest that the water was completely still, as in an oxbow. The plant community is a natural one that is virtually unaffected by direct human activities apart from pollution, although the river environment seems to have differed from today's (see below). The prehistoric plant community represented by these remains is then likely to have been similar to the present-day one.

The remains of these plants could have come from the vegetation of shallow water deposited near where it grew, or could have floated downstream and been deposited in flood debris on the riverbank, so this part of the deposit could be largely natural in origin. This evidence corresponds with that from the beetles and molluscs which feed upon these aquatic plants and others indicating slowly flowing water, evidently the conditions under which the material collected. In the WF1b pollen diagram the record of *Potamogeton* type (pondweeds) becomes rare above 80 cm, which might be an indication of less aquatic (or less regularly flooded) conditions.

WATERSIDE PLANTS (1.5 PHRAGMITETEA) (PLATE 60)

These are also well represented, by records of *Ranunculus* cf. *lingua* (greater spearwort), *Rorippa* sp. (pennycress), *Nasturtium officinale* (watercress), cf. *Apium nodiflorum* (fool's watercress), *Oenanthe aquatica* (water dropwort), *Lycopus europaeus* (gypsywort), *Alisma* sp. (water plantain), *Sagittaria sagittifolia* (arrowhead), *Sparganium* sp. (bur-reed) macrofossils and *Sparganium/Typha angustifolia*-type pollen, *Iris pseudacorus* (yellow flag), *Schoenoplectus* (club-rush), *Eleocharis* sp. (spike-rush), and various species of *Carex* (sedges).

This vegetation is characteristic of permanently wet places such as river banks and pond edges, called 'bankside' (Lambrick and Robinson 1979). It would have grown by the body of water in which the aquatic plants lived, along the riverside. *Sparganium* can also be found growing in deeper water with a fairly strong current (Haslam *et al.* 1982) but generally waterside vegetation acts to slow a river almost to a standstill. Although some of the plants can be used by man, this flora also seems to represent part of the natural vegetation of the river edge by the site. The remains would then have accumulated directly from plants growing on the spot, or brought with flood debris. There is a corresponding fauna of beetles which feed upon these plants, or which live on wet river banks. The Neolithic flora consists of only five taxa compared with some 20 in the Bronze Age samples. It is possible that forest clearance and farming in the Bronze Age led to more soil erosion into the river, and hence muddier river bank conditions with more habitats for such taxa.

MARSH VEGETATION (1.7)

Three taxa, *Ranunculus flammula* (lesser spearwort), *Hydrocotyle vulgaris* (pennywort) and *Menyanthes trifoliata* (bogbean), were identified from macrofossils, and a grain of pollen from pennywort. There was a trace of pollen of *Pedicularis* type (lousewort), although, surprisingly, no macrofossils, even though they do occur on other sites. Occasional leaves and spores of *Sphagnum* moss were also found. The modern vegetation with such taxa is usually characteristic of wetlands which are either acidic mires or base-rich fens. *Menyanthes* and *Sphagnum* are most characteristic of oligotrophic (nutrient-poor, acid) conditions, the other taxa representing a more mesotrophic (neutral) environment. Of course, the soils under the wildwood may well have been acid to neutral brown forest soils, allowing such communities as this to flourish on boggy land. The calcareous sediment may only have been exposed through erosion following forest clearance and farming, leading to the formation of more base-rich soils and the spread of the calcicolous flora. It is not clear whether there could have been suitable habitats right on the site, or if this might represent something brought from elsewhere, perhaps with *Sphagnum* moss. Other marshy vegetation is represented by some of the weed vegetation.

DISCUSSION OF WETLAND VEGETATION

The wetland vegetation detailed above (apart from the damp woodland discussed below under class 8), is fairly well represented at Runnymede. The aquatic and wetland plant communities represented by these remains are perhaps the 'natural background' vegetation which would have been associated with the river, its edge and banks and perhaps with other damp places. The vegetation appears to have been similar to that which grows in and near rivers today (apart from the recent additions to our flora). There is no direct sign of human influence in this wetland assemblage.

Aquatic and wetland vegetation is much less in evidence in some of the archaeological layers; so, for example, in the midden (L19) only *Rorippa* cf. *palustris*, *Nasturtium officinale* and *Schoenoplectus lacustris* were present.

Group 3 Weed and wasteland vegetation (Plate 61)

These communities characteristically consist of plants with requirements for rather open conditions and which colonise bare ground well. In contrast to the comparatively well defined wetland habitats and plant communities described above, weedy vegetation is very hard to classify into communities, because it is by nature transient. The weed taxa from Runnymede are hard to group even before one starts to think about the differences between prehistoric and modern weed communities, which are likely to be very great. They are very well represented by seed records because weeds are productive, but hardly at all in the pollen diagrams because of the low level of identification possible (Caryophyllaceae) as well as the low level of pollen dispersal.

WET SPRINGS (3.1)

Montia fontana spp. *chondrosperma* (blinks) found in the midden (L19) grows on wet stony ground, although it is so insignificant that the plant is not often seen; nevertheless the seeds are not uncommonly found in archaeological material. *Isolepis setacea* (bristle scirpus) is also in this group.

MUDDY WATERSIDE VEGETATION (3.2)

Ranunculus sceleratus (celery-leaved crowfoot) is characteristic of rather muddy conditions, and often found now in ditches. Only a few seeds were found, in one layer sample, in one SS1 and one WF1b column sample. The small amount of evidence for muddy bank vegetation suggests that these were not the general conditions, which were instead of sandy or gravelly banks, as argued above.

SPRING-GERMINATING ANNUAL WEEDS (3.3)

These plants grow on dry land, in contrast to the ones already discussed. They are especially common on disturbed ground, as in gardens, and in fields. The Neolithic flora contains a number of weeds in this modern vegetation grouping, such as *Brassica rapa* spp. *campestris* (wild turnip), the exact identity of which was suggested by Mark Robinson (some of the large Cruciferae pollen record may be from this), *Solanum nigrum* (black nightshade), *Linaria vulgaris* (yellow toadflax) and *Sonchus asper* (spiny sow-thistle).

The Bronze Age weed flora is much greater, bringing the number of taxa up to 24, and the seeds represented are sometimes very abundant: for example, those of *Stellaria media* (chickweed), *Chenopodium* cf. *album* (goosefoot) and *Urtica urens* (small nettle), which occur in hundreds. There are also significant Caryophyllaceae, *Chenopodium* and *Urtica* pollen records. Some of the taxa grow best on light sandy soils – for example, *Fumaria* (fumitory) and *Thlaspi* (pennycress) – while others are simply common weeds which have remained ubiquitous. Some sediment from the site was certainly very light and sandy, and it may at least partly represent the state of the prehistoric soil. The weeds may have grown on the sand and gravel banks thrown up by the changing river course (see Chapters 11 and 23) or on disturbed ground in and around the occupied site, or they could have been brought in with plant materials. Another weed, *Hyoscyamus niger* (henbane) is notably thermophilous, and much less common now than its fossil record would suggest it was in the past.

POSSIBLE CORNFIELD WEEDS (3.4 SECALIETEA)

A few weeds are now classified as being more associated with autumn-sown cornfields than with gardens and open land, although the difference between 3.3 and 3.4 is very blurred, especially in the present oceanic climate of Britain, where many weeds succeed from germinations throughout much of the winter. The Neolithic evidence for this class is small, including *Aphanes arvensis*, *A. microcarpa* and *Valerianella locusta*. In the Bronze Age floras typical taxa are *Papaver rhoeas/dubium/lecoqii* (poppy), *P. argemone* (long prickly-headed poppy), *Aphanes arvensis* (parsley piert), and *Polygonum convolvulus* (bindweed). Also found was cf. *Anagallis* (possible pimpernel) and *Valerianella locusta* (corn salad). There are very few pollen records that can be attributed to this class, for reasons of poor pollen dispersal and identifiability. Many of the taxa grow particularly on sandy or light soils.

The weed seeds that are found in a charred state provide clues that those particular weeds may have grown among cereal crops and then been processed together with cereals and finally burnt with the remains, leaving a few charred fragments in the ashes. This is not an infallible rule, since all sorts of things get burnt, and conversely, not quite all the cereal remains were charred. However, among the plants classified as potential cornfield weeds on modern ecological grounds, *Vicia* cf. *hirsuta*, *Polygonum convolvulus* (black bindweed), *Galium* sp. (cleavers), and *Tripleurospermum inodorum* were found charred. *P. convolvulus* was especially abundant in the midden, L19. Charred *Bromus* (brome) was also present in many of the samples, with traces of *Avena* (oat) and *Secale* (rye), which would appear to have been weeds, although their seeds may well have been gathered up and consumed together with those of the crops themselves. *Lapsana communis* (nipplewort), which was found charred, may also have grown as a cornfield weed in the prehistoric period although not now classified as such (see below). Bindweed was already growing on site during excavation and the other plants grow on open ground, so their presence does not necessarily indicate cereal cultivation.

CROP PLANTS (PLATES 62–67)

The cultivated plants and other useful ones are a prime feature of interest in a site such as this. One of the first pieces of environmental work on site was to mix some sediment in a bucket of water and scoop off charred grain, thus proving its abundance in the layers being excavated. The waterlogging of the site and its plant remains has provided charred cereal remains in an exceptional state of preservation, which Lisa Moffett helped identify. Some of the cereals were partly charred, and there were some waterlogged remains as well. Only a fairly small proportion of the cereal remains were exactly identifiable, notably well preserved chaff.

No identifiable charred cereals have been found among the Neolithic material so far, but since only a trace of cereal pollen was present, there were probably not many cereals around. There was a possible charred pea.

The Late Bronze Age material contained enough good chaff and rachis material to show clearly that *Triticum spelta* (spelt wheat) and *T. dicoccum* (emmer wheat) were both present, in a ratio of about 3:1, according to the identifiable chaff. A small amount of *Hordeum vulgare* (barley; possibly both two- and six row) was found. *Avena* (oats) and *Secale cereale* (rye), were both present in trace quantities, although it is not clear whether these last two were more than weedy contaminants in the wheat and barley crops. There was a slight cereal pollen record throughout the waterfront profile, with moderate amounts at 112 cm and 128 cm. The coincidence of macrofossil (at 120 cm) with pollen evidence of cereals shows that this pollen, at least, may represent what was brought to the site with grain or straw for processing there. The smaller pollen records may represent transport of pollen by wind and water from nearby cornfields, with less brought in with corn and straw. *Linum usitatissimum* (flax) seed and capsule were also present in the Bronze Age material, but no pollen (production is extremely low).

The crops would have been grown on well-drained open land. One can speculate that if the occupied site was in a woodland clearing, the fields were probably close by so that they could be protected against domestic and wild animals, and birds. After harvest the crops would have been stored and then processed in small batches when needed. Products such as cereal straw may have had a number of uses, including perhaps the feeding of stock.

The cereals could have been sown in autumn or in spring, but there is no indication of either season. Emmer and spelt are normally autumn-sown – indeed this is the natural season for wild plants to sow themselves. Some barley and all flax are spring-sown: the spring sowing allows more land to be cleared and sown, or land occupied by failed winter crops to be re-cultivated and reused.

The flax straw was probably used for making linen fibre but linseed may have been eaten as well. Peas and beans may have been grown but have failed to become preserved.

NITROPHILOUS PERENNIAL WEEDS (3.5 ARTEMISIETALIA)

There are also records of a number of perennial weeds such as *Conium maculatum* (hemlock), *Urtica dioica* (stinging nettle), *Artemisia* (mugwort) from pollen alone, which is assumed to represent *A. vulgaris* and is mainly in the middle part of the waterfront pollen diagram, and species of *Arctium* (burdock) and *Cirsium* (thistle). In the past, members of this community, such as *Artemisia* and the *Cirsium* thistles, may have persisted in arable land, for their roots may have proved hard to destroy with the tools available, such as ard ploughs. Other taxa grow in rather damp and shady places, such as valley scrub, for example: *Rubus idaeus* (raspberry). *Eupatorium cannabinum* (hemp agrimony) may be responsible for the *Anthemis*-type pollen records (mainly in WF1), since it is the only plant with a significant macrofossil record that produces this pollen type. *Lapsana communis* (nipplewort) occurs here, although its consistent occurrence in charred-grain assemblages here and elsewhere (Knörzer 1971) shows that it was probably another weed of cornfields.

This vegetation may have grown on the site as well, particularly if areas were abandoned for more than a year or so. The wild raspberries, and the brambles as well, may have been gathered as food, although there is no supporting evidence – the excrement found was apparently all dog-turds rather than from humans, so there is no direct evidence of human diet.

PATHWAYS AND TRODDEN PLACES (3.7) (PLATE 68)

There is evidence of trodden vegetation in the plants of class 3.7 (Plantaginetea), such as *Potentilla anserina* (silverweed) and *P. reptans* (creeping cinquefoil), as well as *Plantago major* (great plantain). *P. anserina* is a coloniser of sandy river-beaches, and would therefore have been part of the natural vegetation.

Group 5 Heathland and grassland vegetation

HEATHLAND

There is a single Neolithic pollen record of Ericales (heathers, etc.) and rather more from the Bronze Age WF1 diagram, along with a single heather-feeding weevil; there is thus only slight evidence for heathland. Some soils on site were light and sandy (shown by the preferences of some of the weed taxa), although at the same time somewhat base-rich (all pollen samples were strongly calcareous), certainly at river level; it is not clear whether they would easily become podzolised to heathland after forest clearance and erosion. The sandy and gravelly soils of the Bagshot Beds, which easily support heathland, outcrop about 1.5 km from Runnymede, and Tertiary sandstone was `brought to the site. Heathland products might have been brought to the site in various forms and the pollen could easily have blown in the wind.

GRASSLANDS (PLATE 68)

There are a few taxa which occur in a large range of different kinds of grasslands, such as the species of *Leontodon* (hawkbit). These could partly be the source of the Compositae (L) pollen, which is abundant, especially in the WF1b pollen diagram. A large Compositae (L) record is occasionally found in archaeological deposits and there is often very little corresponding macrofossil record. Sometimes the pollen is simply over-represented by differential preservation (which could be the case with the upper part of the WF1b pollen diagram). Otherwise the record seems associated with other evidence for short grassland (Greig 1982a).

Sample L24* contained two seeds of *Dianthus armeria* (Deptford Pink), which is a plant of rather dry grassland on light soils. It is rare and decreasing in Britain now, but has recently been found at various other sites.

DRY ACID GRASSLAND AND HEATHLAND (5.1)

There were some macrofossil records of plants of rather acid, sandy soils, such as *Potentilla erecta* (tormentil) and *Rumex acetosella* (sorrel). The pollen record of *Polygala* (milkwort) is included here, as some species grow in this habitat. *Centaurea nigra* (knapweed) pollen is also included here, although in Britain it grows widely in neutral grasslands.

DRY CHALK GRASSLANDS (5.3) (PLATE 69)

There is a small chalk grassland flora from the Neolithic material, represented by *Plantago media* (hoary plantain) and more specifically by *Sanguisorba minor* (small burnet). The Bronze Age flora is larger, with macrofossils of *Medicago*

lupulina (black medick) and *Scabiosa columbaria* (small scabious) as well.

GRASSLANDS ON MOIST AND WET SOILS (5.4) (PLATE 69)

There is plenty of evidence of grassland even in the Neolithic; some represents a distinctly damp habitat, with *Caltha* (kingcup) pollen, *Hypericum* cf. *tetrapterum* (square-stemmed St John's Wort), *Lychnis flos-cuculi* (ragged robin) and *Filipendula ulmaria* (meadowsweet). The abundant Gramineae pollen could represent grassland, or aquatic grasses such as *Phragmites* (reed), which do not leave a good macrofossil record.

The Bronze Age material has an increased flora with *Thalictrum flavum* (meadow rue) and *Sanguisorba officinalis* (greater burnet).

The grasslands indicated have affinities with the water meadows of the Thames such as Picksey (or Pixey) Mead near Oxford, although with only two of the taxa present in this fossil record, compared with the large flora of the modern meadows. At Runnymede it is uncertain whether such grassland could have grown in a natural plant community along the damp river edge, or whether it was affected by human occupation and especially by grazing, as seems likely. Further comparison is possible in the mollusc faunas, since Mark Robinson has found that these can also be characteristic of different kinds of grassland (Lambrick and Robinson 1988); certainly many of the Picksey Mead taxa are also present at Runnymede, while the molluscs are more characteristic of grazed pasture on Port Meadow, such as *Anisus leucostoma*, are uncommon, suggesting more meadow-like than pasture-like conditions at Runnymede.

Grassland on less obviously damp ground seems to be indicated by the Neolithic records of *Ranunculus* cf. *acris* (meadow buttercup), pollen of *Trifolium repens* and *T. pratense* (white and red clovers), of *Plantago lanceolata* (ribwort plantain) and seeds of *Prunella vulgaris* (self-heal). The *Rhinanthus*-type pollen records seems to be confirmed by a Bronze Age macrofossil; otherwise pollen of Scrophulariaceae can be hard to identify exactly. There is also a Bronze Age record of *Taraxacum* (dandelion). The records of *Centaurea nigra*-type pollen (knapweed) also probably belong in this mesotrophic grassland assemblage.

Beetles that feed on grass roots and on members of the Leguminosae are also present, providing additional evidence for this vegetation.

Traditionally, meadows and pastures were mainly in the part of the river valley which regularly became flooded in winter and was therefore unsuitable for growing autumn-sown cereals. In the early Neolithic, use was made of leaf fodder (Welten 1967), but later in the prehistoric period grassy material was used, which could have been obtained in woodlands and on the grasslands and heathlands, developing on abandoned fields. In fact grazing pressure may have been an important factor in preventing forest regeneration. This certainly seems to have been the case at Runnymede, where the signs of grasslands increase with time.

Table 28: Percentage tree cover indicated by pollen.
Calculated according to Andersen 1970. With *Alnus* included in the pollen sum (+*Alnus*), and excluded (−*Alnus*). Based on SS1 at 130 cm

	Number of grains	Factor	Corr. no.	% cover +Alnus	%cover −Alnus	
Pinus	23	×4	92	16	20	pine
Tilia	20	×8	160	28	36	lime
Acer	1	×8	8	1	2	maple
Ulmus	9	×4	36	6	8	elm
Betula	5	×1	5	1	1	birch
Alnus	124	×1	124	22	—	alder
Quercus	106	×1	106	19	24	oak
Fraxinus	5	×8	40	7	9	ash
Totals	293		607	100	100	

Part of the (marshier) grassland could have been growing on site or very close by. Grassland seeds and pollen could also have been brought into the site with fodder (if it was gathered) or with dung (for which there is substantial beetle evidence). The stock could have been brought in to the site from time to time, perhaps for safety, and could have dropped dung containing evidence of grazing pastures that were some distance away. Whether this assemblage represents managed grasslands as early as the Bronze Age is a matter of debate (Greig 1988a; Lambrick and Robinson 1988), but one can certainly say that some of the characteristic taxa of our present-day traditional meadow and pasture plant communities were present then.

Group 6 Woodland herbs and understorey

There are only a few records; *Hypericum* cf. *perforatum* (common St John's wort) occurs in woodland clearings (but also in grassland). *Fragaria vesca* (wild strawberry) also grows in woodlands, but may well have been gathered for food. *Torilis japonica* (upright hedge parsley) grows in woods and along hedgerows now, also in open places. *Sambucus nigra* (elder) also grows under woods as its natural habitat. However, it has a strong association with places enriched by human occupation, and the continuous pollen record in the upper part of the SS1 pollen diagram might be a sign that the site became overgrown after Neolithic occupation.

Group 8 Forest, woodland, scrub (Plates 70 and 71)

ALDER CARR (8.2)

In the SS1 profile there are plentiful macrofossil records of *Alnus* (alder), with seeds and catkins present, as well as a substantial pollen record throughout, averaging 66% land pollen sum. In the WF1b profile there is much less pollen, usually less than 10% LPS. There were also records of alder-feeding insects. The records of *Salix* (willow) pollen could represent willows growing along the river bank.

Alder carr seems to be one of the most widespread kinds of vegetation on the site, although some of the evidence could have been borne there by the river. There is a considerable difference between the amount of evidence of alder

carr in the Neolithic, and its reduced but still important presence in the Late Bronze Age sequence. This may be the result of a general decrease in alder carr, or just a change in the way it is represented, which would be affected by local clearance, and the amounts of other plant materials deposited at the site.

BROAD-LEAVED WOODLAND AND FOREST (8.4)

The Middle Neolithic woodland and forest is rather poorly represented in the macrofossil record, with a little *Rhamnus catharticus* (buckthorn), *Crataegus* (hawthorn), a few buds and many unidentified twigs in the sediment. The wood report also provides evidence for a range of readily available wood, apart from *Tilia* (lime) which is not readily preserved.

The pollen diagram (Figs. 112 and 113) gives a somewhat different picture, and particularly the tree pollen diagram (Fig. 114), which shows tree and shrub pollen (except *Alnus* and *Corylus*) averaging 56% total dry land pollen. This was mainly of *Quercus* (oak), *Ulmus* (elm) and *Tilia* (lime), with some *Fraxinus* (ash), *Pinus* (pine), *Betula* (birch), *Acer* (maple) and *Hedera* (ivy), and traces of pollen of *Crataegus* type (hawthorn) and *Taxus* (yew). This represents fairly forested conditions, which are also indicated by the old forest beetle fauna.

When one calculates the tree cover represented by these pollen records according to Andersen (1970), one gets the figures shown in Table 28, with and without alder.

The main woodland tree was lime. If one considers it grew in a lime/elm/oak mixture on good soils it would have been responsible for about 40% of the total tree cover, and the alder/oak would have occupied the damper parts of the river valley. Even considering all the woodland together (including alder), the forest cover is still mainly of lime. *Corylus* (hazel) has not been included, but the large amounts of pollen show that it was certainly present as a forest understorey. Other taxa, such as *Crataegus* (haw) and *Taxus* (yew), are not allowed for in the calculation, and their pollen is likely to be very poorly represented, yet they may even have been locally dominant because there is a pollen and macrofossil record.

The representation of trees and shrubs by pollen, seeds and buds/twigs is very different according to each kind of evidence and is also hard to interpret in terms of forest composition, cover and nearness to the site. Further evidence of afforestation comes from the snails in terrestrial group B, which are somewhat more abundant in the lower part of the SS1 sequence (see Evans, Chapter 15).

In the Bronze Age WF1b samples (Plates 70 and 71) there is a modest macrofossil record of trees and shrubs. Seeds or fruitstones of *Taxus baccata* (yew), *Rhamnus catharticus* (purging buckthorn), *Cornus sanguinea* (dogwood), *Crataegus* sp. (hawthorn), *Prunus spinosa* (blackthorn), *Sorbus* cf. *torminalis* (possible wild service) were found. Philippa Tomlinson identified a number of buds and bud-scales of *Quercus* sp. (oak) and one of cf. *Betula* (birch).

Pollen records add *Ulmus* (elm), *Tilia* (lime), *Fraxinus* (ash), *Fagus* (beech), *Betula* (birch), *Acer* (maple), and *Pinus* (pine). There was no *Hedera* (ivy). The diagram showing the percentage of tree pollen (Fig. 114) shows a great reduction in the Bronze Age WF1b column results compared with those in the Neolithic sequence from the SS1 column.

The arrival of *Fagus* (beech) pollen represents an important horizon; it was not found at all in SS1, but there are scattered records in WF1b. Beech spread across Europe during the prehistoric period, perhaps by invading cleared land or secondary woodland, and maybe also favoured by warmer winters (Huntley 1988); it reached Britain by the Bronze or Iron Age. In Britain there are few sites so far showing signs of large amounts of beech woods.

Some evidence of wooded conditions is also provided by the macrofossil records of woodland understorey plants such as *Rosa* sp. (wild rose) and *Humulus lupulus* (hop), and herbs such as *Stellaria* cf. *nemorum* (wood stitchwort), *Moehringia trinervia* (three-veined sandwort), *Mercurialis perennis* (dog's mercury) and *Glechoma hederacea* (ground ivy).

The pollen records seem to show that there was much less forest in the immediate surroundings of Runnymede Bridge by the Late Bronze Age. Even *Quercus* (oak) pollen does not reach 10%, and the other records are much less, with *Tilia* and *Ulmus* discontinuous. The signs of woodland in the flora are not enough to represent a forested surrounding to the site, although there does seem to have been woodland close by, with enough oak wood to provide the timber for the piles on the site. The presence of buckthorn, dogwood, blackthorn and hawthorn could represent either scrub, or the propagation of these shrubs for fencing or hedging, botanical evidence of which has been found at other sites from the Neolithic onwards (Groeman-van Waateringe 1978); stock-raising at Runnymede does seem to have been important, judging from Geraldene Done's report on the animal bones; hedges may have been necessary to confine such animals. There is also a hint of woodland in the find of possible Neolithic beaver. The beetle evidence suggests a great reduction in woodland cover (Chapter 17), although the woodland/shade-indicating molluscs are somewhat more abundant in WF1b from 140 cm to the bottom (Chapter 15).

Some of the pollen would have arrived by natural dispersal with wind and water. The area represented by these pollen results (pollen catchment) is probably fairly local, since the deposit seems to have been like a slowly running stream, or pool catching flood debris. The catchment would extent upstream along the river some way, although this might be a uniform environment causing the riverbank vegetation such as the alder carr to be especially well represented. Pollen may also have been brought to the site with plant materials, and this is shown by the peaks of cereal pollen together with cereal macrofossils. It is debatable how much pollen of non-riverside vegetation, such as that of the dry calcareous grassland, could have arrived naturally or not; the pollen of taxa from this habitat such as *Sanguisorba minor* is found in 'natural' riverside deposits also (Greig 1987).

Discussion

Change at Runnymede; comparing the Neolithic with the Bronze Age

The pollen results from the Neolithic SS1 profile show substantial signs of forest in the Late Neolithic. Although the sequence is rather uniform, there is a slight increase in *Tilia*, *Pinus*, *Hedera* and *Polypodium* towards the top, which could be a sign of forest re-growth, matching the reduction in signs of an open environment noted by Mark Robinson (Chapter 17). The great drop in tree pollen between the Neolithic and the Bronze Age is shown in Figure 114. The Bronze Age WF1b pollen diagram seems to consist of more or less a single pollen assemblage. Although there is a clear change in sediment type, from peaty and shelly sand to alluvium, the plant remains in it seem to have remained essentially the same. It shows that by the Late Bronze Age all woodland was much reduced compared with the Neolithic, and signs of grasslands and other open vegetation are correspondingly greater, although some of this could be the result of pollen from imported material. Even the ubiquitous alder and hazel are reduced to a fraction of their former percentages. Beech appears in the Bronze Age, and ivy disappears, while among herbs there are many more records, partly because there were some well preserved pollen samples that allowed large counts.

Aquatic and wetland vegetation, alluviation

The river environments in which the aquatic and wetland flora grew were greatly affected by sedimentary changes. The Mesolithic landscape seems to have been in an equilibrium, with stable vegetation, mainly of forest – the 'wildwood' – maintaining stable soils and sediments. When Neolithic farming and forest clearance began, the balance was disturbed and erosion started, very gradually at first. The human activities would have started soil-wash down into hollows and valleys, thus causing alluvial deposits to start forming, with perhaps an effect on aquatic and wetland vegetation; such a mechanism appears to have caused the deposits at West Heath Spa to start accumulating in the early (pre-elm decline) Neolithic (Greig 1991). The present deposits at Runnymede do not cover the Mesolithic–Neolithic change. The Neolithic sequence has plenty of evidence of aquatic and waterside plants, of which Ceratophyllum was only found then. This flora does not appear to have developed much by the Bronze Age, as there are then only three more taxa, *Hydrocotyle vulgaris*, *Zannichellia palustris* and *Iris pseudacorus*.

Organic deposits of Bronze to Iron Age date, though lacking the obvious signs of occupation seen at Runnymede, have been found along the river Avon in Warwickshire (Shotton 1978, Osborne 1988) and along the river Chelmer at Little Waltham (Peglar and Wilson 1978), and they have been exposed in the valleys of even quite small streams, as at Beckford (Greig and Colledge 1988). One might have thought of these organic river sediments as natural oxbow fills or similar, but their date range and open-landscape faunas and floras seem to connect them with human activity and with the consequent soil erosion and build-up of sediment in rivers caused by it (Shotton 1978). The biological remains in these organic deposits contain evidence of an occupied landscape, even if not of direct occupation itself. The alluvium seems to have hindered drainage so that these organic sediments could collect and then in turn become buried and thus preserved. At these sites, the local wetland floras are as might be expected from river bank and marshland, so they tell us little about the occupied landscape. The only sign of human activities may be an indirect one in the formation of such deposits as a side-effect of erosion.

It is a little hard to visualise the appearance of these rivers in prehistoric times, since almost all watercourses are now carefully controlled by the water authorities. The results from the Avon suggest a river running clean and shallow over a stony bed, in contrast to the modern turbid stream with a muddy bottom, flowing between and constricted by walls of alluvium. Of course, these floras of damp habitats do not represent, we assume, the usual human environment of the Bronze Age: a more typical surrounding is perhaps shown by the results from the Wilsford shaft, a deep well sunk into chalkland, in which remains of very few wetland plants were found (Robinson 1989).

Weed floras and occupation
The Middle Neolithic weed and wayside flora from Runnymede, although small in number of taxa, is actually large compared with the weed floras found at most other sites, and contains *Valerianella locusta*, which does not seem to have been found at other Neolithic sites. The typical range of cornfield weeds, judging by those found charred at The Stumble, consists of *Vicia* sp., Chenopodiaceae, *Polygonum aviculare*, *Rumex* sp., and *Galium aparine* (Murphy 1989).

In the Late Bronze Age levels at Runnymede many of the summer annual weeds that are still common today are present, and most of these have also been found at other Bronze Age sites with good waterlogged weed floras, such as those from the well at Wilsford and ditches at Berinsfield,

Oxfordshire (Robinson 1989 and forthcoming). A peculiar absence at Runnymede compared with most of the other sites appeared for some while to be *Tripleurospermum inodorum* (scentless mayweed), although it does not seem to preserve well when waterlogged. It was finally found charred in L19. Two cornfield weeds, *Lithospermum arvense* (corn gromwell) and *Sherardia arvensis* (field madder) (at Berinfield) were not found at Runnymede. The former was found at Black Patch, near Uckfield, East Sussex (Hinton 1982) and the latter was found charred at Abingdon (Jones 1978). At Potterne there were also found *Capsella bursa-pastoris* (shepherd's purse), *Lithospermum arvense* (corn gromwell), *Veronica hederifolia* (ivy-leaved speedwell) and *Odontites verna* (red Bartsia) (Straker forthcoming), which were not found at Runnymede and are perhaps connected with heavier soils around Potterne. *Ranunculus parviflorus* (small-flowered buttercup) is present at a number of Bronze Age sites as well as at Runnymede – for example at Little Waltham (Peglar and Wilson 1978). It may have grown as a cornfield weed on light dry soils.

Weeds characteristic of light soils have been found at many of these Bronze Age sites in addition to Runnymede, and may indicate that light or sandy soils were being cultivated. At Wilsford *Fumaria* (fumitory) and *Arenaria* (sandwort) were found (Robinson 1989), at Potterne mineralised *Thlaspi* (penny-cress) and *Spergula* (spurrey) (Carruthers 1986). Light soils are certainly easier to cultivate, and being 'warm' might have caused fewer problems with the introduction of originally Near-Eastern crops into a region with a rather oceanic climate, albeit possibly in an 'optimum'. Prehistoric occupation was soil-determined to some extent, as the distribution of the *Bandkeramik* in Europe seems to follow loess soils, and the quality of the soils may have affected the occupation of the landscape of Britain as well. It is sometimes difficult to study this, as wholesale erosion has removed or truncated many sites, and the subsequent alluviation has then buried many others, such as Runnymede itself.

The actual weed communities in the Bronze Age probably differed from those of later times – 'completely different from the crop arable weed communities of modern phytosociology' (Willerding 1988) – not only because the flora was smaller then (lacking many of the typical 'winter corn weeds') but because the possible habitats offered by the activities of people and animals may have been peculiar to the Bronze Age or at least to the prehistoric period. Thus *Lapsana communis* (nipplewort) seems to have been a cornfield weed then (Knörzer 1971). If charring is a guide to the weeds most likely to have been burnt along with crop-processing waste, the following, found as charred remains in the Wilsford shaft, may indicate some of the cornfield weeds typical of the Bronze Age: *Fumaria*, *Stellaria media*, *Chenopodium*, *Plantago lanceolata*, *Galium aparine*, *Tripleurospermum*, and *Bromus* (Robinson 1989). The different weed flora, compared with now, means that the balance of competition between the various taxa in this smaller prehistoric flora would have been different (Willerding 1988).

Many of the weeds could flourish wherever the ground was disturbed and enriched, both in fields and around a settlement, or where livestock walked to drink at the river, or where they were penned, perhaps forming combinations not seen much now. It is not hard to imagine suitable habitats for weeds right on the eyot where the site stood.

Even Bronze Age organic deposits with no sign of occupation on the spot could contain large weed floras of arable weeds, as at Little Waltham (Peglar and Wilson 1978), Beckford (Greig and Colledge 1988) and Bidford upon Avon (Greig 1987). These may perhaps represent the occupied nature of the landscape as a whole, even though there was no evidence of actual settlement at the sites (apart perhaps from some charred grain at Beckford). The seeds and pollen from the weeds could have become preserved in a number of ways: either the arable dry land was close enough to the rivers and marshes for the seeds to have been deposited there by natural dispersal, or all the marshes had enough human activity to transport material containing these seeds there, or the material was borne downstream by the river and deposited by floods. Perhaps all three factors played a part.

The weed floras are also interesting in that they have provided earlier records of a number of plants hitherto only recorded from Iron Age or later deposits; at Runnymede the presence of *Conium maculatum* (hemlock) is early. Too little was previously known about such prehistoric vegetation, and the few plants recorded from Bronze Age sites said as much about the scarcity of information as about the limited nature of the floras themselves. Now that rich sites are beginning to be investigated, the true extent of the Bronze Age flora can be appreciated, although there is always room for surprises in future results.

Cultivated plants

Before the Runnymede excavation the evidence of Neolithic and Bronze Age crops was so slight that there was scarcely any further information than that provided by Jessen and Helbæk (1944). More recently there has been a flood of good data, mainly on the Bronze Age.

The Neolithic levels of Runnymede have so far only contributed two possible peas to our knowledge of crops at this time. More evidence has been compiled by Moffett *et al.* (1989) showing that emmer, bread wheat and barley were certainly present during the Neolithic, but the actual remains found were very scarce at many of these sites – wild food plants such as crab apples and hazelnuts are often more in evidence than cereals, emphasising the process of transition between hunting/gathering and farming. From the Neolithic site at The Stumble, Peter Murphy has identified charred remains of mainly emmer wheat, with a little naked barley and a trace of einkorn, along with hazelnuts, sloe stones and unidentifiable root fragments that may represent food remains (Murphy 1989).

The Late Bronze Age crops at Runnymede and other sites are principally emmer and spelt wheats, barley, and flax. The main newcomer is spelt, and the status of this was uncertain until recently; it was not recorded at Abingdon (Jones 1978), only tentatively at West Row, Mildenhall, Suffolk (Murphy 1983; Martin and Murphy 1988), and there were only traces found at Black Patch (Hinton 1982). Spelt has been found at Potterne, Wiltshire (Carruthers 1986), and Lofts Farm, Maldon, Essex (Murphy in Brown *et al.* 1988). Vanessa Straker also found bread wheat at Potterne, identified from rachis internodes, but found few other Bronze Age records for it (Straker forthcoming). Neither peas, beans, nor their pollen were detected in Bronze Age Runnymede, although they may simply not have been preserved. Finds of these legumes are generally rare, although there were several *Vicia faba* (field bean) found at Black Patch, Sussex (Hinton 1982). The rye and oats appear to be from weeds rather than crops, although, together with *Bromus*, they may have been consumed with the cultivated grains.

The spread of prehistoric farming across Europe is shown by pie diagrams of the crops found at the sites (Körber-Grohne 1981). This shows that emmer, barley and flax are the usual crops found preserved (as at Runnymede). Spelt does occur, although less frequently and mainly in the sub-alpine lakeshore settlements. Bread wheat (not found at Runnymede) is also found in some places. There are occasional finds of einkorn, peas and beans (and sometimes bitter vetch and lentils too), at these continental sites. Only a few peas and beans seem to have been found so far in Britain, and of these only a possible pea at Runnymede.

Other food plants

The remains of edible fruit of wild plants, including bramble, raspberry, wild strawberry, sloe, possible service tree and elder, were found at Runnymede, although there is no proof that any of these were actually eaten. Rose hips and hops could also have been used. There are generally fewer signs of this floral element at other sites, although *Prunus* and *Crataegus* were found at Wilsford (Robinson 1989), and hazel at West Row (Murphy 1983).

Heathland

The single Neolithic pollen record of Ericales from the Runnymede SS1 column represents slight signs of heathland, perhaps rather distant, compared with the much greater signs from West Heath Spa just after the elm-decline forest clearance, also probably about Middle Neolithic in date. This is probably site-related, since West Heath Spa is up on the sandy Bagshot soils, while the other Thames riverside sites show rather little sign of heathland filtering through the alder carr, as might be expected (Greig 1991). Evidently the early farming on some of the lighter soils started podzolisation, and perhaps continued grazing of such land prevented its regeneration. Traces of heathland development are to be seen in a number of pollen diagrams, and soil pollen analyses show this especially well, since the acid soils in which pollen is preserved are also those on which heathland could easily develop: results from Ascot dated to around 1900–1600 cal BC (3430 ± 70 BP, HAR-478) show well developed heathland there (Bradley and Keith-Lucas 1975).

Grasslands

As yet there is little comparative information on Neolithic grasslands. By the Middle Neolithic at Runnymede the indications are of large openings in the forest and developing grasslands, as shown by the SS1 results.

The signs of grassland floras are very much better represented in some Bronze Age remains. The insect remains often provide further evidence of grassland in the form of large dung-beetle faunas, which show that pasture (or meadow or indeed undifferentiated grassland) was probably present, notably at Wilsford, but also at Bidford, Pilgrim Lock and elsewhere (Osborne 1982, 1988).

Evidence of calcicolous grassland similar to that found at Runnymede came from the Wilsford shaft for example: *Sanguisorba minor* (salad burnet) and *Scabiosa columbaria* (small scabious), together with a number of additional taxa uch as *Agrimonia eupatoria* and cf. *Gentianella* (gentian) (Robinson 1989). *Agrimonia* was present at Potterne; otherwise there was little grassland evidence there, as would be expected from a mainly charred flora (Straker forthcoming). The fen grassland taxa at Runnymede, such as *Thalictrum flavum* (meadow rue) and *Sanguisorba officinalis* (greater burnet), have not yet been found at other sites. Only a few possible grassland plants have been found at other Bronze Age sites.

The development of these semi-natural grassland communities seems to have taken place in the Middle Neolithic–Bronze Age periods of agricultural expansion, especially the latter (Greig 1988). By the Bronze Age the signs of this rather open and grassy landscape are very clearly shown at a number of sites by pollen, seeds, beetles (dung beetles and root feeders) and molluscs, which adds up to some convincing evidence. Such an open landscape seems to have existed at least around settlements in the valleys of rivers such as the Thames and the Warwickshire Avon. Of course, the results do not show anything of the proportion of arable land to grassland, but it is likely that the farming was of a mixed nature, since there is evidence of both.

It is hard to tell whether these grasslands were managed, and how. The presence of tall herbs suggests that there was not just closely cropped pasture but taller more meadow-like vegetation as well. It is very hard to prove that the Bronze Age people were using such grassland for hay, in the way that Neolithic communities had gathered tree branches for leaf hay in Switzerland (Welten 1967). Since there is evidence of fairly sophisticated woodland management fairly early in the prehistoric period (Rackham 1980), perhaps grasslands were similarly well organised at this early stage (Greig 1988). Other opinions are more cautious (Lambrick and Robinson 1988).

Trees and woodland

WILDWOOD

At Runnymede, the Middle–Late Neolithic SS1 column has an average of 56% tree pollen and an old forest beetle fauna. It is perhaps a little surprising for an apparently occupied site to have so much evidence of forest. Other pollen sites also show signs of forest, with *Tilia*, *Ulmus* and *Quercus* as well as carr with *Alnus* in the London region. For example, at Hampstead Heath there was 95% tree pollen (dry-land pollen sum without *Alnus* or *Corylus*), down to 25–50% after the elm decline (Greig 1991, Devoy 1979). This forest is not so well represented in the macrofossil evidence: thus only a few *Betula* seeds were found at Hampstead Heath, despite the abundant pollen evidence. However, the main wildwood component, *Tilia*, was identified among the macrofossils at The Stumble (Murphy 1989).

Wildwood evidence has been found at some Bronze Age sites. The amount of tree pollen in the Later Bronze Age WF1b river channel deposits at Runnymede, containing 5–15% tree pollen, can be compared with 17% at Bidford and 15% at Little Waltham. This points to considerable deforestation along such river valleys by this stage. One does need to be very careful, though, because although a site may give signs of *relative* deforestation in reduction of tree pollen, this may have been influenced by factors such as changes in pollen dispersal caused by thinning of the forest canopy, or even in-wash of pollen from disturbed soils. One needs evidence from many sources, particularly beetles. It is very hard to prove *absolute* deforestation and say how much forest remained near a particular site. One can instead, however, generalise and say that the dry land along river valleys seems to have been utilised during the Bronze Age – hence the signs of a rather open landscape with grassland, dung beetles, weeds and perhaps a trace of cereals. The levels of tree pollen suggest that they had, as might be expected, less wildwood remaining in the immediate surroundings of the sites than was the case at less occupied places such as West Heath Spa, and indeed many of the pollen-analysed sites. Thus Bronze Age Runnymede was probably quite deforested if compared with the Early to Middle Neolithic, but rather forested compared with later times.

ALDER WOODS

The other probable primary woodland at Runnymede seems to have been alder carr (with oak) growing along the river banks. *Alnus* (alder) pollen rises before 8000 BP in the lower Thames valley and together with oak accounts for most of the tree pollen there (Devoy 1979). In the probable Early Neolithic sequence at West Heath Spa alder is fairly low, around 10%, but it rises steeply with the elm decline, apparently spreading with forest clearance. At Runnymede, alder is very well represented from pollen, macrofossils, wood and a beetle, which suggests that it grew on the spot or upstream, probably in a carr together with *Quercus* (oak) and *Salix* (willow), which were part of the natural or semi-natural riverside vegetation. In the Neolithic SS1 column there is an average 66% *Alnus* pollen, and any spread in alder would probably already have taken place.

The Bronze Age sequence at Runnymede has much less alder pollen, perhaps because of the settlement of the site. The Little Waltham river channel had considerable evidence of alder pollen and macrofossils; likewise Anslow's Cottages, and West Row, Mildenhall, but at Bidford-on-Avon there was only a trace of alder pollen.

SECONDARY WOODLAND

Assessing the remains of secondary woodland and scrub is difficult because certain species, such as *Malus sylvestris, Prunus spinosa and Crataegus* sp., are poorly represented in pollen records. It is possible, therefore, that these species were more important relative to wildwood than might appear to be the case; indeed they might already have gained some prominence during the Neolithic.

The Bronze Age sites usually have more signs of secondary woodland and scrub than the Neolithic ones. This can be seen in pollen records with the appearance of *Acer* (maple) pollen at Hampstead Heath, and maple macrofossils were found in the old river channel at Anslow's Cottages (Carruthers, forthcoming). At Hampstead there were slight increases in pollen from other secondary woodland trees such as *Fraxinus*. Macrofossil remains at most sites include thorny scrub plants such as *Prunus spinosa, Crataegus* and occasionally others. These may have become more frequent, either because they were protected from grazing by their thorns or because they were grown specially as hedging to contain stock, an idea advanced by Groenman-van Waateringe (1978) for Neolithic sites onwards. Even at Wilsford, a chalkland region thought to have been deforested early on, macrofossils of *Prunus, Crataegus* and *Corylus* were still present (Robinson 1989). *Rhamnus catharticus* (purging buckthorn) and *Taxus baccata* (yew) seem to have been found only at Runnymede so far. It is not clear whether the seeds found on site are the result of a particular use of yew, or occur because it grew close by.

BEECHWOODS

At West Heath Spa, *Fagus* (beech) records start just after the initial forest clearance/elm decline. The Neolithic results from Runnymede have no sign of beech, and nor do the Early–Mid Bronze Age Little Waltham results. The Late Bronze Age Runnymede results have scattered beech pollen records although no macrofossils of beechwood were found. Beech seems to have been a coloniser of suitable land already cleared of wildwood, and the river valleys are unlikely to have provided a good habitat. There are few pollen diagrams with substantial beech pollen records like those from Denmark, apart from the one from Epping Forest (Baker *et al.* 1978). Its rather poor pollen record, with just scattered grains, makes it hard to tell when beech arrived in this country; originally it was thought to be in the Iron Age, but now it seems to have been earlier.

HOLLY WOODS

Ilex (holly) also formed woods and was used for wood-pasture (Rackham 1980). These appear after elm decline clearance (at the same time as heath development) at West Heath Spa (Greig 1991). Holly seems to have been present in single-grain amounts during the Atlantic period, according to evidence from some Thames-side sites (Devoy 1979). There does not seem to have been much at Runnymede, where the sole evidence was some holly wood, but poor pollen and seed dispersal seems to cause holly to be generally under-represented. Holly shows more evidence from acid sandy sites, and therefore features in soil pollen analyses such as those from Ascot (Bradley and Keith-Lucas 1975) as well as in many other such results (Dimbleby 1985).

Summary

The Middle–Late Neolithic and Late Bronze Age botanical evidence is very good from this waterlogged material, which is rich in plant remains. There are waterlogged and charred macrofossils and an extensive pollen flora too. The flora indicates the following main vegetation groups. Aquatic plants include both bankside and marshland ones, which are likely to have been growing close by or at the river's edge. There are many weeds, especially those which grow on light sandy soils. There are grassland plants with habitat indications ranging from damp fen or marshy grassland through to dry calcicolous grassland, the latter possibly having been brought to the site with animal fodder. Woodland includes alder/oak forest and some scrub around the site, and lime/elm wildwood on drier land; its extent was reduced between the Neolithic and the Late Bronze Age. There is some pollen evidence of heathland. Crop plants were emmer and spelt wheats, a little barley and some rye, flax and perhaps peas. These may have been brought there from a distance.

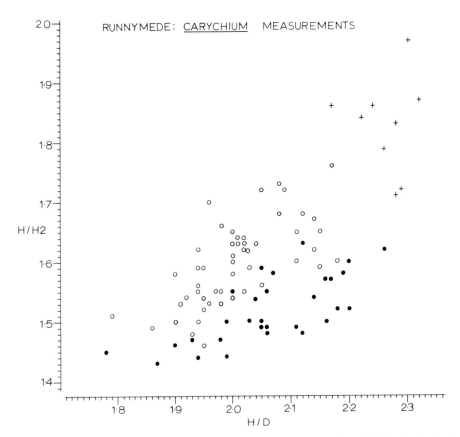

Fig. 116 Measurements of shell shape for Carychium. *Open circles:* C. minimum *from SS1; closed circles:* C. minimum *from* WF1; *crosses:* C. tridentatum.

Chapter 15
The land and freshwater Mollusca

John G Evans

The samples

For details of the lithostratigraphy, see Chapter 11.

SS1 120–195 cm, 15 samples (Fig. 109). The samples were sediment and had not been pre-treated. The weights are listed in Table 29.

WF1b 40–175, 25 samples (Fig. 109). The samples were shells floated off from the sediment and stored in alcohol at the Ancient Monuments Laboratory of English Heritage. There were no residues and no shells that had been picked out from residues. Most of sample 135–140 cm and all of 50–55 cm were missing.

WF1a 15–50 cm, 7 samples (Fig. 109). There is a small overlap with the upper part of WF1b at 40–50 cm, but the matching is not precise because there was a step in the section.

Identification

Extraction and preliminary identification were done by Vivian Evans. All the final identifications were done by me aided in the case of difficult material by Michael Kerney. 32,379 shells were counted. Identification posed a number of problems because I was previously familiar only with terrestrial shells from dry chalkland sites. The river and wetland terrestrial assemblages of Runnymede contained freshwater species, of which I had little experience. More alarmingly, the forms of a few common land species were different from those of drier habitats, and this presented special problems when closely similar wetland species were present as well – for example, the two species of *Carychium* and *Vallonia pulchella* and *Vallonia excentrica*. Here are a few comments on certain species.

Valvata. The possibility of *V. macrostoma* was considered and some shells were compared with reference material provided by Mark Robinson, but there were no convincing specimens.

Bithynia. Although difficult, it was possible to separate all specimens of apices and operculae into the two species.

Carychium. Measurements were made as defined by Watson and Verdcourt (1953) (Fig. 116):

H = maximum height
H2 = height of body whorl
D = minimum diameter (of body whorl excluding lip)

Several combinations of these measurements and ways of plotting them were tested by my research assistant, Rosina Mount, and she found that H/H2 against H/D provided the clearest separation of the two species (Fig. 116). Most of the shells identified as *C. minimum* are fairly tightly clustered and separated from those identified as *C. tridentatum*. Identification of juveniles is approximate.

An interesting feature of the measurements is that there is a difference between the *C. minimum* shells from SS1 and those from WF1, the latter being more swollen and with a relatively shorter spire.

Lymnaea truncatula and *L. palustris*. Both species are present, the former in the great majority. The separation of small apices is very difficult.

Lymnaea peregra. There are three forms, although they have not been listed. They are: (a) a normal form, regularly coiled; (b) a small form, bearing a superficial resemblance to *L. truncatula* but certainly not that species, having a larger apex; and (c) an elongate form, a bit like *Succinea*, but smaller (not *L. stagnalis*).

Myxas glutinosa. A few certain specimens, and one or two adult shells of this beautiful species.

Planorbis. Both *P. planorbis* and *P. carinatus* are present, but it is impossible to separate small juveniles.

Gyraulus acronicus and *G. albus*. Several features were used to separate the two species, and these can be used for the full range of sizes. They are:

With regard to the expansion of the whorls, the ratio of maximum diameter to minimum diameter is 1.15 in *G. albus* and 1.22 in *G. acronicus*. However, there is a variation in both species. One form of *G. acronicus* lacks the keel and has rounded whorls and fairly prominent striae; yet it expands in the manner of a true *G. acronicus* and lacks the flared aperture of *G. albus*. One form of *G. albus* has practically no sculpturing, and some are more tightly coiled than normal, sometimes with quadrangular rather than rounded whorls. Similar variations in both species are described by other workers, e.g. Lozek (1964). In general, identification took considerable time, and there is still probably room for revision. The shells are sufficiently well preserved and numerous for a programme of multivariate analyses to be done on these various shell characters.

	G. albus	G. acronicus
Expansion of whorls	More rapid	Less rapid
Transverse profile of individual whorls	Rounded	Quadrangular
Keel	Less prominent	More prominent
Aperture	Drooping	In line with body
Umbilicus (assuming shell is dextral)	Deeper	Shallower
Spiral ridges	Strong	Weak to absent
Colour	Lighter	Darker

Armiger crista. At least two forms are present: a prominently ribbed or spiny form, sometimes called *A. crista f. cristatus* (Draparnaud) or *A. crista f. spinulosus* (Clessin); and an unribbed form, *A. crista f. nautileus* (Linné) (or var. *laevigata Adam*). In the Runnymede material the ribbed forms predominate by about 2:1, but the distinction was not always clear and quantification, although recorded, is too uncertain to publish.

There is room for further work, especially if the different forms reflect different environments.

Vallonia pulchella. The majority are *V. pulchella* seg. but a few belong to *V. excentrica.* Some specimens are difficult to assign, these being small, with the same number of whorls as *V. excentrica* but with a reflected lip.

Vitrea. No attempt was made to separate *V. crystallina* and *V. contracta,* although most specimens belong to the former.

Euconulus. Both *E. alderi* and *E. fulvus* are present, but some specimens are too small or worn to assign specifically.

Perforatella rubiginosa. Specimens were identified by Michael Kerney, from shells which I had originally identified as *Trichia plebeia.* This is the first subfossil record of the species in Britain (Evans 1987).

Trichia hispida. The shells are large, often flattened, dark and strongly and regularly ribbed. The size and ribbing led me at first to consider them as *T. striolata,* but the individual ribs are not as precisely parallel and evenly spaced as in *T. striolata,* nor as consistently continuous. The characteristic keeled profile of *T. striolata* is never present and there were no adults with typical *T. striolata* features. Although niggling doubts kept returning through the analysis, all are considered to be a form of *T. hispida.*

The identification, characterisation and quantification of these sub-species, varieties or ecophenotypes is not just an academic exercise. If quantified, and if the different forms can be related to environments, then there will be more information to characterise the ancient environments. This is important in these fluvial sites, where all the assemblages are allochthonous and the identification of former communities tricky.

Interpretation

Most of the deposits were laid down either in permanent fast-flowing water or during the flooding of land surfaces, and the molluscan assemblages are therefore not equivalent to former communities but are a mixture of species from a variety of habitats. They are, as the geologist say, allochthonous. It is therefore necessary to consider the assemblages with reference to the present-day ecology of their constituent species, and this means an immediate division into land and aquatic. Even this distinction is not clear-cut because there are one or two species, notably *Lymnaea truncatula,* that can live equally well in both major environments, even within the life-cycle of a single individual.

Within each of the two major groups there is further allochthony, with local mixing of, for example, river-edge and deep-water communities. The identification of ecological subgroups is difficult owing to the range of habitats and associations that a species may adopt. Furthermore, there is no certainty that associations or communities have been permanent through time, with the situation possibly changing through even the short sequences present at Runnymede. This is especially so where there are constant punctuations of environmental change, a feature which might arrest or

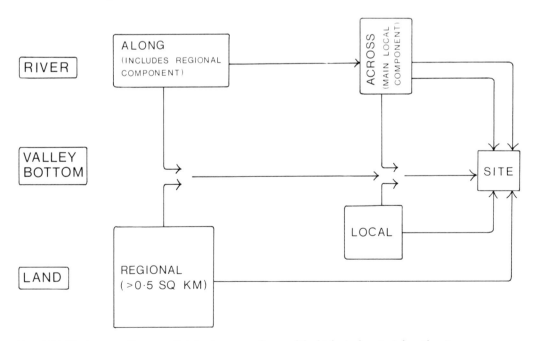

Fig. 117 Taphonomy diagram. Origins in terms of area of the biological material on the site.

slow the establishment of adjusted communities. The composition of communities may often be a result more of chance colonisations and associations than of environment.

The steps in the analysis are as follows:

1. Separation of the land and freshwater groups on the basis of their present-day ecology.
2. Detailing of molluscan assemblages, based on their diversity, the main species, and the presence of certain species which are characteristic of particular environments but which are not necessarily abundant.
3. Identification of ecologically meaningful assemblages or former living communities. The evidence is as follows:
   (a) present-day ecology
   (b) subfossil associations
   (c) patterns of behaviour through time in the subfossil sequences.
4. Environmental interpretation. The environment needs characterizing not only as aquatic or land but also at various scales, namely site, local and regional (Fig. 117; Chapter 24).
4a. Identification of site environments. There are two main site, or depositional environments, permanent aquatic and flood-plain. Their identification is based on the proportions of land to aquatic shells and species composition. The ratio of *Bithynia* shells (three-dimensional hollow bodies that are transported easily) to operculae (two-dimensional solid bodies that are not transported easily) is also used. The way this works is that in an autochthonous river context one would expect a one-to-one ratio (although there will actually be less operculae than shells because at the smallest end of the scale there is a differential loss of operculae in the sieving); in the allochthonous context of a flood-plain or lake edge there are concentrations of shells in a few places, especially at the very edge of the flooded area, but the operculae are more uniformly distributed and therefore predominate over shells. The deposits themselves are also a guide. Thus a sandy deposit with a high proportion of aquatic shells, in which the main species are characteristic of running water, implies a river environment. On the other hand, a clay loam with a high proportion of land shells, in which the main species are of damp grassland, implies marsh or flood-plain. The presence of arionid slug granules is a good indication of terrestrial conditions, especially in fine deposits where they are unlikely to have been transported.
4b. Identification of site and local environments. Consistent changes in composition are an indication. Thus in the two main river sequences there are changes in diversity from low to high and back to low, and these probably reflect the changing nature of the river environment itself. Other examples are the changes that take place in the land assemblages in the upper part of the SS1 and WF1 sequences. As the abundance of land shells increases, both relative to the freshwater shells and in

absolute terms, the sequences pass through a mudflat stage in which *Lymnaea truncatula* is the dominant species, before the ultimate grassland stage of the flood-plain is attained (Fig. 124).

4c. Identification of local and regional environments. In each major site context, there are allochthonous shells, land shells in the river deposits, and freshwater shells in the flood-plain deposits. These give information about local and regional environments. More information can be obtained by comparing the allochthonous and autochthonous components of either the land or aquatic groups between and within assemblages. For example, it is noticeable in the land sequences that there is a higher diversity in the allochthonous assemblages, strongly suggesting that the species that contribute to this are of local or regional, but not site, origin. It applies especially to the SS1 sequence, where there is a higher diversity of open-country dry-ground species, *Vallonia costata* and the terrestrial B group (mostly woodland species) in the allochthonous assemblages (Figs. 119 and 124)

The arrangement of species in the histograms

For the aquatics I have followed Sparks (1961; 1964) except that I have put the amphibious species *Lymnaea truncatula* with the land species.

Group 1. Slum species. Poorly oxygenated environments and/or periodic drought. *Anisus leucostoma, Pisidium casertanum, P. personatum, P. obtusale.*

Group 2. Catholic species. Wide range of conditions, excluding slum. *Lymnaea palustris, L. auricularia, L. peregra, Armiger crista, Bathyomphalus contortus, Gyraulus laevis, G. albus, Hippeutis complanatus, Sphaerium corneum, Pisidium milium, P. subtruncatum, P. nitidum.*

Group 3. Ditch species. Slow-moving, plant-rich streams. *Valvata cristata, Myxas glutinosa, Planorbis planorbis, P. carinatus, Gyraulus acronicus, Acroloxus lacustris, Pisidium pulchellum, P. hibernicum.* In retrospect, and judging by its behaviour in the sequences, *Gyraulus acronicus* should go in group 2.

Group 4. Moving-water. Large streams and ponds where currents or winds ensure water movement. *Theodoxus fluviatilis, Valvata piscinalis, Bithynia tentaculata, B. leachii, Physa fontinalis, Lymnaea stagnalis, Planorbarius corneus, Ancylus fluviatilis, Unio sp., Pisidium amnicum, P. henslowanum, P. moitessierianum.*

For the land species, the following grouping is used:

Mudflat species, amphibious. *Lymnaea truncatula.*

Marsh species, damp grassland. *Carychium minimum*, Succineidae, *Zonitoides nitidus.*

Terrestrial A species (largely following Kerney *et al.* 1980). Wide range of habitats, and often common in marsh. *Trichia hispida, Perforatella rubiginosa, Cochlicopa lubrica, Punctum pygmaeum, Vitrina pellucida, Vitrea crystallina, Nesovitrea hammonis*, Limacidae, *Euconulus, Arianta arbustorum, Cepaea hortensis*.

Terrestrial B species (again largely after Kerney *et al.* 1980). Deciduous woods and other shaded places. *Carychium tridentatum, Vertigo pusilla, Lauria cylindracea, Discus rotundatus, Aegopinella pura, Ae. nitidula, Oxychilus cellarius, Cochlodina laminata, Clausilia bidentata*.

Open-country species. A range of habitats from marsh to dry calcareous grassland, although *Helicella itala* is usually confined to the latter. *Vallonia costata* can also live in shaded environments. *Vertigo pygmaea, Pupilla muscorum, Vallonia costata, V. pulchella, V. excentrica, Helicella itala*.

Arionidae. These are the granules of slugs, and the various species live in a variety of terrestrial habitats.

It must be noted that for both land and aquatic species these are general habitat ascriptions. An individual species may behave quite differently according to climate or other environmental factors, and it may not reflect the same environment through a single sequence.

Presentation

For each sequence, three diagrams have been prepared. The aquatic diagram shows each species or group as a percentage of total aquatic shells, arranged under Sparks' groups. *Bithynia* operculae are not included in the totals. The land diagram shows each species or group as a percentage of total land shells. The Arionidae are not included in the totals, and are presented as a percentage over and above the total land. The third diagram illustrates the summary changes in aquatic and land shells and in the environment at the site, in the river and on land.

Percentages have been used because of the different sample sizes of SS1 and the unknown sample sizes of WF1, and to enable ease of comparison between the two sequences. Ideally, however, actual numbers per unit weight or volume of sample should be used because they indicate changing abundances more realistically (Thomas 1985).

Column SS1 120–195 cm (Table 29)

AQUATIC SEQUENCE (FIGS. 118 AND 120)

160–195 cm. The aquatic assemblage is highly diverse. Six species occur consistently, each at above 10%, and five others, each at between 2 and 5%. There is a mixture of ecologies, with one or more representatives of all of Sparks' groups, except group 1, occurring at above 10%.

Well oxygenated, permanent, fast-flowing water is indicated by the moving-water species, group 4, around 40%,

and especially by the occurrence of the freshwater limpet, *Ancylus fluviatilis*. The group 2 species are also well represented, around 40%, with *Gyraulus, Armiger* and *Pisidium nitidum* being distinctive. *Gyraulus* and *Armiger* live especially in standing and slow-moving plant-rich water. All of these species from these two groups were probably living more or less together, although there was probably some partitioning of the river in terms of, for example, muddy bottom (*Pisidium*), stony bottom (*Ancylus*) and weed (*Gyraulus, Armiger*), and edge areas (*Gyraulus, Armiger*) against middle areas (*Ancylus, Bithynia, Valvata piscinalis*).

On the other hand, *Valvata cristata*, the only major component of Sparks' group 3, probably derives from a different biotope altogether, because it favours shallow, richly vegetated water, slow-flowing or still.

120–160 cm. The aquatic assemblage is less diverse than previously. There is a reduction of insignificant proportions in several species, mostly of Sparks' group 2, and a significant increase in only two, *Valvata cristata* and *Pisidium casertanum*. The only other point to note is the slight but sustained increase of *Bathyomphalus* and *Pisidium subtruncatum*.

Interpretation needs to relate to the site environment, which in this part of the sequence was becoming increasingly terrestrial (Chapter 11). The river shells are derived largely from overbank flooding, so species like *Ancylus* and *Pisidium*, which are not transported far because of their form may be absent for this reason. On the other hand, some fully aquatic *Pisidium* species are present in abundance, so the assemblages cannot be too asymmetric. We can therefore say that the river was well-oxygenated, permanent and fast-flowing, but lacked the previous diversity of vegetated habitats. It can be suggested that the use of the river by man, especially the sharpening of the distinction between land and water, may have been responsible. A contributing factor may have been the discharge into the river of sediment from cultivated land, which clouded the water and, in reducing the rate of photosynthesis and plant productivity, affected adversely the plant communities and the molluscan communities which depended on them.

LAND SEQUENCE (FIGS. 119 AND 120)

155–195 cm. The main species are *Lymnaea truncatula, Carychium minimum* and *Vallonia pulchella*. These are species of open marshland or damp grassland, although *Carychium* can occur in shaded habitats and *Lymnaea truncatula* is an amphibious species. Other marsh species are *Zonitoides nitidus* and the heliophile group, Succineidae.

Also present is a small proportion of strictly terrestrial species that indicate drier places, both woodland (Terrestrial B) and grassland. It has already been suggested (above) that these, being in an allochthonous context, are of regional rather than site significance.

135–155 cm. The predominant species is *Lymnaea truncatula*. This indicates mudflats or open marshland with sparse vegetation, an interpretation supported by the reduction of *Vallonia pulchella. Perforatella rubiginosa* is also typical of

Table 29: Runnymede Neolithic Mollusca, column SS1.

depth (cm):	190	185	180	175	170	165	160	155	150	145	140	135	130	125	120
to:	195	190	185	180	175	170	165	160	155	150	145	140	135	130	125
Air-dry weight (g)	25	25	20	50	57	46	65	69	82	107	255	300	199	126	40
Theodoxus fluviatilis	1	3	1	—	2	13	1	—	1	—	1	1	—	9	—
Valvata cristata	35	33	18	66	153	259	26	11	53	82	69	63	65	45	12
Valvata piscinalis	61	71	32	90	211	346	86	55	102	91	76	36	37	13	25
Bithynia tentaculata, shells	55	87	20	149	282	499	141	90	132	109	105	106	82	24	11
Bithynia tentaculata, operculae	46	36	19	52	84	168	41	65	67	86	111	124	96	33	14
Bithynia leachii, shells	40	39	18	96	187	263	55	38	50	115	78	56	26	4	4
Bithynia leachii, operculae	14	18	11	43	46	75	17	14	22	34	61	34	24	6	2
Carychium minimum	10	8	2	15	28	37	7	1	4	5	17	35	43	57	238
Carychium tridentatum	1	—	—	1	2	4	—	—	—	1	—	—	—	9	1
Physa fontinalis	—	1	—	1	1	2	2	—	—	—	—	—	—	—	—
Lymnaea truncatula	1	6	2	11	20	42	8	6	30	51	71	110	50	26	90
Lymnaea palustris	—	—	—	—	—	—	—	—	—	—	—	—	1	—	2
Lymnaea stagnalis	1	2	—	1	1	—	—	—	1	—	3	—	1	2	1
Lymnaea peregra	7	18	8	33	65	74	17	12	9	3	4	11	4	—	3
Myxas glutinosa	1	3	—	—	3	2	—	—	—	—	1	—	—	—	—
Planorbis planorbis	—	—	—	—	—	—	1	1	1	—	1	—	—	—	4
Planorbis sp.	—	—	—	1	1	6	—	—	—	—	—	—	—	—	—
Anisus leucostoma	—	—	—	—	4	—	—	—	—	—	1	1	—	—	—
Bathyomphalus contortus	5	7	5	22	43	51	4	10	29	34	21	14	7	2	4
Gyraulus acronicus	14	14	6	21	33	104	5	1	3	2	3	—	—	—	—
Gyraulus albus	25	56	13	111	214	364	36	15	14	6	5	3	1	1	2
Armiger crista	29	35	22	75	172	268	43	21	11	22	5	—	3	—	2
Hippeutis complanatus	1	1	—	1	7	6	3	—	4	7	5	3	—	—	—
Ancylus fluviatilis	10	10	7	5	48	45	7	6	1	—	1	2	—	—	—
Acroloxus lacustris	1	—	1	1	8	6	1	1	4	2	1	3	1	1	—
Succineidae	—	3	—	1	4	9	8	—	2	8	16	21	11	10	16
Cochlicopa lubrica	—	1	1	2	6	8	2	1	3	4	7	8	20	9	23
Vertigo pygmaea	—	1	—	1	1	3	—	1	—	—	—	1	1	—	1
Pupilla muscorum	—	1	—	—	—	—	—	—	—	2	—	1	—	—	—
Lauria cylindracea	—	—	—	—	—	1	—	—	—	—	—	—	—	—	—
Vallonia costata	3	—	—	4	6	7	—	2	—	1	1	—	4	—	—
Vallonia pulchella	2	3	—	5	7	3	1	2	4	4	1	9	8	13	33
Vallonia excentrica	1	—	—	—	—	—	—	—	—	—	—	—	1	4	1
Vallonia sp. (not *V. costata*)	14	15	2	27	35	82	5	3	5	8	16	32	23	50	81
Punctum pygmaeum	—	—	—	—	1	—	—	—	—	—	—	—	—	—	—
Discus rotundatus	—	1	—	—	—	1	—	—	1	—	1	—	2	—	1
Arionidae	—	3	1	1	3	4	1	5	2	21	91	325	231	464	1548
Vitrina pellucida	—	—	—	—	—	—	—	—	1	—	—	—	—	—	—
Vitrea crystallina agg.	—	1	1	1	2	8	1	—	2	3	2	—	—	3	10
Nesovitrea hammonis	—	—	—	1	1	—	—	—	—	—	—	1	1	—	—
Aegopinella pura	—	—	—	—	—	—	—	—	—	—	1	—	—	—	—
Aegopinella nitidula	1	—	—	—	—	—	—	—	—	—	—	—	—	—	—
Zonitoides nitidus	3	1	—	8	5	13	5	7	4	9	32	53	45	43	97
Limacidae	1	—	—	1	—	—	—	2	—	—	1	4	5	10	1
Euconulus fulvus	—	—	—	—	—	—	—	—	—	—	—	—	—	—	2
Euconulus alderi	—	—	—	—	—	—	—	1	—	—	—	1	5	2	4
Euconulus fulvus agg.	—	—	—	—	2	—	—	—	—	—	1	—	—	—	3
Helicella itala	—	—	—	—	—	—	—	—	—	—	—	—	—	—	1
Perforatella rubiginosa	—	—	—	—	—	1	—	—	4	—	3	1	6	8	3
Trichia hispida	3	7	1	9	9	19	7	7	7	7	20	19	69	58	59
Arianta arbustorum	1	1	—	—	—	—	1	—	2	—	—	11	14	9	4
Arianta/Cepaea	—	—	—	—	—	—	—	—	—	—	2	1	2	1	12

Table 29: Runnymede Neolithic Mollusca, column SS1 (continued).

| depth (cm): | 190 | 185 | 180 | 175 | 170 | 165 | 160 | 155 | 150 | 145 | 140 | 135 | 130 | 125 | 120 |
to:	195	190	185	180	175	170	165	160	155	150	145	140	135	130	125
Sphaerium corneum	—	—	—	1	1	—	—	—	—	—	—	—	—	—	—
Pisidium amnicum	—	—	—	—	1	1	—	—	3	1	—	—	—	—	—
Pisidium casertanum	3	7	1	5	12	10	13	11	15	26	29	47	23	32	3
Pisidium personatum	—	1	—	—	—	—	—	—	—	—	—	—	—	—	—
Pisidium obtusale	1	1	—	1	3	1	1	—	—	—	—	—	—	—	—
Pisidium milium	2	4	2	1	8	12	1	—	1	—	—	1	—	—	—
Pisidium subtruncatum	5	8	5	17	41	60	18	11	17	16	19	35	14	1	2
Pisidium henslowanum	—	—	2	1	9	6	3	—	—	—	—	—	—	—	—
Pisidium hibernicum	1	2	—	3	5	5	1	—	—	—	—	—	—	—	—
Pisidium nitidum	18	15	14	21	71	113	18	5	3	3	2	2	—	—	1
Pisidium nitidum var. crassa	2	—	—	2	2	1	—	—	—	—	—	—	—	—	—
Pisidium pulchellum	—	1	—	1	1	2	1	—	—	—	—	2	1	—	—
Pisidium moitessierianum	1	—	—	—	4	6	—	1	—	—	—	—	—	—	—

Nomenclature after Kerney (1976) and Kerney and Cameron (1979). All *Pisidium* and *Sphaerium* counts have been divided by 2.

mudflats. The marsh species *Carychium minimum* and *Zonitoides* initially fall but then recover.

There is a general drop in species diversity, the terrestrial B group and *Vallonia costata* being practically absent.

120–135 cm. A reversal of some of the previous trends takes place, especially with regard to the site component. *Lymnaea truncatula* decreases, while species of damp grassland increase. There is a notable increase in the Arionidae slugs. The land surface was becoming stabilised, vegetated with open marsh and less frequently flooded.

SITE ENVIRONMENT (FIG. 120)

155–195 cm. The low percentage of land shells and the high abundance of aquatic shells indicate an aquatic site environment. The low ratio of *Bithynia* operculae to shells points in the same direction. This was a fast-flowing river, an interpretation supported by the sediments.

120–155 cm. Land shells increase from 10% to 90% of the total assemblage and there is an absolute decrease of freshwater shells to, ultimately, very low values. These changes indicate the progression of the site environment from aquatic to land. Other taphonomic indications are the absence of *Ancylus*, a species not readily transported by floodwater because of its limpet form, the steady increase of *Bithynia* operculae relative to shells, and the increase in arionid granules. The ecological changes from open water through a mudflat stage (135–155 cm) to, ultimately, marsh are confirmatory evidence of the autochthonous nature of the land sequence. The interpretation is supported by the sediments, which are fairly uniform fine sandy loams.

Column WF1a and 1b (Table 30)

There are asymmetries in the assemblages owing to the fact that only floated shells were provided. The main absences and reasons for these absences are: *Ancylus fluviatilis* because of its limpet form; *Bithynia* operculae because they are flat; arionid granules and limacid plates because they are solid; and *Pisidium* species because of their dished form.

AQUATIC SEQUENCE (FIGS. 121 AND 123)

150–175 cm. Group 4 species predominate. At the base, *Valvata piscinalis* and *Bithynia* are the main species, amounting to 80%. By the top they have fallen to 65%, and *Gyraulus* and *Valvata cristata* have assumed importance. *Ancylus*, *Pisidium nitidum* and *P. subtruncatum* were probably more abundant than shown, but their shells would have been victims of the extraction process.

The environment was fast-flowing, highly oxygenated water that was permanent. *Theodoxus fluviatilis*, a typical inhabitant of rivers, is consistently present. The only anomaly is *Valvata cristata*, a member of Sparks' group 2, the ditch species. This species probably lived in well weeded habitats in quieter areas of the river than the rest of the assemblage.

There is an increase in diversity from 175–150 cm.

120–150 cm. This is the zone of maximum aquatic assemblage diversity. In addition to the species already present, two others, of group 2, become important. They are *Armiger crista* and *Lymnaea peregra*.

Again we are dealing with a site environment of permanent, highly oxygenated aquatic status, but there was more vegetation, a greater diversity of habitats in the catchment, and perhaps slower-flowing water.

WF1b 40–120 cm, WF1a 15–50 cm. The environment of deposition was becoming increasingly terrestrial, with the shells being derived from over-bank flooding (see below, under 'site environment'). The absence of certain species, for example *Theodoxus fluviatilis*, may be related to this fact. Additionally, the low totals make detailed interpretation difficult and little can be made of the various fluctuations.

In general, the assemblage is similar to that below but less diverse. This suggests a river environment that was becoming increasingly impoverished and, as with the upper

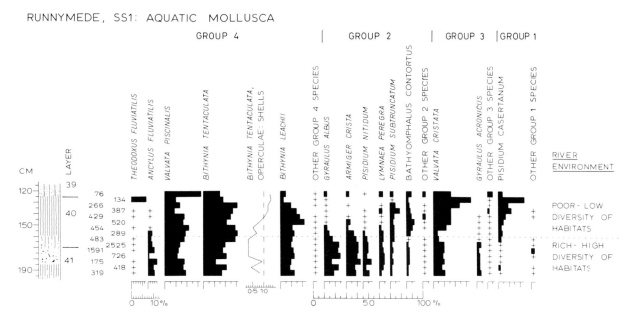

Fig. 118 *Runnymede SS1, aquatic Mollusca. Species and groups as percentages of total aquatic assemblage.*

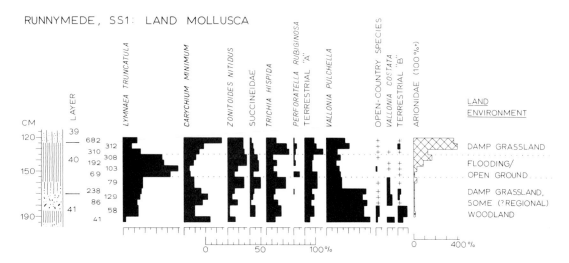

Fig. 119 *Runnymede SS1, land Mollusca. Species and groups as percentages of total land assemblage.*

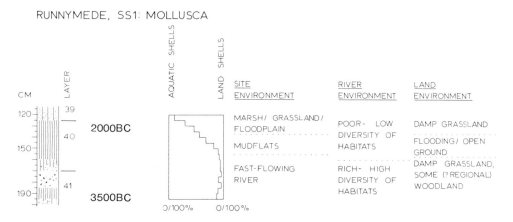

Fig. 120 *Runnymede SS1. Site, river and land environments as indicated by the Mollusca.*

Table 30: Runnymede Late Bronze Age Mollusca, column WF1.

	WF1b																									WF1a						
depth (cm) / to:	170–175	165–170	160–165	155–160	150–155	145–150	140–145	135–140	130–135	125–130	120–125	115–120	110–115	105–110	100–105	95–100	90–95	85–90	80–85	75–80	70–75	65–70	60–65	55–60	40–50	45–50	40–45	35–40	30–35	25–30	20–25	15–20
Theodoxus fluviatilis	60	63	24	18	21	13	44	—	3	15	24	4	1	—	—	2	3	—	—	—	—	—	—	—	—	—	—	—	—	—	—	—
Valvata cristata	73	162	106	119	106	119	91	2	63	87	168	34	13	2	5	2	3	6	8	3	14	22	35	79	9	1	1	—	1	1	1	4
Valvata piscinalis	773	794	375	195	363	225	240	—	97	153	465	71	49	21	11	12	5	7	16	8	7	25	29	12	15	3	1	—	—	2	1	1
Bithynia tentaculata, shells	718	717	400	318	225	221	284	154	227	600	194	81	49	71	17	28	11	15	15	10	14	44	59	69	19	7	—	—	—	—	—	—
Bithynia tentaculata, operculae	3	4	2	2	1	—	—	—	2	2	6	1	2	2	2	2	1	1	—	—	2	4	2	2	—	—	—	—	—	—	—	—
Bithynia leachii, shells	624	755	371	143	297	163	181	57	112	396	111	51	3	11	3	11	5	6	7	1	14	11	14	13	8	1	—	1	—	—	—	1
Bithynia leachii, operculae	—	2	—	—	2	2	2	1	—	1	2	—	2	1	1	—	—	1	1	—	1	—	—	—	—	—	—	—	—	—	—	—
Carychium minimum	9	17	6	15	12	11	26	21	21	27	27	3	1	1	—	1	—	2	2	—	1	1	3	1	4	2	—	28	19	4	11	10
Carychium tridentatum	3	3	4	3	5	4	17	2	2	2	3	3	1	—	—	—	—	—	—	1	2	—	1	—	—	—	1	—	1	1	1	5
Physa fontinalis	1	2	2	2	—	—	2	1	1	—	2	5	1	—	3	—	—	1	—	—	3	—	—	—	—	—	—	—	—	—	—	—
Lymnaea truncatula	8	15	6	4	7	6	4	1	11	11	8	4	1	1	4	4	1	4	4	1	10	1	6	3	5	2	1	4	27	74	29	19
Lymnaea palustris	1	2	—	—	—	2	—	—	—	1	1	1	1	1	—	—	—	—	1	—	—	—	2	—	—	—	—	—	—	—	—	—
Lymnaea stagnalis	—	1	—	1	3	1	2	—	2	2	—	—	1	—	—	—	1	—	—	1	2	—	—	2	—	—	1	1	—	—	—	—
Lymnaea auricularia	2	1	1	1	—	2	—	2	—	—	—	—	—	—	—	—	—	—	—	—	—	—	—	—	—	—	—	—	—	—	—	—
Lymnaea peregra	32	42	23	7	23	27	48	18	31	41	11	2	2	—	2	3	5	3	4	1	10	10	6	3	5	2	1	—	—	1	—	—
Myxas glutinosa	1	—	—	—	—	—	—	2	2	—	2	2	—	—	—	—	—	—	—	—	—	2	2	—	—	—	—	—	—	—	—	—
Planorbis planorbis	6	8	4	4	4	4	—	—	—	3	3	—	—	—	3	1	1	—	1	1	—	—	—	—	—	—	—	1	—	—	—	—
Planorbis carinatus	11	7	4	3	6	6	—	—	—	5	5	3	—	—	1	1	1	1	—	1	1	2	—	2	1	—	—	1	1	—	—	—
Planorbis sp.	10	10	7	—	5	—	15	3	3	2	6	3	—	—	2	—	2	6	1	—	—	—	—	—	—	—	—	—	—	—	—	1
Anisus leucostoma	6	14	8	11	5	2	4	4	4	4	8	1	2	—	4	4	4	—	1	—	—	1	—	—	—	—	1	1	1	1	—	—
Bathyomphalus contortus	70	133	68	68	62	51	62	33	22	78	26	19	7	—	3	2	3	—	3	—	4	12	10	7	5	—	1	—	—	—	—	1
Gyraulus laevis	—	?1	—	?1	—	—	—	—	—	—	—	—	—	—	—	—	—	—	—	—	—	—	—	—	—	—	—	—	—	—	—	—
Gyraulus acronicus	81	115	42	33	65	39	27	22	15	56	56	18	4	3	3	—	1	6	1	—	—	1	—	2	2	1	1	—	—	—	—	—
Gyraulus albus	142	252	124	90	184	136	197	75	145	311	57	34	13	16	16	5	3	—	20	10	5	1	1	1	3	1	1	2	—	2	1	8
Armiger crista	1	12	7	4	13	38	84	40	61	45	13	4	1	3	3	—	1	1	2	2	1	1	1	1	1	1	1	—	—	—	—	—
Hippeutis complanatus	1	—	—	—	2	2	8	5	5	2	1	—	—	—	—	—	—	1	1	2	—	—	—	—	—	—	1	1	—	—	—	—
Planorbarius corneus	—	—	—	—	—	—	?1	—	—	—	—	—	—	—	—	—	—	—	—	—	—	—	—	—	—	—	—	—	—	—	—	—
Ancylus fluviatilis	—	—	—	—	—	?1	—	—	—	—	—	1	—	—	—	—	—	—	—	—	—	1	1	2	—	2	—	1	1	1	2	1
Succineidae	—	1	1	1	2	1	—	—	2	2	2	1	2	1	—	2	2	—	—	1	1	—	—	—	—	—	—	1	1	1	3	3
Cochlicopa lubrica	17	14	12	2	1	2	8	2	4	13	12	7	1	1	—	—	—	—	1	—	—	3	—	—	—	3	—	4	3	3	9	8
Vertigo pusilla	—	—	—	—	1	—	—	—	—	—	—	—	—	—	—	—	—	—	—	—	—	—	—	—	—	—	—	—	—	—	—	—
Vertigo pygmaea	1	1	—	—	—	1	1	—	1	1	1	1	—	—	1	—	1	—	—	1	1	—	1	1	—	1	—	—	—	—	—	1
Pupilla muscorum	8	6	3	3	5	7	2	3	4	4	3	2	1	—	—	—	1	1	2	1	1	2	—	1	—	2	—	2	1	—	2	1
Lauria cylindracea	—	1	—	—	—	—	—	—	—	13	1	1	1	1	—	—	—	—	—	—	1	—	—	—	—	—	—	—	—	—	—	—
Vallonia costata	5	9	8	4	9	3	8	2	2	1	9	5	4	1	1	—	1	1	1	1	1	—	1	—	1	1	—	1	1	1	1	3
Vallonia pulchella	24	46	24	29	43	27	6	11	13	51	9	8	2	2	1	1	1	3	3	4	3	4	1	1	—	7	3	21	34	9	28	29
Vallonia excentrica	1	5	?4	—	—	?1	?1	?1	1	2	2	1	1	—	—	—	—	—	—	—	1	—	—	—	—	—	—	—	2	1	—	—
Vallonia sp.(not V.costata)	19	37	16	19	37	32	48	24	42	53	6	7	1	2	1	2	2	1	3	8	1	2	2	2	3	5	3	28	53	25	55	78
Punctum pygmaeum	—	—	—	—	—	—	2	1	—	1	—	—	—	—	—	—	—	—	—	—	1	—	—	—	—	—	—	—	—	—	—	—

Table 30: Runymede late Bronze Aage Mollusca, column WF1 (continued).

	WF1b																								WF1a							
depth (cm) to:	170–175	165–170	160–165	155–160	150–155	145–150	140–145	135–140	130–135	125–130	120–125	115–120	110–115	105–110	100–105	95–100	90–95	85–90	80–85	75–80	70–75	65–70	60–65	55–60	50–55	45–50	40–45	35–40	30–35	25–30	20–25	15–20
Discus rotundatus	11	15	9	–	10	4	2	–	2	5	6	2	1	–	–	–	–	–	–	–	1	–	–	–	1	–	–	–	–	1	–	–
Vitrina pellucida	–	1	–	–	–	–	–	–	–	–	–	1	–	–	–	–	–	–	–	–	1	–	–	–	–	–	–	–	–	1	–	–
Vitrea crystallina agg.	10	7	3	1	6	4	5	–	7	11	–	2	2	1	–	–	1	1	3	3	2	2	–	–	–	3	–	–	–	–	–	–
Nesovitrea hammonis	2	2	1	–	1	–	–	–	2	–	1	1	1	–	–	–	–	–	1	1	–	–	–	–	–	–	–	–	–	–	–	1
Aegopinella pura	–	1	–	–	–	–	–	–	–	–	–	–	–	–	–	–	–	–	–	–	1	–	–	–	–	–	–	–	–	–	–	–
Aegopinella nitidula	2	3	3	–	2	–	1	–	3	1	1	1	1	–	–	–	–	–	1	1	–	–	–	–	–	–	–	–	–	–	–	–
Oxychilus cellarius	2	–	–	–	1	–	1	–	1	1	–	–	–	–	–	–	–	–	–	1	–	–	–	–	–	–	–	–	–	–	–	–
Zonitoides nitidus	13	11	3	4	4	5	4	–	10	1	4	4	1	1	1	–	–	1	–	3	3	13	13	3	3	31	–	–	–	–	3	5
Limacidae	–	–	–	–	–	–	–	–	1	–	–	–	–	–	–	–	–	–	–	–	–	–	–	–	–	–	–	–	–	–	–	–
Euconulus alderi	–	1	–	–	2	1	–	–	–	–	1	–	1	–	–	–	–	–	–	–	–	–	–	–	–	–	–	–	–	–	–	–
Euconulus fulvus agg.	–	–	1	–	–	–	–	–	–	–	–	–	–	–	–	–	–	–	–	–	–	–	–	1	–	–	–	–	–	–	–	–
Cochlodina laminata	–	–	–	–	–	–	–	–	1	–	1	–	–	–	–	–	–	–	–	1	–	–	–	–	–	–	–	–	–	–	–	–
Clausilia bidentata	3	–	–	3	1	1	1	–	–	–	–	–	–	–	–	–	–	–	–	–	–	–	–	–	–	–	–	–	–	–	–	–
Helicella itala	5	4	3	–	2	–	1	–	1	3	–	–	1	–	–	–	–	–	–	–	–	–	–	–	–	–	–	–	–	–	–	–
Perforatella rubiginosa	4	–	–	2	2	2	–	–	3	3	3	1	–	1	–	–	–	–	1	1	1	1	–	–	–	19	3	1	1	–	–	1
Trichia hispida	160	121	65	45	76	51	16	1	26	40	107	30	10	3	3	1	–	2	2	7	5	7	3	6	5	26	6	12	67	37	84	88
Arianta arbustorum	1	–	1	–	–	–	–	–	1	–	–	–	–	–	–	–	–	–	–	1	–	1	–	–	–	1	–	–	–	–	–	–
Cepaea hortensis	–	–	–	–	–	–	–	–	3	–	–	–	–	–	–	–	–	–	–	–	–	–	–	–	–	–	–	–	–	–	–	–
Unio sp.	–	1	–	–	–	–	–	–	–	–	–	–	–	–	–	–	–	–	–	–	–	–	–	–	–	–	–	–	–	–	–	–
Sphaerium corneum	–	–	–	–	–	–	–	–	2	3	–	–	–	–	–	–	–	–	–	–	–	–	–	–	–	–	–	–	–	–	–	–
Pisidium amnicum	2	3	–	–	–	–	–	–	–	–	–	–	–	–	–	–	–	–	–	–	–	–	–	–	–	–	–	–	–	–	–	–
Pisidium casertanum	2	–	–	–	–	–	–	–	–	1	–	1	–	–	–	–	–	–	–	1	–	–	–	–	–	–	–	–	–	–	–	–
Pisidium milium	2	6	2	–	–	–	–	–	–	–	–	–	–	–	–	–	–	–	–	–	–	–	–	–	–	–	–	–	–	–	–	–
Pisidium subtruncatum	2	2	–	–	–	–	–	–	–	–	–	–	–	–	–	–	–	–	–	–	–	–	–	2	–	–	–	–	–	–	–	–
Pisidium henslowanum	2	–	–	–	–	–	–	–	–	–	–	–	–	–	–	–	–	–	–	–	–	–	2	2	1	–	–	–	–	–	–	–
Pisidium nitidum	2	–	2	1	1	–	–	–	1	–	5	–	2	–	–	–	–	–	–	–	2	–	–	–	–	–	–	–	–	–	–	–
Pisidium nitidum var. crassa	–	–	1	–	–	–	–	–	–	–	–	–	–	–	–	–	–	–	–	1	–	–	–	–	–	–	–	–	–	–	–	–
Pisidium sp.	–	–	–	–	1	–	–	1	–	–	–	–	–	–	–	–	–	–	–	–	–	–	–	–	–	–	–	–	–	–	–	–

Nomenclature after Kerney (1976) and Kerney and Cameron (1979). Shells extracted in the Ancient Monuments Laboratory of English Heritage by floating only.

272

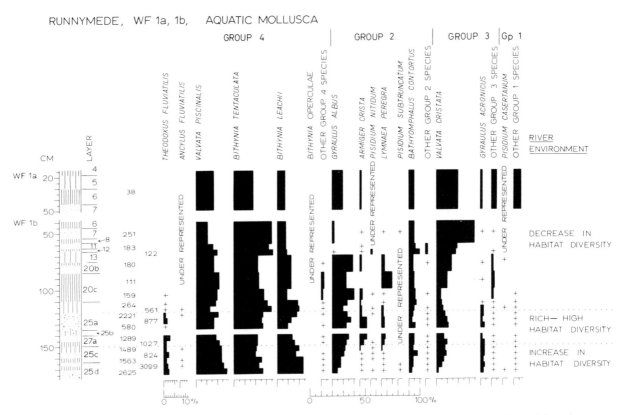

Fig. 121 Runnymede WF1, aquatic Mollusca. Species and groups as percentages of total aquatic assemblage. Note that some species are under-represented because of the method of extraction by floating only.

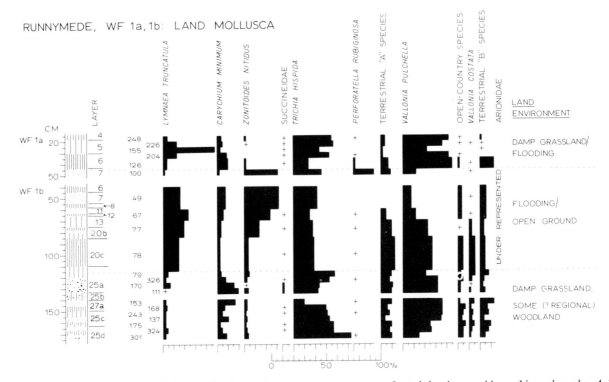

Fig. 122 Runnymede WF1, land Mollusca. Species and groups as percentages of total land assemblage. Note that the Arionidae (and Limacidae in Terrestrial A) are under-represented because of the method of extraction by floating only.

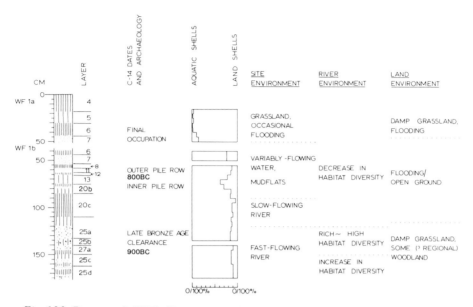

Fig. 123 Runnymede WF1. Site, river and land environments as indicated by the Mollusca.

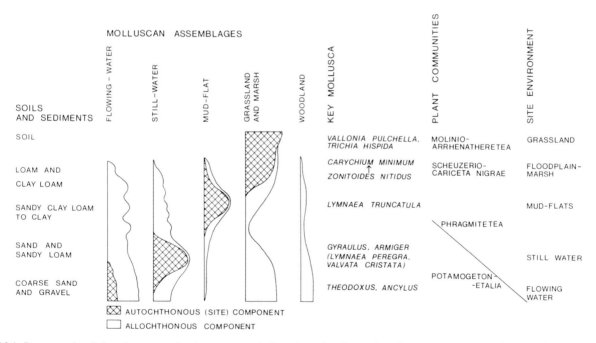

Fig. 124 Runnymede. Selected curves showing suggested changing abundance (numbers, not percentages) of molluscan groups and the variations of the autochthonous and allochthonous components within them as the site environment changes.

association of adults with one or two pre-adult moult stages (70–80, 90–100) can be taken as indicating quiet bottom conditions, and an *in situ* value for this species.

Of the other ostracods listed, *Prionocypris serrata* (90–100, 100–110), is a species which can occur in shallow-water settings such as spring-fed bournes (fossil at Marsworth, Green *et al*. 1984, and Isleworth, Kerney *et al*. 1982). A comparatively large ostracod (up to 1.7 mm long in adults), the Runnymede specimens are all immature, and could have been swept into the otherwise lacustrine environment from a stream or spring flow source nearby. *Cypridopsis vidua* is an active, free-swimming ostracod found in streams with a low current flow as well as in lakes and ponds. Much the same mode of life would apply to *Cypria ophthalmica* (90–100), although this species is almost always found in standing water bodies. *Candona fabaeformis* (90–100) is a species with a preference for bottom conditions rich in plant debris, so backing up the evidence of the more frequently occurring *Candona marchica* and *Candona caudata*.

Ponded water conditions could be supported by the occurrence of a single valve of *Ancylus* cf. *lacustris*, the freshwater limpet, in sample 90–100. The lower samples (150–160, 140–150, 110–120) contained several robust operculae, thought to belong to the gastropod *Bithynia*. The same samples carried the greatest quantities of charcoal debris. Fish scales and fragments of bone, possibly of perch, occurred in the upper samples.

In summary, between 140 and 50 cm of the recorded profile, conditions seem to have prevailed which allowed the development of a ponded drainage association of ostracods dominated by the species *Limnocythere inopinata*.

A modern parallel could be drawn with the ponds on Hampstead Heath, tree-margined, with soft, silty bottoms, fed by the streams draining from the Bagshot Sand high ground, although this model would not be too appropriate for the Thames flood-plain setting of Runnymede. The conclusion, however, is for a pond or lake-basin setting rather than the flowing-water stream course which might have been anticipated from knowledge of the Runnymede site.

Chapter 17
The Neolithic and Late Bronze Age insect assemblages

MARK ROBINSON

Introduction

Excavations in 1978 revealed waterlogged channel sediments adjacent to the Middle Neolithic and Late Bronze Age sites on the banks of the River Thames at Runnymede Bridge. The organic deposits were rich in insect as well as other biological remains. The waterlogged deposits were clearly of considerable importance and extensive sampling was undertaken, as described in Chapter 10.

The samples (Fig. 109)
SS1 column. A series of samples from a column through Neolithic riverine sediments divided at 5 cm vertical intervals. Insect remains were preserved in the column from a depth of 1.25 m to the bottom, at a depth of 1.95 m. The approximate date range spanned by this part of the column was from 3500 to 2000 cal BC.

Layer 40. Bulk sample from the upper part of the same waterlogged Neolithic sediments sampled in the SS1 column. Corresponds to the depth range 1.25–1.70 m in the column.

Layer 41. Bulk sample from the lower part of the same waterlogged Neolithic sediments sampled in the SS1 column. Corresponds to the depth range 1.70–1.95 m in the column and extended below the column.

A4 column. A series of samples from a column through Neolithic riverine sediments divided at 0.2 m intervals. Insect remains were preserved in the column from a depth of 1.10 m to the bottom at 1.90 m. The lowest waterlogged sample in the column was Middle Neolithic, the remainder were Late Neolithic.

WF1b column. A series of samples from a column through riverine sediments adjacent to the Late Bronze Age waterfronts, divided at 5 cm intervals. Insect remains were preserved in the column from a depth of 0.70 cm to the bottom at 1.75 m. The sediments below 1.40 m pre-dated the Bronze Age settlement. The first phase of waterfront timbers were inserted through the sediments from a depth of 0.85 m but the waterlogged sediments did not continue into the second phase of waterfront timbers. The approximate date range spanned by the waterlogged part of the WF1b column was from 1000 to 850 cal BC.

WF bird pellet. A spot sample of an agglomeration of beetle sclerites about 2 cm in diameter which was noticed during the excavation of layer 20 of the WF sediments. It was apparently a pellet of insect remains which had been regurgitated by a bird. Layer 20 corresponds to 0.75–1.20 m

in the WF1b column.
    Midden samples (ca. 8E/13N):
    Layer 19. Spot sample from the waterlogged Late Bronze Age midden debris from the edge of the channel.
    Layer 24*. Spot sample from waterlogged Late Bronze Age midden debris under Layer 19 from the edge of the channel.

Laboratory procedure
A subsample from each of the samples was taken for insect analysis. Records were not found for the weight of all the insect subsamples, but most were about 4 kg although some were as small as 2 kg. Each was soaked in a solution of sodium carbonate to aid breakdown, gently disaggregated in running water and washed onto a 0.3 mm aperture sieve. The fraction retained by the sieve was subjected to paraffin flotation to recover the insect remains. It was drained and mixed with paraffin, and cold water was added to produce a flotant containing most of the insect fragments. The flot was strained on a 0.3 mm sieve, washed in hot water and detergent, then alcohol, and sorted microscopically. The insect remains were stored in 70% ethanol. The residues from flotation were also checked for insect remains, then in some cases combined with the sorted flot for sorting for other biological remains by the relevant specialists. The samples were floated and most of the flots were sorted in the Ancient Monuments Laboratory under the supervision of Dr M. Girling.

Following the death of Dr Girling, the remaining flots were sorted and the insects from all the samples identified by the author in the University Museum, Oxford, using the Hope Entomological Collections. This work was funded by HBMC (England).

Results

The results have been listed in Tables 32–40, giving the minimum number of individuals represented by the fragments of each species for each sample. The nomenclature follows the Royal Entomological Society's revised checklists of British Insects (Kloet and Hincks 1964; 1976; 1977; 1978) and, for Coleoptera now extinct in Britain, Freude et al. (1964–1983).

Along with the identifications is given a short description of the habitat or food of each species. The abbreviations used are as follows:

A: aquatic; B: bankside/water's edge; C: carrion; D: disturbed/bare ground; F: dung; G: grassland; M: marsh; P: pest of stored farinaceous foods; T: terrestrial and occurring in several habitats; V: decaying plant remains; W: woodland or scrub. Less normal habitats are given in brackets.

A wide range of sources has been used for ecological information about the Coleoptera. The main references are as follows:

Balfour-Browne (1940–1958), Donisthorpe (1939),

Fowler (1887–1913), Freude *et al.* (1964–83), Hoffmann (1950; 1954; 1958), Horion (1941–1947), Joy (1932) and the Royal Entomological Society (1953–1986). Other references are given in Robinson (1981a, 70; 1983).

Food and habitat information for Heteroptera is from: Southwood and Leston (1959), Homoptera from Le Quesne (1969), Trichoptera from Marshall (1978) and Formicidae mostly from Boulton and Collingwood (1975).

Notes on identifications
Some of the more significant species are illustrated in Plate 72. Most identifications are straightforward and the main difficulty experienced was that many reference specimens, including non-British taxa, had to be examined in order to ascertain the identity of some species.

Helophorus arvernicus. Remains of this species were recorded from both Neolithic and Bronze Age deposits, eight samples in all. In six of the samples only elytra were recorded and identifications based on elytra alone might be regarded as contentious. However, pronota of this species, identified by their sinuate margins, were present in SS1 1.45–1.50 and 1.30–1.35. Their identity has been confirmed by Dr R. B. Angus.

Aphodius varians. Some elytra of *Aphodius* in WF1b 1.20–1.25 and 1.15–1.20 could be assigned to this species (Plate 72a). Each had a single large reddish mark on an otherwise black background.

Onthophagus taurus. Remains of *O. taurus* were present in four of the Neolithic samples as follows: SS1 1.85–1.90, one male head, one left elytron, one fragment of pronotum; SS1 1.80–1.85, one male head (Plate 72b), one possible right elytral fragment; SS1 1.70–1.75, one left elytron; layer 41, one right elytral fragment. The two heads showed the greenish metallic reflection which characterises the subspecies *illyricus* (Scop.) (Freude *et al.* 1969: 287). The pair of horns on the heads of male *O. taurus*, which give the species its name, were very much reduced in the examples from Runnymede. The head from SS1 1.85–1.90 possessed two small bumps, while there was little more than a transverse ridge on the head from SS1 1.80–1.85. Considerable variation of horn size in *O. t.* ssp. *illyricus* is described by Paulian (1959: 88–89).

Dromaeolus barnabita. The tip of a left elytron from SS1 1.60–1.65 (Plate 72f) was compared with a wide range of European Elateridae and Eucnemidae but could only be matched with *D. barnabita.*

Pelta grossum. Fragments were found in SS1 1.60–1.65 of the left elytron of what at first was thought to be a large member of the Silphidae but was eventually established to be from *P. grossum*, a member of the Peltidae.

Analysis of the data

Two orders of insects, the Trichoptera (caddis flies) and the Coleoptera (beetles), were particularly abundant in the samples from Runnymede. The former, represented by larval remains, were not identified, with the exception of *Ithytrichia* sp., and all have aquatic larvae. The identifiable remains of the Coleoptera, however, could mostly be taken to generic if not specific level and they came from many different habitats. The problem for the statistical manipulation of the Coleopteran results is that, although large assemblages were identified in terms of minimum number of individuals, their species diversity was so great that most species were only represented by a few individuals. It is not possible to present readily intelligible results for each taxon in the manner of a pollen diagram. Some synthesis is required.

An attempt was made to overcome this problem with Coleoptera by the use of species groupings (Robinson 1981b: 279–282) with additional species groupings subsequently being added (Robinson 1983: 33–39). There is now a large enough corpus of results available for comparative purposes to gain some idea of the importance of the habitat of a particular grouping from its percentage value.

The percentages for the species groupings found to be useful are given in Fig. 125 for the SS1 and the WF1b columns and in Table 41 for the SS1 total and samples 40 and 41, A4 column total, WF1b total, and the midden samples total. The results, as is usual, are expressed as a percentage of the minimum number of individuals of terrestrial Coleoptera in each assemblage, excluding the aquatic. This is because the assemblages accumulated under water and it enables some of the differences due to the environment of the deposit itself to be eliminated. About 40% of the terrestrial Coleoptera have been classified into one of the categories. Most of the samples in the columns, which had been sampled at 5 cm intervals, contained insufficient individuals for consideration and therefore the results were combined into units of 10 or 15 cm according to numerical representation.

1. Aquatic
These beetles are all species which can spend much of their adult life under water. Some difficulty arises with the Chrysomelidae and Curculionidae, which feed on aquatic plants. Only *Macroplea appendiculata*, *Eubrychius velutus* and *Litodactylus leucogaster* have been included in the aquatic group.

2. Pasture/dung
Scarabaeoid dung beetles of the genera *Geotrupes*, *Colobopterus*, *Aphodius*, *Copris* and *Onthophagus*, which mostly occur in the dung of large herbivores in the field rather than manure heaps. *Oxyomus sylvestris* has been excluded because it rarely occurs in dung other than manure heaps (Jessup 1986: 19), as has been *Aphodius villosus*, which does not usually occur in animal droppings (Landin 1961: 186, 213). A value of below 1% for this group can be expected for closed woodland, rising to about 10% in a largely pastoral landscape away from the concentrations of domestic animals

RUNNYMEDE COLEOPTERA

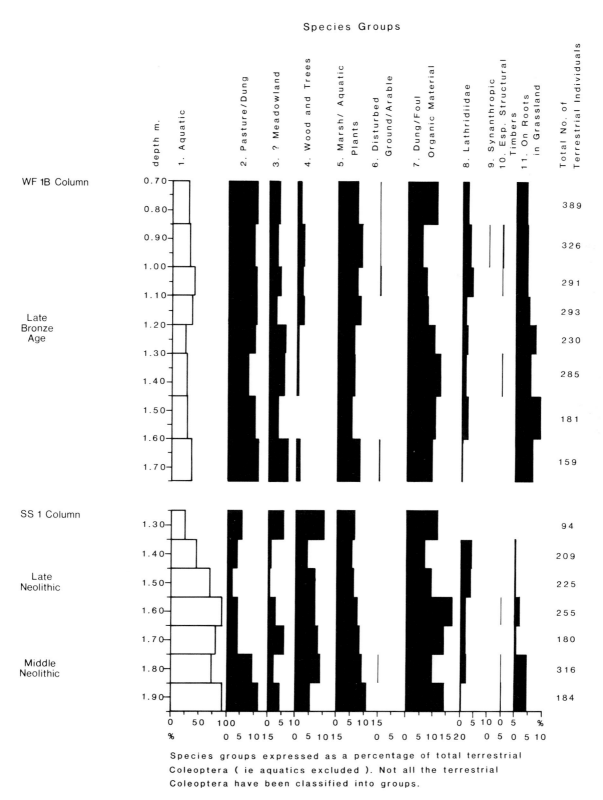

Fig. 125 The percentages of Coleoptera from the SS1 and WF1b columns belonging to various species groups. For details of the habitats of the groups and their species compositions see text.

which occur around settlements. The proportion of these beetles can reach 20 to 25% or more in samples from the ditches of Iron Age enclosures used to corral stock, but can be as low as 6% from a settlement primarily engaged in arable agriculture.

3. ?Meadowland

Members of the genera *Apion* and *Sitona*, which mostly feed on vetches, clovers and other grassland trefoils. Some members of the genus *Apion* feed on other plants, for example mallows and nettles, but many of these can be identified from fragments and so excluded from the total. This group is particularly favoured by hay meadow conditions, reaching values of 8–12%, but can also reach quite high values where there is ungrazed wayside vegetation. Grassland which is not so heavily grazed as to prevent the flowering of *Lotus* (bird's foot trefoil) and *Trifolium* (clover) results in values of 2.5–5% from archaeological assemblages, but values fall to 1% for overgrazed pasture. Values for closed woodland fall below 1%. Caution must be applied to interpretation of this grouping because some species of *Sitona* also attack peas and broad/field beans.

4. Wood and trees

Coleoptera which feed on wood in various stages of decay, leaves, fruits, bark and live wood of trees and shrubs, plus fungal feeders and predators which are strictly associated with wood, such as *Cis* sp. and *Pediacus* sp. General woodland beetles, such as the predatory carabid *Pterostichus oblongopunctatus*, have been excluded. *Anobium punctatum* and *Lyctus linearis* have also been excluded because they have been placed in a separate category. The following families have some members included in Species Group 4 at Runnymede:

Lucanidae	Cucujidae	Chrysomelidae
Elateridae	Cerylonidae	Curculionidae
Eucnemidae	Mycetophagidae	Scolytidae
Anobiidae	Colydiidae	Platypodidae
Peltidae	Tenebrionidae	
Sphindidae	Cerambycidae	

The proportion of this species grouping can be as high as 20% where closed old woodland overhung the deposit and even higher if most of the trees were moribund. However, many of the tree-dependent beetles do not have very good dispersive powers and so this aspect of the landscape can be underrepresented if the woodland is some distance from the deposit. For example, values as low as 10% have been recorded for somewhat open woodland of Boreal date separated from the deposit by an extensive reedswamp. The value for a hedged but otherwise open landscape tends to be around 0.5 to 1.5% but values as low as 0.1% have been obtained from Iron Age sites on the treeless landscape of areas of the Upper Thames flood-plain. It must be remembered that some of the wood-dependent beetles can be introduced in imported timber, particularly firewood.

5. Marsh/aquatic plants

Chrysomelidae and Curculionidae species which feed exclusively on marsh and aquatic plants. Their value can be as high as 50% from fen deposits to 0.5–1.5% from a flood-plain landscape where marsh and aquatic plants did not fringe the deposit.

6. Disturbed ground/arable

Divided into two categories: 6a, species of weedy disturbed ground (*Agonum dorsale* and *Harpalus rufipes*); and 6b, species of *Amara* of bare ground and arable on sandy soils (*A. apricaria*, *bifrons*, *similata* and *tibialis*). Neither grouping is particularly abundant, even when their favoured habitat seems to have been well represented, 1.5% being a high value for 6a and 3.0% being a high value for 6b. Unfortunately it is not possible to use the coleopteran evidence to differentiate arable from other types of bare or disturbed ground, and the members of this grouping do not have such good dispersive powers as the members of the various grassland groupings: therefore Coleoptera are not as reliable for detecting arable.

7. Dung/foul organic material

Certain members of the Hydrophilidae and Staphylinidae which live in various types of foul organic material, including dung, manure heaps, compost and other categories of decaying vegetation: *Cercyon* spp., *Megasternum* sp. *Cryptopleurum* spp., *Anotylus rugosus*, *A. sculpturatus* and *Platystethus arenarius*. Many rural archaeological assemblages show values between 7.5 and 15%, seemingly independently of the percentage of scarabaeoid dung beetles and the intensity of human habitation at the sites. Naturally occurring accumulations of decaying plant debris along the edge of the deposit seem also to be significant contributors of members of this grouping and this may be a major factor explaining the strong presence at Runnymede. On some urban sites with large accumulations of decaying refuse, however, values rise considerably higher than 15%.

8. Lathridiidae

A family of beetles, most of which feed on surface mould on decaying plant material. Values of 0–2.5% are quite normal for assemblages from prehistoric occupation sites and semi-natural deposits, but Roman and more recent occupation sites often produce values in excess of 9%, where the abundance of this family seems to be related to concentrations of old thatch, vegetation used as bedding for animals, etc.

9. Synanthropic

Various members of the Anobiidae, Ptinidae, Endomychidae, Mycetophagidae and Tenebrionidae which usually live in buildings or are associated with human habitation (Robinson 1981b: 265, 268). They can occur in granary refuse and are often associated with hay waste, straw or decaying parts of timber buildings; some are stored-product pests.

In Britain they also have habitats away from human habitation, such as birds' nests, but are very rare unless in their synanthropic habitats. Values for this grouping vary between 0–0.2% from prehistoric and semi-natural deposits, but values of 2–5% are commonly found in Roman rural occupation sites. Urban sites often give even higher values. The only member of this grouping from the Runnymede samples was *Stegobium paniceum*. Those synanthropic members of the Cucujidae, Silvanidae, Tenebrionidae and Curculionidae, such as *Sitophilus granarius*, which can be very serious pests of stored grain and only occur in Britain under artificial conditions ought to be placed in a new category. The wood-boring synanthropic species belong to Species Group 10.

10. Especially structural timbers

Anobium punctatum (the woodworm beetle) and *Lyctus linearis*. They are native members of the British woodland fauna, but they live in dry dead wood, which is not particularly common under natural conditions. These beetles, especially *A. punctatum*, can proliferate in structural timbers. Natural woodland assemblages normally have values below 1% although percentages up to 3% have been recorded. Values from prehistoric occupation sites usually fall below 1% unless the deposit itself contained woodworm-infested timber. The values for Roman rural occupation sites, at 1.5 to 2.5%, probably reflect a greater density of buildings, and on urban sites *A. punctatum* is usually even more abundant.

11. On roots in grassland

Various Scarabaeidae and Elateridae with larvae which live on the roots of herbs in permanent grassland. The species belonging to this grouping which occurred at Runnymede were:

Serica brunnea	*Agrypnus murinus*
Hoplia philanthus	*Athous* spp.
Phyllopertha horticola	*Agriotes* spp.

Amphimallon solstitalis and *Melolontha* sp. have not been included because their adults congregate in woodland. Under conditions of closed woodland their value is below 0.5% but it rises in open woodland. An open landscape of permanent grassland can give a value up to about 7% when the grassland is well drained, but this falls to about 1% if the grassland is ill-drained, although there are some Elateridae which do require waterlogged conditions.

Table 32: Runnymede Neolithic Coleoptera, column SS1 and bulk samples.

	— Minimum numbers of individuals																	
depth (cms) to:	190 195	185 190	180 185	175 180	170 175	165 170	160 165	155 160	150 155	145 150	140 145	135 140	130 135	125 130	L41	L40	Total	Habitat or food
CARABIDAE																		
Carabus granulatus L.	1	–	–	–	–	–	–	–	–	–	–	–	–	–	–	–	1	T – often near water, in rotten trees
C. moniis F.	–	–	–	–	–	–	–	–	–	–	–	–	–	–	–	1	1	WGD
Nebria brevicollis (F.)	–	2	2	1	–	–	–	–	–	–	–	–	–	–	1	–	6	WGD
Loricera pilicornis (F.)	–	–	–	1	–	–	–	–	–	–	–	–	–	–	–	3	4	T – usually moist
Dyschirius globosus (Hbst.)	1	4	1	3	2	2	2	4	1	2	3	7	5	–	1	6	43	T – moist ground, M
Dyschirius sp.	–	–	–	1	–	–	–	–	–	–	–	–	–	–	–	–	1	T – moist ground, M
Clivina collaris (Hbst.) or fossor L.)	–	1	1	1	–	1	1	4	2	–	1	–	–	–	2	3	14	Moist T, often under dung
Patrobus atrorufus (Ström)	–	1	1	–	–	–	–	–	–	–	–	–	–	–	–	–	1	W
Trechus obtusus Er. or quadristriatus (Schr.)	–	–	1	1	–	–	–	1	–	–	–	–	–	–	–	–	3	T
T. secalis (Pk.)	–	1	1	1	–	–	–	1	–	–	–	–	–	–	–	2	4	Moist G and W, B
T. micros (Hbst.)	1	–	–	–	1	–	1	–	–	–	–	1	1	–	1	1	4	B – usually of flowing water
Bembidion properans Step.	1	1	–	1	1	2	–	1	–	–	–	–	–	–	–	–	4	T – damp heavy soil and mud
B. dentellum (Thun.)	1	–	1	1	–	–	–	1	–	–	–	–	–	–	–	–	3	M&(G) – well vegetated
B. semipunctatum Don.	–	–	–	–	–	–	–	–	–	–	–	–	–	–	1	–	1	B – on sand
B. tetracolum Say	–	–	–	–	–	1	–	–	–	–	–	–	–	–	–	2	2	TM
B. quadrimaculatum (L.)	–	–	–	–	–	–	1	–	–	–	–	–	–	–	–	–	1	GD
B. gilvipes Sturm	–	2	1	1	–	–	–	1	1	1	1	2	1	–	1	1	13	(W) B also wet meadowland
B. assimile Gyl.	1	1	–	1	–	–	2	2	1	4	1	1	1	–	2	1	13	BM – well vegetated and close to water
B. doris (Pz.)	–	1	–	–	1	1	1	2	–	1	1	–	–	–	–	–	5	BM
B. biguttatum (F.)	–	2	2	2	–	1	1	–	1	1	1	1	–	–	1	1	10	BG and W, usually near water
B. guttula (F.)	–	1	1	1	1	2	2	3	1	1	2	1	1	–	–	5	19	MG and W – moist
Tachys sp.	–	1	1	–	–	–	–	–	–	–	–	–	–	–	–	1	2	B – at waterside
Pterostichus anthracinus (Pz.)	–	–	–	–	–	–	1	–	1	–	–	1	–	–	–	1	4	M&B – shaded
P. cf. anthracinus (Pz.)	–	1	1	–	–	–	1	–	–	–	–	–	–	–	–	–	2	M&B – shaded
P. cupreus (L.)	–	1	–	–	–	–	1	–	–	–	–	–	–	–	–	–	1	G(D W) – moist, sometimes near water
P. diligens (Sturm)	–	1	1	1	–	–	–	–	–	–	–	–	–	–	–	–	3	MG – wet
P. gracilis (Dej.)	1	–	–	1	1	–	–	–	–	–	1	–	1	–	–	–	6	G&W – wet, M
P. cf. gracilis (Dej.)	–	1	–	–	–	–	–	1	–	–	–	–	–	–	1	–	2	G&W – wet, M
P. melanarius (Ill.)	–	–	–	1	–	–	1	–	–	–	–	–	–	–	–	–	1	DG (W)
P. minor (Gyl.)	–	–	2	–	–	–	1	1	–	–	–	–	–	–	–	–	3	M&B – both wooded and open
P. niger (Schal.)	–	–	–	1	–	–	–	–	–	–	–	–	–	–	–	–	1	W (GD)
P. cf. niger (Schal.)	–	–	–	–	–	–	–	–	1	–	–	–	–	–	1	–	1	W (GD)
P. nigrita (Pk.)	–	–	1	1	–	–	–	1	–	–	–	–	–	–	–	–	2	MB
P. oblongopunctatus (F.)	–	–	–	1	–	–	–	–	–	–	–	–	–	–	–	–	1	W
P. strenuus (Pz.)	–	–	–	1	–	–	–	1	1	–	1	–	–	–	–	–	3	T – often near water
P. vernalis (Pz.)	–	–	–	–	–	–	–	1	–	1	–	–	–	–	–	–	1	DG & (W) – moist, often near water
P. cupreus (L.) or versicolor (Sturm)	–	1	1	1	–	–	–	1	–	–	–	–	–	–	1	–	4	G(DW)
Abax parallelepipedus (P. & M.)	–	–	–	–	–	–	1	1	–	–	–	–	–	–	1	1	3	W (GDC)

Table 32: Runnymede Neolithic Coleoptera, column SS1 and bulk samples (continued).

Taxon														Ecology
Calathus fuscipes (Gz.)	1	—	—	—	—	—	—	—	—	—	—	1	2	WD & G – often in meadowland
C. melanocephalus (L.)	—	—	—	—	—	—	—	—	—	—	—	—	1	GD (W)
Olisthopus rotundatus (Pk.)	—	—	—	—	—	—	1	2	—	—	—	—	2	GD
Agonum albipes (F.)	1	1	—	—	1	2	—	—	1	1	—	—	9	BW (DG)
A. marginatum (L.)	—	—	—	—	—	—	—	—	—	—	—	—	1	MB & G – usually wet
A. muelleri (Hbst.)	—	—	—	—	—	1	—	—	—	—	1	—	2	MGD (W)
A. viduum (Pz.)	1	—	—	—	1	1	—	1	—	—	—	—	2	B – rich vegetation (W)
Amara sp.	—	2	—	1	1	1	—	1	1	—	—	—	6	T
Harpalus rufipes (Deg.)	—	1	—	—	—	—	—	—	—	—	—	—	1	D – often cultivated (G)
Harpalus S. Harpalus sp.	—	—	—	1	—	—	—	—	—	—	—	—	1	T
Chlaenius nigricornis (F.) or nitidulus (Schr.)	—	1	—	—	1	—	—	—	—	—	—	—	1	B – sometimes on mud or under reed debris
Metabletus obscuroguttatus (Duft.)	—	—	—	1	—	1	1	—	—	—	—	—	2	V
HALIPLIDAE														
Brychius elevatus (Pz.)	—	—	—	1	—	—	—	—	—	—	—	—	1	A – moving water on Veronica and Nasturtium spp.
Haliplus sp.	1	—	—	—	1	—	—	—	1	—	—	—	3	A
DYTISCIDAE														
Hygrotus sp.	—	—	—	—	—	—	—	—	—	1	—	—	2	A – stagnant or slowly moving, plant-rich
Graptodytes pictus (F.)	1	1	—	1	—	—	1	—	—	—	—	—	3	A – ponds and slowly moving water
Potamonectes depressus (F.)	1	—	—	—	—	—	—	—	—	—	—	—	1	A
Stictotarsus duodecimpustulatus (F.)	—	—	—	4	—	—	—	—	1	—	1	—	5	A – running water and lakes
Platambus maculatus (L.)	—	—	1	—	—	1	1	—	—	—	—	—	1	A – running water and lakes
Agabus sp. (not bipustulatus)	1	—	—	—	1	—	—	—	—	—	—	—	2	A
GYRINIDAE														
Gyrinus sp.	—	—	—	1	—	—	—	—	—	—	—	—	1	A
Orectochilus villosus (Müll.)	1	2	2	—	—	1	1	—	1	—	1	—	10	A – running water
HYDROPHILIDAE														
Hydrochus sp.	1	—	1	—	—	1	—	—	1	—	—	—	2	A – mostly stagnant
Helophorus arvernicus Muls.	—	—	—	1	—	1	1	2	—	—	2	—	9	A – clean, flowing
H. grandis Ill.	—	—	—	1	—	—	1	—	—	—	—	—	1	A – puddles, ponds rarely flowing water
H. aquaticus (L) or grandis Ill.	1	—	—	—	1	1	—	1	—	—	—	2	6	A – puddles, ponds rarely flowing water
Helophorus spp. (brevipalpis size)	2	1	2	3	3	2	1	—	—	2	—	6	33	A – but readily leave water
Coelostoma orbiculare (F.)	1	—	2	1	3	—	—	—	1	—	—	1	2	V – esp. in wet places, often at water's edge, A – ponds
Sphaeridium bipustulatum F.	1	—	1	—	—	—	—	—	—	—	—	—	1	FVC
S. lunatum F. or scarabaeoides (L.)	1	1	—	—	—	—	—	1	—	1	—	—	5	F – esp. cow dung (CV)
Cercyon analis (Pk.)	—	—	1	1	—	1	—	—	—	—	—	—	1	FV
C. haemorrhoidalis (F.)	2	1	—	2	—	1	1	—	—	2	—	2	13	FV
C. cf. haemorrhoidalis (F.)	1	—	—	1	—	—	—	—	—	—	—	—	1	FV

Table 32: Runnymede Neolithic Coleoptera, column SS1 and bulk samples (continued).

	Minimum numbers of individuals																	Habitat or food
depth (cms) to:	190 195	185 190	180 185	175 180	170 175	165 170	160 165	155 160	150 155	145 150	140 145	135 140	130 135	125 130	L41	L40	Total	
C. cf. *lateralis* (Marsh.)	—	—	—	—	—	—	—	1	—	—	—	—	—	—	—	—	1	FV
C. pygmaeus (Ill.)	2	—	—	—	1	1	—	1	—	—	—	—	—	—	—	—	5	Mostly F
C. sternalis Sharp	3	1	3	1	2	2	2	2	1	3	5	4	2	1	1	4	35	MB – on damp ground
C. tristis (Ill.)	—	—	—	—	—	—	—	—	—	—	—	—	—	1	1	—	2	Under plant detritus
C. ustulatus (Pres.)	—	1	—	1	—	1	1	—	1	—	—	—	—	—	—	—	4	V in moist places (F)
Cercyon spp.	1	—	1	1	—	—	1	—	—	1	1	—	—	—	—	—	6	FVC, some species on wet mud
Megasternum obscurum (Marsh.)	2	8	7	9	6	13	13	4	3	3	1	1	1	1	6	8	93	FVC
Cryptopleurum minutum (F.)	1	—	1	—	1	1	3	—	—	—	—	—	1	—	—	—	6	FVC
Hydrobius fuscipes (L.)	—	—	—	—	—	—	—	—	—	—	—	1	—	—	—	1	2	A – stagnant water often with detritus bottom
Anacaena globulus (Pk.)	—	—	—	1	—	—	—	—	—	—	—	—	—	—	—	—	1	G & W in wet places, VA
A. bipustulata (Marsh.) or *limbata* (F.)	—	—	—	—	—	—	1	—	—	—	—	—	—	—	1	—	2	G & W in wet places, VA
Laccobius sp.	—	—	—	1	1	1	1	1	1	2	1	—	—	—	—	1	10	A
Enochrus sp.	—	—	1	—	—	—	—	—	—	—	—	—	—	—	—	—	1	A – mostly ponds and ditches
Chaetarthria seminulum (Hbst.)	—	—	—	1	—	—	—	—	—	—	1	—	—	—	—	1	3	B – wet vegetation and mud at water's edge (A)
HISTERIDAE																		
Hister bissexstriatus F.	—	—	1	—	—	—	—	—	—	—	—	—	—	1	—	—	2	FV
Paralister sp.	—	—	—	—	—	—	1	—	—	—	—	—	—	—	—	—	1	FVC
Hister or *Paralister* sp.	1	—	—	—	—	—	—	—	—	—	—	—	—	—	—	—	1	FVC
Atholus duodecimstriatus (Schr.)	—	—	—	1	—	—	—	—	—	—	—	—	—	—	—	—	1	FV
HYDRAENIDAE																		
Ochthebius bicolon Germ.	—	—	1	—	—	—	—	—	—	—	—	—	—	—	—	—	1	B – mud and decaying vegetation at water's edge. A
O. cf. *bicolon* Germ.	1	2	2	1	1	1	2	2	2	2	—	1	1	—	—	4	16	B – as above. A
O. minimus (F.)	—	1	4	3	3	3	3	3	4	7	3	2	1	—	1	2	40	A – often stagnant
O. cf. *minimus* (F.)	3	9	10	11	11	20	20	27	8	27	18	9	4	1	8	14	186	A – often stagnant
Hydraena minutissima Step.	—	—	—	—	—	1	—	—	—	—	—	—	—	—	—	—	1	A – flowing
H. cf. *nigrita* Germ.	—	—	—	—	—	—	1	1	—	—	—	—	—	—	—	—	1	A – flowing
H. pulchella Germ.	1	2	1	—	—	1	—	1	2	2	1	—	1	—	1	1	10	A – flowing
H. riparia Kug.	1	4	3	2	4	8	10	9	5	4	1	1	1	2	2	1	58	A
H. testacea Curt.	—	1	—	—	—	—	—	—	—	—	—	1	—	—	1	—	2	A – usually stagnant
Limnebius nitidus (Marsh.)	—	1	1	—	1	1	1	—	—	—	—	—	—	—	—	—	2	A B – mud at water's edge
L. papposus Muls.	—	—	—	1	1	—	—	—	—	—	1	—	—	—	—	—	4	A B – mud at water's edge
PTILIIDAE																		
Ptenidium sp.	—	—	2	1	—	—	—	—	1	2	—	1	2	—	1	2	13	Dung heaps, rotten wood, VM
Ptiliidae gen. et sp.indet. (not *Ptenidium*)	—	3	—	—	1	1	2	—	2	—	3	—	—	—	—	1	13	VM (TF)
LEIODIDAE																		
Agathidium nigrinum Sturm.	1	1	—	—	—	—	—	—	—	—	—	—	—	—	—	—	1	W – in V and under bark

Table 32: Runnymede Neolithic Coleoptera, column SS1 and bulk samples (continued).

Taxon	Total	Ecology
LEIODIDAE (continued)		
Choleva or Catops sp.	3	C (G) V – often leaf litter or fungi in woods
Colon sp.	1	Inc. under bark, grassy places near trees, leaf litter
SILPHIDAE		
Silpha atrata L.	3	mostly under bark or in rotten wood (GDV)
S. obscura L.	1	C
SCYDMAENIDAE		
Scydmaenidae gen. et sp. indet.	5	TV
STAPHYLINIDAE		
Anthobium atrocephalum (Gyl.)	1	Esp. in leaf litter, also B and decaying fungi.
Lesteva sp.	3	B – often at water's edge, M
Phyllodrepa sp.	1	V
Omalium sp.	5	V – all sorts. CFT
Carpelimus bilineatus Step.	18	B – on wet mud (GV & F on wet soils)
C. cf. corticinus (Grav.)	8	B – on wet mud and sand M
C. rivularis (Mots.)	34	B&M on mud or in V
C. cf. rivularis (Mots.)	1	B&M on mud or in V
Platystethus arenarius (Fouc.)	2	FV
P. cornutus gp.	3	M & B – often on mud (VF)
P. nitens (Sahl.)	1	FVB
P. nodifrons (Man.)	12	V
Anotylus rugosus (F.)	27	FV (C)
A. sculpturatus gp.	15	FVC (also T)
Oxytelus sculptus Grav.	6	FV (C)
Stenus spp.	47	TM
Paederus littoralis Grav.	2	G&D – mostly dry
Lathrobium cf. brunnipes (F.)	3	M
L. longulum Grav.	10	T
Lathrobium sp. (not longulum)	18	TV (C)
Sunius sp.	2	V
Rugilus cf. geniculatus (Er.)	1	V (G)
R. orbiculatus (Pk.)	4	V (G)
Gyrohypnus angustatus Step.	2	V – sometimes at water's edge
G. fracticornis gp.	2	FV (C)
Xantholinus linearis (Ol.)	6	WGV (FC)
X. longiventris Heer	4	WGV (FC)
X. linearis (Ol.) or longiventris Heer	15	WGV (FC)
Philonthus spp.	25	FVC (T)

Table 32: Runnymede Neolithic Coleoptera, column SS1 and bulk samples (continued).

depth (cms) to:	Minimum numbers of individuals																	Habitat or food
	190/195	185/190	180/185	175/180	170/175	165/170	160/165	155/160	150/155	145/150	140/145	135/140	130/135	125/130	L41	L40	Total	
Gabrius sp.	–	–	1	1	1	3	1	2	1	1	–	3	2	–	–	2	18	WG FVC
Staphylinus aeneocephalus Deg. or fortunatorum (Wol.)	–	–	–	–	–	–	–	–	–	–	–	1	–	–	–	–	1	WG
Tachyporus spp.	–	2	2	1	–	2	3	1	2	1	1	1	–	–	1	2	19	T
Tachinus spp.	–	2	2	–	–	–	3	3	1	1	1	–	–	–	–	2	10	T
Aleocharinae gen. et sp. indet.	–	2	5	4	4	3	7	2	8	3	9	7	5	2	2	15	75	TFCV
PSELAPHIDAE																		
Brachygluta sp.	–	–	–	–	–	1	1	–	–	1	1	1	–	–	–	–	5	V(GWM)
LUCANIDAE																		
Sinodendron cylindricum (L.)	–	1	1	–	–	–	–	–	–	–	–	1	–	–	–	2	4	Rotten hardwood
GEOTRUPIDAE																		
Geotrupes sp.	1	1	1	1	–	–	–	1	–	–	–	–	–	–	1	–	6	F
SCARABAEIDAE																		
Colobopterus erraticus (L)	–	–	–	–	–	–	–	–	–	–	–	–	–	–	1	–	1	F(C)
C. haemorrhoidalis (L.)	–	1	–	–	–	–	–	–	–	–	–	–	–	–	–	–	1	F
Aphodius equestris (Pz.)	–	–	1	–	–	–	–	–	–	–	–	–	–	–	–	–	1	F
A. fimetarius L.	–	–	1	–	–	–	–	–	–	–	–	–	–	–	–	–	1	FV
A. cf. fimetarius L.	–	1	1	–	–	–	–	–	–	–	–	–	–	–	–	–	1	FV
A. granarius (L.)	3	1	2	1	–	–	1	–	–	1	–	–	–	–	1	1	12	FV
A. porcus (F.)	–	–	–	–	–	–	–	–	1	–	–	–	–	–	–	–	1	F – in Geotrupes burrows
A. cf. prodromus (Brahm)	–	–	–	–	–	–	–	–	–	–	–	–	–	–	–	1	1	FV
A. cf. pusillus (Hbst.)	–	2	2	2	–	–	–	–	–	–	–	–	–	–	–	–	6	FV
A. rufipes (L.)	1	1	1	–	1	1	1	–	–	–	–	–	1	–	1	1	6	F
A. rufus (Moll)	–	–	–	–	–	–	–	–	–	–	–	–	–	–	–	1	1	F
A. cf. sphacelatus (Pz.)	–	1	5	4	–	2	1	3	1	1	2	2	2	–	1	2	26	FVC
A. villosus Gyl.	1	–	–	–	–	–	–	–	–	–	–	–	–	–	–	–	1	V(F)
Aphodius spp.	4	2	2	2	–	–	1	–	–	1	3	1	–	2	–	–	16	Mostly F
Oxyomus sylvestris (Scop.)	1	1	1	1	–	–	1	–	1	1	1	1	–	–	1	1	9	F – mostly as dung heaps VC
Copris lunaris (L.)	–	–	1	–	–	–	–	–	–	–	–	–	–	–	–	–	1	F
Onthophagus ovatus (L.)	3	1	3	–	–	–	–	1	1	–	–	–	–	–	–	1	10	FCV
O. taurus (Sch.)	–	1	–	1	–	–	1	–	–	–	–	–	–	–	1	–	4	F
Onthophagus sp.(not ovatus or taurus)	–	–	1	–	–	–	1	–	–	–	–	–	–	–	–	–	1	F(C)
Serica brunnea (L.)	–	1	1	–	–	–	–	–	–	–	–	–	–	–	–	–	1	Larvae on grass roots in sandy places
Melolontha sp.	1	1	2	–	–	–	–	1	–	–	–	–	–	–	–	–	5	Larvae on roots of grass and trees, adults on tree leaves
Phyllopertha horticola (L.)	2	1	6	–	–	1	2	3	1	1	1	1	–	–	1	3	25	Larvae on roots in permanent grassland
DASCILLIDAE																		
Dascillus cervinus (L.)	–	1	1	–	–	–	1	2	–	2	–	–	–	–	1	1	9	On flowers and bushes

Table 32: Runnymede Neolithic Coleoptera, column SS1 and bulk samples (continued).

Taxon															Ecology
SCIRTIDAE															
cf. *Cyphon* sp.	—	—	—	1	1	1	1	—	1	2	1	2	2	12	Larvae A, adults T, but close to water and M
BYRRHIDAE															
Byrrhus sp.	—	—	—	—	—	—	—	—	—	1	—	—	—	1	T
HETEROCERIDAE															
Heterocerus sp.	—	—	—	—	—	3	—	3	1	—	1	—	3	3	B&M – on mud at water's edge
DRYOPIDAE															
Helichus substriatus (Müll.)	2	8	3	3	2	—	3	1	1	1	—	1	1	26	A & water's edge
Dryops sp.	1	2	1	—	1	2	1	1	1	—	—	—	—	14	BA & M in or close to water (V)
ELMIDAE															
Elmis aenea (Müll.)	—	1	1	1	—	—	—	—	—	—	—	—	—	3	A – clean flowing water, clinging to stones and aquatic plants
Esolus parallelepipedus (Müll.)	1	7	5	7	3	5	2	4	2	3	1	1	6	52	A – clean flowing water, clinging to stones and aquatic plants
Limnius volkmari (Pz.)	1	2	2	2	2	—	1	4	1	1	1	—	1	18	A – clean flowing water, clinging to stones and aquatic plants
Macronychus quadrituberculatus Müll.	—	2	4	2	3	2	1	1	1	1	—	1	1	17	A – on submerged decaying wood
Normandia nitens (Müll.)	26	36	28	36	23	20	10	7	11	6	2	2	15	251	A – clean flowing water clinging to stones and aquatic plants
Oulimnius sp.	13	39	40	41	33	49	32	26	24	21	4	5	28	400	Mostly clean, flowing
Riolus sp.	1	—	—	1	1	—	—	—	—	1	—	—	1	4	Mostly clean, flowing
Stenelmis canaliculata (Gyl.)	2	—	1	1	2	1	1	—	—	—	1	—	3	11	A – clean flowing, also large lakes
ELATERIDAE															
Agrypnus murinus (L)	—	1	1	1	1	2	—	—	—	—	—	1	1	7	G
Melanotus erythropus (Gm.)	—	—	—	—	—	—	—	—	—	—	—	—	—	1	Rotten wood
Athous hirtus (Hbst.)	—	—	1	—	1	—	—	—	—	—	—	1	—	2	WG – esp. meadowland, larvae esp. on the roots of grasses, also trees and shrubs
A. haemorrhoidalis (F.)	—	3	2	—	—	—	—	—	—	—	1	—	—	6	WG – esp. meadowland, larvae esp. on the roots of grasses, also trees and shrubs
Selatosomus bipustulatus (L.)	—	—	—	—	1	—	—	—	—	—	—	—	—	1	Larvae in rotton wood
Agriotes sp.	1	—	—	—	—	—	—	—	—	—	—	—	—	1	Larvae mostly on roots of grassland plants
Synaptus filiformis (F.)	—	—	—	1	—	—	—	—	—	—	—	—	—	1	G – damp. M.
THROSCIDAE															
Trixagus dermestoides (L.)	—	—	—	—	—	2	—	—	—	—	—	—	—	2	Rotten wood, leaf litter
T. obtusus (Curt.)	—	—	—	—	1	—	1	—	—	—	—	—	—	1	Inc. rotten wood, G
T. cf. *obtusus* (Curt.)	—	—	1	—	—	—	—	—	—	—	—	—	—	1	Inc. rotten wood, G
EUCNEMIDAE															
Dirhagus pygmaeus (F.)	—	1	—	—	—	1	—	—	—	—	—	—	—	2	Dead hardwood

Table 32: Runnymede Neolithic Coleoptera, column SS1 and bulk samples (continued).

	Minimum numbers of individuals																
depth (cms) to:	190 195	185 190	180 185	175 180	170 175	165 170	160 165	155 160	150 155	145 150	140 145	135 140	130 135	125 130	L41	L40	Total	Habitat or food
EUCNEMIDAE (continued)																		
Dromaeolus barnabita (Villa)	—	—	—	—	—	—	1	—	—	—	—	—	—	—	—	—	1	Dead dry branches of hardwood
Melasis buprestoides (L.)	—	—	—	—	—	—	—	—	—	—	—	—	—	—	—	1	1	In rotten hardwood
CANTHARIDAE																		
Cantharis sp.	—	—	1	—	—	—	—	1	1	—	—	—	—	—	—	—	3	Adults on flowers of herbs and shrubs
ANOBIIDAE																		
Ptinomorphus imperialis (L.)	—	—	—	—	—	—	—	1	—	—	—	—	—	—	—	—	1	Dead hardwood twigs
Grynobius planus (F.)	—	—	—	—	—	—	1	—	—	—	—	—	—	—	1	—	2	Dead hardwood
Gastrallus immarginatus (Müll.)	—	—	—	—	—	—	2	1	—	—	—	—	—	—	—	—	3	Dead wood of old deciduous trees esp. Acer and Quercus
Anobium cf. punctatum (Deg.)	—	1	—	1	—	—	—	1	—	—	—	—	—	—	—	—	3	Dead wood
PELTIDAE																		
Pelta grossum (L.)	—	—	1	—	—	—	—	—	—	—	—	—	—	—	—	—	1	Dead wood with the bark on
NITIDULIDAE																		
Brachypterus urticae (F.)	—	1	3	—	—	—	1	—	1	—	—	—	—	—	—	—	6	Urtica sp.
Meligethes sp.	1	4	3	4	3	1	4	4	2	5	4	1	—	—	2	1	39	Herbs and trees – mostly on flowers
Epuraea sp.	1	1	1	—	—	—	—	—	—	—	—	—	—	—	—	—	3	In fungi, under bark, at sap, on flowers
Omosita colon (L.)	—	—	—	—	—	—	—	—	—	—	—	—	—	—	—	1	1	C – dry
SPHINDIDAE																		
Aspidiphorus orbiculatus (Gyl.)	—	—	—	—	—	—	—	—	1	—	—	—	—	—	—	—	1	Slime moulds and powdery fungi of wood
CRYPTOPHAGIDAE																		
Cryptophagidae gen. et sp. indet. (not Atomariinae)	—	—	1	—	—	—	—	—	—	—	—	—	—	—	—	—	1	V – of all sorts, T
Atommaria mesomela (Hbst.)	—	2	1	2	—	1	1	1	—	1	—	—	—	—	—	—	7	Wet G, M – often on V
Atomaria spp.	—	2	2	1	—	1	1	2	2	1	—	—	1	—	1	2	12	VT (F)
PHALACRIDAE																		
Phalacrus sp.	—	1	1	—	—	—	—	—	—	—	—	—	—	—	—	1	2	Larvae on grasses & Carex smuts, adults on flowers
Stilbus sp.	—	—	1	—	—	—	—	—	—	1	1	—	—	—	—	—	3	In dry grass, hay and on Typha sp.
CERYLONIDAE																		
Cerylon histeroides (F.)	—	—	—	—	—	—	—	—	—	—	—	—	—	—	—	1	1	In rotten wood and under bark
CORYLOPHIDAE																		
Corylophus cassidoides (Marsh.)	—	—	1	—	—	1	1	—	1	1	3	1	1	1	—	4	11	V – esp. decaying reeds
Orthoperus sp.	—	1	1	—	—	1	—	1	—	—	—	—	—	—	—	—	4	V

Table 32: Runnymede Neolithic Coleoptera, column SS1 and bulk samples (continued).

Taxon											Total	Ecology
COCCINELLIDAE												
Coccidula sp.	—	—	—	—	—	—	—	—	—	—	1	Aphids of marsh and aquatic plants
Stethorus punctillum (Weise)	—	—	—	—	—	—	—	—	—	—	1	Mites esp. of *Tilia* spp.
Chilocorus bipustulatus (L.)	—	1	1	—	1	—	—	—	—	—	1	T
LATHRIDIIDAE												
Enicmus transversus (Ol.)	—	1	1	1	—	2	1	—	1	—	10	V (GW)
Corticariinae gen. et sp. indet.	1	3	2	1	1	4	5	1	1	—	22	Mostly V
COLYDIIDAE												
Colydium elongatum (F.)	—	—	—	—	—	1	1	—	—	—	1	Under loose bark and in rotten wood
Teredus cylindricus (Ol.)	—	1	1	—	—	—	—	—	—	—	1	In tunnels of other insects and under loose bark of *Quercus* and *Fagus*.
TENEBRIONIDAE												
Lagria atripes (Muls.) or *hirta* (L.)	—	—	—	—	—	1	—	—	—	—	1	Larvae in leaf litter, adults on flowers
Prionychus melanarius (Germ.)	1	—	1	—	—	—	—	—	—	—	1	Wood mould in hollow trees, esp. old *Quercus*
SCRAPTIIDAE												
Anaspis sp.	—	1	—	1	—	—	—	—	1	—	2	Adults on blossom esp. shrubs
BRUCHIDAE												
Bruchus loti Pk.	—	—	—	—	1	—	—	—	—	—	1	*Lotus* and *Lathyrus* spp.
CHRYSOMELIDAE												
Macroplea appendiculata (Pz.)	—	1	1	—	—	—	—	1	—	1	3	*Potamogeton* and *Myriophyllum* spp.
Donacia aquatica (L.)	—	1	1	—	—	—	—	—	—	1	3	*Sparganium*, *Carex* & aquatic *Ranunculus* spp.
D. bicolora Zsch.	—	—	—	—	—	—	1	1	—	—	1	*Sparganium erectum* L.
D. cinerea Hbst.	1	1	1	1	—	1	3	—	2	1	4	Various reedswamp monocotyledons
D. clavipes F.	2	1	1	1	2	1	3	1	2	4	21	*Phragmites australis* (Cav.) (? & *Phalaris* sp.)
D. crassipes F.	—	—	2	—	1	2	—	—	1	—	6	*Nymphea alba* L. & *Nuphar lutea* (L.) Sm.
D. dentata Hoppe	4	1	1	—	—	—	—	—	1	—	1	*Sagittaria sagittifolia* L. & *Alisma* sp.
D. impressa Pk.	2	9	3	3	4	3	1	1	2	3	41	*Schoenoplectus lacustris* (L.) Pal.
D. marginata Hoppe	1	—	—	—	—	—	1	—	1	1	3	*Sparganium erectum* L.
D. simplex F.	—	1	1	1	—	1	—	—	—	—	3	Various reedswamp monocotyledons
D. versicolorea (Brahm)	—	1	1	—	1	—	—	1	—	—	3	Floating-leaved species of *Potamogeton*
D. cf. *vulgaris* Zsch.	1	1	—	—	—	—	—	—	—	1	2	Various reedswamp monocotyledons
Donacia spp.	1	1	—	—	1	—	—	1	—	—	3	Various reedswamp monocotyledons
Plateumaris braccata (Scop.)	—	—	1	—	—	—	—	—	—	—	1	*Phragmites australis* (Cav.)
Oulema cf. *melanopa* (L.)	—	—	—	—	1	—	1	—	1	—	2	Grasses
Chrysolina hyperici (Forst.)	—	—	—	1	—	—	—	—	—	—	1	*Hypericum* spp.

Table 32: Runnymede Neolithic Coleoptera, column SS1 and bulk samples.

	Minimum numbers of individuals																	
depth (cms) to:	190 195	185 190	180 185	175 180	170 175	165 170	160 165	155 160	150 155	145 150	140 145	135 140	130 135	125 130	L41	L40	Total	Habitat or food
C. polita (L.)	–	–	1	–	–	–	–	–	–	–	–	–	–	–	–	–	1	Labiatae – often in marshes
Gastrophysa viridula (Deg.)	–	–	1	–	–	–	–	–	–	–	–	–	–	–	1	1	3	*Rumex* & *Polygonum* spp.
Phaedon tumidulus (Germ.)	–	–	–	–	–	–	–	–	–	–	–	–	–	–	1	–	1	Umbelliferae esp. *Heracleum* sp.
Phaedon sp. (not *tumidulus*)	–	–	1	1	–	1	1	–	–	1	3	–	–	–	–	2	10	Various herbs
Hydrothassa glabra (Hbst.)	–	1	1	1	–	1	–	–	–	–	–	–	–	–	–	1	5	*Ranunculus* spp.
H. marginella (L.)	–	1	–	–	–	–	–	1	–	–	–	–	2	–	–	–	4	*Ranunculus* spp.
Prasocuris phellandrii (L.)	–	–	–	1	1	–	–	–	–	–	–	–	–	–	–	1	3	Aquatic Umbelliferae
Agelastica alni (L.)	1	3	1	1	–	1	–	1	–	2	–	1	–	–	2	–	11	*Alnus glutinosa* (L.) Gaert.
Phyllotreta nigripes (F.)	–	1	1	2	–	1	–	–	–	–	1	–	–	–	–	–	5	Cruicfera & *Reseda* sp.
P. ochripes (Curt.)	–	–	–	–	–	–	–	–	–	–	–	–	–	–	–	2	2	Cruicfera & *Reseda* sp.
P. nemorum (L.) or *undulata* Kuts.	–	2	1	–	1	2	1	–	–	1	1	1	–	–	–	–	10	Cruicfera & *Reseda* sp.
P. vittula Redt.	–	1	1	–	–	–	–	–	–	–	–	1	–	–	–	–	3	Cruicfera & *Reseda* sp.
Aphthona nonstriata (Gz.)	–	1	–	–	–	–	–	–	1	–	–	–	–	–	–	–	2	*Iris pseudacorus* L.
Longitarsus spp.	–	1	2	2	2	1	1	–	–	2	1	–	2	–	–	2	16	Various herbs
Altica sp.	–	1	1	1	–	–	–	1	1	–	–	–	–	–	–	1	5	Includes *Corylus, Salix, Rumex* & *Epilobium* spp.
Crepidodera ferruginea (Scop.)	–	1	–	–	–	1	–	2	–	1	1	–	–	–	–	–	6	Various herbs
Chalcoides sp.	–	–	–	1	1	–	–	–	–	–	–	–	–	–	–	–	1	*Salix* and *Populus* spp.
Epitrix pubescens (Koch)	–	–	–	1	3	1	5	1	1	1	–	–	1	–	–	4	17	*Solanum* spp., *Hyoscyamus* sp.
Chaetocnema concinna (Marsh.)	–	1	1	–	1	1	–	1	1	–	–	–	–	–	–	1	5	Polygonaceae esp. *P. aviculare* agg.
Chaetocnema sp. (not *concinna*)	2	1	–	–	–	–	–	–	–	–	–	–	–	–	–	–	3	Various herbs
Psylliodes sp.	–	2	2	1	1	1	1	1	–	2	1	–	–	–	1	2	15	Various herbs
APIONIDAE																		
Apion rufirostre (F.)	–	1	–	–	–	–	–	–	–	–	–	–	–	–	–	–	1	Various Malvaceae
A. aeneum (F.)	–	–	–	1	1	–	–	–	–	–	–	–	–	–	–	–	1	Various Malvaceae
A. urticarium (Hbst.)	–	–	–	1	–	–	–	–	1	–	–	–	–	–	–	–	1	*Urtica dioica* L. & *U. urens* L.
A. cerdo Gerst.	–	–	–	–	–	–	–	–	–	1	–	1	–	–	–	1	1	Larva *Vicia cracca* L., adult *Vicia* and *Lathyrus* spp.
A. craccae (L.)	–	–	–	2	2	–	–	–	–	–	–	–	–	–	–	–	2	*Vicia* and *Lathyrus* spp.
Apion spp. (not above)	4	2	4	1	2	6	3	4	–	1	1	1	2	1	1	1	34	Various herbs
CURCULIONIDAE																		
Caenopsis waltoni (Boh.)	–	–	–	–	–	–	–	–	–	–	–	–	2	–	–	–	2	*Plantago coronopus* L.
Phyllobius roboretanus Gred. or *viridiaeris* (Laich.)	–	–	–	–	–	–	–	–	–	1	–	–	–	–	–	–	1	Various trees and shrubs
Phyllobius sp.	–	–	–	–	–	–	–	–	1	1	–	–	1	–	–	–	2	Trees, grasses and *Urtica* sp.
Polydrusus mollis (Ström)	–	–	–	–	–	–	–	–	–	1	–	–	–	–	–	–	1	Deciduous shrubs and trees
Barypeithes pellucidus (Boh.)	–	–	1	–	–	–	–	–	–	–	–	–	–	–	1	–	1	Various plants
Sciaphilus asperatus (Bons.)	–	–	–	–	–	–	–	–	–	–	–	–	2	1	–	–	4	Woodland herbs esp. *Primula vulgaris* L. and *Sanicula* sp.
Strophosomus melanogrammus (Forst.)	–	–	–	–	–	–	–	–	–	–	1	–	5	–	–	–	6	*Rumex* sp. and various trees

Table 32: Runnymede Neolithic Coleoptera, column SS1 and bulk samples (continued).

Taxon												Total	Food plant / habitat
Barynotus moerens (F.)	—	—	—	—	—	—	—	—	1	—	—	1	esp. *Mercurialis perennis* L.
Barynotus sp.	—	1	1	—	—	—	—	—	—	—	—	4	T
Sitona hispidulus (F.)	1	2	—	—	2	—	1	—	1	1	—	5	Papilionaceae esp. *Medicago* and *Trifolium* spp.
Sitona sp.	1	—	—	—	1	—	—	—	—	—	—	1	Papilionaceae esp *Trifolium* sp.
Rhinocyllus conicus (Frö.)	—	1	—	1	—	—	—	—	—	—	—	2	*Carduus, Cirsium* and *Centaurea* spp.
Hypera punctata (F.)	1	—	—	—	—	1	—	—	1	—	—	4	Papilionaceae esp. *Trifolium* sp.
Hypera sp. (not punctata)	—	1	2	1	—	—	1	—	—	—	—	4	Various herbs
Tanysphyrus lemnae (Pk.)	—	—	—	—	—	—	—	—	—	1	—	1	*Lemna* spp.
Rhyncolus lignarius (Marsh.)	1	—	—	1	—	—	—	—	—	—	—	2	Sapwood of various hardwoods
R. truncorum (Germ.)	1	1	—	—	—	—	—	—	—	—	—	1	Sapwood of various hardwoods in large forests
Acalles turbatus Boh.	—	—	—	—	1	—	—	—	—	—	—	1	Dead *Crataegus* and *Corylus* esp.in hedges
Bagous spp.	2	3	2	3	4	2	2	1	—	1	3	29	Aquatic plants
Notaris acridulus (L.)	1	—	1	—	—	1	—	—	—	—	—	4	Marsh and aquatic plants
N. bimaculatus (F.)	—	—	—	—	—	—	—	—	—	1	—	1	Aquatic grasses, sedges and *Typha* sp.
Coeliodes dryados (Gm.)	—	—	—	—	1	—	1	—	—	—	—	2	*Quercus* spp. leaves
Micrelus ericae (Gyl.)	1	1	—	1	—	—	—	—	—	—	—	1	*Calluna* and *Erica* spp.
Cidnorhinus quadrimaculatus (L.)	2	2	—	—	—	1	1	—	2	2	2	12	*Urtica* spp.
Ceutorhynchidius troglodytes (F.)	—	1	—	—	—	—	1	—	1	—	—	—	*Plantago lanceolata* L.
Ceutorhynchus erysimi (F.)	1	1	—	1	—	1	—	—	—	—	—	3	Cruciferae
C. litura (F.)	—	—	—	—	—	—	—	—	—	—	—	1	*Carduus* and *Cirsium* spp.
C. pollinarius (Forst.)	—	1	1	—	1	—	1	—	—	1	—	2	*Urtica dioica* L.
Eubrychius velutus (Beck.)	—	—	1	—	—	—	1	—	—	—	—	1	Submerged plants esp.*Potamogeton* and *Myriophyllum* spp.
Phytobius sp.	1	—	1	—	—	5	—	—	—	—	—	1	esp. *Polygonum* and *Lythrum* spp.
Ceuthorhynchinae gen. et sp.indet.	2	4	1	2	5	1	4	3	1	2	5	41	Various herbs
Anthonomus sp. (not rubi)	—	—	—	1	1	1	1	—	1	—	—	1	Mostly Rosaceous trees and shrubs
Anthonomus sp.	—	1	—	—	—	1	—	—	—	1	—	3	Mostly Rosaceous trees and shrubs
Curculio nucum L.	—	1	—	1	—	—	—	—	—	—	—	1	*Corylus avellana* L. nuts
C. pyrrhoceras Marsh.	—	1	2	—	1	—	—	—	—	1	—	5	Galls on *Quercus* sp.
Tychius cf. tibialis Boh.	—	—	—	1	—	—	—	—	1	—	—	1	*Trifolium* spp. esp. *T. campestre* Sch.
Tychius sp.	1	—	1	2	1	1	—	—	—	—	—	7	Mostly Papilionaceae
Mecinus pyraster (Hbst.)	4	4	—	2	1	1	—	1	—	1	1	18	*Plantago lanceolata* L. and *P. media* L.
Gymnetron labile (Hbst.)	1	1	1	—	—	—	—	—	—	—	1	4	*Plantago lanceolata* L.
G. pascuorum (Gyl.)	—	—	1	1	—	1	—	—	—	—	—	1	*Plantago lanceolata* L.
G. rostellum (Hbst.)	1	1	—	1	—	—	—	—	—	1	—	5	Various herbs
G. villosum Gyl.	1	—	1	—	1	—	1	—	1	1	1	4	Various *Veronica* spp. esp. aquatic ones
Rhynchaenus avellanae (Don.)	1	—	—	—	1	—	—	—	—	—	1	3	*Quercus* leaves

Table 32: Runnymede Neolithic Coleoptera, column SS1 and bulk samples (continued).

								Minimum numbers of individuals										Habitat or food
depth (cms) to:	190 195	185 190	180 185	175 180	170 175	165 170	160 165	155 160	150 155	145 150	140 145	135 140	130 135	125 130	L41	L40	Total	
R. pilosus (F.)	—	—	—	—	—	—	—	—	—	—	—	1	—	—	—	—	1	Quercus leaves
R. cf. pilosus (F.)	—	1	1	—	—	—	—	1	—	—	—	—	—	—	—	—	3	Quercus leaves
R. quercus (L.)	1	2	4	1	5	—	2	4	3	2	—	4	7	2	1	2	40	Quercus leaves
Rhynchaenus spp.(not pratensis)	—	—	2	4	—	—	—	—	—	—	1	—	—	—	1	—	8	Leaves of various trees
Ramphus pulicarius (Hbst.)	—	—	—	—	—	1	—	—	—	—	—	—	—	—	—	—	1	Salix spp., also Populus & Betula spp.
SCOLYTIDAE																		
Scolytus intricatus (Ratz.)	—	—	1	1	—	1	—	—	—	1	—	—	—	—	—	—	4	Mainly young Quercus, also other hardwood
S. rugulosus (Mull.)	—	—	—	—	—	1	—	—	—	—	—	—	—	—	—	1	2	Rosaceous trees and shrubs
Scolytus sp.	1	—	—	—	—	—	—	—	—	—	—	—	—	—	—	—	1	Under bark of moribund hardwood
Leperisinus varius (F.)	—	—	—	—	1	—	—	—	1	—	—	—	—	—	—	—	2	Mainly Fraxinus, also other trees
Acrantus vittatus (F.)	—	—	—	—	—	—	—	—	—	—	1	—	—	—	—	—	1	Mainly decaying Ulmus, also other trees
Ernoporus caucasicus Lind.	—	—	—	—	—	—	1	—	—	—	—	—	—	—	—	1	2	Tilia cordata Mill.
Xyleborus saxesini (Ratz.)	—	—	—	—	—	—	—	—	—	1	—	—	—	—	—	—	1	Dead wood
X. dryophagus (Ratz.) or saxesini (Ratz.)	—	—	—	—	—	—	—	1	—	—	—	—	—	—	1	—	2	Dead wood
PLATYPODIAE																		
Platypus cylindrus Hbst.	—	—	—	—	—	—	—	1	—	—	—	—	—	—	—	—	1	Recently dead hardwood esp. Quercus
Totals	130	225	314	233	191	134	242	259	144	214	197	105	97	20	137	292	2934	

Table 33: Runnymede Neolithic other insects, column SS1 and bulk samples.

depth (cms) to:	190 195	185 190	180 185	175 180	170 175	165 170	160 165	155 160	150 155	145 150	140 145	135 140	130 135	125 130	L41	L40	Total	Habitat or food
ODONATA																		
Agrion splendens (Har.) or virgo (L.)	–	–	1	–	–	–	1	–	–	–	–	–	–	–	–	–	2	Nymphs A
Odonata gen.et sp.indet.	–	–	1	–	–	–	–	–	–	–	–	–	–	–	–	1	2	Nymphs A
DERMAPTERA																		
Forficula auricularia L.	–	1	–	–	–	–	–	–	–	–	–	–	–	–	–	–	1	T
HEMIPTERA																		
Sehirus luctuosus (Muls.)	1	–	–	–	–	–	–	–	–	–	–	–	–	–	–	–	1	Myosotis spp.
Pentatoma rufipes (L.)	–	1	–	–	–	1	–	–	2	–	–	–	–	–	–	1	5	Deciduous trees esp. Quercus sp.
Eurydema oleracea (L.)	–	–	1	–	–	–	–	–	–	–	–	–	–	–	–	–	1	Cruciferae
Scolopostethus sp.	–	–	1	–	–	–	–	–	–	–	–	1	–	–	1	–	3	T
Derephysia foliacea (Fal.)	–	–	1	–	–	–	–	–	–	–	–	–	–	–	–	–	1	Hedera helix L.
Anthocorinae gen.et sp.indet.	–	1	–	–	1	–	–	1	1	–	–	1	–	–	–	1	6	T
Miridae gen.et sp.indet.	–	–	–	–	–	–	–	–	–	–	–	–	–	–	–	1	1	T
Saldula S. Saldula sp.	–	–	1	1	–	–	–	–	–	–	–	–	–	–	–	–	2	M & B – at water's edge
Gerris sp.	–	–	–	–	–	–	–	1	1	–	–	–	–	–	1	–	3	A – on water's surface
Aphrodes flavostriatus (Don.)	–	–	–	–	–	–	–	–	1	1	1	–	–	–	1	–	4	Grasses
Aphrodes sp.	–	–	–	–	–	–	–	–	–	1	1	–	–	–	–	–	2	Grasses
Aphidoidea gen.et sp.indet.	–	–	–	–	1	–	1	–	–	1	–	1	–	–	–	–	4	
Homoptera gen.et sp.indet.	–	–	–	–	1	–	–	–	1	1	1	–	1	–	–	–	5	
NEUROPTERA																		
Sialis sp.	–	–	–	–	–	–	–	–	–	–	–	–	1	–	–	–	1	Larvae A – muddy bottom
TRICHOPTERA																		
Ithytrichia lamellaris Eat. or clavata Mort. – larval case	8	11	9	13	13	8	14	3	2	–	1	–	–	–	21	14	117	A – running water
Trichoptera gen.et sp.indet. – larvae	23	49	23	73	71	58	117	109	44	27	31	8	4	4	31	119	641	A
HYMENOPTERA																		
Bethylus sp.	–	–	–	–	–	–	1	–	–	–	–	–	–	–	–	–	1	T
Stenamma westwoodii West. – worker	–	–	–	2	–	1	–	–	–	–	–	–	–	–	–	2	5	Nests under large stones or tree roots in shady woodland or hedges
Lasius niger gp. – worker	–	–	–	–	–	–	–	–	–	–	1	–	–	–	–	–	1	T
Lasius sp. (not fuliginosus) – female	–	1	–	–	–	–	–	–	–	1	–	–	–	–	–	–	2	T
Lasius sp. (not fuliginosus) – male	–	–	–	1	–	–	–	–	–	–	–	–	–	–	–	–	1	T
Hymenoptera gen.et sp.indet.	6	4	11	11	–	4	11	9	12	9	1	1	1	–	1	11	82	T
DIPTERA																		
Bibionidae	–	1	–	–	–	–	–	–	–	–	–	–	–	–	1	–	2	V
Diptera gen.et sp.indet. – adult	–	1	1	2	–	4	5	5	7	5	1	–	2	–	1	9	43	
Diptera gen.et sp.indet. – puparium	1	1	1	–	–	3	2	5	10	3	9	4	4	–	–	34	77	

Table 34: Runnymede Neolithic Coleoptera, Area 4 column.

			Minimum no. of individuals			
depth (cms):	170	150	130	110	Total	Habitat or food
to:	190	170	150	130		

CARABIDAE						
Carabus granulatus (L.)	—	1	—	—	1	T – often near water, in rotten trees
Nebria brevicollis (F.)	—	1	—	—	1	WGD
Dyschirius globosus (Hbst.)	1	1	1	—	3	T – moist ground, M
Clivina collaris (Hbst.) or fossor (L.)	2	1	—	—	3	moist T, often under dung
Trechus secalis (Pk.)	—	1	—	—	1	moist G&W, B
Bembidion properans Step.	1	—	—	—	1	T – moist heavy soil and mud
B. gilvipes Sturm	—	1	—	—	1	B(W) also wet meadowland
B. guttula (F.)	1	—	—	—	1	M G&W – moist
B. lunulatum (Fouc.)	1	—	—	—	1	DBM&W – well vegetated often clay soil
Abax parallelepipedus (P.& M.)	—	1	—	—	1	W(GDC)
Calathus fuscipes (Gz.)	1	—	—	—	1	WDG – often in meadowland
Harpalus rufipes (Deg.)	1	—	—	—	1	D – often cultivated (G)
H. affinis (Schr.)	—	1	—	—	1	DG(W)
Bradycellus sp.	1	1	—	—	2	T
Chlaenius nigricornis (F.) or nitidulus (Schr.)	—	1	—	—	1	B – sometimes on mud or under reed debris
HALIPLIDAE						
Haliplus sp.	2	1	—	—	3	A
DYTISCIDAE						
Potamonectes depressus (F.)	—	1	1	—	2	A
Colymbetes fuscus (L.)	—	1	—	—	1	A – stagnant water, pond and ditches with much vegetation
GYRINIDAE						
Orectochilus villosus (Müll.)	1	1	—	—	2	A – running water
HYDROPHILIDAE						
Helophorus arvernicus Muls.	—	—	—	1	1	A – clean flowing
H. aquaticus (L.) or grandis Ill.	—	1	—	—	1	A – puddles, ponds, rarely flowing water
Helophorus spp. (brevipalpis size)	—	1	—	—	1	A – but readily leaves water
Coelostoma orbiculare (F.)	1	—	—	—	1	V – esp. in wet places, often at water's edge; A – ponds
Sphaeridium lunatum F. or scarabaeoides (L.)	—	1	—	—	1	F – esp. cow dung (CV)
Cercyon atomarius (F.)	—	1	—	—	1	FV
Megasternum obscurum (Marsh.)	2	2	1	—	5	FVC
Anacaena bipustulata (Marsh.) or limbata (F.)	1	—	—	—	1	G&W in wet places, VA
HISTERIDAE						
Histerinae gen.et sp.indet.	1	—	—	—	1	FVC
HYDRAENIDAE						
Ochthebius minimus (F.)	—	1	—	—	1	A – often stagnant
O. cf. minimus (F.)	—	2	1	—	3	A – often stagnant
Hydraena pulchella Germ.	—	—	1	—	1	A – flowing
H. riparia Kug.	—	4	—	—	4	A
SILPHIDAE						
Silpha atrata L.	1	—	—	—	1	Mostly under bark or in rotten wood (GDV)
STAPHYLINIDAE						
Lesteva punctata Er.	—	1	—	—	1	B – in splash zone, esp.in W

Table 34: Runnymede Neolithic Coleoptera, Area 4 column (continued).

		Minimum no. of individuals					
depth (cms):	170	150	130	110	Total	Habitat or food
to:	190	170	150	130		
Carpelimus bilineatus Step.	—	1	—	1	2	B – on wet mud (GV&F on wet soils)
Anotylus rugosus (F.)	1	1	—	—	2	FV(C)
A. nitidulus (Grav.)	—	—	1	—	1	FVC(M)
Stenus spp.	1	2	—	—	3	TM
Lathrobium sp.	2	1	—	—	3	TV(C)
Rugilus orbiculatus (Pk.)	—	1	—	—	1	V(G)
Gyrohypnus angustatus Step.	—	1	—	—	1	V – sometimes at water's edge
Xantholinus linearis (Ol.) or *longiventris* Heer	1	—	—	—	1	WGV(FC)
Philonthus sp.	—	1	—	—	1	FVC(T)
Gabrius sp.	—	1	—	—	1	WGFVC
Aleocharinae gen.et sp. indet.	—	5	—	—	5	TFVC
GEOTRUPIDAE						
Geotrupes sp.	—	1	—	—	1	F
SCARABAEIDAE						
Aphodius foetidus (Hbst.)	—	1	—	—	1	FV
A. cf. *prodromus* (Brahm)	—	1	—	—	1	FV
Aphodius sp.	1	—	—	—	1	Mostly F
Onthophagus ovatus (L.)	1	—	—	—	1	FCV
Melolontha sp.	—	1	—	—	1	Larvae on roots of grass and trees, adults on tree leaves
Phyllopertha horticola (L.)	1	1	1	1	4	Larvae on roots in permanent grassland
SCIRTIDAE						
cf. *Cyphon* sp.	—	2	1	—	3	Larvae A. adults T, close to water & M
DRYOPIDAE						
Helichus substriatus (Müll.)	—	1	—	—	1	A & water's edge
Dryops sp.	—	1	—	—	1	BA&M in or close to water (V)
ELMIDAE						
Elmis aenea (Müll.)	—	1	—	—	1	A – clean flowing water, clinging to stones and aquatic plants
Esolus parallelepipedus (Müll.)	—	3	1	—	4	(as above)
Limnius volckmari (Pz.)	—	1	—	—	1	(as above)
Macronychus quadrituberculatus (Müll.)	3	—	—	—	3	A – on submerged decaying wood
Normandia nitens (Müll.)	4	10	—	1	15	A – clean flowing
Oulimnius sp.	7	21	3	1	32	A – mostly clean, flowing
Stenelmis canaliculata (Gyl.)	2	2	—	—	4	A – clean flowing
ELATERIDAE						
Agrypnus murinus (L.)	1	1	—	—	2	G
Agriotes obscurus (L.)	—	1	—	—	1	Larvae mostly on roots of grassland plants
Agriotes sp.	1	—	—	—	1	(as above)
CANTHARIDAE						
Ragonycha sp.	—	1	—	—	1	Adults on flowers
ANOBIIDAE						
Grynobius planus (F.)	—	1	—	—	1	Dead hardwood
NITIDULIDAE						
Meligethes sp.	—	1	—	—	1	Mostly on flowers
SPHINDIDAE						
Aspidiphorus orbiculatus (Gyl.)	—	—	1	—	1	Slime moulds and powdery fungi of wood

Table 34: Runnymede Neolithic Coleoptera, Area 4 column (continued).

	depth (cms): to:	170 190	150 170	130 150	110 130	Total	Habitat or food
			Minimum no. of individuals				
CRYPTOPHAGIDAE							
Cryptophagidae gen. et sp. indet.							
(not Atomariinae)		—	1	—	—	1	V of all sorts, T
CERAMBYCIDAE							
Alosterna tabacicolor (Deg.)		—	1	—	—	1	Larvae under bark of deciduous trees, esp. *Acer* and *Quercus*
CHRYSOMELIDAE							
Donacia clavipes F.		—	2	1	1	4	*Phragmites austriacus*
D. crassipes F.		1	—	—	—	1	*Nymphaea* and *Nuphar* sp.
D. impressa Pk.		1	1	—	—	2	*Schoenoplectus lacustris* (L.)P.
D. vulgaris Zsch.		—	—	1	—	1	Reedswamp monocotyledons
Chrysolina graminis (L.)		—	1	—	—	1	Compositae, ? other herbs
C. haemoptera (L.)		1	—	—	—	1	*Plantago* spp. in sandy places
C. hyperici (Forst.)		1	—	—	—	1	*Hypericum* spp.
Gastrophysa viridula (Deg.)		—	1	—	—	1	*Rumex* and *Polygonum* spp.
Phyllotreta nemorum (L.) or *undulata* Kuts.		—	—	1	—	1	Cruciferae and *Reseda* sp.
Psylliodes sp.		1	—	—	—	1	Various herbs
APIONIDAE							
Apion sp.		1	2	—	—	3	Various herbs
CURCULIONIDAE							
Phyllobius pyri (L.)		1	1	—	—	2	Various herbs and trees
Bagous sp.		1	2	—	—	3	Aquatic plants
Ceuthorhynchinae gen. et sp.indet.		1	—	1	—	2	Various herbs
Anthonomus sp.		—	1	—	—	1	Mostly rosaceous trees and shrubs
Miccotrogus picirostris (F.)		—	1	—	—	1	*Trifolium* spp.
Mecinus pyraster (Hbst.)		1	—	—	—	1	*Plantago lanceolata* L. and *P.media* L.
Gymnetron pascuorum (Gyll.)		—	1	—	—	1	*Plantago lanceolata* L.
Rhynchaenus quercus (L.)		2	1	—	—	3	*Quercus* leaves
SCOLYTIDAE							
Scolytus rugulosus (Müll.)		—	1	—	—	1	Rosaceous trees and shrubs
Hylastinus obscurus (Marsh.)		—	1	—	—	1	Dead roots of Papilionaceae
Taphrorychus bicolor (Hbst.)		—	—	1	—	1	Decaying hardwoods
Totals		56	112	18	6	192	

Table 35:   Runnymede Neolithic other insects, Area 4 column.

	depth (cms): to:	170 190	150 170	130 150	110 130	Total	Habitat or food
ODONATA							
Odonata gen.et sp.indet.		—	1	—	—	1	Nymphs A
HEMIPTERA							
Anthocorinae gen.et sp.indet.		—	1	—	—	1	T
Gerris sp.		—	1	—	1	2	A – on water's surface
TRICHOPTERA							
Ithytrichia lamellaris Eat. or							
clavata Mort. – larval case		4	7	—	—	11	A – running water
Trichoptera gen.et sp.indet. – larvae		7	16	3	3	29	A
HYMENOPTERA							
Myrmica rubra (L.) or *ruginodis* Nyl.							
– worker		1	—	—	—	1	T
Hymenoptera gen.et sp.indet.		2	1	—	—	3	T
DIPTERA							
Bibionidae gen.et sp.indet.		—	1	—	—	1	V
Musca cf. *domestica* (L.) – puparium		1	—	—	—	1	FVC
Diptera gen.et sp.indet. – puparium		3	2	—	—	5	

Table 36: Runnymede Late Bronze Age Coleoptera, column WF1b.

Minimum numbers of individuals

depth (cms) / to:	170/175	165/170	160/165	155/160	150/155	145/150	140/145	135/140	130/135	125/130	120/125	115/120	110/115	105/110	100/105	95/100	90/95	85/90	80/85	75/80	70/75	Total	Habitat or food
CARABIDAE																							
Carabus monilis F.	—	—	—	—	—	—	—	—	—	—	—	1	—	—	—	—	—	—	—	—	—	1	WGD
Nebria brevicollis (F.)	—	1	—	—	—	—	1	—	—	—	—	1	1	1	1	—	—	—	—	—	—	6	WGD
Notiophilus aquaticus (L.)	—	1	—	—	—	—	—	—	—	—	1	—	1	1	—	2	—	—	—	—	—	2	GD
Notiophilus sp.	—	—	—	—	—	—	—	—	—	—	—	1	—	—	—	—	—	—	—	—	—	1	MWGD
Elaphrus riparius (L.)	—	—	—	—	—	—	1	—	—	—	—	1	—	—	—	—	—	—	—	—	—	1	B – waterside mud
Dyschirius globosus (Hbst.)	—	1	1	1	—	1	1	—	—	—	—	1	—	2	1	1	—	1	—	—	—	10	T – moist ground, M
Clivina collaris (Hbst.) or fossor (L.)	—	—	1	—	1	—	2	1	1	1	4	1	1	2	1	1	—	1	—	1	1	15	Moist T, often under dung
Patrobus atrorufus (Strm)	—	—	—	—	—	—	—	—	—	—	1	1	1	—	1	1	1	—	—	—	2	W
Trechus obtusus Er. or quadristriatus (Schr.)	—	1	—	—	1	3	—	—	2	1	—	1	1	1	3	1	2	—	—	2	1	18	T
T. secalis (Pk.)	—	1	—	—	—	—	—	1	1	—	—	1	—	—	2	1	1	1	—	1	—	7	Moist G and W, B
T. micros (Hbst.)	1	—	1	1	—	—	—	—	—	—	—	—	—	—	—	2	—	—	—	—	—	4	B – usually of flowing water
Asaphidion flavipes (L.)	—	1	1	—	—	—	1	—	—	—	—	—	—	1	—	1	—	1	—	—	—	3	G – damp, BMW
Bembidion lampros (Hbst.)	—	—	—	—	—	—	—	—	—	—	—	—	—	—	1	—	—	—	—	—	—	1	G & D – dry open soil (W)
B. properans Step.	—	1	—	—	1	—	1	1	1	—	1	1	3	—	1	—	1	1	—	—	1	11	T – damp heavy soil and mud
B. lampros (Hbst.) or properans (Step)	1	—	—	—	—	—	—	—	—	—	—	—	—	—	—	—	1	—	—	—	—	2	T
B. tetracolum Say	—	—	—	1	—	—	—	—	2	1	—	—	—	1	1	1	1	1	—	—	—	7	TM
B. gilvipes Sturm	—	—	—	—	—	—	—	—	1	1	—	1	—	—	—	—	1	—	—	—	1	5	B (W) also wet meadowland
B. cf. gilvipes Sturm	—	—	—	—	—	—	—	—	—	—	1	—	—	—	—	—	—	—	—	—	—	1	B (W) also wet meadowland
B. obtusum Serv.	—	—	—	—	—	—	1	—	—	—	1	1	—	—	—	—	—	—	—	—	—	1	T – open, clayish
B. biguttatum (F.)	—	—	—	1	1	—	—	—	—	1	—	—	1	1	1	1	1	—	—	—	—	4	BG and W, usually near water
B. guttula (F.)	—	1	1	1	—	1	2	—	1	1	1	1	2	1	1	1	1	1	—	—	—	13	MG and W – moist
B. lunulatum (Fouc.)	—	1	—	—	—	—	—	—	—	—	1	1	1	1	—	—	—	—	—	—	—	2	DBM&W -well vegetated, often clay soil
Bembidion sp.	—	—	—	—	—	—	—	—	—	—	—	—	—	—	—	1	—	—	—	—	—	1	Mostly in wet or marshy places
Tachys sp.	—	—	—	—	—	—	—	—	1	—	—	—	—	1	—	—	1	1	1	1	—	3	B – at waterside
Stomis pumicatus (Pz.)	1	—	—	—	—	—	—	—	1	1	—	—	—	—	—	—	—	—	—	—	—	1	GD(BW)
Pterostichus anthracinus (Pz.)	—	1	—	—	—	—	2	—	2	—	1	1	1	—	—	—	—	—	—	—	—	4	M&B – shaded
P. cupreus (L.)	1	—	—	—	1	—	—	—	—	—	1	1	1	1	—	—	—	—	—	—	—	3	G(DW) – moist, sometimes near water
P. gracilis (Dej.)	—	1	—	—	—	—	—	—	—	—	—	—	1	—	1	—	—	—	—	—	—	2	G&W – wet, M
P. cf. gracilis (Dej)	—	1	—	—	—	—	—	—	—	—	—	—	—	1	—	—	—	1	1	—	—	2	G&W – wet, M
P. melanarius (Ill.)	—	—	—	—	—	—	1	—	1	1	1	1	1	1	1	1	1	—	2	—	—	10	DG (W)
P. minor (Gyll.)	—	—	—	—	—	—	—	—	—	—	—	—	—	1	1	—	—	—	—	—	—	4	M&B – both wooded and open
P. niger (Schal.)	—	—	1	—	1	—	—	—	—	—	—	—	—	1	1	—	—	—	—	—	—	1	W(GD)
P. nigrita (Pk.)	—	—	1	1	—	—	—	—	—	—	1	—	—	—	—	—	—	—	—	—	—	2	MB
P. strenuus (Pz.)	—	—	1	—	—	—	—	—	2	—	—	—	—	—	—	—	—	—	—	—	—	4	T – often near water
P. vernalis (Pz.)	—	—	—	—	—	—	—	—	1	1	—	—	—	—	—	—	—	—	—	—	—	2	G&(W) – moist, often near water

Table 36: Runnymede Late Bronze Age Coleoptera, column WF1b (continued).

Taxon	No.	Ecology
P. versicolor (Sturm)	2	G(D)
P. cupreus (L.) or versicolor (Sturm)—		
Abax parallelepipedus (P. & M.)	8	G(DW)
Calathus fuscipes (Gz.)	1	W(GDC)
C. melanocephalus (L.)	5	WD&G – often in meadowland
Agonum albipes (F.)	10	GD(W)
A. dorsale (Pont.)	4	BW(DG)
A. fuliginosum (Pz.)	1	D(G) – usually open, often cultivated
A. livens (Gyll.)	1	W – moist, M – usually shaded
A. muelleri (Hbst.)	1	W – marshy, often *Alnus*
A. viduum (Pz.)	3	MGD(W)
Amara aulica (Pz.)	2	B – rich vegetation (W)
A. cf. plebeja (Gyll.)	1	G&D – often feeding on seeds of Compositae
Amara spp.	4	T
Harpalus rufipes (Deg.)	19	T
Harpalus S. Ophonus sp.	4	D – often cultivated,(G)
H. affinis (Schr.)	5	T – mostly dry and open
Harpalus S.Harpalus sp.(not affinis)	2	DG(W)
Bradycellus sp.	3	T
Acupalpus sp.	1	T
Chlaenius nigricornis (F.)	2	Mostly wet places
	1	B – sometimes on mud or under reed debris
Lebia chlorocephala (Hofseg.)	1	G – larvae mostly on *Hypericum*-feeding chrysomelids
Dromius linearis (Ol.)	1	G(M)
D. quadrimaculatus (L.)	1	W – often on trees
Metabletus obscuroguttatus (Duft.)	2	V
HALIPLIDAE		
Brychius elevatus (Pz.)	2	A – moving water on *Veronica* and *Nasturtium* spp.
Haliplus sp.	13	A
DYTISCIDAE		
Hydroporus sp.	1	A
Graptodytes pictus (F.)	9	A – ponds and slowly moving water
Deronectes latus (Step.)	1	A – clear, flowing
Potamonectes depressus (F.)	13	A
Stictotarsus duodecimpustulatus (F.)	6	A – running water and lakes
Platambus maculatus (L.)	10	A – running water and lakes
Agabus sp. (not bipustulatus)	2	A
Rhantus sp.	3	A

Table 36: Runnymede Late Bronze Age Coleoptera, column WF1b (continued).

depth (cms) to:	170–175	165–170	160–165	155–160	150–155	145–150	140–145	135–140	130–135	125–130	120–125	115–120	110–115	105–110	100–105	95–100	90–95	85–90	80–85	75–80	70–75	Total	Habitat or food
Colymbetes fuscus (L.)	—	—	—	—	—	—	—	—	—	—	—	—	—	1	—	—	1	—	1	—	—	3	A – stagnant water, ponds and ditches with much vegetation
Dytiscus sp.	—	—	—	—	—	—	—	—	—	—	—	—	—	—	—	—	1	—	—	—	—	1	A – mostly stagnant
GYRINIDAE																							
Gyrinus sp.	—	—	—	—	—	1	1	—	—	—	—	—	—	—	—	—	—	1	1	—	—	4	A
Orectochilus villosus (Müll.)	—	1	—	—	1	3	—	3	—	1	—	3	2	2	2	1	1	2	1	1	1	25	A – running water
HYDROPHILIDAE																							
Georissus crenulatus (Rossi)	—	—	—	—	—	—	1	—	—	—	—	—	—	—	—	—	—	—	—	—	—	1	Damp places in mud
Helophorus aquaticus (L.)	—	—	1	—	—	—	—	—	—	—	1	—	—	—	—	—	1	—	—	—	—	3	A – puddles, ponds, rarely flowing water
H. arvernicus Muls.	—	—	—	—	—	—	—	—	—	—	—	—	—	—	—	1	—	—	—	—	—	1	A – clean, flowing
H. aquaticus (L.) or grandis Ill.	—	1	—	—	—	—	—	—	1	—	—	1	1	1	1	1	—	—	—	—	—	7	A – puddles, ponds, rarely flowing water
H. nubilus F.	—	—	—	—	—	—	—	—	—	—	—	1	—	1	—	—	—	—	—	—	—	2	T
H. porculus Bed. or rufipes (Bosc.)	—	—	—	—	—	—	—	—	—	—	1	—	—	—	—	—	—	—	—	—	—	1	T – often on Cruciferae
Helophorus spp. (brevipalpis size)	1	3	1	—	1	2	2	1	1	2	3	5	3	5	2	2	3	4	4	—	2	47	A – but readily leaves water
Coelostoma orbiculare (F.)	—	—	—	—	—	—	—	—	1	—	—	—	—	—	—	—	—	—	—	—	—	1	V – esp. in wet places, often at water's edge. A – ponds
Sphaeridium bipustulatum F.	1	—	1	—	—	2	—	—	1	—	1	1	—	—	1	—	—	—	—	—	—	8	FVC
S. lunatum F. or scarabaeoides (L.)	—	—	—	—	2	—	—	1	1	—	—	—	—	—	—	—	—	—	—	—	—	4	F – esp. cow dung (CV)
Cercyon analis (Pk.)	—	—	1	—	2	2	2	5	2	—	1	2	1	1	1	—	—	—	—	—	—	20	FV
C. atricapillus (Marsh.)	—	—	—	—	2	1	—	—	1	2	1	—	—	1	—	—	—	—	—	—	—	8	FV
C. haemorrhoidalis (F.)	—	—	—	—	2	1	1	2	2	2	3	1	2	2	2	—	—	—	—	—	—	20	FV
C. melanocephalus (L.)	—	—	1	—	—	—	1	—	1	—	1	—	3	1	—	—	—	—	—	—	—	8	Mostly F
C. pygmaeus (Ill.)	—	—	—	—	1	—	—	—	1	1	1	—	1	1	—	—	1	—	—	—	—	7	Mostly F
C. sternalis Sharp	1	—	—	—	—	1	—	1	—	1	—	—	—	—	—	—	—	—	—	—	—	4	MB – on damp ground under plant detritus
C. terminatus (Marsh.)	—	—	—	—	—	—	—	—	—	—	—	—	—	—	—	—	—	—	1	—	—	1	FV
C. tristis (Ill.)	—	—	—	—	—	—	—	1	—	—	—	—	1	—	—	—	—	1	2	1	—	6	MB – on damp ground under plant detritus
C. unipunctatus (L.)	—	—	—	—	—	—	1	—	—	—	—	—	—	—	—	—	—	—	—	—	—	1	F(V)
C. ustulatus (Pres.)	—	1	—	—	2	—	—	—	—	—	2	1	—	—	—	—	—	—	—	—	—	6	V in moist places (F)
Cercyon spp.	—	—	1	—	—	1	1	—	1	1	—	—	—	2	—	—	—	—	—	—	—	7	FVC, some species on wet mud
Megasternum obscurum (Marsh.)	—	8	1	—	1	2	3	4	4	4	4	3	4	4	—	1	5	4	2	2	—	56	FVC
Cryptopleurum minutum (F.)	—	—	1	—	1	—	—	—	2	—	1	—	—	—	—	—	—	1	1	—	—	7	FVC
Hydrobius fuscipes (L.)	1	—	—	—	—	—	1	—	2	—	1	—	1	—	—	—	1	1	—	—	—	8	A – stagnant water often with detritus bottom
Anacaena bipustulata (Marsh.) or limbata (F.)	—	—	—	—	1	—	—	—	1	—	1	1	—	2	—	1	1	1	2	—	—	11	G & W in wet places, VA
Laccobius sp.	—	—	—	1	—	—	1	—	—	—	1	—	—	1	1	3	2	2	1	—	—	13	A

Table 36: Runnymede Late Bronze Age Coleoptera, column WF1b (continued).

Taxon	Count	Habitat / notes
Chaetarthria seminulum (Hbst.)	4	B – wet vegetation and mud at water's edge (A)
Hydrochara caraboides (L.)	1	A – ponds, pools and ditches
Hydrophilus piceus (L.)	1	A – well vegetated ponds & marsh dykes
HISTERIDAE		
Acritus nigricornis (Hoff.)	9	V – often haystack refuse
Sapinus aeneus (F.)	1	FC(V)
Onthophilus striatus (Forst.)	1	FVC
Hister bissexstriatus F.	7	FV
Hister sp.	1	FVC
Paralister purpurascens (Hbst.)	1	FV
Hister or *Paralister* sp.	2	FVC
Athoulus duodecimstriatus (Schr.)	1	FV
HYDRAENIDAE		
Ochthebius bicolon Germ.	1	B – mud and decaying vegetation at water's edge. A
O. cf. *bicolon* Germ.	8	as above
O. exsculptus Germ.	2	A – on stones in clean flowing water
O. minimus (F.)	7	A – often stagnant
O. cf. *minimus* (F.)	48	A – often stagnant
Hydraena minutissima Step.	1	A – flowing
H. pulchella Germ.	7	A – flowing
H. riparia Kug.	19	A
H. testacea Curt.	4	A – usually stagnant
Limnebius aluta (Bed.)	1	B – mud at water's edge, M(A)
L. truncatellus (Thun.)	1	A
PTILIIDAE		
Ptenidium sp.	1	Dung heaps, rotten wood, VM
Ptiliidae gen. et sp.indet. (not *Ptenidium*)	9	VM (TF)
LEIODIDAE		
Choleva sp.	2	V – often leaf litter or fungi in woods C(G)
Choleva or *Catops* sp.	2	as above
SILPHIDAE		
Thanatophilus rugosus (L.)	2	C
Silpha atrata L.	6	Mostly under bark or in rotten wood GDV)
S. tristis Ill.	4	Esp. C, also DGW
S. cf. *tristis* Ill.	1	Esp. C, also DGW

Table 36: Runnymede Late Bronze Age Coleoptera, column WF1b (continued).

Minimum numbers of individuals

	170	165	160	155	150	145	140	135	130	125	120	115	110	105	100	95	90	85	80	75	70	Total	Habitat or food
depth (cms) to:	175	170	165	160	155	150	145	140	135	130	125	120	115	110	105	100	95	90	85	80	75		
SCYDMAENIDAE																							
Scydmaenidae gen. et sp. indet.	—	—	—	1	—	—	—	—	—	1	—	—	—	—	1	—	1	—	—	1	—	5	TV
STAPHYLINIDAE																							
Metopsia retusa (Step.)	—	—	—	—	—	—	—	—	—	1	—	—	—	—	—	—	—	—	—	—	—	1	GV
Acidota cruentata (Man.)	—	—	—	—	—	—	—	—	—	—	1	—	—	—	—	—	—	—	—	—	—	1	Moss, leaf litter etc.
Lesteva longoelytrata (Gz.)	—	—	1	—	—	1	—	1	—	1	1	1	1	1	2	1	1	2	—	—	1	13	B – often at water's edge, M
Dropephylla ioptera (Step.)	—	—	—	—	—	—	—	1	—	1	—	—	—	—	—	1	—	—	—	—	—	1	Often under bark
Omalium sp.	—	1	—	—	—	—	—	—	—	—	—	—	—	—	1	1	—	—	2	—	—	5	V – all sorts. CFT
Carelimus bilineatus Step.	—	—	—	1	—	1	1	—	—	6	—	2	2	1	1	1	1	1	—	1	1	18	B – on wet mud (GV & F on wet soils)
C. rivularis (Mots.)	—	—	—	—	—	—	—	—	—	3	—	—	—	—	—	—	—	—	—	—	—	3	B&M on mud or in V
Platystethus arenarius (Fouc.)	—	—	—	1	—	1	1	—	—	1	—	—	—	—	1	1	1	2	—	2	—	6	FV
P. cornutus gp.	—	—	1	1	—	1	1	—	4	4	4	9	8	2	1	1	1	1	1	1	2	40	M & B – often on mud (VF)
P. nitens (Sahl.)	—	—	—	1	—	1	1	—	1	1	1	1	2	1	1	1	1	1	1	—	—	10	FVB
P. nodifrons (Man.)	—	—	—	—	—	1	1	—	—	1	1	—	1	1	—	—	—	—	—	1	—	2	V
Anotylus nitidulus (Grav.)	1	1	2	—	—	1	1	—	—	1	1	3	2	1	—	2	2	1	—	1	—	25	VFC(M)
A. rugosus (F.)	1	1	1	—	—	2	1	—	—	1	—	2	3	2	—	—	—	3	4	4	1	25	FV(C)
A. sculpturatus gp.	1	1	—	—	—	—	—	4	—	—	—	—	1	—	—	2	—	3	—	1	—	13	FVC (also T)
Oxytelus sculptus Grav.	1	1	—	—	—	—	2	—	—	3	—	1	2	2	2	—	2	1	—	—	—	16	FV (C)
Stenus guttula Müll.	—	—	—	—	—	—	—	—	—	—	—	—	1	—	1	—	—	—	—	—	—	1	B – often on mud
Stenus spp.	3	—	1	1	—	2	1	2	—	3	—	2	—	3	2	2	1	2	3	3	1	34	TM
Paederus littoralis Grav.	—	—	—	—	—	—	—	—	—	—	—	1	—	—	1	1	1	1	—	—	—	4	G&D – mostly dry
Lathrobium sp.	2	—	—	—	—	1	1	—	—	1	1	—	1	1	1	—	—	1	1	1	—	10	TV (C)
Sunius sp.	—	—	—	—	—	—	1	1	—	—	1	1	—	—	—	—	—	—	—	—	—	4	V
Astenus sp.	—	—	—	—	1	—	—	—	—	—	—	—	—	—	—	—	—	—	—	—	—	2	VF
Rugilus orbiculatus (Pk.)	1	1	—	—	—	—	—	—	—	1	—	—	—	—	—	—	1	1	—	—	—	5	V (G)
Leptacinus batychrus (Gyll.)	1	—	—	2	—	2	—	—	—	1	—	—	—	1	1	—	1	—	—	—	—	10	FV
Gyrohypnus angustatus Step.	—	—	—	—	—	—	—	—	—	—	—	1	1	—	—	—	—	1	—	—	—	3	V – sometimes at water's edge
G. fracticornis gp.	—	—	—	—	—	1	1	—	—	2	—	1	—	2	1	—	—	—	1	1	—	12	FV (C)
Xantholinus glabratus (Grav.)	—	—	—	1	—	—	—	—	—	—	—	—	—	—	—	—	—	—	—	—	—	1	GDFV
X. linearis (Ol.)	—	—	—	1	—	—	—	1	—	—	—	1	—	—	—	—	—	2	—	1	—	5	WGV (FC)
X. longiventris Heer	—	—	1	—	—	2	2	1	—	—	—	—	1	1	—	—	—	—	1	1	—	7	WGV (FC)
X. linearis (Ol.) or longiventris Heer	—	2	—	—	—	1	—	2	—	1	1	4	—	—	2	1	—	—	—	—	—	14	WGV (FC)
Philonthus spp.	1	1	1	1	2	2	2	2	—	3	1	1	2	1	1	2	1	2	—	2	2	27	FVC (T)
Gabrius sp.	1	—	1	1	—	1	—	2	—	1	1	1	1	—	1	—	—	—	—	—	—	7	WG FVC
Staphylinus aeneocephalus fortunatorum (Wol.)	—	—	—	—	—	—	—	—	—	—	—	—	—	—	—	—	—	1	—	—	—	1	WG
S. caesareus Ced. or dimidiaticornis Gem.	—	—	—	—	—	—	—	—	—	—	—	1	—	—	—	—	—	—	—	—	—	1	T

Table 36: Runnymede Late Bronze Age Coleoptera, column WF1b (continued).

										Minimum numbers of individuals													
depth (cms) to:	170 175	165 170	160 165	155 160	150 155	145 150	140 145	135 140	130 135	125 130	120 125	115 120	110 115	105 110	100 105	95 100	90 95	85 90	80 85	75 80	70 75	Total	Habitat or food
S. olens Müll.	–	–	–	–	–	1	–	–	–	–	–	–	–	–	–	–	–	1	1	–	–	2	WG(D)
Mycetoporus sp.	–	1	–	–	–	–	–	–	–	–	–	–	–	–	–	–	1	1	1	1	2	5	V – moss, leaf litter
Tachyporus spp.	–	1	1	1	–	3	–	2	–	1	–	1	–	2	2	2	1	3	3	2	1	25	T
Tachinus spp.	–	–	–	–	–	2	1	1	–	1	–	1	2	1	–	–	1	2	2	–	1	12	T
Aleocharinae gen. et sp. indet.	1	1	–	1	1	2	–	4	1	4	2	3	3	5	2	2	2	4	4	2	3	44	TFCV
PSELAPHIDAE																							
Brachygluta sp.	–	–	–	–	–	–	–	–	–	–	–	–	–	–	1	–	–	–	–	–	–	1	V(GWM)
GEOTRUPIDAE																							
Geotrupes sp.	–	2	–	–	–	2	–	2	1	3	3	1	1	2	1	1	–	1	1	1	1	20	F
SCARABAEIDAE																							
Colobopterus erraticus (L.)	1	1	–	1	1	–	–	1	–	–	–	1	–	–	–	–	–	–	–	–	1	7	F(C)
C. haemorrhoidalis (L.)	–	–	–	–	–	–	–	–	–	–	–	–	–	–	–	1	1	–	–	–	–	1	F
Aphodius contaminatus (Hbst.)	1	2	–	1	2	2	–	1	–	–	–	–	2	–	2	2	2	5	5	2	–	22	F
A. fimetarius L.	–	–	–	–	–	–	–	–	–	–	–	–	–	–	–	1	–	–	–	–	1	2	FV
A. cf. *fimetarius* L.	–	–	–	–	1	1	1	–	1	1	1	2	1	3	3	–	1	1	1	1	–	3	FV
A. foetidus (Hbst.)	–	–	–	1	1	1	–	3	1	4	1	5	2	3	5	5	2	3	1	1	3	13	FV
A. granarius (L.)	–	–	–	1	1	1	1	1	1	4	4	1	1	3	5	–	4	1	2	1	3	46	FV
A. luridus (F.)	–	–	–	–	–	–	–	–	–	1	1	1	1	–	1	2	1	2	–	–	–	7	F
A. porcus (F.)	–	–	–	–	–	–	–	2	–	–	–	–	–	1	–	–	–	–	–	1	–	2	F – in *Geotrupes* burrows
A. cf. *prodromus* (Brahm)	–	–	1	–	–	–	–	–	–	–	–	1	1	1	–	–	–	1	1	2	2	7	FV
A. cf. *pusillus* (Hbst.)	1	–	–	1	2	2	–	1	2	2	2	–	2	–	1	2	–	1	–	–	1	6	FV
A. putridus (Fouc.)	–	–	–	–	–	–	–	–	–	–	–	–	–	–	1	1	–	–	–	–	–	1	F
A. rufipes (L.)	–	–	–	1	1	–	–	1	–	–	–	–	2	2	1	1	–	–	–	–	–	4	F
A. cf. *sphacelatus* (Pz.)	1	2	1	1	1	1	1	1	1	1	1	–	3	1	2	2	1	2	2	–	2	23	FVC
A. varians Duft.	–	–	–	–	–	–	–	–	–	2	2	–	–	1	–	–	–	–	–	1	–	3	FV
Aphodius spp.	1	2	–	2	3	1	–	2	2	2	2	1	1	1	1	–	1	2	2	1	1	27	Mostly F
Oxyomus sylvestris (Scop.)	–	–	–	1	1	1	–	1	1	2	1	2	2	–	–	–	1	–	–	1	2	14	F – mostly as dung heaps VC
Onthophagus ovatus (L.)	–	–	1	1	–	2	–	1	1	2	1	1	1	–	–	1	1	1	1	3	1	17	FCV
O. similis (Scriba)	–	–	–	1	1	–	–	–	–	–	–	–	–	–	–	–	–	–	–	–	–	–	F
O. vacca (L.)	1	–	–	–	1	–	1	–	1	–	–	–	–	2	–	–	–	–	–	1	–	4	F – mostly
Onthophagus sp.(not *ovatus*)	–	–	–	–	–	–	–	–	–	–	–	–	–	–	–	–	–	–	–	–	1	1	F(C)
Amphimallon solstitialis (L.)	–	–	–	–	–	–	–	–	–	–	–	–	–	–	–	–	–	1	1	–	–	1	Larvae on roots, adults fly to trees and bushes
Hoplia philanthus (Fues.)	–	1	–	–	1	1	1	1	–	1	–	2	–	1	1	–	–	–	–	–	–	9	Larvae on roots in permanent grassland
Phyllopertha horticola (L.)	3	2	1	2	4	3	–	3	2	4	1	1	1	4	2	1	–	3	5	1	1	44	Larvae on roots in permanent grassland
DASCILLIDAE																							
Dascillus cervinus (L.)	–	–	–	1	–	–	–	–	–	–	1	–	–	–	–	1	–	–	–	1	1	5	On flowers and bushes

Table 36: Runnymede Late Bronze Age Coleoptera, column WF1b (continued).

Taxon		Total	Ecology
CLAMBIDAE			
Calyptomerus dubius (Marsh.)		1	V esp. old hay and straw
Clambus sp.		2	V
SCIRTIDAE			
cf. *Cyphon* sp.		8	Larvae A, adults T, but close to water and M
BYRRHIDAE			
Cytilus sericeus (Forst.)		1	T
Byrrhus sp.		6	T
Syncalyptera setigera (Ill.) or *striatopunctata* Steff.		1	T
HETEROCERIDAE			
Heterocerus sp.		1	B&M – on mud at water's edge
DRYOPIDAE			
Helichus substriatus (Müll.)		9	A & water's edge
Dryops sp.		9	BA & M in or close to water (V)
ELMIDAE			
Elmis aenea (Müll.)		11	A – clean flowing water, clinging to stones and aquatic plants
Esolus parallelepipedus (Müll.)		52	A – as above
Limnius volckmari (Pz.)		17	A – as above
Macronychus quadrituberculatus Müll.		2	A – on submerged decaying wood
Normandia nitens (Müll.)		114	A – clean flowing water clinging to stones and aquatic plants
Oulimnius sp.		152	A – mostly clean, flowing
Riolus sp.		1	A – mostly clean, flowing
Stenelmis canaliculata (Gyl.)		18	A – clean flowing, also large lakes
ELATERIDAE			
Agrypnus murinus (L.)		21	G
Ampedus nigerrimus (Lac.)		1	Rotten wood
Cidnopus minutus (L.)		1	G
Athous hirtus (Hbst.)		5	WG – esp. meadowland, larvae esp.on the roots of grasses, also trees and shrubs
Athous sp.		1	WG – as above
Agriotes acuminatus (Step.)		1	Larvae mostly on roots of grassland plants
A. lineatus (L.)		2	as above
A. obscurus (L.)		10	as above
A. pallidulus (Ill.)		2	as above
A. sputator (L.)		10	as above

Table 36: Runnymede Late Bronze Age Coleoptera, column WF1b (continued).

Minimum numbers of individuals

depth (cms) to:	170–175	165–170	160–165	155–160	150–155	145–150	140–145	135–140	130–135	125–130	120–125	115–120	110–115	105–110	100–105	95–100	90–95	85–90	80–85	75–80	70–75	Total	Habitat or food
Agriotes spp.	1	–	–	1	1	1	1	–	–	1	–	–	–	–	1	–	–	–	1	–	1	9	as above
Denticollis linearis (L.)	–	1	1	–	–	–	–	–	–	–	–	–	–	–	–	–	1	–	–	–	–	3	larvae in rotten wood, adults on flowers
THROSCIDAE																							
Trixagus obtusus (Curt.)	–	–	–	–	–	1	–	–	–	–	–	–	–	–	–	–	–	–	–	–	–	1	Inc. rotten wood, G
CANTHARIDAE																							
Cantharis rustica Fal.	–	–	–	–	–	–	–	–	–	–	–	–	–	1	1	–	–	–	–	–	–	2	Adults on flowers of herbs and shrubs
Cantharis sp.	–	–	–	–	–	1	–	–	1	–	–	–	–	1	1	1	–	2	2	–	–	9	Adults on flowers of herbs and shrubs
Rhagonycha sp.	–	–	–	–	–	–	–	–	–	–	–	–	–	–	–	–	–	1	–	–	1	2	Adults on flowers of herbs and shrubs
Cantharis or *Rhagonycha* sp.	–	–	–	–	–	–	1	–	–	–	–	–	–	–	–	–	–	–	–	–	–	1	Adults on flowers of herbs and shrubs
DERMESTIDAE																							
Dermestes lardarius L.	–	–	–	–	–	–	–	–	–	–	–	–	–	–	–	–	–	–	–	–	1	1	C
ANOBIIDAE																							
Grynobius planus (F.)	–	–	–	–	–	–	–	–	–	–	–	–	–	–	1	–	2	–	–	–	1	4	Dead hardwood
Stegobium paniceum (L.)	–	–	–	–	–	–	–	–	–	–	–	–	–	–	–	–	1	–	–	–	–	1	P – flour, bread, grain and other dried products
Anobium punctatum (Deg.)	–	–	–	–	–	–	1	–	–	–	–	–	–	–	1	–	–	1	–	–	–	3	Dead wood
LYCTIDAE																							
Lyctus linearis (Gz.)	–	–	–	–	–	–	–	–	–	–	–	–	–	–	–	–	–	1	–	–	–	1	Dead hardwood
MELYRIDAE																							
Malachius bipustulatus (L.)	–	–	–	–	–	–	–	–	–	–	–	–	–	1	–	1	–	–	–	–	–	2	Adults often on flowers
M. cf. *viridis* F.	–	–	–	–	–	–	–	–	–	–	–	–	–	–	2	–	–	–	–	–	–	2	Adults often on flowers
Malachius sp.	–	–	–	–	–	1	–	–	–	–	–	–	1	1	–	–	–	–	1	–	–	4	Adults often on flowers
NITIDULIDAE																							
Brachypterus urticae (F.)	–	–	–	–	–	–	–	–	1	1	–	1	1	1	–	1	–	–	–	3	–	9	*Urtica* sp.
Brachypterolus pulicarius (L.)	–	–	–	–	–	–	–	–	–	1	–	–	–	–	–	–	–	–	–	1	–	2	*Linaria* spp.
Meligethes sp.	–	1	–	–	1	1	–	–	1	–	1	–	–	1	–	1	–	–	1	3	–	11	Herbs and trees – mostly on flowers
Epuraea sp.	–	–	–	–	–	1	–	–	–	–	–	–	–	–	–	–	–	–	1	–	–	2	On flowers, under bark, at sap, in fungi
Omosita colon (L.)	–	–	–	–	–	–	1	–	1	–	–	1	1	–	–	–	–	–	–	–	–	4	C – dry
O. discoidea (F.)	–	–	–	–	–	1	–	–	–	–	–	–	–	–	–	–	–	–	–	–	–	1	C – dry
RHIZOPHAGIDAE																							
Monotoma spinicollis Aubé	–	–	–	–	–	–	–	–	–	–	–	–	–	1	–	–	–	–	–	–	–	1	V

Table 36: Runnymede Late Bronze Age Coleoptera, column WF1b (continued).

Taxon	Total	Ecology
Monotoma sp.	4	V (manure C)
CUCUSIDAE		
Pediacus dermestoides (F.)	1	Under loose bark & in scolytid tunnels
CRYPTOPHAGIDAE		
Crypotphagidae gen. et sp. indet. (not Atomariinae)	6	V – of all sorts, T
Atomaria spp.	24	VT (F)
PHALACRIDAE		
Phalacrus sp.	4	Larvae on grasses & *Carex* smuts, adults on flowers
Olibrus sp.	5	Adults on flowers of Compositae
Stilbus sp.	8	In dry grass, hay and on *Typha* sp.
CORYLOPHIDAE		
Corylophus cassidoides (Marsh.)	4	V – esp. decaying reeds
Orthoperus sp.	8	V
COCCINELLIDAE		
Coccidula rufa (Hbst.)	1	Aphids of marsh and aquatic plants
C. scutellata (Hbst.)	1	Aphids of marsh and aquatic plants
Rhyzobius litura (F.)	1	T
Scymnus frontalis (F.)	1	G – esp. dry, sandy
S. haemorrhoidalis (F.)	1	G – wet, M
Platynaspis luteorubra (Gz.)	2	On trees and in dry grassland
Propylea quattuordecimpunctata (L.)	2	T
LATHRIDIIDAE		
Lathridius minutus gp.	5	V, also manure heaps (CGW)
Enicmus transversus (Ol.)	11	V (GW)
Corticaria punctulata Marsh.	4	V
Corticariinae gen. et sp. indet.	29	Mostly V
CISIDAE		
Cis sp.	1	Tree fungi
COLYDIIDAE		
Synchita sp.	1	Under bark of old hardwood trees
SCRAPTIIDAE		
Anaspis sp.	1	Adults on blossom, esp. shrubs
MORDELLIDAE		
Mordellistena sp.	2	On flowers
OEDEMERIDAE		
Oedemera lurida (Marsh.)	1	Adults on flowers in meadows & on shrubs

Table 36: Runnymede Late Bronze Age Coleoptera, column WF1b (continued).

Minimum numbers of individuals

	170/175	165/170	160/165	155/160	150/155	145/150	140/145	135/140	130/135	125/130	120/125	115/120	110/115	105/110	100/105	95/100	90/95	85/90	80/85	75/80	70/75	Total	Habitat or food
MELOIDAE																							
Meloe proscarabaeus L.	–	–	–	–	–	–	–	–	–	–	–	–	–	–	–	1	–	–	–	–	–	1	G
M. cf. *violaceus* Marsh.	–	–	–	–	–	–	–	–	–	–	–	–	–	–	1	–	–	–	–	–	–	1	G
ANTHICIDAE																							
Anthicus antherinus (L.)	–	–	–	–	–	1	–	–	–	1	–	–	–	–	1	–	1	–	–	–	–	4	V
A. bifasciatus (Ros.)	–	–	–	–	–	–	–	–	–	–	–	–	–	–	–	–	–	1	–	–	–	1	V and old manure heaps
A. formicarius (Gz.)	–	–	–	–	–	–	–	–	2	–	–	–	–	–	–	–	–	–	–	–	–	2	V and in manure heaps
A. floralis (L.) or *formicarius* (Gz.)	–	–	–	–	–	–	1	–	–	–	1	–	–	–	–	–	–	–	–	–	–	2	V and in manure heaps
CERAMBYCIDAE																							
Phymatodes alni (L.)	–	–	–	–	–	–	–	–	–	–	–	–	1	–	–	–	–	–	–	–	–	1	Recently dead hardwood with the bark on esp. *Quercus*
P. testaceus (L.)	–	–	–	–	–	–	–	–	–	–	–	1	–	–	–	–	–	–	–	–	–	1	as above
BRUCHIDAE																							
Bruchus atomarius (L.)	–	–	–	–	–	–	–	–	–	–	1	–	–	–	1	–	–	1	–	–	–	3	*Vicia* spp.
B. loti Pk.	–	–	–	–	1	–	–	–	1	–	–	–	1	–	–	–	–	–	–	–	–	3	*Lotus* and *Lathyrus* spp.
Bruchus (not *rufimanus*) or *Bruchidius* sp.	–	–	–	–	–	–	–	1	–	–	–	1	1	–	–	–	1	–	–	–	–	4	On Papilionaceae
CHRYSOMELIDAE																							
Macroplea appendiculata (Pz.)	–	–	–	–	–	–	1	–	–	–	1	–	–	1	1	1	–	–	1	–	–	6	*Potamogeton* and *Myriophyllum* spp.
Donacia cinerea Hbst.	–	–	1	–	1	–	–	–	–	1	–	–	–	–	–	–	2	2	–	–	–	7	Various reedswamp monocotyledons
D. clavipes F.	–	–	2	1	2	2	–	–	–	2	2	–	2	3	3	–	2	6	3	2	2	33	*Phragmites australis* (Cav.) (? & *Phalaris* sp.)
D. crassipes F.	–	–	1	–	–	–	–	1	–	–	–	1	1	–	–	–	–	1	–	–	–	5	*Nymphea alba* L. & *Nuphar lutea* (L.) Sm.
D. dentata Hoppe	–	–	1	1	1	–	1	2	–	–	2	–	–	1	–	1	–	–	–	–	–	10	*Sagittaria sagittifolia* L. & *Alisma* sp.
D. impressa Pk.	–	1	1	1	1	–	3	1	–	3	3	–	4	2	–	1	2	2	1	–	–	27	*Schoenoplectus lacustris* (L.) Pal.
D. simplex F.	–	–	–	–	–	–	–	–	–	1	–	–	1	–	–	–	–	1	–	2	1	6	Various reedswamp monocotyledons
D. versicolorea (Brahm)	–	–	1	–	–	–	–	–	–	–	–	–	–	–	–	–	–	–	–	–	–	1	Floating-leaved species of *Potamogeton*
D. vulgaris Zsch.	–	–	–	–	–	–	–	–	–	–	–	–	1	1	–	–	–	1	–	–	–	2	Various reedswamp monocotyledons
Donacia sp.	–	1	–	–	–	–	–	–	–	–	–	1	–	–	–	–	–	–	–	–	–	2	Various reedswamp monocotyledons
Plateumaris affinis (Kunze)	–	–	1	–	–	–	–	–	–	–	–	–	–	–	–	–	–	1	–	1	–	2	*Carex* spp.
P. cf. *sericea* (L.)	–	–	–	–	–	–	–	–	–	1	–	–	–	–	–	–	–	1	–	–	–	1	*Carex* spp. and *Iris pseudacorus* L.
Lema cyanella (L.)	–	1	–	–	–	–	–	–	–	–	–	–	–	1	–	–	–	–	–	–	–	1	Various plants
Cryptocephalus moraei (L.)	–	–	–	–	–	1	1	–	–	–	–	–	–	–	–	–	1	1	–	–	–	3	*Hypericum* spp.
Cryptocephalus sp.	–	–	–	–	–	–	–	–	–	–	1	–	–	1	–	–	–	–	–	–	–	1	Herbs and trees
Chrysolina cf. *banksi* (F.)	–	–	–	–	–	–	–	–	–	–	–	–	–	1	–	–	1	–	–	–	–	1	*Ballota nigra* L. & *Teucrium* spp.
C. fastuosa (Scop.)	1	–	–	–	–	2	2	–	1	1	–	–	–	–	–	–	–	1	–	–	–	4	Labiatae esp. *Galeopsis* sp.
C. haemoptera (L.)	1	1	–	–	–	1	1	1	–	–	–	–	–	–	–	–	–	–	–	–	–	2	*Plantago* spp. in sandy places
C. polita (L.)	1	1	–	1	–	–	–	–	–	–	–	–	–	–	–	1	–	–	–	–	–	3	Labiatae – often in marshes

Table 36: Runnymede Late Bronze Age Coleoptera, column WF1b (continued).

Taxon	Total	Ecology
C. violacea (Müll.)	1	Labiatae and Rubiaceae
Gastrophysa polygoni (L.)	3	*Rumex* & *Polygonum* spp.
G. viridula (Deg.)	4	*Rumex* & *Polygonum* spp.
Phaedon sp.	2	Various herbs
Hydrothassa glabra (Hbst.)	4	*Ranunculus* spp.
Prasocuris phellandrii (L.)	3	Aquatic Umbelliferae
Galeruca tanaceti (L.)	2	Various herbs
Phyllotreta atra (F.)	2	Cruciferae & *Reseda* sp.
P. cruciferae (Gz.)	1	Cruciferae & *Reseda* sp.
P. cf. *diademata* (Foud.)	1	Cruciferae & *Reseda* sp.
P. nigripes (F.)	3	Cruciferae & *Reseda* sp.
P. ochripes (Curt.)	1	Cruciferae & *Reseda* sp.
P. nemorum (L.) or *undulata* Kuts.	4	Cruciferae & *Reseda* sp.
P. vittula Redt.	42	Cruciferae & *Reseda* sp.
Aphthona nonstriata (Gz.)	3	*Iris pseudacorus* L.
Longitarsus spp.	87	Various herbs
Altica sp.	4	Includes *Corylus*, *Salix*, *Rumex* & *Epilobium* spp.
Chalcoides sp.	2	*Salix* and *Populus* spp.
Epitrix pubescens (Koch)	5	*Solanum* spp., *Hyoscyamus* sp.
Podagrica fuscipes (F.)		Various Malvaceae
Chaetocnema concinna (Marsh.)	43	Polygonaceae esp. *P. aviculare* agg.
Chaetocnema sp. (not *concinna*)	18	Various herbs
Psylliodes affinis (Pk.)	1	Solanaceae
P. dulcamarae (Koch)		*Solanum dulcamara* L.
Psylliodes sp.	11	Various herbs
APIONIDAE		
Apion malvae (F.)	1	Various Malvaceae
A. rufirostre (F.)	1	Various Malvaceae
A. aeneum (F.)	9	Various Malvaceae
A. radiolus (Marsh.)		Various Malvaceae
A. urticarium (Hbst.)	4	*Urtica dioica* L. & *U. urens* L.
A. cf. *carduorum* Kb.	1	*Onopordum*, *Carduus*, *Cirsium* & *Centaurea* spp.
A. craccae (L.)	6	*Vicia* and *Lathyrus* spp.
Apion spp. (not above)	49	Various herbs
CURCULIONIDAE		
Trachyphloeus bifoveolatus (Beck)	2	T
Phyllobius roboretanus Gred. or *viridiaeris* (Laich.)		Various trees and shrubs
Phyllobius sp.	3	Various trees and shrubs
Polydrusus sp.	7	Trees, grasses and *Urtica* sp.
Barypeithes araneiformis (Schr.)	3	Trees, bushes and a few herbs / T

Table 36: Runnymede Late Bronze Age Coleoptera, column WF1b (continued).

Minimum numbers of individuals

depth (cms) to:	170/175	165/170	160/165	155/160	150/155	145/150	140/145	135/140	130/135	125/130	120/125	115/120	110/115	105/110	100/105	95/100	90/95	85/90	80/85	75/80	70/75	Total	Habitat or food
Sciaphilus asperatus (Bons.)	—	—	—	—	—	—	—	—	—	—	—	—	—	—	—	—	1	—	—	—	—	1	Woodland herbs esp. *Primula vulgaris* L. and *Sanicula* sp.
Strophosomus sp.	—	—	—	—	—	—	—	—	—	—	—	—	—	—	—	1	—	—	—	—	—	1	T
Liophloeus tessulatus (Müll.)	—	—	1	—	—	—	—	—	—	1	—	—	—	—	—	—	—	—	—	1	—	3	Adults esp. *Hedera helix* L.
Barynotus sp.	—	—	—	—	—	—	—	—	—	—	—	—	1	—	—	—	—	—	—	—	1	2	T
Sitona hispidulus (F.)	—	1	1	—	—	—	5	2	3	—	1	1	—	—	—	1	—	1	1	2	—	19	Papilionaceae esp. *Medicago* and *Trifolium* spp.
S. lepidus Gyll.	—	—	—	—	—	—	2	—	—	—	—	—	—	—	—	—	—	—	—	—	—	2	Papilionaceae
S. cf. lineatus (L.)	—	—	—	—	—	—	—	—	—	—	1	—	—	—	—	—	—	—	—	—	—	1	Various Papilionaceae
S. cf. macularius (Marsh.)	—	—	—	—	—	—	—	—	—	1	—	—	—	—	—	—	—	—	—	—	—	1	Various Papilionaceae
S. sulcifrons (Thun.)	—	—	—	—	—	—	—	—	—	2	—	—	—	—	—	—	—	—	—	—	—	2	Papilionaceae esp. *Medicago* and *Trifolium* spp.
Sitona sp.	1	—	—	—	—	—	—	—	—	—	—	—	2	1	1	1	—	—	—	—	1	7	Papilionaceae esp *Trifolium* sp.
Cleonis piger (Scop.)	—	—	—	—	—	—	—	—	—	1	—	—	—	—	—	—	—	—	—	—	—	1	*Carduus, Cirsium* and *Onopordum* sp.
Hypera punctata (F.)	1	—	—	—	1	—	1	—	—	—	1	—	—	1	1	1	1	2	—	—	—	10	Papilionaceae esp. *Trifolium* sp.
Hypera sp. (not punctata)	1	—	—	—	1	—	—	—	1	—	—	—	—	—	—	1	1	—	—	1	—	6	Various herbs
Alophus triguttatus (F.)	1	—	—	1	1	—	—	—	—	1	—	—	2	—	—	—	—	—	—	1	—	7	Various herbs
Liparus coronatus (Gz.)	1	—	—	—	—	—	—	—	—	—	—	—	—	—	—	—	—	—	—	—	—	1	Umbelliferae
Magdalis ruficornis (L.)	—	—	—	—	—	—	—	—	—	—	—	—	—	1	—	—	—	—	2	—	—	3	Larvae on bark of Rosaceous trees esp. *Crataegus* and *Prunus* spp.
Trachodes hispidus (L.)	—	—	—	—	—	—	—	—	—	—	—	—	—	—	—	—	1	—	—	—	—	1	Dead hardwood
Acalles turbatus Boh.	—	—	—	—	—	—	—	—	—	—	—	1	—	—	—	—	—	—	—	—	—	1	Dead *Crataegus* & *Corylus* esp.in hedges
Bagous spp.	1	1	—	—	1	—	1	—	2	1	1	2	5	1	3	3	1	1	2	3	2	31	Aquatic plants
Notaris acridulus (L.)	—	—	—	1	—	—	—	—	—	—	—	1	1	—	—	—	—	—	—	—	—	3	Marsh and aquatic plants
N. bimaculatus (F.) or scirpi (F.)	—	—	—	—	—	—	—	—	—	—	1	—	—	—	—	—	—	—	—	—	—	1	Aquatic grasses, sedges and *Typha* sp.
Orthocaetes setiger (Beck)	—	—	—	—	—	—	—	—	—	—	—	—	—	—	1	—	—	—	—	—	—	1	T
Stenocarus umbrinus (Gyll.)	—	—	—	—	—	—	—	—	—	—	1	—	1	—	—	—	—	1	—	1	—	4	Papaver spp.
Micrelus ericae (Gyll.)	—	—	—	—	—	—	—	—	—	—	—	—	—	—	—	—	—	1	—	—	—	1	*Calluna* and *Erica* spp.
Cidnorhinus quadrimaculatus (L.)	—	1	—	—	—	—	—	—	—	—	—	—	—	—	—	—	—	—	—	—	—	1	Urtica spp.
Ceutorhynchidius troglodytes (F.)	—	1	—	—	1	—	1	—	2	1	—	—	—	2	—	—	—	2	1	—	—	11	*Plantago lanceolata* L.
Ceutorhynchus atomus Boh.	—	—	—	—	—	—	—	—	—	—	—	—	—	—	—	—	2	—	—	—	—	2	Cruciferae
C. erysimi (F.)	—	—	1	—	—	—	—	—	—	—	1	1	—	—	—	—	2	—	—	—	—	5	Cruciferae
C. pollinarius (Forst.)	—	—	—	—	—	—	—	1	1	—	—	—	—	—	—	—	—	—	—	—	—	2	*Urtica dioica* L.
Eubrychius velutus (Beck.)	—	—	—	—	—	—	1	—	—	—	1	—	1	1	—	—	—	1	—	—	—	5	Submerged plants esp. *Potamogeton* and *Myriophyllum* spp.
Litodactylus leucogaster (Marsh.)	—	—	—	—	—	—	—	—	—	—	—	—	—	—	—	1	—	—	—	—	—	1	as above
Rhinoncus bruchoides (Hbst.)	—	—	—	—	—	—	—	—	—	—	1	—	—	—	—	—	—	—	—	—	—	1	*Polygonum* S. *Persicaria* spp.
Ceuthorhynchinae gen. et sp.indet.	—	2	2	2	2	—	4	1	4	1	1	3	3	4	4	2	2	3	3	4	2	45	Various herbs

309

Table 36: Runnymede Late Bronze Age Coleoptera, column WF1b (continued).

Taxon																						Count	Habitat
Baris lepidii Germ.	—	—	—	—	—	—	—	—	—	—	—	—	—	—	—	—	—	1	—	—	—	1	Various Cruciferae in marshy places
Limnobaris pilistriata (Step.)	—	—	—	—	—	—	—	—	—	—	—	—	—	—	—	—	—	—	1	—	—	1	Larvae esp. *Schoenoplectus* sp.
Anthonomus cf. *rubi* (Hbst.)	—	—	—	—	—	—	—	—	2	—	—	—	—	1	—	—	—	—	1	—	—	4	*Fragaria* and *Rubus* spp.
Anthonomus sp.	—	—	—	—	—	—	—	—	1	—	—	—	—	1	—	—	—	—	1	1	—	2	Mostly Rosaceous trees and shrubs
Tychius sp.	1	4	2	—	2	—	3	—	1	1	—	1	—	1	1	—	—	3	1	—	—	19	Mostly Papilionaceae
Miarus plantarum (Germ.)	—	—	1	—	1	—	—	—	1	1	—	—	—	—	—	—	—	—	—	—	—	1	Campanulaceae
Mecinus pyraster (Hbst.)	—	—	1	2	1	—	—	—	1	1	—	—	—	—	—	—	—	—	—	—	—	5	*Plantago lanceolata* L. and *P. media* L.
Gymnetron labile (Hbst.)	—	—	1	—	1	—	—	—	—	—	1	—	—	1	—	—	—	—	1	—	—	4	*Plantago lanceolata* L.
G. pascuorum (Gyll.)	—	—	—	—	—	1	—	—	1	—	1	—	—	1	—	—	—	—	—	2	—	6	*Plantago lanceolata* L.
G. veronicae (Germ.)	—	—	—	—	—	—	—	—	—	—	—	—	—	—	—	—	—	—	—	—	1	1	Marsh and aquatic *Veronica* spp.
G. villosulum Gyll.	1	—	—	—	—	—	—	—	—	—	—	—	—	—	—	—	—	—	—	—	—	1	Various *Veronica* spp. esp. aquatic ones
Ramphus pulicarius (Hbst.)	—	—	—	—	—	—	—	—	—	—	—	—	1	—	—	—	—	1	1	—	—	3	*Salix* spp., also *Populus* & *Betula* spp.
SCOLYTIDAE																							
Scolytus intricatus (Ratz.)	—	—	—	—	—	—	—	—	—	—	—	—	—	—	—	1	—	—	—	—	—	1	Mainly young *Quercus*, but also other hardwoods
S. rugulosus (Müll.)	2	—	—	1	—	1	—	—	—	—	1	—	—	—	—	—	1	—	—	—	—	5	Rosaceous trees and shrubs
Leperisinus varius (F.)	—	—	—	—	—	—	—	—	—	—	—	—	—	1	—	—	—	—	—	—	—	1	Mainly *Fraxinus*, also other trees
Hylastinus obscurus (Marsh.)	—	—	—	—	—	—	—	—	—	—	—	—	—	1	1	—	—	—	1	1	—	3	Dead roots of Papilionaceae
Xyleborus saxesini (Ratz.)	—	—	—	—	—	—	—	—	—	—	—	—	—	—	—	—	—	—	—	—	1	1	Dead wood
Totals	41	138	36	36	57	147	170	9	182	124	159	169	230	207	204	143	116	177	191	195	112	2843	

Table 37: Runnymede Late Bronze Age other insects, column WF1b.

Minimum numbers of individuals

depth (cms) to:	170–175	165–170	160–165	155–160	150–155	145–150	140–145	135–140	130–135	125–130	120–125	115–120	110–115	105–110	100–105	95–100	90–95	85–90	80–85	75–80	70–75	Total	Habitat or food
ODONATA																							
Agrion splendens (Har.)	–	–	–	–	–	–	–	–	–	–	–	–	–	–	1	–	–	–	–	–	–	1	Breeds in and flies over muddy-bottomed streams in open areas
Agrion splendens (Har.) or *virgo* (L.)	–	–	–	–	–	–	1	–	–	–	–	–	–	–	–	–	–	1	1	–	–	3	Nymphs A
DERMAPTERA																							
Forficula auricularia L.	–	–	–	–	–	1	–	–	1	–	–	–	1	–	–	1	–	–	–	–	–	3	T
HEMIPTERA – CYDNIDAE																							
Sehirus bicolor (L.)	–	–	–	–	–	–	–	–	–	–	–	1	–	–	–	–	–	–	–	–	–	1	*Lamium album* L. & *Ballota nigra* L.
Thyreocoris scarabaeoides (L.)	–	–	–	–	–	–	–	–	–	–	–	–	1	–	–	–	–	–	–	–	–	1	Perhaps *Viola* spp.
– PENTATOMIDAE																							
Palomena prasina (L.)	–	–	–	–	–	–	1	–	–	–	–	–	–	–	–	–	–	–	–	1	–	2	T
Pentatoma rufipes (L.)	–	–	–	1	–	–	–	–	–	1	–	1	–	–	–	1	–	–	–	–	–	4	Deciduous trees esp. *Quercus* sp.
– LYGAEIDAE																							
Heterogaster urticae (F.)	–	1	–	–	–	–	–	–	–	–	–	–	–	–	–	1	–	1	–	1	–	4	*Urtica dioica* L.
Megalonotus praetextatus (H.S.)	–	–	–	–	–	–	–	–	–	–	–	–	–	1	–	–	–	–	–	–	–	1	T
Stygnocoris fuligineus (Geof.)	–	–	–	–	–	–	–	–	–	–	–	–	–	–	–	–	–	1	–	–	–	1	T
Drymus sylvaticus (F.)	–	1	–	–	–	–	–	–	–	1	–	1	–	–	–	–	1	–	–	–	–	4	T
Scolopostethus sp.	–	–	–	–	–	1	1	2	–	–	–	1	–	1	–	–	–	–	–	1	1	7	T
– BERYTINIDAE																							
Berytinus sp.	–	1	–	–	–	–	–	–	–	–	1	–	–	–	–	–	–	–	–	–	–	2	T – open, dry places
– TINGIDAE																							
Campylosteira verna (Fal.)	–	–	–	–	–	–	–	1	–	–	–	–	–	1	–	–	–	–	–	–	–	2	Esp. amongst moss
– CIMICIDAE																							
Anthocorinae gen. et sp.indet.	–	–	–	–	–	1	–	–	–	1	1	–	–	–	–	–	–	1	–	–	–	4	T
– SALDIDAE																							
Saldula S. *Saldula* sp.	–	–	–	–	–	1	–	–	–	–	–	–	2	1	1	1	–	1	–	–	–	7	M&B at water's edge
– GERRIDAE																							
Gerris sp.	–	1	–	–	–	–	–	–	–	–	–	1	–	1	–	–	1	1	–	–	–	5	A – on water's surface
– Heteroptera gen. et sp.indet.	–	–	1	1	–	–	–	–	–	–	–	1	1	1	–	–	–	–	1	–	–	6	
– CERCOPIDAE																							
Philaenus or *Neophilaenus* sp.	–	–	–	–	–	–	1	–	–	–	–	–	1	–	–	1	–	–	–	–	–	3	Various plants
– CICADELLIDAE																							
Megophthalmus scabripennis Ed. or *scanicus* (Fal.)	–	1	–	–	–	–	–	–	–	–	–	–	–	–	–	–	–	1	–	–	–	2	Esp. grasses
Aphrodes cf. *albifrons* (L.)	–	–	–	1	–	1	–	1	1	1	–	–	2	–	–	–	1	1	1	–	–	9	Grasses
A. bicinctus (Schr.)	–	1	–	1	–	2	–	2	2	–	–	1	–	–	–	–	–	–	–	–	–	9	Grasses

Table 37: Runnymede Late Bronze Age other insects, column WF1b (continued).

A. flavostriatus (Don.)	—	1	1	—	—	—	—	—	—	—	—	1	—	1	—	—	1	—	—	—	—	5	Grasses
– Aphidoidea gen.et sp.indet.	—	—	—	1	—	1	—	—	2	—	—	—	1	—	—	—	—	—	—	—	—	5	
– Homoptera gen.et sp.indet.	—	—	—	—	—	—	—	—	—	—	1	—	—	—	—	—	—	—	—	—	—	1	
TRICHOPTERA																							
Ithytrichia lamellaris Eat. or *clavata*																							
Mort. – larval case	5	8	8	4	7	5	6	3	13	11	11	7	16	17	20	13	8	9	7	10	—	188	A – running water
Trichoptera gen.et sp.indet.-larva	11	29	8	10	5	18	23	7	18	19	26	18	36	33	51	34	3	61	18	36	1	465	A
– larval case	—	—	—	—	—	—	—	—	—	—	1	—	—	—	—	—	—	—	1	—		2	A
HYMENOPTERA – BETHYLIDAE																							
Bethylus sp.	—	—	—	—	—	—	—	—	—	—	—	1	—	—	—	—	—	—	1	—		2	T
– FORMICIDAE																							
Myrmica rubra (L.) or *ruginodis* Nyl.																							
– worker	—	1	—	—	—	—	2	—	—	1	1	—	—	1	—	1	—	—	—	2	—	8	T
– female	—	—	—	—	—	—	—	—	—	—	—	1	—	—	—	—	—	—	—	—	—	1	T
M. scabrinodis gp. – female	—	—	—	1	—	—	—	—	—	—	—	—	—	—	—	—	—	—	—	—		1	T
– male	—	—	—	—	—	1	—	—	—	—	—	—	—	—	—	—	—	—	—	—		1	T
Stenamma westwoodii West.																							
– worker	—	—	—	—	—	—	—	—	—	—	1	—	—	—	—	—	—	—	—	—		1	Nests under large stones or tree
West. – female	—	—	—	—	—	—	—	—	—	—	—	—	—	1	—	—	—	—	—	—		1	roots in shady woodland or hedges
Lasius flavus gp. – worker	2	—	—	—	3	1	2	—	—	5	—	—	1	—	—	1	—	—	1	3	—	19	Mounds in old pasture and at the edge of woodland
L. niger gp. – worker	—	—	—	—	—	—	—	—	—	1	1	—	1	1	—	—	—	2	—	—		6	T
Lasius sp.(not *fuliginosus*) – female	—	—	—	—	—	—	—	—	—	1	—	—	1	1	1	—	—	—	—	—		4	T
Lasius sp.(not *fuliginosus*) – male	—	—	—	—	—	—	—	—	—	1	—	—	—	—	—	—	—	—	—	—		1	T
– Hymenoptera gen.et sp.indet.	1	2	2	1	4	8	7	1	8	4	15	3	9	21	15	16	6	9	9	5	—	146	T
DIPTERA																							
Bibionidae gen.et sp.indet. – adult	—	1	—	—	1	—	—	—	5	1	—	1	1	2	—	2	—	—	—	1	1	16	V
Musca cf. *domestica* (L.) – puparium	—	—	—	—	—	—	—	—	—	1	2	1	1	—	—	—	—	—	—	—	—	5	FVC
Diptera gen.et sp.indet. – adult	—	1	2	—	1	5	5	1	5	9	8	2	3	6	5	4	2	4	2	1	—	66	
Diptera gen.et sp.indet. – puparium	3	4	3	—	—	2	5	1	11	11	9	5	1	—	7	1	—	2	—	2	—	67	

Table 38: Runnymede Late Bronze Age Coleoptera, Area 6, midden samples.

	Minimum no. of individuals			
	layer: 24*	19	Total	Habitat or food
CARABIDAE				
Nebria brevicollis (F.)	—	1	1	WGD
Trechus obtusus Er. or *quadristriatus* (Schr.)	2	2	4	T
T. micros (Hbst.)	1	—	1	B – usually of flowing water
Bembidion tetracolum Say	1	1	2	TM
B. biguttatum (F.)	—	1	1	BG&W, usually near water
Bembidion sp.	—	1	1	Mostly in wet or marshy places
Pterostichus versicolor (Sturm)	—	1	1	G(D)
Agonum albipes (F.)	2	2	4	BW(GD)
Badister bipustulatus (F.)	—	1	1	Mostly wet places
GYRINIDAE				
Orectochilus villosus (Müll.)	4	—	4	A – running water
HYDROPHILIDAE				
Helophorus spp. (*brevipalpis* size)	—	1	1	A – but readily leave water
Cercyon analis (Pk.)	8	6	14	FV
C. atricapillus (Marsh.)	2	—	2	FV
C. lugubris (Ol.)	2	2	4	FV
C. melanocephalus (L.)	—	1	1	Mostly F
Cercyon sp.	—	1	1	FVC, some species on wet mud
Megasternum obscurum (Marsh.)	1	—	1	FVC
Hydrobius fuscipes (L.)	—	1	1	A – stagnant
HISTERIDAE				
Hister sp.	—	1	1	FVC
HYDRAENIDAE				
Ochthebius cf. *minimus* (F.)	—	1	1	A – often stagnant
LEIODIDAE				
Choleva or *Catops* sp.	1	—	1	V – often leaf litter or fungi in woods, C(G)
STAPHYLINIDAE				
Coprophilus striatulus (F.)	—	1	1	V
Carpelimus bilineatus Step.	1	4	5	B – on wet mud (GV&F on wet soil)
Platystethus cornutus gp.	2	1	3	M&B – often on mud (VF)
P. nitens (Sahl.)	—	1	1	FVB

	Minimum no. of individuals			
	layer: 24*	19	Total	Habitat or food
STAPHYLINIDAE (continued)				
Anotylus nitidulus (Grav.)	2	1	3	VFC(M)
A. rugosus (F.)	—	3	3	FV(C)
Oxytelus sculptus Grav.	6	1	7	FV(C)
Stenus sp.	—	1	1	TM
Leptacinus pusillus (Step.)	7	2	9	FV
Gyrohypnus angustatus Step.	1	—	1	V – sometimes at water's edge
G. fracticornis gp.	3	3	6	FV(C)
Xantholinus linearis (Ol.) or *longiventris* Heer	—	1	1	WGV(FC)
Philonthus sp.	1	2	3	FVC(T)
Quedius sp.	—	2	2	T
Tachyporus sp.	—	1	1	T
Aleocharinae gen.et sp.indet.	5	3	8	TFVC
SCARABAEIDAE				
Aphodius foetidus (Hbst.)	—	1	1	FV
A. granarius (L.)	1	1	2	FV
A. cf. *prodromus* (Brahm)	1	—	1	FV
A. cf. *sphacelatus* (Pz.)	—	1	1	FVC
Aphodius sp.	2	1	3	Mostly F
Onthophagus ovatus (L.)	—	1	1	FCV
Phyllopertha horticola (L.)	1	—	1	Larvae on roots in permanent grassland
ELMIDAE				
Esolus parallelepipedus (Müll.)	—	1	1	A – clean flowing water, clinging to stones and aquatic plants
Normandia nitens (Müll.)	—	1	1	A – as above
Oulimnius sp.	1	2	3	A – mostly clean flowing
ELATERIDAE				
Agrypnus murinus (L.)	—	1	1	G
Agriotes sp.	—	1	1	Larvae on roots of grassland plants
CANTHARIDAE				
Cantharis sp.	—	1	1	Adults on flowers of herbs & shrubs

Table 38: Runnymede Late Bronze Age Coleoptera, Area 6, midden samples (continued).

	Minimum no. of individuals layer: 24*	19	Total	Habitat or food
ANOBIIDAE				
Anobium punctatum (Deg.)	1	—	1	Dead wood
LYCTIDAE				
Lyctus linearis (Gz.)	—	1	1	Dead hardwood
NITIDULIDAE				
Meligethes sp.	1	—	1	Herbs and trees – mostly on flowers
Omosita colon (L.)	—	1	1	C – dry
RHIZOPHAGIDAE				
Monotoma sp.	1	1	2	V (manure C)
CRYPTOPHAGIDAE				
Cryptophagidae gen.et sp.indet. (not Atomariinae)	2	—	2	V – of all sorts, T
PHALACRIDAE				
Stilbus sp.	1	—	1	In dry grass, hay and on *Typha* sp.
LATHRIDIIDAE				
Lathridius minutus gp.	—	1	1	V, also manure heaps (CGW)
Enicmus transversus (Ol.)	—	1	1	V(GW)
Corticaria punctulata Marsh.	—	1	1	V
Corticariinae gen.et sp.indet.	—	3	3	Mostly V
MYCETOPHAGIDAE				
Litargus connexus (Fouc.)	1	—	1	Wood fungi and under mouldy bark
ANTHICIDAE				
Anthicus formicarius (Gz.)	1	—	1	V and in manure heaps
CERAMBYCIDAE				
Phymatodes testaceus (L.)	1	—	1	Recently dead hardwood with the bark on
CHRYSOMELIDAE				
Donacia dentata Hoppe	—	2	2	*Sagittaria sagittifolia* L. & *Alisma* sp.
Chrysolina cf. *menthastri* (Suf.)	1	—	1	Labiatae esp. *Mentha* spp.
Phyllotreta cf. *ochripes* (Curt.)	1	—	1	Cruciferae and *Reseda* sp.
P. vittula Redt.	1	1	2	Cruciferae and *Reseda* sp.
Aphthona nonstriata (Gz.)	1	—	1	*Iris pseudocorus* L.
Longitarsus spp.	1	1	2	Various herbs
CHRYSOMELIDAE (continued)				
Chaetocnema concinna (Marsh.)	—	1	1	Polygonaceae esp. *P. aviculare* agg.
Psylliodes sp.	—	1	1	Various herbs
APIONIDAE				
Apion aeneum (F.)	—	1	1	Various Malvaceae
Apion sp. (not *aeneum*)	1	1	2	Various herbs
CURCULIONIDAE				
Phyllobius sp.	1	—	1	Trees, grasses and *Urtica* sp.
Barynotus obscurus (F.)	—	1	1	T
Sitona sp.	1	1	2	Papilionaceae esp. *Trifolium* sp.
Hypera punctata (F.)	—	1	1	Papilionaceae esp. *Trifolium* sp.
Bagous sp.	1	1	2	Aquatic plants
Ceuthorhynchinae gen.et sp.indet.	1	2	3	Various herbs
Limnobaris pilistriata (Step.)	1	—	1	Larvae esp. *Schoenoplectus* sp.
Mecinus pyraster (Hbst.)	—	1	1	*Plantago lanceolata* L. & *P. media* L.
Totals	78	87	165	

Table 39: Runnymede Late Bronze Age other insects, midden samples

	Minimum no. of individuals			
layer:	24*	19	Total	Habitat or food
HEMIPTERA				
Pentatoma rufipes (L.)	1	—	1	Deciduous trees esp. Quercus sp.
Aphrodes cf. albifrons (L.)	—	1	1	Grasses
TRICHOPTERA				
Ithytrichia lamellaris Eat. or clavata Mort. – larval case	17	36	53	A – running water
Orthotrichia sp. – larval case	—	2	2	A – standing or slowly moving
Trichoptera gen.et sp.indet. – larva	—	6	6	A
HYMENOPTERA				
Hymenoptera gen.et sp.indet.	1	—	1	T
DIPTERA				
Bibionidae gen.et sp.indet. – adult	—	1	1	V
cf. Sepsidae gen.et sp.indet. – puparium	1	—	1	FV
Sphaeroceridae gen.et sp.indet. – puparium	16	—	16	FV
cf. Scathophaga stercoraria (L.) – puparium	4	2	6	Fresh dung
Musca cf. domestica (L.) – puparium	51	15	66	FVC
Stomoxys calcitrans (L.) – puparium	24	2	26	V – usually contaminated with excreta
Diptera gen.et sp.indet. – adult	1	2	3	
Diptera gen.et sp.indet. – puparium	28	5	33	

Table 40: Runnymede Late Bronze Age Insecta, layer 20 bird pellet

	Minimum no. of individuals	Habitat or food
HEMIPTERA – HETEROPTERA		
Odontoscelis fuliginosa (L.)	1	Sandy places
COLEOPTERA		
Patrobus atrorufus (Ström)	1	W
Pterostichus melanarius (Ill.)	4	DG(W)
P. niger (Schal.)	1	W(GD)
Calathus fuscipes (Gz.)	1	WDG – often in meadowland
Amara apricaria (Pk.)	3	D – dry
Harpalus rufipes (Deg.)	8	D – often cultivated, (G)
H. affinis (Schr.)	2	DG(W)
Silpha atrata L.	1	Mostly under bark or in rotten wood (GDV)
Total Coleoptera	21	

Interpretation of the insect assemblages: their taphonomy

The insect assemblages from Runnymede accumulated under water in riverine sediments. They showed no evidence of sorting according to size (apart from the insects in the bird pellet). They appeared to be representative samples of the insects which lived in the river and those which entered it from various terrestrial habitats, biased only by the usual differential preservation between some taxa. Preservation of Coleoptera was good except in the topmost sample of each of the SS1 and WF1b columns and differential preservation does not present a problem at Runnymede.

The aquatic insects primarily comprised a fauna of clean, well oxygenated, flowing water with a well developed flora of submerged, floating leaved and emergent vegetation, although some stagnant water elements were present. Although almost all the aquatic insects could have lived in the channels at the place of deposition, presumably the majority of insect fragments had been carried some distance by the river before deposition.

The non-aquatic component of the assemblages, with the exception of the midden samples, mostly comprised insects from the various habitats to be found in grazed grassland, and woodland and along the margin of a river. Most of the terrestrial individuals probably fell or inadvertently flew into the river. It is possible that some of them were washed in by flooding (but see below for evidence that probably little flooding occurred). There is no evidence that any of the Neolithic insect remains experienced human transport. For the Late Bronze Age, comparison between the assemblages from the WF1b column and the midden samples (see below) suggests that only a small proportion of the insects from the column had experienced human transport; indeed only a small proportion of the insects from the WF1b column came from the settlement itself. Even though the midden material contained abundant fly puparia and beetles of foul organic material, and it had been dumped into the channel several metres from the location of the column as it was accumulating, this was only reflected by an occasional puparium of *Musca* cf. *domestica* (housefly) in the contemporaneous column samples.

Whereas the majority of rural archaeological insect assemblages that have been studied have come from deposits with a concentric catchment of a rather limited area, the effect of river flow would have been greatly to increase the catchment. The environmental picture given by the terrestrial insect would thus have been of a substantial strip of landscape extending upstream on either side of the river. It is believed that something of the order of 50% of the terrestrial Coleoptera had their origins in a strip extending only 50 m on either side of the river and 0.5 km upstream. This assumption is based upon a consideration of these and other lowland riverine assemblages rather than on direct experimental evidence.

The midden insect assemblages comprised about 50% individuals which lived in the decaying organic material while it was accumulating on land. The remainder was an assortment of terrestrial and aquatic species which probably entered the deposit as the midden material was being incorporated into the riverine sediments.

A close-packed mass of insect (mostly beetle) exoskeletons was discovered during the excavation of the WF sediments. It has been interpreted as a bird pellet, perhaps regurgitated by a member of the Corvidae. The insects would clearly have been selected by the bird which consumed them, but the bird pellet was so different from the other assemblages that it probably had its origin beyond their main catchment areas.

The Neolithic environment

The aquatic and waterside environment

Somewhat over 40% of the Coleoptera from the SS1 and A4 samples were water beetles (i.e. they were at a level of over 70% of the total terrestrial Coleoptera, Table 41). Furthermore, 8% of the terrestrial Coleoptera are species which feed on marsh or aquatic plants.

The aquatic insects comprised a balanced fauna of a well vegetated river with clean calcareous water in all its aspects, both rapids and almost still pools. Most of the Trichoptera (caddis) larval remains were not identified, but cases of the caddis *Ithytrichia* sp. were present in most of the samples. Both members of the genus require running water. The Coleoptera included species which cling to stones under well oxygenated flowing water (*Esolus parallelepipedus*), climb the stems of submerged plants (*Brychius elevatus*), swim actively in running water (*Stictotarsus duodecimpustulatus*), skim over the surface of turbulent water at night (*Orectochilus villosus*) and live in slowly moving shallow water at the margin (*Ochthebius minimus*).

The most abundant aquatic beetles belong to the family Elmidae. They occur in clean flowing water (and large lakes), clinging to stones and aquatic plants. Some of these species are so fastidious in their requirement for clean, well oxygenated water that in most of the major English lowland river systems, if they occur at all, they are restricted to weir outflows and the fast-flowing tributary streams – as, for example, *Esolus parallelepipedus* in the upper Thames (Walker 1911: 8). One of them, *Stenelmis canaliculata*, was only added to the British list about 30 years ago, when it was discovered living in Lake Windermere (it is a distinctive medium-sized beetle) (Claridge and Staddon 1960). Another, *Macronychus quadrituberculatus*, now only occurs in the upper reaches of the Trent basin. Its larvae feed on decaying submerged wood in flowing water (Freude *et al.* 1979: 294; Olmi 1976: 209). Other water beetles from Runnymede which apparently no longer occur in the Thames include *Helephorus arvernicus* and *Helichus substriatus*.

A very similar fauna of water beetles, including *S. canaliculata*, *M. quadrituberculatus*, most of the other elmids, *H. arvernicus* and *H. substriatus* was discovered in sediments dated to 4010 ± 90 BP from a main channel of the Thames at Buscot Lock, on the Oxfordshire–Gloucestershire border (Robinson 1981a: 308–313). Such a fauna probably occurred throughout much of the length of the Thames while it remained in its unpolluted and unmanaged state.

Amongst the phytophagous Coleoptera were a few species which feed on submerged aquatic plants. They included the weevil *Eubrychius velutus*, which lives in stagnant or slowly moving water and whose larvae develop in the submerged stems of *Potamogeton* and *Myriophyllum* spp. (Harde 1984: 12). The very rare chrysomelid beetle *Macroplea appendiculata*, which lives on river beds amongst the roots of those two plants on which it feeds, was also present. There are early 19th-century records of this species from the Thames near Windsor (Donisthorpe 1939: 90).

A floating-leaved element to the aquatic flora is also suggested by the phytophagous Coleoptera. Water lilies, either *Nymphaea alba* or *Nuphar lutea*, are indicated by *Donacia crassipes*, and *D. versicolorea* feeds on the floating-leaved species of *Potamogeton*. The majority of the beetles which feed on marsh and aquatic plants, however, are those members of the genus *Donacia* which are dependent on tall emergent and reedswamp monocotyledons. Their larvae live on the submerged parts of their hosts while the adults feed on the leaves above the water. Most abundant of these beetles was *Donacia impressa*, which is restricted to *Schoenoplectus lacustris* as a host plant, followed by *D. clavipes*, which feeds on *Phragmites australis*. Other reedswamp and waterside plants indicated by the Coleoptera include *Sparganium erectum* (*D. marginata*), *Sagittaria sagittifolia* or *Alisma* sp. (*D. dentata*), aquatic Umbelliferae, probably *Oenanthe aquatica* gp. (*Prasocuris phellandrii*), *Iris pseudacorus* (*Aphthona nonstriata*) and perhaps species of *Rorippa* or *Nasturtium* (*Phyllotreta* spp.).

The phytophagous Coleoptera do not give much evidence of extensive riverside marshes with reeds of *Carex* spp. etc. This is illustrated, for example, by *Plateumaris sericea*, which can be very abundant in deposits which accumulated under ungrazed sedge fens or marshes but was absent at Runnymede. Similarly, *Notaris acridulus*, which often favours grazed marshes, was poorly represented. Likewise the Carabidae (ground beetles), even though they include many species of waterside or wet grassland and woodland habitats, do not comprise a full marshland fauna. Members of the family Scirtidae, which have larvae that live in pools in fens and marshes, were not well represented, whereas they were some of the most abundant beetles from the Somerset Levels excavations (e.g. Girling 1976).

There was, however, a rich amphibious and waterside fauna from the Neolithic samples, comprising *Dryops* spp., *Ochthebius* spp. and other members of the Hydraenidae, which readily leave water and venture onto exposed mud. Non-aquatic inhabitants of mud included *Carpelimus rivularis*, which often occurs in decaying plant debris on exposed mud, and *Dyschirus globosus*, which burrows in mud and wet sand near water. The bankside species of Carabidae included *Bembidion assimile*, which favours well vegetated conditions, *Agonum albipes*, which favours bare ground, some of the smaller members of the genus *Pterostichus* and other species of *Bembidion*.

The overall picture that emerges of the River Thames at Runnymede in the later Neolithic is of a river with stretches of turbulent rapids with a stony bed, perhaps fringed by sand banks, and lengths of deep, slowly moving water covered with water lilies and fringed by muddy shallows, from which emerged almost impenetrable stands of true bulrush and reed. There do not seem to have been

Table 41: Summary of the representation of the Coleoptera species groups in the various sample locations.

Runnymede Coleoptera: Species groups

	Neolithic			Late Bronze Age	
	SS1 column (+other A6 samples)	A4 column	WF1b column	Midden samples	Bird pellet
(1. Aquatic	71.3	78	31.1	8	0)
2. Pasture/dung	5.6	5	10.0	6	0
3. ? Meadowland	2.5	3	4.0	3	0
4. Wood and trees	7.0	7	1.6	1	0
5. Marsh/aquatic plants	7.9	9	7.0	4	0
6a. General disturbed ground/arable	0.1	1	0.2	0	38
6b. Sand/dry disturbed ground/arable	0	0	0	0	14
7. Dung/foul organic	12.3	7	9.0	17	0
8. Lathridiidae	1.9	0	2.3	4	0
9. Synanthropic	0	0	0.1	0	0
10. Esp. structural timbers	0.2	0	0.2	1	0
11. On roots in grassland	2.5	7	5.3	2	0
12. Unclassified	60.1	60	60.4	54	48
Total number of terrestrial individuals	1713	108	2168	153	21

See text for further details of the habitats of the groups and their species composition. Figures are percentages of terrestrial species.

extensive fringing marshes but areas of mud were probably exposed when the water level dropped during the summer.

Such conditions seem to have prevailed throughout the deposition of the SS1 and A4 columns. However, the proportion of water beetles and phytophagous beetles which feed on aquatic plants declined towards the top of the SS1 column from a depth of about 1.55 m upwards. It is possible that this was related to the silting up of the channel so that a greater proportion of the insects had a local terrestrial origin. The individual assemblages from the A4 column were too small for assessment, but the percentages of aquatic beetles from the column as a whole corresponds with the results from the lower half of the SS1 column.

Woodland and scrub

Over 7% of the terrestrial Coleoptera from the SS1 and A4 samples fall into Species Group 4, wood and tree-dependent species. In addition, many of the ground-dwelling Carabidae and Staphylinidae from these samples can occur in woodland, indeed some are restricted to it, whilst various of the other Coleoptera can be members of woodland communities – for example, some of the phytophagous species feed on woodland herbs. It is clear from these results that woodland was a major aspect of the terrestrial catchment area from which the insects had been derived. It is more difficult to assess the degree of cover. With reference to the comments made above about the representation of wood and tree-dependent Coleoptera, the figure of 7% is regarded as reflecting over one-third woodland cover and possibly as much as two-thirds cover if the open areas tended to be alongside the river bank and thus over-represented in the samples.

Some of the tree- and shrub-feeding beetles from the site are host-specific (Table 42).

The relative abundance of the different groups of beetles shown in Table 42 is not in direct proportion to the degree of representation of each tree species. Oak, for example supports a diverse and abundant beetle fauna, whereas there are few beetles exclusive to hazel. What these results do provide, however, is a corrective to the over-representation of alder in the botanical evidence. This tree, which probably grew up to the channel edge, is prolific in its production of pollen and seeds but does not support an abundant beetle fauna.

When due allowance is made for differential representation, it is clear that most of the tree and shrub cover was from potential woodland trees rather than thorn or willow scrub. In contrast, beetles of potential woodland trees were very much in the minority amongst the impoverished group of host-specific tree- and shrub-feeding beetles from the Bronze Age deposits at Runnymede.

Alder and oak woodland seems to have predominated. It must be remembered that during the Neolithic the water table was probably lower than at present in the valley bottom at Runnymede and that much of the alluvium on the flood-plain is of post-Neolithic date. The extent of Neolithic alder

woodland cannot simply be correlated with the modern flood-plain. Some areas of the flood-plain would formerly have been more akin to the terrace gravels, with only a thin covering of soil over the gravel. However, the silt-filled former channels of the Colne and Thames, the banks of the Neolithic channels and those parts of the flood-plain which now have the deepest alluvial covering over gravel would all have readily supported alder woodland.

Recent palynological studies have emphasised the former prevalance of lime woodland over much of southern England and the Midlands during the Atlantic period prior to clearance, but only two specimens of the lime-feeding scolytid *Ernoporus caucasicus* were recovered from the Neolithic samples from Runnymede. In contrast *E. caucasicus* greatly outnumbered the oak leaf-feeding weevils from deposits dating to around the time of the elm decline at West Heath Spa, Hampstead, on the acid Bagshot sands and clays (Girling, forthcoming). The abundance of the oak-leaf feeding weevils in the samples from Runnymede suggests that oak probably dominated woodland on the terrace gravels, with ash, elm and perhaps lime being of lesser importance. Some support for the view that oak woodland represents the natural Atlantic climax vegetation on the Thames gravel terraces, at least where the soil cover was thin, comes from the analysis of charcoal from Neolithic tree clearance at Drayton, Oxfordshire, where oak predominated (Robinson, in prep.).

Lime-related insects were not entirely absent from Runnymede and, in addition to *E. caucasicus*, the coccinellid *Stethorus punctillum* was present. It feeds on plant mites, especially on trees, and shows a close association with the mite *Tetranychus* sp. on the underside of lime leaves. It is possible that lime dominated the woodland on the nearby

Table 42: **Host plants of the more host-specific of the tree- and shrub-feeding Coleoptera from the SS1 and Area 4 samples.**

Tree or shrub	Beetle species	% of total
Alnus glutinosa (alder)	*Aegelastica alni*	13
Corylus avellana (hazel)	*Curculio nucum*	1
mostly *Fraxinus excelsior* (ash)	*Leperesinus varius*	2
Prunoideae and Pomoideae (sloe, hawthorn, apple, whitebeam, etc.)	*Scolytus rugulosus*	4
Quercus sp. (oak)	*Coeliodes dryados* *Curculio pyrrhoceras* *Rhynchaenus avellanae* *R. pilosus* *R. quercus*	69
mostly *Quercus* sp. (oak)	*Scolytus intricatus*	5
Salix or *Populus* sp. (willow or poplar)	*Chalcoides* sp. *Ramphus pulicarius*	2
Tilia cordata (small-leaved lime)	*Ernoporus caucasicus*	2
mostly *Ulmus* spp. (elm)	*Acrantus vittatus*	1
	N = 83	100%

Table 43: Extinct or very rare woodland Coleoptera from the SS1 column and Area 4 samples.

	NCC old woodland grade 1	Extinct in Britain	Modern localities	Other archaeological records
Dromaeolus barnabita		+		
Gastrallus immarginatus	+		W	SL TM MD
Pelta grossum		+		TM
Colydium elongatum	+		NF	TM
Teredus cylindricus	+		W S	TM
Prionychus melanarius	+		A S	TM
Agelastica alni		?	1	MD SL
Ryncolus truncorum	+		2	B SL
Ernoporus caucasicus	+		3	MD SL

A: Arundel Park (Elton 1960); NF: New Forest; S: Sherwood Forest; W: Windsor Forest; 1: early 19th-century records from London, Bristol and Exeter; 2: various large forests in Southern England; 3: Moccas Park and some other Midland localities; B: Buscot Lock (Robinson 1981a 308–313); MD: Mingies Ditch (Allen and Robinson, in prep.); SL: Somerset Levels (Girling 1976; 1977a; 1979; 1980; 1984); TM: Thorne Moors (Buckland 1979).

Tertiary Sands, which probably did not experience extreme acidification until after clearance, and on the London Clay. These geologies would have been on the edge of the main catchment area for the insect remains.

There would have been transitional zones between areas of woodland and cleared areas, which are perhaps, where the thorny members of the Prunoideae and Pomoideae grew. Other beetles of this type of scrub community identified from the Neolithic samples included *Anthonomus* spp., which are associated with rosaceous shrubs, particularly *Rubus* spp., and *Epitrix pubescens*, which favours *Solanum dulcamara*.

The woodland assemblage of Coleoptera comprised a balanced fauna. The tree-feeding species range from leaf-eating beetles (e.g. *Rhynchaenus quercus*) through a beetle which bores into recently dead wood containing fermenting sap (*Platypus cylindrus*), to beetles of rotten wood, such as *Sinodendron cylindricum*. Others hunt for their prey under loose bark (*Silpha atrata*) or feed on tree fungi (*Aspidiphorus orbiculatus*). There are predators which hunt on the forest floor (*Pterostichus oblongopunctatus*) and phytophagous species which feed on woodland herbs: for example, *Sciaphilus asperatus* is partial to *Primula vulgaris*. The assemblage differs from the faunas of most modern British woodlands in that it contains a strong 'old woodland' element – that is, beetles which are associated with over-mature trees or areas which have retained their woodland cover, albeit in a much altered form, since before the Neolithic. Many of these species occur in categories of decaying wood only to be found in neglected woodland and have little ability to withstand intensive forest management or to colonise new areas once their woodland habitat has become fragmented. Some of these species from Runnymede are now extinct in the British Isles, others are extremely rare. The most significant of these species are given in Table 43.

All the species in Table 43 which still occur in Britain have been classified as Grade 1 in the Nature Conservancy Council's list of Coleoptera associated with mature timber habitats: that is they are species which are known to have occurred in recent times only in areas believed to be primary woodland or parkland. Most are now restricted to a very few localities, and it is noticeable that some of these sites are mostly parkland, as is Windsor Forest, rather than dense woodland. This is because the over-mature timber habitats that some of these beetles require can now only be found in the very old pollards of huge girth which occur in these parks, sometimes actual survivors of the primary woodland which was cleared around them. *Prionychus melanarius*, for example, occurs in hollow trees, particularly oaks, full of wood mould (Joy 1932: 316); *Teredus cylindricus* occurs in Windsor Great Park in old oaks infested by wood-boring beetles and in nests of the ant *Lasius brunneus* in old trees (Donisthorpe 1939, 60–61).

Two, possibly three, of these beetles are now extinct in Britain. *Dromaeolus barnabita* occurs in dry dead wood of deciduous trees, such as damaged branches which have not been shed, in scattered localities throughout central and southern Europe (Freude *et al.* 1979: 192). *Pelta grossum* is a large beetle which occurs in rotten wood of both deciduous and coniferous trees. It has a boreo-montane distribution in Europe, occurring in Scandinavia, Prussia, the Alps and the Pyrenees (Buckland 1979: 78; Freude *et al.* 1967: 17). The third species, *Agelastica alni*, is now probably extinct in Britain (Harde 1984: 280). It feeds on alder leaves and is common in parts of continental Europe. *A. alni* is not as obviously an old woodland species as the other beetles in Table 43. However, it is possible that on the edge of its range it is only capable of maintaining a viable population in large, undisturbed alder woods.

The 'old woodland' fauna is a familiar element of most of the archaeological insect assemblages that have been examined from between about 7000 and 4000 BP and it is clear that it reflects the character of the primary woodland which formerly covered most of Britain. There are previous archaeological records from Britain of all the species in Table 43 except *Dromaeolus barnabita*. The other archaeological records given in the table are not exhaustive, but cover the other two Thames Valley sites which have produced large woodland insect faunas: Buscot Lock, Oxon./Glos. (4010 ± 90 BP), Mingies Ditch Sample O, Oxon. (6540 ± 80 BP). They also include the Neolithic deposits on the Somerset Levels and Thorne Moors, Humberside, a Late Bronze Age trackway site amidst moribund woodland, killed by a rising water table (2980 ± 110 BP).

The sequence of samples from the SS1 column does not suggest any changes in the woodland environment during the period of deposition.

Grassland and the open environment

Open areas were also a significant aspect of the Neolithic landscape around Runnymede, and they seem primarily to have supported grassland. The Scarabaeidae and Elateridae, with larvae which feed underground on roots in grassland, Species Group 11, comprised 2.5% of the terrestrial Coleoptera from the SS1 samples. The most abundant of the elaterids in this category was *Agrypnus murinus*, which, unlike some grassland elaterids, does not seem to be able to tolerate flooding very well. It is more characteristic of well aerated soils.

The weevils of the genera *Apion* and *Sitona*, which feed on grassland trefoils and comprise Species Group 3, also made up 2.5% of the terrestrial Coleoptera from the SS1 samples. They were not so abundant as to suggest hay meadow conditions, but the rich phytophagous fauna of grassland beetles from the site does seem to indicate somewhat flowery herb-rich grassland, rather than overgrazed pasture.

Some of the more host-specific phytophagous grassland Coleoptera from these samples and their favoured foods include:

Ceuthorhynchidius troglodytes	*Plantago lanceolata*
Gymnetron labile	
G. pascuorum	
Mecinus pyraster	*P. lanceolata* and *P. media*
Hydrothassa glabra	*Ranunculus* spp.
Hypera punctata	*Trifolium* spp.
Apion cerdo	*Vicia* and *Lathyrus* spp
A. craccae	

The scarabaeoid dung beetles of Species Group 2 comprised 5.7% of the terrestrial Coleoptera from the SS1 samples, which indicates a significant presence of the larger herbivorous mammals. Most scarabaeoid dung beetles present in Britain are not restricted to the dung of any one large herbivore, although *Aphodius zenkeri* tends to be associated with deer dung (Britton 1956: 15). *A. zenkeri* is now abundant in deer dung in Windsor Great Park (Donisthorpe 1939: 75) but was not amongst the ten species of *Aphodius* identified from the Runnymede Neolithic samples. The dung beetles can be regarded as indicating that the areas of grassland were used as pasture for domestic animals.

Some of the dung beetles are still common in the area: for example, the most numerous species, *Aphodius granarius* and *A. sphacelatus*, are common in cow dung around Wind-

sor (Donisthorpe 1939: 74). However, one species, *Onthophagus taurus*, represented by four individuals, is now extinct in Britain, and another, *Copris lunaris*, is very rare and perhaps on the verge of extinction in Britain (Jessup 1986: 26). *O. taurus* is common in southern and central Europe, where it tends to occur in cow dung, but it is rare and of sporadic occurrence further north (Harde 1984: 232; Paulian 1959: 88–89). The subspecies *illyricus*, which the four Runnymede specimens most closely resemble, has been recorded from Belgium. There are specimens of *O. taurus* in early 19th-century collections of British beetles, and although many of them probably came from the Channel Islands, where this species still occurs, the claimed captures from the New Forest are accepted (Fowler 1890: 12; Jessup 1986: 26). However, there have been no records of its capture in Britain for over 130 years and it is regarded as extinct. A single individual of *O. taurus* was identified from Late Bronze Age deposits at Bidford-on-Avon, Warwick. (Osborne 1982: 71). A single specimen of *Copris lunaris* was identified from Runnymede. This species occurs under cow and sheep dung on sandy and chalky soils, now being restricted to a few localities in southern England (Paulian 1959: 73; Jessup 1986: 26). It was, however, identified from a Late Bronze Age pond near Dorchester, Oxon. (Robinson, unpublished). There was one notable absence from the Runnymede Neolithic assemblage of scarabaeoid dung beetles: *Aphodius contaminatus*. It is common in the area at present and is usually one of the more numerous members of the genus in archaeological assemblages from the Thames Valley, the Late Bronze Age deposits from Runnymede included.

It is uncertain as to why there should be these differences from more recent dung faunas. It is not as if the Neolithic assemblages are solely reflecting pasture under conditions of park woodland. *A. contaminatus*, for example, is now common in deer dung at Windsor under these conditions (Donisthorpe 1939: 75) and *O. taurus* only occurs in dung in warm places exposed to the sun in the north of its range. Possible climatic implications are considered below.

Various other beetles from the Hydrophilidae, such as *Cercyon* spp. and *Megasternum obscurum*, and the Staphylinidae, such as *Anotylus rugosus* and *Philonthus*, which also comprise part of the fauna of dung were present in appropriate numbers. One of the hydrophilids, *Sphaeridium lunatum* or *scarabaeoides*, usually occurs in cow-pats. The Carabidae and Staphylinidae from the Neolithic samples included many species which commonly occur in grassland, such as *Pterostichus cupreus* and *Xantholinus linearis*, but few are exclusive to it. The smaller families not so far mentioned also contained appropriate elements of a grassland fauna.

Grassland species were not uniformly represented throughout the SS1 column. The scarabaeoid dung beetles were more than twice as abundant in the bottom four samples of the column, from 1.75 to 1.95 m. They averaged over 10% of the terrestrial Coleoptera, as opposed to 3.5% throughout the remainder of the column. The scarabs and elaterids with larvae that feed on roots in grassland were also twice as abundant in the four samples below 1.75 m as in the samples above them. Given that much of the catchment seems to have remained woodland throughout the period of deposition of the SS1 column, these results suggest that a substantial clearing grazed by domestic animals existed close to the site during the period of deposition of the sediments between 1.95 and 1.75 m, but subsequently this area of grassland was substantially reduced. It is possible that the clearing, which could have been several hundred or more metres in diameter, was replaced by another, equally large, more distant in the catchment.

There was no recognisable arable component to the Neolithic insect assemblages from Runnymede and few of the phytophagous species are associated with annual weeds. There were a few individuals of *Ceutorhynchus erysimi*, which feeds on Cruciferae such as *Brassica rapa*, and *Chaetocnema concinna*, which feeds on Polygonaceae, particularly *Polygonum aviculare*, but both could have been feeding on grassland or waterside herbs. However, a small arable plot in one of the clearings could easily have remained undetected from the insect evidence, especially inland away from the river.

Beetles which feed on *Urtica* spp. were rather more abundant, and included *Apion urticarium*, *Cidnorhinus quadrimaculatus* and *Ceutorhynchus pollinarius*. Nettles probably grew along the river bank and on the edge of wooded area. There were also a few beetles which feed on plants of ungrazed grassland perhaps transitional to scrub, such as *Apion rufirostre* and *A. aeneum* on Malvaceae, *Chrysolina hyperici* on *Hypericum* spp., and *Phaedon tumidulus* on Umbelliferae, particularly *Heracleum sphondylium*.

Most of the woodland and grassland beetles from the Neolithic samples occur on circumneutral to somewhat calcareous loams, ranging from wet to well drained. A few of the beetles fall outside this description. There was a single individual weevil, *Micrelus ericae*, which feeds on *Erica* spp. and *Calluna vulgaris*. Either the heathlands of the Tertiary sands were beyond the main catchment area of the Runnymede deposits or they had yet to develop. There was also a group of beetles which tends to be associated with insolated (sun-warmed) habitats on sandy and sometimes chalky soils. Most now tend to have a somewhat coastal distribution:

Aphodius villosus	*Caenopsis waltoni*
Serica brunnea	*Barypeithes pellucidus*
Chrysolina banksii	*Rhynocyllus conicus*
C. haemoptera	*Tychius* cf. *tibialis*

Each species was only represented by one or two individuals. There are at least sporadic recent inland records of most of them. *Rhynocyllus conicus*, however, is now very rare in Britain, being known from only a few localities on the south coast (Fowler 1891: 238; Harde 1984: 292). *Caenopsis waltoni* is restricted to the plantain *Plantago coronopus*, which is usually regarded as a coastal plant, but does also occur inland on bare sandy and gravelly soils. There is a specimen of this beetle in the Hope Collections at Oxford, which was captured at Woking, Surrey. It is possible that during the Neolithic these beetles were living in newly cleared areas on the Tertiary sands, or possibly the terrace gravels if the soil cover was thin. There is evidence from the Thames gravels at Drayton, Oxon., that clearance of large trees was achieved by killing them, allowing them to fall and then burning the remains (Lambrick and Robinson, in prep.). This results in considerable disruption of the soil and exposure of the subsoil to erosion, hence providing a potential habitat for *C. waltoni*.

Other habitats
There is no evidence provided by the insect remains from the SS1 and A4 samples for human habitation on the site. Synanthropic species belonging to Species Group 9 were absent, numbers of Lathridiidae were no higher than might be expected away from settlement, and the three individuals of *Anobium punctatum* (Species Group 10) could easily have been derived from woodland. The percentage of beetles which occurs in dung/foul organic material and comprises Species Group 7 was not excessively high and need not imply settlement refuse. Indeed the most abundant member of the genus *Cercyon* from this group was *C. sternalis*, which occurs on damp ground in places such as river banks, under plant detritus, rather than in middens or dung heaps (Freude *et al.*, 1971: 139).

A few of the water beetles, such as *Helophorus aquaticus* or *grandis*, more usually occur in small bodies of stagnant water such as puddles, ponds or ditches and rarely occur in rivers. It is likely that some of them had their origin in the bodies of water in the catchment.

The Late Bronze Age environment

The aquatic and waterside environment

Water beetles did not form as high a proportion of the Coleoptera from the WF1b column as they did from the Neolithic samples, 24% of the Coleoptera from the WF1b column being water beetles (i.e. they were at a level of 31% of the total terrestrial Coleoptera, Table 41). Of the terrestrial Coleoptera, 7% feed on marsh or aquatic plants. The aquatic insect fauna was very similar to that from the Neolithic channel sediments. There was the same range of species of clean flowing water, and Elmidae were again the most abundant aquatic beetles. However, *Macronychus quadrituberculatus* was not nearly so well represented, which might suggest that there was not so much fallen wood entering the Thames. A similar range of phytophagous Coleoptera, particularly donaciine chrysomelids, suggested the same submerged, floating leaved and emergent vegetation. Muddy shallows along the banks of the more slowly moving stretches of water still supported dense stands of true bulrush and reed; but reed (*Phragmites australis*) had perhaps increased at the expense of bulrush (*Schoenoplectus lacustris*), because *Donacia clavipes*, which feeds on the former, had displaced *D. impressa*, which feeds on the latter, as the most abundant member of this genus. Almost all the aquatic and reedswamp plants suggested by the Neolithic Coleoptera are again indicated by phytophagous Coleoptera from the Bronze Age deposits, although there were no longer any beetles solely dependent on *Sparganium erectum*. As before, there was a rich marginal and bankside fauna, but otherwise there was not a significant marshland element. The sequence of samples gave no evidence of changing aquatic conditions during the period of deposition of the column.

Woodland and scrub

Wood- and tree-dependent beetles comprised under 2% of the terrestrial Coleoptera from the WF1b column. This suggests that woodland cover in the catchment had been greatly reduced since the Late Neolithic. The percentage value is similar to those from insect assemblages from Mingies Ditch and Watkins Farm, Iron Age sites in the upper Thames valley where, although the landscape seems predominantly to have been open, there was some scrub or woodland (Robinson 1981b: 280–281; Allen and Robinson in prep.).

A somewhat different range of tree- and shrub-feeding beetles was present compared to the Neolithic samples (Table 44).

Not only was the number of beetles greatly reduced, they mostly comprised species which do not feed on the major trees of primary woodland. About half feed on rosaceous shrubs and trees such as hawthorn and sloe. Perhaps there were areas of thorn scrub on the grassland around the site, but they could also have been growing in hedgerows. Beetles that feed on willow and poplar were also better represented. It is possible that once the alders, which cast dense shade, had largely been removed from the flood-plain, more light-demanding willows grew up along the water courses.

Oak woodland, or at least old oak trees, were not entirely absent from the catchment. A few of the beetles usually occur on oak and two species from the WF1b column, *Ampedus nigerrimus* and *Pediacus dermestoides*, are classified by the Nature Conservancy Council as Grade 1 indicators of primary woodland or parkland. *A. nigerrimus* has been captured from the rotting wood of old damaged oaks in Windsor Great Park, the only locality where it is now known to occur (Donisthorpe 1939: 78). There is a possible record of it from Late Bronze Age deposits at Thorne Moors, Humberside (Buckland 1979: 32). *P. dermestoides* is a predator which hunts scolytid larvae under loose bark and in scolytid tunnels. It also occurs in Windsor Forest, but is of more widespread occurrence in southern England today than the previous species. The woodland from which these beetles derive could have been that part of the primary woodland cover which survived the onslaughts of agricultural clearance, ultimately to become the parkland of Windsor Forest.

Various other woodland beetles were identified from the WF1b column but the woodland carabid *Patrobus atrorufus* seemed somewhat more abundant than might be expected from the proportion of other woodland insects. It is possible that it was managing to survive, perhaps in company with *Pterostichus niger* and *Abax parallelepipedus*, in areas that had largely been cleared of woodland but had yet to be intensively exploited agriculturally.

A considerable quantity of timber was brought to the site for the construction of the waterfront structures when silting in the WF1b column was at *circa* 0.80 to 0.85 m. However, this was not reflected by the insect fauna.

Grassland, arable and the open landscape

The Late Bronze Age landscape around the site was largely open. The abundance of scarabaeoid dung beetles (Species Group 2) and scarab chafers and elaterid click beetles (Species Group 11) suggests that it was mostly grazed grassland. Members of Species Group 11, which have larvae that feed on roots in grassland, made up 5.3% of the terrestrial Coleoptera from the WF1b column. The chafer *Phyllopertha*

Table 44:　Host plants of the more host-specific of the tree- and shrub-feeding Coleoptera of the WF1b column.

Tree or shrub	Beetle species	% of total
mostly *Fraxinus excelsior* (ash)	*Leperesinus varius*	6
Prunoideae and Pomoideae (sloe, hawthorn, apple, whitebeam, etc.)	*Magdalis hispidus* *Scolytus rugulosus*	47
mostly *Quercus* sp. (oak)	*Phymatodes alni* *P. testaceus* *Scolytus intricatus*	18
Salix or *Populus* sp: (willow or popular)	*Chalcoides* sp. *Ramphus pulicarius*	29
	N = 17	100%

horticola was the most abundant and *Agrypnus murinus* was again the most numerous of the elaterids. They had, however, been joined by various species of *Agriotes*. Just as in the Neolithic, the fauna appears to have been one of well drained permanent pasture, although much greater expanses existed by now.

The clover and vetch-feeding weevils of the genera *Apion* and *Sitona* (Species Group 3) comprised 4% of the terrestrial Coleoptera, which is insufficient to indicate meadowland – i.e. grassland mown for hay. The phytophagous Coleoptera again show the grassland to have been very herb-rich. All the species listed on p. 320, which feed on *Plantago lanceolata*, *Ranunculus* spp., *Trifolium* spp. and *Vicia* or *Lathyrus* spp. were present, with the exception of *Apion cerdo*. Other members of the grassland flora suggested by the Coleoptera are *Lotus corniculatus*, the favoured host of *Bruchus loti*, and grassland Compositae, on which the adults of *Olibrus* sp. occur.

The scarabaeoid dung beetles of Species Group 2 comprised 10% of the terrestrial Coleoptera from the WF1b column, which is similar to the level of abundance shown by this group from the bottom of the SS1 column. *Aphodius granarius* and *A. sphacelatus* were again the most numerous species, but they had been joined by a significant presence of *A. contaminatus*. *Onthophagus taurus* was absent but there were three individuals of another extinct dung beetle, *Aphodius varians*. This is widely distributed in France and Germany (Freude *et al.* 1969: 328; Paulian 1959: 171). In France it is usually associated with sheep droppings. There are specimens of *A. varians* in some old collections of British Coleoptera, but they are without data and their origins are suspect. Stephens (1830: 197) reported that the only indigenous specimens that he had ever seen were taken near Windsor many years before. A single specimen of *A. varians* was identified from an Iron Age deposit at Mingies Ditch, Oxon. (Allen and Robinson, in prep.).

The dung beetles from the Hydrophilidae and Staphylinidae which are not included in Species Group 2, because they do not occur only in droppings on pasture, occurred in sufficient numbers to present a balanced fauna with the Scarabaeidae. In addition to the phytophagous species and dung beetles already mentioned, most of the other terrestrial Coleoptera from the WF1b column can occur in grassland, and nowadays can be captured in areas of widespread grassland in the upper Thames valley (e.g. Robinson 1983: 50–55). There was an even representation of grassland Coleoptera throughout the waterlogged sample column.

There was not an obvious arable component to the insect assemblages from the WF1b Column although several specimens of *Agonum dorsale* and *Harpalus rufipes* (Species Group 6a) were present. Some of the phytophagous Coleoptera can feed on arable weeds, such as *Phyllotreta vittula* on cruciferous weeds and *Chaetocnema concinna* on *Polygonum aviculare*. These beetles were much more abundant than they were in the Neolithic deposits, but this was probably due in part to the Late Bronze Age environment being more open, since

none of these species is restricted to arable weeds.

The bird pellet of insect remains from layer 20 in the river channel sediments, however, presents a different picture. Just over half the beetles from it fell into the two categories that make up Species Group 6 (Table 41). Most abundant was *Harpalus rufipes*, which was represented by more individuals than were discovered in the entire WF1b column. It is a ground beetle that appears to be well adapted to conditions of arable cultivation, feeding on fallen annual weed seeds and aphids. It is often very abundant on weedy disturbed ground, particularly arable (Robinson 1983: 28–29). *Amara apricaria*, which normally occurs in weedy, open, dry places where it feeds on fallen seeds, was also represented by several individuals. It is a member of Species Group 6b. Most of the remaining insects from the bird pellet were Carabidae, which can occur in arable fields, although there were single individuals of two of the woodland carabids mentioned earlier, *Patrobus atrorufus* and *Pterostichus niger*. *P. niger* does, however, occasionally occur in arable fields. There was also a specimen of the heteropteran bug *Odontoscelis fuliginosa*, which in England is a rare species of sandy soils with a mostly coastal distribution (Southwood and Leston 1959: 31). It does, however, occur inland in certain sandy areas in Europe.

The bird which regurgitated the pellet was probably a member of the Corvidae, the crow family, because the sclerites of the large beetles were more or less intact. Corvids, which readily feed on beetles, swallow them whole, whereas owls and kestrels, which also hunt beetles, tear their prey to pieces. (Sclerites of large beetles remain intact in toad droppings but the pellet did not contain the small species also taken by toads.) The range of species in the pellet suggests the bird had been feeding on arable land before it flew to the site. Corvids do not fly long distances with a full crop, so the area of arable was probably not far beyond the catchment of the beetles in the WF1b column. There have been other archaeological finds of bird pellets containing insect remains, again probably cast by corvids (Girling 1977b).

The same species of beetles which feed on *Urtica* spp. were present as in the Neolithic, *Brachypterus urticae* being the most abundant. There was a greater range of species and also number of individuals from the genus *Apion* which feed on members of the Malvaceae than in the Neolithic samples. They had been joined by the mallow-feeding chrysomelid *Podagrica fuscipes*, *Brachypterolus pulicarius*, which feeds on *Linaria* spp., *Cryptocephalus moraei* on *Hypericum* spp. and a couple of species of *Chrysolina* on Labiatae. *Urtica dioica* and various Labiatae such as *Stachys palustris*, probably grew along the steeper parts of the river bank, to which cattle did not have access. All these herbs would have been capable of growing in neglected corners of the Late Bronze Age settlement itself, as well as at the edge of scrub or along hedgerows, where coarse herbage would experience some protection from the grazing and trampling of domestic stock.

There was again only a single specimen of the heathland

weevil *Micrelus ericae*, suggesting that there had not been any significant encroachment of heathland in the catchment. There were fewer insects from the Late Bronze Age deposits that nowadays tend to occur in sandy, coastal areas than from the Neolithic samples, but this group was not entirely absent. In addition to the bug *Odontoscelis fuliginosa* from the bird pellet, the following beetles from the WF1b columns have such a distribution: *Chrysolina* cf. *banksi* and *C. haemoptera*.

The Late Bronze Age settlement and other habitats

The insect remains of the WF1b column give little indication of the proximity of the Late Bronze Age settlement. This is probably partly because the sediments yielding insects had been deposited under flowing water conditions, so that the insect remains would have been derived from a large catchment upstream, of which the settlement comprised just a small part. Partly, however, this may be due to the samples belonging to the early phases of Late Bronze Age activities on the site, when little cultural refuse (with the exception of the localised midden several metres away) was finding its way into the channel fill. The layers were mostly cleanish flood silts until channel stage E, which lies *above* the insect preservation level.

The percentage of hydrophilids and staphylinids which occur in dung/foul organic material (Species Group 7) was lower than in the Neolithic samples, while the Lathridiidae (Species Group 8) were only slightly more abundant. Despite the presence of substantial timberwork on the site, there were very few woodworm beetles (Species Group 10) and there was only a single synanthropic beetle (Species Group 9). These four species groups showed little variation in their abundance throughout the WF1b column.

There were, however, some differences between the Neolithic and the Late Bronze Age faunas of dead and decaying plant and animal remains. The two most abundant species of *Cercyon* from the WF1b column were *C. analis* and *C. haemorrhoidalis*, which occur in dung and various other types of decaying vegetable material, whereas the most abundant species in the Neolithic samples, *C. sternalis*, which occurs on damp ground under plant detritus, was only represented by a few individuals. *Lathridius minutus* gp., which seems to show a closer association with human habitation than the other Lathridiidae identified from the site (*Enicmus transversus* and the Corticariinae), only occurred in the Late Bronze Age samples. Other beetles associated with habitats such as haystack refuse and 'sweet' compost heaps, which were noticeably present in the Late Bronze Age samples but absent from the early ones, were *Acritus nigricornis*, *Anthicus antherinus* and *An. bifasciatus*. The latter species now has a very restricted distribution in Britain, only being known from a few counties in central England (Buck 1954: 24).

Carrion beetles belonging to the following species were identified from the WF1 Column:

Thanatophilus rugosus   *Omosita colon*

Silpha tristis   *O. discoidea*
Dermestes lardarius

They only comprised 0.6% of the terrestrial Coleoptera from the column but were entirely absent from the Neolithic samples. The silphids attack carrion in its early stages of decay, whereas *Omosita* spp. are late in the succession of carrion beetles. *D. lardarius* is the bacon beetle, which nowadays most commonly occurs in buildings, where it can be a pest feeding on skins or dried meat (Hinton 1945: 284). It does, however, have outdoor habitats in Britain, such as dead animals (Fowler 1889: 358). The single synanthropic beetle from the WF1b column was *Stegobium paniceum*. It is uncertain whether it has outdoor habitats in Britain. I have identified it from rotted wood frass from inside an old hollow beech tree at Wytham Wood, Oxon. The other insects from this assemblage had been identified some years earlier, but included the rare *Prionychus ater* (Elton 1960). There is also another outdoor record of this beetle (Allen 1965a). It develops in various farinaceous materials and can be a minor pest in granaries or bakeries. However, it can also infest a great variety of other stored plant and animal products, such as spices (Harde 1984: 212). *S. paniceum* is the only grain pest to have been identified from pre-Roman sites in Britain, having been recorded from an Iron Age context at Tattershall Thorpe, Lincs. (Chowne *et al.* 1986: 177) and the Middle Bronze Age deposits at the bottom of Wilsford Shaft, Wilts. (Osborne, pers. comm.).

Although individually the presence of any one of *Lathridius minutus* gp., the 'sweet' compost beetles, the carrion beetles or even *Stegobium paniceum* could not be taken to indicate the proximity of a settlement, collectively they probably are of significance. They perhaps reflect the accumulation of refuse such as crop-processing waste and debris from butchery around the settlement. All these species first make their appearance in the column at or above a depth of 1.45–1.50 m and thereafter are of sporadic occurrence until the top of the zone of organic preservation. The first archaeological evidence for activity related to the settlement comes at a depth of about 1.40 m in the WF1b column, with the occurrence of charred debris from what appears to be clearance of localised scrub on the site. The uppermost limit for the survival of insect remains in the column was at a depth of 0.70 m, which is about 0.20 m of silting above the level at which the first pile row was inserted.

The midden

A Late Bronze Age deposit of waterlogged midden debris was found on the edge of the river channel around grid 8E/13N. The midden samples contained many beetles and fly puparia which had lived in the midden on land before the material had become incorporated into the channel sediments. Beetles from the midden were not evident in the WF1b column samples. However, samples from the column between depths of 1.25 and 1.10 m contained a few puparia of *Musca* cf. *domestica*, the housefly. Puparia of this fly were absent from the remainder of the column samples but numerous in the midden. The column sediments containing these puparia show some stratigraphic correlation with the midden deposits.

Many of the beetles from the midden samples were terrestrial and aquatic species that had not been living in the midden. However, a significant decomposer community of beetles was present. Species Group 7, which comprises certain Hydrophilidae and Staphylinidae of foul organic material, made up 17% of the terrestrial Coleoptera from the midden. The most numerous beetles of decaying organic material were:

Cercyon analis	*Leptacinus pusillus*
Oxytelus sculptus	*Gyrohypnus fracticornis*

There were numerous fly puparia in the midden, *Musca* cf. *domestica* being the most abundant, followed by *Stomoxys calcitrans*, the stable fly. The beetle community is one associated with foul rotting matter including dung (Kenwood 1982). *M. domestica* breeds in a wide range of decaying plant and animal remains (Pont 1973: 262–263, 266). *S. calcitrans* usually lays eggs on old straw or hay which has been enriched with urine and faeces, as, for example, occurs around a cattle feeding trough (Edwards *et al.* 1939: 116–117). In exceptional cases oviposition may take place on decaying vegetable material which is uncontaminated, and also on pure horse manure. Phipps (1987) notes that the association between the puparia of these two flies in archaeological deposits appears to result from oviposition by *M. domestica* in a mass of decomposing material and by *S. calcitrans* on the drying surface of the mass. The presence of a few puparia resembling those of *Scopeuma stercorarium*, the yellow dung fly, whose larvae live in fresh dung (Colyer and Hammond 1951: 252), suggests that the contents of the midden included dung. However, the plant remains from the midden included *Pteridium* frond fragments, *Sphagnum* leaves and *Linum* capsule fragments, showing that imported plant material had also been incorporated. The adult of *S. calcitrans* bites both humans and domestic animals. It can be a considerable nuisance when present in numbers.

The midden assemblage did not contain any synanthropic species such as members of the Ptinidae, and there was only a single specimen of *Anobium*. There were also few members of the Lathridiidae. If a high proportion of the debris in the midden had come from houses on the site – for example, if strewn plant material from floors had been incorporated – a much higher proportion of these species would have been expected. Such midden assemblages of indoor refuse are familiar from Roman and medieval sites.

The only other habitat suggested by the insects is that of small bodies of stagnant water. Just as in the Neolithic, a few of the water beetles from the Late Bronze Age samples are characteristic of such conditions and rarely occur in rivers.

General landscape and climatic implications

The Neolithic and Late Bronze Age landscapes

Pollen evidence suggests that at the start of the Bronze Age the British Isles were still largely wooded, although in some areas the Atlantic forest had been permanently altered and in a few places greatly reduced (Tinsley 1981: 231). However, pollen evidence is slight for some of the areas of Lowland England which in the later prehistoric period seem to have been most intensively exploited, such as the chalkland of Wessex, the terraces of the Thames and some of the major river valleys of the south Midlands. Indeed, in the case of the Wessex chalkland, land snail analysis had provided evidence for large permanent clearances from the middle of the fourth millennium cal BC onwards (Evans 1971; 1972; 1975: 116–119) which raised the possibility that these other areas could have been extensively cleared at an early date. Runnymede is situated amidst what would have been potentially useful agricultural land on the gravel terraces in an area where there is much evidence of Neolithic activity. The insect evidence from Runnymede, however, suggests that the middle Thames landscape conforms to the usual pattern for Neolithic Britain, with the survival of much woodland. Waterlogged remains from Buscot Lock, at the top of the upper Thames, suggested an even more thoroughly wooded landscape in the Late Neolithic (Robinson 1981a: 113–127; Robinson and Wilson 1987: 31–32).

The Late Neolithic insect assemblages from Runnymede are particularly interesting because they contain substantial faunal elements of open grassland as well as old woodland. Old woodland faunas, which are characterised by beetles dependent on certain habitats related to overmature or dead trees that no longer occur in modern, managed woodland, have been identified from all the sites of later Mesolithic to Neolithic date on which insect analysis has been undertaken (Girling 1982; Osborne 1978). Apart from Runnymede, the earliest substantial open country insect assemblage to have been investigated was from the Wilsford Shaft, Wilts., and dated from the Middle Bronze Age (Osborne 1969). Open country elements were also present in some of the Neolithic assemblages from the Somerset Levels (e.g. Girling 1984: 87) but these sites were set in extensive wetlands, so do not reflect typical Neolithic agricultural activities against a woodland background.

The grassland fauna from the Neolithic deposits at Runnymede, while showing some differences from more recent faunas, was well developed and species-rich. It is clear that grassland had been a feature of the landscape for a long time, and even if some of the differences from more recent faunas were due to problems of colonisation, most 'native British' potential colonists had already arrived. Apart from in Wessex and those ecologically fragile upland areas which were permanently cleared during the Neolithic, the usual pattern shown by pollen diagrams spanning the Neolithic is of a series of clearances, some small and perhaps only lasting a few decades, others large and lasting more than a century. However, even those pollen diagrams which show a gradual rise of herb pollen also show episodes of woodland regeneration. The insect sequence is consistent with such a picture of new clearances being made and colonised as other open areas were abandoned to woodland, perhaps with a few areas remaining permanently open. The old woodland beetles would have been able to colonise the regenerated areas once the trees on them had reached an appropriate state, provided populations of them existed in adjacent woodland (Elton 1966: 52).

It has been argued elsewhere that while hunting was of secondary importance to the raising of domestic stock, the gathering of wild food plants, such as hazelnuts, remained of importance alongside cereal cultivation throughout the Neolithic (Moffett *et al.* 1989). The open areas at Runnymede do indeed seem from the evidence of dung beetles to have been used for pasture but plenty of woodland remained for the collection of fruit and nuts and for the herding of pigs.

The Late Bronze Age was a period of increasing clearance and agricultural intensification over much of southern England (Robinson 1984: 9). The insect results from the deposits of this period at Runnymede duly reflected an agricultural landscape. The river seems to have been flanked by pasture, but arable was also present, perhaps on the higher ground of the gravel terraces. The middle Thames and lower Kennet gravels showed a proliferation of occupation sites in the Late Bronze Age. Insect remains have so far been examined from four of the sites: Dorney, Bucks., on the Thames gravels, and Reading Business Park, Anslow's Cottages and Knight's Farm, on the Kennet gravels in Berkshire (Bradley *et al.* 1980: 282; Robinson, unpublished). Only small assemblages were examined but these sites too seem to have been surrounded by largely open agricultural landscapes.

The insect faunas and climate
The Neolithic assemblages from Runnymede include some species that now only occur further south in Europe. Most are old woodland species whose extinction can be explained on grounds of habitat loss without any need to invoke climatic change. There remains *Onthophagus taurus*. Osborne (1982; 1988) suggested that the presence of *O. taurus* and *O. nutans*, another member of the genus now extinct in Britain, in organic silt dated between 2880 ± 100 BP and 3006 ± 117 BP at Pilgrim Lock on the River Avon, Warwicks., is evidence for warmer summer temperatures than at present. Osborne regards the habitat of this genus, dung in pastureland, as one which, unlike that of the woodland beetles, has not been greatly reduced by human activities.

Girling (1984: 80–82, 86–87) argued from the European distribution of two fenland beetles, *Chlaenius sulcicollis* and *Oodes gracilis*, which are now extinct in Britain but which she identified from Neolithic deposits in the Somerset Levels, for more continental conditions in Somerset during the Early Neolithic than today. She suggested that the mean July temperature was perhaps 2–3°C higher than at present but that the mean January temperature was depressed by a corresponding amount.

The Late Neolithic is usually regarded as a period of warm climatic conditions in England, with the overall mean temperature about 2°C warmer than at present (Lamb 1981: 53–55). It is believed that a fall in temperature occurred between about 2950 and 2700 BP to a level slightly lower than at present (Lamb 1981: 54–55).

The climatic implications of the Neolithic insect faunas from Runnymede do not support the evidence for more continental conditions, and even the evidence of the extinct *Onthophagus* spp. for warmer conditions is by no means unambiguous. One of the beetles from Runnymede, *Chrysolina banksii*, now has an Atlantic distribution in NW Europe. It does not occur in Germany but has been recorded from the coastal counties of the southern half of England. It also occurs in southern Europe (Fowler 1891: 304; Freude *et al.* 1966: 157). Its presence at Runnymede might be argued as suggesting winter temperatures no colder than at present. Most members of the genus *Onthophagus* seem to have shown a decline in numbers in England over the past 150 years unrelated to any climatic deterioration, possibly in part due to the loss of their habitat of well drained permanent pasture. There are 19th-century claims of the capture of *O. taurus* and *O. nutans* in England and while Osborne (1982; 1988) is undoubtedly correct in regarding some as dubious, there are reliable records for *O. nutans* (Allen 1965b).

The presence of many species which now have a markedly southern distribution in the Neolithic insect assemblages from Runnymede suggests that mean summer temperature was unlikely to have been any lower than at present, while the presence of *Onthophagus taurus* would not be inconsistent with summer temperatures 2–3°C higher than at present.

The Late Bronze Age insect assemblages from Runnymede also contained species with a southerly distribution in England, such as the very large weevil *Liparus coronatus* (Fowler 1891: 249). None of the beetles, however, requires warmer conditions than at present occur at Runnymede. The waterlogged deposits of the WF1b column spanned the period 1000–850 cal BC, which was during the presumed period of the most rapid climatic deterioration in the Late Bronze Age (Turner 1981: 251–261). However, there were no changes in the insect faunas which could be related to climatic change.

Chapter 18
The animal bone

Geraldene Done

Introduction: materials and methods

This account of the Runnymede animals is based on bone from the Middle and Late Neolithic and Late Bronze Ages. Of a total weight of slightly more than 100 kg, approximately two-thirds are Late Bronze Age. Late Neolithic bone consists of a small butchery deposit in silt (L40 in Area 6, trench 2). Most bone from contexts of uncertain date has been excluded from this assessment but a single beaver tibia in layer 41* must be mentioned in view of the drastic effects beavers can have on riverine landscapes.

In appearance the LBA bone was generally consistent throughout its period, as was the Neolithic bone, which was uniformly much darker, probably on account of the dark enveloping silts. Late Bronze Age bones from certain organic-rich contexts, such as the dog skeleton (F111/111A) and bones from the deeper layers of F6 and parts of L25, were closer in colour to Neolithic than to other LBA material. Preservation was generally good.

Sieving was possible only on a very limited scale on site, but recovery by hand of a number of the smaller sesamoids, cyprinid pharyngeal teeth and enough minute fragments to make the 'unidentified' count in some areas awesome suggest a high retrieval from trowelling. There remains the possibility that some of the fauna, such as small wild mammals, amphibia and fish, are missing.

The Neolithic bones were from ox, sheep/goat, pig and dog, with a fish vertebra classifiable as far as flatfish.

About 9000 LBA fragments include horse, ox, sheep and goat, pig, dog, red and roe deer, water vole, a small mustelid (one mandible in F6), duck, goose, cyprinid pharyngeal teeth, and a single fish vertebra of unknown species. The horse and dog bones included one virtually complete skeleton of each. A small amount of bone from residues from environmental sampling consisted mainly of eel vertebrae, a not unexpected finding given the location.

Fragments were counted and weighed by species or, failing that, as 'large' or 'small' animal. Ribs, which featured prominently, being often large fragments, were treated separately and also categorised as large or small animal, though it is probable that most of the large ribs are from cattle. Measurements were made whenever possible, using the system of von den Driesch (1976); withers heights were calculated from factors of Kiesewalter, Foch, Matolcsi or Teichert, quoted in von den Driesch and Boessneck (1979); Harcourt's factors (1974) were used for the dogs.

Minimum numbers were assessed on handedness of most frequently occurring bone, with adjustment for pairing on grounds of age and/or size. They were calculated for each

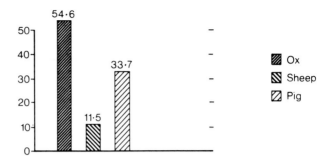

Fig. 126 Relative fragment numbers for Middle Neolithic bones from Areas 4 and 6.

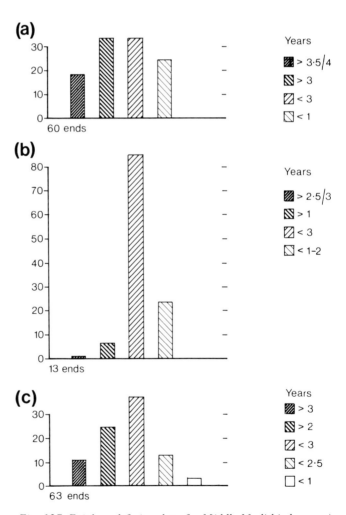

Fig. 127 Epiphyseal fusion data for Middle Neolithic bones: a) cattle; b) sheep/goats; c) pigs.

phase of the LBA and for each period as a whole (i.e. LBA or Neolithic).

Wear on teeth was classified according to Grant (1975); where age in years is given, it is based on eruption data of Sisson and Grossman (1938); epiphyseal fusion times applied are those of Silver (1963).

Middle Neolithic

Bone was recovered from Area 4 and Area 6, the former associated with artifacts and structures. The latter, forming the major part, was from stream channel deposits. Fragment counts are summarised in Table 45 and Fig. 126. A small amount of unstratified bone (A4 U/S) is tabulated separately but is probably to be considered as associated with A4 stratified material from layers 117a, 120, 121. As no characteristics of size, type, age or butchery differentiate between the groups, and as relativities between species are more or less constant, the bones are considered as one assemblage in the following account.

The species identified were ox, sheep/goat, pig, dog, red deer and an unidentifiable flatfish represented by a single vertebra.

The animals

THE CATTLE

A minimum number of seven includes one newborn and

two calves of *c.* six months. Teeth being almost totally absent, age estimates depended on fusion data (Fig. 127a). There were 29 adult bones, i.e. with late-fusing or vertebral central epiphyses completely integrated, and 24 immature bones. Dental evidence from A4 L121a consisted of one full-mouthed mandible with PM4 and M3 at wear stage b, and a pair of calf mandibles containing deciduous molars only.

A few measurements allow limited comparison with Bronze Age bones. As far as they go they show the Neolithic bones to be consistently bigger than the Runnymede LBA (Tables 46 and 47). One strikingly large calcaneum is possibly aurochs.

THE SHEEP/GOATS

Though the sheep/goat is poorly represented and the bones are uninformative, the few fragments indicate at least four animals. One-third of the bones were immature. Measurements are given in Table 48 and fusion data in Fig. 127b.

THE PIGS

As with the sheep, a relatively small number of fragments represents an unexpectedly large minimum number, in this case five. Size variation is notable (humerus Bd 34–43 mm). As to age, dental evidence consists of a single adult mandible worn as follows:-

PM3, PM4, M1 k, M2 f/g, M3 d.

About one-third of fragments were from pigs killed at less

Table 45: Animal bone fragment distribution for Middle Neolithic contexts, Areas 4 and 6.

	Ox	Sheep/Goat	Pig	LA	SA	LR	SR	Other	Unknown	Total
A4, L117a, 120, 121										
Fragment number	74	7	22	25	—	29	5	9	5	174
Fragment %	42.5	4	12.5	14.2	—	16.5	2.9	5	2.9	
Fragment wt. in g.	4075	55	555	545	—	345	20	100	175	5870
Fragment wt. %	69	0.9	9.5	9.3	—	5.9	0.3	1.7	3.0	
Av. Fragment size in g.	55	7.8	25.2	21.8	—	11.9	4	11	35	
Minimum numbers	2	1	1							
A4, U/S										
Fragment number	34	12	18	14	—	12	—	4*	—	94
Fragment %	36	12.8	19	14.9	—	12.8	—	4.3	—	
Fragment wt. in g.	3525	192	690	500	—	555	—	2580	—	8042
Fragment wt. %	43.8	2.4	8.6	6.2	—	6.9	—	32	—	
Av. Fragment size in g.	103.7	16	38.3	35.7	—	46.3	—	645	—	
Minimum numbers	3	3	2							
A6, L40, 41										
Fragment number	103	26	90	4	6	48	16	8	29	330
Fragment %	31.2	7.9	27.8	1.2	2	14.5	4.8	2	8.8	
Fragment wt. in g.	7016	418	2867	116	31	1857	108	171	170	12754
Fragment wt. %	55	3.3	22.5	0.9	0.3	14.6	0.8	1.3	1.3	
Av. Fragment wt. in g.	68	16	32	29	5	39	7	21.4	6	
Minimum numbers	7	2	5							

* Includes 3 large antler fragments.
Abbreviations: LA - large animal (horse/ox/red deer), SA - small animal (sheep/goat, pig, dog)
            LR - large animal rib, SR - small animal rib

Table 50: Measurements for Middle Neolithic dog bones (in millimetres)

Humerus	Bd 26		
Ulna	GL 152, DPA 20, SDO 11.5		
Tibia	GL	Bp	Bd
	139	28	17.5
	150	—	19
	160	27	18.5

Late Neolithic

This isolated deposit, F125 (Plate 19; Fig. 19), in L40 consisted of 111 fragments plus *c.* 116 scraps; 95 fragments were identified, all from ox and conceivably from a single beast. Bones identified were:

a pair of horn cores
a pair of maxillae/premaxillae
a pair of mandibles
parts of cervical, thoracic and lumbar vertebrae
two rib heads
left radius
left femur

Dental and fusion evidence gave an age of *c.* 3 years (I1 in wear, I2U, I3V, DI3, and 4 present, PM4 1/2, M1g, M2f, M3c). The third molars of the upper jaw were unworn though well up, all vertebral centra were unfused, as were rib heads, and the head and distal epiphysis of femur.

Both mandibles had been chopped through at the level of PM2/3; the left was missing behind this point but the right had been chopped, again behind M3. This pattern of butchery is not uncommon in archaeological bone, but its objective is by no means clear, as an easier way to dismantle the jaw is to split it through the symphysis. Four fragments of thoracic centrum were almost sagittal halves. Long-bone shaft fragments resulting from butchery were well enough preserved in some cases to allow chopped or split surfaces to be accurately fitted together. Other pieces were chipped and flaked, as though the butchering had been laborious.

Late Bronze Age

The bones were examined in the following context groups initially, in order to identify any spatial or, in the river channel, temporal trends. However, they are considered below as a single group unless stated otherwise. Table 52 summarises the fragment distribution.

River channel
Units A–B
Units C–D
Units E–D
Units H–J
Occupation
Pit F6

Table 51: Bone frequency for Middle Neolithic bones (based on fragment number)

	Ox	A4, L117a, 120, 121 Sheep/Goat	Pig	Ox	A4, U/S Sheep/Goat	Pig	Ox	A6, L40, 41 Sheep/Goat	Pig
Horn core	—	1	—	2	—	—	—	—	—
Skull	6	1	6	—	—	—	2	3	5
Maxilla	3	—	1	1	—	—	—	—	—
Mandible	8	1	2	1	—	1	2	1	3
C. vertebra	5	—	—	2	—	2	4	1	5
T. vertebra	12	—	—	2	1	—	20	1	9
L. vertebra	—	—	3	—	—	—	—	—	3
Sacrum	1	—	—	—	—	—	1	—	—
Scapula	2	—	2	2	—	1	1	2	6
Humerus	2	—	1	5	—	2	1	4	10
Radius	1	—	2	2	—	2	4	4	8
Ulna	1	—	—	—	—	—	1	3	3
Metacarpal	—	2	1	1	3	1	5	1	2
Innominate	2	—	1	1	1	—	8	2	9
Femur	1	1	—	2	1	1	8	2	9
Tibia	—	—	—	1	3	4	5	2	5
Calcaneum	2	—	—	—	—	—	4	—	3
Astragalus	1	—	—	1	—	—	3	—	2
Metatarsal	1	—	1	—	—	1	1	—	5
1st phalanx	—	—	—	2	—	—	1	1	—
2nd phalanx	2	—	—	—	—	—	1	—	—
3rd phalanx	—	—	1	—	—	—	2	—	—

Table 52: Animal bone fragment distribution for Late Bronze Age contexts, Area 6, divided into major context groups.

	Horse	Ox	Sheep/Goat	Pig	LA	SA	LR	SR	Other	Unknown	Total
Units A–B											
Fragment number	4	51	21	23	16	1	16	11	2	31	176
Fragment %	2	29	12	13	9	0.5	9	6	1	17.5	
Fragment wt. in g.	407	4022	248	674	459	1	148	27	43	164	6193
Fragment wt. in %	6.5	64.9	4	11	7	0.2	2.4	0.5	0.7	2.7	
Av. fragment size in g.	102	79	12	29	28.5	1	9	2.5	21	5	
Minimum numbers	P	3	2	2							
Units C–D											
Fragment number	1	79	74	62	29	5	38	14	29	148	479
Fragment %	0.2	16.4	15.4	12.9	6	1	8	3	6	31	
Fragment wt. in g.	205	5563	681	998	836	66	698	145	354	288	9834
Fragment wt. %	2	57	7	10	8.5	0.7	7	1.5	3.5	3	
Av. fragment size in g.	205	70	9	16	29	13	18	10.5	9	1.5	
Minimum numbers	P	3	2	3							
Units E–G											
Fragment number	26	164	125	178	67	5	61	75	58	1606	2365
Fragment %	1	7	5	7.5	3	0.2	2.5	3	2.5	68	
Fragment wt. in g.	1389	4778	490	1745	1206	6	593	76	536	3240	14059
Fragment wt. %	9	34	3.5	12.5	8.5	0.04	4	0.5	4	23	
Av. fragment size in g.	53	29	4	10	18	1	10	1	9	2	
Minimum numbers	2	4	3	7							
Units H–J											
Fragment number	5	89	152	204	127	248	31	78	19	1083	2036
Fragment %	0.25	4	7.5	10	6	12	1.5	4	1	53	
Fragment wt. in g.	200	2477	597	1611	1250	470	455	183	263	1209	8715
Fragment wt. %	2	28	7	18.5	14	5.5	5	2	3	14	
Av. fragment size in g.	40	28	4	8	10	2	14.5	2.5	14	1	
Minimum numbers	P	4	3	6							
Occupation											
Fragment number	39	201	169	248	135	55	57	76	12	2195	3187
Fragment %	1	6	5	8	4	2	2	2	0.4	69	
Fragment wt. in g.	1631	5790	675	2046	1707	152	816	232	403	5144	18596
Fragment wt. %	9	31	3.5	11	9	1	4	1	2	28	
Av. fragment size in g.	42	29	4	8	12.5	3	14	3	33.5	2	
Minimum numbers	?2	5	6	8							
Pit F6											
Fragment number	3	109	65	89	134	64	42	27	4	475	1020
Fragment %	0.3	11	6	9	13	6	4	3	0.4	47	
Fragment wt. in g.	37	3716	323	1076	956	152	418	85	10	870	7643
Fragment wt. %	0.5	49	4	14	12.5	2	5.5	2	0.1	11	
Av. fragment size in g.	12	34	5	12	7	2.5	10	3	2.5	2	
Minimum numbers	1	4	3	3							

(F6 figures exclude horse skeleton)

Table 53: Measurements for the Late Bronze Age horse skeleton from pit F6 (in millimetres).

Axial skeleton:

Skull (L5)
Atlas (L5)

BFcr	87
GLF	80
H	76.5

Axis (L5)

LCDe	142.5
BFcr	80
SBV	40

Cervical vertebrae (L5)

	C3	C4	C5	C6	C7
PL	90	83	79	75	58
GLPa	109	115.5	111.5	95.5	—
BPacr	69	69	71	72.5	—
BPacd	—	65	67.5	73	78
BFcr	31	31	32	32	31
BFcd	c. 41.5	44.5	46	45.5	60
Hcr	30	29	32	32	35.5
Hcd	47	43	—	—	40

Thoracic vertebrae (L5)

	T1	T2
PL	46	43
BFcr	29	62.5
BFcd	59	57
Hcr	31	31
Hcd	35.5	—

Lumbar vertebrae (L5)

	L1	L2	L3	L4	L5
PL	—	44	46	47	45
BFcr	—	42.5	47	51	47.5
BFcd	43	45	50	51	48.5
Hcr	—	35	35.5	30.5	29
Hcd	35	34	32	26	22

Sacrum (L5)

BFcr	46
Hcr	20

Appendicular skeleton:

Fore limb

Scapula

	L (L5)	R (L5)
SLC	67	—
GLP	91	92
LG	53.5	55
BG	46.5	c. 45

Humerus

	R (L5)
Bd	c. 75
BT	71

Radius

	L (L5)	R (L5)
Gl	330	328
GL1	318	316
Bp	80	80
BFp	71	71
SD	36.5	36
CD	104	103
Bd	75	75.5
BFD	63	63

Ulna

	L (L5)	R (L5)
GL	—	390
SDO	—	44.5
DPA	c. 61	63
BPC	41	43

Carpals (L5)

Metacarpal

	L (L5)	R (L5)
GL	210	210
GL1	208	208.5
L1	202	204
Bp	46	—
SD	31.5	31.5
CD	91	92
Bd	47	47
Dd	34	34.5

1st Phalanx

	L (L5)	R (L5)
GL	83	83
Bp	55	55
BFp	49.5	48.5
SD	35	35
Bd	47	47.5
BFd	43.5	44

2nd Phalanx

	L (L5)	R (L5)
GL	45	44
Bp	54.5	54.5
BFp	46	47
Dp	30	29.5
SD	46	46.5
Bd	50	50.5

3rd Phalanx

	L (L5)	R (L5)
GL	70	70
GB	81	81
LF	24.5	25
BF	50.5	50
LD	49	50
HP	38	38

Hind limb

Pelvis (L5)

	L	R
LA	65	—
LAR	60.5	—

Femur

	L (L5/6)	R (L5)
Bp	116	117
DC	54	54
SD	36	36
CD	148	148
Bd	87	—

Patella

	L (L5)	R (L5)
GL	64.5	65
GB	64	64.5

Tibia

	L (L5/6)	R (L5)
GL	343	341
L1	307	—
Bp	94.5	—
SD	38	38
CD	111	112
Bd	73	73
Dd	44.5	44

Fibula (L5)

Astragalus

	L (L6)	R (L6)
GH	58	58
GB	60	60
BFd	50.5	50
LmT	60.5	60

Calcaneum

	L (L6)	R (L6)
GL	107.5	106.5
GB	50.5	51

Central tarsal

	R
GB	49

Metatarsal

	L (L6)	R (L6)
GL	—	254
GL1	—	251
L1	—	246.5
Bp	—	47.5
SD	30	29
CD	95	95
Bd	47	47
Dd	45.5	46

1st Phalanx

	L
GL	76
Bp	55
BFp	51
Dp	33
SD	33
Bd	45
BFd	42

3rd Phalanx

	L
GL	66
GB	74
LF	26
BF	48
LD	53
HP	42

The animals

THE HORSES

Pit F6 contained the almost complete skeleton of one horse (other horse bones are described below). The measurements of its bones and their location in the pit are given in Table 53.

The F6 horse stood somewhat over 13 hands – 1332 mm – and was probably male, with well developed canine teeth in the upper jaw (lower jaw missing). Its age was judged to be about 10 years, though irregularity of wear has produced an atypical appearance. As Plate 74 shows, wear on the occlusal surfaces of the central and lateral incisors has continued on to the labial surface. This sort of wear pattern would not result from mere browsing but would be caused by persistent gnawing of some solid fixed object, perhaps the bark of a tree or, if the horse were in any way housed, a wall, hitching post or manger. The horse bones in F6 mainly lay in layer 5, with parts of pelvis and hind limb dropping down into layer 6, where they became darker in colour. In the left hind limb the third tarsal was ankylosed with the proximal end of the metatarsal, with exostoses extending towards the muscle insertion on the cranial face of the metatarsal (Plate 75). The lesion would have caused pain and lameness while developing, probably settling down in time to leave a degree of stiffness or disability. The skull (in pieces), the cervical and lumber vertebrae, the sacrum, the entire forelimbs, a proximal femur and some rib and pelvic fragments were lodged in layer 5 with two thoracic vertebrae. The remaining 16 thoracic vertebrae were missing.

The skull lay palate uppermost, parts of maxilla and maxillary molars being in layer 3. There was no mandible; a molar-in-jaw fragment and another molar in layer 3 are of the right age but cannot be ascribed with certainty to this horse.

The forelimbs were found in articulation, lying on top of each other as though the 'arms' were crossed, i.e. left proximal metacarpal to right distal metacarpal. This is a position the horse is incapable of attaining in life, or even after death. As Plate 50 shows, the arrangement seems too neat to have happened by chance after a degree of decomposition had freed the bones from their surrounding soft tissues sufficiently to allow them to adopt a bizarre relationship. If they were placed deliberately, for whatever reason, dismemberment must have preceded burial. The remaining bones are not entirely random, though disturbed, and ritual burial, subsequently interfered with, cannot be ruled out. It is, however, quite easy to remove forelimbs and when getting even a moderate-sized horse into a hole it may be helpful to do so.

A further 78 fragments of horse bones were distributed through all context groups. An estimate of withers height made from a metatarsal was 1236 mm; the available teeth indicate at least one young horse (premolar with most of reserve crown unused), and at least one horse aged 15 years or more. These fragments are from at least three individuals, the F6 horse making a minimum of four.

THE CATTLE

693 fragments of ox bone were identified representing 376 possible bones and at least 13 beasts overall, or 23 if a running total is made over all context groups. Withers heights ranged from 1003 mm to 1225 mm (seven measurements, see Table 54), the spread being similar to that observed previously at Runnymede (Done 1980) and body size is again probably generally small. Six of nine mandibles with teeth contained deciduous molars at various wear stages and two had attained adult dentition (Table 55). The loose teeth included both deciduous and very worn permanent teeth, but the indications are that most cattle were killed as young adults at an age for economic meat production. The m_3 wear stage data might suggest killing at a younger age than this – milk production provides one possible explanation. The patterns of epiphyseal fusion shown in Fig. 128a are derived from relatively small numbers, but might indicate some change in killing age in the later group, when the proportion of cattle killed at less than three years increases sharply.

All parts of the skeleton are represented in all context groups without major discrepancy, and indeed with a good overall correlation (Table 56). Two almost complete horn cores from F6 exhibited slight downward and forward curve. Two more horn core stumps from F6 were possibly a pair and apparently the consequence of horn removal from the living animal, as both cavities were sealed with cancellous bone resulting from a healing process (Plate 76). A similar stump was found among fired bones in the occupation levels. Accidental loss of horns is not uncommon and evidence is occasionally seen in excavated material (Grant 1975; Baker and Brothwell 1980), but three instances from a relatively small excavated area must reduce the probability of accident, and the neatness and symmetry of the unburnt stumps strongly suggest deliberate removal.

There is possible weapon damage to an ox scapula from L25 (units A–B). The position of the hole is right for an attack on the vital organs of the thorax (Noe Nygard 1974) and the damage itself is not, in the writer's opinion, the sort of break to which excavated shoulder blades are vulnerable. While weapon damage to a deer scapula is readily acceptable, in the ox it is a puzzle. Was the beast wild, unapproachable for some reason or a victim of poaching?

THE SHEEP/GOATS

An overall minimum number of 12 was calculated, the running total by context group being 20. Sheep and goats were identified. Three complete metacarpals gave withers heights which slightly extend the range of five heights calculated from bones from the preceding excavation (1976: 568–604 mm; 1978: 590–619 mm). The measured bones (Table 57) with few exceptions outscore those of a five-year-old farm-bred Soay ewe in the writer's reference collection,

Table 54: Measurements for Late Bronze Age cattle bones (in millimetres)

Horn core	BC	GL				Context/unit
	130	c.120				F6
	146	165				F6
	113					F6
	116					F6

Scapula	GLP	LG	BG	SLC		
	61	52	45	45		A–B
		55	50.5	53		A–B

Humerus	BT	Bd	SD		
	71		29.5		A–B
	65.5				C–D
	65.6	68			E–G
	67.5	72			E–G
	75	79			E–G
	52.5	53			E–G
	62.5	77.5			Occ
	63				F6
	76.5				H–J
	57.5				H–J

Radius

GL	Bp	BFp	Bd	BFd	SD	
246	69	63	c.54		32.5	A–B
	72.5	66.5			36	A–B
244	71	65	57.5	54	31	C–D
285	81	73	79	73	37	C–D
251	74	66.5	60.5	55		Occ

Metacarpal	GL	Bp	Bd	SD	
		45		25	A–B
	174	48	50	26	E–G
		50			E–G
		49			Occ
		50			Occ
		51		30	Occ
			61		Occ
		46			F6
	193	60	61	33.5	H–J

Pelvis	LA		
	59		E–G
	69		E–G
	58		Occ
	55		F6

Femur	DC	Bd	
	39		A–B
		78	C–D
	36		Occ

Tibia	Bp	Bd	
		50	C–D
		57	C–D
		56.5	E–G
	84.5		Occ
		57	F6

Table 54: Measurements for Late Bronze Age cattle bones (in millimetres) (continued).

Calcaneum	GL	GB		
	83.5	23		Occ
	108	38		Occ
	110	38		Occ
	122	36		F6

Astragalus	GLl	GLm	PW*	DW*	
	58	52.5	37.5	36.5	A–B
	58	54.5	39	36.5	A–B
	56	52	36	35	C–D
	58	53.5	38	36	C–D
	57.5	52	35	34.5	C–D
	58	54.5	38	36	E–G
	58	52	37	34.5	E–G
	61.5	53.5	39	39.5	E–G
	56	50	35.5	33.5	E–G
	58	54	37	38	Occ
	58.5	52	35.5	35.5	Occ
	61	56	38	38	Occ
	61	54.5	42.5	41	Occ
	57.5	53	36.5	36.5	Occ
				40.5	Occ
	61	54	41	37.5	F6
	57.5	54	32	35	F6
	59	54	40	38.5	H–J

Metatarsal	GL	Bp	Bd	SD	
		46.5		26	A–B
				25	A–B
		47		26.5	E–G
		43		23.5	E–G
		40		23	E–G
		49		27	Occ
		46		26	F6
	184	40	51	22	H–J
		39.5		25	H–J

* These dimensions are equivalent to PW and DW of Runnymede 1976 (Done 1980).

Table 55: Mandibular tooth wear data for Late Bronze Age cattle

m_1	m_2	m_3	PM_2	PM_3	PM_4	M_1	M_2	M_3
a	a	e						
—	U	—						
/	/	—						
—	/	a						
/	/	c	—	—	—	V	—	—
/	/	d	—	—	V	—	—	—
/	/	g	—	—	—	1/2	—	—
—	—	—	—	/	c	g	g	c*
—	—	—	—	/	e	k	k	j
—	—	—	/	/	—	k	j	f

Loose teeth:
m_3 a, 2c, f, 2g
M_1 1 g.
M_2 1 U.
$M_{1/2}$ a, q, h, k, o
M_3 1 U, 1 E, 1 b, 2 f, 2 g, 1 l, 1 j.

* Two cusps only.
/ present

Table 56: Bone frequency for Late Bronze Age bones (based on fragment number.)

	Ox	Sheep/goat	Pig	Horse
Skull	67	34	99	2
Horn core	10	7	—	—
Maxilla	9	11	68	1
Mandible	27	42	59	—
Atlas	4	2	7	—
Axis	2	4	5	—
C. vertebra	32	16	9	5
T. vertebra	27	22	20	7
L. vertebra	28	13	7	2
Sacrum	3	5	—	1
Scapula	11	34	36	—
Humerus	22	28	28	—
Radius	21	24	23	—
Ulna	14	9	29	—
Carpal	25	10	7	3
Metacarpal	24	16	17	1
Pelvis	30	27	22	—
Femur	22	34	9	4
Patella	1	8	4	—
Tibia	22	29	27	1
Fibula	—	—	4	1
Malleolus	1	—	—	—
Astragalus	20	12	10	—
Calcaneum	21	6	8	—
Tarsals	12	12	3	3
Metatarsals	19	26	24	4
1st Phalanx	39	16	46	3
2nd Phalanx	18	18	27	4
3rd Phalanx	8	7	16	2
Sesamoids	8	—	—	1
Loose teeth:				
Incisor	10	6	44	3
Canine	—	—	14	—
Molar	66	79	63	2
Deciduous I.	1	1	3	—
Deciduous M.	9	1	3	1

Notes
F6 skeleton excluded from horse fragments.
Ox skull figure includes as 1 one almost complete skull.
Ox – 376 possible bones + one skull.
Sheep/goat – 293 possible bones.
Pig – 449 possible bones.

Table 57: Measurements for Late Bronze Age sheep/goat bones (in millimetres).

Horn core	GL	BC						
(Goat)	c.70	73						C–D
(Goat)	135	c.200						C–D
(Goat)	75	93						C–D

Scapula							
HS	DHA	LD	SLC	GLP	BG	LG	
130	136	80	15	26.5	17	20	A–B
				26	15	21	Occ
				25		19	Occ
				29	17	23	H–J

Humerus	BT	Bd	
	26		C–D
	21.5	24	C–D
	25		E–G
	24		Occ
	26		Occ

Radius	Bp	BFp	Bd	
			25	E–G
	25			F6
	26			F6
	25	24		H–J
	25			H–J

Metacarpal	GL	Bp	Bd	SD	
	128	19	19.5	9	A–B
	119	17.5	20	9	C–D (Plate 52)
		18.5		10.5	C–D
	122	19	21		E–G
		19		10	E–G
			23		H–J

Pelvis	GL	LA	SH	SB	LF	
	162	23	12	6.5	33	A–B
		28.5				C–D
		28				E–G
		25				E–G
	c.159	25	13	8		F6
		25				H–J

Femur	DC	Bd	
	16.5		A–B
		35	A–B
		31.5	A–B
	19.5		E–G
	20		Occ
	18.5		H–J
	18		H–J

Tibia	GL	Bp	Bd	
			21	A–B
	196	35.5	24.5	C–D
			23	H–J

Calcaneum	GL	GB	
	49	18	A–B
		15	Occ

(continued)

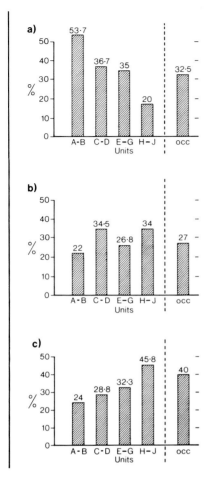

Fig. 129 Changing bone fragment percentages of the main domestic species through the Late Bronze Age river channel sequence, and in the occupation deposits on the levee for comparison: a) cattle; b) sheep/goats; c) pigs.

Table 57: **Measurements for Late Bronze Age sheep/goat bones (in millimetres) (continued).**

Astragalus	GLI	GLm	PW*	DW*	
	25	23	18	16	C–D
	26	24	16	17.5	C–D
	25	24	16	16	C–D
	26	25.5	17	17	E–G
	23	22	14	14	Occ
	25.5	24	15	16	Occ
	25.5	25	17	16	Occ
	27	27	18	16	H–J
Metatarsal	Bd				
	21				Occ
	21				Occ

* These dimensions are equivalent to PW and DW of Runnymede 1976 (Done 1980).

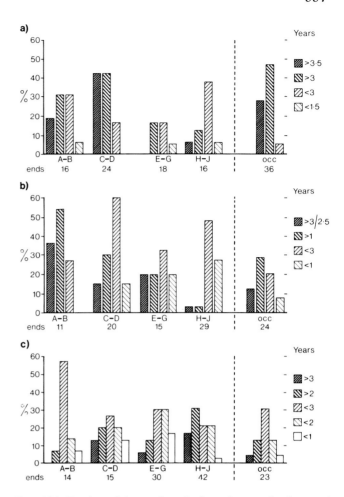

Fig. 128 Epiphyseal fusion data for Late Bronze Age bones: a) cattle; b) sheep/goats, c) pigs.

Table 58: **Mandibular tooth wear data for Late Bronze Age sheep/goats.**

m_1	m_2	m_3	PM_2	PM_3	PM_4	M_1	M_2	M_3
/	/	f						
—	/	f						
—	/	g						
—	/	g						
—	/	g	—	—	—	U	—	—
—	—	g	—	—	—	U	—	—
—	/	g	—	—	—	f	—	—
/	/	g	—	—	—	f	V	—
—	—	g	—	—	—	g	1/2	—
—	/	g	—	—	—	g	—	—
—	—	/	—	—	—	—	f	U
—	—	h	—	—	—	g	f	—
/	/	—	—	—	—	g	b	—
/	/	—	—	—	—	g	c	—
—	—	—	—	—	1/2	g	f	E
—	—	—	—	—	—	g	g	c
—	—	—	—	—	—	g	f/g	d
—	—	—	—	—	—	—	g	e
—	—	—	—	—	g	h	h	d
—	—	—	—	—	h	j	g	f

Key to Table 58   Loose teeth:
$M_{1/2}$ c, 2e, f, 3h, l
M_3 3g, h
/ present

338

Table 59: Measurements for Late Bronze Age pig bones (in millimetres)

M_3
L

30, 31, 32.5, 33, 33, 36.		Occ
32, 33, 35.		F6
29		E–G
30, 32, 35.		H–J

Mandible
(A–B)
(2) 258, (4) 172, (6) 130.5, (7) 124, (7a) 102, (8) 63, (9) 58, (9a) 38.5, (11) 48, (12) 72, (16c) 44, (21) 12.5.
(E–G)
(6) 114, (7) 111.5, (7a) 98, (8) 62, (9) 47, (9a) 34, (16a) 45.5, (16b) 37.5, (16c) 38.

Scapula	GLP	LG	BG	
			25.5	C–D
	34	27	24	C–D
	35	29.5	23	E–G
	31.5	25	20	Occ
			23	Occ
	36	29.5	26	H–J
	35	28.5	23.5	H–J

Humerus	Bd	
	36	A–B
	47, 48	C–D
	33	E–G
	38, 38, 39	Occ
	36.5, 48.5	F6

Radius	GL	Bp	Bd	SD	
		31			A–B
		25			C–D
		27.5			E–G
		29			E–G
		29.5			E–G
	159.5	32.5	35	22	H–J
		32	34	19	H–J
		30		18	H–J

Ulna	GL	DPA	SDO	
	190	39	29.5	A–B
		33		F6
		40	32	F6
	223	41	31.5	H–J
		40	31	H–J

3rd metacarpal	GL	Bp	Bd	
		16.5		C–D
	81.5	16.5	17.5	H–J
		19.5		H–J

4th metacarpal				
		14.5	15	F6
	70	16	16.5	H–J

Pelvis	LA	LAR	SH	
	34	31	22	A–B
	34			C–D
	32			E–G
	35			E–G
	32	30		Occ
	35.5	34		H–J
	35	33.5		H–J

Femur	DC	
	24	Occ

Tibia	Bd	
	29	E–G
	29.5	Occ

Astragalus	GLl	GLm	
	42.5	40	C–D
	39	37	C–D
	40	38	E–G
	43	40	E–G
	47	43	Occ
	42	39	H–J
	39	34.5	H–J
	43	40.5	H–J

3rd metatarsal	GL	Bp	LeP	Bd	B	
	105	17.5				A–B
		15				A–B
		14				E–G
		15				E–G
		15.5				E–G
	89	23.5	86	25.5		Occ
	86	17	83	16	14	F6
	83	12	81	15	11	H–J
		18.5				H–J

4th metatarsal	Bp	
	15	Occ
	13	H–J
	15	H–J
	16	H–J

which was killed in good condition at 21.8 kg, carcase weight 11.5 kg, withers height 527 mm.

Wear stages of teeth in 19 mandibles are set out in Table 58. The pattern tends towards killing young, for the pot, but the available data are inconclusive. Epiphyseal fusion is also equivocal (Fig. 128b).

There were bones from all parts of the skeleton (Table 56), with no sign of disease except for gross exostosis of a first phalanx (Plate 77). There is also the inexplicable damage to a distal metacarpal done by a bone point (B4; Chapter 7) found tightly embedded in the condyle (Plate 52). The incident happened after death, or conceivably at the time of death.

THE PIGS

The pig features prominently in this collection – minimum numbers 18 overall, running total 29 – and exhibits none of the uniformity of size of the ruminant species. Distal humeri from 33 mm to 48.5 mm (eight bones), with wide variation in size of other bones, confirm that the pig was by no means stabilised as a type and that the population was in a state of variation over a large range (Table 59).

Pig was present in all context groups, fragments outnumbering those of cattle in occupation levels and in the post-waterfront stages of the river channel (Table 52 and Fig. 129). Half of 23 mandibles presenting ageable teeth were probably less than two years old, with only one instance of heavily worn molars among the rest. The known variability of tooth wear in the pig prevents dependable construction of a pattern of age at death, but that young adulthood is a likely norm is supported by the fusion data (Fig. 128c). Dental wear stages are set out in Table 60.

THE DOGS

A complete dog skeleton, F111/111A, was found isolated from the general scatter of bone in trench 2. Its disposition is shown in Plate 43 and Fig. 29: though the head appears well separated from the rest it is not a decapitation. The spinal column was breached between the fourth and fifth thoracic vertebrae, i.e. at the level of the shoulder, and there are no cut or chop marks. It is likely that separation happened after decomposition was well advanced and the bones were no longer held firmly together by ligaments, etc. The disruption of the skeleton is perhaps too great to be attributed to earthworms or soil movement but explanatory scenarios such as an inrush of flood water, pigs prospecting for food or fishermen seeking maggots come readily to mind.

The dog, which was male, stood about 56 cm high at the shoulder (measurements Table 61), appears strongly built, with a 'retrieving' rather than a 'racing' head and had undoubtedly been afflicted with toothache, culminating in 'death' of the lower right carnassial. Judging by the excessive wear on the teeth of the normal left mandible, the tooth had been a long-standing seat of pain, though it is unlikely to have caused death as the sufferer had plainly managed to eat avoiding it. The dead tooth is 3 mm shorter than the corresponding tooth (lower left carnassial) and grey in colour rather than ivory (Plate 78). Radiographs showed no underlying lesion to account for this condition.

In addition to this skeleton, dog bones were present in all context groups except pit F6. Half of the 56 fragments identified (there were a further 54 possible bones) were from the waterfront stages in the channel (units E–G) and from at least four dogs. No sound length measurements were possible but one incomplete radius is plainly that of a very small dog. Harcourt (1974), discussing dogs of the Bronze Age as a whole, expresses misgivings as to the provenance of two small skulls as such a degree of variation was unexpected in a pre-Roman period. A single damaged bone may not dispel such doubts but it is perhaps pertinent to add that

Table 60: Mandibular tooth wear data for Late Bronze Age pigs.

I_1	I_2	I_3	C	m_1	m_2	m_3	PM_2	PM_3	PM_4	M_1	M_2	M_3
U	—	—	U	—	—	—	E	—	—	—	—	—
U	U	U	U	—	—	—	—	—	—	—	—	—
U	U	U	—	—	—	—	—	—	e	m	g	b
—	V	—	E	/	/	—	—	—	—	—	—	—
—	—	—	—	—	—	—	—	V	E	—	—	—
—	—	—	—	—	/	g	—	V	V	b	—	—
—	—	—	—	—	—	—	—	V	V	d	—	—
—	—	—	—	—	—	—	—	—	U	d	a	—
—	—	—	—	—	—	j	—	—	—	b	E	—
—	—	—	—	—	/	j	—	—	—	d	E	—
—	—	—	—	—	—	—	—	—	c	c	a	—
/	/	/	/	—	—	—	—	/	c	f	e	a
/	—	—	/	—	—	—	—	/	c	j	—	—
—	—	—	—	—	—	—	—	—	d	f	c	—
—	—	—	—	—	—	—	—	—	—	e	c	V
—	—	—	/	—	—	—	/	/	e	l	f	a
—	—	—	—	—	—	—	—	—	—	—	e	a
—	—	—	—	—	—	—	/	/	f	l	—	—
—	—	—	—	—	—	—	/	/	/	l	g	a
—	—	—	—	—	—	—	/	/	e	—	f	c
—	—	—	—	—	—	—	—	—	f	j	h	c
—	—	—	—	—	—	—	—	—	—	—	h	e
—	—	—	—	—	—	—	/	/	d	—	g	e
—	—	—	—	—	—	—	—	—	—	—	h	f
—	—	—	—	—	—	—	—	—	—	—	l	k

Loose teeth:
M_1 1 U, 2 h.
M_2 2 U, 1 E, 3 b, 2 d, 2 d/e, 2 f.
M_3 3 U, 2 E, 2 a, 1 b, 2 d/e, 1 e.

/ present

throughout the examination of the waterfront assemblage unidentifiable fragments of a small mammal were noted; cat was suspected, a diagnostic fragment hoped for and in due course the dog radius of appropriate size presented itself.

The remaining fragments are unremarkable except for a humerus with considerable callus formation on the proximal shaft, probably in response to a fracture.

THE DEER

A small number of red deer bones occurred in all context groups except the early channel deposits (units A–B). They were mainly distal limb bones, along with five antler fragments, three of which were worked. Unless a large proportion of pieces classified as large animal are in fact deer, rather than ox or horse, it seems that red deer was in the nature of a fringe benefit. Two roe deer fragments were identified.

Relationships and uses

Excursions over the shifting sands of quantitative analysis are based on data summarised in Table 52. There are many much-discussed caveats about interpretation of archaeo-

Table 61: Measurements for the Late Bronze Age dog skeleton, F111/111a (in millimetres)

Skull

(1)	c.198	(15)	69	(27)	21
(2)	c.171	(15a)	15	(28)	18.5
(3)	171	(16)	21.5	(29)	57
(4)	48	(17)	52	(30)	—
(5)	c.121	(18)	20	(31)	37
(6)	—	(18a)	9.5	(32)	55
(7)	102	(19)-		(33)	41
(8)	86	(20)	14x17	(34)	73
(9)	c.106	(21)	7x10	(35)	42
(10)	—	(23)	—	(36)	45
(11)	49	(24)	72	(37)	—
(12)	78	(25)	39	(38)	66
(13)	95	(26)	55.5	(39)	60.5
(14)	—	(27)	21	(40)	51

Left Mandible

(1)	150	(8)	71	(15)	10x6
(2)	153	(9)	67	(16)	—
(3)	143	(10)	72	(17)	13
(4)	123	(11)	38	(18)	59
(5)	121	(12)	34	(19)	28
(6)	130	(13)	26x9*	(20)	22
(7)	76	(14)	22.5	(21)	44 (L 43)

* R 23x9

Appendicular Skeleton

Scapula GLP 33, LG 29, BG 19, HS 144.
Humerus GL 169, GLC 165, Dp 43.5, SD 14, Bd 36.5.
Radius GL 165, Bp 20, SD 14, Bd 26.
Ulna GL 196, DPA 28, SDO 24.
Pelvis GL 157, LA 24, SH 21, SB 10.
Femur GL 182, GLC 180, DC 19, Bp 40, SD 14, Bd 33.5.
Tibia GL 181, Bp 37.5, SD 12.5, Bd 24.
Calcaneum GL 47, GB 18.5.

Note:

Right bones listed. Left bones as above except for L. humerus Bd 37 and L. calcaneum GB 21.

zoological numbers; the difficulties can be illustrated by estimating the expected total bone weight for the minimum numbers proposed.

Assuming a live weight of 350 kg for each of the cattle, of which about 7% would be bone, we might expect over 300 kg of bone from 13 cattle; in fact 27 kg was positively identified, rising to 36 kg if all large animal fragments and large ribs are regarded as ox. Much has been lost, as might indeed be expected with the nearby river as a handy waste receptacle. However, using the data at face value, the standing of the pig in the economy is striking (Fig. 129). Both in fragment count and minimum number it proceeds towards eventually outscoring cattle, the weight difference reflecting only the intrinsic difference in size between ox and pig bones.

Relatively few instances of carnivorous chewing (and two of rodent gnawing) are in themselves insignificant, except as indicators of another possible cause of bone loss.

No estimate of the male/female ratio could be made for any of the food animals. The apparent age structure of the cattle population militates against postulation of a dairying aspect to the economy: some firmer indication of cows being kept on over a period of years might be expected if that were the case. In terms of meat, cattle would have been the main source, with pig contributing about one-quarter of the supply. Horse is included in the meat weight assessment as there are signs of butchery on horse bones. Although it appears to contribute significantly to the meat supply, it was probably not primarily a food animal, the number of fragments being small compared with the other meat producers. A meat weight guesstimate might be proposed as follows:

13 cattle at 350 kg live wt. – 175 kg killed wt. – 2275 kg meat; 58%

12 sheep at 25 kg live wt. – 12.5 killed wt. – 150 kg meat; 4%

18 pigs at 100 kg live wt. – 50 kg killed wt. – 900 kg meat; 23%

3 horses at 400 kg live wt. – 200 kg killed wt. – 600 kg meat; 15%

Acceptance of these possible meat yields leaves the sheep contributing so small a share as to bring in to question its role as a food staple. Milk and wool may well have been important but cannot easily be reconciled with the killing of an apparently high proportion of young adults. It might be that sheep meat had some special status, akin to the Christmas turkey, which made sheep-keeping worthwhile even when output could only be relatively low. On the other hand, the sheep is the subsistence animal *par excellence* and was perhaps worth maintaining as a prudent insurance against hard times.

While ruminants and horses have more to offer the economy than food, the pigs are not to be dismissed solely as a source of meat. They also efficiently clear and break up uncultivated land, a pioneering quality which may have been very useful to the Runnymede farmers. Their capacity for

rootling exploration of the soil can be useful in improving tilth, breaking pan and defending cleared land from encroachment by bracken.

Butchery

Marks from cutting, chopping and splitting were noted on 292 fragments from ox, sheep and pig, affecting bones from all parts of the skeleton and presenting no readily discernible pattern of favoured procedure. The number of butchery incidents is small (ca. 3% of all fragments), tending to support the proposal that butchery was minimal and meat cooked in large 'joints'. The butchered horse bones were two split and two chopped femoral fragments, a chopped metacarpal and a metatarsal which had been chopped and split. Some significance might be attributed to the absence of the thoracic sector of spine from the horse in F6 as there is a similar deficiency in the horse spinal remains in layer 8 (see below). Coincidence, or rib roast of horse?

Notable groups

PIT F6

The horse bones of this pit are described above. The unphysiological disposition of the forelimbs raises possibilities of ritual burial, though other bone was also present, and in amounts much as might be expected of an 'ordinary' pit. If disposal was the sole object, the use of the pit rather than the nearby river might seem unnecessarily complicated, unless there was either a special need for pit burial or, alternatively, the pit was open and redundant.

F111/111A

The dog skeleton is described fully above.

BURNT BONE IN OCCUPATION LEVELS

A relative concentration of burnt bone occurred in the occupation levels. Though most fragments proved unidentifiable, ox, sheep/goat, pig and horse were recognised. A right hind limb of horse may have been burnt/cooked complete. There were also traces of a right forelimb and left hind. The other species provided no evidence that bones were in articulation when placed on the fire (except for three articulating lumbar vertebrae of ox). However, articulated limb bones from other food animals were recorded in the 1976 assemblage (Done 1980), and it is likely that the articulated horse bones in Area 6 are simply another example of cooking in large lumps, meatless foot being thrown in with the rest of the leg.

An ox horn core similar to the dehorned stumps in F6 was reconstructed from burnt fragments.

Several unidentified pieces, including part of a large animal long bone, were blackened on the 'inside' i.e. the walls of the marrow cavity, but not on the outside; presumably these bones were broken before being heated and behaved as chimneys.

LAYER 8 11–13E/10N

Within river channel units E–G one area yielded a concentration of bone from cattle, sheep, pig, and dog similar in character to the assemblage in general. There was in addition a group of horse vertebrae consisting of cervical 3–7, thoracic 2 with parts of four other cranial thoracics, possibly in articulation, and lumbar 1–5. As the middle thoracic section is missing, the lumbar section cannot with certainty be said to belong to the rest, but the association of the bones could be consistent with a body, or part of it, being caught behind the waterfront piles. Four more horse bones may be related to this group but another cervical vertebra must belong to another horse.

Comment

Comments are offered with caution in the knowledge that much material from Runnymede has yet to be examined.

The animal bones hint at a sophisticated livestock husbandry and, by implication, a standard of agriculture above subsistence level. The change in emphasis as between cattle and pigs which the bones appear to show (Fig. 129) argues for a flexibility of stocking, with adjustment being made to changing circumstances. As already suggested (Done 1980), ruminants at times may have failed to thrive. Among the many ills they no doubt encountered, liver fluke infestation might with reason be cited as a problem which might account for the apparent increase in the use of the pig. Though susceptible to fluke, the pig is less likely to suffer acutely, for reasons thought to be associated with the microscopic structure of the liver (Nansen *et al.* 1972). The parasite's intermediate host, *Limnaea truncatula*, is found at Runnymede, so the chance of infestation must be quite high. The observed pattern of livestock use, with the apparent trend away from cattle, would also be consistent with a change (?development) from grassland to arable. Evidence for hedging plants may point to a need to contain livestock rather than allow free range, and the increasing prominence of the pig favours postulation of an agriculture in some degree of surplus, as the omnivorous pig, unlike the ruminants, competes with man in times of scarcity.

The comparable relationships at Potterne (Locker 1988) show the sheep/pig pattern reversed, with sheep rising relative to cattle while the pig fragment count shows little variation. Although both assemblages have in common the decline in cattle, the particular disease postulation given above will not serve for Potterne. Data from many sources (see Grigson 1981) indicate a rise in the use of sheep in southern England in the Middle and Late Bronze Age; Potterne and Runnymede together suggest that the change may be a decline in cattle rather than an increase in sheep.

Although it is possible that pigs were brought in to Runnymede at the behest of rich and powerful residents, the possibility of a ceremonial function, as at Durrington (Harcourt 1971), is at present unlikely on this settlement site. A more appealing interpretation to the writer is that the livestock situation is the result of a competent and prosperous agriculture from which wealth and power might develop, the pigs being part of the origins of prosperity rather than an effect of it.

Three instances of de-horning could imply confinement of cattle in limited space, precautions against unruly beasts, or treatment of damaged horn. Deliberate removal of horn requires an organised effort, some technique, but little technology. The animal must be caught and restrained while the horn is cut, which would need manpower; a cutting tool and ropes would be helpful but not essential. Bleeding would occur which, if control were thought necessary, could be stopped effectively by searing.

The possibility that animals were housed receives some support from the dental abnormality of the F6 horse (above). Though not the classic crib-biting pattern, the wear on these incisors could well result from a horse using its immediate, solid surroundings to alleviate boredom or pica (depraved appetite). Detailed evidence for the stalling of cattle and sheep/goats in the Early Iron Age is reported by Therkorn *et al.* (1984), and certainly the provision of even minimal shelter would have greatly improved the performance of the food animals and their contribution to farming prosperity.

Chapter 19
Neolithic food residues on pottery

JOHN EVANS

Thirteen Neolithic sherds which bore charred deposits were sampled for analysis. In the first stage the charred matter itself was carefully scraped off the pot surface, wherever possible leaving half of the deposit *in situ* for future investigation. The charred matter was in 12 cases attached to the inner face of the pot (e.g. Plate 58a), in one case to the outside. Seven of the former yielded positive results (Table 62), five from Area 4 and two from Area 6. In a second stage of the programme six of the sherds bearing identifiable substances (not sample no. 6) were themselves sampled to test for impregnation by, and survival of, residues in the body of the pot. A corner of each sherd was detached and crushed for analysis. Theoretical aspects of the preservation of foodstuffs and the success of extraction have recently been discussed in Needham and Evans (1987).

Experimental

The quantities of charred material analysed ranged from 50 mg to 300 mg. Samples FR3, FR7 and FR10 had a vesicular structure commonly associated with such residues. The remaining samples appeared to be amorphous systems. No samples contained detectable biological debris.

The charred samples were gently crushed to open up the vesicules, and placed in a Soxlet apparatus. The residue was then extracted sequentially with hexane, chloroform, 2-propanol and water. Each extract was evaporated to dryness under reduced pressure. Any residues obtained were examined by infrared spectroscopy. The extracts, if sufficient in quantity, were then investigated using thin-layer chromatography (TLC). This technique is especially useful for the hexane (oils and fats) and chloroform (resins) extracts, as it enables the various major constituent components of the oils etc. to be detected. For instance, fats and oils are composed in part of triglycerides which are unique to a particular fat or oil.

The next stage of the procedure was to examine the residue by gas (GLC) and high-performance liquid chromatography (HPLC), the actual procedure depending on the nature of the extract. For instance, the hexane extracts were hydrolysed and the resulting free fatty acid methylated and/or naphthacylated, depending on their quantity. The methylated systems were examined by GLC and the naphthacylated esters by HPLC. In this way it was possible to identify and quantify the levels of fatty acids present in the extracts. These data, coupled with the TLC data, enabled fats etc. to be identified with a reasonable degree of certainty. Examination of the aqueous extract for sodium levels was also done routinely. In this way the use of salt preservation etc. could be inferred.

After extraction the samples were divided into two portions. One portion was digested with hydrochloric acid in order to release amino acids for any proteinaceous material present. The liberated acids were then identified by appropriate chromatographic methods. In this way proteinaceous material could be detected. Occasionally it was possible to

Table 62: Neolithic pottery sherds with identified food residues attached: descriptions and findings.

Sample number	Area and context	Description	Average wall thickness (mm)	Food residues
FR1	A4 L121a	Fineware body sherd; fine flint filler, smoothed surfaces, especially interior	5.5	Triglyceride pattern (TLC) and fatty acids (GLC, HPLC), suggestive of adipocere
FR2	A4 L121a	Coarseware, body sherd, medium–large flint filler	10.5	Glucose (TLC, HPLC) traces of beeswax (ir, GLC) and resin (ir)
FR6	A6 L41 sump	Fineware body sherd; medium flint filler; smoothed surfaces with decoration (catalogue NP 23)	6	Fructose, maltose (TLC, HPLC)
FR7	A6 L41	Coarseware body sherd; large flint filler	7	Triglyceride pattern (TLC) and fatty acids (GLC, HPLC) suggestive of fish
FR8	A4 L121a	Coarseware body sherd; medium flint filler	9	Triglyceride pattern (TLC) and fatty acids (GLC, HPLC) suggestive of fish
FR12	A4 L121a	Coarseware body sherd; medium–large flint filler; exterior with seed impression	8	Triglyceride pattern (TLC) and fatty acids (GLC, HPLC) suggestive of pork fat
FR14	A4 L121a	Coarseware body sherd; medium–large flint filler	10.5	Resin, most probably from wood

isolate the protein by extracting the sample with a buffer and investigating the extract by electrophoresis. Additionally the acid extract was investigated for calcium and magnesium levels. This information was used to indicate the original presence of aqueous systems. Where sufficient sample was available it was examined by scanning electron microscopy (SEM) for the presence of any identifiable biological debris. In none of the Runnymede samples investigated was any such debris seen. (SEM is more useful than optical microscopy for this type of material, as its black coloration makes it difficult to view.)

Discussion

The positive results are shown in Table 62. Certain substances readily lend themselves to identification. Beeswax is very stable and its infrared spectrum is very characteristic. Fish and other marine products contain substantial amounts of palmitoleic acid. As other substances contain little or none of this substance, its presence is exceedingly useful for the identification of such products. As several of the residues gave no detectable substances, the possibility of ground contamination appears to be unimportant on this site, and this finds further support in the fact that the actual pottery samples all gave negative results.

The presence of beeswax on one sherd (FR2) and the consequent implications for the early exploitation of bee-products in this country has been explored in some depth elsewhere (Needham and Evans 1987). On ecological grounds there is no good reason to doubt the presence of the honeybee, *Apis mellifera*, in post-glacial Britain – the case has been well stated recently by Limbrey (1982). There is thus no need to make extravagant claims for the importation of wax from the Continent.

The more immediate significance of the beeswax present in sample FR2 is difficult to assess. Obviously the use of wax to impregnate the pottery vessel and hence make it watertight is an alternative to its derivation from the contained foodstuffs. This sample also produced evidence for glucose and resin. The combination of wax and glucose in the residue is highly suggestive of honey constituent, especially since wax, which is very stable, was not found in the body of the pot, where it would be expected if introduced as a sealant.

The other identifications are of less interest individually, but show the potential for building up a useful picture of foodstuffs consumed. The pork fat inferred from sample FR12 occasions no surprise; pig is well attested in the Neolithic levels as well as in the Late Bronze Age. We can take this a little further, however, since the presence of pork fat without protein would suggest either frying or storage of the fat, i.e. dripping. Again the lack of results from the pot sherd itself argues against use as a sealing agent.

The presence of probable fish-based foods in two vessels (FR7, FR8) is perhaps more revealing, from the site perspective. As yet, despite excellent conditions for the preservation of bone, wet sieving has produced no more than a handful of fish bones. Evidence of the fishing economy on which the food remains are based is therefore negligible.

The evidence for adipocere, salt and protein in FR1 raises the possibility of salted meat. The practice of salting meat is entirely to be expected in prehistoric economies, but organic residues are likely to be the only direct evidence for this process.

SECTION D: SCIENTIFIC DATING

Summary

Three methods of scientific dating were applied to the 1978 material. Radiocarbon dating (Chapter 20) has yielded most information, giving in particular a solid framework for the Late Bronze Age occupation with 31 measurements. Attention was focused on four main events which offered samples of high contextual integrity and which could be interrelated stratigraphically. Multiple dating of each event, and the statistical evaluation and calibration of each date group, has allowed a fairly refined chronology to be elucidated for the river channel. The date sequence runs from the clearance horizon (unit B), ca. 900 cal BC, through to unit F, ca. 800 cal BC. Other LBA dates are for pits and an articulated bone group.

Six dates were run on Neolithic samples thereby establishing broadly contemporary activity, in the early 4th millennium cal BC, in Areas 4, 6 and 8. The later-stratified bone group in Area 6 was found to have a later calibrated age span.

The Neolithic dates correspond relatively well with the independent palaeomagnetic dating of silts in column SS2, Area 6 (Chapter 21). The magnetic measurements seem to fit the master curve best for the end of the 5th to the early 4th millennium cal BC.

A pilot scheme of dendrochronological work on the timber piles showed that they were not suitable for dating purposes (Chapter 22). However the tree-ring patterns mapped do cross-match for five piles of the outer row, lending weight to the supposition that the set was felled over a short period of time, perhaps in one season.

Table 63: Runnymede Neolithic radiocarbon dates.

Area and sample		Context	Sample no.	Date BP	Date cal BC
Area 4	MN pile	A4 S1(b)	HAR-6132	4630 ± 70	3621–3105
	MN pile	A4 S4(b)	HAR-6128	4920 ± 80	3950–3524
Area 6	MN worked timber	A6 F202(a)	HAR-6130	4830 ± 70	3780–3381
	MN worked timber	A6 168(a)	HAR-6131	4930 ± 90	3970–3520
	LN butchered bone	A6 F125(a)	HAR-6136	4270 ± 110	3302–2580
Area 8	tip of pile	A8 3B(a)	HAR-6133	4690 ± 110	3770–3100

Note: All samples waterlogged wood, except HAR-6136 (bone).

Table 64: Runnymede Late Bronze Age radiocarbon dates.

Event	Context	Sample no.	Date BP	Date cal BC
Group 1	A6 L24/3*	HAR-3114	2690 ± 80	1010–780
Clearance [unit B]	A6 L24/1*	HAR-3115	2720 ± 80	1050–790
	A6 L24/2*	HAR-3120	2690 ± 80	1010–780
	A6 F163/1(a)	HAR-3752	2970 ± 70	1410–1000
	A6 F163/1(b)	HAR-3751	2800 ± 60	1126–830
	A6 F195(a)	HAR-3116	3090 ± 120	1630–1010
	A6 F195(b)	HAR-3117	2700 ± 70	1000–790
Group 2	A6 F276(a)	HAR-4257	2650 ± 70	930–770
Waterfront 1 [unit C/D]	A6 F276(b)	HAR-4275	2820 ± 70	1253–830
	A6 F236(a)	HAR-4268	2750 ± 70	1060–800
	A6 F236(b)	HAR-4413	2790 ± 90	1256–800
	A6 F285(a)	HAR-4341	2780 ± 80	1161–800
	A6 F285(b)	HAR-4274	2770 ± 90	1212–800
	A6 F117(a)	HAR-4269	2690 ± 70	1000–790
	A6 F117(b)	HAR-4277	2730 ± 70	1040–800
Group 3	A6 F210(a)	HAR-4267	2640 ± 70	920–607
Waterfront 2 [unit E]	A6 F210(b)	HAR-4273	2920 ± 90	1410–900
	A6 F144(a)	HAR-4265	2630 ± 60	910–770
	A6 F144(b)	HAR-4340	2810 ± 90	1260–810
	A6 F215(a)	HAR-4264	2640 ± 70	920–607
	A6 F215(b)	HAR-4270	2580 ± 80	900–421
	A6 F187	HAR-4272	2690 ± 80	1010–780
Group 4	A6 F155/3(a)	HAR-3762	2580 ± 60	839–540
Hardstandings	A6 F155/3(b)	HAR-3759	2540 ± 70	830–410
against waterfront 2,	A6 F164/1(a)	HAR-3761	2530 ± 70	820–410
[unit F]	A6 F164/1(b)	HAR-3750	2690 ± 80	1010–780
Articulated bone group L8a [unit G]	A6 L8a	HAR-6138	2830 ± 110	1376–800
Pit F6 [post unit D]	A6 F6L4(a)*	HAR-3113	2670 ± 80	1000–770
	A6 F6L4(b)*	HAR-3112	2700 ± 70	1000–790
Pit F11	A6 F11L3(a)*	HAR-3118	2720 ± 90	1090–780
	A6 F11L3(b)*	HAR-3119	2710 ± 130	1256–530

* Charcoal; all other samples waterlogged wood, except HAR-6138 (bone); (a), (b) denote duplicate determinations on same sample.

Chapter 20
Radiocarbon dating

Sampling strategy and the radiocarbon measurements

The Area 6 excavation, supplemented by salvage work elsewhere, offered a good range of potential material for radiocarbon dating. It was possible to make a strong case for a good series of dates for three reasons: i) a deep stratigraphy was involved; ii) a large artifact assemblage was associated; iii) the range of datable material available allowed the selection of mainly short-lived samples (young wood) from contexts in which the chances of residuality were considered small. In this way a close relationship could be expected between the date of the sample material and the date of the archaeological event or horizon. This tight contextual control encouraged optimism that, by multiple dating of key contexts, a meaningful and fairly refined radiocarbon chronology could be attached to the site sequence. That the project in fact proved to be successful was also partly due to the nature of the calibration curve covering the major period of occupation at Runnymede; between 1000 and 800 cal BC the curve falls steeply, with only minor wiggles (Pearson and Stuiver 1986: 843 fig. 1A). This means that there is a better than usual chance of establishing that two dates separated by only a short interval (say less than 100 calendar years) are significantly different. The steepness of the curve also gives the best possible refinement of calendar dates for a given precision in the radiocarbon measurements.

In choosing samples for measurement the following principles were followed:

1. Samples were, wherever possible, taken from an actual structure, or otherwise from a deposit believed to represent a restricted time-span.
2. Samples were mostly taken from wood known to be young, thus minimising the risk of any significant discrepancy between date obtained and date of felling.
3. Each context chosen was multiply dated, to allow the possible identification of residual elements or aberrant measurements.

Table 65: Prior succession hypotheses for the dated Late Bronze Age river channel contexts.

Group	2	3	4	succeeds group
	**	***	***	1
		**	**	2
			*	3

*** No doubt about a stratigraphic succession
** Strong arguments for a succession
* Weaker arguments for a succession

4. Wherever possible, each element in the context (e.g. branch or pile within a structure) was split to provide two samples, in the hope of either isolating aberrant measurements or, more usually, producing a mean with improved precision from a compatible pair of measurements.

The Middle Neolithic material in Area 6 was mainly in secondary contexts and so just two worked timbers were dated (one sample each) to give a broad chronology. This was given further context by the dating of an *in situ* bone group (F125) from a higher stratigraphic position. Middle Neolithic material in Area 4, was, however, associated with *in situ* timber, including brush and piles. Two piles were singly dated; a further sample taken from a horizontal branch was submitted, but no result is available. Finally, one pile in Area 8 was sampled to provide an indication of the age of certain structural remains in that area.

For the Late Bronze Age phase, for which a wealth of datable material existed, most samples were taken from the deep river channel sequence of Area 6. Four contexts at different stratigraphic positions met all the criteria set out above:

Group 1: two branches and three charcoal samples associated with a single layer (L24) interpreted as a clearance horizon and taken from different locations within it: seven measurements.
Group 2: four piles distributed along the length of the inner pile row: eight measurements.
Group 3: four piles distributed along the length of the outer pile row: seven measurements.
Group 4: two branches from hardstandings (F155, F164) situated outside the outer pile row: four measurements.

The archaeological evidence for the chronological relationships of the Late Bronze Age groups is summarised in Table 65. Also dated were two discrete deposits of charcoal from pits (two measurements each) and an articulated group of vertebrae in river channel layer 8a (one measurement). Thirty-one samples from the 1978 campaign were measured by Harwell between 1979 and 1984. The complete set of dates with their 'one-sigma' errors is given in Tables 63 & 64. The tables also give the corresponding 95% calibrated confidence limits, obtained using the 'intercept' method (method A) in the computer program of Stuiver and Reimer (1986).

Statistical analysis of Late Bronze Age dates

MORVEN LEESE

Introduction

The following topics are considered: the agreement between duplicate measurements on the same sample; the interpretation of each group of dates separately; and, finally, the overall picture based on all the acceptable dates. The significance tests are those described by Ward and Wilson (1978). Uncalibrated radiocarbon measurements are used both for testing the consistency of duplicate measurements on the same sample and for considering the homogeneity of groups of objects dating single events. This procedure is justifiable in the latter case only if the events can be considered to have durations which are negligible compared to the measurement and calibration errors involved. This assumption seems reasonable in view of the sampling strategy described earlier. The uncalibrated dates are discussed under the heading relating to the particular group involved. Calibration is necessary for the final synthesis, in which different dates are to be used to establish a chronology for distinct events, and this synthesis is discussed in the summary at the end.

Figure 130 shows a summary of the raw data, with duplicates linked together. To avoid prejudging which individual of any discrepant pair is the outlier, both have been shown. The diagram suggests that for both group 1 and group 3 there are two possible interpretations: either the discrepant dates are too early and the acceptable dates represent a single event or the acceptable dates represent two distinct events which had nevertheless become incorporated into a single archaeological horizon in each case. In other words, Fig. 130 allows the interpretation that each group of dates represents at most two events. However, it seems intrinsically more likely that the data represent only one event, with one or two discrepant determinations. The interpretations are discussed in more detail below.

A third model, in which each group of dates represents a random sample of individual events occurring over a significant span of time, is not considered here. The problem in that case would be to estimate the beginning and end of each phase, using all the available data and taking into consideration calibration from the outset. It is a far more complex problem, requiring special methods, and as it seems intrinsically less plausible for the Runnymede contexts dated, it is deferred for consideration until such methods have been developed.

Group 1: clearance (stratigraphic unit B)
Three singleton dates have values 2690 ± 80 BP, 2720 ± 80 BP and 2690 ± 80 BP. Neither of the two duplicate pairs agree within measurement error at the 10% level. As noted above, a number of statistically acceptable divisions of the data are possible, and these are summarised in Table 66: the division suggested in (a) implies a single event, those in (b)–(d) double events. The χ^2 values, based on the variation among the acceptable dates, indicate the relative merits of the various models. They are not used as the basis for χ^2 tests as such, because the basic conditions for the validity of the test cannot be met when it is successively reapplied to different models on the same data.

The dating evidence alone supports the possibility of two events at 2700 ± 46 BP and 3001 ± 61 BP, with 2700 and

Table 66:   Four possible divisions of the clearance dates (unit B).

	Outlier (BP)	Acceptable dates (BP)	Weighted mean date of event(s)	χ^2
(a)		2690		
		2720		
		2690	2729 ± 32	2
	2970———— 2800			
	3090———— 2700			
(b)		2690		
		2720		
		2690	2737 ± 37	2
	2970———— 2800			
	2700———— 3090		3090 ± 120	—
(c)		2690		
		2720		
		2690	2700 ± 39	<1
	3090———— 2700			
	2800———— 2970		2970 ± 70	—
(d)		2690		
		2720	2700 ± 46	<1
		2690		
	2800———— 2970			
	2700———— 3090		3001 ± 60	<1

2800 BP as the discrepant dates in their respective pairs, since there is high internal homogeneity for both subsets ($\chi^2 < 1$ in both cases; see Table 66d). However, this would imply that the two charred branches (F163/1, F195) would date to 300 years earlier than the other burnt deposits they lie within, a hypothesis which can probably be rejected on archaeological grounds. The other double-event hypotheses can be similarly rejected, and the most plausible model for the clearance dates is therefore of a single event at 2729 ± 32 BP, with 3090 and 2970 BP being the result of sampling or measurement errors (Table 66a).

One possibility that should be considered is that the errors have been underestimated, which would have the effect of exaggerating the apparent significance of differences between duplicates. This could explain the rejection of F163/1a and b (though not F195a and b) as a homogeneous pair: an increase of 10 years in the errors would allow their acceptance at the 10% level. In these circumstances their mean age would be realistically estimated at 2872 ± 84 BP, the error being derived from the difference between them rather than from their quoted errors. In fact the inclusion of both of these dates makes a negligible difference to the overall mean date of the clearance, which would then be 2740 ± 41 BP. However, we accept 2729 ± 32 BP as the best estimate available on the preferred single-event model.

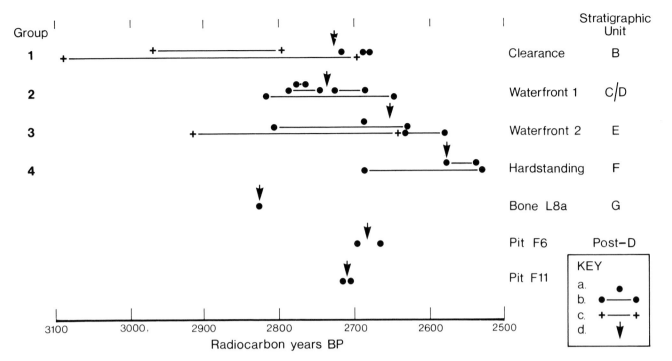

Fig. 130 *Central values of Late Bronze Age radiocarbon results with duplicate pairs linked (see Table 64 for associated errors). Key: a) singleton date; b) consistent duplicates; c) inconsistent duplicates; d) mean value, assuming single radiocarbon event within group.*

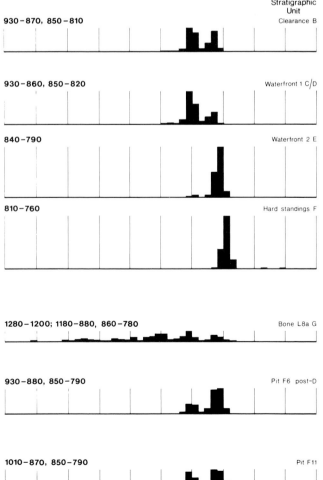

Fig. 131 *Calibrated radiocarbon date ranges for Late Bronze Age events. The numerical date ranges (on left) are the 95% most probable bands, to the nearest 10 years, or, for L8a, the nearest 20 years. Each histogram represents the complete distribution of possible calendar dates, given the weighted mean radiocarbon date and associated error for that event.*

Group 2: waterfront 1 (stratigraphic unit C/D)
All four sets of duplicates show good agreement, and each pair has been averaged to give weighted means 2735 ± 50 BP, 2770 ± 64 BP, 2776 ± 60 BP, 2710 ± 50 BP. These means show good agreement with one another and are consistent with a single event dated at 2742 ± 28 BP.

Group 3: waterfront 2 (stratigraphic unit E)
The single determination has a value of 2690 ± 80 BP, and two of the sets of duplicates agree sufficiently well to give weighted means of 2685 ± 50 BP and 2614 ± 53 BP. The third pair shows a significant difference at the 5% level, and we conclude that one of the pair is likely to be in error. If we retain 2640 ± 70 BP, the four acceptable dates (two being means) are in good agreement with one another and give a final single-event date of 2655 ± 30 BP. Alternatively, if 2640 BP is the outlier, we would have to accept a double-event interpretation, with one event at 2920 ± 90 BP and another at 2658 ± 33 BP. Statistical measures do not help in assessing the earlier date (2920 BP) since it is a singleton, and an overwhelming preference must anyway be given to a single event at 2655 ± 30 BP.

Group 4: hardstandings (stratigraphic unit F)
The duplicates are in good agreement and give weighted means 2563 ± 46 BP and 2599 ± 53 BP. These are consistent with a single event at 2579 ± 35 BP.

The remaining dates
The duplicates agree well for both pits and give weighted means of 2687 ± 53 BP and 2717 ± 74 BP; the single date on L8a (articulated bone group, Unit G) is 2830 ± 110 BP.

Summary of the Late Bronze Age radiocarbon evidence
The balance of evidence, archaeological and statistical taken together, leads us to reject the earlier members of discrepant pairs as outliers. (It is noteworthy that all three outliers, if they are such, differ from their acceptable counterparts by approximately the same amount, i.e. they are too old by 200–400 radiocarbon years.) Thus, although none of the possibilities suggested by the data shown in Figure 130 can be absolutely ruled out, our preferred interpretation of the uncalibrated radiocarbon dates is as shown in Table 67. The numbers of samples and measurements refer to the dates actually used, i.e. excluding outliers. The summary dates are the weighted means of all the acceptable dates, duplicates on the same sample having first been averaged as described in the appropriate section above.

The summary dates in Table 67 have been converted into calendar date bands by taking the (normal) distribution implied by the accepted mean date and its error and calibrating a discretized version of that distribution represented as a histogram (Leese 1987). The resulting calibrated distribution is generally multimodal, its shape depending on interaction between the size of the error and the behaviour of the calibration curve in the region of interest, and to a lesser

Table 67: Summary of preferred mean radiocarbon dates for Late Bronze Age events at Runnymede.

Group	Samples	Determinations	Weighted mean date BP	Error
1 Clearance	5	5	2729	±32
2 Waterfront 1	4	8	2742	±28
3 Waterfront 2	4	6	2655	±30
4 Hardstandings	2	4	2579	±35
Articulated bone	1	1	2830	±110
Pit F6	1	2	2687	±53
Pit F11	1	2	2717	±74

extent on the bin-sizes used to represent the distributions as histograms. Histograms for each event are shown in Fig. 131; these indicate the most probable ranges of calendar dates, given the relevant mean radiocarbon date and error.

The histograms are not representations of duration, which, according to our basic single-event model, is negligible for each event dated. The peaks and troughs show that there are relatively unlikely periods within each calibrated range, though a more realistic model, assuming *a priori* equiprobable calendar dates, has since suggested the peaks to be less extreme than indicated here. Approximate 95% probability bands based on the histograms are also quoted numerically, to the nearest 10 years in most cases.

Interpretation of the radiocarbon dates

Neolithic
HAR-6128 and HAR-6132 date two piles (S4 and S1) penetrating the brush consolidation platform in Area 4 (L120 and 121). They do not have to be of one phase, but this structure was not expected to have been long-lived. The difference between the two measurements (at 290 radiocarbon years, significantly greater than expected on the basis of their errors) is therefore a little surprising. Samples of a branch from the platform itself were submitted in the hope of comparative dating, but no results have been possible.

The calibrated ranges suggest that S4 dates from the early half of the 4th millennium cal BC and S1 from mid to late 4th millennium BC. The calibrated 2σ ranges only overlap between 3620–3520 cal BC (Fig. 132).

The two dated timbers from Area 6 (F168, F202) were both prostrate in secondary contexts within the sediments of L41, but the radiocarbon measurements are in reasonable agreement with one another at 1σ and provide *termini post quos* for the deposits. The overlap in the 95% calibrated ranges for the two measurements is *c.* 3780–3520 cal BC (Fig. 132). Assuming that these timbers entered the channel deposits as rubbish along with the associated pottery, flint and bone, then they give a date for the Middle Neolithic assemblage. It is thought likely that deposition of this assemblage was more or less contemporary with occupation (Chapter 2).

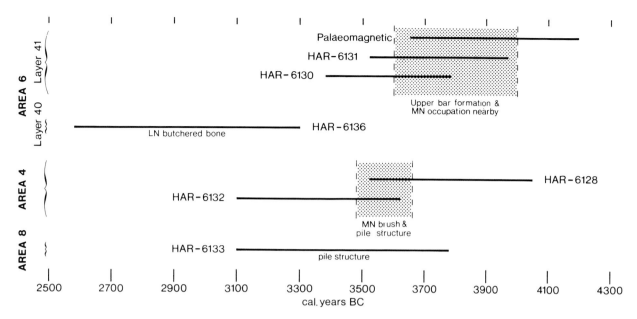

Fig. 132 Neolithic dating evidence from Runnymede Bridge, based on calibrated radiocarbon results at 2σ and the palaeomagnetic result.

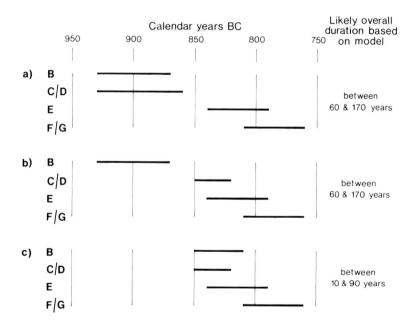

Fig. 133 Alternative interpretations of calendar date spans for the Late Bronze Age events represented in the river channel, based on radiocarbon and stratigraphic evidence; (a) is preferred.

The third sample from Area 6, HAR-6136 (bone), provides a useful indication of the chronology of the silts between the two main cultural horizons. The group of butchered bones (F125) which was sampled was unquestionably *in situ*, and the measurement of 4270 ± 110 BP, giving a calibrated range of 3300–2580 cal BC, therefore dates that level fairly high in L40. This result, in conjunction with the earlier ones, suggests that there was a substantial passage of time, perhaps several hundred years, between the respective episodes of human activity. During this interval part of layer 41 and much of layer 40 accumulated.

The sample from Area 8 was one of several timber piles recovered from the base of a drawn section (Fig. 12), almost 2 m below the Late Bronze Age horizon and also below a pre-LBA thick bed of gravel (L84). It was felt rather unlikely that the piles had been driven through this gravel, and on this basis they would be somewhat earlier than Late Bronze Age. The measurement of HAR-6133, 4690 ± 110 BP, is in fact well within the range of dates associated with Middle Neolithic activity in Areas 4 and 6 and therefore suggests a wider geographical spread of that activity.

In conclusion, it is possible to say on the current radiocarbon evidence that Middle Neolithic activity was taking place at Runnymede Bridge between *c.* 4000 and 3500 cal BC (Fig. 132). An isolated Late Neolithic deposit of butchered bone was dumped in the silt between *c.* 3300 and 2600 cal BC.

Late Bronze Age

The policy of multiple dating and the choice, for the most part, of short-lived material have paid off. The statistical evaluation of the date series when used in conjunction with archaeological evidence allows a useful and reasonably confident statement to be made about the chronology of certain channel deposits.

CLEARANCE

Interpretation (a) in Table 66 is favoured on archaeological grounds; this would allow the two charred branches to be roughly contemporary with the mixed charcoal in which they lie, with a mean date of 2729 ± 32 BP. This results in a bimodal calibrated probability distribution (Fig. 131) with a slight preference for the earlier of the two peaks, i.e. that within the range 930–870 cal BC. If any of the other, double-event, possibilities are entertained, then the date of the horizon is always best approximated by the later date, based on three or four determinations, since the risk of intrusion of stratigraphically higher material is thought to be very low. Given this, use of any of the less favoured alternatives for grouping the clearance dates would not substantially alter the distribution against the calendar chronology, but (c) and (d) (Table 66) would give much more weight to the later peak.

WATERFRONT 1

Statistical evaluation of eight dates allows that all are compatible with one event, dated 2742 ± 28 BP. The 95% most probable date bands on the calendar scale are similar to those for clearance, but with a rather greater probability attached to the peak within the earlier range, 930–860 cal BC, than to that within the later, 850–820 cal BC. Unless the waterfront 1 timbers had been stored for any length of time prior to use (i.e. for some decades), the ^{14}C measurements should give dates less than 15 years discrepant from felling and construction, for the timbers have less than 30 growth rings. In fact unseasoned wood was probably used (Heal, Chapter 7) and it seems most likely therefore that waterfront 1 was constructed at some time around the end of the 10th and beginning of the 9th centuries cal BC. On stratigraphical evidence clearance would have occurred beforehand, but not long enough before to show significantly in the radiocarbon assay. Indeed, it is possible that some of the clearance debris of branches etc. and the oak trunks used for waterfront 1 belonged to the same plants.

It is rather less likely that waterfront 1 should be dated to the latter half of the 9th century cal BC. If it were, however, clearance could either have been effectively contemporary, or up to a century earlier (Fig. 133). The silt which accumulated between the two stratigraphic events could represent virtually any duration and thus does not help choose between interpretations.

WATERFRONT 2

Again most determinations give good agreement and a central date of 2655 ± 30 BP, or 2658 ± 33 BP, for the outer pile row. These give a single-peak range of calendar dates when calibrated, 840–790 cal BC, which can be applied to waterfront 2 construction, again assuming that the timber was not stored long between felling and use. If one accepts the hypothesis that F210 was genuinely earlier, then the timber would clearly be reused from a much earlier phase.

HARDSTANDINGS

A consistent set of determinations on young wood gives the mean weighted date of 2579 ± 35 BP and a single-peak calibrated range of 810–760 cal BC. It is noteworthy that, owing to the steepness of the calibration curve in the relevant stretch, a difference of some 75 years in radiocarbon dates between groups 3 and 4 contracts to a difference of about 30 calendar years. This does not affect the level of significance that can be attached to the separation, but instead allows an unusually refined chronology to be elucidated.

ARTICULATED BONE GROUP, L8A

This date shows the pitfalls of too much reliance on single dates, especially those with poor standard deviations. Its calibrated distribution curve is widely spread and multi-peaked. Only the latest of the peaks, 860–780 cal BC, corresponds properly to the hardstanding range which it should equate with or slightly post-date.

PITS

Pit F6 is stratigraphically related to the channel sequence, having been dug after stratigraphic unit D and therefore after waterfront 1 construction. The two dated samples come from one deposit of charcoal of unknown maturity, this deposit lying in the upper fill, but pre-dating a secondary cut. F6 gave a bimodal calibrated date range similar to that for the clearance and waterfront 1 groups, but this time with the higher probability attached to the later peak, 850–790 cal BC. These results are thus in good agreement with the stratigraphy.

The pit F11 combined date, 2717 ± 75 BP, gives a multi-peak calibrated range. The main peaks span those for channel groups 1–3.

OVERALL SPAN

The radiocarbon-dated part of the channel sequence (stratigraphic units B–F) does not cover all of the occupation evidence, which continues until unit I. Through careful examination of associated groups of dates it has been possible to refine the chronology of the four dated stratigraphic groups.

The preferred calibrated dates of B–F cover, at most, little more than 100 calendar years (160 radiocarbon years), from *c.* 900 to 790 cal BC (Fig. 133a). On a minimalist view this same sequence could cover as little as, say, 40 years, *c.* 830 to 790 cal BC. Three possible chronological sequences are shown schematically in Fig. 133. Any of these give an important indication of the approximate duration of certain events represented in the river channel sequence which could not have been assessed on archaeological grounds alone. It is more difficult to assess the chronology of later settlement following on from the dated sequence. Even had suitable radiocarbon material been available, problems develop after *c.* 700 cal BC owing to the plateauing of the calibration curve giving rise to very ill-defined calendar date ranges.

Chapter 21
Palaeomagnetic dating

ANTHONY CLARK AND ANDREW DAVID

A column of samples for palaeomagnetic directional measurement was taken through the stream-channel deposits (41c–41i: column SS2), and another through the overlying grey-black alluvium (40: column SS1).

The method of sampling was the standard one used in the Ancient Monuments Laboratory for firm silts (Clark *et al.* 1988). Starting at the top, a step is carved into the silt, and this is further cut away, leaving a pillar of material, which is then encapsulated with plaster of Paris in a levelled plastic tube of 5 cm diameter by 5 cm length. The top of the tube and plaster are levelled to provide a reference for angle of magnetic dip or inclination of the sample. The top of the plaster is then marked with a line accurately related to north as a declination reference, in this case by means of a magnetic trough compass. Two samples were taken at each of seven levels in the stream channel deposits, and the results from each pair were averaged. The alluvium was sampled with a single column of five samples. The samples in each series were taken at 0.1 m vertical intervals.

The samples were measured in a Digico spinner magnetometer and partially demagnetised in an alternating field with a peak amplitude of 5 millitesla to remove viscous magnetic components; they were then compared with the curve derived from lacustrine sediments by Turner and Thompson (1982). Because of drying out and shrinkage, the three uppermost samples of the grey-black alluvium had to be discarded, and the uppermost pair from the stream-channel deposits were rejected because of excessively discrepant results, possibly due to disturbance. The mean demagnetised declination values of the remaining six pairs of samples from the stream channel coincide closely with the shape of the Turner and Thompson curve between 6150 and 5600 cal BP (4200 and 3650 cal BC). A distinctive feature of this part of the curve is the sharp, brief movement eastward shown by samples 9/10. This is especially clear in the Loch Lomond curve LLRD 1, the best of the lake sediment cores (Turner and Thompson 1979). Little could be deduced from the directional values of the remaining two layer 40 samples, and these are not discussed further.

Precise magnetic intensity measurements were not made, but the approximate relative values are given in Table 68,

that given for samples 9/10 may be taken as being of the order of 13×10^{-3} Am^{-1}. There is a fall in intensity toward the top of the stream channel with increasing clay content. No magnetic susceptibility measurements were made, but these would have varied roughly in proportion to the intensity values.

The average directional value of the Runnymede samples is about 10° west of those used in the reference curve, and the inclinations are about 8° too steep, after correction for latitude and longitude differences have been made. Comparable discrepancies have been observed at other sites. There is a lack of reference data for establishing absolute declination values for lake cores such as those used by Turner and Thompson in constructing the curve, and archaeomagnetic data subsequently acquired suggest that the curve should be moved further to the west. Recent measurements on a sediment column beside Brean Down, Somerset (Clark 1990), gave inclinations that also appeared to be too steep by 5.4°. It is possible that the sediments used for the reference curve were affected by an inclination-shallowing effect, which is not uncommon in sediments, but more data need to be accumulated to check this suggestion.

The palaeomagnetic date span of about 4200 to 3650 cal BC correlates well with radiocarbon determinations on timbers from the stream channel, which span 3970 to 3380 cal BC (see Chapter 20). However, the magnetic result must be accepted with caution, being based on only a small number of samples.

Table 68: Palaeomagnetic results on Neolithic sediments in Area 6.

In stratigraphic order from top (latest) to bottom (earliest). Declination and inclination are in degrees.

Sample(s)	Direction after 5 mT AF demag. Dec.	Inc.	Relative NRM intensity (approx.)	m OD (sample base)
Alluvium (L40) – column SS1				
18	12.4 W	71.6	12	12.33
19	11.4 W	76.0	6	12.23
Stream channel (L41c–41i) – column SS2				
1/2	–	–	1	12.97
3/4	11.2 W	73.5	1	12.87
5/6	6.4 W	68.5	5	12.77
7/8	0.3 W	66.9	7	12.67
9/10	11.3 E	70.3	10	12.57
11/12	6.6 W	66.7	5	12.47
13/14	3.5 W	71.5	8	12.37

Chapter 22
Tree-ring analysis

Jennifer Hillam

Eleven oak piles (*Quercus* spp.) from the Area 6 Late Bronze Age waterfronts were sectioned to evaluate their potential for tree-ring dating. Because the piles were relatively small in diameter (Table 69), it was uncertain whether they would contain sufficient rings for dating purposes and, as many of the piles were to be conserved, only a small number were sampled for this pilot study. The samples, thin slices taken from the top of the piles just below the rotten part, were examined in the Sheffield Dendrochronology Laboratory in January 1980. Six (F189, F230, F231, F240, F243, F285) were from the inner row of piles, whilst the remaining five (F215, F217, F218, F222, F223) came from the outer row.

The samples were prepared and measured following the method set out by Hillam (1985). The piles had between 13 and 34 rings, and all contained sapwood. Three samples (F218, F222, F223) had bark. The most recently formed ring, that beneath the bark, was not complete, indicating that these trees were felled in late spring or early summer. Of the remaining samples, F243 had been worked since the sapwood was removed from one side. Others (e.g. F230) may also have been trimmed, but the bark and outer sapwood may have been damaged prior to or during excavation.

The complete samples (F218, F222, F223) came from trees aged 32, 15 and 18 years respectively. The other samples also came from young oak trees. The oldest of these (F189) had 34 rings, including 14 sapwood rings, and was probably under 40 years old when felled.

The annual ring widths of all the samples were measured and plotted as graphs, known as tree-ring curves. The curves were tested against each other for similarity, although nor-mally tree-ring dating is carried out on ring sequences with more than 50 rings, and samples of at least 100 years are preferred. More recently, however, some success has been obtained using shorter sequences of 30–50 rings (Hillam 1985; Hillam *et al.* 1987). Tests on samples from modern oaks suggest that sequences under 30 years cannot be dated with any reliability (Hillam, unpublished).

Seven of the curves appeared to crossmatch, but it was felt that the curves were too short to be certain. If the cross-matching is correct, the relative positions of the ring sequences (Fig. 134) suggest that the seven matching samples came from trees felled in the same year. The tree samples with bark end in year 32 on the arbitrary time scale. They were felled in year 33, but the widths of the incomplete outer rings were not measured. The heartwood–sapwood transitions for all the samples are very similar, varying from year 20 to 23, which could suggest that at least seven out of the 11 piles sampled are contemporary.

These results were obtained in 1980, when it was thought that the inner row and the outer row of piles were contemporary. The tree-ring results seemed to support this supposition. However, evidence from the radiocarbon dating and the stratigraphic analysis now suggests that there was an interval of time between the insertion of the two rows of piles, which would suggest that at least some of the above tree-ring 'matches' are spurious correlations, since F230 and F240 are from the inner row and the other 'matching' curves are from the outer row. It is noteworthy, however, that F230 and F240 terminate earlier than the outer row piles in this supposed correlation. If these are separated from the others (on archaeological grounds), we are left with the correlations for five outer row piles shown in Fig. 134. In view of the shortness of their ring patterns, however, these cannot be considered reliable. As no larger timbers were recovered, it must be concluded that the Runnymede piles are not suitable for dendrochronology.

Table 69: Details of the tree-ring samples from Late Bronze Age piles. 'Felled summer' indicates that the wood was felled in late spring or early summer.

Context number	Diameter (mm)	Total no. of rings	Sapwood rings	Comment	Pile Row
F189	100–110	34	14	not bark edge	inner
F215	100–115	22	12	near bark edge	outer
F218	95–110	32	12	felled summer	outer
F217	105–110	15	9	not bark edge	outer
F222	85–100	15	10	felled summer	outer
F223	90–95	18	10	felled summer	outer
F230	130–145	18	5	not bark edge	inner
F231	110–125	14	9	not bark edge	inner
F240	115–125	17	5	not bark edge	inner
F243	100–120	13	7	not bark edge	inner
F285	125–140	17	8	not bark edge	inner

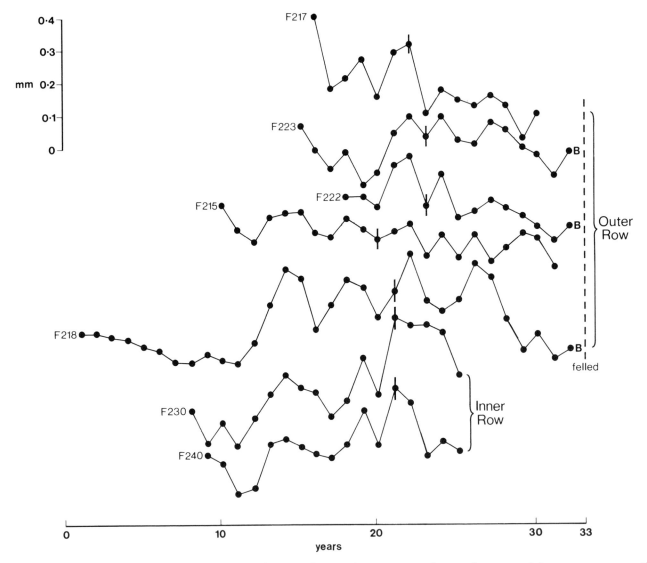

Fig. 134 Apparent cross-matching for seven of the Runnymede tree-ring sequences; the top five curves belong to outer row piles; the lower two are for inner row piles and may only be spuriously correlated with those above. The timescale is an arbitrary one; the dotted line would indicate the year in which F128, F222 and F223, and perhaps the remaining outer row piles, were felled. Heartwood-sapwood transition is represented by a vertical line; B: bark present.

SECTION E: SYNTHESES

Summary

This section offers three chapters of synthesis on different aspects of the site and its setting. The beginning of Chapter 23 is given to description of the physiography of the region with some comments on the evidence for prehistoric use of the zones. This is essential background for understanding the sources of naturally and anthropogenically introduced material to the site. The 1978 campaign on the site began to demonstrate the extent to which the flood-plain topography, at least, had altered in recent millennia. An essay on current interpretation of river channel changes is offered.

The volume and complexity of the environmental data require careful distillation if an overview is to be produced from sometimes apparently conflicting interpretations. Chapter 24 is divided into two: 1) a discussion of essential principles such as the transformation of life assemblages into sub-fossil ones, consideration of the different spheres of origin of the various ecofacts, and mechanisms of transportation; 2) integration of all of the 1978 results into a synthesis of environmental change in the Runnymede locality.

The final discussion in Chapter 25 attempts to bring together all of the strands of evidence presented in the volume as a whole. In addition to depicting the site in terms of its natural landscape and the imposed human structures, it touches on more speculative views on the behaviour and customs of the occupants. The possibilities of special feasting and certain ritual activities are raised for the Late Bronze Age in Area 6, which lies on the north-eastern edge of a settled area up to two hectares in extent. The conceptual values of the LBA occupants, in terms of site boundary definition and choice of site location are also explored.

Some tentative views on shifts in Neolithic settlement patterns in the region are formulated through consideration of other sites and their settings. The abandonment of this phase of settlement at Runnymede Bridge might be part of a broader drift, including, a little later, the abandonment of Yeoveney Lodge causewayed enclosure nearby.

Chapter 23
Geological and geomorphological aspects of the Runnymede region

The physiography of the region

Runnymede Bridge lies at the eastern, downstream end of the tract of flood-plain known as Runnymede and opposite the confluence of the Thames and a tributary, the Colne

Brook (Fig. 135). This small river is one of a network of channels which drain the broad Colne Valley from the north and today meet the Thames at points distributed through a kilometre and a half between Egham and Staines. The broad multiple confluence thus created is the junction between two complexes of flood-plain alluvium, occupying respectively the Colne valley stretching northwards and the Thames valley running south-eastwards from Staines to Walton-on-Thames. In contrast, the Thames flood-plain west of the confluence is much more restricted by terraces.

In the environs of the site the river system and its immediate flood-plains are mainly flanked by wide expanses of gravel and brickearth forming the terrace of Shepperton age, and further afield, higher, earlier terraces (Gibbard 1985). The Shepperton or 'flood-plain' gravel underlies the alluvial

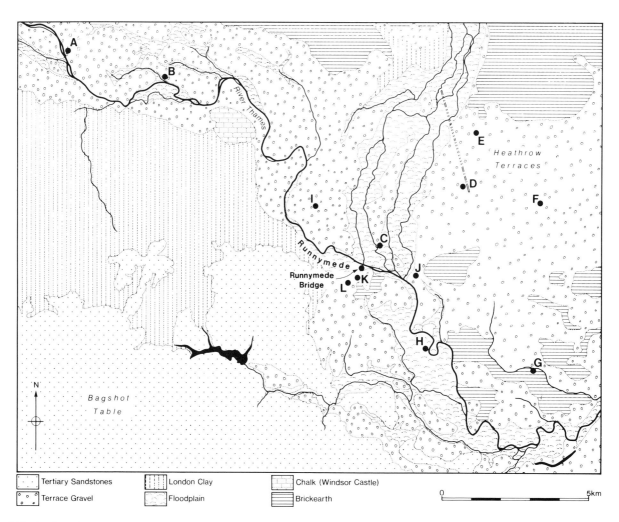

Fig. 135 Drift geology of the region around Runnymede with selected prehistoric sites A: Dorney causewayed enclosure; B: Eton Wick causewayed enclosure; C: Yeoveney Lodge causewayed enclosure; D: Stanwell cursus and LBA field system; E: Heathrow Neolithic segmented ring ditch; F: Mayfield Farm hengiform monument and LBA ring-fort; G: Shepperton Neolithic ring ditch; H: Mixnam's Farm Neolithic pottery and EIA settlement; I: Wraysbury Manor Farm Neolithic pottery; J: Staines Town Neolithic and Bronze Age pottery; K: Petters LBA settlement; L: Egham High Street LBA feature.

floors of the valleys but, where it is exposed on the flanks, tends to stand proud of even the modern alluvium surface, thus being less prone to flooding. Such terraces spread north and south of Runnymede and east from Staines as the extensive Heathrow Terraces. However, to the south-west and abutting directly the meadows at Runnymede, a range of hills betrays a geology distinct from that of the flat and low-lying valley. Cooper's Hill, overlooking Runnymede, lies on the northern edge of the Bagshot Table formed by Tertiary sandstones, capped, in places, with plateau gravels. The Tertiaries closest to the Thames are Bagshot sands, and these are fringed, above Runnymede, by a tongue of London clay. Further west the clay expands into a 7 kilometre broad belt which dominates the land south of the Thames just as the gravel and brickearth deposits dominate the land to the north. These two terrains therefore constitute the immediate up-valley catchment for the site, but it is worth noting that, although the present Thames runs close to the edge of the London clay belt, it is considered unlikely that Flandrian river systems have at any point in these reaches significantly eroded that geology. Only minor streams run off the clay into the Thames. With the exception of the small knoll on which Windsor Castle stands, the nearest chalk outcrop to Runnymede lies 16 km to the west.

Four main ecological zones will, then, have contributed in varying ways to the bulk of the environmental, economic and artifactual records at Runnymede Bridge: the flood-plain, the terraces, the Bagshot Table and the London clay belt (Fig. 135). In order to assess their contributions better it is worth summarising our knowledge of later prehistoric exploitation of the respective zones. In keeping with major river valleys everywhere, the lower Thames has yielded evidence for recurrent settlement of its terraces during later prehistory from Neolithic times onwards. Increasingly, however, there is the suggestion that this pattern is complemented by equally dense utilisation and settlement of the flood-plains, which, unlike the gravel areas, rarely give up evidence of their sites through the simple medium of aerial photography. Runnymede and other sites in the region suggest a focal concern with the flood-plain and the terrace bluffs which overlook it (e.g. Needham and Trott 1987: 482). These need to be considered as potentially part of an interdependent network with sites spread across the gravel and brickearth terraces. It is these areas that have given evidence for land division, presumably for agricultural purposes, most notably a large field system dated to the early 1st millennium BC at Stanwell (O'Connell 1986b, and pers. comm.), but also a fragment of ditch system exposed at Petters Sports Field, which neighbours Runnymede Bridge and dates to before the LBA settlement phase (O'Connell 1986a: 9). It may reasonably be surmised that sizable areas of the terraces were already not only cleared, but also boundary-organised landscapes. Again, the Stanwell/Heathrow cursus, extending for a distance of at least 4 km, (Field and Cotton 1987: 81–82) might suggest the existence of long clear vistas as early as the Late Neolithic.

The evidence for settlement on the Bagshot Table, much of it circumstantial, points to only a short-lived phase of significant utilisation during the mid–late 2nd millennium BC (Needham 1987: 130–2). Communities may have been forced to abandon arable agriculture on the sandy soils by the 1st millennium BC, owing to repetitive soil degradation. Cleared land would have reverted to light scrub, or been maintained as rough grazing, with heather establishing an ever stronger stranglehold on the ecosystem. It is clear that, however little agriculture may have been taking place in Late Bronze Age times, the Table was still exploited, since Runnymede yields large quantities of Tertiary sandstone, brought in as grinding stone. Prospecting for useful stone might perhaps have accompanied a pattern of grazing on the sandy hills. Sheep and goats would have taken best advantage of the poor vegetation.

Later prehistoric evidence from the London clay continues to be sparse even where, in neighbouring East Berkshire, systematic fieldwalking has attempted to identify surface flint scatters (Ford 1987). Elsewhere in the region the paucity of stray finds from London clay seems to support the traditional assumption of an under-used, indeed uncleared, environment. If we are right to envisage large tracts of primary woodland on London clay, then these might be one source of the selected young oak trunks used in the Late Bronze Age waterfront structures. They might also have offered good feeding grounds for an evidently flourishing population of pigs which the Runnymede community enjoyed.

The changing river system and flood-plain topography at Runnymede during the Flandrian

The river system on and around the site has clearly changed its configuration on more than one occasion during the Flandrian period. A complicated situation may be inferred, possibly resulting from the confluence of three channels at Runnymede Bridge: the Colne Brook draining from the north, and perhaps two branches of the Thames draining across Runnymede from the west towards Runnymede Bridge. The modern course of the Thames is assumed to have a long history in some shape or form; this will be referred to as the north meadows branch. On the southern edge of the meadows a relict channel is indicated by Langham's Pond and a linear depression stretching out from it towards Glanty roundabout; this is referred to as the south meadows, or Langham's channel. At times when both these channels flowed, the whole of Runnymede meadows would have been a large island. At certain points in its history the plot of land occupied by prehistoric settlements at Runnymede Bridge also appears to have been an island, created by cut-off channels scoured between established channels. Channels flowing along the north-eastern side of the site at various times are referred to generally as northern channels, whilst those round the south of the occupied site are known as southern channels, and the specific course of

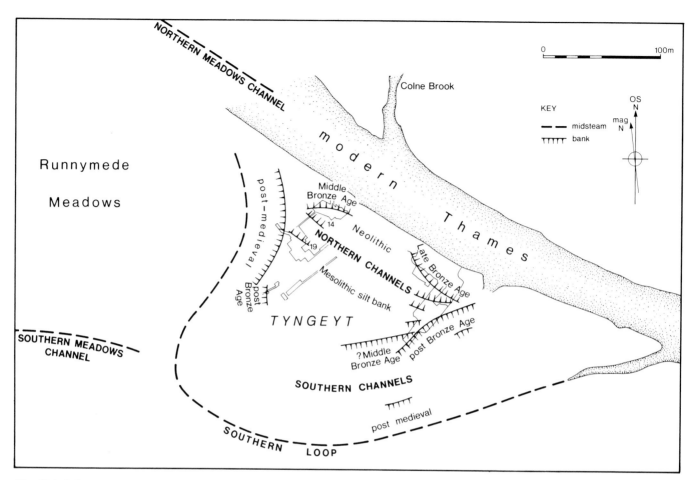

Fig. 136 Schematic plan of known river channel axes around the site at various stages of the past 6000 years.

medieval and later times as the southern loop (Fig. 136).

Before embarking on an elucidation of possible changes, it is important to stress the hazards of such a project when considering a long time trajectory. Firstly, although relevant topographic observations have been made in a number of archaeological sections across the site, and others have been gleaned from cartographic, historical and place-name sources, such observations tend by their nature to be extremely fragmented. Partly this is due to the considerable cumulative loss of information on the courses of ancient channels as they themselves migrated across the flood-plain, eroding as they went. The second difficulty arises from the behaviour of rivers when occupying broad flood-plains. They may for long periods conform to classic patterns of meander development, then suddenly change course due to unexpected flow conditions and sediment discharges, notably in the course of floods. If we add to these natural phenomena the possibilities of interference with drainage patterns by man or beavers, any reconstruction may seem a daunting prospect. It is hardly surprising, therefore, that interpretations of river changes in the locality have been continually reassessed since the 1978 excavation and may continue to be modified as archaeological investigations proceed. In these circumstances the present provisional account will be confined to description, without detailed reconstruction plans.

The Middle Neolithic bearing sediments in Area 6 are channel deposits formed under active flow within the northern channel, and they are interpreted as a mid-channel bar (Chapter 2). A comparable sequence was present in the Area 4 section with a horizon of *in situ* Middle Neolithic settlement. It is possible to interpolate the line of a Middle Neolithic channel broadly parallel to, and just to the south of, the modern river Thames. The fill of this channel is alluvial parcel 2A. The evidence of the Area 7 section suggests that this channel had migrated northwards to the Middle Neolithic position, thus leaving an earlier south bank buried under silt layer 75. This bank therefore reflects the southern edge of the channel prior to the Middle Neolithic, when it was cutting back earlier, probably Mesolithic, flood-plain deposits, 88–96 (alluvial parcel 1A). In its pre-Middle Neolithic stage this channel was apparently laying tufa down across its base. South of this channel the earlier flood-plain offered a dry bank for activity which culminated in a Middle Neolithic settlement, as witnessed in later excavations. A north-west/south-east watershed is discernible, with the land surface dipping both north-east, towards the channel already described, and south-west to a possible parallel river, an early form of the southern channel.

During the Late Neolithic the channel activity in the investigated areas diminished and the later stages of alluvial parcel 2A saw steady silting under quiet-water conditions. One possibility is that the earlier pattern of northward migration of the channel or channels continued, so that by the Late Neolithic the main water flow passed to the north-east of Areas 4, 5 and 6, which were left as a swampy backwater. At some stage, however, the northern channel may have choked up entirely, in which case the feeding river upstream would have been diverted into another course around the site. It may not be entirely coincidental, then, that the first good evidence for channel activity to the south of the occupation site dates close to the Neolithic/Bronze Age transition. Indeed the earliest identifiable channel, that filled with alluvial parcel 1B, is associated with a large influx of moderately heavy gravel (84), implying a high water-energy event. It has been suggested that such an event, or set of events over a restricted period, may also account for the truncation observed at the parcel 2A/2B interface (Chapter 1).

During the 2nd millennium BC (Early–Middle Bronze Ages), the relict of the early, Mesolithic, flood-plain remained as the highest ground within the explored site. The well investigated areas to be north-east of this watershed show a broad spread of relatively homogeneous alluvium, which steadily accumulated to depths of over a metre and characterises alluvial parcel 2B. Similar alluviation was probably taking place to the south-west of the watershed, as suggested by silts lapping up towards the high spine in Area 8 (83) and in similar stratigraphic positions in trenches on the west side of the site. The parcel 2B alluvium is eroded by river channels which cut back into the likely island from two sides. The 'cutting back' of both channels is likely to have occurred late in the second millennium, but their relative chronology cannot be established in detail.

On the southern side of the site alluvial parcel 2B was eroded by a narrow channel filled with parcel 3. This channel has been interpreted as running west–east, and was perhaps only a sub-channel of a major southern branch of the Thames. At the very least it may suggest that a channel had been flowing in the near vicinity since the earlier activity attested by alluvial parcel 1B. The parcel 3 channel had become largely choked with silt before Late Bronze Age occupation covered the remaining depression, in *c.* 900 cal BC.

Also late in the 2nd millennium BC we find renewed evidence for a northern channel which runs through Areas 4, 5, 6 and 7 (alluvial parcel 4) and has also been found in later excavations at the northern tip of the site to the north-west (Fig. 136).

This 'new' northern channel, which remained open, partially at least, into LBA times, not only appears to have cut back into the thick second millennium flood-plain deposit (38, 62, 114) but also, at its base, it dissected the underlying Neolithic channel deposits. It is difficult at the moment to reconcile the 'cutting back' action with the overall line of the bank, which is convex. In detail, however, the A5–A6–A4 stretch of the bank describes a locally concave line (Fig. 16) and the fact that this curve projected northwards lines up with the west bank of the Colne Brook could suggest that a forerunner of that tributary occupied roughly the same position. The influence of the tributary's current may well be a factor to help explain the difficulty noted in understanding the full line of the bank, whilst gross changes in the discharge of this northern channel may also have to be considered.

It should be considered that there is as yet no clear indication of a flowing northern channel between the Late Neolithic and the late Middle Bronze Age, while the Area 8 evidence suggests major channel activity to the south at times during the 2nd millennium BC. It is possible, therefore, that a southern channel system alone drained the Thames while part of the relict Neolithic northern channel was impinged upon by an early form of the Colne Brook. The two would have met somewhere beneath the woods immediately east of the site. In this scenario the western part of the new (late MBA) northern channel would have been a cut-off channel bridging the neck of the land between the Colne Brook and the north meadows branch just to the west, which may earlier have been diverted into the southern loop. If so, this cut-off, which partially exploited a buried channel course, would have created a true island late in the 2nd millennium BC.

Whatever the difficulties of interpreting the origins of the convex bank documented for the northern channel, the history of subsequent aggradation seems more straightforward. The gravel/sand bar running alongside the bank through Areas 4, 7 and 6 probably continued all the way round to the Area 14 zone, where a comparable formation occurred. This would appear to be a typical bar formation along an aggrading convex bank. Formation began, as would be expected, at the upstream (A14) end, where not only the bar, but also a series of stratified sands in its lea, had accumulated before Late Bronze Age occupation. In contrast, downstream at Area 6, occupation began while the bar was still growing.

All of the excavated evidence for the parcel 4 river channel is confined to the channel edge incorporating the gravel bar and the trough trapped in its lea. It is therefore impossible to ascertain whether the slack-water silting pattern of the trough was just a function of the protection of the gravel bar, while the main river still flowed just beyond, or whether it reflected a more general trend in a renewed choking of this northern channel. If choking took place at the upstream end of the proposed cut-off channel, it would not have caused total blocking of the downstream end, assuming that this still carried the Colne Brook waters into the Thames system. Even here, though, starved of Thames current, flow would have been severely abated.

If the cut-off channel did indeed choke up shortly prior to Late Bronze Age occupation, then the relatively recently formed island would have again become linked to the land as a peninsula, although the isthmus might still have been a marshy belt. In this situation a continuing north meadows branch of the Thames would probably have diverted once more into the southern loop around the site.

The southern loop may well have been the only open channel, or at least the major channel, by early Saxon times, for the county boundary was laid to follow it, whereas it followed the north meadows branch of the river westward from the site across Runnymede. By the 13th century AD the prehistoric occupied plot was known as *Tyngeyt* (Turner 1926: 7 fig. 9, 64) – the eyot, or island, component referring perhaps to a true island with a now flowing northern channel, or conceivably to what was effectively an island, delimited on the north by a still recognisable marshy ribbon. Whichever is the case, the northern channel must have been well established, if not re-established, in a form similar to the present straight course by the 18th century AD, as shown in early maps, and by this stage advanced silting of the southern loop was finally reducing it to a marshy belt. The south meadows branch, which had presumably emptied into the southern loop, must have stopped carrying water somewhat earlier.

An important repercussion of the Runnymede excavations is the ability to date more or less closely various sequences of alluvium owing to the inter-stratification of the remains of occupation and other activities. It is premature to say much about the detailed history of alluviation and its causes in this report, which must await analysis of subsequent investigations. However, a few general points are worth advancing at this stage. It will have become apparent from the stratigraphic discussion that a long history of alluviation, spanning, intermittently, most of the Holocene, is represented on the site. To what extent the sequences recognised at Runnymede might or might not reflect wider patterns in the lower Thames basin remains to be seen. It is perhaps of considerable interest that the earliest substantial body of alluvium to survive on the site appears to be due to over-bank flooding and dates to the Mesolithic, or certainly before any widespread agriculture was being practised. One is intrigued to know under what circumstances, in particular vegetation cover, such a deposit could develop. Again, the ultimate origin of the sediment being transported and reworked is of great interest; indeed such bodies may help corroborate Catt's perceptive suggestion that much presumed but now vanished loess has ended up in altered form in valley bottoms (1978: 18). What must surely be accepted is that there is unlikely to be any mono-causal explanation for alluviation, even in a particular catchment. Causes are likely to be varied, including, along with climatic, hydrologic and anthropogenic factors, such topics as beaver activity. It is now known that beaver were active in the Runnymede area well into later prehistory and account therefore needs to be taken of their potential impact on drainage patterns and the geomorphologic effects.

Chapter 24
Syntheses of the environmental evidence

John G. Evans

The formation and interpretation of the environmental record

The main aim of the environmental work at Runnymede has been to detail the ancient environment at various spatial scales around the site and through time. The primary data are the on-site samples of soils and sediments and their contained biological material, with interpretation being based on present-day analogues. The plant and animal remains are studied in their major taxonomic and preservational groups – vertebrates, molluscs, pollen, wood and so on – because this is practical, but ultimately it is necessary to transcend these groups and look at more natural groupings such as trophic levels or, at least, ecological communities. Before this, however, the formation of the environmental record at Runnymede must be discussed, because there is variation between and within the various kinds of data, and their significance in palaeoenvironmental terms also varies.

Scales of space
With reference to the archaeological site, information is obtained at various spatial scales, site, local and regional (Fig. 117). Roughly, the *site* encompasses an area of up to a few hundred square metres, it can be a single soil sample, an archaeological entity such as a midden or waterfront, or a fossil biological community. The *locality* is an area of up to about 0.5 km sq. and may be seen as the main catchment area for the site. The *region* is an area greater than that of the locality, and from which only a small amount of data reaches the site.

Of course, this is the artificial viewpoint of environmental archaeology, in that the environment and the dispersal of organisms within it are a continuum. Nevertheless, discrete units of deposition – e.g. river channels, flood-plains and middens – provide a basis for such a concept, as do differences in the dispersal area of different organisms (compare molluscs and pollen) and of the soils and sediments. So from the point of view of the natural world, the site, locality and region have at least some basis in fact.

Likewise for human communities there are different scales of activity which constitute different intensities and areas of land use; the concept of studying regional arboreal history, local activities such as those in a single river valley catchment, and the environment of a site through, respectively, regional, local and site pollen is a familiar one. Again, the extent and nature of our conception of the site vary, both with the archaeological viewpoint and the activities of former human communities, from being of a relatively localised and concentrated area of activity such as a habitation to a more extensive area such as farmland or hunting tracts, or even areas hardly or not at all exploited by people.

So there are three aspects to scale in space: the real scale of the former environment, the real scale of former human activity, and the partial scale of each to which the evidence relates. The first two are natural; the last is an artefact, at least partly a function of the constraints of fieldwork and excavation and of the biases of preservation.

Taphonomy
In the strict sense, taphonomy is concerned with the way in which dead organisms or parts of organisms become fossilised. It is especially concerned with the processes that result in asymmetries of fossil assemblages by comparison with the death assemblages from which they derive. An appreciation of these processes, through a knowledge of the way organisms decay and disperse after death and the formation of the soils and sediments in which they occur, can help us interpret the fossil record.

But in environmental archaeology, a broader view is useful. From the start, there are problems with using the species concept of biological classification. We can never be certain that the geological specimens, identified solely on their anatomy – as opposed to their behaviour, calls, biochemistry or capacity to produce fertile offspring – are the same as those of today, on whose ecology we base our interpretations. In most cases there has probably been no change, but it is sensible to be aware of the problem. A complementary approach to using the present-day ecology of individual species is to consider assemblages in terms of their diversity and structure, which at least will tell us something about general aspects of the environment, if not its detail.

Asymmetries in the record arise prior to death. All plants and animals are mobile in at least some stage of their life cycle, and the arrangement of biological material at death is thus only one of a range of possibilities. Furthermore, on or even before death organisms, or bits of them, are moved about by scavengers or humans, introducing more asymmetry.

At the other end of the progression are asymmetries introduced by archaeologists: the selection of a site, the way it is excavated and sampled, the nature of the post-excavation work, and the publication. None is complete or objective. All introduce bias.

The formation of death assemblages
Other than by multiple sampling, we can make statements about the area beyond the sampling site from the facts that all organisms are mobile in some of their life stages and that the formation of sediments usually involves transport. Taking the former, and thus excluding post-death transport for the time being, we can propose a scale of mobility in which 'site', 'local' and 'regional' refer to the maximum areas of distribution of the various organisms in life (the biocoeno-

sis), and thus to areas to which the death assemblage (the thanatocoenosis) relates.

Site
Vegetative parts and flowers of plants
Some pollen and macrofossil taxa
Some species of insects
Molluscs
Ostracods

Local
Seeds
Some pollen taxa
Small vertebrates
Predatory and scavenging mammals
Insects

Regional
Medium and large mammals
A few insects
Predatory birds (pellets)
Many pollen taxa

Interpretation is based on present-day behaviour, for the place in which the individual dies may not be especially representative of the environment of life. Temporal variation on a small scale – diurnal, seasonal, annual – is not revealed, nor is small-scale spatial variability, such as the vertical distribution of organisms in a wood. The resulting two-dimensional and atemporally structured death assemblage can be contrasted with the three-dimensional and temporally structured living community from which it derives.

The formation of subfossil assemblages

We now consider the processes between the formation of the death assemblage and its deposition as a subfossil assemblage.

There are two aspects: i) how the various categories of biological material were transported to the site and incorporated into a deposit; ii) what area of land they represent. As with behaviour in life, there is a range of scales of movement. The basic distinction is between soils, in which there is no lateral post-death movement and in which the death and subfossil assemblages are essentially the same, and sediments, in which there is post-death movement resulting in the alteration of the death assemblage. In the former situation the assemblage is said to be autochthonous, in the latter allochthonous.

Material distributed by human beings also relates to all spatial scales. Biological remains may be brought onto the site from elsewhere both deliberately and accidentally, e.g. on clothing or in dung. Recurring movements of these kinds could obviously change patterns significantly, but probably in quite a different way than other processes. Such effects are likely to be most pronounced in the deposits relating to the occupation of the site, but one cannot exclude the possibility that during the longer intervening periods human activity elsewhere in the catchment will be recorded in the site sediments themselves.

Understanding death assemblages is not just an aid to the interpretation of the data in terms of its environment of origin; the mode of transport and the environment of deposition are integral parts of environmental history as well. Consider a mixed land and freshwater mollusc assemblage in a freshwater deposit: from this we can say something about the terrestrial environment from which the land component derived, something about the aquatic environment in which the assemblage as a whole was transported, and something about the site environment in which it ended up. So a single set of data can tell us about different components of the palaeoenvironment – land and freshwater – and at a range of spatial scales.

SOILS AND SEDIMENTS

There are two main types of sediment at Runnymede. One consists of organic sand with discontinuous layers of sandy loam, generally distinctly stratified and confined to channels. Sediments of this type are river channel deposits, laid down in permanently flowing water and not subjected to pedogenesis. On the whole, they occur in the lower part of the SS1 and WF1 sequences.

The other type of deposit is finer, with texture ranging from sandy clay-loam to clay. Macro-stratification is apparent but the layers are vertically more uniform and horizontally more continuous and extensive than those of the channel deposits, and some layers are consistently uniform throughout. These deposits were laid down in a variety of environments, from permanent, slowly moving water to over-bank flooding. On the whole this type of deposit occurs in the upper part of the SS1 and WF1 sequences.

Pedogenesis is apparent in both sequences, especially in the upper parts.

PLANT AND ANIMAL REMAINS

In the coarser river channel deposits, the sands and finer gravels, all the biological material is, on *a priori* grounds alone, allochthonous. Of the various taxonomic groups, the ostracods are the most nearly autochthonous because their shells are fragile, and indeed the assemblages are ecologically uniform. The molluscan assemblages are also fairly pure, with 85–90% of the total individuals being aquatic. By contrast, not more than 25% of the total minimum number of individuals of Coleoptera are aquatics. For the plant macrofossils only about seven species out of more than 100 are specified as living in flowing water.

The terrestrial component in the channel deposits is incorporated from the river edge and the flood-plain, being either swept in (molluscs and seeds) or aerially derived (insects and pollen). Mark Robinson suggests that in general terms the major land biological groups may be arranged in order of decreasing catchment area upstream and either side of the river; 50% of each group derive from this catchment, as follows, assuming no significant human interference:

Pollen – 2 km upstream and 100 m each side of river
Beetles – 0.5 km and 50 m
Waterlogged seeds – 0.5 km and 10 m
Molluscs – 0.2 km and 2 m

These are guesses, not yet substantiated by experiment or detailed observation, but they are an indication of the regional to local to site significance of the various groups. The figures would not apply if most of the remains entered the water as a result of extensive flooding or human dumping of organic material. The latter can be eliminated (especially Chapters 14, 15, 17) as a significant contribution, but the former cannot.

There may also be a component reworked from older deposits, introduced by scouring and bank collapse. This is clearest in the case of the wood pebbles noted by Susan Limbrey (Chapter 11).

In the finer deposits, the loams and clay-loams, there is also a mixture of ecological groups, although it is likely, in view of the low energy of deposition, that the assemblages are more nearly autochthonous. In fact the situation is complicated, because there are two genetic types of deposit.

First there are the finer units of the channel deposits (layers 41, 27a and the lower part of 20c), probably formed in permanently still or gently flowing water, as indicated by the high proportion of freshwater shells (Chapter 15). It was in this environment that most of the ostracods and aquatic vegetation and many of the aquatic molluscs lived. They include, however, a terrestrial mollusc and plant component, so the assemblages are not entirely autochthonous.

Second, higher up, in both the SS1 and WF1 sequences, there are flood-plain deposits, laid down in an environment that supported an essentially land vegetation and molluscan fauna (the upper part of layers 40 and 38, and layers 7–4), as indicated by the high proportion of land shells. (This is probably true for layer 38, although the molluscs were not analysed.) By comparison with the situation in the channel deposits, the land component is more nearly autochthonous and the freshwater component allochthonous. A complication with flood-plains is that under certain conditions amphibious and land groups of Mollusca live in the same place but at different times of the year: the amphibious live and breed in the standing waters of the winter, the land species do so in the drier conditions of the summer, as demonstrated by Robinson (1988) for modern meadows in the upper Thames. Thus in addition to spatial mixing on flood-plains (true allochthony) there is small-scale temporal mixing.

In land surfaces, the midden, and human structures, such as the waterfronts, there is a further component, that introduced by man. Comparison of the insect assemblages from the WF1 sequence with the contemporary LBA midden shows that this component is confined to certain contexts, for hardly any insects associated with settlements and middens occur in the river channel fill. Most of the timber on the site is thought to have been brought in by people for a variety of purposes, such as structures, small artifacts and firewood, although there is also driftwood in some layers (Chapter 13).

The other main source of biological material is that which relates to activities in life rather than the transport mechanisms, mainly fluvial and human, discussed so far. There is an aerial component which includes mainly insects and pollen, some arriving passively, some actively; Mark Robinson suggests that most of the terrestrial insects arrived in this way, either falling or inadvertently flying into the river, rather than by being swept in by floodwaters. There are small vertebrates which could have arrived by a variety of means – swimming, walking, and as bird of prey pellets; and some of the insect remains were deposited in a corvid pellet. It is possible that some of the non-structural timber is from the activity of beavers.

The overall differences in the proportions of land and freshwater components for different taxonomic groups relate to ecology and taphonomy. Also, the pool of available species in each habitat varies. For example, there are no (or extremely few) land ostracods, so their assemblages will be totally aquatic; the number of species of aquatic plants and beetles relative to terrestrial ones in the biocoenosis is much less than for molluscs; and the numbers of plant species in the river edge communities is greater than the numbers of molluscs in the same habitat. Thus, because of the artificial way in which the evidence is studied, by taxonomic rather than ecological groups, such asymmetries emerge.

Summary and conclusions
The origins of the biological and other components are summarised below (see also Fig. 117):

1. Channel deposits
   (a) Organisms living in the river (some local mixing but mainly autochthonous)
   (b) Organisms living on the river bank and flood-plain (all allochthonous)
   (c) Organisms re-worked from earlier deposits (probably slight)
2. Flood-plain deposits
   (a) Organisms living on the flood-plain (slight mixing but mainly autochthonous)
   (b) Organisms derived from flooding, land and freshwater (all allochthonous)
3. Middens, other human structures and soils
   (a) Material derived directly from human activity and brought from off-site
   (b) Organisms living on the site
4. In all there is a component deriving from transport that has to do with the biology of the organisms themselves. This applies especially to mobile groups like pollen, insects and vertebrates, and to human activity.

So the origin and environmental significance of the biological material vary according to the environments of deposition and the transport mechanisms (Fig. 117). Sometimes they relate to the site environment – that is, the site of deposition – and sometimes to a wider sphere of influence. This is important when considering changes of abundance through time, in that these may relate to taphonomic processes rather than to population density. At Runnymede, there are two main components of the environment at almost every level, the aquatic and the land, one of which is always equivalent to the site of deposition or pedogenesis, and both of which may reflect local and regional environments. Thus in a change from river channel to flood-plain, an aquatic species changes from being autochthonous and of site significance to allochthonous and of local or regional significance; and the reverse is true for a land species (Fig. 124).

In general, the aquatic biota indicate a range of slow- and fast-moving water environments in a well oxygenated permanent river. There was undoubtedly spatial variation at different scales, such as vegetated and non-vegetated areas in a few square metres and differences of flow rate along the length of the river over a few kilometres, but these can only be inferred from the ecological groups. Almost still water is indicated by some of the plants and the ostracods, probably at the river's edge, but there were no completely still-water bodies such as ox-bow lakes.

In the land component, similar spatial variation at a range of scales is implied. The molluscs are fairly uniform, both as autochthonous and allochthonous assemblages, usually indicating wet grassland, and this is supported by the plants and insects, with species of richer, fen habitats being rare. Such uniformity suggests either that wet grassland was widespread or that there was little mixing, or both. Woodland is indicated by the plant macrofossils, insects and pollen, but while the pollen suggests mixed lime/oak woods, the insects suggest oak as the main species, probably the result of pollen having a greater range than beetles. The likely picture is that there was alder carr on the wetter soils close to the site, oak on the gravel terrace, and mixed lime/oak/elm woodland further away. The land molluscs do not reflect these woodland environments strongly, although there is greater diversity in the allochthonous assemblages than in the autochthonous ones, suggesting that the elements contributing to this increased diversity are from habitats further away (Chapter 15). They indicate woodland and dry grassland. In the Bronze Age there is plentiful evidence for cereal cultivation, not least from cereal grains themselves, and it is likely that the fields were on dry ground close to the site, although how close is uncertain. There was also dry calcareous grassland, as indicated by the occasional presence of the snail *Helicella itala* and plants such as *Scabiosa columbaria*, and heathland, as indicated by the pollen of Ericales.

Synthesis of environmental history at Runnymede Bridge

The environments at Runnymede in the Neolithic and Bronze Age can be classified in various ways, for example, as on hydrology or vegetational structure. In terms of hydrology, there are three main groups: aquatic, intermediate and terrestrial.

Aquatic environments are mainly the river and its edge habitats, both being well represented in the fossil record.

Intermediate environments are those strongly influenced by the water table but in which there is usually dry land for at least part of the year. They include alder carr, for which there is abundant evidence of local growth, and a number of open vegetations. Of the latter, wet grassland, probably flooded in winter and possibly managed, was abundant, while other, wetter environments such as marsh, wet springs and muddy waterside areas were not. Herb-rich sedge fen was absent.

Terrestrial environments were mostly further away from the site than the aquatic and intermediate ones, although in the case of some of the dry open habitats were perhaps still fairly local, for example, where crops were grown. They include various kinds of mixed deciduous woodland, cultivated land and wasteland. There was also heathland and dry calcareous grassland.

SS1 and Neolithic contexts
Between about 195 and 170 cm the sediments indicate a rapidly flowing river, laterally mobile and depositing banks of sand and fine gravel; in slacker pools between finer organic deposits accumulated. The molluscs and insects indicate a rich diversity of aquatic habitats, with well oxygenated still water, rapids with stony substratum and stagnant areas. Among the beetles of clean flowing water, the Elmidae are particularly abundant, often clinging to stones, and the gastropod limpet, *Ancylus fluviatilis*, probably co-existed in the same habitat. At the river's edge there was reedswamp of tall emergent monocotyledons, especially *Schoenoplectus lacustris* and *Phragmites austriacus*, as indicated by host-specific beetles of the genus *Donacia*, with areas of exposed mud, as indicated by various amphibious and non-aquatic mud-dwelling insects and the small gastropod *Lymnaea truncatula*.

The land at this stage was grassland and woodland, the latter constituting maybe one-third of the cover, or perhaps two-thirds if the grassland was only along the river. The molluscs show little trace of woodland, so the land closest to the site was grassland. This was wet and herb-rich, as indicated by the most abundant land snail, *Vallonia pulchella*, and the associated fauna of marsh species. The plants and insects indicate a similar environment of flowery herb-rich grassland, used as lightly grazed pasture rather than meadow. Insects and molluscs point to the absence of extensive wet marsh and sedge fen, so the junction between land and river at this stage was fairly sharp.

The woodland was mainly lime and oak, with oak predominant nearer to the site, and alder on the wetter soils of the flood-plain and river's edge, as indicated by the main host-specific insects – for example, the alder leaf beetle, *Agelastica alni*. Ash and elm were of lesser importance. There were transitional areas between the woodland and grassland in which shrub and small tree species of the Prunoideae and Pomoideae grew. The timber on the site, some of it from human activity, came from a variety of environments at a greater or lesser distance. Oak and alder were the main species used for the Neolithic structures. Timber from Area 5, not certainly due to human activities, included hazel, willow/poplar, *Prunus* and oak; the age of the timbers suggests that the material was not coppice wood but chosen from branches or mature stems.

Between about 170 and 125 cm (layer 40) the sediments indicate continuing aquatic conditions at the site of deposition, but with less rapidly flowing water. There is a decline of water beetles and phytophagous species feeding on aquatic plants from 155 to 125 cm. In the upper part of the layer, from about 150 cm, the molluscs show increasing dryness, and by 125 cm there was land. The pattern of change in the land assemblages is especially convincing, both in the steady increase in shell numbers and slug granules and in the environmental sequence, which shows an ecological progression from river channel, through mudflat to intermittently flooded grassland (Figs. 118 and 124). The river channel had shifted away from Area 6.

In addition to the drier conditions indicated by the changing ratio of land to aquatic shells, the aquatic molluscs and beetles indicate that the river environment between 155 and 125 cm was poorer and less diverse than previously. This may be due to human interference, both in sharpening the distinction between land and water and in introducing sediment into the water from agricultural erosion. However, major human activity on the site was probably long since over, so it is more likely that the changes are due to the shifting river course, as already proposed, with the assemblages deriving from areas of gentler flow rather than the main channel.

Significant changes in the land assemblages in the SS1 sequence are a decrease in grassland molluscs, especially *Vallonia pulchella*, from 165 cm to 125 cm, and a decrease in grassland insects from 175 cm to 125 cm, especially scarabaeoid dung beetles and species with larvae that feed on roots in grassland. These changes suggest a decrease in grassland immediately adjacent to the site, and are consistent with the pollen evidence for forest regrowth in the SS1 sequence (at 170–150 cm).

Truncation of layer 40 by renewed river action took place (Figs. 21 and 23) and clayey alluvium (layers 39 and 38) was deposited. Here we have only the sediments. Initially the depositional environment was aquatic, a perennially stagnant, muddy water body. There was no subaerial weathering. With time conditions became drier, leading to the development of a gleyed soil in wet, rushy grassland. Above 65 cm, the land was better drained and the soil was aerobic, at least

in summer.

Intense pedogenesis took place from the dried-out surface of layer 38, and there was LBA occupation (layers 31 to 37).

WF1 and Late Bronze Age contexts

Layers 25 and 27 were laid down in a swiftly flowing river. Once again the river had shifted its course and, in doing so, it cut a channel into the deposits of the SS1 sequence, laying down initially shingle lenses, sand and sandy loam above a gravelly river bed (Figs. 20–23). The insects suggest a well vegetated channel fringed with tall reedswamp, similar to that in the earlier stages of the SS1 sequence. The botanical evidence includes at least six species of rooted aquatics that grew in the river, equivalent to today's Potamogetonetalia (pondweed) community, with tall emergent monocotyledons of the Phragmitetea community at the edges. The molluscan assemblages are rich, and fully in keeping with the plant and insect evidence, with *Theodoxus fluviatilis*, a species of rapidly flowing water, abundant. There is an increase in aquatic habitat diversity, as indicated by the molluscs, as the deposits built up. In the lower deposits ostracods are richest in layer 27a, a shelly sandy loam with finer loamy areas. The main species is *Limnocythere inopinata*, a species generally of lakes, so this horizon perhaps represents a period of abatement in river flow.

On land, the insect and plant macrofossils point to a generally open landscape with a much reduced woodland cover by comparison with the Neolithic. The open land was mainly well drained permanent pasture, lightly grazed and herb-rich. The plant remains, in addition to grassland generally, indicate a range of types such as wet grassland, mineral-rich fen and perhaps semi-managed flood-plain communities of pasture and meadow. The molluscs indicate wet grassland. There was some riverside marsh, but it was not extensive. There is no indication of arable in the main catchment, but the insect remains in a corvid pellet indicate cultivation not far beyond.

Woodland, in addition to having been reduced since the Neolithic, was made up of a different range of species. The major species of the primary woodland, especially lime, were rare, and in their place grew various shrubs such as hazel, hawthorn, sloe, holly and buckthorn; many were spiny or prickly species, possibly planted as hedges. There was more willow/poplar and less alder. Other trees included ash, field maple and yew (both possibly from the chalk, although field maple does not need to be, given the calcareous nature of the alluvium here) and elm. Timber remains on the site indicate the exploitation of vast quantities of young oak trunks, with in addition the employment of young stems on a seven-year cycle, suggesting coppicing.

Further afield there is evidence from molluscs, insects and plants of other habitats, such as dry calcareous chalk grassland and heath, but these indications are very slight.

Layer 25a (WF 120–132 cm) marks the beginning of LBA occupation. From this level upwards to layer 7 the biological remains indicate still-water conditions, with perhaps periodic influxes of sediment; the environment became increasingly terrestrial. The molluscs are in agreement, with *Theodoxus fluviatilis* dying out and total shell abundance falling. Peaks of ostracod abundance occur in layer 20c, with the species indicating standing permanent water. The water became shallower, with intermittent drying at the level where the preservation of the piles deteriorates (layers 20b to 13; 80–65 cm) and there is a nice peak of land shells here. This may have been a mudflat, and the gastropod *Lymnaea truncatula* is characteristic. Layers 20b to 13 span the period of the inner pile row. The period of the outer pile row (layer 11) sees a slight increase in aquatic influence, but from layer 6 to the top of the sequence the site environment was wet grassland subject to flooding.

The aquatic environment, as detailed by the molluscs, saw a decrease in diversity similar to that in the SS1 sequence. Again one can propose a change in the river regime due to human interference, and there is direct evidence for this in the timber waterfronts and the botanical evidence for cereal cultivation, although the latter was probably not in the river catchment. Or again, one can suggest that the changing river environment is a function of the shifting river course itself, and that the molluscan assemblages are derived from a slow-moving or still-water part of the river rather than from the main channel.

Chapter 25
Overall discussion

In this concluding discussion it is important to attempt to interrelate the evidence stemming directly from human activity on the site (mainly structural and artifactual) with that based on environmental data. This is not a straightforward matter. Even at a site like Runnymede, which benefits from a wealth and diversity of environmental evidence, allowing composite pictures to emerge from substantial, not ephemeral, traces of human occupation and from an immediate juxtaposition of the two, it is all too easy to slip into a compartmentalist mode and regard each kind of data in isolation. Part of the problem is that in spite of the closeness of the association, there does seem to be a certain lack of impact, one upon the other. There could almost be two separate stories to tell, and this phenomenon in itself deserves consideration, aside from the detailed questions of interrelationship, where these may be addressed. It is the more surprising, perhaps, when it is considered that the bulk of the environmental data is believed (by and large by all the specialists) to derive from a rather small tract of land in the bottom of the valley around (and mainly upstream of) the site.

Some fundamental issues to come under consideration in the discussion are:

1. Anachronism: does the main settlement activity date differently from the activity generating the environmental remains?
2. Processes by which residues (of whatever kind) enter permanent deposits, while others escape local traps.
3. The rapidity with which the mark of settlement itself becomes lost in the immediate environs.

This last bears on the question which has been raised in recent years of whether a 'site' can be defined closely in spatial terms. It could be argued that, although they appear to reflect very different spheres of the contemporary cultural landscape, the two branches of evidence nevertheless both bear largely on one system, but on different 'sites' as defined by distinct activity sets. Indeed, a potential advantage of riverine situations like Runnymede is that evidence from a somewhat wider catchment can 'come home to roost' in the settlement site deposits themselves, owing to the geomorphological processes at play. This is a positive asset. In a sense the artifactual and structural debris in Area 6 is telling us what was happening on site, being the north-eastern perimeter of the settlement, whereas the environmental debris speaks largely of what was happening off-site in the surrounding countryside. This does not mean that there are no complexities in interpretation, nor a lack of contribution from external and unrelated ecologies; but the assuredly local nature of the great bulk of the evidence gives plausibility to the claim that the contemporary environmental record found on the site belongs largely to the activities of the Runnymede occupants or their immediate neighbours, who are likely to have been interdependent groups in the same community.

Perhaps the most serious bias in the environmental data *en masse* is the linearity of the zone represented, as deduced from a dominance of river, river bank and adjacent low-lying habitats – in other words, a strip along the river system. Here 'local' might only mean that in terms of similarity of terrain, the flood-plain 4 km upstream may be better represented than the terraces 400 m inland. This could well be a significant distortion, and hints from a wider pollen rain and a contribution from wind-swept insects have to be teased out as a minimal counterbalance. Far more positive and compelling evidence, however, comes from the fortuitous find of a corvid pellet (LBA). Robinson has argued that, although the beetle spectrum within bears witness to an arable landscape hardly detectable in the other records, the arable fields would not have been far off, since corvids do not fly far with a full crop. Similarly, the contrast between the assumed culturally introduced grain and the paucity of any other unequivocal indications of arable agriculture is striking. This evidence, however, does not answer the question of *where* the corn was grown, and for this one needs to turn to the evidence from other sites in the locality, such as the field systems mentioned below.

Grain adds new dimensions to the map of 'catchment', as does more general cultural refuse; worked stone is a case in point. Taking the predominant Tertiary sandstone, it is clear that there was frequent access to the low hills of the Bagshot Table, yet this zone appears to be extremely distant in the environmental records, although it must be admitted that this is based on a preconception of that terrain's vegetational cover.

The geomorphological processes at work in a fluvial environment will obviously have a potentially marked effect on any kind of remains, and the importance of such effects has been clearly addressed in the environmental reports and synthesis through discussion of the autochthonous/allochtonous contributions to assemblages. Extra-site material will have been swept in; site residues will often have been swept out. The Area 6 river channel illustrates the latter well. The density of charcoal in layers 8a and 8b thinned rapidly beyond the inner and outer pile rows respectively, probably owing to scouring of the foreshore up to the waterfront structures. Again, the distinctive and informative insect assemblage of the localised midden around 8E/12N was rapidly dissipated, to the extent that only a pale shadow survived in the WF1 column a few metres away. Only the fickleness of survival (waterlogging) allowed the midden constituents to be recognised, and these make an unusually direct statement on an 'environmental' product of human occupation. This specific insight, like the corvid pellet, is at total variance with the general ecological background and it illustrates how easily individual circumstances usually blend and blur in the archaeological record.

The question of chronological association is not simply one of having useful stratigraphies and identifying physical relationships. Account must be taken of possible time lapses, and here the discrimination of allochtonous from autochtonous elements becomes the more essential. Sediments may contain records of a historical nature even at the moment of their deposition. Even after these allowances are made further difficulties of interpretation can occur. Evans, for example, points out that a group of snail species present at a given point of a sequence and deduced to be cohabitants need not always represent a significant association. Some may instead result from chance and transitory colonisations in a quickly changing local environment.

The origin of the sediments themselves, particularly those accumulating at this site during the later Neolithic and Early–Middle Bronze Age, is of wider interest. There have been past suggestions of accelerated alluviation due to later prehistoric tilling of valley slopes (e.g. Limbrey 1983), or impedance of river flow associated with sea-level rises (Needham 1985: 133), whilst beavers, now shown to be present during later prehistory in the lower Thames valley, could have had significant regional impact on patterns of erosion and aggradation. The build-up of alluvium is shown at Runnymede to have a long history, going back to the Mesolithic period. Explanation of particular silt bodies is unlikely to be easy in the absence of broader three-dimensional evidence on sedimentation in the middle reaches of the Thames Valley. Soil micromorphological studies should also help here.

Neolithic

Relative chronology is essential to the integration of the Runnymede Neolithic evidence, as also is some idea of the scale of occupation. This has been brought to light better by the later excavations on the site. There is evidence for activity on the site during the later Mesolithic and Early Neolithic but, apart from the group of flints salvaged from Area 8, this did not come through in the 1978 campaign. This early activity is attested on a high spine of silt, 100 m to the west, and is overlain by dense evidence for Middle Neolithic settlement. In contrast, the main contexts yielding Middle Neolithic material in Areas 4 and 6 occupied low-lying levels, some 2 m lower, where the underlying tufa bed implies a water margin environment already present at an earlier stage of the Holocene. Although the Area 4 remains clearly included *in situ* structural elements, their altitude at *c.* 12.20–12.40 m OD (cf. Area 6 channel deposits with finds concentrations, 11.95–12.17 m) suggests that they could only have been utilised transiently or seasonally. The Neolithic evidence covered in this report therefore stems from activities and effects somewhat marginal to the main settlement nucleus on the silt bank a little distance away. Interpreted changes in activity and the environment are summarised diagrammatically in Fig. 137.

The main feature of the Area 6 Neolithic deposits, a bar of interleaved sands, silts and shingles, is dated most directly, perhaps, by the palaeomagnetic column which penetrated it in trench 2. These sediments are best placed within the span 4200–3650 cal BC, while the dated worked timbers, which lie on or near the top of the bar, give ranges of 3970–3520 cal BC and 3780–3380 cal BC. In broad terms it would seem that this bar developed and then became dormant some time during the earlier half of the 4th millennium cal BC. The cultural refuse recovered in excavation comes, like the timbers, from a late phase of this sequence, mainly 41a–e. This could suggest that activity peripheral to the main settlement encroached at a time when the river had shifted away to leave this bar periodically dry. There may, however, have been some material in lower stratigraphic positions: for example, some pottery from the sump dug into the southeast corner of trench 1 deep is likely to have come from below 41e, as also are sherds from the north-east corner of trench 1 deep.

The Area 4 and Area 6 deposits containing Middle Neolithic material need not be closely contemporaneous; unfortunately stratigraphic conclusions do not allow any fine assessment of this. Both groups lie within variegated sediments which underlie more homogeneous material, layers 40 and 116, which are probably of the same depositional phase. The Area 4 deposits, however (117–121) are basically horizontally bedded, perhaps bespeaking a different depositional regime from the tipping shoal deposit of L41 in Area 6; this could be partly or entirely due to relative position in the channel system (Fig. 16). A temporal difference might be indicated by the limited pottery assemblages, with Area 4 earlier than Area 6, but the radiocarbon results point if anything the other way (Fig. 132). Although there is a possibility of the redeposition of the Area 6 cultural debris, it has been argued that there can have been no appreciable time lapse since initial discard, nor, indeed, since the felling of the dated timbers (p. 53). It is not improbable that the finds were early-stage refuse dumped quickly into the channel edge.

It would appear from the recorded section of Area 4 that there was something of a depth of cultural deposits of which only the lower elements were excavated in plan (120c and around). The withies in 120a and 120b seem likely to be further dumps of brush similar to that excavated, perhaps deliberate consolidation, which was augmented by the addition of stone material in 118. It is regrettable that more of this structure could not be investigated.

At least four of the piles penetrating this brush platform belong to the Neolithic, for they were worked with stone axes. In fact it is more than likely that most of the piles in Area 4B belong, to judge from certain alignments and regularity of spacing. The two dated examples have produced rather different radiocarbon measurements, perhaps indicating some time depth to these deposits, although their calibrated ranges overlap at 2σ around the 36th century cal BC.

The associated artifacts, including pottery, a bone point, stone axes, various flint types and worked bark, clearly point

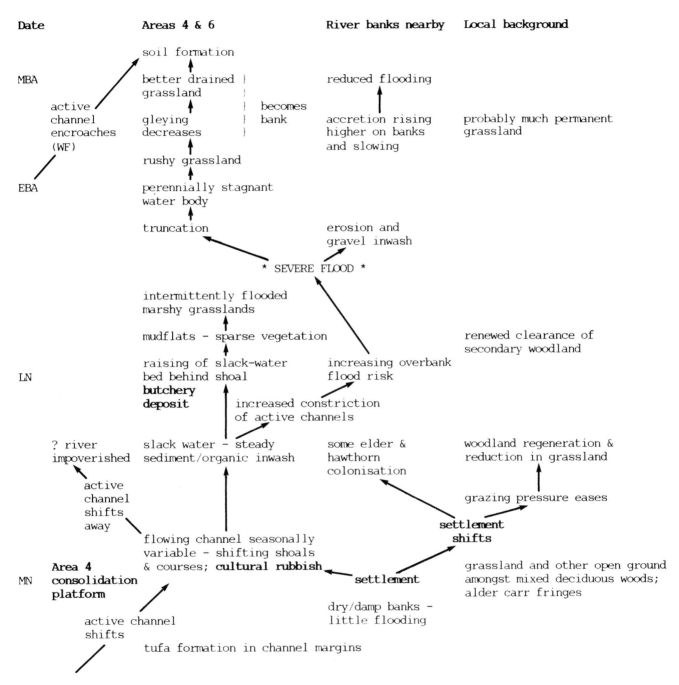

Fig. 137 Neolithic settlement activity within the context of environmental and geomorphological changes in the vicinity of Runnymede Bridge.

to certain domestic activities having taken place in this low-lying setting in Area 4, but the assemblage is too small to assess whether any specialisation was involved. The condition of certain finds, however, might well reflect the physical circumstances of this zone; two complete stone axes (S2, S3) and the greater part of a pottery bowl (NP5) may witness the easy loss of material amongst dense sub-structure or in soft mud, or indeed speedy abandonment if the river level rose unexpectedly. Permanent waterlogging of the sub-structure is shown by the survival of a worked bark artifact (W4), as well as by the more resilient structural timbers.

Another set of branch wood, in Area 5, is stratigraphically placed in the Neolithic channel sediments (Figs. 7–8) which survive, in dissected form, beneath the Late Bronze Age river channel. Although superficially similar to the Area 4 brushwood, no worked timbers were recovered, nor were there any indications from arrangement or species selection to suggest that they derived from human activity.

If Neolithic activity in both Areas 4 and 6 is to be regarded as marginal, then it is necessary to enquire where the nearest ground suitable for a settlement nucleus might have been. It is likely that the high silt spine known to have supported settlement in Areas 19 etc. would have extended south-east-wards as a dry bank to the junction of Areas 7 and 8, where similar underlying sediments exist as alluvial parcel 1A (Fig. 136). The overlying gravel deposit in Area 8 is almost certainly the same as gravel elsewhere on the site which sealed the Neolithic surface in about Beaker or Early Bronze Age times. The interface beneath (84/88) truncates earlier silt bodies, embedded in which were the bases of *in situ* Neolithic piles, one dated to 3770–3100 cal BC. These piles themselves suggest structures located within a low-lying setting or at a river bank during the Middle Neolithic, and if any drier bank rose to the north-east, it was unfortunately truncated in the southern part of Area 7 above about 13.40 m OD by the A30 floodway and by contractors, although it is possible that the bases of some dug features were still present at the top of the section.

The rest of the Area 7 section shows a sequence of silts which, broadly speaking, are part of the same channel system as the Neolithic sediments in Areas 4 and 6. The south-western bank of this system is seen clearly under contexts 75/76 and early channel fill deposits lie against it in succession (75/76, 73/74, 68), while further out horizontally bedded deposits accumulated in the remaining broad channel (70–72). This suite of sediments is probably broadly coeval with the Early–Middle Neolithic ones in Areas 4 and 6, and it may be significant that a patch of possible burnt clay was noted in section in layer 73, where it could easily have derived from occupation on the adjacent bank. On balance, however, it would seem that at least 15 m separated Areas 4 and 6 from a 'dry' occupied river bank.

Quieter water conditions came to settle on the syncline to the south-west of the Area 6 bar and steady, probably slower, silt accumulation trapped a variety of environmental fossils. The sequence they document probably picks up late

within or after the Middle Neolithic activity in the immediate vicinity, depending on whether the nearby refuse is regarded as having been redeposited. The lowest samples of column SS1, below 170 cm, are therefore closest in time to the settlement phase, and a similar situation obtains in the A4 column, again below about 170 cm. These low samples have in fact yielded environmental remains that would tie in well with nearby activity (see below). Although the ensuing sequence interpreted for these columns does show change, generally throughout the Neolithic sediments a fairly consistent pattern of habitats is presented. In the immediate catchment, habitats of both water and land would appear to have been mixed. There is abundant evidence of different water conditions in terms of speed of flow or lack of it, kind of growing vegetation, presence or absence of plant detritus or type of river bed. Wherever there was flow, the water was well oxygenated. The damper parts of the valley were characterised by variety; while alder fringe and stands of sedges or bulrushes existed around the land/water interfaces, there is little if any indication of monotonous and extensive wetland ecozones of alder carr or sedge fen. There were probably many patches of 'waste' ground, perhaps especially along the river banks, amongst them marshy grassland. Although plant taxa specifically associated with such habitats were rather few, this may be partly due to small sample sizes of plant remains examined for the Neolithic. It is probable that elements of this habitat diversity may have been caused by changes associated with the introduction of agriculture to the region a little earlier, but the overall picture of the wetter valley area is one of lack of pressure and failure to impose monocultures (however inadvertently) on the landscape for economic gain. This low-scale impact and lack of 'management' is reinforced by the associated picture of a full cycle of natural decay in the background vegetation: plant detritus along the water's edge and over-mature wood in the still substantial wooded areas. The woods themselves may have fallen into fairly neat biozones according to drainage and surface geology across the valley floor, with the dominance of alder on the wetter parts, perhaps oak on the drier terraces and mixed lime/oak/elm elsewhere. A certain amount of impact there was: good tracts of open land existed, perhaps mostly cleared during the earlier Neolithic, although this sequence is not yet documented for the Runnymede area. Even here, though, the signs are of herb-rich, insect-rich grasslands, grazed, but not heavily, and there is a sense of stability well below the level of a maximising economy. As we shall see, however, stability does not mean stasis. Overall it may be concluded that there was for the duration of the SS1 waterlogged silts probably sufficient variety of habitat associated with a relatively low demand by local inhabitants to allow them to select resources as need be without dramatically affecting the environment.

A lack of grazing pressure on the grassland could have been for one of two reasons. Either there was, prior to the SS1 sequence, a real decline in grazing owing to a reduction in livestock density in the catchment, or the lack of pressure was not a new phenomenon but instead a feature of cleared land since its clearance at whatever earlier time. The latter would be an important conclusion, somewhat at variance with the current perception of clearance taking place in a framework of immediate needs, with the consequent heavy exploitation of available cleared land. On the other hand, the first possibility could tie in with a shift of the settlement nucleus away from the site, which can be argued on other grounds. Unfortunately, at present there is not sufficient evidence to be sure whether grazing pressure seen in the post-occupation phase represents a decrease on previous grazing. Robinson does, however, note a big decline in Coleoptera Species Grouping 2 (Chapter 17) which depend on the dung of large herbivores from lower to upper SS1, and, perhaps related to this, there is evidence between 190 and 160 cm for some forest regeneration (Chapter 14). This regeneration follows on from the most open conditions witnessed in the SS1 column, in sample 190 at its base. Apart from having the lowest arboreal pollen percentage, it alone has a good presence of *Plantago lanceolata*, whilst cereals occur in this and the overlying sample (180 cm). This combination of features suggests strongly that the bottom of the SS1 column records the environmental and agricultural situation associated with the Middle Neolithic settlement phase, although perhaps in its closing phases.

Woodland regeneration seems to peak between 170 and 150 cm depth, with the major species of tree or shrub peaking (in pollen production) at slightly different stages. Thereafter those same major species – oak, alder and hazel – decline rapidly to give way to a renewal of more open conditions. To some extent it would seem that the new onslaught was on regenerated woodland, rather than primary woodland, but the cultural context of this phase is not yet known.

It is unlikely that the local grassland had ever been abandoned wholesale during this progression. More probably the grassland was a little remote from the contemporary settlement nuclei and was subjected to less persistent grazing than it experienced when the settlement was nearby. During this period the site appears to have received only intermittent visitations, to judge by a thin scatter of Late Neolithic finds, amongst them the butchered bone group (F125) in Area 6. These cattle bones (possibly one beast) are likely to relate to a prevalence of cattle grazing on the valley bottom areas, which one might postulate continuing from Middle Neolithic times.

It has been suggested that abandonment of the settlement need not have been accompanied by abandonment of the countryside around. There doubtless were areas which fell into neglect and it has been suggested by Greig (Chapter 14) that areas like the settlement site itself could have sprouted hawthorn and elder scrub. Regeneration was probably not very widespread, and there is no sense of enclosed clearings in the forest which were gradually swallowed up after abandonment, as in classic *Landnam* sequences. Rather the evidence gives the impression of more interconnected tracts of open land spreading away from settlements in which

shifts in demographic patterns set in train a complex pattern of habitat modifications, each in itself perhaps small, gradual or localised, but which overall altered the balance and distribution of habitat. This essentially stable, but not static, situation enabled the habitat-specific flora and fauna to maintain themselves by colonisation in keeping with the habitat drifts.

Other changes seem to be recorded in the SS1 sequence. Although at an early stage there was plenty of damp grassland, there was little regular flooding. There are signs, however, of increased over-bank flooding in the catchment. This is not necessarily directly attested early on in Area 6, where the build-up of sediment, L40, was probably a natural consequence of seasonal flooding in the lee of the shingle bar – flooding that ironically simultaneously caused a shift towards more terrestrial conditions at this spot, by way of an intermediate mud-flat stage. However, the noticeable truncation across all earlier deposits before the deposition of L39 may have been a consequence of increasing flood events, as too could have been the gravel deposit thrown across the adjacent bank to the south-west. These serious events seem to occur around the Neolithic/Bronze Age transition, and it might not be coincidence that they correlate with the early stages of Devoy's marine transgression Thames III in the Thames estuary (cf. Needham 1985: 134). An alternative suggestion in considering possible impoverishment in the aquatic assemblages in SS1 is that increased silt loads in the river were due to erosion of agricultural land in the valleys upstream, and that these caused more constriction and choking of channels and more rapid floods. Constriction of the channels in the region of the site at this time cannot be demonstrated, but is feasible. Certainly a broad tract of former 'channel' seen in the Area 7 section was silting up during the Late Neolithic, and, unless considerable erosion took place along the north (now lost) bank of this system, overall channel width might well have decreased. The situation is complicated by the likelihood that a second channel was flowing a little to the south at this time as part of a braided system, and Evans's impoverishment of fauna above 160 cm in the SS1 sequence (Chapter 15) could perhaps stem from the main water flow by-passing what had become a backwater in Areas 4 and 6. More than one factor may have contributed to silting, channel constriction and increased flooding. In addition to changing estuarine water levels and agriculturally generated silt loads, there is the further possibility that much more local factors were at play, namely consequences of human interference with the topography and flow patterns at the site itself during occupation.

A final area of discussion of the Neolithic evidence concerns the food economy. As has already been made clear, the biases in the environmental remains recovered will not have favoured the drier land of the valley terraces, which are perhaps likely to have been the major locations of arable farming. This makes it difficult on present evidence to assess the role of arable, although its contribution relative to other sources is always notoriously difficult to gauge. Some current views of the earlier Neolithic see cereal production in a subordinate role to livestock, with gathering also as an element in the food economy. If this was the case at Runnymede there was nevertheless some cereal farming going on in the locality and flour was being ground on site (cf. the later finds of quernstones).

The animal bone assemblage (Chapter 18) shows the presence of the main domestic species expected in the Neolithic, but more revealing, perhaps, are the results of food residue analysis (Chapter 19). These suggest contents based on fruit and malt (FR6), meat (FR1, FR12) – in the latter case most likely only as pork dripping – and more importantly, honey-based products (FR2) and fish substances (FR7, FR8), neither of which would otherwise have been detected (since no sieving for fish bones was possible for Area 4 deposits). These show that there was some exploitation of wild food resources, as also do finds of hazelnuts (later excavations), but there is surprisingly little indication of hunting mammals or fowl. Two of the identifiable food residues occur on fineware sherds (FR1, FR6); most interesting, perhaps, is the association of the fruit/malt material with decorated sherd NP23. One imagines these to have been vessels for serving or consuming, in which case the charring of residues would be the result of accidents.

Some consideration needs to be given to how the suggested settlement drift in the Runnymede locality might fit into the regional situation. Evidence of Neolithic settlement in the reaches of the river systems around Runnymede is not abundant. Many finds cannot be dated to a particular phase of the Neolithic and do not, therefore, help in assessing changes during this long period. Furthermore, most finds are small groups of artifacts which say little about the nature of the sites whence they came.

The Early Neolithic, as defined by true Grimston bowl pottery (Herne 1988) is sparsely represented; vessels are known closest at Cannon Hill, Bray, Berkshire, to the west (Bradley *et al.* 1975–6) and Clapham, Greater London, to the east (Densem and Seeley 1982). Middle and Late Neolithic sites are, however, rather better represented and have been discussed recently by Field and Cotton (1987) and Needham and Trott (1987). Field and Cotton, considering Surrey and its immediate environs, noted that earlier Neolithic (Early–Middle) pottery was seldom found far from the Thames, whilst later pottery had a less restricted distribution (1987: 89). Looking more specifically at the Thames valley around Runnymede, it was possible to suggest that the location of Middle Neolithic monuments and other sites showed a focal concern with the valley bottom, the flood-plain and immediately adjacent terraces (Needham and Trott 1987). In particular, three causewayed enclosures show consistent siting on the edge of gravel terraces overlooking the flood-plain. The fourth possible example, inland at East Bedfont, has since been shown to be a later site (Jon Cotton – pers. comm.) and is therefore no longer relevant to Neolithic patterns. There are also a few Middle Neolithic sherds from Staines town (Barrett 1984: 31; Steve Dyer – pers. comm.). There are, however, indications of some activity

during this phase on the extensive Heathrow terraces north of the Thames: for example, a single sherd amongst the LBA/EIA assemblage from Heathrow runway 1 site (Museum of London) and a new find at Shepperton (Phil Jones – pers. comm.). By contrast, the evidence for the Late Neolithic in this zone is abundant. Many pit groups containing flintwork, pottery and other remains have been discovered, the Stanwell cursus has yielded Mortlake-style pottery in its secondary fills, and a segmented ring ditch at Heathrow probably also belongs to this period (Cotton *et al.* 1986: 33–40; O'Connell 1986b; Grimes 1960). There is also a newly discovered hengiform monument at Mayfield Farm, Bedfont (Jon Cotton – pers. comm.). A further group of Late Neolithic pottery occurs at Iver (Bucks.), to the west of the Colne valley (Lacaille 1937).

While there are finds of Late Neolithic material alongside the Thames river system, they tend to be isolated finds in this region: for example, the occasional sherds and flints from Runnymede mentioned, a single Mortlake sherd from Petters Sports Field (Longworth 1986) and a transverse arrowhead from Egham High Street (David Barker – pers. comm.). It would appear that there was a shift in the focus of settlement and activity during the Neolithic in this region, and the Runnymede evidence for movement of settlement might reflect such a trend in microcosm. However, consideration needs to be given to the chronology of this process. While settlement appears to have moved away from Runnymede Bridge during the currency, or at the end, of Middle Neolithic decorated styles, this was evidently not the case at Yeoveney Lodge causewayed enclosure, just 1 km to the north-east. Following abundant Middle Neolithic evidence, there would appear to have been a continuation of activity on the site through to the Ebbsfleet phase, regarded as the beginning of Late Neolithic developments. The Ebbsfleet pottery on the site appears to mark the closing stages of the lifetime of the causewayed monument, occurring in the upper silts of a restricted part of the outer ditch. This distribution directly mirrors that of decorated Middle Neolithic wares (Robertson-Mackay 1987: 35, 58), which may suggest continuity in functional or behavioural terms. Other Ebbsfleet finds from close to the Thames are presently confined to a group from Mixnam's Farm, Thorpe (Grimes 1960), and an isolated sherd from Wraysbury Manor Farm (Windsor and Wraysbury Archaeological Group). It is possible, then, that the shift in settlement and its environmental consequences documented at Runnymede Bridge were an early stage of, or even unrelated to, a broader shift during or after the Ebbsfleet stage.

The 2nd millennium BC interlude

The L39/40 interface happens to occur close to the water table and hence the deep alluvial sequence above (L38 and L39) is deprived of the rich array of environmental remains found below. These deposits seem consistently to represent over-bank flooding and are dated broadly to the span of the 2nd millennium cal BC. No human activity is represented on the site during this long period, even on the higher ground to the south, and we are left with sediment studies to tell us something of conditions on the flood-plain at this time (Fig. 137).

Low down in the SS1 sequence (L39), when deposition was still just within the contemporary water table, the environment was perennially stagnant. A relatively high proportion of non-calcareous sand (as distinct from the ubiquitous shell sand) could, it is suggested, have been reworked from the lower sediments during their truncation. Obviously this could also apply to some of the snails, but it is noteworthy how the molluscan assemblage shows a major change around the L39/40 boundary (125 cm), suggestive of a major discontinuity (Figs. 118–120).

Apart from perhaps slight variation in the rate of accretion, the clay-loam of L38 seems to represent deposition under a long-standing alluvial regime, which by steady alluviation built up riverside areas such as Area 6 into banks that were dry most of the year. It would seem that the first significant arrest in this cycle occurred at the upper surface of L38, just below Late Bronze Age levels. The accretion of new mineral sediment became so slight as to allow the humic matter in the soil that the riverbank now supported to survive, unaltered by whatever processes had removed it lower down. The LBA deposits on the bank showed no sign of significant inwashes of silt during the occupation, and it may be that the bank was virtually free of flooding during the Late Bronze Age. That this dry condition did not obtain much earlier is suggested by the lack of decalcification which Limbrey observed in the soil.

These observations are of the utmost importance to explanations of the siting of the settlement. Whatever other reasons there may have been for the choice of location (below), there would appear to have been a recognition that during this period occupation of the flood-plain banks at Runnymede Bridge would be relatively untroubled by flooding. This would presumably have been knowledge gained gradually through experience, beginning with intermittent use of the land from home bases on drier terraces or hills nearby.

Although there is no direct evidence from pollen, insects or (as yet) snails for this period, sedimentology points to the later history of L38 as one of fairly well drained grassland, which would be more attractive for grazing than the somewhat rushy grassland inferred for the lower sequence. At most it seems likely that the site itself had some light scrub amongst grassland rather than any full woodland regeneration, for no tree hollows have been recognised in the old ground surface beneath the LBA settlement. Regeneration was presumably kept at bay during the MBA by regular grazing.

The Late Bronze Age settlement and its setting

The rich Late Bronze Age evidence of the excavated area of the 1978 campaign in Area 6 needs to be viewed against earlier and later work on the site. In addition to the salvage section records of LBA occupation deposits surviving in Area 8 up to 60 m to the south, Area 1/2 (Longley 1980) extends the known distribution 110 m to the south-west, while later excavations have revealed equivalent deposits in trenches between 80 and 140 m away in western to north-western directions. These trenches are spread across an area of approximately 1.5 ha and it is believed that the bulk, if not all, of this zone, and more, would have yielded Late Bronze Age settlement evidence. Making allowance for parts of the site known to have been truncated by post-Bronze Age channel erosion, particularly on the west and south-east (Area 8) sides, the occupied area could easily have covered some 2 ha, not to mention contemporary structures on the adjacent terrace site of Petters (Needham 1990; O'Connell 1986a).

Area 6 occupies a peripheral position on the north-east side of this apparently intensive settlement zone. Its peripheral nature is made abundantly clear by the contemporary river bank, reinforced by waterfront structures thought to represent enclosure barriers. In fact all the margins of the site that it has been possible to explore are bordered by relict river channels. Their active phases range from shortly before the LBA to considerably later, but interpretation of changes in the river network around the site suggests strongly that the plot of land settled in the Late Bronze Age was either an island or a near-island. In the latter case a land bridge across a newly filled river channel, perhaps still represented by a marshy belt, would have approached the site from the north. Area 6, however, is currently unique and likely to remain so, in that the adjacent bank of the river was silting up *during* occupation, not before or after as has been observed elsewhere. Consequently it preserves a unique record of highly relevant change through a deep stratigraphic sequence, made the more distinctive by the decision of the Late Bronze Age occupants to site certain timber structures in the waterlogged silts of the channel edge. The kinds of information yielded and the potential for identifying correlations between them will be hard to surpass.

Before entering into discussion about the nature of Late Bronze Age activity in and around Area 6 it is necessary to deal with two matters: firstly, to summarise the precise form of the parcel 4 channel fill; secondly, to recognise the limitations in correlating the channel sequence with events occurring alongside on the dry bank.

Layers 4–30 are incontrovertibly sediments filling part of a river channel, and they lie up against an old bank, which would formerly have been eroding, or at least stable. However, those layers above layer 25 also rise to the north-east away from the old bank, in effect sitting in a trough created between the bank and a shoal of sand and gravel. This shoal may well have risen higher than the maximum recorded in the drawn sections (A6–33, A7–SA5, A4–SA11). It sits on top of the horizontal gravel band representing the river bed itself and was almost certainly a mid-channel bar – that is a bar that initially developed within the flowing water body, rather than against one bank. In all probability the shoal formation and subsequent silting in its lee are very local features, and a river (though possibly the Colne Brook alone) continued to flow on the north-eastern side. Once it had become a permanent feature of the channel because currents close to the south-western bank were insufficient to move it on, the shoal formed an effective barrier between the main channel and the former river's edge. The base of the intervening trough so created was filled with interleaved sediments of highly variable character, implying variable flow conditions, perhaps seasonal. Already flow here against the edge was becoming intermittent, but the snails and insects show rich aquatic assemblages in part suited to flowing water habitats, although notably with elements (*Valva cristata*) suggesting some quieter weeded habitats upstream. During this active channel stage (stratigraphic units A–B) the river was reworking earlier deposits, wood pebbles and, doubtless, some earlier cultural material eroded from the banks. Natural deposition of, for example, Neolithic material is probably a significant problem only at this early stage. (The Neolithic flint cores from higher stratigraphic levels were more probably brought up into LBA levels by human agency – Chapter 5.) Thereafter the trough rapidly became a backwater (WF1 column 120 cm upwards), as testified by the dominant ostracod species and mudflat-favouring snails. Fast water species, now in the minority, suggest flowing water, in close proximity with periodic inwashes to the trough. This change coincides remarkably with the level at which human activity first becomes apparent in the sequence (L24/L25b), and it may be wondered whether certain changes in an otherwise natural succession were precipitated by human interference. The 'clearance' horizon was followed by a marked abatement in flow, but there was nonetheless still a degree of alternation between fine and coarser sediment early in the deposition of L20, which became more homogeneous only in its upper part. The question of the imposition and impact of human evidence on an essentially natural sequence will be returned to. During occupation the trough became steadily more terrestrial, eventually to become part of the river bank itself, but it was nevertheless always subject to intermittent flooding, with consequent off-loading of silt and detritus, and at times shallow standing water in wet seasons. The story of the post-active channel stage basically concerns detailed changes in frequency and character of waterborne contributions dependent on geomorphological changes, coupled, perhaps, with human actions. Some of the important changes are discussed below.

The second issue requiring preliminary discussion concerns the relative chronologies of LBA deposits in the channel and on the bank. Stratigraphic correlations alone soon made it clear that the well separated stratigraphic horizons of the channel were not going to find strict equivalents on

the levee. Instead, the impression gained was that a mass of layers converged and mingled into one at the top of the slope, so that, if anything, the levee occupation deposits could only be related to a homogenised, or at least drastically conflated, sequence. This problem was compounded by the truncation of the actual junction of the two sets of deposits throughout trench 1. Evaluation of the chronology of the levee deposits has therefore proceeded independently of stratigraphic correlations, being based instead on comparisons in the pottery assemblages and on pottery joins. This has confirmed initial suspicions that the bank deposits may be not only conflated, but also partial, with the possibility of substantial gaps in the record for occupation. Such gaps must be assessed against the yardstick of the channel sequence, itself doubtless not fully representative of all phases, but nevertheless the most complete sequence retrieved. The bank deposits seem to be generally lacking in early-phase material and it is envisaged that such debris was removed by clearance before the accumulation of layers 32–35 and 37 (Fig. 138). Secondarily, they have suffered truncation by later flooding, whereas the channel deposits have generally been more quickly protected by flood silts. This leads to some difficulties in the interpretation of the 'late' pottery assemblage in L6 (below). Many of these points are shown graphically in Fig. 138, which offers in schematic form the interpreted sequence of major events across Area 6 during the Late Bronze Age, based on the evidence of stratigraphy, radiocarbon and pottery joins.

The stratified sequences in Area 6, especially the river channel, provide one of the best opportunities to assess change in the local pottery assemblage during the Late Bronze Age. The internal stratigraphic sequences of both the channel and the levee show that over the 9th–8th centuries cal BC the percentage of decorated pottery increased significantly, perhaps approximately doubling. This tallies with previously published schemes of succession from essentially plainware assemblages to decorated assemblages (notably Barrett 1980). In detail, however, site and activity area dictate the absolute percentages of decoration, which may vary by a factor of two for contemporary deposits, even within a small area such as Area 6. Longley (Chapter 9) notes, furthermore, that there is a gross distinction between the 1976 and 1978 assemblages, and it would appear that this stems largely from the lack of any early (units A–D) material in the 1976 groups. Nevertheless, the decorated components of the 1976 trench, set within the occupied island, compare most favourably with those in the mid to late channel deposits, rather than the contemporary occupation deposits on the Area 6 levee. This suggests functional distinctions in the 'occupation' of the two areas. It is clear that there will be no simple seriation possible on the basis of decorated proportions, even at the intra-site level, let alone at a regional scale. Specific forms of pot and decoration may help us out of this difficulty in the future.

The expansion of decoration from unit E upwards in the channel seems to be associated primarily with a new trend to decorate the fineware bowls, Longley's type 4. This is accompanied by a, perhaps simultaneous, partition of the finer bowls (type 4) from the coarser ones (type 5), where formerly type 9 bowls had served in both fine and coarseware. Elaboration of particular ceramics, as well as increase in form range, seems, therefore, to go hand in hand with more specific definition of function. If these changes relate closely to social behaviour, they constitute perhaps the most important turning point yet documented within the LBA occupation period at Runnymede.

The new decorative repertoire concentrated on combed curvilinear and incised geometric designs, and it dates broadly from the latter part of the 9th century cal BC. Certain specific pot forms change in popularity through the sequence, though rarely are there enough positive identifications to give statistical significance to these changes. Longley notes, however, that the dominant type 9 bowl of early stages loses ground to other bowl forms after unit D, while S-profiled jars (type 11) only appear from unit E on. Although generally based on few examples, the following additional associations may be noted: omphalos bases are early (A–D); foot-rings are mid–late (E–I); pronounced carinations on bowls are mid (E–G); high-and-wide shouldered jars are mainly early (A–D); tall-necked jars and slack-shouldered jars are mainly mid–late (E–I); cabled rims are also predomi-nantly E–I; finger-treated necks, neck cordons and all-over (body) finger-tipping are largely late (I). There may be important pointers here to changing preferences of form and style.

The environmental backdrop to Late Bronze Age occupa-tion shows certain changes from that in the Neolithic. How these changes came about during the 2nd millennium BC is not as yet documented. The water environment itself was again quite varied, as might be expected, with oxygen-rich flowing water in the main channels through to weedy, near-still water along margins and in backwater creeks. Small bodies of stagnant, acidic water are also attested in the catch-ment, and these must have been divorced from the cal-careous-rich active river system; perhaps they represent much earlier cut-off channels. There is argued to have been less fallen wood debris in the water than in the Neolithic, although some such material was present in the excavated silts (notably in L20 under F164–Fig. 27A), even after making allowance for wood pebbles from earlier deposits and wood debitage introduced by the Late Bronze Age occu-pants.

Along the riverside, intermittent muddy bank habitats with associated soil erosion are indicated. Partly this may reflect immediate site conditions, where river bank collapse marks an extreme consequence of occupation (see below), but away

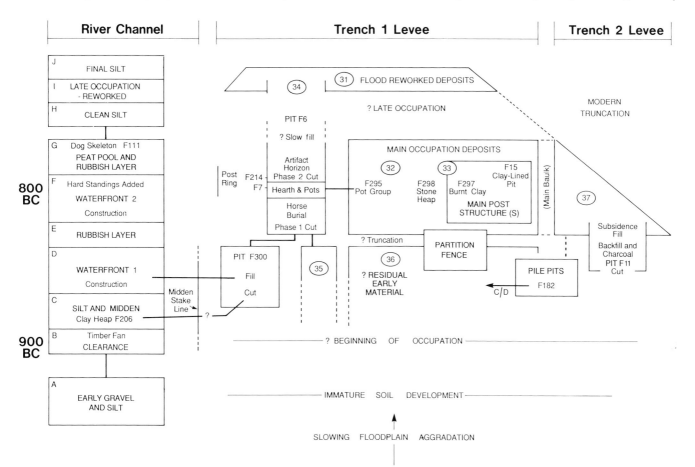

Fig. 138 Suggested sequence of major events and structures in Area 6 during the Late Bronze Age.

from the settlement the watering places of the livestock would have contributed substantially to such habitats. Reeds may now have become more important than bulrushes, the converse of the Neolithic balance between these two taxa. Alder, which was probably extant in good stands fringing the rivers in the Neolithic, had by the Late Bronze Age mainly been cleared, with the consequence that more willow had been left in to the more open conditions that prevailed. Further attacks on alder may be attested by the alder pieces identified in channel stages A–C. Much of the valley bottom was now well drained, permanent grassland. As in the Neolithic, there is a chance that the percentage of woodland pollen will have been under-represented if woodland was generally further away from the settlement than the open land used for farming. Nevertheless it is clear that there had been substantial reductions in the woodland cover of the catchment since the late Neolithic. Gale observes that much of the Late Bronze Age wood and charcoal assemblage comprises species typical of secondary woodland (Chapter 13), and so a good proportion of the extant woodland may actually have been due to regeneration of previously cleared land. Undisturbed primary woodland evidently did survive in places, as borne out by the occurrence of beetles dependent on mature/over-mature oaks. Other trees significantly present in the landscape were elm, lime, ash, birch, field maple and pine, with hazel and one or two other shrubs.

The composition of the woodland is of great importance to the selection of timbers for the waterfront structures. The foundation piles of the waterfront were almost exclusively of oak in both of its phases. Young tree trunks, almost all of less than 30 years' growth, were consistently chosen for this purpose. Interestingly, however, the piles from waterfront 2 seem to have come from trees grown under different environmental conditions than those used in waterfront 1 (Chapter 3). It should be remembered that by their very nature these structures may give a biased view of timber selection, and in particular more mature timber may well have been preferred for superstructural components, such as planks and beams, which have not survived. Similarly, in the superstructure emphasis need not have been placed on a wood which withstood the permanently damp ground conditions required of the piles. Nevertheless, whatever other demands of the local woodland were made by the settlement, the pile foundations placed a high demand on young oaks. With a spacing of four to five per metre, even the established 50 m length of riverbank piling would have required some 200–250 piles in each phase. Given a strong chance that piling continued round much more of the periphery of the site, a minimum distance of 500 m, substantial timber resources would have been exploited. Up to 2500 piles could have been employed in each waterfront phase, although these could have come from fewer tree trunks. Each tree trunk could have supplied a few piles, if the reconstructions offered here are correct to the extent that the foundations were tied by beams raised only a little above the river level. The presence of a significant aspect of secondary

woodland might have allowed the harvesting of the required young oak trunks without roaming too far afield. The demands made of woodland in the course of establishing the settlement may well be recorded by a dip in the pollen spectra for certain woodland and scrub species (oak, alder, hazel) in WF1 column samples 112 and 128 cm. That there was some coppicing of oak and hazel is indicated by rods in the river channel, notably in structure F164, the hardstanding; this is hardly surprising, and not in itself evidence of any great investment in that form of exploitation.

Although much has been said about the slightness of the human impact on the environmental evidence, at least insofar as the microfauna and flora are concerned, one can point to certain humanly-generated effects on the local environment. Amongst the most obvious are the discontinuities created in the sedimentary strata by the emplaced pile rows. These structures and the opening stages of the settlement ('clearance') also have other perceptible effects. Interpretation of the so-called 'clearance' horizon is interlinked with its chronological relationship to the first pile row. The charcoal was at first thought to be literally clearance debris – that is, the burnt remains of the vegetation on the site to be occupied; its identification as primarily oak now suggests that this deposit results instead from human selection. One interpretation would be to link the deposits with the oak trees that were used for the first waterfront by suggesting that it results from the burning of all the trimmings. This might find support in the very similar mean radiocarbon measurements obtained for 'clearance' charcoal and waterfront 1 timbers, although it should be recognised that even the 'most probable' calibrated ranges for the two events are broad enough to allow an interval measured in terms of decades. Furthermore, the intervening deposition of L20c is thought to be steady alluviation, with indications of seasonal variation in its lower part. This implies a passage of some years, perhaps decades, between the two events. The suggested link would seem difficult to sustain if the interval were any more than two or three years, even accepting the possibility that an enclosure may have been constructed in stages as the agricultural regime allowed.

The dominance of oak wood (non-structural) in the channel is maintained during stratigraphic units B and C, associated with a fair amount of ash in C, but is in marked contrast to a much more balanced representation of several wood species (non-structural) in units D–G. Even this later assemblage is unlikely to represent the composition of local woods. Over half the identifications are on charcoal rather than waterlogged wood, suggesting their deliberate introduction for the most part as firewood. Some wood may, of course, have been utilised for the manufacture of artifacts, and it is noteworthy that a number of pieces of *Prunus* were recorded, in addition to the small cup or ladle (W1), which is probably of that species.

Establishment of the settlement created some disturbance of the bank and its communities, as seen both in the physical effect of localised slumpage of the crest of the bank (section

38; Fig. 23) and, perhaps, in rapid fluctuations in the abundance of two land snails around 115–145 cm depth in WF1b (*Carychium minimum; Trichia hispida*). Although certain changes occur at about the construction of waterfront 1, around 80 cm depth, some or all may be part of the natural succession of vegetation and micro-habitat, with human interference acting at most as a trigger for thresholds to be crossed. The demise of *Potamogeton* at 80 cm is doubtless linked to the increasingly terrestrial nature of the trough behind the bar. Apparently significant changes also occur in snails at this point, as *Zonitoides nitidus* starts a rapid increase at the expense of *Vallonia pulchella*. However, the degree of comparability between the changing mollusc assemblages against similar geomorphological sequences in the SS1 and WF1 columns, which involve these amongst other key species, is a warning that natural processes may be largely responsible.

The landscape around Runnymede at this time has been compared (by M. Robinson – Chapter 17) to those indicated around contemporary sites in the Kennet and Thames valleys. There was now a considerable amount of open land, some of which would have been partitioned by 'field systems'. One of the ditches at Petters Sports Field nearby (O'Connell 1986a), if not connected with the enclosure phase, is likely to have been a field boundary. More substantial is a large tract of a 'celtic' field system datable to around the LBA/EIA transition at Stanwell, 5 km north-east (O'Connell 1986b). In the implied organised valley landscape there would be plenty of need for hedging to divide arable from pasture, and Greig suggests that the right shrubs are in evidence to allow the existence of hedges (Chapter 14). The permanent, well drained and apparently extensive grasslands of the valley probably offered the best-quality grazing, ideal for cattle. This grassland was being sufficiently well grazed to prevent regeneration but, as in the Neolithic, not overgrazed. Poorer grasslands or heaths on unstable parts of the flood-plain or exhausted soils would be left to the sheep and goats; included here might be nearby parts of the Bagshot Table, potentially already supporting much heathland (Needham 1987: 130–2). Certainly the quantity of Tertiary rocks on the site suggests the frequent collection of raw materials from the Table. The success of pig in the settlement's agricultural practice was dependent only on surplus of foodstuffs of almost any kind, and a desire to propagate the species. If the population of the settlement was significantly above that of an extended family group, then slops left from human meals may well have been a significant contribution to the pig diet. Beyond the site there was still scope for endless browsing in varied woodland and scrub areas.

Positive evidence for livestock having been brought in to the settlement area is rare, yet two pieces of information point this way in the assemblage under discussion. Both the dehorned cows and the crib-biting horse (Chapter 18) could relate to the confinement of beasts to stalls or closed compounds. Furthermore, there is just a hint that the organic contribution to the midden deposits (Layers 19, 24*–26) was in fact horse manure, perhaps excreted nearby.

For the arable side of the food economy, Greig (Chapter 14) has found a variety of cereals to be present – spelt wheat, emmer wheat, barley and flax were crops, whilst rye and oats were more likely just to have been weeds in the corn-fields.

As has already been pointed out, Area 6 probably occupies one edge of the settled area; activities were in all probability strongly conditioned by this peripheral position, in particular the structural demarcations of the palisades and attendant structures. Deciding what aspects of occupation are best represented here will depend not only on interpretation of the structures, but also on the nature of the refuse and on comparisons with other parts of the site. Part of this consideration must obviously await further analysis of the later excavations, but a number of points may be made.

The rubbish in the river channel deposits does not present anything approaching a uniform distribution over the duration of occupation; rather there were just a few horizons which were rich in refuse, and even these may not have been so for similar reasons. One possibility to be considered is that the 'cleaner' layers reflected a very rapid accumulation of sediment, but the nature of the sediments themselves did not indicate any gross alternation between fast and slow accumulation, and a steady (although seasonally varying) rate is implied throughout. The interpretation favoured here is that the differences related mainly to the history of intensive activity and structural change on this part of the site. The slope of the silting-up bank may well have been an obvious site for dumping or natural collection. At times, during the palisade phases, the 'trap' would have been almost perfect behind the pile foundations, and this effect was clearly demonstrated by groups of large bone caught immediately behind the piles. All but the last refuse-rich (layer 6) can be attributed to human actions. The 'clearance' horizon of burnt debris was so concentrated as surely to have been dumped directly on the slope, albeit followed by a little water reworking; some branches may even have been placed to define the zone of midden dumping. Continuing from this, but far more localised, was the series of midden dumps around 8E/12N incorporating large crocks of pottery along with burnt clay and manure, at first on the slope (unit C), then in the trough on the crest (F300–unit D). Silts accumulating elsewhere were relatively barren over this period, and it was not until unit E, then again at unit G, that large-scale domestic refuse occurred. Unit E coincides with the replacement of waterfront 1 by waterfront 2, while G is likely to fall around the end of the latter's lifetime, given that the overlying layer buried piles that were already reduced to stumps. It has been suggested that in both cases the abundance of refuse relates not simply to human activity nearby but more specifically to the accessibility of the river bank to rubbish. Accessibility at the end of structural phases could allow the corollary that access was restricted during the lifetime of a structure, and this has been tied in with the idea of a fairly continuous horizontal structural component, i.e. a walkway suspended across the slope of the bank. Structural alterations in themselves might intensify the rubbish horizons, if, for example, ground clearance was necessary on the adjacent plot in readiness for rebuilding. If clearance was involved, this has implications for the time-span of the rubbish being redeposited. However, the large size of some sherds and the occurrence of joining groups argue for at least an element of primary deposition, while the high percentage of certain ceramic classes cannot be matched on the levee, suggesting derivation from different activities (see below).

The interpretation of the waterfront foundations as supporting, *inter alia*, walkways bears on their function, to which contemporary water conditions in the river channel are also relevant. The shallowness and likely intermittency of water immediately outside the structures argues against a specific mooring function, even if at times circumstances and boating practices led to opportunistic mooring against or close to them (cf. Needham and Longley 1980). More emphasis is now placed on the act of enclosure as a primary determinant for the waterfronts, in keeping with the broader pattern of enclosing settlements. 'Enclosure' requires a solid obstacle, something tangible, whether for reasons of defence, screening, ostentation or demarcation, and a high stockade rising above the piled foundations is inherently likely. Possible reconstructions in some detail have been advanced, based on theoretical structural considerations in conjunction with the evidence for tie beams across sets of six piles. The cusping structure of the waterfront remains inadequately explained but would seem to relate functionally or aesthetically to the focally outlying posts. These could have served as mooring posts, supports for planked walkways, display posts or even devices to constrict the channel.

The piles themselves were generally prepared in a fairly standard manner, the tips sharpened with bronze axes, the remainder of the shaft left with bark intact for maximum protection against decay, but with side-branches removed. The lack of impact deformation has suggested that fairly soft silts were penetrated, in Area 6 at least, and that wooden mallets were used for driving, although another possibility is the use of some of the large blocks of stone that were recovered from the channel sediments. On the few occasions when piles were inserted into the dry bank, a pit was dug first, before pile-driving began.

During most of the use spans of the waterfront, layers of sediment which built up behind the piles (units D–F) are barely represented just outside. This would again suggest sufficient water flow at times to scour sediment from the trough in front of the palisade, or otherwise a deliberate policy of silt clearance by the occupants. Conditions did, however, become steadily drier and more terrestrial, culminating in a period (unit G) when water flow over the bar carried a little sediment in, to deposit it within the developing peat bed, but was rarely, if ever, strong enough to scour. It is noteworthy that it was late in this sequence (unit F),

when conditions were fairly dry, just before the inception of peat growth, that the hardstanding was laid on the foreshore (F164) in a depression. A hollow mainly free of flowing water, behind the protection of a gravel bar, may have seemed an ideal spot for beaching a small craft. Its use around 800 cal BC and late in the currency of waterfront 2 was soon to be curtailed by the development of the peat pool in the hollow.

The debris on the levee is likely to have differed in its depositional history from that on the slope. Interpreting rubbish directly in terms of the pursuit and location of specific activities is always a difficult matter. The vast majority of the debris from Area 6 would broadly be categorized as domestic, and much is doubtless 'background noise', in which any primary spatial structure had long since been diffused prior to permanent incorporation in the 'occupation deposits' excavated. Certain aspects, however, shine through this screen and are worthy of attention as the most direct testimony to the role of Area 6. Some such aspects have already been mentioned but are also relevant to this discussion: the wood debitage of stratigraphic unit B, and the manure-rich midden of units C and D associated with F300. Some evidence seems to be of special deposits and possibly related special consumption, as distinct from the everyday consumption assumed to be represented by the bulk of the preparation, cooking and eating debris (animal bones, burnt flints, pottery, quern fragments).

These 'special' contexts need some definition. They are merely defined as those that appear to stand out from an established norm of behaviour seen at either the site level or in wider contemporary societies. They should not automatically be taken to be of ritual significance, although some may be; in other cases they may have related to events or circumstances which were only enacted by society (for whatever reason) at infrequent intervals, or in restricted locations. They nevertheless give the potential for distinguishing further elements of a given settlement complex, on the grounds that special events may take place at specific times and places, determined by the 'order of things'.

Horse remains and fine pottery bowls are central planks in this interpretation. The burial of a dismembered horse in pit F6, the association with it of horse harness gear, including manufacturing evidence, and the evident care of horses into old age allow it to be envisaged that the standing of the horse, over and above its undoubted intrinsic value, may have extended to veneration beyond death, accompanied by measures to protect its interests and its man-linked fate in the after-life. We should not overlook the possibility that eating horses, if expedient at times, could nevertheless have been done in reverence to the beasts. With this thought in mind it is worth recalling the three or four articulated groups of horse vertebrae from Area 6, which have led to the speculation of a liking for rib-roast joints. It may not be irrelevant also that the organic component of the midden is likely to have been horse manure, suggesting stabling or corralling nearby. The evidence for 'crib biting' on the F6 horse jaw is of relevance here.

Although it has been possible to suggest temporal correlations between river channel and levee deposits on the basis of pottery joins and assemblage characteristics, some important aspects of ceramics on the site are seen as gross differences between these two broad context groups. Although there can be little doubt that their respective assemblages represent broadly the same occupation, they would seem to attest quite different balances, of activities. The higher proportion of bowls, fineware and decorated vessels (probably all to some degree interlinked) from the river channel shows that the assemblage there did not derive wholesale from deposits like those that formed on the adjacent bank. A significant minority, at least, seems to have a different source, and the large portions of bowls often present might suggest their more immediate discarding. These vessels imply food consumption, perhaps on some scale, perhaps even feasting. Whatever the scale, broken tableware was preferentially being disposed of in the channel edge. The wooden cup or ladle bowl seems likely to tie in with this phenomenon and might be solitary testimony to a more common vessel class, which was less breakable, more reducible by fire or decay, or more prone to floating away on entering water, and thus rarely preserved in on-site deposits (cf. Evans C 1989). Bowls feature strongly throughout the river channel sequence, but predominate over jars most markedly in channel phases C–D. This suggests that a long-lived pattern of behaviour lay behind their deposition, but it need not have been continuous. As explained above, the concentrations of material in the channel may well represent bursts of activity, some being connected to major episodes of structural change. Could ritual and feasting have accompanied these episodes?

In considering the food economy the relative importance of cultigens and animal product is, as always, difficult to assess. More can be said of the balance between different meats consumed on this part of the site. Assuming that similar proportions of meat were stripped from the carcasses of the different species it is estimated that cattle contributed 50%, pig 23%, horse 15% and sheep/goat 4% to the meat supply (Chapter 18). Very little came from non-domesticates. This balance, however, was not static through time. Most striking is the steady growth in the percentage of pig bones through the river channel sequence, at the expense of cattle. Secondarily, there are downward shifts in the age distributions for cattle and sheep (but not pig) late in the sequence. Although apparent changes in the proportions need to be considered carefully in terms of changing depositional process, it is not clear that selective redeposition in the late stages of the river channel sequence (H–J) would create the pattern observed, and cultural explanations are therefore favoured. In particular, it seems probable that during the lifetime of the occupation there was a sustained increase in the butchery and perhaps consumption of pig relative to cattle in the zone of Area 6. This need not have been a site-wide trend and should not automatically be assumed to reflect changes in herd structures, although this is clearly a possibility. Such changes emphasise the potential dynamism of patterns of butchery and the discard of food remains.

Carbonised grain and cereal pollen levels, generally at a low but consistent ebb through the river channel sequence, show a curious strong peak at 112–128 cm, equating broadly with units B–C. While it is difficult to suggest the precise significance of this peak, it would seem to relate to a source of storage or processing which was very close by for a period. In contrast, the otherwise low percentages can be taken to be the typical 'background' reaching this part of the site. Their consistency and their occurrence at levels below the 'clearance' horizon might suggest that this is typical 'rain' generated by the agricultural practices of the immediate catchment during the early 1st millennium BC and did not stem directly from the settlement.

The grinding of grain may have been going on nearby, for a number of quern fragments and one virtually intact quernstone (S39) were recovered, especially from channel units C–D. It is possible that these and the cereal evidence peak derive from interrelated food-processing activities on the adjacent bank, even if some of the stones had been put to a secondary use, as suggested above. There is evidence from flakes that previously dressed stones were being re-fashioned or incidentally chipped. The quernstones at Runnymede were regularly made of lower greensand, which was far more durable than the local Tertiary sandstones and must have come from at least 25 km away. Indeed, Freestone has compared some examples (Chapter 6) to the rock at Lodsworth quarry, West Sussex, still further afield (50 km); this would mean an early exploitation of that source, which is now well documented as having been in use in the Iron Age and Roman periods (Peacock 1987). If this identification holds, it will provide not only the earliest secure contexts for Lodsworth stone but also the most northerly limit for saddle querns in this stone yet found (*ibid.*: 73 fig. 6).

There is little evidence for the practice in or close to Area 6 of any specialised craft activities, although the usual range of related artifacts were recovered: spindlewhorls, loomweights, antlerworking debris, metalworking debris, grinding stones and a possible anvil stone. Most noteworthy, perhaps, are the few pieces of metallurgical refuse, of both clay and metals, particularly the fragment of a large crucible or furnace lining with a bronze residue attached. The possibility has been raised that the small clay-lined bowl pit (F15) might have been concerned with metalworking which would give a rare 'structural' and locational context for this practice. The compositional analyses (to be reported on in detail in a future volume) show the introduction to the site of unalloyed copper material, as well as lead and a lead–tin mix. The non-leaded bronze blob on the crucible/furnace is also important, given the rare usage of non-leaded bronze for artifacts in the Late Bronze Age. It may imply either the on-site alloying of tin with copper, prior to the addition of lead or scrap leaded bronze, or the local refining of imported tin-bronze ingots, again before adulteration with lead.

Attention has already been drawn to the likelihood that pit F6, with its horse burial, had a ritual aspect to it, and that pit F11 may have belonged to the same activity set. It has also been suggested that a fence may have divided the ground between these pits. A further pit of similar proportions has since been discovered to the north-west in Area 14; it also occurs on the periphery of the settlement, whilst no such pits have been discovered 'inland' on the site. The Area 14 pit contained placed objects, including two antler fittings for horse harness, again suggesting a ritual aspect connected with horses. An intriguing contextual comparison can perhaps be made between these large pits at Runnymede and a series of pits found at Danebury hillfort, in positions close to the 425-foot contour on the eastern side of the hill (Cunliffe 1984: 11 fig. 2.1). The Danebury pits are not closely dated, but should precede the 4th century BC (*ibid:* 12) and may therefore be contemporary with Runnymede or only a little later. Pit morphology is not closely comparable between the two sites, the Danebury examples being flat-bottomed and much larger in ground plan. What draws the two together, however, is a combination of factors: their apparently peripheral positions on the two sites, the inclusion of standing posts in some at least, the occurrence of disarticulated animal skeletons and a general 'ritual' interpretation. The primary animal remains at Danebury are two disarticulated dog skeletons low in the fill of pit A. It seems possible that these represent similar ways of demarcating boundaries on the respective sites, though it is not known whether such pits fully encircle either site.

The main timber structure interpreted on the levee is clearly incomplete, which makes functional assessment difficult. The arrangement does not conform to any as yet known for domestic buildings of the period. Its proximity to, and shared alignment with, the waterfronts could favour a function ancillary to the enclosure: for example, a raised platform or a tower. In this context it may be significant that dense refuse spreads, including feasting debris and remains of hearths, were allowed to build up around its footings while the structure stood, sometimes evidently right up against the posts. This might suggest a largely 'open' structure at ground level, although the possibility of a wall line between F96 and F39 has been raised to account for the L32/L33 soil distinction. The main post structure belongs broadly to the middle part of the occupation span and is interpreted as superseding an open area divided by a light fence running perpendicular to the river bank.

No structural evidence has been recognised to belong with the late-phase deposits (H–J), either in the channel or on the bank, and this is one of the problems in interpreting the nature of any late occupation. This late period is usefully defined as beginning with the demise of waterfront 2 during stage G and therefore after about 800 cal BC, to which the hardstandings (unit F) are dated. The peat pool itself occu-pied a pre-existing hollow (Fig. 28C) and was in places up to 15 cm thick; probably representing an accumulation over some decades. Artifactual material within the peat (L9) suggests occupation continuing for some of this period at least. Layer 8a seems most obviously to mark the end of the water-front 2 phase. A tail of this layer filtered through the piles or their stumps and spread over the peat. This was perhaps due to erosion from the main slope deposit of 8a prior to the renewed aggradation seen in layer 7. This new silt inwash showed some lensing and was probably therefore a progressive aggradation over a number of years. It sealed the stumps of waterfront 2 and was virtually clean of rubbish, suggesting little activity nearby. It also sealed a dog skeleton (F111) lying in the top of the peat outside the pile row. The skeleton was fully articulated apart from the separation by 1 m of the skull and adjacent vertebrae; these also remained in articulation, presumably having been dragged away by an animal at an intermediate stage of decay. Otherwise the skeleton was undisturbed and was conceivably representative of a more frequent disposal of dead dogs in this waterfront zone, to judge from the good number of dog bones from the channel layers.

By this late stage the channel edge trough had effectively become a shallow ditch which only intermittently carried standing water. This 'ditch' environment was admirably suited to the mollusc *Valvata cristata* which was very abundant from 70 cm upwards in the WF column. Its strongest peak, at around 40–65 cm, coincides roughly with stratigraphic units F–H and brackets the formation of peat outside the outer pile row. The peat pool phase may mark a slight rise in the mean water table, but it saw only limited intrusions over the bar of flood silt from the main channel. Further rises in water levels and/or increases in the flood risk changed the situation, however, and led to the frequent breaching of the bar. Higher water flows are indicated by the increase in medium sand in layers 6, 5 and 4, and probably began with layer 7, where sandiness was also noted (though not at the column position).

The last artifact-rich layer (L6) occurred within this sequence. Layer 6 is a flood silt rather than a soil; this, in conjunction with the predominantly small sherd size and lack of structures, *in situ* groups or features, points to the assemblage being derived. On the basis of its density, the finds probably came from deposits on a river bank nearby. The trends identified in the pottery report suggest that this stratigraphically late assemblage contains elements not present in the underlying channel stages (A–G), nor in the main occupation deposits surviving on the levee in Area 6. The latter were clearly truncated, with the loss of an unknown depth of deposits, reworked remnants of which are probably represented in layer 31. This allows for the possibility of a late phase of occupation on the levee, but if this was genuinely later than the stage E–G assemblage, it must have taken place after layer 8a formed in the channel. As already noted, there is little sign of occupation during stage H, and it is possible that the reworking of material into flood silt layer 6 was more or less simultaneous with its initial disposal. Taking this further, it is therefore possible that a late phase of occupation post-dated the demise of waterfront 2 and even followed a hiatus in activity in immediate proximity. An altered settlement pattern might well have followed the inception of a new flood regime. That such a phase can be recognised at all is entirely due to the 'trap' created by the hollow in the channel edge.

The stage J deposits in the top of the channel fill contained a much smaller quantity of artifacts; with signs of even greater attrition. During this period it is likely that the previously eroded surface of the levee was beginning to become covered by fresh alluvium and, simultaneously, artifacts were being worked down from surfaces into the pre-existing profiles by worm action.

The archaeological importance of the areas reported on in this volume has been perceived to lie, firstly, in rich and diverse evidence relating to a specific part of a settlement complex, and, secondly, in a crucial background of information relating to the natural and farmed habitats of the immediate environs. The result is a discussion totally focused on such parochial issues. The wider significance of the Runnymede–Petters complex has received much previous discussion (e.g. Needham and Longley 1980, Needham 1989) and renewed consideration will advisedly await a more thorough understanding of the later excavation campaign. Much has been made of the trading role played by the settlement in its regional system; it has been tied in to site location and waterfront function. This needs careful evaluation. Certainly exotic goods were being brought to Runnymede from far and wide (Longley 1980: 1; Needham 1980; Needham and Bimson 1989), but these constitute a very small percentage of the material record surviving on the site and their importance should not be exaggerated. The site is well positioned on a good communications network (the river system); sites back on the river terraces nearby, however, were almost as well placed. The site does appear to have supported a relatively sizeable occupation and some specialised crafts, and it can also be interpreted as having a special status (Needham and Sorensen 1988). These are all potentially factors that could help explain why this settlement was in regular *receipt* of far-displaced items. However, they are far from being evidence that the site had the primary purpose of engaging in, promoting or controlling exchange. Powerful and well positioned sites may have incidentally or intentionally enhanced exchange networks, but could equally have obstructed or regulated them. I am assuming a non-commercial basis for the contemporary exchange network, in which case the actual siting of the settlement on the river bank is something of a red herring. Socially demanded exchange networks would operate whether or not they had sites located on arterial routes and such sites could anyway be bypassed if the social etiquette of the period allowed it. If, on the other hand, the hierarchy of the time decreed the centrality of a particular settlement in exchange mechanisms, then its exact location would, in strictly functional terms, have been immaterial. Proximity to a major route of exchange may, if anything, have been nothing more than an overt demonstration of association, as though enshrining the perceived order. If, however, we are to think in terms of a community needing to express its close association with a river through siting of its settlement, then we may do well to consider other potential attractions of this particular body of water, thought to have been highly revered in the Late Bronze Age. I would argue, however, that either of these possible explanations is prone to be overridden by the harsh reality of flood-plain conditions, which for a brief interlude in the Late Bronze Age left the Runnymede island relatively flood-free.

384

References

Abbreviations

BAR   British Archaeological Reports series

CBA   Council for British Archaeology

HBMC   Historic Buildings and Monuments Commission for England

HMSO   Her Majesty's Stationery Office

PPS   Proceedings of the Prehistoric Society

RES   Royal Entomological Society of London; handbooks for the identification of British insects.

Absolon, A. 1973. 'Ostracoden aus einigen Profilen spät- und postglazialer Karbonatablagerungen in Mitteleuropa', *Mitteilung der Bayerischen Staatssammlung für Paläontologie und Historische Geologie*, 13: 47–94.

Allen, A. A. 1965a. 'Stegobium paniceum L. (Col., Anobiidae) becoming established in the open (?)', *Entomologist's Monthly Magazine*, 101: 115.

Allen, A. A. 1965b. 'Is Onthophagus nutans F. (Col., Scarabaeidae) still taken in Britain?', *Entomologist's Monthly Magazine*, 101: 30.

Allen, T. G. and Robinson, M. A. in prep. *The prehistoric landscape and Iron Age enclosed settlement at Mingies Ditch, Hardwick-with-Yelford, Oxon.*

Andersen, S.Th. 1970. 'The relative pollen productivity and pollen representation of north European trees, and correction factors for tree pollen spectra', *Danmarks geologiske Undersøgelse*, 2. Række, 96: 1–99.

Baker, C. A., Moxey, P. A. and Oxford, P. M. 1978. 'Woodland continuity and change in Epping Forest', *Field Studies*, 4: 645–69.

Baker, J. and Brothwell, D. 1980. *Animal diseases in archaeology*. London, Academic Press.

Balfour-Browne, F. 1940–58. *British water beetles*, 1–2. London, Ray Society.

Barrett, J. 1980. 'The pottery of the later Bronze Age in lowland England', *PPS*, 46: 297–319.

Barrett, J. 1984. 'The prehistoric pottery', in K. R. Crouch and S. A. Shanks, *Excavations in Staines, 1975–76: The Friends' Burial Ground Site*. London and Middlesex Archaeological Society with Surrey Archaeological Society: 31–3.

Batterbee, R. W. 1984. 'Diatom analysis and the acidification of lakes', *Philosophical Transactions of the Royal Society, London*, B 305: 451–77.

Bird, J. and Bird D. G. (eds) 1987. *The Archaeology of Surrey to 1540*. Surrey Archaeological Society, Guildford.

Boulton, B. and Collingwood, C. A. 1975. *Hymenoptera: Formicidae*. RES 6, pt. 3c.

Bradley, R., Lobb, S., Richards, J. and Robinson, M. 1980. 'Two Late Bronze Age settlements on the Kennet gravels: excavations at Aldermaston Wharf and Knight's Farm, Burghfield, Berkshire', *PPS*, 46: 217–95.

Bradley, R. and Keith-Lucas, M. 1975. 'Excavation and pollen analysis on a bell barrow at Ascot, Berkshire', *Journal of Archaeological Science*, 2: 95–108.

Bradley, R., Over, L., Startin, D. W. A. and Weng, R. 1975–6. 'The excavation of a Neolithic site at Cannon Hill, Maidenhead, Berkshire, 1974–5', *Berkshire Archaeological Journal*, 68: 5–19.

Brewster, T. C. M. 1963. *The Excavation of Staple Howe*. The East Riding Archaeological Research Committee, Malton, Yorkshire.

British Standards Institution 1975. *Methods of testing soils for civil engineering purposes*. BS 1377, British Standards Institution, London.

Britton, E. B. 1956. *Coleoptera: Scarabaeoidea*. RES, 5, pt. 11.

Brown, N. 1988. 'A Late Bronze Age enclosure at Lofts Farm, Essex', *PPS*, 54: 249–302.

Buck, F. D. 1954. *Lagriidae to Meloidae*. RES, 5, pt. 9.

Buckland, P. C. 1979. *Thorne Moors: A paleoecological study of a Bronze Age site*. Birmingham University Department of Geography, Occasional Publication 8.

Carruthers, W. J. 1986. 'The Late Bronze Age midden at Potterne', *Circaea*, 4(1): 16–17.

Carruthers, W. J. (forthcoming). Anslow's Cottages: the carbonised and waterlogged plant remains.

Catt, J. A. 1978. 'The contribution of loess to soils in lowland Britain', in S. Limbrey and J. G. Evans (eds), *The effect of man on the landscape: the lowland zone*. London, CBA Research Report no. 21: 12–20.

Cheetham, G. H. 1976. 'Palaeohydrological investigations of river terrace gravels', in D. A. Davidson and M. L. Shackley (eds), *Geoarchaeology*. London, Duckworth: 335–44.

Childe, V. G. and Smith, I. F. 1954. 'Excavation of a Neolithic barrow on Whiteleaf Hill, Bucks', *PPS*, 20: 212–30.

Chowne, P., Girling, M. A. and Greig, J. R. A. 1986. 'Excavations at an Iron Age defended enclosure at Tattershall Thorpe, Lincolnshire', *PPS*, 52: 159–88.

Clapham, A. R., Tutin, T. G. and Warburg, E. F. 1962. *Flora of the British Isles*. 2nd edition. Cambridge University Press.

Claridge, M. F. and Staddon, B. W. 1960. 'Stenelmis canaliculata Gyll. (Col. Elmidae): A species new to the British List', *Entomologist's Monthly Magazine*, 96: 141–4.

Clark, A. J. 1990. 'Archaeomagnetic measurements', in M. Bell, *Brean Down excavations 1983–87*. London, English Heritage Archaeological Report no. 15: 113–16.

Clark, A. J., Tarling, D. H. and Noël, M. 1988. 'Developments in archaeomagnetic dating in Britain', *Journal of Archaeological Science*, 15: 643–67.

Clark, J. G. D., Higgs, E. S. and Longworth, I. H. 1960. 'Excavations at the Neolithic site at Hurst Fen, Mildenhall, Suffolk (1954, 1957 and 1958)', *PPS*, 26: 202–45.

Colyer, L. N. and Hammond, C. O. 1951. *Flies of the British Isles*. London, F. Warne.

Cotton, J., Mills, J. and Clegg, G. 1986. *Archaeology in West Middlesex*. Hillingdon Borough Libraries.

Cunliffe, B. 1984. *Danebury: an Iron Age hillfort in Hampshire. Volume 1, The excavations, 1969–1978: the site*. London, CBA Research Report no. 52.

Cunnington, M. E. 1923. *The Early Iron Age inhabited site at All Cannings Cross Farm, Wiltshire*. Devizes, George Simpson.

Densem, R. and Seeley, D. 1982. 'Excavations at Rectory Grove, Clapham, 1980–81', *London Archaeologist*, 4: 177–84.

Devoy, R. J. N. 1979. 'Flandrian sea level changes and vegetational history of the lower Thames estuary', *Philosophical Transactions of the Royal Society, London*, B 285: 355–406.

Dewey, H. and Bromehead, C. E. N. 1915. *The Geology of the Country around Windsor and Chertsey*. Memoir of the Geological Survey. London, HMSO.

Dimbleby, G. W. 1985. *The palynology of archaeological sites*. London, Academic Press.

Done, G. M. 1980. 'The animal bone', in D. Longley, 1980: 74–9.

Donisthorpe, H. St. J. K. 1939. *A preliminary list of the Coleoptera of Windsor Forest*. London, Nathaniel Lloyd.

von den Driesch, A. 1976. *A Guide to the Measurement of Animal Bones from Archaeological Sites*. Peabody Museum Bulletin 1,

Harvard University.

von den Driesch, A. and Boessneck, J. 1974. 'Kritische Ammerkungen zur Widerrist-hohenberechnung aus Langenmassen vor-und frühgeschichtlicher Tierknochen', *Saugetierkundliche Mitteilungen*, 22: 325–48.

Edlin, H. L. 1949. *Woodland crafts in Britain*. London, Batsford.

Edwards, F. W., Oldroyd, H. and Smart, J. 1939, *British bloodsucking flies*. London, British Museum.

Ellenberg, H. 1979. 'Zeigerwerte der Gefäßpflanzen Mitteleuropas', *Scripta Geobotanica*, 9. 2nd edition. Göttingen Erich Goltze.

Ellenberg, H. 1982. *Vegetation Europas mit den Alpen*. Stuttgart, Ulmer.

Ellenberg, H. 1988. (tr. G. K. Strutt) *Vegetation ecology of central Europe*. Cambridge University Press.

Elton, C. S. 1960. '*Prionychus ater* (F.) (Col., Alleculidae) in Wytham Woods, Berkshire'. *Entomologist's Monthly Magazine*, 96: 176–7.

Elton, C. S. 1966. *The pattern of animal communities*. London, Methuen.

Evans, C. 1989. 'Perishables and worldly goods – artifact decoration and classification in the light of wetlands research', *Oxford Journal of Archaeology*, 8: 179–201.

Evans, J. G. 1971. 'Habitat change on the calcareous soils of Britain: the impact of Neolithic man', in D. D. A. Simpson, (ed), *Economy and settlement in Neolithic and Early Bronze Age Britain and Europe*. Leicester University Press: 27–73.

Evans, J. G. 1972. *Land snails in archaeology*. London, Seminar Press.

Evans, J. G. 1975. *The environment of early man in the British Isles*. London, Elek.

Evans, J. G. 1987. '*Perforatella rubiginosa* (Schmidt 1853) in the Late Bronze Age at Runnymede, Egham, Surrey', *Conchologists' Newsletter*, no. 102: 27–8.

Field, D. and Cotton, J. 1987. 'Neolithic Surrey: a survey of the evidence', in Bird and Bird 1987: 71–96.

Folk, R. L. and Ward, W. C. 1957. 'Brazos River Bar: A study in the significance of grain size parameters', *Journal of Sedimentary Petrology*, 27: 3–26.

Ford, S. 1987. *East Berkshire Archaeological Survey*. Dept of Highways and Planning, Berkshire County Council, Occasional Paper 1.

Ford, S., Bradley, R., Hawkes, J. and Fisher, P. 1984. 'Flintworking in the metal age', *Oxford Journal of Archaeology*, 3 (2): 157–73.

Fowler, W. W. 1887–1913. *The Coleoptera of the British Islands*, 1–6. London, L. Reeve.

Fowler, W. W. 1889. *The Coleoptera of the British Islands*, 3. London, L. Reeve.

Fowler, W. W. 1890. *The Coleoptera of the British Islands*, 4. London, L. Reeve.

Fowler, W. W. 1891. *The Coleoptera of the British Islands*, 5. London, L. Reeve.

Freude, H., Harde, K. W. and Lohse, G. A. 1964–1983. *Die Käfer Mitteleuropas*, 1–11. Krefeld, Goecke and Evers.

Freude, H., Harde, K. W. and Lohse, G. A. 1966. *Die Käfer Mitteleuropas*, 9. Krefeld, Goecke and Evers.

Freude, H., Harde, K. W. and Lohse, G. A. 1967. *Die Käfer Mitteleuropas*, 7. Krefeld, Goecke and Evers.

Freude, H., Harde, K. W. and Lohse, G. A. 1969. *Die Käfer Mitteleuropas*, 8. Krefeld, Goecke and Evers.

Freude, H., Harde, K. W. and Lohse, G. A. 1971. *Die Käfer Mitte-*

leuropas, 3. Krefeld, Goecke and Evers.

Freude, H., Harde, K. W. and Lohse, G. A. 1979. *Die Käfer Mitteleuropas*, 6. Krefeld, Goecke and Evers.

Gibbard, P. L. 1985. *The Pleistocene history of the Middle Thames Valley*. Cambridge University Press.

Girling, M. A. 1976. 'Fossil Coleoptera from the Somerset Levels: The Abbot's Way', *Somerset Levels papers*, 2: 28–33.

Girling, M. A. 1977a. 'Fossil insect assemblages from Rowland's Track', *Somerset Levels Papers*, 3: 51–60.

Girling, M. A. 1977b. 'Bird pellets from a Somerset Levels trackway', *Naturalist (Hull)*, 102: 49–52.

Girling, M. A. 1979. 'Fossil insects from the Sweet Track', *Somerset Levels Papers*, 5: 84–90.

Girling, M. A. 1980. 'The Fossil insect assemblage from the Baker Site', *Somerset Levels Papers*, 6: 36–42.

Girling, M. A. 1982. 'Fossil insect faunas from forest sites', in M. Bell and S. Limbrey (eds), *Archaeological aspects of woodland ecology*. BAR International Series 146, Oxford: 129–46.

Girling, M. A. 1984. 'Investigations of a second insect assemblage from the Sweet Track', *Somerset Levels Papers*, 10: 79–91.

Girling, M. A. (forthcoming). Mesolithic and later landscapes interpreted from the insect assemblages of West Heath Spa, Hampstead. In D. Collins and D. H. Lorimer (eds), *Excavations at a Mesolithic site on Hampstead Heath, 1976–81*. Oxford, BAR 217.

Grant, A. 1975. 'The animal bones', in B. Cunliffe. *Excavations at Portchester Castle*, 1. Society of Antiquaries of London: 378–408.

Green, C. P. and McGregor, D. F. M. 1978. 'Pleistocene gravel trains of the River Thames', *Proceedings of the Geological Association*, 89: 143–56.

Green, C. P., Coope, G. R., Currant, A. P., Holyoak, D. T., *et al* 1984. 'Evidence of two temperate episodes in Late Pleistocene deposits at Marsworth, U.K.', *Nature*, 309: 778–81.

Greig, J. R. A. 1982a. 'The interpretation of pollen spectra from urban archaeological deposits', in A. R. Hall and H. K. Kenward (eds), *Environmental archaeology in the urban context*. London, CBA Research Report 43: 47–65.

Greig, J. R. A. 1987. The late prehistoric surroundings of Bidford upon Avon, Warwickshire. Ancient Monuments Laboratory Unpublished Report 170/87, London.

Greig, J. R. A. 1988. 'Some evidence of the development of grassland plant communities', in M. K. Jones (ed), *Archaeology and the flora of the British Isles*. Botanical Society of the British Isles, Conference Report 19, Oxford: 39–54.

Greig, J. R. A. 1991. 'The Deforestation of London', *Review of Palaeobotany and Palynology*.

Greig, J. R. A. and Colledge, S. M. 1988. The prehistoric and early medieval waterlogged plant remains from multiperiod Beckford sites 5006 and 5007 (Worcestershire), and what they show of the surroundings then. Ancient Monuments Laboratory Unpublished Report 54/88, London.

Grigson, C. 1979. In M. Kubesiewicz, (ed), *Archaeozoology 1*. Szczecin, Academy of Agriculture: 365–74.

Grigson, C. 1981. 'The Bronze Age Fauna', in I. G. Simmons and M. J. Tooley, (eds), *The Environment in British Prehistory*. London, Duckworth: 217–20.

Grimes, W. F. 1960. *Excavations on defence sites, 1939–45, part I: mainly Neolithic–Bronze Age*. Ministry of Works, Archaeological Report 3, London, HMSO.

Groenman-van Waateringe, W. 1978. 'Neolithic man in the

Netherlands', in S. Limbrey and J. G. Evans (eds), *The effect of man on the landscape: the lowland zone*. London, CBA Research Report 21, 135–46.

Hanworth, R. and Tomalin, D. J. 1977. *Brooklands, Weybridge: the excavation of an Iron Age and Mediæval site 1964–65 and 1970–71*. Surrey Archaeological Society Research Volume no. 4, Guildford.

Harcourt, R. 1971. 'Animal Bones from Durrington Walls', in G. Wainwright and I. Longworth, *Durrington Walls 1966–68*. Society of Antiquaries Research Report no. 29, London: 338–50.

Harcourt, R. 1974. 'The Dog in Prehistoric and Early Historic Britain', *Journal of Archaeological Science*, 1: 151–75.

Harde, K. W. 1984. *A field guide in colour to beetles*. London, Octopus.

Haslam, S., Sinker, C. and Wolsey, P. 1982. *British water plants*. Taunton, Field Studies Council.

Hedges, J. and Buckley, D. 1978. 'Excavations at a Neolithic causewayed enclosure, Orsett, Essex, 1975', *PPS*, 44: 219–308.

Herne, A. 1988. 'A time and a place for the Grimston bowl', in J. C. Barrett and I. A. Kinnes (eds), *The Archaeology of context in the Neolithic and Bronze Age: recent trends*. University of Sheffield: 9–29.

Hillam, J. 1985. 'Theoretical and applied dendrochronology: how to make a date with a tree', in P. Phillips (ed), *The Archaeologist and the Laboratory*. London, CBA Research Report 58: 17–23.

Hillam, J., Morgan, R. and Tyers, I. 1987. 'Sapwood estimates and the dating of short ring sequences', in R. G. W. Ward (ed), *Applications of tree-ring studies: current research in dendrochronology and related areas*. Oxford, BAR International series, 333.

Hinton, H. E. 1945. *A monograph of beetles associated with stored products*, 1. London, British Museum.

Hinton, P. 1982. 'Carbonised seeds', in P. Drewett, 'Late Bronze Age Downland economy and excavations at Black Patch, East Sussex', *PPS*, 48: 321–400.

Hjulstrom, F. 1935. 'Studies of the morphological activity of rivers as illustrated by the River Fyris', *Bulletin of the Geological Institute of the University of Uppsala*, 25: 221–37.

Hodgson, J. M. (ed) 1976. *Soil Survey Field Handbook*. Technical Monograph no. 5, Soil Survey, Harpenden.

Hoffmann, A. 1950. *Coléoptères curculionides*, 1. Faune de France 52, Paris: Lechevalier.

Hoffmann, A. 1954. *Coléoptères curculionides*, 2. Faune de France 59, Paris: Lechevalier.

Hoffmann, A. 1958. *Coléoptères curculionides*, 3. Faune de France 62, Paris: Lechevalier.

Horion, A. D. 1941–67. *Faunistik der Mitteleuropäischen Kafer*, 1–11. Uberlingen-Bodensee, Frankfurt am Main, Krefeld, Munchen: Aug. Feyel.

Huntley, B. 1988. 'Europe', in B. Huntley and T. Webb III (eds), *Vegetation History*. Handbook of vegetation science 7. Dordrecht, Kluwer: 341–83.

Jessen, K. and Helbæk, H. 1944. 'Cereals in Great Britain and Ireland in prehistoric and early historic times', *Det Kongelige Danske Videnskabernes Selskab, Biologiske Skrifter*, 3(2): 1–68.

Jessup, L. 1986. *Coleoptera: Scarbaeoidea*. RES 5, pt. 11 (new edition).

Jones, M. 1978. 'The plant remains', in M. Parrington, *The excavation of an Iron Age settlement, Bronze Age ring-ditches and Roman features at Ashville Trading Estate, Abingdon, (Oxfordshire) 1974–76*. London, CBA Research Report 28: 93–110.

Joy, N. H. 1932. *A practical handbook of British beetles* 1. London,

Witherby.

Kenward, H. K. 1982. 'Insect communities and death assemblages, past and present', in A. R. Hall and H. K. Kenward (eds), *Environmental archaeology in the urban context*. London, CBA Research Report 43: 71–8.

Kerney, M. P. 1976. *Atlas of the Non-marine Mollusca of the British Isles*. Cambridge, Institute of Terrestrial Ecology.

Kerney, M. P. and Cameron, R. A. D. 1979. *A field Guide to the Land Snails of Britain and North-West Europe*. London, Collins.

Kerney, M. P., Preece, R. C. and Turner, C. 1980. 'Molluscan and plant biostratigraphy of some Late Devensian and Flandrian deposits in Kent', *Philosophical Transactions of the Royal Society, London*, B 291: 1–43.

Kerney, M. P., Gibbard, P. L., Hall, A. R. and Robinson, J. E. 1982. 'Middle Devensian river deposits beneath the "Upper Floodplain" terrace of the river Thames at Isleworth, West London', *Proceedings of the Geological Association*, 93: 385–93.

Klie, W. 1938. 'Ostracoda; Muschellkrebse'. *Tierwelt Deutschland*. Jena: 1–230.

Kloet, G. S. and Hincks, W. D. 1964. *A checklist of British insects, 2nd edition (revised): Small Orders and Hemiptera*. RES 11, pt. 1.

Kloet, G. S. and Hincks, W. D. 1976. *A checklist of British insects, 2nd edition (revised): Diptera and Siphonaptera*. RES 11, pt. 5.

Kloet, G. S. and Hincks, W. D. 1977. *A checklist of British insects, 2nd edition (revised): Coleoptera and Strepsiptera*. RES 11, pt. 3.

Kloet, G. S. and Hincks, W. D. 1978. *A Checklist of British insects, 2nd edition (revised): Hymenoptera*. RES 11, pt. 4.

Knörzer, K-H 1971. 'Urgeschichtliche Unkräuter im Rheinland. Ein Beitrag zur Entstehungsgeschichte der Segetalgesellschaften', *Vegetatio*, 23: 89–111.

Körber-Grohne, U. 1981. 'Pflanzliche Abdrucke in Eisenzeitlicher Keramik – Spiegelbild damaliger Nutzpflanzen?', *Fundberichte aus Baden-Württemberg*, 6: 165–210.

Lacaille, A. D. 1937. 'Prehistoric pottery found at Iver, Bucks', *Records of Buckinghamshire*, 13: 287–99.

Lamb, H. H. 1981. 'Climate from 1000 BC to 1000 AD', in M. Jones, and G. W. Dimbleby, (eds), *The environment of man: the Iron Age to the Anglo-Saxon period*. BAR 87, Oxford: 53–65.

Lambrick, G. and Robinson, M. 1979. *Iron Age and Roman riverside settlements at Farmoor, Oxfordshire*. London, CBA Research Report 32.

Lambrick, G. and Robinson, M. 1988. 'The development of floodplain grassland in the Upper Thames Valley', in M. Jones (ed), *Archaeology and the Flora of the British Isles*. Oxford University Committee for Archaeology Monograph 14: 55–75.

Landin, B. O. 1961. 'Ecological studies on dung-beetles', *Opuscula Entomologica Supplementum*, 19: 1–227.

Le Quesne, W. J. 1975. *Hemiptera: Cicadomorpha*. RES 2, pt. 2a.

Leese, M. N. 1988. 'Calendar date bands from multiple valued radiocarbon calibration curves', in C. L. N. Ruggles and S. P. Q. Rahtz (eds), *Computer and quantitative methods in Archaeology, 1987*. BAR International Series, 393, 147–51.

Legge, A. J. 1981. 'Aspects of Cattle Husbandry', in R. Mercer (ed), *Farming Practice in British Prehistory*. Edinburgh University Press: 169–81.

Limbrey, S. 1983. 'Archaeology and palaeohydrology', in K. J. Gregory (ed), *Background to palaeohydrology: a perspective*. Chichester, John Wiley: 189–212.

Limbrey, S. 1982. 'The honeybee and woodland resources', in M. Bell and S. Limbrey (eds), *Archaeological aspects of woodland ecology*. BAR International Series, 146: 279–86.

Locker, A. 1988. 'The animal bones from the 1984 excavations of the Late Bronze Age midden at Potterne, near Devizes, Wiltshire. Ancient Monuments Laboratory Unpublished Report 88, London.

Longley, D. 1980. *Runnymede Bridge 1976: excavations on the site of a Late Bronze Age settlement*. Surrey Archaeological Society Research Volume no. 6, Guildford.

Longworth, I. H. 1986. 'The Pottery', in O'Connell 1986a: 9.

Ložek, V. 1964. 'Quartärmollusken der Tschechoslowakei', *Rozpr. ústréd. Úst. geol.*, 31: 1–374.

Mace, A. 1959. 'An upper palaeolithic open-site at Hengistbury Head, Christchurch, Hants', *PPS*, 25: 233–59.

Marciniak, B. 1973. 'The application of the diatomological analysis in the stratigraphy of the Glacial Deposits of the Mikolajskie Lake' (in Polish), *Studia Geologica Polonica*, 31.

Marshall, J. E. 1978. *Trichoptera: Hydroptilidae*. RES pt. 14a.

Martin, E. & Murphy, P. 1988. 'West Row Fen, Suffolk: a Bronze Age fen-edge settlement site', *Antiquity*, 62: 353–8.

Mercer, R. J. 1981. *Grimes Graves, Norfolk: excavations 1971–72*, vol. I. Department of the Environment Archaeological Report no. 11, London, HMSO.

Moffett, L. C., Robinson, M. and Straker, V. 1989. 'Cereals, fruit and nuts: charred plant remains from Neolithic sites in England and Wales and the Neolithic economy', in A. Milles and D. Williams (eds), *Ancient agriculture*. BAR International series, 496: 243–61.

Murphy, P. 1983. 'Studies of the environment and economy of a Bronze Age Fen-edge site at West Row, Mildenhall, Suffolk: a preliminary report', *Circaea*, 1(2): 49–60.

Murphy, P. 1989. 'Carbonised Neolithic plant remains from The Stumble, an intertidal site in the Blackwater estuary, Essex, England', *Circaea*, 6(1): 21–38.

Nansen, P., Anderson, S., Harmer, E. and Riising, H. J. 1972. 'Experimental Fascioliasis in the Pig', *Exp. Parasitol.*, 31: 247–54.

Needham, S. P. 1980. 'The bronzes', in Longley 1980: 13–27.

Needham, S. P. 1985. 'Neolithic and Bronze Age settlement on the buried floodplains of Runnymede', *Oxford Journal of Archaeology*, 4: 125–37.

Needham, S. P. 1987. 'The Bronze Age', in Bird and Bird 1987: 97–137.

Needham, S. P. 1990. *The Petters Late Bronze Age Metalwork: an analytical study of Thames Valley metalworking in a settlement context*. British Museum Occasional Paper no. 70, London.

Needham, S. P. and Bimson, M. 1988. 'Late Bronze Age Egyptian Blue at Runnymede', *Antiquaries Journal*, 68: 314–15.

Needham, S. P. and Evans, J. 1987. 'Honey and dripping: Neolithic food residues from Runnymede Bridge', *Oxford Journal of Archaeology*, 6: 21–8.

Needham, S. P. and Hook, D. R. 1988. 'Lead and lead alloys in the Bronze Age: recent finds from Runnymede Bridge', in E. A. Slater and J. Tate (eds), *Science and Archaeology, Glasgow, 1987*. BAR 196, Oxford: 259–74.

Needham, S. P. and Longley, D. 1980. 'Runnymede Bridge, Egham: A Late Bronze Age riverside settlement', in J. Barrett and R. Bradley (eds), *Settlement and society in the British later Bronze Age*. 2 vols. BAR 83, Oxford: 397–436.

Needham, S. P. and Sorensen, M. L. 1988. 'Runnymede refuse tip: a consideration of midden deposits and their formation', in J. C. Barrett and I. A. Kinnes (eds), *The archaeology of context in the Neolithic and Bronze Age: recent trends*. Dept of Archaeology

and Prehistory, University of Sheffield: 113–26.

Needham, S. P. and Trott, M. 1987. 'Structure and sequence in the Neolithic deposits at Runnymede', *PPS*, 53: 479–82.

Noe-Nygard, N. 1974. 'Bone injuries caused by Human Weapons in Mesolithic Denmark', in A. T. Clason (ed), *Archaeological Studies*. North Holland Publishing Co: 151–9.

Nüchterlein, H. 1969. 'Süsswasserostracoden aus Franken. Ein Beitrag zur Systematik und Ökologie der Ostracoden', *Internationale Revue Gesamt Hydrobiologie*, 54: 223–87.

O'Connell, M. 1986a. *Petters Sports Field, Egham: excavation of a Late Bronze Age/Early Iron Age site*. Surrey Archaeological Society Research Volume no. 10, Guildford.

O'Connell, M. 1986b. 'The Heathrow/Stanwell cursus', *Current Archaeology*, 9: 122–5.

Olmi, M. 1976. *Faune D'Italia 12: Coleoptera, Dryopidae, Elmithidae*. Bologna, Edizioni Calderini.

Osborne, P. J. 1969. 'An insect fauna of Late Bronze Age date from Wilsford, Wiltshire', *Journal of Animal Ecology*, 38: 555–66.

Osborne, P. J. 1978. 'Insect evidence for the effect of man on the lowland landscape', in S. Limbrey and J. G. Evans (eds), *The effect of man on the landscape: the lowland zone*. London, CBA Research Report 21: 32–4.

Osborne, P. J. 1982. 'Some British later prehistoric insect faunas and their climatic implications', in A. F. Harding, (ed), *Climatic change in later prehistory*. Edinburgh, University Press: 68–74.

Osborne, P. J. 1988. 'A Late Bronze Age insect fauna from the River Avon, Warwickshire, England: its implications for the terrestrial and fluvial environment and for climate', *Journal of Archaeological Science*, 15: 715–27.

Paulian, R. 1959. *Coléoptères scarabeides*. Faune de France, 63. Paris, Lechevalier.

Peacock, D. P. S. 1987. 'Iron Age and Roman quern production at Lodsworth, West Sussex', *Antiquaries Journal*, 67: 61–85.

Pearson, G. W. and Stuiver, M. 1986. 'High precision calibration of the radiocarbon time scale, 500–2500 BC', *Radiocarbon*, 28, 839–62.

Peglar, S. M. and Wilson, D. G. 1978. 'The abandoned river channel', in P. J. Drury *et al.*, *Excavations at Little Waltham 1970–1*. CBA Research Report, 26: 146–8.

Phipps, J. 1987. 'The archaeological remains of flies', *Circaea*, 5: 65–6.

Pont, A. C. 1973. 'Musicidae', in K. G. V. Smith, (ed) *Insects and other arthropods of medical importance*. London, British Museum: 251–69.

Rackham, O. 1980. *Ancient Woodland*, London, Arnold.

Rackham, O. 1986. *The history of the countryside*. London, Dent.

Robertson-Mackay, R. 1987. 'The Neolithic causewayed enclosure at Staines, Surrey: excavations 1961–63', *PPS*, 53: 23–128.

Robinson, M. A. 1981a. 'Investigation of palaeoenvironments in the Upper Thames Valley, Oxfordshire'. University of London, PhD thesis.

Robinson, M. A. 1981b. 'The Iron Age to early Saxon environment of the Upper Thames Terraces', in M. Jones and G. Dimbleby, (eds), *The environment of man: the Iron Age to the Anglo-Saxon period*. BAR, 87, Oxford: 251–86.

Robinson, M. A. 1983. 'Arable/pastoral ratios from insects?', in M. Jones (ed), *Integrating the subsistence economy*. BAR International Series 181, Oxford: 19–55.

Robinson, M. A. 1984. 'Landscape and environment of Central Southern England during the Iron Age', in B. W. Cunliffe and D. Miles (eds), *Aspects of the Iron Age in Central Southern Britain*.

University Committee for Archaeology Monograph 2, Oxford: 1–11.

Robinson, M. A. and Wilson, R. 1987. 'A survey of environmental archaeology in the South Midlands', in H. C. M. Keeley (ed), *Environmental archaeology: a regional review*, 2. HBMC, Occasional Paper 1, London: 16–100.

Robinson, M. 1988. 'Molluscan evidence for pasture and meadowland on the floodplain of the upper Thames basin', in P. Murphy and C. French (eds), *The Exploitation of Wetlands*. BAR, 186, International Series, Oxford: 101–12.

Robinson, M. 1989. 'Macroscopic plant remains from the Wilsford shaft, Wiltshire', in P. Ashbee, M. Bell and E. Proudfoot (eds), *Wilsford Shaft excavations 1960–2*. HBMC Archaeological Report no. 11, London: 78–90.

Robinson, M. (forthcoming). Waterlogged plant remains from Berinsfield, Oxfordshire.

Round, F. E. 1957. 'The late glacial diatom succession in the Kentmere Valley deposit. I, Introduction, methods and flora', *New Phytologist*, 56: 98–126.

Royal Entomological Society, 1953–86. *Handbooks for the identification of British insects*. London.

Salisbury, C. R., Whitley, P. J., Litton, C. D. and Fox, J. L. 1984. 'Flandrian courses of the river Trent at Colwick, Nottingham', *The Mercian Geologist*, 9: 189–207.

Saville, A. 1977/78. 'Five flint assemblages from excavated sites in Wiltshire', *Wiltshire Archaeological Magazine*, 72/73: 1–27.

Saville, A. 1981. *Grimes Graves, Norfolk, excavations 1971–72: Vol. II, The flint assemblage*. Department of the Environment Archaeological Report no. 11, London, HMSO.

Shotton, F. W. 1978. 'Archaeological inferences from the study of alluvium in the lower Severn-Avon', in S. Limbrey and J. G. Evans (eds), *The effect of man on the landscape: the lowland zone*. London, CBA Research Report 21: 27–82.

Silver, I. A. 1963. 'The Ageing of the Domestic Animals', in D. Brothwell, and E. S. Higgs (eds), *Science in Archaeology*. London, Thames and Hudson.

Sisson, S. and Grossman, J. D. 1938. *The Anatomy of the Domestic Animals*. Philadelphia, Saunders.

Smith, I. F. 1956. The Decorative Art of Neolithic Ceramics in South-Eastern England and its Relations. University of London, unpublished PhD thesis.

Smith, I. F. 1965. *Windmill Hill and Avebury: excavations by Alexander Keiller, 1925–1939*. Oxford.

Southwood, T. R. E. and Leston, D. 1959. *Land and water bugs of the British Isles*. London, F. Warne.

Sparks, B. W. 1961. 'The ecological interpretation of Quaternary non-marine Mollusca', *Proceedings of the Linnean Society of London*, 172: 71–80.

Sparks, B. W. 1964. 'Non-marine Mollusca and Quaternary ecology', *Journal of Animal Ecology*, 33 (suppl.): 87–98.

Stephens, J. F. 1830. *Illustrations of British entomology* 3. London, Baldwin and Cradock.

Straker, V. (forthcoming). Carbonised cereals, weeds and charcoal from the Bronze Age midden and settlement at Potterne, Wiltshire.

Stuiver, M. and Reimer, P. J. 1986. 'A computer program for radiocarbon age calibration', *Radiocarbon*, 28: 1022–30.

Tansley, A. G. 1968. *Britain's Green Mantle*. London, Allen & Unwin.

Therkorn, L. L., Brandt, R. W., Pals, J. P. and Taylor, M. 1984. 'An Early Iron Age Farmstead: Site Q of the Assendelver Polders Project', *PPS*, 50: 351–73.

Thomas, K. D. 1985. 'Land snail analysis in archaeology: theory and practice', in N. R. J. Fieller, D. D. Gilbertson and N. G. A. Ralph (eds), *Palaeobiological Investigations: Research Design, Methods and Data Analysis*. Oxford, BAR International Series, 266, 131–56.

Tinsley, H. M. 1981. 'The Bronze Age', in I. G. Simmons and M. G. Tooley, (eds), *The environment in British prehistory*. London, Duckworth: 210–49.

Turner, F. 1926. *Egham, Surrey: a history of the parish under church and crown*. Egham.

Turner, G. M. and Thompson, R. 1979. 'Behaviour of the Earth's magnetic field as recorded in the sediment of Loch Lomond', *Earth and Planetary Science Letters*, 42: 412–26.

Turner, G. M. and Thompson, R. 1982. 'Detransformation of the British geomagnetic secular variation record for Holocene times', *Geophysical Journal of the Royal Astronomical Society*, 70: 789–92.

Turner, J. 1981. 'The Iron Age', in I. G. Simmons and M. D. Tooley (eds), *The environment in British prehistory*. London, Duckworth: 250–81.

Walker, J. J. 1911. 'Preliminary list of the Coleoptera observed in the neighbourhood of Oxford from 1819 to 1907: third supplement', *Ashmolean Natural History Society of Oxfordshire Report*: 45–54.

Ward, G. K. and Wilson, S. R. 1978. 'Procedures for comparing and combining radiocarbon age determinations; a critique', *Archaeometry*, 20: 19–31.

Watson, H. and Verdcourt, B. 1953. 'The two British species of *Carychium*', *Journal of Conchology*, 23: 306–24.

Welten, M. 1967. 'Die pollenanalytische Erforschung des Wohnplatzes Burgäschisee-süd; Ergänzungen', in K. Brunnacker *et al*, *Seeberg Burgäschisee-süd, Teil 4: Chronologie und Umwelt*. Acta Bernensia 2: 11–20.

Willerding, U. 1988. 'Zur Entwicklung von Ackerunkrautgesellschaften im Zeitraum vom Neolithikum bis in die Neuzeit', in H-J. Küster (ed), *Der prähistorische Mensch und seine Umwelt (Festschrift für U. Körber-Grohne)*. Forschungen und Berichte zur Vor- und Frühgeschichte in Baden-Württemberg, 31: 31–41.

1. *The south bank of the Thames with iron-piled coffer dam early in the bridge construction, from the 1959–60 bridge.*

2. *Salvage section SA4 with Area 4 in background. Area 6 was later excavated in the undisturbed ground beneath the pump.*

3. *Salvage section SA4 showing early discovery of timber pile row (left) and dark midden earth (centre).*

4. *Part of Area 4 and salvage section SA11 with channel sediments to the left of the pile rows and the Neolithic stone concentration to the right. Truncated piles can be picked out to the left of the puddle.*

6. *Area 8 sections SA6 & 7 with embankment spoil at top. The dark LBA horizon with associated features can be identified across the middle of the plate.*

8. *Area 7 salvage section SA5; the parcel 1/2 interface occurs at the ranging rod.*

5. *The northern corner of Area 4; the section destroyed prior to recording.*

7. *Looking north-west across the contractor's pit and bridge foundations to the 1959–60 bridge and Area 5 below it.*

10. Area 6 trench 2 deep (foreground) from the east; the top of layer 40 and the tail of the Neolithic bar is exposed in the base.

9. Area 6 trench 1 deep (foreground) from the west; the top of layer 40 is exposed at the base.

11. *Neolithic cobble structure in salvage section SA11, Area 4.*

12. *Neolithic brush structure, Area 4B.*

13. *Detail of Neolithic brush structure, Area 4B.*

14. *Detail of Neolithic brush structure, Area 4B.*

15. *Late Bronze Age pile rows and driftwood across Area 4.*

16. *Late Bronze Age inner pile row in Area 4 section SA11.*

17. *Neolithic worked bark piece, W4 (F89)* in situ *in Area 4A.*

18. *Neolithic worked bark piece, W4 (F89) – radiograph after reconstruction.*

19. Area 6, Late Neolithic butchered bone group F125.

20. Area 6, Middle Neolithic timber F184 in prostrate position.

21. Area 6 trench 1, excavation of the river channel leaving soil columns around pile rows.

22. Area 6 trench 2, section 37 showing dense charcoal deposits lying on slope of ancient river bank.

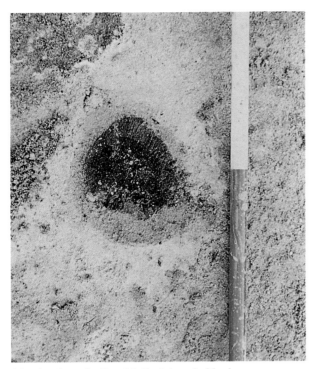

23. *An Area 4 pile with 'halo' probably due to drag effect.*

24. *An Area 4 pile tip sectioned showing cone or drag-line at top.*

25. *Area 6 pile F268 with enveloping silts sectioned to show drag-lines of paler silt into darker silt.*

26. *Area 6 pile F209 with enveloping silts sectioned to show drag-lines of paler silt into darker silt.*

27. *Late Bronze Age channel sediments and piles from the two rows in section 38, trench 1 Area 6.*

28. *Late Bronze Age channel sediments and piles from the two rows in section 37, trench 2 Area 6.*

30. *Late Bronze Age piles, trench 2: F239, 286, 285.*

29. *Late Bronze Age inner row pile F117 in section 38.*

31. *Outer row piles, central baulk: F170–173.*

32. *Outer row piles, trench 2: F277–284, F241.*

33. *Tip of pile F224 penetrating buried wood.*

34. *Hole created in wood lump by tip of pile F224.*

35. *Rear brace pile F126.*

36. *Inner row pile F129.*

37. *Inner row pile F240 (F223 in background).*

38. *Inner row pile F122.*

40. Branches of hard standing F164 poking out of silt layer 20.

42. Detail of rods and branches in F164.

39. Bone refuse including articulated vertebrae in layer 8a trapped behind line of inner pile row.

41. Hard standing F164 from the east.

43. *Dog skeleton F11/111A in the river channel.*

45. *Section 35 through F300 and midden deposit in channel edge.*

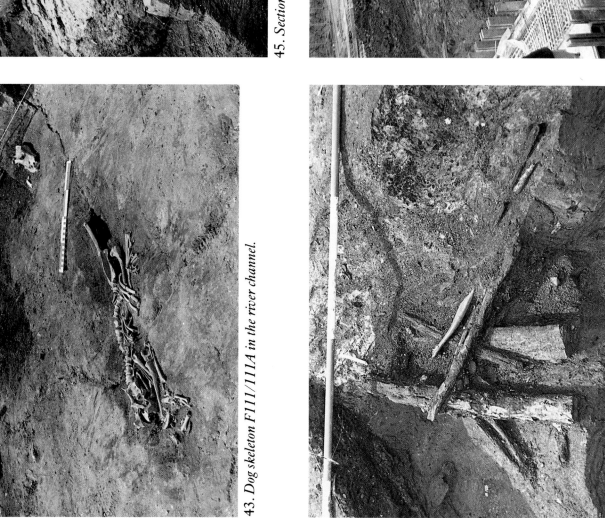

44. *Wooden elements F163 bordering west side of midden deposit in channel edge.*

46. *Area 6 trench 1 after machining of overburden and cleaning, to show channel edge.*

47. *Pot group F295 in layer 32.*

48. *Pot group in F6 including portion of vessel 558.*

49. *Inverted hearth deposit in section in southern part of F6.*

50. *Parts of the horse skeleton in south-west quadrant of pit F6.*

52. Bone point embedded in drilled condyle of metacarpal bone (B4), in situ and removed.

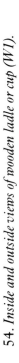

54. Inside and outside views of wooden ladle or cup (W1).

51. The polished stone axes (S2, S3) from Area 4A.

53. Whittled antler tine (B12).

55. *Inner row piles (left to right: 2 views of each) F132, 235, 287, 239.*

56. Left: inner row piles (2 views of each) F122, 188. Right (top to bottom): outer row piles F170, 171, 165 and outlier F212.

57. Outer row piles (2 views of each) F216, 279, 215, 283.

58a. *Neolithic sherds with attached charred food residues and tufa encrustation. Area 4.*

58b. *Sampling the Late Bronze Age river channel sediments, column WF1. Maureen Girling is on the far left.*

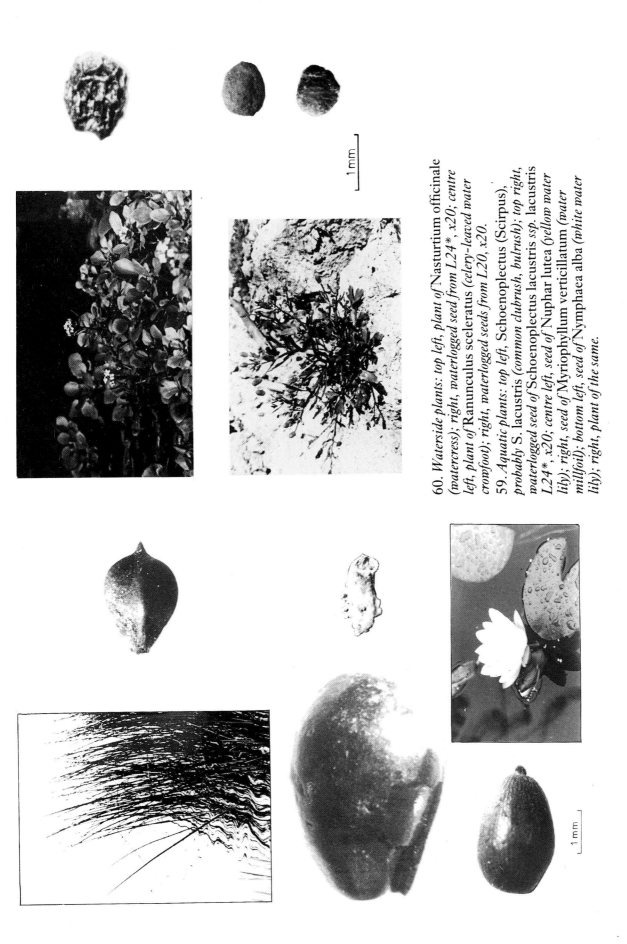

60. *Waterside plants: top left, plant of Nasturtium officinale (watercress); right, waterlogged seed from L24*, x20; centre left, plant of Ranunculus sceleratus (celery-leaved water crowfoot); right, waterlogged seeds from L20, x20.*

59. *Aquatic plants: top left, Schoenoplectus (Scirpus), probably S. lacustris (common clubrush, bulrush); top right, waterlogged seed of Schoenoplectus lacustris ssp. lacustris L24*, x20; centre left, seed of Nuphar lutea (yellow water lily); right, seed of Myriophyllum verticillatum (water millfoil); bottom left, seed of Nymphaea alba (white water lily); right, plant of the same.*

1mm

61. *Weeds (all waterlogged) L24*, x20: top left, plant of* Fumaria officinalis *(fumitory); middle, seed of* Fumaria sp. *(above), seeds of* Spergula arvensis *(below); right, plant of* Spergula arvensis *(corn-spurrey); middle left, plant of* Linaria vulgaris *(yellow toadflax); centre, seed of same (L24*); right, seed of* Lamium purpureum *(purple dead-nettle); bottom left and centre, seedcoat and seed of* Malva sylvestris *(common mallow); right, plant of* Lamium purpureum.

57. *Outer row piles (2 views of each) F216, 279, 215, 283.*

58a. *Neolithic sherds with attached charred food residues and tufa encrustation. Area 4.*

58b. *Sampling the Late Bronze Age river channel sediments, column WF1. Maureen Girling is on the far left.*

62. *Crops; wheat (all remains charred), L24* x20: top two, grain of* Triticum cf. dicoccum *(cf. emmer) from above and from the side; bottom two rows,* Triticum dicoccum *(emmer) spikelet forks and a single rachis segment.*

63. *Crops; wheat (all remains charred), L24* x20: top row, glume bases of* Triticum dicoccum *(emmer); middle row, emmer spikelet forks; bottom row, emmer rachis segments.*

64. *Crops; wheat (all remains charred), L24* x20: top,* Triticum cf. spelta *(spelt wheat) grain; middle and bottom,* Triticum spelta *spikelet forks.*

65. *Crops: barley, all charred from L24* x20: top row, left and centre,* Hordeum vulgare *(6-row barley) rachis segments, right* H. vulgare; *bottom,* Hordeum vulgare *grain enclosed in glumes.*

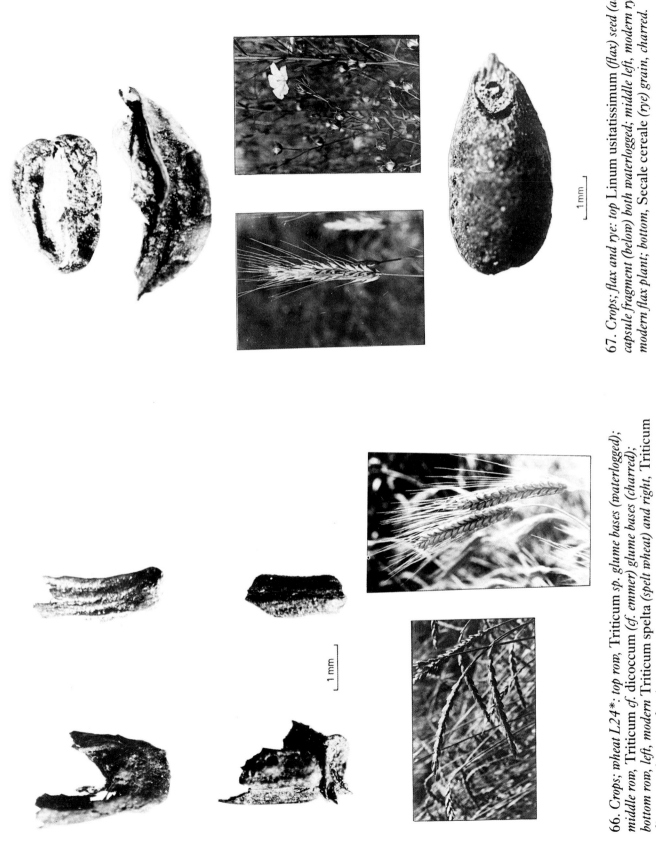

67. *Crops; flax and rye: top* Linum usitatissimum *(flax) seed (above) and capsule fragment (below) both waterlogged; middle left, modern rye ear, right, modern flax plant; bottom,* Secale cereale *(rye) grain, charred.*

66. *Crops; wheat L24*: top row,* Triticum *sp. glume bases (waterlogged); middle row,* Triticum cf. dicoccum *(cf. emmer) glume bases (charred); bottom row, left, modern* Triticum spelta *(spelt wheat) and right,* Triticum dicoccum *(emmer wheat).*

68. *Plants of waysides, paths and various open habitats (waterlogged) x20: top row,* Dianthus armeria *(Deptford pink) plant, modern seed and subfossil; middle row,* Dipsacus fullonum *(teasel) plant and seed; bottom row,* Potentilla anserina *(silverweed), plant and seed.*

69. *Grassland plants (waterlogged): from the top, seed opposite picture of the appropriate plant:* Scabiosa columbaria *(small scabious)*, Thalictrum flavum *(meadow rue)*, Sanguisorba officinalis *(greater burnet)*, Prunella vulgaris *(self-heal)*, Plantago major *(rat-tail plantain)*.

71. *Plants of woodland and scrub (waterlogged): from the top, picture of modern plant opposite seeds:* Prunus spinosa *(sloe),* Crataegus sp. *(hawthorn),* Taxus baccata *(yew) (modern seed left and fossil one right), cf.* Sorbus aria *(cf. whitebeam).*

70. *Plants of woodland and scrub (waterlogged): top from left:* Cornus sanguinea *(dogwood) seed,* Humulus lupulus *(hop) seed and modern plant; middle,* Rhamnus catharticus *fossil seed; below* Mercurialis perennis *(dog's mercury) seed,* Rosa *(wild rose) pip with plant above the seed; bottom,* Fragaria vesca *(wild strawberry) left, plant, right, fossil seed.*

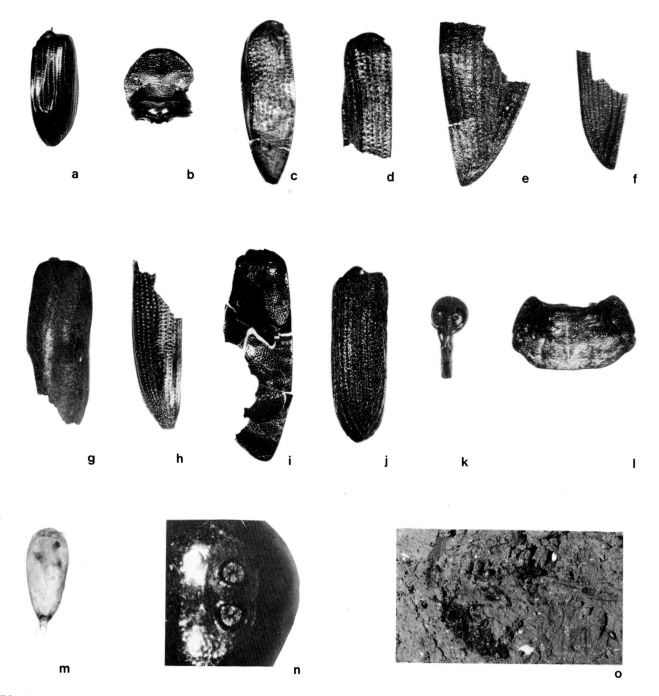

72. *Insects from Runnymede:*

a Aphodius varians *rt. elytron;*
b Onthophagus taurus *head;*
c Macronychus quadrituberculatus *lt. elytron;*
d Stenelmis canaliculata *lt. elytral frag.;*
e Agrupnus murinus *rt. elytral frag.;*
f Dromaeolus barnabita *lt. elytral frag.;*
g Gastrallus immarginatus *rt. elytron;*
h Donacia impressa *lt. elytral frag.;*
i Aegelastica alni *lt. elytral frags.;*
j Mecinus pyraster *rt. elytron;*
k Rhynchaenus quercus *head;*
l Odontoscelis fugiginosa *pronotum;*
m Ithytrichia *sp. larval case;*
n Musca *cf.* domestica *posterior spiracles of puparium;*
o *Bird pellet in sediment.*

Magnification: a–b, o, h–i, l–m x8.5; c–d, f, j–k x17; g x24; n x34; o x0.8.
Contexts: a WF1b 1.20–1.25m; b–e, h–k SS1 1.80–1.85m; f–g SS1 1.60–1.65; l, o WF bird pellet; m WF1b 1.50–1.55; n midden layer 24*.

73. *Neolithic Ox sacrum, cranial aspect, with severe osteitis/arthrosis; Area 4 L121a.*

74. *Horse: upper incisors showing abnormal wear on labial edge of tables; Area 6 F6.*

75. *Ox horn cores with cavities filled with healing bone; Area 6 F6.*

76. *Horse: metatarsal showing fusion with third tarsal and exostoses on insertion of hock flexors; Area 6 F6.*

77. *Sheep/goat first phalanx with extensive exostoses; Area 6 L20 18E ION.*

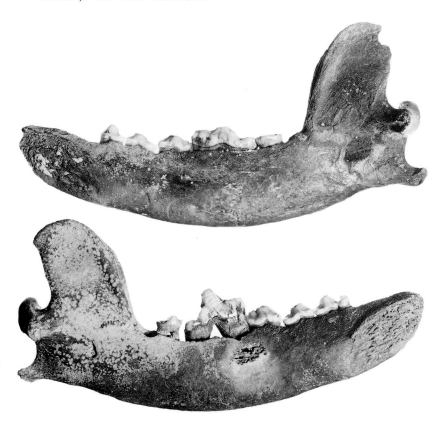

78. *Dog: left and right mandibles. The dead carnassial in the left (lower) mandible compared with the normal right (upper) carnassial. Area 6 F111A.*